BORDER AND TERRITORIAL
DISPUTES

KEESING'S PUBLICATIONS

Other Keesing's Reference Publications (KRP) titles (all published by Longman Group UK Limited) include the following:—

The Radical Right: A World Directory, compiled by Ciarán Ó Maoláin (1987)

Revolutionary and Dissident Movements of the World, compiled by Henry W. Degenhardt (1987)

Trade Unions of the World, edited and compiled by F. John Harper (1987)

The World Financial System, compiled and written by Robert Fraser (1987)

Political Parties of the World (2nd edition), edited by Alan J. Day & Henry W. Degenhardt (1984)

State Economic Agencies of the World, edited by Alan J. Day (1985)

Maritime Affairs: A World Handbook, compiled by Henry W. Degenhardt (1985)

Latin American Political Movements, compiled by Ciarán Ó Maoláin (1985)

Communist and Marxist Parties of the World, compiled by Charles Hobday (1986)

OPEC, Its Member States and the World Energy Market, compiled by John Evans (1986)

Treaties and Alliances of the World (4th edition), compiled by Henry W. Degenhardt (1986)

Peace Movements of the World: An International Directory, edited by Alan J. Day (1986)

The following titles are currently available in the Keesing's International Studies series (all published by Longman Group UK Limited):—

China and the Soviet Union 1949–84, compiled by Peter Jones and Siân Kevill (1985)

Conflict in Central America, by Helen Schooley (1987)

From the Six to the Twelve, by Frances Nicholson and Roger East (1987)

Keesing's Record of World Events (formerly *Keesing's Contemporary Archives*), the monthly worldwide news reference service with an unrivalled reputation for accuracy and impartiality, has appeared continuously since 1931. Published by Longman Group UK Limited on annual subscription; back volumes are also available.

BORDER AND TERRITORIAL DISPUTES

DISPUTES

2nd Edition

A KEESING'S REFERENCE PUBLICATION

Edited by
ALAN J. DAY

**Contributors: Judith Bell, Henry W. Degenhardt, Roger East,
Ella Gleisner, Gillian Goodhind, Charles Hobday, Susan Mushin,
Darren Sagar, Michael Wilson, Martin Wright**

Longman

BORDER AND TERRITORIAL DISPUTES

1st Edition 1982
2nd Edition (revised and updated) 1987

Published by Longman Group UK Limited, Longman House,
Burnt Mill, Harlow, Essex CM20 2JE, United Kingdom

Distributed exclusively in the United States and
Canada by Gale Research Company, Book Tower,
Detroit, Michigan, 48226, United States of America

ISBN 0-582-00987-1   (Longman)
ISBN 0-8103-2543-8   (Gale)
Library of Congress Catalog Card Number 87–23770

British Library Cataloguing in Publication Data
Border and territorial disputes.——2nd ed.
    ——(A Keesing's reference publication).
    1. Boundary disputes——History
    I. Day, Alan J. II. Bell, Judith III. Series
    341.4′09   JX4111

ISBN 0-582-00987-1

Library of Congress Cataloging-in-Publication Data
Border and territorial disputes.

    (A Keesing's reference publication)
    Bibliography: p.
    Includes index.
    1. World politics——1945– . 2. Boundary disputes——
History——20th century. 3. Territory, National——
History——20th century. I. Day, Alan J. (Alan John)
II. Bell, Judith. III. Series.
D843.B623   1987   341.4′09   87–23770
ISBN 0-8103-2543-8

Typesetting by Quorn Selective Repro Limited, Loughborough
Printed in the United Kingdom by Page Bros (Norwich) Limited

CONTENTS

LIST OF MAPS

INTRODUCTION

When the first edition of this work went to press in June 1982, three major armed conflicts were in progress in different parts of the globe, each to do in one way or another with opposing territorial claims by states or peoples. These conflicts were the Falklands/Malvinas war in the South Atlantic, the Iran-Iraq war and the Israeli invasion of Lebanon. Five years on, none has been resolved in any fundamental sense. The South Atlantic war quickly resulted in British forces repossessing the Falklands, but Argentina has continued to assert its claim to sovereignty over these and other British possessions in the region. The Iran-Iraq conflict shows no sign of reaching a military conclusion, notwithstanding huge physical losses on both sides and interminable efforts at mediation. The Israelis eventually withdrew from Lebanon, where they had sought to disperse Palestinian forces posing a threat to their own territorial sovereignty; yet the state of Israel remains a territorial entity that is unacceptable to most Arabs outside and inside its borders.

Each of these three conflicts has its own special ingredients and its own particular historical and geographical dimensions. But all are instances of a problem, namely territorial dispute, which continues to generate severe strains in relations between states in all parts of the world, despite the considerable efforts made in the post-war era to create international or regional channels for the peaceful resolution of inter-state disagreements.

The present edition is an expanded and updated version of the first, aiming to present concise but informative accounts of some 80 contemporary border and territorial disputes between states. Arranged alphabetically in five sections covering broad geographical areas, each account seeks to explain the historical background of the particular dispute and to pinpoint the territorial elements involved, as well as to cover diplomatic exchanges and negotiations between the interested parties. In this last respect, the new edition gives particular attention to relevant developments since 1982 and also includes accounts of several new disputes which have arisen, or become active again, over the past five years.

It should be explained that the situations described in the present volume are those deemed to be of territorial and/or political significance and do not, for example, include boundary demarcation problems where these do not involve contentious territorial claims by one state against another. Moreover, the book is concerned essentially with disputes over land and thus does not cover those concerned with maritime boundaries and jurisdictions unless these arise from, or are interrelated with, competing landward claims.[1]

A particular word should be said about the problem of defining what constitutes a contemporary territorial dispute. In the introduction to his masterly work on African boundaries,[2] Prof. Ian Brownlie took certain earlier writers to task for

---

[1]For maritime boundary disputes, see Henry W. Degenhardt, *Maritime Affairs: A World Handbook* (Longman, Harlow, 1985), pp. 183-220.

[2]Ian Brownlie, *African Boundaries—A Legal and Diplomatic Encyclopaedia* (G. Hurst & Company, London; University of California Press, Berkeley & Los Angeles; for the Royal Institute of International Affairs, London, 1979).

including in their lists of current African disputes several which had already been settled or which had never existed under a proper legal definition of the concept of an inter-state dispute. The present work may not be immune from similar criticism, in that some of the situations included do not currently involve the active prosecution of claims at governmental level and others have been officially declared to be settled. However, in defence of the judgments made in the following pages, it should be noted that territorial claims which seem to be resolved or dormant are notoriously liable to acquire unexpected new life, especially where regional political alignments are unstable or where internal political conditions are susceptible to rapid change. The Iran-Iraq dispute, ostensibly resolved in 1975 but five years later the cause of war between the two countries, is a case in point.

On these grounds, the present work contains accounts not only of existing official disputes between governments but also of a number of situations where unofficial or popular aspirations to territorial change exist. In some of these latter instances, there is a question-mark over the durability of agreements between governments; in others, actual peoples, or sections thereof, have demonstrated dissatisfaction with territorial dispositions made by governments on their behalf. In other words, the book has been compiled not from a legalistic perspective but as a contribution to greater political understanding of the strains in relations between states arising from territorial factors of several different types.

In the work of expansion and updating, as with the original compilation, extensive use has been made of the editorial resources of *Keesing's Record of World Events* (formerly *Keesing's Contemporary Archives*). The authors and updaters are almost all present or former members of the *Keesing's* editorial team, and every effort has been made to achieve *Keesing's*-style objectivity and balance in the presentation of conflicting claims and divergent historical accounts received from government departments. As listed in the select bibliography at the end of the book, published works dealing with border and territorial questions have also been drawn upon for historical background.

The editor wishes to express his gratitude to the many government officials who took the trouble to comment on the content of the first edition and to supply new material; he should also record that the way in which such comments and additional material has been utilized in the present volume is entirely his responsibility. Thanks are also due to Richard German for the index to the present work and to Allan Lamb of Longman for the maps.

London, June 1987   *AJD*

ABOUT THE EDITOR. Alan J. Day was from 1974 to 1982 deputy editor of *Keesing's Contemporary Archives* (now retitled *Keesing's Record of World Events*) and has written or edited several titles in the Keesing's Reference Publications series (see page facing main title page for list). He became an independent publishing consultant and reference work compiler in 1987 and will become editor of *The Annual Register* in 1988.

1. EUROPE

Introduction

In the course of history the continent of Europe has been the scene of countless territorial disputes between dynasties and states, with the result that until very recent times the political map of Europe has been subject to a continual process of change. However, over four decades have now passed since the last major territorial adjustments were made at the end of World War II, and Europe today probably has the lowest incidence of inter-governmental dispute over territory of any continent in the world. In this context, it should be noted that the general acceptance by European governments of the post-war status quo was officially enshrined in the Final Act of the Conference on Security and Co-operation in Europe (CSCE) signed in Helsinki on Aug. 1, 1975, by all European sovereign states except Albania and also by the United States and Canada. In Article III of a "declaration on principles guiding relations between participating states" contained in Basket One, the Final Act specified that the signatories "regard as inviolable all one another's frontiers as well as the frontiers of all states in Europe" and therefore "will refrain now and in the future from assaulting these frontiers"; accordingly, the signatories undertook to "refrain from any demand for, or act of, seizure and usurpation of part or all of the territory of any participating state".

Nevertheless, there remain among the 34 sovereign states of Europe a number of unresolved issues which can be defined as having a territorial element notwithstanding the signature of the Helsinki Final Act by 33 of them. The Northern Ireland question has as one of its central ingredients the Irish Republic's aspiration to the unity of Ireland, which remains implicit in the Republic's constitution despite the signature in 1985 of the historic Anglo-Irish Agreement on Northern Ireland. The United Kingdom is also a party to another major European territorial issue, namely the status of Gibraltar, to which Spain has long laid claim. There are also issues, such as the Trentino-Alto Adige (South Tyrol) question, which are not fully resolved to the satisfaction of all interested parties notwithstanding the dropping of actual territorial claims. And in south-eastern Europe traditional territorial rivalries between Greeks and Turks underlie the current dispute between Greece and Turkey in the Aegean Sea and also the unresolved question of Cyprus.

As regards the post-war territorial changes in Eastern Europe, many of them cannot be regarded as involving any current inter-state dispute. For example, the Soviet Union's absorption of the formerly independent Baltic republics of Estonia, Latvia and Lithuania, although not formally recognized by a number of countries, is not a direct issue between sovereign governments; and Finland's cession of territory to the Soviet Union is regarded as final by both sides. On the other hand, the post-war territorial changes involving Germany, Poland and the Soviet Union—under which the Soviet Union acquired large tracts of former Polish and German territory, while Poland's western border was moved to the Oder-Neisse line in former German territory—remains contentious in West Germany notwithstanding

1

the Bonn government's signature of bilateral and multilateral agreements recognizing current frontiers. Moreover, the demographic dimensions of some 20th-century territorial transfers in central and south-eastern communist Europe, notably in the Balkans, continue to involve the governments concerned in strains which reflect historical territorial antagonisms. It remains an open question, therefore, whether a transformation of existing power relationships in Eastern Europe would leave post-war territorial arrangements unchallenged.

Map 1   Present-day territorial relationship between Albania, Greece and Yugoslavia, showing Epirus and Kosovo.

Albania-Greece

A dispute between Greece and Albania over the southern part of Albania inhabited by ethnic Greeks has been referred to in Greece as "the Northern Epirus question", implying that the disputed area should be regarded as part of the Greek region of Epirus on both historical and ethnic grounds. The question is officially regarded as settled by the governments of the two countries, any residual official Greek aspiration to territorial change being dropped when the Athens government in August 1985 acknowledged that it was not in a state of war with Albania. Nevertheless, the existence of an ethnic Greek minority in Albania remains a factor in relations between the states of the Balkan region.

History of the Dispute

An independent state of Albania was first proclaimed on Nov. 12, 1912, during the First Balkan War which resulted in the loss, by the Ottoman Empire, of all its territory in Europe except an area around Constantinople (Istanbul). The Albanian state was recognized by a peace conference of European powers held in London in December 1912, when the delimitation of its frontiers was reserved for a future decision of the Great Powers. Agreement in principle on Albania's borders was subsequently reached at an ambassadors' conference in London in the summer of 1913.

During World War I Greece occupied southern Albania in October 1914 (while the northern and central parts were occupied by Austro-Hungarian troops in 1915). In the secret treaty of London of 1915, designed to bring Italy into the war on the side of the Allies, Italy was promised a protectorate over the greater part of Albania, with the north going to Serbia and the south to Greece. This was rejected by the Albanians, who declared their own independent state in 1920. After armed Albanians had attacked an Italian-held port, Italy withdrew from Albania in August 1920 and recognized Albania's independence and territorial integrity. Following Albania's admission to the League of Nations in 1920, a boundary commission composed of Britain, France and Italy delimited Albania's frontiers and completed its work in 1926. A final demarcation act was signed by the above powers and also Greece and Yugoslavia in Paris on July 30, 1926.

After the advent of the Fascist regime in Italy and the conclusion of a treaty of friendship and security between Italy and Albania in November 1926, Italian influence increased greatly in Albania, culminating in the occupation of the latter by Italian forces as from April 17, 1939. From Albanian soil Italian forces attacked Greece in October 1940, but they were defeated by the Greeks who subsequently took over about half of Albania. However, in April 1941 Hitler's forces overran both Greece and Yugoslavia, and Italy again obtained control over all of Albania.

During the period of resistance by the Albanians against the Italian (and later German) occupation forces, there emerged a National Front formed by Albanian Communists and nationalists. The provisional government set up by the Front under the leadership of Col. Enver Hoxha was recognized by the Allies towards the end of 1945, but the Greek government protested against the Allies' recognition on Nov. 10, 1945, and at the demand of all Greek political parties except the Communists declared its claim "for the union of North Epirus with the Greek motherland".

This Greek claim was supported by the US Senate which in July 1946 passed the "Pepper resolution" in favour of ceding "Northern Epirus" to Greece. However, when the Greek claim was raised at a Paris meeting of Allied Foreign Ministers in August-September 1946, it was removed from the agenda by James Byrne (the US Secretary of State) after Col. Enver Hoxha, representing Albania, had declared that "neither the Paris conference nor the conference of the Big Four nor any other gathering can review the frontiers of my country, which has no foreign territory of any kind under its jurisdiction". The Allies thus de facto reaffirmed Albania's 1913 frontiers.

Rapprochement between Albania and Greece

No mention of the Greek claim was made when the Foreign Ministers of Greece, Turkey and Yugoslavia (then members of a tripartite grouping which became the Balkan Pact) met in Athens on July 7-11, 1953, and agreed that "the independence of Albania constitutes an important element of peace and stability in the Balkans".

On July 2, 1958, the Albanian government expressed its desire to establish "normal and good-neighbourly relations" with Greece, but at the same time it rejected a Greek statement to the effect that there was still a state of war between the two countries resulting from Albanian participation in Italy's attack on Greece in 1940. The Greek response to Albania's proposal was said to have included a reiteration of Greece's claim to "Northern Epirus" but also an offer to seek a settlement of this problem through normal channels. The Albanian side rejected the Greek reply on Aug. 14, 1958, denying again that there was "a state of war" between the two countries and rebutting the Greek territorial claim on the ground that "the question of Northern Epirus does not exist, as this is Albanian territory".

On Jan. 9, 1962, the Albanian government again expressed its readiness to establish diplomatic relations with Greece, provided the Greek government abandoned its "baseless" claim to part of southern Albania. A first trade agreement between the two countries at non-governmental level was concluded on June 2, 1970. It was followed by the establishment of diplomatic relations on May 6, 1971, this step being understood to imply Greek recognition of Albania's existing borders. Further trade agreements or protocols were signed in later years, and on March 28, 1978, a direct airlink was set up.

During a visit to Albania (the first by a Greek minister since World War II) by Karolos Papoulias, the Greek Alternate Minister of Foreign Affairs, on Dec. 3-6, 1984, agreements were signed on transport, postal services, telecommunications, cultural relations and scientific exchanges. Papoulias, who was himself born in Albania, also met representatives of the Greek community in Albania.

The border crossing at Kakavia, which had been closed since 1940, was reopened on Jan. 12, 1985, although mainly for official traffic only. An economic co-operation agreement was signed on Jan. 25, 1985, and a cultural exchange programme for 1985-86 on March 8, 1985. In July of that year a protocol was signed on the restoration of border markers and procedures for the settlement of border disputes and violations.

The territorial claim previously made by Greece against Albania was effectively annulled by an official Greek announcement made on Aug. 23, 1985, terminating the state of war which in the Greek view had existed between the two countries since Oct. 25, 1940.

The Situation of the Greek Minority in Albania

Enver Hoxha, then First Secretary of the Party of Labour of Albania, stated in a speech addressed to the Greek minority in Albania on March 23, 1978, that no harm would come to Greece from Albania and that the Greek minority in Albania should speak and study the Greek language and maintain its Greek culture.

This minority had before World War II been estimated (by Greek consular authorities) at 300,000 (or about 20 per cent of Albania's total population). However, during and immediately after the war many Greeks left Albania for Greece, and in 1981 the minority was estimated at 200,000. According to Greek sources, 62 of Albania's 250 members of Parliament were of Greek origin or Greek-speaking (including three Cabinet ministers, two under-secretaries and one Deputy Speaker of Parliament). There was a Greek newspaper published twice a week (as the only paper published by any minority in Albania); the functioning of Greek schools and the publication of books in Greek for the use of the Greek minority were allowed in two strictly defined areas; there was also a teaching academy for the training of teachers for the Greek schools; and there were cultural exchanges.

Among Greek nationalists, however, the claim for "Northern Epirus" has continued to be made. In particular, the Northern Epirus Society, led by Xenophon Kountouris, and the Pan-Epirus Federation of America and Canada, led by Menelaos Tzelios, have campaigned

4

for the cause of the Greeks in Albania, alleging that they were suffering repression, with 20,000 of them being held in prisons and concentration camps; that they were prevented from having free access to their relatives in Greece; and that the suppression of all religion in Albania (since 1967) had prevented the Greek Orthodox Church from operating in Albania. In July 1981 Greek nationalists were reported to have introduced in the Greek Parliament a motion calling on the government to "reaffirm in all directions Greece's persistent national rights in Northern Epirus".

In 1983 a "Committee for the Protection of the Rights of the Greek Minority in Northern Epirus" claimed that up to 25,000 ethnic Greeks had been imprisoned in Albania and that the Greek minority in that country numbered up to 400,000 (whereas Enver Hoxha gave a figure of 28,000). Following a hunger strike by two Greek refugees from Albania, detained by the Greek police in Athens, the Greek Prime Minister declared on Feb. 21, 1984, that his government would not tolerate "the violation of human rights of Greeks in Albania", but added that Greece had no territorial claim against that country.

Alleged Albanian Aspirations to "Greater Albania"

The question of Greek-Albanian relations was again raised when a map was published in Yugoslavia in May 1981, purporting to show that the Communist government of Albania had claims to a "Greater Albania" incorporating territories currently parts of Yugoslavia and of Greece; it was found, however, that this map had been produced by Albanian exiles in the West in 1971.

George Rallis, then Greek Prime Minister, stated in mid-1981 that the Greek government was opposed to "any attempt to disturb the status quo in the area", while in an eight-page document issued by the Albanian embassy in Athens it was emphasized that Albania desired the continuation of good relations between the two countries, to which was added: "The healthy sections of Greek public opinion know that the so-called Northern Epirus issue is long dead and has no future."

HWD

Albania-Yugoslavia (Kosovo)

Since the end of World War II relations between Albania and Yugoslavia have been periodically strained by questions surrounding the predominantly Albanian population of Kosovo, a province currently forming part of the Yugoslavian Federation. Particularly since 1968 a resurgence of Albanian nationalism has been in evidence in the province, leading to the expression of demands for the establishment of Kosovo as a full republic within the Yugoslavian Federation, but also on occasions to direct demands for secession from Yugoslavia and union with Albania. Whereas until 1981 Yugoslavia refrained from direct accusations against Albania (alleging generally that "Stalinist" and "Cominformist" elements from abroad were involved in the Kosovo unrest), in that year relations deteriorated to the point where direct Yugoslavian allegations were made of Albanian involvement, both financially and organizationally, in the Kosovo disturbances. Albania for its part has consistently denied any role in the Kosovo unrest, which it sees as a spontaneous rebellion against the allegedly oppressive rule of the Serbs in the province, and has countered the Yugoslavian arguments with claims that during the post-war years Yugoslavia itself entertained the idea of annexing Albania. (For map of Balkans showing Kosovo, see page 2.)

5

The relationship between Albania and Yugoslavia has been particularly complicated in the post-war period by the series of fundamental changes of policy and alignment which both countries have undergone since 1945. Whereas up to 1948 both countries owed their principal allegiance to the Soviet-dominated Cominform, in that year Yugoslavia was expelled from the Cominform and adopted an independent and non-aligned policy which has frequently involved ideological and political conflict both with the Soviet Union and with Albania. Albania, for its part, broke its links with Moscow in the early 1960s to adopt a Maoist line and intensified its political and economic contacts with China; this policy was in turn abandoned in the late-1970s amid strong Albanian criticism of China's post-Mao policies and against a background of improved Chinese-Yugoslav relations. Although Albania and Yugoslavia resumed full diplomatic relations in 1971 after their breach in 1948, and although after 1976 they greatly intensified their economic contacts, a strongly nationalist and anti-Yugoslavian propaganda campaign remained evident in Albania.

The Albanians in Kosovo have maintained a distinctive culture and in many cases have retained their Albanian dialects. The strains in their relations with the Serbs of Kosovo originate partly from specific circumstances arising from the war-time occupation of Albania and Kosovo by the Italians, but more particularly from the alleged imposition of pan-Serbian principles on the Albanian population of Kosovo. This situation changed dramatically in the 1960s, however, with the denunciation and removal of Alexander Rankovic, a strongly pan-Serbian Vice-President of the Republic, organizational secretary of the League of Communists of Yugoslavia and former chief of the security police; since the promulgation of the 1963 Yugoslavian constitution (under which Kosovo achieved the status of an autonomous province with appropriate powers), Albanian influence in the local administrative and Communist party apparatus has grown to an extent which has even been described as oppressive by the Serbian and other non-Albanian elements in the province.

Geographical and Demographic Aspects of the Kosovo Issue

Kosovo, or Kosovo-Metohija (Kosmet) as it was known until 1968, is generally regarded as the most economically backward part of the Yugoslavian Federation. The country is partly mountainous (although agriculture is dominant in the Metohija lowlands) and copper, coal and chromite are mined. It has received a considerable proportion of the regional development assistance given by the central government in Belgrade since World War II, but remains chronically underdeveloped in relation to other areas of Yugoslavia, a fact which has repeatedly given rise to bitter complaints from its predominantly Albanian population that it has been neglected by Belgrade. This sentiment became particularly apparent in 1968-69, when large-scale riots broke out in Pristina, the provincial capital, and again in the late 1970s, when the economic pressures affecting the national economy as a whole coincided with a wave of Albanian irredentism to provoke an increasing number of anti-Yugoslavian and anti-Tito activities in the region. These culminated in 1981 in further riots in the course of which a state of emergency was declared. Paradoxically, much of the unrest centred on the University of Pristina, the fourth largest in Yugoslavia, which was set up by the central government with the aim of raising the general level of culture in the area (it being reported in 1963 that only about 30 per cent of schoolchildren were completing the official minimum of eight years' schooling).

Kosovo has the highest population density in the Yugoslavian Federation, with 140 persons per square kilometre (1977 figures), compared with the national average of 86. About 85 per cent of its 1,486,000 inhabitants (1981) are Albanian, this proportion having risen steadily since the late 1960s due partly to the extensive emigration of Serbs to other parts of Yugoslavia but also to the unusually high annual birth rate, particularly among Albanians as compared with Serbs and Magyars. The results of the 1981 census showed that, whereas Yugoslavia's population as a whole had increased in size by 9.3 per cent since 1971, the country's Albanian population had grown by about 30 per cent over the same period.

Development of the Dispute since 1944

The constitution promulgated on Jan. 31, 1946, by the Federal People's Republic of Yugoslavia incorporated the region of Kosovo-Metohija within the republic of Serbia, giving it the status of an autonomous region, or oblast, with a number of administrative organs and competences of its own. The region had in fact belonged to Yugoslavia since before World War II but from 1941, the year of the German/Italian occupation of Yugoslavia, until the liberation in 1944 it had been integrated into the administrative structure of Albania (which had itself been in effect controlled by Italian economic interests since 1926 and which had in 1939 been occupied by Italy).

The period 1944-48 was marked by extensive co-operation, both economic and administrative, between the new Communist regimes of Albania and Yugoslavia, which in 1946 briefly formed a customs union; in consequence, the question of Kosovo was effectively dormant. On the expulsion of Yugoslavia from the Cominform in 1948, however, the Albanian government adopted a hostile attitude to Yugoslavia: Yugoslavian advisers, politicians and military staff were pressurized to leave or actually expelled from Albania, and in 1949-50 a series of shooting incidents took place along the Albanian border with Macedonia and Kosovo, leading in November 1950 to the closure of the Yugoslavian legation in Tirana, the Albanian capital. In December 1953, as the attacks along the border continued, it was agreed by the two countries to mark their communal border with demarcation posts, and relations were to some extent normalized.

The nationality issue in Kosovo was re-opened in August and September 1958, however, by the news of the death of an Albanian who was attempting to escape from a Yugoslavian detention camp. Like many others of his countrymen, the Albanian in question had collaborated during the war with the Italian Fascists and German Nazis and had spent the period since the war in refuge in West Germany, but had been arrested in Belgrade in May 1958 while returning to Albania. In this connexion the Albanian press also made allegations that up to 36,000 Albanians in Yugoslavia had been massacred by the Titoist partisan forces directly after the liberation in 1944, and that severe repression by the Serbs still continued in Kosmet. Yugoslavia responded with a series of trials of alleged Albanian spies, claiming in a White Paper circulated to members of the United Nations on April 7, 1961, that between 1948 and 1960 Albania had sent 657 agents, mostly armed, into Yugoslavia, of whom 115 had been caught and convicted, and also that 649 frontier incidents involving 12 deaths had occurred.

In the federal constitution promulgated in Yugoslavia in 1963 Kosmet was elevated to the status of an autonomous province, and in 1968 the designation Metohija was dropped from its name so that it became simply Kosovo. By this time there was growing evidence of nationalist and secessionist unrest in the province which had been heightened by the removal from office in 1966 of Vice-President Rankovic for the propagation of pan-Serbian ideals and for the violent repression of Albanians in Kosovo through the UDBA (State Security Administration), which he had controlled. The troubles, further exacerbated by economic difficulties which followed the reforms introduced throughout Yugoslavia in 1965, led on Nov. 29, 1968, to the first major wave of rioting in Kosovo, when students at the University of Pristina led well-co-ordinated but often violent demonstrations calling inter alia for the designation of Kosovo as an autonomous Yugoslavian republic in which Albanians would have a dominant role. The demonstrations coincided with others in Macedonia and also with Albania's national day (Nov. 27). Certain Serbian members of the Kosovo League of Communists who protested at what they saw as Albanian irredentism were in turn subjected to criticism for alleged Serbian nationalism.

In addition to Rankovic, many of his associates were also removed from power, including Vojin Lukic, the Serbian Minister of the Interior, who was in 1973 imprisoned for pan-Serbianism and for describing the Albanians of Kosovo as "an unsafe element"; moreover, a major purge of the Serbian League of Communists was instituted, involving some 2,000 dismissals. Nevertheless, the tensions in the province persisted and were regarded as particularly serious in view of a general re-awakening of nationalism in various Yugoslavian republics, notably in Serbia and Croatia. In February 1973 greatly increased penalties, including the death penalty, were introduced for crimes such as terrorism and "hostile propaganda", while trials of both Albanian separatists and Serbian nationalists continued.

The third federal constitution since World War II was promulgated on Feb. 21, 1974, and provided inter alia that each socio-political community (the autonomous provinces, the republics and the Federation) would have an assembly enjoying a considerable degree of autonomy within the context of its respective community; it also specified that 20 delegates from Kosovo were to form part of the Federal Chamber, which was to have the power to decide inter alia on any alterations to Yugoslavia's boundaries. The number of members of the collective presidency (created in 1971 in order primarily to minimize inter-republican quarrelling on President Tito's death or retirement) was reduced from 23 to nine, in which the Kosovo representative had equal status with those of the six full republics and with the other autonomous province of Vojvodina. The ninth member was the president of the League of Communists, then President Tito, who was appointed President for an unlimited term.

In a significant development on Sept. 20, 1974, the Federal Public Prosecutor issued a statement on the recent trials of 27 persons on Kosovo and of five in Montenegro (north of Albania and directly north-west of Kosovo) who had been charged with "conspiring against the people and the state", and who had received prison sentences of up to 14 years. The statement referred to 'pro-Cominform emigrés who are engaged in hostile activities abroad against our country", and who had distributed "propaganda and other material of a seditious nature". President Tito had himself described the "Cominformists" on Sept. 12 as undertaking "an attempt . . . to create a new communist party which disputes all our actions and all our successes" and which was "evidently some kind of Stalinist party". (It was known at this time that, apart from the still tense relationship with the Soviet Union, fears were being expressed in Yugoslavia that post-Maoist Albania might revert to the Soviet model of communism.)

In December 1974 over 100 demonstrators at Pristina were reported to have been detained for promoting the concept of a "Greater Albania" including Kosovo, and for directly accusing President Tito and the government of persecuting Yugoslavian Albanians; five persons were subsequently imprisoned in January 1975 for "attempting to overthrow the constitutional order and attacking the territorial integrity of Yugoslavia". Further incidents continued to be reported in the Yugoslav and foreign press, although as relations between Yugoslavia and Albania improved in the latter's post-Maoist period the disturbances evidently became increasingly embarrassing to Yugoslavia and led in early 1980 to a highly confused situation surrounding the apparent arrest of some 50 Yugoslavian Albanians in connexion with demonstrations in December 1979.

The weekly Yugoslavian journal *Politika* reported in March 1980 that the nationalists had been charged with "crimes against the state and against public security", the trials being held, as was usual, in camera. The then president of the Kosovo League of Communists, Mahmut Bakali, reacted angrily on April 4 to the *Politika* report, which he described as false and unfounded, while it was claimed elsewhere that only relatively few persons had been charged. Eight of the accused were on June 9, 1980, sentenced to prison terms of up to eight years for distributing "anti-state propaganda with conspiratorial intent".

The Albanian embassy in Belgrade, while issuing its usual denial of involvement in the disturbances, described the timing of the incident as unfortunate. In early July 1980 Nedin Hoxha, the Albanian Minister of Commerce, undertook an official tour of the Yugoslavian republics (the first such ministerial visit since 1948), including a visit to the province of Kosovo, while on July 14 the two countries signed a five-year trade agreement which provided for a significant increase in their bilateral trade. A second plan, finalized in 1986, provided for mutual trade of some US$680,000,000 in 1986-90, a 20 per cent increase on the total for 1981-85. Moreover, a new railway link was opened in August 1986, connecting Shkodër (Scutari) in northern Albania with Titograd (in the Yugoslavian republic of Montenegro) and thus linking Albania with the European railway network for export purposes; it was envisaged, initially at least, that the new line would be used solely for freight.

Kosovo Tensions in the 1980s

Tensions in Kosovo itself have remained high since the spring of 1981, when a wave of serious rioting occurred in Pristina, the provincial capital, in pursuit of demands for full republic status for Kosovo. Some 250 people were injured and nine killed during the first round of protests, which centred on the University at Pristina, and 500 people were arrested. The Yugoslavian authorities followed through with a series of measures against dissident groups in the province, claiming by late 1986 to have unearthed and disbanded eight "irredentist" organizations comprising over 90 separatist groups.

Official sources revealed in early 1987 that over 1,200 ethnic Albanians had been sentenced to jail, often for very long terms, for "counter-revolutionary nationalism and irredentism", and that another 3,000 had been convicted of more minor offences. Early in 1986, the Yugoslavian police claimed to have found arms and ammunition in the hands of a 150-member separatist group which they suspected of planning an armed insurrection.

The 1981 arrests evoked a strong reaction from the Albanian authorities, still led at the time by Enver Hoxha. Tensions were further raised by the explosion on May 24, 1981, of two small bombs outside the Yugoslavian embassy in Tirana, coinciding with Yugoslavia's "Youth Day" (formerly the late President Tito's official birthday), for which Albania rejected all responsibility with the counter-accusation that the explosions had been set up by Yugoslavia as a provocation.

In Yugoslavia, the 1981 disturbances led to a major reshaping of the political structures in Kosovo and in Serbia, in which many senior ethnic Albanians, and especially activists, were removed from office. The provincial Communist leader, Mahmut Bakali, the provincial president, Dzavid Nimani, and the provincial premier, Bahri Oruci, were all removed in 1981-82. Changes at lower level continued throughout the next five years, and another round of senior-level changes got under way in 1986; Fadil Hoxha, a prominent Albanian politician, failed to gain a nomination for any party office in either Kosovo or Belgrade, while those Albanians selected for election included such long-standing opponents of "irredentism" as Ali Sukrija, Sinan Hasani and Kolj Siroka.

These political measures failed, however, to defuse the growing mistrust and hostility between Serbs and Albanians in Kosovo. In October 1985, 2,000 prominent Serbs sent a petition to Belgrade demanding greater protection from what they complained was a rising tide of attacks by ethnic Albanians; moreover, in February 1986, 212 Serbian intellectuals in Belgrade issued a complaint describing Albanian policy in Kosovo as one of "genocide" against them. It was estimated in 1986 that as many as a third of the Serbs in the province had moved away since the onset of the 1981 disturbances.

The mid-1980s have seen a relative normalization of bilateral relations, as Albania has sought to improve its external links not only with Yugoslavia but also with Greece and Italy. Since the death in 1985 of Enver Hoxha, the hard-line leader of the Albanian Party of Labour (ALP), the Albanian authorities appear to have stepped back from the extreme positions of the late 1970s (when, for example, Hoxha was still demanding the overthrow of the Yugoslavian government). Although Albania still complains of "persecution and chauvinist violence" against Albanians in Yugoslavia, there have been indications on both sides of a wish to limit the damage, and Yugoslavia has come forward with a number of economic incentives to Albania, including preferential import arrangements and offers of finance for joint development projects.

MW

Austria-Italy (South Tyrol)

Since the end of World War I relations between Italy and Austria have been affected by the problem of the large proportion of native German speakers living in the northern part of the Italian region of South Tyrol (i.e. in the province of Bolzano, formerly known as Oberetsch and now part of the autonomous region of Trentino-Alto Adige). The territory was ceded to Italy by Austria in 1919 following Italy's intervention on the side of the Allies in World War I. Although Austria has raised no territorial claims as such on the province since 1946, it has gained the acknowledged right to oversee the treatment of the German speakers in the region and on many occasions has expressed strong concern at what was felt to be a serious threat to the German-speaking community and its language in the form of prejudicial treatment by successive Italian governments.

Map 2   The autonomous region of
Trentino-Alto Adige.

Austria has campaigned both in bilateral negotiations and within the United Nations for the establishment of a separate statute of autonomy for Bolzano province, in accordance with its interpretation of an agreement signed by the two countries in 1946. Italy for its part has maintained that the autonomy guaranteed by the agreement has in fact been fulfilled by the creation in 1948 of the autonomous region of Trentino-Alto Adige, which comprises the predominantly German-speaking province of Bolzano (334,000 inhabitants in 1948 and 432,073 in 1980) and the almost entirely (98 per cent) Italian-speaking province of Trento (394,000 inhabitants in 1948 and 444,176 in 1980). The latter lies directly to the south of Bolzano and was also ceded to Italy by Austria in 1919.

Regional and Demographic Characteristics

The province of Bolzano (740 sq km) is delineated in the north by the Italian Alpine border with Austria (including the Brenner Pass), in the south-east by the Dolomites and in the south-west by the Adige river valley; its southernmost point is near Salurn. The province is predominantly agricultural in character, though industry and commerce are developing rapidly in Bolzano and Merano. Trento province (621 sq km), apart from a strip running north-east along the southern edge of the Dolomites, centres on the middle reaches of the Adige, to the south of Bolzano province.

A census conducted in Bolzano province in October 1981 showed that the number of Italian speakers had fallen since 1971 by 3.9 per cent, while German speakers had increased by 3.4 per cent. Ladin speakers were found in the census to represent 4.2 per cent of the population, compared with 3.6 per cent in 1971. An earlier census of 1971 had shown strong regional discrepancies in the distribution of linguistic groups; whereas Italian speakers had represented only 5 per cent of the agricultural workforce, they had occupied 72 per cent of all posts in public administration, partly because of their generally higher standard of education but also because of the general pattern of employment in the public sector; currently the great majority live in the urban centres, more than two-thirds in Merano and Bolzano alone.

10

The region has benefited in the early 1980s from preferential treatment deliberately applied by central government, and especially from the arrival of new technology-oriented industries. Standards of living are high in comparison to other parts of Italy and the 1981 census revealed that the proportion of professional and executive people in the workforce was well above average. On the one hand, this relative prosperity has helped to defuse some of the worst complaints from the local German-speaking population, while on the other, the high level of immigration from southern Italy has made the economically inferior local Italian speakers particularly bitter about allegedly irredentist sentiments among German speakers.

The South Tyrol Question to 1946

Although most of the possessions of the Habsburg empire in northern Italy were incorporated into the unified Italian state established by 1870, the predominantly Italian-speaking region of Trento remained under Austrian control as part of the Tyrol, in which Habsburg rule dated back to the 14th century. Italian irredentist aspirations towards Trento (which had come under Austrian rule as recently as 1803) were clearly expressed by many Italians towards the end of the 19th century, supported by numerous nationalist groups in Trento itself.

At the outbreak of World War I, Italy declared itself neutral and negotiated briefly with Austria for the acquisition of the *terre irredente* in recognition of its neutrality; however, in a secret treaty signed in London on April 26, 1915, Italy agreed to enter the war on the side of the Allies, in return for which Great Britain, France and Russia offered the cession to Italy not only of Trento but also of the whole of southern Tyrol as far north as the Brenner Pass (as well as Trieste, Gorizia and Istria and part of Dalmatia). Consequently, on May 23, 1915, Italy declared war on Austria-Hungary and the following year also opened hostilities against Germany. In the major battle of Caporetto in 1917, the Italian army was routed by combined Austrian and German forces. An armistice was signed with Austria on Nov. 3, 1918, and in February 1919 the Italian government submitted to the Paris peace conference a memorandum claiming substantially the same territories which had been agreed under the Treaty of London; subsequently, in Article 27 of the Treaty of St Germain-en-Laye, signed on Sept. 10, 1919, Italy received, among other territories, the South Tyrol as far north as the Brenner Pass.

Austria protested strongly at the loss of South Tyrol, but immediately after its annexation by Italy in 1919, both the Italian monarchy and the commander of the army occupying the region gave assurances that the customs and language, the local institutions and the self-determination of the South Tyrol would be respected. Nonetheless, the province of Bolzano was immediately united with Trento to form the Italian province of Venezia Tridentina, and although the new province was in 1927 re-divided into the provinces of Bolzano and of Trento, the latter retained numerous lowland areas previously administered from Bolzano.

Particularly decisive in the development of the South Tyrol region was the advent to power of the Italian Fascists under Benito Mussolini in 1922. Mussolini embarked upon an intensive policy of "italianization" of the South Tyrol, in the course of which the Italian population of Bolzano province (which according to the 1921 census comprised only 20,000 of the total population of 243,000) grew steadily in numbers and in significance. The German-speaking communal administrative offices in Bolzano province were dissolved and were replaced by mayors brought in from other parts of Italy; German-speaking schools were abolished and even private German tuition banned; German ceased to be recognized as a legitimate medium for legal transactions; virtually all place names were changed and many families were obliged to "Italianize" their surnames; and the active policy of appointing Italians to public service posts was accompanied by an influx of Italian labour brought about by the expansion of industries in the province.

A major resettlement of German-speaking South Tyroleans occurred at the beginning of World War II as a result of the pact signed by Hitler and Mussolini in May 1939. An

11

agreement was published by the two powers on Oct. 21, 1939, relating to the "return of Germans of the Reich and emigration of ethnic Germans from the Alto Adige" and in effect obliging the Germans and Ladines of the South Tyrol to choose either German nationality (meaning compulsory resettlement in Germany or in Austria) or acceptance of Italian nationality (which in itself offered no effective guarantee of the right to remain in the province). Some 212,000 persons accepted the first option (although in fact only about 75,000 were moved, due to the disturbances caused by the war) and about 34,000 opted for Italy; of the Ladine population, about 45 per cent opted for Italy. Although after the war Italy offered the right of return to the resettled persons, only a relatively small proportion were thought to have accepted.

German troops occupied the South Tyrol in late 1943, receiving the general support of much of the population, many of whom collaborated in the handing over of fugitive Italian soldiers to the Nazi authorities. Germany made no attempt to annex the South Tyrol, however.

The Paris Agreement of 1946

Pressure for the return of the South Tyrol to Austria mounted again at the end of World War II. The Austrian Chancellor, Leopold Figl, was on April 22, 1946, presented with a petition bearing the signatures of 159,628 South Tyrolean citizens and calling for its return to Austria. Three days later the Austrian government submitted a memorandum to the member states of the United Nations reiterating Austria's claims to the South Tyrol. However, on April 30 a conference of Allied Foreign Ministers in Paris decided to make no major changes to the Italian-Austrian border—although it stated that applications for minor adjustments would be considered. An Austrian application was made on May 30 for the return of a border area, but a subsequent Foreign Ministers' conference in Paris rejected this request on June 24, 1946.

Austria's response to the failure of its applications to the Paris conference was to seek a bilateral agreement with Italy whereby it could argue on behalf of the South Tyrol for the achievement of autonomy for the region and for the protection of the German-speaking community. Consequently the Austrian Foreign Minister, Dr Karl Gruber, and the Italian Prime Minister, Alcide de Gasperi, signed an agreement in Paris on Sept. 5, 1946, relating to the province of Bolzano and to the lowland territories lost to Trento in 1927. The first two articles of the agreement read as follows:

"(1) German-speaking inhabitants of the Bolzano province and of the neighbouring bilingual townships of the Trento province will be assured a complete equality of rights with the Italian-speaking inhabitants within the framework of special provisions to safeguard the ethnical character and the cultural and economic development of the German-speaking element.

"In accordance with legislation already enacted or awaiting enactment, the said German-speaking citizens will be granted in particular: (a) elementary and secondary teaching in the mother tongue; (b) parification of the German and Italian languages in public offices and official documents as well as in bilingual topographic naming; (c) the right to re-establish German family names which were Italianized in recent years; [and] (d) equality of rights as regards the entering upon public offices with a view to reaching a more appropriate proportion of employment between the two ethnical groups.

"(2) The population of the above-mentioned zones will be granted the exercise of autonomous legislative and executive regional power. The frame within which the said provisions of autonomy will apply will be drafted in consultation also with local representative German-speaking elements".

Article 3 of the agreement contained a pledge by the Italian government to consult with the Austrian government within one year on the revision of the 1939 citizenship options, on the mutual recognition of academic qualifications, and on the facilitation of goods and passenger transit between the two countries.

The Gruber-de Gasperi agreement became Annex IV of the overall peace treaty signed between the Allies and Italy in Paris on Feb. 10, 1947, and was thus, in accordance with the stipulation of Article 85, to be considered an integral part of the treaty.

Autonomy Statute for Trentino-Alto Adige

On June 27, 1947, the Italian Legislative Assembly decided on the amalgamation of the provinces of Bolzano and Trento in order to create a single region. The autonomy statute for the new region of Trentino-Alto Adige was accordingly approved by the Assembly on Jan. 29, 1948, and came into effect on March 14, 1948. Under the new statute Bolzano province retrieved the lowland and border territories lost to Trento in 1927, but lost much of its legislative and executive authority to the newly-created joint Regional Council for Trentino-Alto Adige. Under the new arrangements, the Regional Council, which was to be returned by general election, would elect the regional government (regional committee) and would be presided over alternately by German and Italian speakers. The Regional Council deputies from Bolzano province would also comprise the Bolzano provincial assembly and would elect the Bolzano provincial government (a parallel arrangement being established in Trento province); the president of the Bolzano provincial assembly was to be elected for a term of two years and was to be alternately an Italian and a German speaker.

Over the following years the Austrian and Italian governments exchanged a series of memorandums relating to the new provisions in terms of the fulfilment of the Paris agreement. Austrian complaints centred on (i) the claim that the overall five-to-two predominance of Italian speakers in the region as a whole precluded the administrative autonomy which had been promised in Article 2 of the Paris agreement; (ii) the allegation that the effective equality of the German and Italian languages in public life, as provided in Articles 1 (b) and 1 (d), had not been adequately implemented in practice; and (iii) the fact that the Italian government had effective rights of veto over the decisions of the Bolzano provincial assembly and that it had imposed certain budgetary measures without consultation. The Italian government, while admitting to certain delays in implementation, maintained that the essential provisions relating to the autonomy of Bolzano province had been fulfilled by the new arrangements.

Particular resentment arose among the German speakers of Bolzano province over the decision of the Italian Council of Ministers, taken on Jan. 16, 1959, to implement a People's Housing Project in Bolzano. The project, which was expected to provide housing for some 20,000 people, was regarded with suspicion in Bolzano, where it was seen primarily as promoting the influx of Italian speakers. Following representations from the widely-supported South Tyrol People's Party (SVP), the Austrian government issued a statement which claimed that according to the provisions of the autonomy statute the decision on the project should have been left to the province of Bolzano.

Meanwhile, a series of explosions and other violent attacks perpetrated by right-wing extremists in South Tyrol caused repeated tensions between the Austrian and Italian governments. The attacks first occurred in late 1956 but continued throughout the 1960s and (to a lesser degree) also through the 1970s, being directed not merely at such material targets as electricity pylons but also at Italian soldiers, border guards and other personnel. In the first Milan trial of persons accused of such attacks, 46 of the 94 defendants were on July 17, 1964, sentenced to prison terms of up to $25\frac{1}{2}$ years (the heaviest sentences being passed against Austrians tried in absentia); in the second and third Milan trials held in 1966 and 1969 respectively, and in a Bologna trial held in 1969, some 80 other defendants were tried, many also in absentia, receiving prison sentences of up to 30 years.

In Austria, however, a court in Graz raised strong Italian protests by its acquittal in October 1965 of 27 Austrians and West Germans accused of attacks in Italy (to which several had freely confessed). The Italian government repeatedly accused the Austrian authorities of aiding and protecting the extremists, and on July 11, 1961, following a particularly sharp exchange of notes, Italy introduced a visa requirement on all Austrians visiting Italy in view of Austria's alleged failure to stop the passage of explosives across the border. This requirement, which gave rise to strong protests from Austria, was lifted on Sept. 14, 1962.

Negotiations leading to 1969 Agreement on South Tyrol

In the period 1959-61 Austria made repeated representations to the United Nations concerning the alleged non-realization of the 1946 Paris agreement, and on Oct. 27, 1960, the UN General Assembly unanimously passed a resolution calling on Italy and Austria to seek a solution bilaterally or, failing this, to seek recourse to any peaceful means of their choice. (Italy had until this point maintained that the International Court of Justice was the only appropriate arbitrator in the dispute.)

In September 1961 the Italian government appointed a mixed "Commission of 19", comprising experts and politicians—some of whom were South Tyrol People's Party (SVP) deputies in the Italian Parliament—to study the problem of the South Tyrol. By 1963 its investigations had reached such a point that Austria and Italy decided to resume bilateral negotiations, and in May 1964, following the final report, the two countries set up a joint committee of experts. The package offered by Italy in December 1964, including extended powers for Bolzano and the creation of a special referee commission (later retracted), was rejected by Austria, however. Following prolonged negotiations a new package of legislation, backed up by a "calendar of operations", or fixed sequence of agreements and reforms, was devised and was published in the autumn of 1969. Although they did not fully satisfy the party's demands for full regional autonomy for Bolzano, these measures went sufficiently far to receive the SVP's approval at a party conference held on Nov. 22-23, 1969.

The new package of reforms provided essentially that, although Bolzano was to remain a province within the Trentino-Alto Adige region, it was to receive extensive additional powers including a number of capabilities previously exercised by the region or by the Italian state.

Economic powers guaranteed by the new package related to responsibilities in agriculture, trade, transport and the promotion of industry. The province was to receive a large degree of self-determination in cultural and educational matters, including a separate director of education to be nominated by the provincial government, and in German-language broadcasting. Detailed clauses also concerned the achievement of linguistic equality, and special provisions were made for the preservation of the rights of Ladines as well as Germans. The package also provided that the right to contest laws at the Italian Constitutional Court, previously held only by regions, should be extended to Bolzano, and that a special permanent commission was to be set up by the presidium of the Italian Council of Ministers to examine any further problems which might arise in the province.

The calendar of operations, which specified no fixed time-span but only a fixed sequence, was designed to offer all parties the maximum security in the realization of the package. Its main stages were as follows: (i) agreement on amendments to Article 27 of the European convention on the peaceful settlement of international conflicts and recognition of the rights of jurisdiction of the International Court of Justice in the dispute; (ii) alteration of the Italian Regolamento to permit inter alia changes in the use of the German and Italian languages; (iii) and (iv) government statements in Austria and Italy; (v) the establishment of an Italian commission to propose formulations for legislative and constitutional amendments; (vi) statements by both countries to the UN General Assembly; (vii)-(ix) the signature of agreement (i) above and its approval, together with constitutional amendments, by the Italian Parliament; (x) development by Italy of individual executive laws; (xi) declaration of the executive laws; (xii) publication of a decree on the transfer of powers to Bolzano; (xiii) concluding declaration by Austria within 50 days of the publication of the last executive law and an exchange of documents ratifying (i) above; (xiv)-(xvii) Italian acknowledgement of (xiii) and notifications of the end of the dispute to the United Nations, the International Court of Justice and the Council of Europe; and (xviii) signature of an Austrian-Italian treaty of co-operation.

By the end of 1969 the sequence had reached stage (v) of the above schedule; the agreement mentioned as (i) above was signed by Austria and Italy on July 17, 1971, and the Italian constitutional reforms came into effect on Oct. 27, 1971. The lengthy and complex process of stage (x) above was still in progress at the end of 1986, though by this date most of the envisaged laws had been agreed. Particular problems still outstanding were those relating to the equality of the German and Italian languages in courts of law, police activities and state administrative bodies. There had also been no definitive ruling on the financing of the bodies responsible for regional autonomy.

Both Austrian and local Italian politicians continued throughout the early 1980s to press their concern on the Italian authorities about the slow pace at which the 1969 autonomy package was being realized. Successive Italian governments followed the example of the 1980 government of Arnaldo Forlani in undertaking to expedite the negotiations; both Giovanni Spadolini and Amintore Fanfani, who headed successive governments in 1981-83, responded with promises to this effect, in response to renewed pressure from Dr Silvius Magnago (the leader of the SVP and head of the provincial government of Bolzano), and from such senior Austrian figures as Dr Fred Sinowatz, then Austrian Chancellor, and Dr Rudolf Kirchschläger, who served as President from 1974 to 1981.

In the first diplomatic action to be taken over the issue by Austria since 1969, the Austrian ambassador in Rome on March 11, 1981, delivered to the Italian Foreign Ministry an aide-mémoire pressing for the rapid realization of the autonomy statutes for the province. Meanwhile, terrorist attacks continued in the province, and in late 1981 a right-wing pressure group developed within the SVP in favour of a provincial referendum to decide the future of Alto Adige. Thereafter the issue seemed to lose some of its impetus during the years 1982-84, at a time when Austria and Italy were concentrating on developing their bilateral trade relations. However, interest revived in 1984, partly as a result of a visit to Austria by the Italian Socialist Prime Minister, Bettino Craxi—the first visit to Austria by an Italian premier for 103 years.

A new challenge to the 1969 package emerged during this period from the neo-fascist Italian Social Movement, which obtained an unexpectedly favourable result in the provincial elections of May 12-13, 1985. Campaigning on a nationalistic and anti-German platform, the party won 22.6 per cent of the vote in Bolzano and raised its representation on the provincial council from three to 11 seats. It then went on to demand formally the repeal of five provisions of the autonomy statute, of which the most important were the clause affirming the legal equality of the German and Italian languages in administrative circles, and the clause establishing a minimum proportion of German speakers in local state bodies. The Supreme Court in Rome, however, ruled later the same year that the disputed statutes should stand unaltered.

In a statement to the UN General Assembly on Sept. 30, 1986, the Austrian Foreign Minister, Dr Peter Jankowitsch, said that although Austria enjoyed friendly relations with Italy, the essential autonomy provisions of the 1969 agreement on South Tyrol still remained to be implemented. He added that this applied in particular to the "centre-piece" of autonomy, namely the use of the German language in courts and in police and civil proceedings, and that there was continuing justified concern among German-speaking South Tyroleans.

Tensions mounted in the South Tyrol region in the run-up to the 1987 Italian general elections (held on June 14-15), amid a series of bombing and shooting attacks on Italian targets in Bolzano and other towns. Whereas police inquiries in connexion with the attacks concentrated on German-speaking extremist groups, the SVP expressed the view that they had been organized as provocation by the neo-fascist Italian Social Movement (MSI) to activate its substantial existing support among the local Italian population.

MW

The Cyprus Question

Cyprus, the third largest island in the Mediterranean after Sardinia and Sicily, is situated in the eastern Mediterranean about 80 miles (130 km) west of Syria, 44 miles (80 km) south of the Turkish coast and some 500 miles (885 km) south-east of the Greek mainland. Having been a Greek island in terms of population and culture since ancient times, Cyprus was taken by the Ottoman Turks in the 1570s and remained under Turkish dominion for more than three centuries, during which it acquired a significant Moslem Turkish population. In the modern era the existence of the two distinct communities in the island, the one gravitating towards Greece and the other towards Turkey, has effectively precluded the establishment of agreed political and constitutional arrangements for Cyprus, which in consequence has proved a major source of strain in relations between the Athens and Ankara governments. Although Cyprus became an independent republic in 1960 after 82 years of British rule, intractable differences between the two communities have led in recent years to the effective division of the island into Greek and Turkish areas—a process consolidated by the intervention of Turkish military forces in 1974 and the proclamation the following year of a Turkish Cypriot Federated State (TCFS) in the northern part of the island. Since then inter-communal talks have been pursued periodically under United Nations auspices; however, although both sides support the principle of preserving Cyprus as an independent state, no resolution has yet been achieved of the complex political, constitutional, territorial and security issues which divide the two communities. In the absence of any such solution, the TCFS declared itself independent in November 1983 as the "Turkish Republic of Northern Cyprus", but received recognition only from Turkey. In the broader context, the Cyprus question represents a major current issue deriving from historical conflict between Greeks and Turks in the eastern Mediterranean region.[1]

The Cyprus question, which has become increasingly contentious since the late 1950s, revolves around a political conflict between the two major ethnic groups in the island, the Greek majority and the Turkish Moslem contingent (which at the time of the last reliable census in 1961 comprised 18 per cent of the population). Turkey has always rejected the term "minority" in respect of this group, claiming rather that it constitutes one of the two dominant and distinct communities on the island, and has assumed the role of protector of the Turkish Cypriots against what it regards as a danger of their being overridden by the Greek Cypriot majority; in particular, Turkey consistently opposed the concept of *enosis* (political union with Greece) traditionally espoused by many Greeks, on the grounds that its fulfilment would be to the serious disadvantage of the Turkish Cypriots.

The 1960 constitution, which came into effect upon the independence of the Republic of Cyprus, made various fundamental allowances for the preservation of the separate cultural and political identities of the two groups, and was initially felt to protect the interests of the Turkish community within the framework of a number of international guarantees and alliances. However, the predominantly Greek Cypriot government under Archbishop Makarios, the first President of Cyprus, soon expressed the view that the maintenance of certain of these distinctions was economically and administratively cumbersome, and adopted a number of steps for their removal. Fierce and often violent confrontations ensued between Greek and Turkish Cypriots, leading to the decision of the United Nations Security Council in 1964 to establish a peace-keeping force in Cyprus. The UN has since then played a

---

[1]For an account of the Greek-Turkish dispute in the Aegean Sea area, see pages 45-52.

16

central role in encouraging and organizing inter-communal debate between the two groups.

In July 1974 the government of President Makarios was overthrown by Greek officers of the Cyprus National Guard, and a strongly pro-*enosis* government was installed under President Nicos Sampson. Within five days Turkish troops had invaded Cyprus, whereupon a period of bitter fighting ensued at the end of which Turkish forces controlled a substantial area in the north of the island. A Turkish Cypriot Federated State was proclaimed in February 1975 and has since then administered the northern occupied area, although it is recognized neither by the official government of Cyprus nor by any other state except Turkey.

President Sampson resigned on July 23, 1974 (the day of the overthrow of the military regime in Greece), and Glafcos Clerides became acting President until Makarios resumed his presidential functions in December of that year; Makarios died in August 1977 and was succeeded as President by Spyros Kyprianou. Meaningful bilateral negotiations between the two communities were resumed in 1977 after the Greek Cypriots accepted in principle the Turkish Cypriot proposal that a bi-communal, federated state of Cyprus should be created rather than the unitary state provided for under the 1960 constitution.

Early Background to the Cyprus Issue

The historical existence of the two distinct communities in Cyprus derived in part from the economic importance of the island, its fertility and its location on eastern Mediterranean trading routes, but more significantly from its strategic importance as a base for military

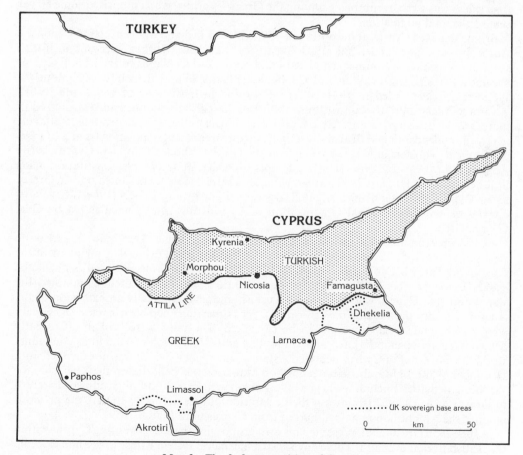

Map 3   The de facto partition of Cyprus.

operations in the Middle East region. These factors explain why Cyprus has been ruled by a succession of foreign powers throughout much of recorded history, which in turn has exposed the island to a continuous series of cultural influences from outside.

The Greek language is believed to have been brought to Cyprus between 1500 and 1200 BC, when first Mycenean and then Achean merchants began to establish themselves. In the fourth century BC Cyprus became part of the empire of Alexander the Great, on whose death it passed to the dominion of the Ptomelaic kings of Egypt. In the first century BC the island was annexed by the Romans, and by the fourth century AD it had become part of the Eastern Roman (Byzantine) empire. Richard I (Coeur de Lion) of England conquered Cyprus during the Crusades in 1191 and used it as a Mediterranean strategic base; it then passed to the dispossessed King of Jerusalem, who ran it as a feudal monarchy. In the early 14th century Cyprus formed an alliance with the Papacy against the Turks, and by the 15th century first the Genoese and then the Venetians had enjoyed periods of possession. The Ottoman Turks conquered Cyprus in 1570-71, however, and the island then remained under Turkish rule for more than three centuries.

The Moslem Turks were at first relatively generous to the Christians, giving them a wide degree of autonomy and restoring the Greek Orthodox archbishopric. However, as the Ottoman empire declined in the 18th and 19th centuries its rule became increasingly oppressive, and a series of revolts took place among the Greek-speaking population, the most important being that of 1821. At the 1878 Congress of Berlin it was agreed that Britain should take over the administration of Cyprus under continued Turkish sovereignty, in return for a British pledge of support for Turkey against any aggression from Russia. By this time *enosis* was a recurrent theme among the Greek Cypriots, who comprised some 80 per cent of the total population.

Britain annexed Cyprus at the outbreak of World War I when Turkey declared war on the Allied powers, and under the 1923 Treaty of Lausanne Turkey recognized British sovereignty as having commenced in 1914 and renounced its claims to the island. Cyprus became a British Crown Colony in 1925, but a rising tide of anti-British feeling among the supporters of *enosis* led in 1931 to serious rioting in the course of which the British government suspended the constitution, abolished the legislative council and transferred all powers to the British governor. After World War II British efforts to restore democratic rule in Cyprus under continued British sovereignty met with constant opposition from the Greek government (who demanded *enosis*) and from the Greek Orthodox Church in Cyprus, led by Archbishop Makarios; consequently attempts to devise an acceptable constitution made little headway until the late 1950s. Meanwhile, anti-British violence mounted both in Greece and in Cyprus, the latter being instigated largely by the pro-*enosis* EOKA (*Ethniki Organosis Kypriakon Agonos*—National Organization of Cypriot Struggle) guerrillas led by Gen. George Grivas.

At a tripartite meeting called in London in late August 1955 and attended by representatives from Greece, Turkey and the United Kingdom (as well as members of the Greek and Turkish Cypriot communities), Archbishop Makarios repeated his calls for *enosis*. However, the Turkish Cypriot representative, Dr Fazil Kütchük, adopted the standpoint that Cyprus was historically Turkish and geographically an extension of the Anatolian peninsula, and that the "so-called Cyprus question" had been invented by Greeks who, he contended, had no right to be consulted. The talks were broken off in early September and two months later, amid mounting anti-British violence and inter-communal strife, the Governor of Cyprus declared a state of emergency (which was not revoked until December 1959). In March 1956 Archbishop Makarios was deported to the Seychelles for "seditious activities" including alleged involvement with EOKA; although allowed to return to Greece in April 1957 (following the declaration of a ceasefire by EOKA the previous month), the Archbishop remained barred from Cyprus until March 1959.

In June 1956 Dr Kütchük presented his own proposals for a self-governing Cyprus within the British Commonwealth. These envisaged a bicameral system whose lower house would comprise one elected member for every 10,000 of the electorate (giving Greek Cypriots an effective 4-1 majority over Turkish Cypriots) and whose upper house, with powers of veto over lower house decisions, would comprise eight Greek Cypriot and eight Turkish Cypriot members. By mid-1957, however, he had adopted the view of the Turkish government that partition of the island between Greece and Turkey (*taksim*) was the only viable solution to the problem. In June 1958, as Turkish Cypriot riots broke out in Nicosia and Larnaca, some 200,000 people demonstrated in Istanbul for *taksim*. Meanwhile, EOKA had resumed its attacks in the autumn of 1957, these provoking the formation of a Turkish Cypriot resistance movement called TMT.

Formulation of the 1960 Constitution

As the hostilities in Cyprus mounted the United Nations adopted a resolution on Dec. 5, 1958, expressing its confidence that all involved parties would reach "a peaceful, democratic and just solution in accordance with the UN Charter". After Greece and Turkey had on Feb. 11, 1959, concluded the "Zürich agreement" on the structure of an independent Cyprus, a trilateral conference in London later in the month (also attended by Greek and Turkish Cypriot representatives) resulted in the initialling on Feb. 19, 1959, of an agreement which formed the basis of the Cypriot constitution of 1960. However, this outcome produced a bitter dispute, never completely resolved, between Archbishop Makarios and Gen. Grivas, the latter accusing the former of making unnecessary and secret verbal concessions to the other parties at the London meeting. The London agreement was ratified on Feb. 28, 1959, by the Greek Parliament and on March 4 by the Turkish Parliament.

The constitution subsequently drafted came into effect on Aug. 16, 1960—the day on which Cyprus became independent. It stipulated that the Republic of Cyprus would be presided over by a Greek Cypriot President and a Turkish Cypriot Vice-President, each of whom would have certain rights of veto over laws relating to foreign affairs, defence or security. The President would nominate a fixed contingent of seven Greek Cypriot Ministers to the Council of Ministers (the chief executive organ) and the Vice-President three Turkish Cypriot Ministers. In general elections the Greek and Turkish Cypriot communities were to vote separately in divided municipalities, the former electing 35 deputies to the House of Representatives and the latter 15. Any modification of the electoral law, or the adoption of any law pertaining to the separate electoral municipalities or to certain areas of financial legislation, would require the approval of simple majorities of both the Greek and the Turkish Cypriot contingents of the House—a situation which made it difficult to raise the necessary majorities on sensitive issues. The Supreme Constitutional Court and the High Court of Justice were to be presided over by a neutral president, the constitution providing that Turkish Cypriot judges should try cases involving only Turkish Cypriots, that Greek Cypriots should try Greek Cypriot cases and that mixed courts should try cases involving both communities. Although the Turkish Cypriot community at this time constituted only 18 per cent of the population it was guaranteed 30 per cent of all civil service posts and 40 per cent of army and police force positions.

Under a Treaty of Guarantee initialled in London by Cyprus, Turkey, Greece and the United Kingdom in February 1959, any or all of the three latter parties retained certain rights of political intervention for the purpose of restoring the conditions specified by the London agreement, if they were deemed to be endangered. A Treaty of Alliance, also initialled in London in February 1959 and signed in 1960 by Greece, Turkey and Cyprus, provided for the maintenance of limited contingents of Turkish and Greek troops in Cyprus. The United Kingdom also negotiated its retention of sovereignty—which it still maintains—over two military bases totalling 99 square miles (256 sq km) at Akrotiri (south-western coast) and Dhekelia (south-eastern coast).

On Dec. 13, 1959, Archbishop Makarios was elected as the first President of Cyprus and Dr Kütchük as Vice-President. Cyprus joined the United Nations on Aug. 24, 1960, and became a member of the British Commonwealth on Sept. 20, 1960. The Maronite, Roman Catholic and Armenian communities of Cyprus, who between them comprised some 5 per cent of the population, voted on Nov. 13, 1960, in favour of association with the Greek majority for constitutional purposes.

Constitutional Crises and the Turkish Involvement of 1964

Despite the specific recommendations made by the 1960 constitution in relation to the respective rights of the Greek and Turkish Cypriot populations, a series of differences arose during 1961 and 1962 over their interpretation, leading to a constitutional crisis and to fullscale inter-communal hostilities in which, it was claimed, the Turkish armed forces were involved. The situation was eventually contained by the installation in March 1964 of a United Nations peace-keeping force in Cyprus (UNFICYP).

The first dispute arose in March 1961 over a Greek Cypriot bill which the Turkish Cypriots feared would erode certain community rights embodied in the tax system; the Turkish Cypriot deputies in the House of Representatives used their veto to block the passage of the bill, and for two years the tax situation remained very uncertain. The second and more significant dispute arose over the maintenance of separate Greek and Turkish Cypriot communities. The government proposed, despite the strong opposition of its Turkish Cypriot members (i) to replace the segregated National Guard units with mixed ones under a Greek Cypriot commander, (ii) to remove the provision guaranteeing Turkish Cypriots 30 per cent of administrative positions in local government, and (iii) to dissolve the divided municipalities in the five largest towns (Nicosia, Limassol, Larnaca, Famagusta and Paphos), replacing them with "improvement boards" appointed directly by the government under a 1950 law passed under British rule.

In opposition to this third and most controversial proposal, the Turkish Communal Chamber on Dec. 29, 1962, approved a bill to preserve the five divided municipalities and to create one more, whereupon President Makarios rejected the decision as "legally non-existent" and issued a decree abolishing the municipalities as from Jan. 1, 1963. The House of Representatives (the Turkish members being absent) approved on Jan. 2, 1963, a bill installing the "improvement boards", and although the Supreme Constitutional Court subsequently rejected this move it caused deep resentment among Turkish Cypriots. On Nov. 30, 1963, President Makarios made 13 proposals for constitutional reform aimed especially at the removal of communal distinctions, including the removal of the presidential and vice-presidential veto, changes in the functions of the Vice-President and a reduction in the proportion of administrative positions allocated to Turkish Cypriots. However, the latter, supported by the Turkish government, rejected the proposals as endangering the preservation of their rights, and in December 1963 the Turkish Cypriot Ministers and parliamentary deputies boycotted sessions of their respective bodies, to which they have never returned.

Serious inter-communal fighting broke out in late 1963, and despite the efforts of all sides to establish a permanent ceasefire it continued periodically throughout most of 1964. Turkish naval units were reported to have left Istanbul during December 1963 for the eastern Mediterranean, giving rise to complaints from Greek Cypriots that a Turkish invasion was imminent. Meanwhile, part of the Turkish Army contingent in Cyprus took up a position outside Nicosia, so as to command the strategically important road linking Nicosia with Kyrenia, the only major port on the north coast of Cyprus. After the Greek and Cypriot governments had rejected a UK-US proposal that a NATO peace-keeping force should be installed on the island, on March 4, 1964, the United Nations Security Council decided to establish a UN force (UNFICYP) in Cyprus. Initially introduced for a three-month period, its mandate was thereafter repeatedly renewed, and at the end of 1986 2,500 UN troops were still present on the island. On April 27, 1964, the then UN Secretary-General, U Thant, also appointed a special representative for Cyprus to oversee and report on the situation.

On the arrival of the UN force in late March 1964, President Makarios asked the Turkish government to withdraw its troops from the Nicosia-Kyrenia road; Turkey replied that its troops were overseeing the restoration of order, whereupon Cyprus unilaterally terminated the 1959 Treaty of Alliance (a step which Turkey refused to recognize). Despite the presence of the UN force the inter-communal fighting continued, and on Aug. 9 the Turkish Air Force bombed Greek Cypriot targets in north-western Cyprus. A ceasefire was declared the next day in accordance with a resolution passed by the UN Security Council, to which Turkey protested concerning the alleged reduction of Turkish Cypriots to "ghetto" conditions by the Greek Cypriot imposition of economic sanctions. The sanctions had been applied particularly to the Turkish Cypriot-controlled villages of Kokkina and Mansoura in north-western Cyprus following Greek Cypriot allegations that they were being used for clandestine landings of Turkish troops and equipment, and had led to acute shortages of food in the area. The blockade was eased on Aug. 18, however, following the intervention of UNFICYP and the International Red Cross.

Turkey at this time claimed that Greece was maintaining some 10,000 troops in Cyprus compared with the 950 specified by the Zürich and London agreements, but it was itself believed to have marginally exceeded its own quota of 650. A further confrontation arose in this connexion during August 1964, when Cyprus refused to allow the regular rotation of one-third of the Turkish contingent of troops on the island, claiming that it had the right to do so in view of its unilateral abrogation of the Treaty of Alliance. The issue was eventually settled, however, and control of the Nicosia-Kyrenia road was handed over to UNFICYP.

Meanwhile Dean Acheson, Secretary of State in the Truman Administration, had proposed in Geneva in July 1964 an arrangement whereby Cyprus was to be allowed union with Greece in return for concessions including (i) the creation of rented areas (amounting to 50 sq km) in north-eastern Cyprus, which were to be used for Turkish military bases and refugee areas; (ii) the cession to Turkey of the small Greek island of Castellorizo, close to the Anatolian coast; (iii) the placing of two of the six districts under Turkish Cypriot administration; and (iv) the creation of a central body under an international commissioner to protect Turkish rights. The Turkish government approved of these measures despite its demand for ownership, not merely tenancy, of the military areas, whereas the Greek Cypriots rejected them as "a betrayal of the whole of Hellenism". Turkey responded to the Greek and Greek Cypriot positions with an escalation of anti-Greek and anti-British feeling, and during 1964 many thousands of ethnic Greeks were expelled from Turkey (particularly from Istanbul and Izmir) under the pretext of alleged espionage or other subversive activities.

Establishment of Turkish Cypriot Autonomous Administration

Despite the stabilization of the internal security situation in late 1964, no real progress was achieved over the next six years in bilateral communal talks which were embarked upon by the two communities. In June 1965 the Cypriot House of Representatives (still without its 15 Turkish Cypriot deputies) unanimously passed bills (i) extending for one year the five-year term of President Makarios in view of the alleged impossibility of conducting proper elections (this exercise being repeated annually until 1968); and (ii) abolishing the separate electoral registration of Greek and Turkish Cypriot voters. It was also announced that Dr Kütchük's post as Vice-President was regarded as having lapsed in view of his continued absence, and that the three Turkish Cypriot Ministers (also absent) had been replaced by Greek Cypriots. Turkish and British protests at these moves were rejected by Cyprus, which told the UN Security Council on Aug. 3-10, 1965, that they represented an interference in its internal affairs.

Initiatives adopted by the United States and the UN led in December 1967 to an undertaking by the Greek and Turkish governments to withdraw from Cyprus all troops in excess of the contingents permitted in the 1959 agreements. This withdrawal was said to have been completed by mid-January 1968, but towards the end of that year the deadlock intensified when Turkish Cypriot leaders announced on Dec. 29 the setting up of a "Turkish Cypriot Autonomous Administration" to run Turkish Cypriot affairs "until such time as the provisions of the 1960 constitution have been fully implemented". A set of 19 "basic laws" on executive, judicial and legislative matters received the support of the Turkish government, and Dr Kütchük was appointed President of the Autonomous Administration and Rauf Denktash as its Vice-President. (Denktash, a former president of the Turkish Communal Chamber, had returned to Cyprus in April 1968 following two periods of exile in Turkey dating back to 1964.) The new administration also set up a Legislative Assembly comprising the Turkish deputies of the House of Representatives and the members of the Turkish Communal Chamber, and established a nine-member Executive Council (i.e. Cabinet). President Makarios described the new Turkish Cypriot administration as "totally illegal", and warned foreign diplomats against attempting to contact it (though this ban was lifted on Dec. 31, 1968). U Thant expressed his misgivings that it could harm relations in Cyprus, but Dr Kütchük claimed that it was non-political, purely administrative and fully constitutional.

Elections for the 35 Greek Cypriot seats to the House of Representatives were held on July 5, 1970 (for the first time since 1960), and passed off quietly; on the same day the Turkish community held elections for its 15 House of Representatives mandates and its 15 Communal Chamber seats. Following the unopposed return of President Makarios as President of the Republic on Feb. 8, 1973, Rauf Denktash was on Feb. 16 declared elected by the Turkish Cypriots as Vice-President in succession to Dr Kütchük. The two leaders were separately inaugurated on Feb. 28, Denktash at an unofficial ceremony held in the Turkish quarter of Nicosia.

Overthrow of President Makarios and Turkish Invasion of 1974

On July 15, 1974, President Makarios was overthrown by a military coup led by officers of the Cypriot National Guard; he fled to Malta, subsequently arriving in the United Kingdom and the United States. For some years the President had faced growing opposition among Greek Cypriots, not only from Gen. Grivas (until his death in January 1974) but also from the National Guard (accused by him of involvement with the EOKA-B movement). He had, moreover, come into conflict with the three Greek Orthodox bishops of Paphos, Kyrenia and Kirium, who objected to his simultaneous functions as Archbishop and President and who had tried to vote him out of his religious office, only to be defrocked at his instigation in July 1973. The President had apparently also survived a number of assassination attempts by extreme supporters of *enosis* since 1960.

Nicos Sampson, the leader of the Progressive Party and a former EOKA leader, was sworn in on July 15 as the new President of the Republic, and the following day formed a government of *enosis* supporters. He immediately announced that the new government would honour all international agreements, continue to strive for an inter-communal solution to the problems of Cyprus and pursue the goal of independence, adding that there was thus no justification for Turkish intervention. Meanwhile, however, a conference was held in London on July 16 at which the then Turkish Prime Minister, Bülent Ecevit, claimed that the Greek government had landed troops on Cyprus—an action which, he said, was tantamount to an invasion by Greece—and announced that "we cannot tolerate a government which has no legal basis".

At an emergency session of the UN Security Council on July 16, Zenon Rossides (the Cyprus permanent representative to the UN) urged "appropriate measures to protect the independence, sovereignty and territorial integrity of Cyprus", while the Greek permanent representative, Emmanuel Megolokonomos, described the matter as purely internal and denied that his government was involved. On the other hand, Osman Olcay (Turkey) claimed that what he called the Greek intervention violated the agreements guaranteeing the independence of Cyprus, and stressed Turkey's obligations to protect the interests of the Turkish Cypriot contingent. President Makarios told the Security Council on July 19 that there had been "an invasion which violated the independence and sovereignty of the Republic", and urged the Security Council to "call on the military regime of Greece to withdraw from Cyprus the Greek officers serving in the National Guard and to put an end to the invasion".

Acting in what Turkey described as its capacity as a guarantor of Cyprus, an armed invasion force of Turkish troops landed near Kyrenia at dawn on July 20, 1974, and engaged immediately in heavy fighting with the Greek Cypriot National Guard for control of the port of Kyrenia. By July 22, when the first ceasefire was declared on the recommendation of the UN Security Council, Turkey had gained control of the entire region surrounding the Kyrenia-Nicosia road as well as a large part of Nicosia itself, which had been taken by paratroopers dropped into the Turkish Cypriot quarter of the city. Between 30,000 and 40,000 Turkish troops were thought to have been involved in the invasion.

The UN Security Council again held an emergency session on July 20, this time to discuss the Turkish invasion, and adopted on the same day a resolution calling on all states to respect the sovereignty, independence and territorial integrity of Cyprus while also urging (i) the declaration of a ceasefire by all parties, (ii) the immediate cessation of foreign military intervention in the Republic and (iii) the withdrawal of all invasion forces, as well as of 650 Greek officers of the Cypriot National Guard (whom President Makarios had accused of plotting his overthrow). Greece, Turkey and the United Kingdom were urged to begin negotiations for the restoration of peace in the area, and a ceasefire was agreed for July 22.

The peace talks were opened in Geneva on July 25, 1974, under the chairmanship of James Callaghan, then British Foreign and Commonwealth Secretary. By July 30 a ceasefire line was agreed, a security zone proclaimed, an exchange of prisoners provided for, the evacuation of Greek Cypriot or Greek forces from Turkish Cypriot enclaves agreed and the convening of a second round of talks initiated. By Aug. 9, when the ceasefire line agreement was signed, the Turks had extended their area of control to the east and west of the Nicosia-Kyrenia road and had more than doubled the extent of the Turkish-controlled coastline.

Meanwhile, following the fall of the military regime in Greece on July 23, Nicos Sampson resigned on that day as President of Cyprus and, in the absence of President Makarios, was replaced by Glafcos Clerides, the Speaker of the Cypriot House of Representatives who had conducted the inter-communal talks with the Turkish Cypriots. On Aug. 8 acting President Clerides appointed a new Cabinet of moderates and liberals.

The second phase of the Geneva talks opened on Aug. 8, but broke down on Aug. 14 following disagreements between Greece, Turkey and Cyprus. It was understood that Denktash had rejected a proposal for a federal system giving a large degree of autonomy to Turkish Cypriots and had proposed instead the creation of an autonomous Turkish Cypriot region in the north of the island, occupying about 34 per cent of the total area of Cyprus. Turkey had proposed a compromise plan which gave the Turkish Cypriots half of the northern part of the island as well as pockets of autonomous territory in other parts of the island, but rejected the requests of Greek and Greek Cypriot representatives for time to discuss the proposals with their respective governments. Two hours after the breakdown of the talks a new Turkish offensive was launched, and by Aug. 16, when a new ceasefire was declared, Turkey controlled 37.6 per cent of the territory of Cyprus, including most of the northern and eastern coastline. The UN Security Council, which had repeatedly deplored the resumption of hostilities, adopted a resolution on Aug. 16 calling on both sides to resume the Geneva peace talks without delay.

Economic, Demographic and Human Consequences of Island's Division

In 1975 the (Greek Cypriot) government of Cyprus published material claiming that the geographical area controlled by the Turks accounted for 65 per cent of the country's tourist accommodation capacity and 87 per cent of hotel beds then under construction, 83 per cent of the general cargo handling capacity (i.e. mainly the port of Famagusta), 56 per cent of the mining and quarrying output, 41 per cent of the livestock production, 48 per cent of agricultural exports and 46 per cent of the total plant production. On the basis of such statistics, Turkey was claimed to be in control of some 70 per cent of the overall gross output of Cyprus.

Since 1974 the Cypriot government has repeatedly claimed that quite apart from refugee migration the demographic pattern of northern Cyprus is being changed by a deliberate Turkish policy of colonization, involving the immigration of large numbers of Turkish families from the Turkish mainland, their registration on arrival as Cypriots and offers of financial assistance. Figures published by the Public Information Office in Nicosia suggest that some 27,000 such Turkish settlers had arrived by late January 1976 and that in 1987 the number was stable at about 60,000. Fears were expressed, however, that as many as 100,000 settlers might eventually arrive, and that the Turkish Cypriots could lose their Cypriot identity and come to regard themselves as Turks. Figures published by the UN on Aug. 29, 1974, showed that 225,600 of the approximately 650,000 inhabitants of Cyprus were at that time classified as displaced, having lost their homes either through military attack or through forced flight to other zones of Cyprus.

On May 16, 1983, it was announced that the Turkish lira would replace the Cyprus pound as the main currency in the Turkish sector of Cyprus.

Proclamation of the Turkish Cypriot Federated State and Subsequent Greek-Turkish Talks

The transitional Turkish Cypriot Autonomous Administration announced on Feb. 13, 1975, that it supported the formation of a "Federal Republic of Cyprus", which was to be a "bi-regional federation" of the two Cypriot communities; it added that, in order to pursue such a federation, it had restructured itself into "a secular and federated state" in the north of the island, to be known as the Turkish Cypriot Federated State. Rauf Denktash was appointed President of the new state, being confirmed in this office in elections held on June 20, 1975, in which his National Unity Party won 30 of the 40 seats in the newly-formed Constituent Assembly. On Feb. 13 the Greek side was sent the new administration's proposals for a bi-communal and bi-regional federated state in which the state itself would be vested "only with the powers necessary for the establishment of the federation, so as to enable the state to function effectively", while "all power" was to be vested in the federated states. The proposals also maintained that the 1959 international treaties of guarantee should remain in force after the formation of the new state.

Archbishop Makarios, who had meanwhile returned in December 1974 to resume the presidency, attempted from 1975 onwards to restart the negotiations with the Turkish Cypriots. Five rounds of talks were held in Vienna between April 1975 and Feb. 1976, but they foundered over the Greek Cypriot insistence that Cyprus should be indivisible, and that foreign troops should withdraw without delay. The deadlock started to loosen in January 1977, when Denktash and Makarios met on the proposal of the UN Secretary-General's special representative for Cyprus, agreeing on Jan. 27 to continue the inter-communal talks. The two subsequently announced on Feb. 13 their agreement on a set of guidelines envisaging the formation of an independent, bi-communal, non-aligned federal republic in which the central government would hold only such powers as required to safeguard the unity of the state. UN Secretary-General Kurt Waldheim, who attended the February talks, applauded the guidelines as a first sign of a willingness to discuss substantive issues such as the size of the areas to be administered by the respective regional bodies.

The new series of talks began in Vienna on March 31, 1977, when the Greek Cypriots published proposals accepting the principle of the bi-communal state, and when they presented a map offering 20 per cent of the total area of Cyprus to the Turkish Cypriots. However, the talks broke down over the issue of Varosha, a largely Greek Cypriot area of Famagusta whose original population (which had largely fled) should, Turkish Cypriots argued, be subject to the administration of the Turkish Cypriot Federated State on their return. The Turkish Cypriots for their part presented proposals based on partition, and offered a minor reduction of the area to be occupied by Turkish troops. This being unacceptable to the Greek Cypriot side, negotiations remained once again stalled for a period of more than two years.

On May 18-19, 1979, however, President Spyros Kyprianou (who had succeeded President

Makarios on the latter's death in August 1977) met Denktash and the two reached agreement on a 10-point programme for the resumption of negotiations which were to give priority to the resettlement of Varosha under UN auspices and to the intensive consideration of a permanent settlement on this area. The programme also defined as its basis the Makarios-Denktash guidelines of February 1977, and envisaged the demilitarization of Cyprus. Talks were resumed on June 15-22, 1979, and have continued at intervals since then, although so far without result on any of the substantive issues.

Declaration of Independent Turkish Republic of Northern Cyprus

Legislative elections were held in June 1981 in the Turkish Federated State of Cyprus (as it described itself), when the National Unity Party formed a government headed by Mustafa Catagay. On Nov. 15, 1983, the new legislature unanimously approved the formation of a "Turkish Republic of Northern Cyprus" (TRNC). The proclamation of independence "before the world and before history" accused the Greek Cypriot administration of deliberately blocking the negotiations. Referring to the May 1983 resolution of the UN General Assembly, in which the UN had called for the withdrawal of all foreign troops, it accused Nicosia of "taking the Cyprus problem to international forums where the Turkish Cypriot people had no opportunity of being heard". The proclamation declared the Turkish side's conviction "that these two peoples, who are destined to coexist side by side in the island, can and must find peaceful, just and durable solutions to all the differences between them, through negotiations on the basis of equality". It also stated its expectation that the declaration of independence would "facilitate the re-establishment of the partnership between the two peoples within a federal framework and [would] also facilitate the settlement of the problems between them".

President Kyprianou accused Denktash, however, of attempting to proceed by fait accompli, in order to promote Turkish expansionist plans and to use Turkish troops for introducing an illegal partition. The British government called the decision tantamount to an act of secession; Turkey, the only state to recognize the TRNC, made it plain that it would rather have seen a just and lasting solution arrived at through the inter-communal talks, instead of by a declaration of independence. The Turkish Cypriot line at the ensuing UN discussions was that the 1960 treaties had been made unworkable for the north of the island because of years of dilution of Turkish Cypriot rights by Greek Cypriots in Nicosia. Nonetheless, the UN Security Council declared on Nov. 18, 1983, that the declaration of the Turkish Cypriot state was invalid and incompatible with the 1960 treaties of establishment and guarantee.

Denktash meanwhile continued his efforts to obtain wider international recognition of the TRNC, but without success. In the mid-1980s, he has accused the United States of pressurizing potential sympathizers among the Moslem states of the Middle East not to recognize his state.

Immediately after the proclamation of the TRNC in November 1983, a new Turkish Cypriot government was sworn in under the leadership of Nejat Konuk, the Prime Minister of the Turkish Cypriot Federated State from 1976 to 1978. On Dec. 2 a 70-member Constituent Assembly was formed from the existing 40 parliamentary representatives and 30 other persons, of whom Denktash nominated 10. A draft constitution was accordingly drafted and was published in May 1984, and it was approved by a referendum held in the Turkish zone on May 5, 1985. A presidential election followed on June 9, in which Denktash won 70.5 per cent of the vote, and elections to the new 50-member Parliament produced a coalition government comprising his own National Unity Party and the left-wing Communal Liberation Party (TKP).

Failure of 1985 Summit and Subsequent Developments

The early 1980s were marked on both sides by a hardening of attitudes to the question of communal reform. On the one hand, strongly nationalist attitudes were expressed by the military administration which ruled in Turkey between 1980 and 1983 (and which described northern Cyprus in 1980, for example, as "the daughter of our motherland ... an integral part of Turkey"). On the other, Greek Cypriot negotiators refused, on the whole, even to sit in the same room as their Turkish Cypriot counterparts, for fear of being seen to have implicitly accepted their legitimacy. Such fears and tensions contributed to the failure in 1981 of a series of inter-communal talks which were initiated by Javier Pérez de Cuellar, the UN Secretary-General, in pursuit of efforts by his special representative in Cyprus, Hugo Gobbi. Although the two sides succeeded in 1980 in opening discussions (i) on the resettlement of Varosha, (ii) on "initial practical measures to promote goodwill, mutual confidence and the return to normal conditions", and (iii) on constitutional and territorial aspects, they faltered fairly quickly and came to an abrupt stop after the declaration of independence in the north. The UN was pressing at this time, regardless of any other disputed issues, for the re-opening of the airport at Nicosia, and for a settlement of the Varosha issue under UN auspices, which it saw as a special priority.

The period following the 1981 breakdown did, however, give increasing credibility on the Greek Cypriot side to the UN Secretary-General's support for a "bizonal" solution, in which Cyprus would become a federation of two relatively autonomous states. A new initiative was launched in late 1984, in which the Secretary-General started a series of bilateral discussions with each of the two sides (the so-called "proximity talks"); by the third round, the Turkish Cypriots had abandoned their insistence on an alternating Greek Cypriot/Turkish Cypriot presidency for the proposed unified state, and they had offered to reduce their territorial hold to 29 per cent, for the sake of what they maintained was a draft agreement on substantive issues.

While the "proximity talks" clearly gave a propaganda advantage to the apparently more flexible Turkish Cypriot side, the resulting summit conference between Presidents Denktash and Kyprianou on Jan. 17-20, 1985, showed that little had changed on either side. Kyprianou refused at once to recognize the UN Secretary-General's draft as implying any kind of draft agreement (a move for which he was then bitterly attacked by other Greek Cypriot bodies), and the talks ended among mutual recriminations against Pérez de Cuellar himself. In mid-1985 the Greek Cypriot government issued a statement saying it was "now obvious that our disagreement with the UN Secretary-General is substantive and not procedural". Meanwhile, Pérez de Cuellar had told the UN Security Council that the Greek Cypriot rejection of his latest draft for a federal solution had created a "dangerous" situation.

In January 1986 the Soviet Union floated a proposal for the withdrawal of "all foreign troops and bases"—meaning Turkish, UN and British forces—and for a large-scale international conference to negotiate a settlement. Any settlement, it maintained, could be guaranteed by the USSR, USA and certain non-aligned countries. But while the Cypriot side approved the idea, it was evident that Turkish Cypriot opposition made it improbable for the foreseeable future.

Early in 1987 (with attempts to revive talks still blocked), tensions in Cyprus rose amid reports that Turkey had increased its military presence by 25 per cent in 1986 to a total of some 36,000 men and had deployed new offensive weapons in the north of the island. However, Turkish Cypriot spokesmen maintained that there were only 20,000 Turkish troops on the island and that this level was necessary as "a deterrent against upsetting the status quo of peace"; they added that the allegations of increased Turkish forces were a "smokescreen" to divert attention from the recent equipment of the Greek Cypriot National Guard (numbering 12,000) with new anti-tank missiles and armoured troop carriers.

MW

Finland-Sweden (Aaland Islands)

Situated at the entrance to the Gulf of Bothnia (between Finland and Sweden), the Aaland Islands (with a Swedish-speaking population of some 23,000) were part of Sweden until 1809 and have been part of Finland since then. Although the islands have not been a cause of dispute between the governments of Finland and Sweden since a 1921 League of Nations decision maintained their status quo as part of Finland, there has been continued dissatisfaction with this decision among the inhabitants of the islands, of whom a majority decided, both during World War I and at the end of World War II, to ask for the islands' return to Sweden. However, their 1945 request was not supported by the Swedish government and has not been met. The issue is of special significance because of the League of Nations decision in favour of the maintenance of the frontiers of an existing state against the expressed wishes of a minority in part of that state. The Finnish name of the islands is Ahvenanmaa.

Historical Background

The Aaland Islands were part of Sweden until 1809, when they were seized by Russia and joined with Finland (which had also been Swedish territory); Finland then became a partially autonomous Grand-Duchy within the Russian Empire, with its own Diet responsible for internal matters, but not for foreign affairs. In 1854 British and French fleets destroyed the islands' fortifications at Bomarsund, and under the 1856 Treaty of Paris, which ended the Crimean War (between the Western powers and Russia), the islands were de-militarized and neutralized, but remained with Finland under Russian suzerainty.

Map 4   The Aaland Islands.

During World War I the Finnish Diet assumed, on Nov. 15, 1917 (i.e. after the October Revolution in Russia), supreme powers and constituted a Republic with a national government, which was recognized by Russia in January 1918 and later also by other states. The communes of the Aaland Islands, however, had, in August 1917, informed the King of Sweden that they had, at a meeting at Finström, adopted a resolution expressing their desire to be reunited with Sweden, and in two plebicites held subsequently an overwhelming majority of the islanders voted in favour of reunion with Sweden. The King of Sweden supported their move and in February 1920 a Swedish military expedition was sent to the islands in order to secure the withdrawal of all Finnish forces, i.e. of the White and Red Guards who were then at war with each other.

The League of Nations Decision

In June 1920 both Finland and Sweden put their cases to the League of Nations Council. As against the islanders' call for self-determination, the Finnish government pointed out that the islands had been part of Finland for over 100 years, and that they were also recognized as part of the independent Finland constituted in 1917, with the result that the destiny of the islands was a purely domestic matter in which the League had no authority to intervene.

27

The Council appointed a commission of jurists to decide whether or not the Council had a right to intervene, and this commission concluded that the issue involved "a situation of doubt and ambiguity concerned with the break-up of nations" and was therefore "a problem of great concern to the international community and of great importance for the growth of international law", and that the League of Nations Council was competent to adjudicate in the matter. The commission also stated that the principle of self-determination had to be balanced against other principles and that a compromise along the lines of minority guarantees might be the best solution.

The Council thereupon sent a commission of rapporteurs to the area and charged it with making specific recommendations. The commission, in its opinion given in April 1921, concluded that "to detach the islands from Finland would be ... an alteration of its status, depriving this country of a part of that which belongs to it". Regarding the principle of self-determination, the commission stated that it was "not, properly speaking, a rule of international law but a general principle expressed in a vague formula", and that it would certainly not apply to "fractions of states" (like the Aaland Islands) in the same way as it applied to "a people with a defined national life" (like the Finns). The commission stated explicitly: "To concede to minorities, either of race or of religion, or to any fractions of a population, the right to withdraw from the community to which they belong, because it is their good will or their good pleasure, would be to destroy order and stability within states and to inaugurate anarchy in international life; it would be to uphold a theory incompatible with the very idea of the state as a territorial and political unity."

The commission also recommended, however, that Finland should be obliged to give a number of guarantees to the Aalanders to preserve their national culture and identity, namely the right of pre-emption of land in the Aalands; five years' minimum residence as a qualification for the franchise; the exclusion of Finnish from the schools in favour of Swedish; the assurance that governors would not be appointed against the wish of the people; and the right of recourse to the League of Nations Council. The commission's report was endorsed by the Council in June 1921, and both Finland (which undertook to give the required guarantees) and Sweden subsequently accepted this decision.

The decision was embodied in a London Convention of Oct. 20, 1921, providing for the islands' regional autonomy within the Finnish Republic and their demilitarization and neutralization, with their inhabitants being exempt from Finnish military service. This convention was signed not only by Finland and Sweden but also by Britain, Denmark, Estonia, France, Germany, Italy, Latvia and Poland (but not by the Soviet Union) and it has remained in force for all the signatories except Estonia and Latvia (which became part of the Soviet Union in 1940).

Temporary Remilitarization of the Islands in 1939-40

When the outbreak of war between Germany and the Soviet Union was considered possible, Finland and Sweden agreed on Jan. 8, 1939, on a plan for limited remilitarization of the islands, including fortification in the south and military service for the inhabitants. The two governments explained their decision in a note addressed to the signatories of the 1921 convention, stating that in case of imminent war in the Baltic, Sweden reserved the right to collaborate, at the request of Finland, in applying measures to safeguard the neutrality of the islands, and that both parties would decline any offer by a belligerent power to "protect" the islands. During April-May 1939 the plan was approved by all the signatories of the convention except Germany. However, the islanders themselves, in a petition bearing 10,800 signatures, protested to the League of Nations Council against the proposed remilitarization.

On a request by Finland and Sweden the League of Nations Council considered the remilitarization plan on May 22-29, 1939, but reached no agreement because the Soviet Union did not consider itself to be in possession of all the information necessary for defining its attitude, although Finland and Sweden claimed that they had supplied the USSR with the same information as had been furnished to all the other powers.

On May 31, 1939, the Soviet Union proposed an effective pact of mutual assistance against aggression to be concluded by Britain, France and the Soviet Union, with the possibility of guarantees against aggression being given to the Baltic states. Sweden thereupon withdrew from the remilitarization plan on June 3, whereas the Finnish Minister of Defence stated on June 5 that his government would proceed with the fortification of some of the Aaland Islands. With regard to the guarantees proposed by the Soviet Union, the Finnish Foreign Minister stated on June 6 that Finland could not accept them but would have to treat as an aggressor every state which, on the basis of such an unasked-for guarantee, intended to give its so-called assistance whenever it considered that the "guaranteed" state required help.

Following the outbreak of war between Finland and the Soviet Union on Nov. 30, 1939, the Finnish government informed the League of Nations on Dec. 4 that it had decided to fortify the Aaland Islands. However, after the conclusion of the Finnish-Soviet peace treaty (ratified by the Finnish Parliament on March 15, 1940), the Finnish government announced on July 18, 1940, that it had begun to demilitarize the islands, and on Oct. 12 of that year Finland and the Soviet Union ratified an agreement under which Finland undertook to demilitarize the islands and not to place them at the disposal of other states.

The Aaland Islanders' Renewed Request for Reunion with Sweden (1945)

At the end of World War II the *Landsting* (Legislative Assembly) of the Aaland Islands unanimously demanded, on Sept. 12, 1945, the islands' reunion with Sweden and the dissolution of the existing union with Finland, and requested an opportunity of putting their case to the Allies in their peace negotiations with Finland. In the *Landsting* resolution it was recorded that the islands had been compulsorily separated from Sweden under the 1809 peace treaty of Frederikshamn but that their inhabitants had never given up hope of a reunion; it was also claimed that the 1921 convention no longer conformed to the existing situation. In Sweden, however, the Foreign Ministry officially denied on Sept. 13 any Swedish initiative in the islanders' demand for a revision of their islands' status.

In the event, the peace treaty concluded between the Allied powers (including the Soviet Union) and Finland—which was signed on Feb. 10, 1947, ratified by Finland on April 18 and effective from Sept. 16, 1947—laid down (in Article 5) that the Aaland Islands would remain demilitarized as part of Finland. Their status as it had obtained between 1921 and 1939 was thus restored.

In answer to a parliamentary question about the rights of the population of the Aaland Islands, the Swedish Foreign Minister said in 1986 that his government regarded the obligations undertaken by Finland as still being valid. He added that the Swedish government believed that the Finnish authorities had dealt with questions concerning the language and culture of the islands' inhabitants in a commendable way.

HWD

East Germany-West Germany-Poland

At intergovernmental level the existing frontiers between the Federal Republic of Germany (FRG), the German Democratic Republic (GDR) and Poland have been agreed (i) as determined first at the end of World War II in Europe, notably under the Potsdam agreement of Aug. 2, 1945; and (ii) as subsequently confirmed in treaties concluded between the GDR and Poland (on July 6, 1950), the FRG and the Soviet Union (on Aug. 12, 1970), the FRG and Poland (on Nov. 20, 1970) and the

FRG and the GDR (on Dec. 21, 1972). The frontiers were, moreover, reaffirmed as being inviolable in the 1975 Helsinki Final Act of the Conference on Security and Co-operation in Europe.

However, the 1970 treaties were ratified by the FRG only with the proviso that its policy was aimed at "the peaceful restoration of national unity" and that the treaties did not affect earlier agreements concluded between the Western powers (Britain, France and the United States) with the Soviet Union, in particular on the status of Berlin. It has therefore been argued that in concluding these treaties the government of the FRG was not acting as a fully sovereign government. Moreover, the treaties were ratified by the West German Parliament only with the abstention of the majority of the (Christian Democratic) opposition, who continued to insist that in terms of the Potsdam agreement the western frontiers of Poland could be finally determined only under a peace treaty formally ending the war between the Allies and Germany (which has never been concluded).

Notwithstanding the 1970 treaties the government of the FRG continued to refuse to recognize the GDR as a "foreign" country, and it also insisted on recognizing only one German citizenship (i.e. it has treated citizens of the GDR as citizens of the FRG). The contradictions in the development of the relationship between the FRG on the one hand and the GDR and Poland on the other have had their origin in the FRG's need of security, which it has sought to achieve by fostering international détente (albeit as a member of the North Atlantic Treaty Organization). This in turn involved the normalization of relations with the Eastern-bloc countries at the cost of postponing the pursuit of the long-term aim of all West German governments of the reunification of all Germans in one state (on the nature of which there has been no unanimity).

Origins of the Present-Day Eastern Frontiers of Germany

Proposals for the frontiers of Germany after World War II were first agreed upon by a European Advisory Council (constituted by Britain, the Soviet Union and the United States) as laid down in two protocols signed in London on Sept. 12 and Nov. 14, 1944. These proposals were finally agreed to by Britain in December 1944, by the United States on Feb. 1, 1945, and by the Soviet Union on Feb. 6 of that year. The protocol of Sept. 12 provided for the division of Germany (within its frontiers as at Dec. 31, 1937, i.e. before Hitler's annexations) into three occupation zones (British, US and Soviet), with Greater Berlin (as defined by a German law of April 27, 1920) to be occupied in separate sectors by the three Allied powers and to be administered by a joint *Kommandatura*. The protocol of Nov. 14 specified the limits of the western zones and laid down (in 11 articles) details of the administration by the three military commanders who would form a Control Council.

At the Yalta conference, held on Feb. 4-10, 1945, the leaders of the three Allied powers (Churchill, Roosevelt and Stalin) agreed that France should be invited to occupy a zone of Germany (including a zone of Berlin) and to co-operate in the Control Council as a fourth member.

The principle of the division of Germany into four occupation zones was embodied in a declaration issued on June 5, 1945, and the London protocol of Sept. 12, 1944, was amended by an agreement signed on July 25, 1945, by the governments of the United States, the Soviet Union and the United Kingdom and the provisional government of the French Republic, providing for a third western zone and a section of West Berlin to be occupied by French forces.

On the question of Poland's frontiers it was stated in the Yalta agreement: "The three heads of government consider that the eastern frontier of Poland should follow the Curzon line (Poland's eastern border in 1919) with digressions from it in some regions of five to eight kilometres in favour of Poland. It is recognized that Poland must receive substantial accessions of territory in the north and west. They feel that the opinion of the new Polish provisional government of national unity should be sought in due course on the extent of these accessions and that the final delimitation of the western frontier of Poland should thereafter await the peace conference."

In accordance with the London protocols, US troops who had advanced to the Elbe river by the end of the war in Europe, withdrew on July 1, 1945, from Saxony and Thuringia, which had been allocated to the Soviet occupation zone. British troops similarly withdrew from parts of Mecklenburg, while British and US units entered sections of Berlin which had been taken by the Soviet Army. In a message to the German people Marshal Stalin declared on May 9 inter alia: "The USSR celebrates victory but it has no intention of dismembering or destroying Germany."

However, the Soviet Union had on April 21, 1945, in an agreement with the Polish provisional government, specified that former German territories to the east of the Oder and the western Neisse should be placed under Polish administration. This agreement did not become known to the Western powers until at least two months later. The British government protested against it, and the US State Department declared on June 29 that the transfer of the territories to Polish control was "an infringement of the Crimea [Yalta]

Map 5 Territorial changes in Eastern Europe following World War II. The territory of the Free City of Danzig, now part of Poland, had been occupied by the Germans in 1939.

decision and of the general tripartite understanding regarding the disposal of occupied German territory".

President Truman, speaking on behalf of the three Western powers, stated in a message to the Polish provisional government on Aug. 1, 1945: "The territorial boundaries have been established. The actual agreement of the three heads of government [of Britain, the Soviet Union and the United States], however, was that the final delimitation of the western frontier of Poland should await the peace settlement and that, pending the final determination of the frontier, Stettin and the area east of the Oder-Neisse line should be under the administration of the Polish state."

In the final communiqué of the Potsdam conference, held by the heads of government of Britain, the Soviet Union and the United States between July 17 and Aug. 2, 1945, it was stated with regard to Poland's western boundaries that their "final delimitation ... should await the peace settlement" but that "pending the final determination of Poland's western frontier the former German territories east of a line running from the Baltic Sea immediately west of Swinemünde, and thence along the Oder river to the confluence of the western Neisse river, and along the western Neisse to the Czechoslovak frontier, including that portion of East Prussia not placed under the administration of the USSR, and including the area of the former Free City of Danzig, shall be under the administration of the Polish state, and for such purposes shall not be considered as part of the Soviet zone of occupation in Germany". In a previous section of the communiqué it was stated that the conference had "agreed in principle to the proposal of the Soviet government concerning the ultimate transfer to the Soviet Union of the city of Königsberg and the area adjacent to it ..." and that the President of the United States and the British Prime Minister would "support the proposal of the conference at the forthcoming peace settlement". Among the Western Allies, France, which was not represented at Potsdam, had earlier tacitly accepted the Oder-western Neisse line as Poland's western frontier.

Between 1945 and 1947 the British and US governments repeatedly stated that they had only reluctantly agreed to the frontier changes insisted upon by the Soviet Union and that they were not committed to supporting the "provisional" arrangements concerning Poland's western borders at a peace conference. The Soviet Union, however, appeared to depart from the position which it had taken at the Potsdam conference (when it had agreed that the transfer of former German territories to Poland was made "pending final determination"). On Sept. 17, 1946, the Soviet Foreign Minister (V. M. Molotov) declared that the Potsdam "decision to shift the western Polish frontier to the Oder and western Neisse" had been taken after prolonged discussion, including also the Polish provisional government, and that the three Allied powers "never envisaged any revision of this decision in the future"; at the same time, he admitted that it was correct that the conference had "believed it necessary to postpone a final definition of the Polish western frontier until the peace conference".

The Polish government has always regarded the Potsdam decision on Poland's western frontiers as quite unambiguous on the following grounds: (i) that it refers, in an introductory section, to "the western frontier of Poland" and not to any provisional line of demarcation; (ii) that it uses the term "former German territories", thereby indicating that they are no longer regarded as belonging to Germany; (iii) that, as these territories were "not part of the Soviet zone of occupation", they were not part of Germany (the whole of which was placed under Allied occupation), and the "administration" referred to in the agreement had nothing in common with the Allied occupation but meant that the parties to the agreement consented to Polish administration in these territories; and (iv) that the transfer of the German population from the territories confirmed that the words "final delimitation" meant only the formal tracing of the border on the ground, which was also, in the Polish view, confirmed by the statement that the "final delimitation" would await a "peaceful settlement"—not a peace treaty.

The US State Department announced on Dec. 7, 1945, that within eight months 6,550,000 Germans had been moved from neighbouring countries to Germany (including 3,500,000 from Poland). According to a West German census of Sept. 13, 1950, almost 8,000,000

German "refugees and expellees" had reached the Federal Republic of Germany so far, and it was said that the majority of them had been integrated and assimilated in an expanding economy. Some of the Germans who entered the FRG from the east organized themselves in *Landsmannschaften* (regional expellees' organizations), which were encouraged by some FRG politicians in their hope of returning one day to their region of origin, perhaps simultaneously with the restoration of a German Reich. Although a Charter of German Expellees, adopted on Aug. 5, 1950, expressed the wish of the *Landsmannschaften* to refrain from any act of revenge or the use of force, there existed in the FRG extremist anti-Polish groups which, among other activities, distributed maps showing Germany's frontiers as being those of 1914.

The Polish government has also regarded the former German territories as part of Poland on historical grounds going back to the existence of a Polish state embracing these areas 1,000 years ago. In January 1949 the *Sejm* (Polish Parliament) passed a law placing the newly-acquired territories under the Ministry of the Interior. Under the Treaty of Zgorzelec (Görlitz), signed on July 6, 1950, the Oder-Neisse line was declared to be the "frontier of peace and friendship" between the GDR and Poland. An agreement on the final delimitation of this frontier was signed on Jan. 27, 1951.

From 1946 onwards developments in the Soviet occupation zone on the one hand and in the Western occupation zones on the other diverged increasingly with the establishment of a communist regime in the East and the gradual integration of the Western zones in the alliance of Western states—first in the Western European Union and later in the North

Map 6   Present-day Poland and its neighbours. The Oder and Neisse rivers forming Poland's western border have the Polish names Odra and Nysa Luzycka respectively.

33

Atlantic Treaty Organization. Owing to these developments the border between the Eastern and Western occupation zones eventually became a border between states, and the city of Greater Berlin was also divided into two separately administered parts.

Development of the GDR

In the Soviet zone the military commander began in 1945 to hand over power to the German Communists, of whom a group led by Walter Ulbricht had arrived in Berlin from Moscow in April 1945. On April 22, 1946, the Communists together with leaders of the "official" Social Democratic Party (SPD) formed the Socialist Unity Party of Germany (SED)—while a reorganized SPD, opposed to the formation of the SED, had been formed in the US sector of Berlin on April 7 (and held its first conference in Hanover on May 9-11, 1946). Both the SED and the SPD were recognized by the Allied Control Council on May 28, 1946.

A new constitution, approved by a "German People's Congress" in East Berlin on May 30, 1949, declared inter alia: "Germany is an indivisible democratic republic built upon the *Länder* . . . . There is only one German citizenship". A new state, the German Democratic Republic (GDR), was proclaimed on Oct. 7, 1949. It was immediately recognized by the Soviet Union whereas the Western powers and the FRG declared it to be "without legal basis" as its government had not been freely elected. On March 25, 1954, the Soviet Union recognized the GDR as a sovereign independent state, in which the functions of the Soviet High Commission would be limited to security questions and to liaison with the Western Allies on all-German questions, with Soviet troops remaining in the GDR under the existing four-power agreements.

The *Bundestag* (Lower House of Parliament of the FRG), however, in a resolution adopted unanimously on April 7, 1954, refused to recognize the Soviet Union's right "to create an East German state" and reiterated the previously expressed West German view that the federal government had the sole right to represent the German people. The three Western High Commissioners declared on April 8 that their governments would continue to regard the Soviet Union as the power responsible for the Soviet zone and would not recognize the government of the GDR but would regard the federal government as "the only freely-elected and legally-constituted government of Germany".

The GDR became a member of the Warsaw Treaty Organization at the latter's establishment on May 13, 1955. A treaty concluded between the USSR and the GDR on Sept. 20, 1955, stated in its preamble that both sides would respect the obligations undertaken by them under "international agreements relating to Germany as a whole" (and thus recognized by implication the four-power status of Berlin). In Article 1 it was stated that the GDR was henceforth "free to decide questions concerning its internal and foreign policy, including its relations with the FRG as well as its relations with other states". In Article 4 it was stated: "The Soviet forces at present stationed in the GDR under international agreements will continue to be stationed there temporarily with the approval of the government of the GDR and on conditions to be settled by an additional agreement between the two governments." In Article 5 the two sides stated that they would "make the necessary efforts towards a settlement by a peace treaty and towards the restoration of the unity of Germany on a peaceful and democratic basis".

In documents published at the same time it was confirmed that the GDR would have control of traffic (other than military traffic) across its territory from the FRG to Berlin and also of the frontiers of the GDR; that all laws and orders issued by the Soviet control organs in 1945-48 were rescinded; and that the Soviet High Commission in the GDR would be replaced by a Soviet embassy.

A new constitution approved by the *Volkskammer* (the Parliament of the GDR) on Jan. 31, 1968, and in a referendum on April 6 (by 94.5 per cent of the voters) and in force from April 9, 1968, stated (in Article 1, first paragraph) that the GDR "is a socialist state of the German nation and the political organization of the working people in town and country who are jointly implementing socialism under the leadership of the working class and its

Marxist-Leninist party". Article 8 stated: "The GDR and its citizens ... strive to overcome the division of Germany imposed upon the German nation by imperialism and support the step-by-step rapprochement between the two German states until the time of their unification on the basis of democracy and socialism."

However, among numerous amendments to this constitution which were approved by the *Volkskammer* on Sept. 27, 1974, and which entered into force on Oct. 7 of that year, the words "of the German nation" were deleted from Article 1, and the whole of Article 8 was also deleted. In Article 6 of the amended constitution it was stated inter alia: "The GDR is linked irrevocably and for ever with the Soviet Union .... The GDR is an inseparable part of the socialist community of states."

On Oct. 16, 1972, the *Volkskammer* passed a bill on citizenship, under which GDR citizens who had illegally left the GDR before Jan. 1, 1972, and had not since resumed residence in the GDR would lose their GDR citizenship; their descendants, if they were resident outside the GDR without the latter's authorization, would also lose their GDR citizenship; but no criminal proceedings would be instituted against these persons for having left the GDR without permission.

Evolution of the Western Occupation Zones into the FRG

The British and US occupation zones were, with effect from Jan. 1, 1947, merged in a single economic zone under an agreement signed on Dec. 2, 1946, and a German Economic Council was set up for this new bi-zone on June 25, 1947 (under an agreement of May 29, 1947). A conference of six Western powers held in London from April 20 to June 1, 1948, decided inter alia that it was necessary to "enable the German people to achieve, on the basis of a free and democratic form of government, the eventual restoration of German unity which does not exist at present" and to prepare the adoption of a constitution.

The Soviet Union denounced all these developments as contravening the Potsdam decisions and as a first step towards the establishment of a West German state. The Soviet representative left the Allied Control Council (set up under the Potsdam agreement) on March 20, 1948, and the Council did not meet again thereafter.

The Basic Law (constitution) of the FRG, finally approved by a Parliamentary Council on May 8, 1949, and in force from May 24 of that year, was (under its Article 23) to apply, in the first instance, not only in the *Länder* of the Western occupation zones but also in Greater Berlin. In a preamble to the law it was stated that its authors had "acted also on behalf of those Germans to whom participation was denied" and that "the entire German people is called upon to accomplish by free self-determination the unity and freedom of Germany". The Foreign Ministers of the three Western powers had made it clear, on April 22, 1949, that Berlin should not, at that stage, be included in the FRG as a *Land*. The Chief Burgomaster of West Berlin, however, signed the Basic Law on May 23. The FRG was inaugurated on Sept. 7, 1949, when its Parliament elected the first Federal President, and on Sept. 14 the *Bundestag* elected the first Federal Chancellor (Dr Konrad Adenauer).

Allied military government in the Western occupation zones was ended on Sept. 21, 1949, with the entry into force of an occupation statute (issued on April 10, 1949), which was "designed to encourage and facilitate the closest integration ... of the German people under a democratic federal state within the framework of the European association". The statute laid down inter alia that any amendment of the Basic Law of the federal state would require the express approval of the occupation authorities before becoming effective.

The Foreign Ministers of the three Western powers, meeting in New York on Sept. 12-14, 1950, declared that their governments "consider the government of the FRG as the only German government freely and legitimately constituted and therefore entitled to speak for Germany as the representative of the German people in international affairs". In a convention on the relations between the three Western powers and the FRG, signed on May 26, 1952, it was laid down (in Article 2) that, in view of the international situation which had until then prevented the reunification of Germany and the conclusion of a peace treaty, the three powers retained the rights and responsibilities which they exercised or held in respect of Berlin and of Germany as a whole, including the reunification of Germany and a settlement through a peace treaty.

The FRG became a full and equal member of the Brussels Treaty Organization (later the Western European Union) and the North Atlantic Treaty Organization (NATO), as laid down in declarations embodied in the Final Act of a nine-power conference which ended in London on Oct. 3, 1954, and in agreements signed in Paris on Oct. 23 of that year. All of these texts subsequently entered into force on May 5, 1955. In a declaration incorporated into the 1954 Paris agreements, the FRG undertook "never to have recourse to force to achieve the reunification of Germany or the modification of the present boundaries of the FRG, and to resolve by peaceful means any disputes which may arise between the Federal Republic and other states". In a simultaneous declaration the three Western powers recorded their belief (i) that "a peace settlement for the whole of Germany, freely negotiated between Germany and her former enemies, ... remains an essential aim of their policy"; (ii) that the "final determination of the boundaries of Germany must await such a settlement"; (iii) that "the achievement through peaceful means of a fully free and unified Germany remains a fundamental goal of their policy"; and (iv) that "the security and welfare of Berlin and the maintenance of the position of the three powers there are regarded by the three powers as essential elements of the peace of the free world" and that "they will treat any attack against Berlin from any quarter as an attack upon their forces and themselves".

Following the establishment of diplomatic relations between the FRG and the Soviet Union during a visit to Moscow by the Federal Chancellor (Dr Adenauer) on Sept. 9-14, 1955, the Soviet government stated on Sept. 15: "The Soviet government regards the FRG as a part of Germany. The other part of Germany is the GDR .... The question of the frontiers of Germany was solved by the Potsdam agreement .... The FRG is carrying out its jurisdiction on the territory under its sovereignty." Dr Adenauer, however, had stated at a press conference in Moscow on Sept. 14 that in the FRG's opinion a final settlement of Germany's frontiers must await the conclusion of a peace treaty and the government of the FRG was "the only legitimate government of all Germany".

In a note sent by the government of the FRG on March 25, 1966, to all governments with which it had diplomatic relations, and also to East European and Arab states, and containing proposals for peace and disarmament, it was asserted that under the 1945 Potsdam agreements the settlement of Germany's frontiers had been "postponed until the conclusion of a peace treaty with the whole of Germany" and that under international law Germany continued to "exist within its frontiers of Dec. 31, 1937, until such time as a freely elected all-German government recognizes other frontiers". In response to this note the Soviet Union declared on May 17, 1966, that the Oder-Neisse frontier was "final and unalterable"; it accused the FRG of trying "to restore the German Reich with all its pretensions"; and it pointed out that not a single European state had territorial claims against the FRG.

However, following the election to the federal chancellorship in October 1969 of Willy Brandt (former SPD Chief Burgomaster of West Berlin and Vice-Chancellor and Foreign Minister in the "grand coalition" government of 1967-69), the government of the FRG embarked on a new "*Ostpolitik*" designed, as the new Chancellor stated on Oct. 28, to "arrive at a modus vivendi [with the GDR] and from there to proceed to co-operation" on the basis of the existing "two states of Germany" which "are not foreign countries to each other". Over the next three years the FRG proceeded to conclude treaties with the Soviet Union, Poland and the GDR respectively and these treaties incorporated various passages relating to the existing German borders.

Article 3 of the treaty of Aug. 12, 1970, with the Soviet Union states: "The USSR and the FRG share the realization that peace in Europe can only be maintained if no one disturbs the present frontiers. They undertake to respect the territorial integrity of all states in Europe within their existing frontiers; they declare that they have no territorial claims whatsoever against anybody, and will not assert such claims in the future; they regard as inviolable now and in the future the frontiers of all states in Europe as they are on the date of the signing of this treaty, including the Oder-Neisse line, which forms the western frontier of the Polish People's Republic, and the frontier between the FRG and the GDR." In Article 4 it is stated: "The present treaty between the USSR and the FRG does not affect any bilateral or multilateral treaties and agreements previously concluded by them."

In a separate letter the FRG expressly stated: "This treaty does not conflict with the political objective of the FRG to work for a state of peace in Europe in which the German nation will recover its unity in free self-determination."

In the treaty with Poland, published on Nov. 20, 1970, Article 1 states: "The FRG and the People's Republic of Poland state in mutual agreement that the existing boundary line, the course of which is laid down in Chapter IX of the decisions of the Potsdam conference of Aug. 2, 1945, as running from the Baltic Sea immediately west of Swinemünde, and thence along the Oder river to the confluence of the western Neisse river and along the western Neisse to the Czechoslovak frontier, shall constitute the western state frontier of the People's Republic of Poland. They reaffirm the inviolability of their existing frontiers now and in the future and undertake to respect each other's territorial integrity without restriction. They declare that they have no territorial claims whatsoever against each other and that they will not assert such claims in the future." Article IV of this treaty states: "The present treaty shall not affect any bilateral or multilateral international arrangements previously concluded by either contracting party or concerning them."

Article 3 of the Basic Treaty of Dec. 21, 1972, between the FRG and the GDR states: "[The FRG and the GDR] affirm the inviolability, now and in the future, of the border existing between them, and pledge themselves to unrestricted respect for each other's territorial integrity." The treaty also states, in Article 6: "The FRG and the GDR proceed from the principle that the sovereign power of each of the two states is confined to its [own] state territory. They respect the independence and sovereignty of each of the two states in its internal and external affairs." Under Article 9 the two sides also "agreed that bilateral and multilateral international treaties and agreements previously concluded by or concerning them are not affected by this treaty". Under a supplementary protocol the two sides agreed to set up a commission to "examine and, so far as is necessary, renew or supplement the demarcation of the border between the two states" and to "compile the necessary documentation on the line of the border".

The treaties with the Soviet Union and Poland entered into force on June 3, 1972, not having been ratified by the *Bundestag* (the Lower House of the FRG Parliament) until May 17, 1972, and then only with the abstention of the opposition Christian Democratic and Christian Social Unions and after the adoption (with only five abstentions and no opposition) of a joint resolution intended to clarify the FRG's position. In this resolution it was stated inter alia that "the treaties proceed from the frontiers as existing today, the unilateral alteration of which they exclude"; that "the treaties do not anticipate a peace settlement for Germany by treaty and do not create any legal basis for the frontiers existing today"; that "the policy of the FRG, which aims at a peaceful restoration of national unity within the European framework, is not inconsistent with the treaties, which do not prejudice the solution of the German question"; that "the rights and responsibilities of the four powers with regard to Germany as a whole and to Berlin are not affected by the treaties"; and that the *Bundestag*, "in view of the fact that the final settlement of the German question as a whole is still outstanding, considers as essential the continuance of these rights and responsibilities".

The Basic Treaty between the FRG and the GDR was approved by the *Bundestag* on May 11, 1973, and by the *Volkskammer* on June 13, and it entered into force on June 21, 1973. The *Bundestag* approved the relevant bill at its second reading by 268 votes to 217 (of the Christian Democratic and Christian Social Unions). An application by the Christian Social *Land* government of Bavaria to the Federal Constitutional Court for a ruling as to whether the treaty was in conflict with the Basic Law (the constitution of the FRG) resulted in a court ruling, given on July 31, 1973, to the effect that the treaty did not conflict with the Basic Law. In this ruling the Court reaffirmed the continued existence in law of the German Reich (a thesis which, in the Court's view, had formed the basis of the 1949 Basic Law, or constitution, of the FRG) and took the view that the FRG was "a state identical with the state of the German Reich". The Court also declared reunification as being "constitutionally imperative" and explicitly referred in its decision to "the borders of the German Reich as at Dec. 31, 1937" as one of several legal possibilities.

The German federal government has since then repeatedly reaffirmed its reunification policy. Thus Dr Helmut Kohl, the Federal Chancellor, stated at a gathering on Aug. 12, 1984 (the 14th anniversary of the 1970 treaty with the Soviet Union), that the treaty would be "fully respected and fulfilled" but that "the goal of unifying the German people" remained "an historic task".

The Final Act of the Conference on Security and Co-operation in Europe, signed in Helsinki on Aug. 1, 1975, by 35 countries (including all those of Europe except Albania), reaffirmed the inviolability of frontiers and the territorial integrity of states. The relevant passages—in Basket One, (A) I and IV—read as follows: "The participating states regard as inviolable all one another's frontiers as well as the frontiers of all states in Europe and therefore they will refrain from now on and in the future from assaulting these frontiers. Accordingly they will also refrain from any demand for, or act of, seizure and usurpation of part or all of the territory of any participating state . . . . The participating states will respect the territorial integrity of any of the participating states."

Under a protocol agreed to at the conclusion of the Helsinki Final Act on Aug. 1, 1975, between 120,000 and 125,000 ethnic Germans were allowed to leave Poland and settle in the FRG during the following four years, with further emigration applications being permitted after the expiry of that period. The protocol was signed on Oct. 9, 1975, and was finally approved on March 15, 1976. In the FRG it was stated that between early 1950 and September 1975 a total of 471,760 ethnic Germans had been allowed to emigrate from Poland to the FRG.

In a treaty signed in Prague on Dec. 11, 1973, by the FRG and Czechoslovakia it was laid down (in Article 1) that the Munich agreement of Sept. 29, 1938 (after which Hitler had annexed the Sudeten areas of Czechoslovakia), was "null and void" because it had been "imposed on the Czechoslovak Republic by the National Socialist regime under the threat of force". Article 4 stated that the two sides "have no territorial claims of any kind against each other and likewise in the future will not raise any such claims".

Continued East-West Disagreement over Berlin

The division of Berlin into an Eastern (Soviet) sector and a Western sector (under the commandants of the three Western powers) was intensified following the introduction of a currency reform by the Western powers in their respective occupation zones on June 18, 1948. The Soviet government in turn announced, on June 23, a currency reform which was to apply to the Soviet zone of Germany as well as to Greater Berlin, and on June 23-24 the Eastern authorities stopped the supply of electric current, coal, food and other goods to Berlin's Western sectors. A slightly modified form of Western mark was introduced by the Western commandants on June 24.

On June 28, 1948, the US government announced the creation of an airlift designed to break the Soviet blockade of West Berlin, and on July 1 all co-operation between the members of the four-power *Kommandatura* (the Allied authority in Greater Berlin) was ended. In an announcement the Soviet chief of staff at the Berlin *Kommandatura* stated that Soviet representatives would no longer attend meetings of any organization of the *Kommandatura*, on the ground, inter alia, of the introduction of the new Western currency into Berlin which, he said, was "part of the economic system of the Soviet zone". The Western powers did not accept this view and explained their position in notes handed to the Soviet side on July 8, stating that Berlin was "not part of the Soviet zone but an international zone of occupation". The notes also made it clear that the Western powers now shared "the responsibility . . . for the physical well-being of 2,400,000 persons in the western sectors of

Berlin" and demanded that the lines of communication between the western zones of Germany and West Berlin should be fully restored.

The Soviet Union rejected this reply of the Western powers on July 14 and accused them of having violated the Yalta and Potsdam agreements, in particular by the introduction of the currency reform and by taking separatist action in West Germany (especially through the London agreement), which had "destroyed the system of quadripartite administration of Germany", with the effect that the Allied Control Council had ceased to function, and had thereby "undermined the legal basis on which rested the right to participate in the administration of Berlin". The Soviet note continued: "Berlin is the centre of the Soviet zone and is part of that zone". It added: "The entire mass of currency notes invalidated in the western zone threatened to pour into Berlin and into the Soviet zone. The Soviet Command was therefore compelled to adopt urgent measures to safeguard the interests of the German population as well as of the economy of the Soviet zone and of Greater Berlin." If necessary, the note declared, the Soviet government would "not object to ensuring sufficient supplies for the whole of Greater Berlin by its own means".

Under a Soviet decree of July 23, 1948, an Eastern Deutschemark was introduced for the Soviet zone and Greater Berlin. The three Western powers accepted this currency for West Berlin until March 20, 1949, when they announced that only the Western Deutschemark would be used as legal tender in West Berlin.

The city of Berlin was effectively divided into two separately administered sectors as from Nov. 30, 1948. On that date the 26 SED members of the City Assembly declared the City *Magistrat* to be deposed, set up a new *Magistrat* and elected a new provisional chief burgomaster, and on Dec. 1 this new *Magistrat* took over what had been the municipal headquarters for the whole city (situated in the Soviet sector). It claimed to represent the whole of Berlin as "the capital of a unified democratic German republic". However, the legally elected City Assembly repudiated the SED-controlled *Magistrat* and set up its own headquarters in the western sector. Elections to a new City Assembly were held on Dec. 5, when the SED abstained from voting. In the event, about 13.8 per cent of the electorate of West Berlin took no part in these elections. (In elections to the City Assembly of Greater Berlin, held on Oct. 20, 1946, the SED had gained 19.8 per cent of the vote and 26 out of the 130 seats.) Under the 1949 Basic Law of the FRG the West Berlin City Assembly (and later the House of Representatives) has appointed 22 delegates to sit as members of the *Bundestag*, although without a vote (except on procedural matters).

The airlift, carried out jointly by the United States and Britain, kept West Berlin supplied with basic needs in food and fuel until the Soviet military government lifted the blockade on May 12, 1949, under an agreement reached on May 4 and laying down that the problem should be discussed at a meeting of the Allied Council of Ministers. However, such a meeting, held between May 23 and June 20, 1949, reached no agreement on the future of Berlin other than that the blockade should not be reimposed.

On May 14, 1949, the three Western commandants in Berlin signed a new charter granting wide powers to the Western City Assembly, with the *Kommandatura* retaining only specified powers in regard to disarmament, demilitarization, reparations, currency and credit policy, banking and foreign trade, protection and security of the Allied forces, relations with authorities abroad and supervision of the police. It was also announced that the power of veto hitherto held by each member of the *Kommandatura* was abolished and that this body would in future take decisions by majority vote.

On Sept. 30, 1949, the *Bundestag* adopted a resolution (opposed only by the 15 Communist members of the House) declaring "solemnly that it is the wish of the German people that Greater Berlin should form an integral part of the FRG and should become its capital". The resolution also appealed to the Allied occupying powers to revise their "negative attitude" towards the integration of Berlin as the twelfth *Land* of the FRG. On Oct. 8 the *Magistrat* of West Berlin formally applied to the Western powers to agree to the integration of Berlin as the twelfth *Land* of the FRG.

On Oct. 21, 1949, however, the Federal Chancellor (Dr Konrad Adenauer) stated in the

Bundestag that Berlin could not, for the present, become the twelfth *Land* of the FRG and that it was "in the interests of Berlin itself" that Article 23 of the Basic Law (relating to the inclusion of Greater Berlin in the territories in which the Basic Law was to apply) should not be invoked, but that the federal government welcomed the city's intention of bringing its laws into conformity with those of the FRG and thereby achieving its de facto membership of the FRG. He also said that the government regarded Berlin as a "distressed area" and were "determined not to abandon Berlin but to do everything to revitalize the city's economy and finances".

A proposal made on April 10, 1950, by the Assembly of West Berlin for the holding of city-wide elections on the basis of the 1948 constitution was not rejected by the Soviet commandant of the eastern zone but was (on May 8) made subject to Soviet conditions—including the withdrawal of all occupation forces from Berlin and the abolition of its division into sectors—most of which were unacceptable to the western City Assembly, which feared that acceptance of these conditions would eventually lead to Soviet occupation of the whole city. The Soviet conditions were also rejected by the Western military commandants who laid down, on June 10, four general principles which, they stated, guided their "approach to the reunification of Berlin": (i) a freely elected city government operating under a constitution drafted by representatives of the people; (ii) city-wide freedom for all democratic political parties before, during and after the elections; (iii) individual freedom of movement, freedom from arbitrary arrest and detention, freedom of association, assembly, speech, press and radio throughout the city; and (iv) the resumption of quadripartite work by the *Kommandatura*, but without the right of veto of any one member.

The West Berlin constitution of Sept. 1, 1950, stated in Article 3 that "(i) Berlin is a German *Land* and at the same time one city; (ii) Berlin is a *Land* of the FRG; (iii) the Basic Law and laws of the FRG are binding for Berlin". In Article 7 it was stated (without any mention of the division of the city into two sectors) that the Berlin House of Representatives (which replaced the City Assembly) was entitled to decide, during a transitional period, that a law of the FRG would be applied without modification in Berlin.

An anti-communist rising by workers in East Berlin and other East German cities was crushed in June 1953 with the help of Soviet occupation troops, casualties being officially stated to include 25 persons killed and 378 injured, whereas the government of the FRG believed that 62 persons had been sentenced to death and 25,000 imprisoned. The number of refugees from East Berlin and the GDR was, in 1956, given as 122,000 in 1952, over 300,000 in 1953, over 184,000 in 1954 and over 252,000 in 1955, with the grand total since 1950 exceeding 1,500,000.

In the joint declaration issued by the Western powers at the end of the London nine-power conference which was held on Sept. 28-Oct. 3, 1954, and which led to the admission of the FRG to the Brussels Treaty Organization (later the Western European Union) and to the North Atlantic Treaty Organization (NATO), it was stated with reference to Berlin: "The security and welfare of Berlin and the maintenance of the position of the three powers there are regarded by the three powers as essential elements of the peace of the free world in the present international situation. Accordingly they will maintain armed forces within the territory of Berlin as long as their responsibilities require it. They therefore reaffirm that they will treat any attack against Berlin from any quarter as an attack upon their forces and themselves."

Developments leading to Construction of Berlin Wall

A new crisis arose over Berlin in 1958 out of what the West regarded as a Soviet attempt to incorporate the whole of Berlin in the GDR. Walter Ulbricht (the First Secretary of the SED) declared on Oct. 27, 1958: "The whole of Berlin lies within the territory of the GDR. The whole of Berlin belongs to the area under the sovereignty of the GDR. The authority of the Western occupying powers no longer has any legal basis in Berlin." Nikita Khrushchev (then USSR Prime Minister) stated in a speech on Nov. 10, 1958, inter alia: "The German question—if this means unification of the two German states now in existence—can be solved only by the German people themselves through the rapprochement of those states. The conclusion of a peace treaty with Germany is another matter." Accusing the Western powers of having violated the Potsdam agreement, he stated that virtually all that remained of that agreement was the "so-called four-power status of Berlin", to which, he said, the Western powers were clinging because it was beneficial to them. He continued: "The time has evidently come for the powers which signed the Potsdam agreement to abandon the remnants of the occupation regime in Berlin and thus make it possible to create a normal atmosphere in the capital of the GDR. The Soviet Union, for its part, will hand over to the sovereign GDR those functions in Berlin which are still wielded by the Soviet organs."

In a note of Nov. 27, 1958, the Soviet government notified the United States that it regarded as "null and void" the protocol of Sept. 12, 1944, on the occupation zones of Germany and the administration of Greater Berlin and also the associated supplementary agreements, including a quadripartite agreement of May 1, 1945, on the control mechanism in Germany; it added that, if no agreement was reached within six months on examining a Soviet proposal to make West Berlin an independent political entity as a Free City, then the Soviet government would carry out its own arrangements with the GDR.

Khrushchev said at a mass rally in East Berlin on March 9, 1959, that the implementation of the proposed inclusion of West Berlin in the GDR would only terminate the occupation status but would not change West Berlin's social system and mode of social life, as Berlin would be a free city, the independence of which would be guaranteed by the great powers. On March 19 he acknowledged that the United States, Britain and France had "lawful rights for their stay in West Berlin".

The Soviet proposals for Berlin were reiterated in a memorandum presented to President John F. Kennedy of the United States and published on June 11, 1961. President Kennedy, however, declared on July 6 that since March 1958 the Soviets had conducted "a new campaign to force the Western Allies out of Berlin" and that the "obvious purpose" of this campaign was "to make permanent the partition of Germany". In a note presented to the Soviet Union on July 17, 1961, the US government stated that it was the USSR which had "blocked all progress towards a peace settlement" in Germany; that the United States supported "the clearly expressed wish of the West Berliners that no change be made in the status of their city which would expose them ... to the domination of the regime which at present controls the surrounding areas". The note also rejected as "entirely without foundation" Soviet references to Berlin being "situated in the territory of the so-called GDR" and emphasized that since the protocol of Sept. 12, 1944 (which had been approved by the USSR on Feb. 6, 1945), there had been "no legal alteration in the special status of Berlin".

On July 25, 1961, President Kennedy announced in a broadcast that he was taking a number of defence measures "based on our need to meet a world-wide threat on a basis which stretches far beyond the Berlin crisis". The measures involved an increase in the strength of the US armed forces and a call-up of reservists "if necessary". Khrushchev in turn announced on Aug. 7 that the USSR would have to call up reservists and move forces to the Western borders in response to the measures taken by the United States. At the same time he called on the Western powers to "sit down sincerely at the conference table" and to "clear the atmosphere".

However, upon a decision by the Political Advisory Council of the Warsaw Treaty Organization, the GDR, on Aug. 13, 1961, closed the border between East and West Berlin (except for 13 official crossing points) and from Aug. 17 onwards it erected a wall along this border. On Aug. 22 the number of crossing points was reduced to six, and a no man's land of 100 metres' width was established on the eastern side of the border. The official grounds for taking these measures were "to put an end to the hostile activities of the revanchist and militarist forces" in West Germany and West Berlin, especially those of "espionage organizations" which were "systematically luring GDR citizens and carrying out a regular slave traffic".

41

On Aug. 17, 1961, the three Western powers delivered strong protest notes to the Soviet Union, stating that the border restrictions were "a flagrant and particularly serious violation of the quadripartite status of Berlin", as reaffirmed by the four-power agreements of May 4, 1949, and the Paris decision of June 20, 1949. These protests were rejected by the Soviet Union on Aug. 19, when the West was specifically accused of spying, of damaging the population and national economy of the GDR by arbitrarily introducing "a speculative rate of exchange of Western marks into GDR currency" and "buying up valuable goods and foodstuffs in the GDR", and of directing "a whole army of recruiters ... to impel part of the GDR population to move to West Germany". (Figures published by the FRG's Ministry of Refugees showed that between 1949 and June 30, 1961, over 2,600,000 refugees had left the GDR, over 300,000 of them during the last 18 months of that period.)

The military forces in the GDR were at that time stated to consist of at least 400,000 Soviet troops equipped with tactical nuclear weapons; the GDR National People's Army of about 65,000 men; and 75,000 armed members of two police forces. On the other hand there were about 11,000 Allied troops in West Berlin (4,000 British, 5,000 US and 2,000 French); 24,000 armed policemen in West Berlin; and NATO forces in the FRG consisting of about 50,000 British, 180,000 US, 30,000 French and 150,000 FRG troops, as well as one Canadian brigade group. There were no Western troops in an 18-mile wide strip along the FRG's border with the GDR—which the GDR subsequently provided with strong fences supervised from watchtowers.

There followed further military preparations of both the NATO and the Warsaw Pact sides, as well as exchanges of notes between East and West. Walter Ulbricht stated on Aug. 25 that the Allied air traffic to West Berlin would remain subject to Soviet—and not GDR—control until a peace treaty was signed. On Sept. 7 he said that after the signing of a peace treaty with the Soviet Union the GDR would have the right to control air entry into Berlin and that visas would be needed to travel between the FRG and the GDR. Khrushchev, speaking before the central committee of the Communist Party of the Soviet Union on Oct. 17, 1961, said that if the Western powers showed readiness to settle the German problem he would not insist on the signing of a peace treaty before Dec. 31, 1961 (as previously envisaged by him).

President Kennedy, visiting Western Europe between June 23 and July 2, 1963, inspected the Berlin wall and declared in a speech in West Berlin on June 26: "Today, in the world of freedom, the proudest boast is *'Ich bin ein Berliner'*." Of the ultimate reunification of Germany he said: "In 18 years of peace and of good faith this generation of Germans has earned the right to be free, including the right to unite their family and nation in lasting peace with the goodwill of all people."

However, towards the end of 1963 there were signs that the tension over the status of Berlin was abating. On Dec. 17, 1963, agreement was reached between the West Berlin authorities and the GDR on one-day visits to East Berlin by West Berliners between Dec. 20, 1963, and Jan. 5, 1964 (for the first time since the building of the Berlin wall in August 1961). On Sept. 24, 1964, a "technical" agreement was signed between the West Berlin Senate (which under the 1950 constitution had succeeded the *Magistrat*) and the GDR government to enable West Berliners to visit their relatives in East Berlin. On the Western side it was emphasized that both these agreements, which had been approved by the FRG, did not imply any recognition of the GDR. Further travel concessions were made by the GDR on March 10, 1964, to enable West Berliners to meet relatives in certain GDR towns, and on Sept. 24, 1964, to allow elderly East Germans to visit relatives in West Berlin and the FRG.

Dr Ludwig Erhard, then Federal Chancellor of the FRG, could declare with satisfaction in a policy statement on Nov. 10, 1965, that the Soviet Union's intention of separating Berlin from West Germany had not been carried out because of "the firm stand of our Allies, our own firm will and above all the gallant attitude of the Berliners". He stated that the future of the city rested on four principles and demands—(i) "the presence of the three Allies in Berlin"; (ii) "unrestricted free access to Berlin"; (iii) Berlin's forming part of free Germany; and (iv) respect for "the unequivocal will of the Berliners" as the basis of any agreement on Berlin.

In a note to the three Western ambassadors in Bonn the Soviet ambassador to the GDR alleged on Feb. 14, 1968, that the FRG had "systematically extended" its "illegal activity" in West Berlin—by holding "regular parliamentary weeks", convening meetings of the FRG Cabinet and of *Bundestag* committees, establishing ministries and other government offices, planning to build an official residence for the Federal President and claiming to exercise state power in West Berlin (whose Chief Burgomaster had been elected president of the *Bundesrat*, the Upper House of the FRG's Parliament). In their reply of March 3 the three Western ambassadors pointed out that the special status of Berlin laid down in the four-power agreements was not limited to West Berlin but covered the whole city, and that in the view of their governments the FRG's concern for "the welfare and validity" of Berlin did not conflict with that status.

On April 13, 1968, the GDR issued an order forbidding FRG ministers and senior officials from travelling through the GDR to Berlin. The Western ambassadors, however, reminded the Soviet government on April 19 that the GDR authorities were "not competent to modify the four-power agreements" on access to Berlin. In further decrees issued on June 11, 1968, the GDR imposed new restrictions on West German and West Berlin citizens and goods, involving the carrying of passports or identity cards, the requirement of visas and payment of taxes. The official GDR motivation for these measures was the 17th amendment to the Basic Law (constitution) of the FRG, granting the government far-reaching powers to deal with any emergency (which had been approved by the *Bundestag* on May 30, 1968, and had thereafter been condemned as "anti-democratic and militaristic" by the GDR and the Soviet government).

Signature of 1971 Quadripartite Agreement on Berlin

As a result of protracted negotiations by the four occupation powers a new quadripartite agreement on Berlin was signed on Sept. 3, 1971. In this agreement it was decided that all disputes should be "settled solely by peaceful means" and that the situation in the area (of Greater Berlin) should "not be changed unilaterally". The agreement provided that transit traffic through the territory of the GDR between the western sectors of Berlin and the FRG should be unimpeded, and that "the ties between the western sectors of Berlin and the FRG will be maintained and developed, taking into account that these sectors continue not to be a constituent part of the FRG and not to be governed by it".

In an annex on the status of West Berlin, Britain, France and the United States agreed that "the provisions of the Basic Law of the FRG and of the constitution operative in the western sectors of Berlin which contradict the above have been suspended and continue not to be in effect", and also that no constitutional or official acts would be performed in the western sectors of Berlin by state bodies of the FRG.

The conclusion of this agreement was followed by further agreements, in particular (i) an agreement between the FRG and the GDR on transit traffic between the FRG and West Berlin, signed on Dec. 17, 1971, and (ii) agreements between the West Berlin Senate and the GDR on the facilitation of visits by West Berliners to East Berlin and the GDR, and another one on an exchange of territory designed to provide West Berlin with access to what had hitherto been an enclave in East Berlin territory—both these agreements being signed on Dec. 20, 1971. All three agreements came into force on June 3, 1972, together with the quadripartite agreement.

A new transit agreement replacing one of Dec. 19, 1975 (providing for annual tolls to be paid by the FRG to the GDR), was signed on Nov. 16, 1978, between the FRG and the GDR involving inter alia the construction of a motorway link between Hamburg and West Berlin at the expense of the FRG. (According to a statement made on March 4, 1979, by the FRG Minister of Inter-German Affairs, about 100,000,000 visitors to West Berlin had used the road and rail transit routes since the entry into force of the four-power agreement on Berlin in 1972.)

After 1975 it became apparent that there were differing interpretations of the 1971 quadripartite agreement on Berlin in East and West. The Soviet ambassador to the GDR declared on Sept. 3, 1976, that the agreement's conditions applied to West Berlin only, and that West Berlin should not be drawn into the process of West European integration (and in particular not be represented in the Parliament of the European Communities).

Under a GDR passport law (published on Dec. 30, 1976, in the *Legal Gazette for Greater Berlin* and entering into force on Jan. 1, 1977), all persons (i.e. also non-Germans) entering East Berlin or the GDR would require a visa valid until midnight on the day of entry. A GDR government spokesman claimed that this law did not infringe the four-power agreement, to which in his view East Berlin was not subject. The GDR at the same time withdrew control points between East Berlin and the GDR. The governments of Britain, France and the United States protested against this action on Jan. 6, 1977, emphasizing that the 1971 agreement applied to the whole of Berlin and calling on the Soviet Union to carry out its obligations under the agreement. However, on Jan. 11 Moscow radio claimed that the four-power status of the whole of Berlin had been destroyed by the unilateral action of the Western Allies in 1948 (at the six-power London conference). Moreover, a spokesman for the government of the FRG said on Jan. 18 that the GDR was not a signatory to the four-power agreement and therefore had no authority regarding West Berlin.

The Western attitude to the 1971 quadripartite agreement on Berlin was strongly reaffirmed by the Presidents of France and the United States, the UK Prime Minister and the Federal Chancellor of the FRG in a statement issued on May 8, 1977, confirming inter alia that the status of the special area of Berlin could not be modified unilaterally, and that the ties between West Berlin and the FRG should be maintained and developed. The statement was subsequently rejected by the Soviet Union, and in *Pravda* (the organ of the central committee of the Communist Party of the Soviet Union) it was claimed on May 15, 1977, that it was "well known that for a long time there has been neither a Germany nor a Berlin; there is the FRG, there is the GDR and there is West Berlin with its occupation regime"; and that the four-power status of Berlin had not existed since 1948, following the London six-power conference and the division of the Berlin *Magistrat*.

Incidents arose on a number of occasions during 1977-78 from GDR refusals to admit FRG political representatives to the GDR or to East Berlin, or even to the West Berlin transit routes. For their part, the Western powers repeatedly protested against the presence (and in particular traditional parades) of units of the GDR's National People's Army, which the West considered to be "illegal" and in contravention of the four-power agreements under which Berlin was to be a demilitarized zone.

The de facto incorporation of East Berlin in the GDR was further confirmed on June 28, 1979, when the *Volkskammer* unanimously decided to extend full status and voting rights to the 66 representatives of East Berlin in the House (who had hitherto been appointed to the *Volkskammer* by the East Berlin Municipal Assembly) and to amend the 1967 electoral law so as to enable them to be directly elected like all other members of the *Volkskammer*. This decision led to protests by the Western powers, the government of the FRG and the *Bundestag*, the Western powers stating in particular that this "unilateral action" was altering the special status of Berlin in contravention of the four-power agreement of Sept. 3, 1971.

HWD

Greece-Turkey

Disputes between Greece and Turkey over the Aegean Sea, which lies between the Greek and Turkish mainlands, have for some years been a source of tension between the two countries and have on several occasions given rise not merely to diplomatic measures but also to states of military alert in either or both states. In the present day the only major islands in the Aegean under Turkish sovereignty are Gökçeada (Imbroz) and Bozcaada (Tenedos) in the northern Aegean close to the mouth of the Dardanelles. Greek sovereignty over most of the others was confirmed in the dismemberment of the non-Turkish parts of the Ottoman empire which followed World War I, while the Dodecanese (Sporades) in the south-eastern Aegean were ceded to Greece by Italy at the end of World War II. Although neither side is officially seeking to challenge the respective sovereignties resulting from these earlier territorial adjustments, an unresolved dispute over the delimitation of the Aegean continental shelf to some extent reflects historical animosities between Greeks and Turks and a continuing feeling among sections of both populations that existing territorial arrangements are unsatisfactory.

The establishment of Greece's sovereignty over most of the Aegean islands in the 20th century has stemmed from its aspiration to bring within the national territory all those areas with longstanding Greek populations which had previously been excluded for various reasons; moreover, the eastern Aegean islands have major strategic importance for Greece in that they command most of the eastern coastline of Turkish Anatolia. Since 1970, however, attention has been increasingly focused on the mineral potential of the continental shelf in the Aegean itself, and consequently questions of maritime, strategic, economic and purely territorial advantage have become intermixed. The arguments surrounding the sovereignty of the continental shelf between the eastern Aegean islands and the Greek mainland remain problematic, insofar as there is as yet no complete or definitive set of international rulings on the law of the sea, but only a complex and often contradictory body of individual rulings and conventions, parts of which can be and frequently are quoted to the advantage of either party.

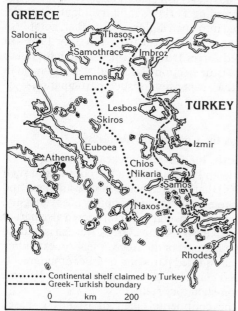

Map 7   The Aegean Sea.

The Aegean dispute, although currently centring on an issue of undefined maritime law, is nonetheless relevant to a consideration of the territorial relationships between Greece and Turkey insofar as it has often been the theatre in which other disputes were enacted. It has been particularly important, for example, at various stages of the Cyprus dispute,[1] whether in terms of military strategy or of actual territorial bargaining; moreover, the resentment still felt by many Turks at the Greek possession of the islands can be seen as a significant factor in the general and continuing

---

[1]For an account of the Cyprus Question, see pages 16-26.

tension between the two countries. Although Turkey has at present no formal claims for their return, the issue remains politically alive in Turkey and has frequently been exploited as a source of electoral support, particularly by extremist nationalist forces. As recently as 1976, the extreme right-wing National Action Party (NAP) leader and then Deputy Prime Minister, Col. Alparslan Türkes, made a series of controversial statements on the alleged Turkish character of the Greek Aegean islands, demanding that all islands within 50 kilometres of the Anatolian coast (including Lesbos and the Dodecanese) should be returned to Turkey.

As far as Greek opinion is concerned, its perception of Turkish intentions remains historically coloured by the disastrous defeat suffered by Greek forces in the 1921-22 war with Turkey, initiated by Greece in an attempt to secure the Ottoman territories which it had been awarded under the 1920 Treaty of Sèvres—i.e. most of Thrace west of Constantinople (Istanbul), the islands of Imbroz and Tenedos and the Dodecanese (except Rhodes), as well as mandated authority over the Anatolian port of Smyrna (Izmir) and its hinterland. Lacking any support from the European powers, the Greek forces were driven out of Anatolia by Kemal Atatürk in 1922 and under the 1923 Treaty of Lausanne Greece recognized Turkish sovereignty over the disputed territories, except that the Dodecanese were ceded to Italy (which had backed the Turks in the recent war). Although the 1922 disaster effectively marked the end of "Greater Greece" aspirations, in many Greek minds the episode is still seen as an avoidable defeat for "Christian Europe" at the hands of the Moslem East.

In the post-World War II era the exigencies of the international balance of power brought both Greece and Turkey into the North Atlantic Treaty Organization (NATO) and the two countries have also come together under the umbrella of the Council of Europe. Nevertheless, their relations have continued to be adversely affected by underlying historical strains and in particular by Greek suspicions concerning Turkey's military intentions in the area. These strains have from time to time escalated into open diplomatic conflict, notably in connexion with the occupation of northern Cyprus by Turkish troops in July 1974—in protest against which Greece withdrew its armed forces from NATO. (Although Greece resumed its military participation in NATO in 1980, the election of a Socialist government in Athens the following year again led to the effective suspension of such participation—see below.)

Basic Greek and Turkish Positions on the Continental Shelf Issue

The argument adduced by Greece as regards the current Aegean Sea dispute is fundamentally based on the theses (i) that every island is entitled to a full continental shelf and 12-mile territorial water limit of its own, and (ii) that the area between such an island and the country of which it forms part should, in the interests of "the indivisibility of sovereignty, political unity and national territory, be it continental or insular", be considered also part of that sovereign area. Accordingly, because of the proximity of many Greek Aegean islands to the Turkish coastline, Greece claims by far the greater part of the Aegean seabed, extending to points east of its easternmost islands. Greece has quoted parts of a number of judgments and conventions in support of this argument, and claims that some of them have become international customary law, binding even on non-signatory states.

The first-mentioned argument concerning the continental shelf of islands is based primarily on a convention adopted by certain nations (including Greece but not Turkey) at the first United Nations Conference on the Law of the Sea, which took place on Feb. 24-April 28, 1958, in Geneva. The convention, which was the first of its type to attempt a definition of a continental shelf, defined the shelf in Article 1 as "(a) the seabed and subsoil of the territorial areas adjacent to the coast, but outside the area of the territorial sea, up to a depth of 200 metres or, beyond that limit, to where the depth of the superjacent waters admits of the exploitation of the natural resources of the said areas; (b) the seabed and subsoil of similar submarine areas adjacent to the coasts of islands". Articles 2 and 3 provide inter alia that the coastal state exercises exclusive rights to the exploitation of mineral resources in the shelf, although these rights "do not affect the legal status of the superjacent waters as high seas, or that of the airspace above those waters" (implying that international shipping, etc., would normally enjoy free passage over the continental shelf).

Greece asserts that the 1958 Geneva convention on the continental shelf has passed into international customary law, and claims in support of this argument that the International Court of Justice, in its February 1969 judgment on the North Sea continental shelf (involving disputes between West Germany, Denmark and the Netherlands), included in Paragraph 63 the observation that Articles 1-3 of the Geneva convention were regarded at least as "reflecting or crystallizing received or emergent rules of customary international law relative to the continental shelf".

The 1958 convention also provided that, in cases where a continental shelf bordered on two or more countries (as, for example, the Aegean borders on Greece and Turkey), the boundary of the shelf was to be determined by mutual agreement; failing that, and unless unusual circumstances justified a different solution, it would, according to Article 6, follow the median line "every part of which is equidistant from the nearest points of the baselines from which the breadth of the territorial sea of each state is measured" (i.e. a line half-way between what could reasonably be described as the broad coastal outlines of the two countries). Failing bilateral agreement, disputes were to be settled by the compulsory jurisdiction of the International Court of Justice (a principle rejected by Turkey as a non-signatory of the convention), or by an independent arbitral tribunal.

The Turkish argument is based on the claim that the Aegean is a special case. While not at present seriously disputing Greek sovereignty over the Greek Aegean islands., Turkey maintains that in geological terms they represent an extension of the Anatolian peninsula and that they thus fall within the scope of a statement made by the International Court of Justice during the 1969 North Sea continental shelf case, to the effect that the rights of the coastal state extend over "the areas of the continental shelf which constitutes a natural prolongation of its land territory". Proceeding on this basis, Turkey has claimed what amounts to half of the Aegean, defining the rightful delineation of the continental shelf as that which follows the north-south median line between the Greek and Turkish mainlands. On Nov. 1, 1973, the Turkish *Official Gazette* published a map based on this principle and showing a line which starts from the mouth of the River Evros (Meric) on the Greek/Turkish mainland border and passes to the west of Samothrace, Lemnos, Aghios Efstratios, Lesbos, Psara and Chios. Turkey allows each of the Greek islands a six-mile territorial waters limit but rejects the Greek view that a 12-mile limit should become the international standard; it has repeatedly expressed the view that a 12-mile limit, coupled with Greek sovereignty over the continental shelf, would effectively turn the Aegean into a "Greek lake".

Greece responds to this argument with the claim that Turkish shipping would enjoy the right to innocent passage both through Greek territorial waters and over the Greek continental shelf, although military shipping would be subject to certain restrictions including a ban on manoeuvres.

Oil Prospecting in the Aegean

Although the prospects of finding significant oil deposits in the Aegean appear modest at present (only one minor oilfield having been tapped so far), the question of Greek and Turkish prospecting rights in the Aegean has prompted the most open manifestations of Greek and Turkish claims in respect of the continental shelf, and has at times led to military tensions and confrontations in the area. Greek prospecting in the Aegean has to date been conducted solely by an international consortium, the North Aegean Petroleum Company (NAPC) led by the Denison Mines Company of Canada—although it is planned to open up the area to other companies such as the Romanian state-owned company Rompetrol, which has already conducted extensive explorations on the Greek mainland. The only productive well so far drilled in the Aegean is in the Prinos oilfield, located in 1973 near Thasos in the northern Aegean; early estimates of a potential production of 50,000-70,000 barrels per day (bpd) proved optimistic, however. A new round of Greek exploration started in 1982, but was abruptly cancelled after threats of reprisals from Turkey.

Turkish prospecting was until early 1980 restricted to the state-owned Turkish Petroleum Corporation (TPAO), which received exclusive exploration rights in November 1973 (from the Turkish government) covering the continental shelf and territorial waters claimed by Turkey. Exploration was first carried out in June 1973 by the Turkish naval vessel *Candarli*, but since then has been conducted under licence by Norwegian, Canadian, American and Turkish vessels, notably the Turkish *Sismik I* [see below]. A new regulation passed by the Turkish Parliament on Jan. 24, 1980, allowed other foreign companies to prospect for oil in the disputed waters, although it was stipulated that 65 per cent of all oil thus obtained should be sold on the Turkish market.

Turkey has on the whole treated its regular seismic exploration of the Aegean as part of the process of registering its claim to the sovereignty of the eastern Aegean continental shelf; Greece on the other hand describes this kind of practice as an attempt to resolve the dispute by fait accompli, and rejects the legitimacy of the Turkish explorations, although it accepts the right of the Turkish seismic vessels to innocent passage when they are not actually prospecting.

Confrontations arising from the Dispute in the 1970s

Following the November 1973 publication of the Turkish map claiming half of the continental shelf, the Turkish government offered on Feb. 27, 1974, to negotiate with Greece on the question of jurisdiction over the Aegean outside the two countries' territorial waters. No Greek reply being forthcoming, work was started in April-May 1974 on the seismic exploration by Turkey of 27 sites in the Aegean. Greece offered on May 25 to negotiate with Turkey on the basis of the 1958 Geneva convention, but repeatedly asserted its claim to any oil found under the continental shelf; however, Turkey rejected the Geneva convention as a basis for discussion, and a deadlock ensued which repeated bilateral discussions at ministerial level failed to resolve.

Relations between the Turkish government and what was then the Greek military regime worsened steadily during the following months, but deteriorated markedly on July 20, 1974, when Turkish troops launched an invasion of northern Cyprus. On that day Turkey issued a Notice to Airmen (Notam 714) in which it declared the air space over the eastern Aegean to be a dangerous zone for international aviation; on Aug. 6, moreover, it unilaterally extended its flight information region to the north-south median line which it claimed to be the just delineation of the continental shelf. Greece, which had under IATA regulations hitherto administered the flight control region over the entire Aegean, was thus obliged to close all Aegean air corridors. This situation prevailed until Feb. 22, 1980, when Turkey withdrew the 1974 instruction, the Aegean air space being re-opened on Feb. 23 to international air traffic.

Turkey resumed its plans to explore the Aegean seabed in January 1975 following the end of the airlift of Turkish Cypriot refugees to Turkey. However, on Jan. 30 the Norwegian vessel *Longva*, which had contracted to undertake the mission, refused to prospect in disputed waters, so that the project was cancelled, causing bitter controversy in Turkish political circles. Seismic research vessels of various nationalities continued the research on behalf of Turkey for the next year, but the most serious military confrontation to arise over the prospecting rights issue involved the Turkish vessel *Sismik I* (a converted ship formerly known as the *Hora*), which began in late July 1976 an exploration of the disputed waters between Lemnos and Lesbos despite calls from several countries, including the United States, for a postponement of its activities. Turkey had already on July 15 threatened that any Greek interference with the mission would be met by force, but when the *Sismik I* sailed on July 23 it was shadowed by the Greek oceanographic research vessel *Naftilos* and by several Greek warships. Greece protested to Turkey on Aug. 7 at the alleged violation of its continental shelf, although Turkey replied that there was neither a Greek nor a Turkish continental shelf while the issue was in dispute.

On Aug. 9, 1976, the Greek government called for an emergency meeting of the United Nations Security Council in view of what appeared to be a threat of war. The Security Council met on Aug. 12 and passed a resolution on Aug. 25 recommending that the two countries should take the dispute to the International Court of Justice (which the following day refused a Greek application for an injunction preventing the Turkish explorations, with the result that the Turkish seismic research continued). A wide range of issues were raised by the two sides in presenting their cases to the UN Security Council. Turkey referred to the "unwarranted harassment" of the *Sismik I*, accused Greece of attempting to annex Cyprus by the overthrow of Archbishop Makarios on July 15, and complained particularly of what it described as the illegal Greek militarization of the eastern Aegean islands (i.e. in contravention of the 1947 Paris peace treaty between the Allies and Italy, under which the Dodecanese had been ceded to Greece).

Particularly after the 1974 Turkish intervention in Cyprus, Greece had engaged in the military development of certain of the eastern Dodecanese in view of what was regarded as a direct military threat from Turkey. Turkey had responded in July 1975 by creating a new Fourth Army division, known as the "Aegean Army", comprising all ground and naval units on the Aegean coast, with its headquarters in Izmir.

Unsuccessful Moves Towards a Settlement

Greece proposed to Turkey on Jan. 27, 1975, that the Aegean dispute should be placed before the International Court of Justice, to which suggestion Turkey immediately agreed. It rapidly became clear, however, that opinions within Turkey were divided on the advisability of this course, and Turkey began later that year to insist that the International Court of Justice should be invited to rule only on matters which could not be decided by bilateral negotiation. Greece, while agreeing to conduct such bilateral discussions, nevertheless continued to propose jurisdiction by the Court, and on July 18, 1977, following the 1976 confrontation and a similar period of tension in March 1977 over Turkish drillings and military manoeuvres in the Aegean, it submitted a memorial to the Court stating its arguments. Turkey, however, refused to recognize the authority of the Court to rule on what it described as a domestic dispute, and consequently refused to attend or to submit memorials to the Court. The Court began an examination of the case in late 1977 but concluded in a decision of Dec. 19, 1978, that it was incompetent to make a ruling on what it described as a matter of "domestic jurisdiction" between the two countries.

Meanwhile, in accordance with Turkey's wishes, the two countries engaged from September 1976 onwards in bilateral discussions with the aim of determining a technical basis for the delineation of Aegean seabed rights. The first such discussions took place in New York in September 1976 between the Greek and Turkish Foreign Ministers, and on Nov. 11, 1976, an agreement was signed in Berne providing for the establishment of a joint standing committee of experts to study "inter-state practice and international rules for the determination of sea-bed boundaries" and also containing an undertaking that both sides would refrain from any initiative or action which might have an adverse effect on the negotiations. Although the talks were broken off in 1977 during a period of particular tension over naval manoeuvres in the Aegean, they resumed in March 1978, when it was agreed by both countries to refrain from publishing details of the discussions in order to avoid disturbance by domestic factors on either side.

The military coup in Turkey in September 1980 had the effect of blocking further substantive discussions. Following the gradual restoration of civilian rule in Turkey from 1983, the authorities in Ankara sought to initiate new talks with Greece on all the issues which divided the two countries. However, preliminary talks in mid-1983 had been cut short by Turkey's recognition of the newly-proclaimed Turkish Republic of Northern Cyprus, and the Athens government ruled out any further direct discussions until Turkey undertook to withdraw its troops from Cyprus and to accept what the Greek side terms "the existing legal regime in the Aegean".

External Discussions at the European Community and NATO

In 1987 Greece was still formally refusing to open negotiations of any sort with Turkey as long as the Cyprus occupation continued. It has, however, repeatedly raised its complaints against Turkey within the forum of the European Community, which it joined as a full member in 1981. The Greek insistence on this issue has been forthright, notwithstanding the European Commission's recommendation at the time of admission that the Community should not be made a party to Greek-Turkish territorial disputes.

Although its main accusations against Turkey centre on violations of human rights, both during and in the aftermath of the period of Turkish military rule, Greece's arguments are widely recognized as being founded on territorial questions. In particular, the country has been trying to force a discussion of Turkey's activities in the Aegean, in Cyprus and in Thrace [see below], with a view to exerting pressure on Turkey through sanctions and through a restriction of its association agreement with the EEC (dating from 1964). Although, as other members of the European Community have pointed out, Greece accepted the Turkish association agreement as a condition of joining the Community, it has moved (i) to block the extension of the agreement to the new Community members, Spain and Portugal, which joined in January 1986, and (ii) to restrict the planned provisions of free movement for Turkish workers within the Community, which were due for full implementation in 1987-88.

As a prelude to its application for full membership of the European Community (lodged on April 14, 1987), the Turkish government confirmed in February 1987 that it intended to lift a decree dating from 1964 preventing ethnic Greeks living in Istanbul (numbering about 7,000) from selling their property. The lifting of this decree had been one of Greece's conditions for accepting the further development of the EEC-Turkey association agreement, but was not expected to make Greece more amenable to full Turkish membership (Greece being the only Community country to vote against the referral of the Turkish application to the European Commission on April 27). Greek charges of Turkish mistreatment of ethnic Greeks in Istanbul (and also in Izmir) were regularly countered by Turkish allegations that Turks on the Greek side of the border in Thrace suffered officially condoned disadvantages.

More serious problems have arisen within the context of the North Atlantic Treaty Organization, where Greek-Turkish aerial and naval tensions have proved a real obstacle to co-operation in security matters. Conflict surrounds the refusal of NATO to use the Greek army and air force bases at Lemnos, or their reconnaissance facilities, in aerial or naval manoeuvres, on the grounds that this would amount to taking sides on the disputed issue of Greece's right to develop military installations on the island. Greece, however, takes the view that the 1923 Lausanne Treaty's demilitarization of Lemnos and Samothrace ended with the signature of the 1936 Montreux Convention, and it has recently made a firm stand for militarization. In 1982, 1983 and 1984 it cancelled its participation in NATO exercises in northern Greece, largely because of the NATO refusal to use Lemnos.

Both sides have repeatedly expressed apprehension over NATO proposals for military development in one or the other country, with Greece insisting that the United States' fixed ratio of assistance (US$7 to Turkey for every US$10 to Greece) must be maintained at all costs. Greece threatened in February 1984 to suspend a recently-concluded agreement with the US unless alleged overspending in Turkey were curtailed. Relations deteriorated further in the first half of 1986, with Greece announcing a new civil defence plan for the eastern Greek islands, which it declared were targets for invasion by the Turkish Fourth Army.

December 1986 Military Clash in Thrace

The area of land between Istanbul and the River Evros, which forms the border between Greece and Turkey, has remained within Turkey's borders since the defeat of Greek forces in the 1921-22 war with Turkey. Although Greece no longer lays any formal claim to any part of the territory, and although relations between the mixed Greek and Turkish elements on either side of the border have been generally peaceful, they have tended to improve or deteriorate in accordance with the climate of bilateral relations. The region's proximity to

Samothrace and Imbroz has lent a particular local currency to the issues of territorial waters and general Aegean security, and the conflicts over the Aegean, Cyprus and other issues have been reflected in the late 1970s and 1980s by considerable tensions which have periodically erupted into violence.

One of the worst of these incidents occurred on Dec. 19, 1986, on the Evros border near the Greek town of Ferrai, when a Greek soldier and two Turkish soldiers were killed in what was described by the Greeks as a calculated ambush of one of its patrols. The shooting developed as Greek troops were attempting to prevent Iranian refugees from crossing the border, it being alleged by the Greek side that the Turkish authorities were assisting such illegal entry. Both sides claimed that the other had committed a territorial infringement.

The Turkish Prime Minister, Turgut Özal, said that the incident proved the need for Greek-Turkish dialogue and renewed an offer made in April 1985 to conclude a treaty of friendship and co-operation with Greece and to guarantee the existing frontiers between the two countries. However, the Greek government rejected the proposal as "a trap".

Further Aegean Tensions, 1986-87

In the Aegean Sea, periodic incidents in the early 1980s developed into further sharp tensions from mid-1986, with each side accusing the other of violations of national airspace by military aircraft and of infringements of territorial waters. On July 29, 1986, the Greek government protested over the alleged violation of its coastal limits by the Turkish scientific research vessel *Piri Reis*, while it was reported the next day that Turkey had complained that Greek aircraft and warships had harassed the vessel in international waters. A further Greek protest was lodged over an incident on Sept. 16, when it was alleged that Turkish warships had fired five volleys close to a Greek patrol boat in international waters near Lesbos. The Turkish authorities rejected the protest, however.

Further incidents occurred in the Aegean in early March 1987 involving the *Piri Reis*, with the Greek authorities protesting that its course near or around Greek islands was provocative and the Turkish side again complaining of harassment of the vessel. Relations were also strained by the tabling of a government bill in the Greek Parliament on March 6 providing for government control of the North Aegean Petroleum Company (NAPC), which exploited the Prinos oilfield off the island of Thasos [see above]. The Athens government justified this step on the grounds that the NAPC's stated intention to begin exploratory drillings outside the Greek territorial limit (but within what Greece regarded as its continental shelf) should be a state responsibility in view of the potential international implications. The Turkish government responded that it would take "the necessary measures to safeguard its rights and interests in the Aegean" if the NAPC proceeded with its plans, claiming that any exploration would be in breach of the 1976 Berne agreement, under which the two sides had undertaken not to search for oil outside their respective territorial waters while the continental shelf issue remained unresolved. The Greek side replied that in its view the Berne agreement was no longer valid and asserted that Greece would decide when, where and how to conduct exploration on the "Greek continental shelf".

On March 25, 1987, the Turkish government decided to issue a permit to the state-owned Turkish Petroleum Corporation (TPAO) for oil exploration outside Turkish territorial waters, off the Greek islands of Lesbos, Lemnos and Samothrace. On the following day the Athens government warned that if the TPAO research vessel *Sismik I* carried out work "in areas where under conventional and customary law the continental shelf belongs to Greece", Greece would take "the necessary measures to ensure its sovereign rights". Greece also reiterated its longstanding offer to submit the Aegean Sea continental shelf dispute to the arbitration of the International Court of Justice.

The Greek Prime Minister, Dr Andreas Papandreou, stated on March 27 that the Greek armed forces would "teach the Turks a very hard lesson" if Turkey continued with its "aggressive acts" in the Aegean, and warned that in the event of hostilities breaking out US military bases in Greece would be closed. Amid reports that the armed forces of Greece and

Turkey had been placed on alert, strenuous mediation efforts were mounted within the NATO framework and produced an announcement by the Turkish Prime Minister later on March 27 that the *Sismik I* would not commence exploratory operation outside territorial waters unless the Greek side did so first. Although the vessel set sail from the Dardanelles on March 28 accompanied by a naval escort, the Turkish government announced later in the day that the escort had been withdrawn and that the *Sismik I* would not operate in disputed waters. For its part, the Greek government also gave assurances that oil exploration would not be conducted in disputed areas and that NAPC plans in that respect had been frozen.

In the period after the March 1987 crisis, the Greek and Turkish Prime Ministers exchanged messages which were believed to relate to the possibility of establishing the basis for submission of the Aegean dispute to the International Court of Justice.

MW

Hungary-Romania (Northern Transylvania)

Under the territorial changes made in Eastern Europe after World War II Hungary ceded Northern Transylvania to Romania, which had acquired the whole of Transylvania in the post-World War I break-up of the Austro-Hungarian empire but had been forced to cede the northern part to Hungary in 1940. To the extent that the post-1945 territorial adjustments made in the Soviet sphere of influence in Europe were accepted by all governments concerned as final, no formal dispute exists between Hungary and Romania over the sovereignty of Northern Transylvania (the majority of whose inhabitants are Romanians). Nevertheless, there have been periodic manifestations of official Hungarian concern at the Romanian government's treatment of the Hungarian inhabitants of the region (who constitute the largest national minority group in Europe), suggesting that territorial issues cannot be regarded as completely closed between two countries.

Historical Background

The province of Transylvania, a naturally well-endowed plateau of some 24,000 square miles (62,000 sq km) separated from the rest of Romania by the Carpathian mountains and the Transylvanian Alps, has been the subject of contending national aspirations for a thousand years. Magyar-speaking settlers (*Szeklers*) began to move into Transylvania in the 10th century and the province was eventually conquered by King Stephen of Hungary in 1003. After a substantial admixture of Germans had arrived in the 12th and 13th centuries, the so-called "three nations" of the province (i.e. Romanians, Magyars and Germans) enjoyed self-government under Hungarian and later (from 1526) Ottoman Turkish suzerainty. At the end of the 17th century Transylvania came under the dominion of the Austrian Hapsburgs and later became an important factor in Hungarian efforts to throw off Austrian rule, notably as the scene of much strife during the Hungarian revolt of 1848-49.

Regarded by the Hungarians as part of their historic national territory, Transylvania was incorporated into the Hungarian part of the Austro-Hungarian empire born in 1867. But the new independent state of Romania which emerged at this time aspired to incorporate the province into its territory, on the grounds that a majority of its inhabitants were Romanians. Having entered World War I on the side of the Allies in 1916 with this end in view, Romania initially suffered humiliation at the hands of the Central Powers, but on the eventual defeat of the latter Transylvania was one of its territorial rewards. After 20 years of Romanian rule, however, the northern half of Transylvania was transferred to Hungary by the August 1940 "Vienna award", under which Romania also lost Bessarabia and Northern Bukovina to the Soviet Union and Southern Dobruja to Bulgaria. The arbitrators on this occasion were Nazi Germany and Italy, to which Axis Hungary was then allied, and their findings were widely believed to reflect secret agreements reached between Hitler and Stalin in the context of their short-lived non-aggression pact of August 1939.

In 1941 Romania joined Germany in its invasion of the Soviet Union and succeeded in recovering Bessarabia and Northern Bukovina (as well as annexing a large adjacent area of Soviet territory), although Northern Transylvania remained under the sovereignty of Hungary. The eventual victory of the Red Army transformed the situation yet again, Romania being obliged to restore Bessarabia and Northern Bukovina to Soviet sovereignty (notwithstanding the former's substantial Romanian majority) and Hungary being constrained to restore Northern Transylvania to Romania.[1] These dispositions were enshrined in the 1947 Paris peace treaties signed by the Allies with Hungary and Romania (treaties which also confirmed Bulgarian sovereignty over Southern Dobruja, the reversion of Eastern Slovakia from Hungary to Czechoslovakia and the transfer of Ruthenia from Czechoslovakia to the Soviet Union).

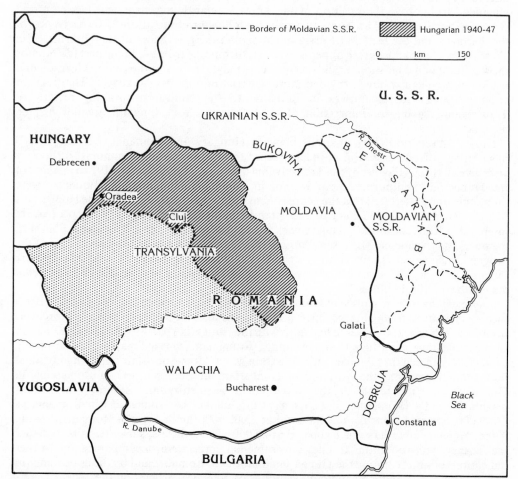

Map 8 Present borders of Hungary, Romania and the Soviet Union, showing Transylvania and Bessarabia.

---

[1]For an account of the Bessarabian question, see pages 85–90.

Post-War Dissension over Minorities Question

In the first post-war decade the Hungarian and German minorities in Transylvania were afforded the protection of the occupying Soviet authorities against attempts to suppress their national identities made by the Romanian government. However, after the departure of Soviet troops in 1956 a number of measures were taken by the Romanian authorities which were regarded by the Hungarian minority as inimical to its interests and which in consequence generated strains in relations between the allied governments of Hungary and Romania. During the 1960s the grievances of the Hungarian minority in Romania included—according to *The Times* of London dated Aug. 12, 1971—"restrictions on instruction in their mother tongue, the forcible merging of universities with Romanian ones, job discrimination, inadequate representation in the higher party and state organs, and isolation from the mainstream of Hungarian cultural life".

The same report continued, however, that President Ceausescu (who had assumed the leadership of the Romanian Communist Party in 1965 and the presidency in 1967) had taken steps to correct "the grosser injustices of his Stalinist predecessor's nationalist policies" and to ease "the suspicions of the minorities"; accelerated in the wake of the 1968 Soviet-led intervention in Czechoslovakia (in which Romania did not participate), such measures were intended "to improve the position of the Transylvanian Hungarians and Germans and cement national unity". The report also made the following observation: "The restiveness of the Germans and the fear that Russia might exploit the grievances of the Hungarians in Transylvania have added fresh impetus to efforts to improve their lot. In the past few months their cultural and educational rights have been strengthened, and the radio, television and mass media generally have provided more material in minority languages. The frequent visits of Soviet representatives in Romania to the Hungarian-speaking regions of Transylvania, giving an impression of Soviet support for Hungary, are not helping matters . . . ."

During this period recriminations between Hungary and Romania over the latter's increasingly forceful assertion of independence from Moscow-line communist orthodoxy were given a special flavour by the Transylvania question. Thus in August 1971 a member of the Hungarian Politburo, Zoltan Komocsin, said that Hungarian Communists were "fundamentally interested that the people of both our countries—including the Hungarians living in Romania—should come to understand that the fate and destiny of our peoples are inseparable from socialism". This remark brought a retort from a Romanian Politburo member, Paul Nicolescu-Mizil, that "no-one can set himself up as an arbiter or judge of the progress of socialism in one country or another", especially not those who in 1956 were "unable to cope with the task of governing their own party and people and registered lamentable political failures".

Such exchanges did not prevent Hungary and Romania from renewing (on Feb. 24, 1972) their 1948 treaty of friendship, co-operation and assistance for a further 20 years. Moreover, in mid-1977 President Ceausescu had talks with the Hungarian party leader, János Kádár, in Debrecen (Hungary) on June 15 and in Oradea (Romanian Transylvania) on June 16, during which it was agreed that the minorities question was a "domestic affair" of each individual host country and that the existence of Hungarians in Romania and of Romanians in Hungary was "the result of the development of history and several centuries of neighbourhood". (Romanian statistics gave the number of Hungarians in Romania as 1,700,000, whereas Hungary put the total at 2,000,000; the number of Romanians living within Hungary's borders was estimated at 20,000.) Nevertheless, such attempts to defuse the Transylvania question at inter-governmental level were accompanied by further indications of unrest among the Hungarian minority in Romania and by the appearance in various Hungarian and Romanian publications of polemical articles on the issue.

Allegations of government repression of the Hungarian minority in Romania were made in an open letter sent in December 1977 to the leadership of the Romanian Communist Party (RCP) by Carol Kiraly, a former high-ranking party official of Hungarian extraction, who maintained in particular that Hungarians living in Romania were subject to discrimination in employment and education. The Romanian government responded by branding Kiraly a traitor, threatening to expel him from the party and denying all allegations that minorities were being repressed—this last contention being quickly endorsed by meetings in Bucharest of both the Hungarian and the German national councils of Romania. Nevertheless, it was reported on April 24, 1978, that three prominent members of the Hungarian community who held leading positions in the RCP—namely Janos Fazekas (a Deputy Premier), Prof. Lajos Takacs (a former chancellor of the University of Cluj in Transylvania) and Andreas Suto (a well-known writer)—had sent separate appeals to the Romanian leadership protesting against the government's alleged discriminatory policies towards its minority groups and demanding a number of improvements.

Although the Hungarian government made no official comment on these developments, its continuing interest in the Transylvania question was indicated by the appearance during this period of a number of articles by individuals expressing dissatisfaction with Romania's treatment of its Hungarian minority. Moreover, in December 1977 the Budapest newspaper *Magyar Hirlap* published comments by a Hungarian historian who called into question official Romanian theories on the origins of the Romanian people and their continued presence in Transylvania. The Romanian authorities responded with their own articles denying allegations of anti-minority discrimination and criticizing Hungary for permitting the publication of material "hostile" to Romania. At the same time (i.e. early May 1978) the official Romanian news agency Agerpres republished in full an article by the Romanian historian Dr Ion Spalatelu dealing in depth with the atrocities perpetrated by Hungary under Admiral Horthy during its occupation of Northern Transylvania in 1940-44. This article concluded with the assertion that, although the overwhelming majority of Hungarian nationals lived in complete harmony and shared equal rights with Romanian citizens, they still had to fight against "fascist and Horthyist elements in various parts of the world" who were attempting "to revive the chauvinistic, irredentist policy which caused so much suffering to broad masses of citizens".

Continued Tensions over Northern Transylvania in the 1980s

From 1982 Hungarian-Romanian relations became increasingly strained over the Northern Transylvanian question, as further allegations were made in Hungary of official Romanian discrimination against the Hungarian population of the region. Although the Foreign Ministers of the two countries agreed in March 1983 that the minority issue must be solved by diplomatic means, during that year polemics developed between newspapers and journals of the two countries, particularly over what was viewed by the Hungarian side as the overtly nationalist tone of Romanian celebrations of the 65th anniversary of the original union of Transylvania with Romania. In September 1984 an official Romanian delegation to Hungary, including three members of the RCP secretariat, was reportedly presented with a 12-page document suggesting ways in which the position of the Transylvanian Hungarians could be improved. However, all allegations of discrimination against the minority were rejected by Romanian officials. Later the same month (September 1984), the parliamentary assembly of the Council of Europe (of West European states) adopted a report on the position of minorities in Romania and called on the Romanian government to ensure respect for their rights.

In December 1984 the Romanian news agency Agerpress twice carried articles from *Romania Literara* (the organ of the Union of Writers) strongly criticizing the Hungarian journal *Kritika* for publishing historical documents which supported Hungary's claim the Hungarian-inhabited areas of Transylvania. In the same month the central committee of the ruling Hungarian Socialist Workers' Party (HSWP) issued guiding policy principles which raised the issue of Hungarian minorities abroad, apparently for the first time in such a context. The documents stated that it was "natural to demand that citizens of Hungarian nationality in neighbouring countries should be permitted to develop fully their national culture and to use their mother tongue". At the end of the month, President Ceausescu responded by defending his government's record on minorities at a joint meeting of the Council of Working People of Hungarian Nationality and its German counterpart, voicing strong opposition to the belief that "the national question in one country ... should be dealt with by parties or governments in other countries".

Official Hungarian concern for the Northern Transylvanian minority did not extend to giving any support to dissident intellectuals who called for more vigorous action vis-à-vis the Romanian government. In fact, restrictive measures were taken against several intellectuals who had once lived in Transylvania, notably Gáspár Miklós Tamás, who in mid-1984 had written to *The Times* of London requesting help from "Western media and elected bodies" for the Hungarian minority and drawing attention to the cases of four Transylvanian Hungarians who had been detained by the Romanian authorities since late 1982 on "apparently absurd grounds". For their part, the Romanian authorities were reported in October 1985 to have searched the homes of a number of Romanians and ethnic Hungarians living in Transylvania and to have confiscated copies of a memorandum protesting about the position of the Hungarian minority. It was understood that the memorandum had been submitted to the European Cultural Forum held in Budapest in October-November 1985 within the framework of the Conference on Security and Co-operation in Europe (CSCE), while a year later Hungary was a joint sponsor with Canada of a resolution on the protection of national minorities submitted to the third CSCE follow-up meeting which opened in Vienna in November 1986.

The issue flared up again in February 1987, when President Ceausescu publicly condemned a three-volume history of Transylvania published in November 1986 by the Hungarian Academy of Science, which apparently challenged the view that the region had been occupied first by ethnic Romanians and only later by Magyars (i.e. Hungarians). Speaking to representatives of Romania's ethnic minorities, the President described the work as reviving "Horthyist, fascist, chauvinist and even racist ideas" and asked "Whom does this science serve, except the most reactionary imperialist circles?" He added that, in his view, such ideas "by no means serve the cause of friendship and collaboration, or the cause of socialism".

In a television interview on March 8, 1987, the Hungarian Secretary of State for Foreign Affairs, Gyula Horn, commented that "one cannot speak of fruitful and truly friendly relations between two communist countries if there are problems with national minorities" and referred to the plight of "millions of Hungarians living in our vicinity", although he did not specifically mention Romania. He added that, while Hungary was using its "right to draw attention to the importance of problems of Hungarian nationals living outside our frontiers", this did not mean that the Hungarian authorities wanted to interfere in the internal affairs of its neighbours.

In the light of such exchanges and other factors, it is the view of many observers that the Transylvania question remains a "live" issue within the context of East European power politics. As stated above, there is no territorial dispute as such between the present governments of Hungary and Romania, each of which remains committed to the territorial adjustments made in the wake of the Red Army's victory in 1945. At the same time, the Soviet guarantee of Romania's existing borders is seen as an important factor in relations between Bucharest and Moscow in that it provides the latter with the option of reopening the Transylvania question should Romania's pursuance of an independent line within the communist fold come to be regarded as unacceptable by the Soviet Union.

In a move to defuse the extreme tension between the two countries, a senior Romanian delegation, led by Emil Bobu (a member of the RCP permanent bureau), had talks in Budapest on June 3, 1987, with a team led by Matyas Szürös (an HSWP secretary); however, this highest-level meeting between the two sides for a decade apparently failed to result in any significant easement of Hungary's concern over the situation in Northern Transylvania. Shortly before the Budapest talks, the Romanian government had ordered the closure of the Hungarian consulate in Cluj (containing the biggest Hungarian community in Romania) because of "unacceptable" behaviour by the consul. **AJD**

The Northern Ireland Question

The partition of Ireland in 1922 into an independent and overwhelmingly Catholic state on the one hand and a northern Protestant-majority province which remained part of the United Kingdom on the other has been the source of serious dispute and conflict ever since. In what was to become the Irish Republic the partition of Ireland has always been regarded as artificial and successive governments have remained committed to reunification as a basic objective, while recognizing that this should be achieved with the consent of the majority of the people in the North. Within Northern Ireland itself the overwhelming majority of the Protestant community have consistently opposed union with the Republic, while successive UK governments have upheld the principle that no change should be made in Northern Ireland's status without the consent of a majority of its population. In recent years this fundamental political deadlock has been accompanied by a serious escalation of violence in the form both of armed struggle between militant pro-unification movements and the security forces on both sides of the border and of sectarian tensions between the Protestant and Catholic communities in Northern Ireland itself. The 1985 Anglo-Irish Agreement represented a new departure at governmental level in that, in return for obtaining a consultative role in Northern Irish affairs, the Dublin government formally accepted that Irish reunification could only be achieved with the consent of the Northern majority. However, the Agreement has been strongly opposed not only by Protestant Unionists in the North but also by the militant Irish nationalist groups.

The existing boundary between the Republic of Ireland and Northern Ireland (a province of the United Kingdom of Great Britain and Northern Ireland) was confirmed in 1925, after the establishment of the Irish Free State as a self-governing dominion under an Anglo-Irish treaty which was signed on Dec. 6, 1921, and which came into force in 1922. Under this treaty the Irish Free State became a co-equal member of the Commonwealth with the rights of an independent country, but its ambassadors were accredited by the British monarch, who was represented in the Irish Free State by a governor-general; moreover, members of the Irish Parliament were required to swear an oath of allegiance to the British Crown.

The conclusion of the treaty was preceded by the passage in Britain of the Government of Ireland Act, which became law on Dec. 23, 1920, and came into operation in June 1921. This act effectively enabled the Protestant Unionists in the north to retain control of six counties of the Irish province of Ulster—i.e. of Antrim, Armagh, Down, Fermanagh, Londonderry and Tyrone, but not of Cavan, Donegal and Monaghan—and reflected their belief (as stated in a report to a cabinet committee) that the inclusion of the latter counties in a separate political entity in the north would "provide such an access of strength to the Roman Catholic party that the supremacy of the Unionists would be seriously threatened". Under the 1921 treaty the six counties were given the option of retaining their status under the 1920 act, and they exercised this option immediately, so that the partition of Ireland became a fact in 1922, with Cavan, Donegal and Monaghan becoming part of a 26-county Irish Free State.

The 1920 act also gave Northern Ireland its own government and parliament (for which a new building was completed at Stormont, Belfast, in 1932). Moreover, the act created a Council of Ireland to encourage co-operation between the two parts of Ireland, but after the settlement of the boundary in 1925 this Council was formally dissolved in 1926. Those parts of the act referring to the Irish Free State were repealed by the British Parliament in 1927. In 1936 the Irish Free State, by its External Relations Act, removed all mention of the Crown from its constitution, and a new constitution adopted in 1937 removed any distinction between the Free State and Northern Ireland. Articles 2 and 3 of the 1937 constitution define "the national territory" as "the whole island of Ireland" (referred to as Eire) but provide that "pending the reintegration of the national territory" the constitution would apply only in the 26 counties.

Under a 1948 act Eire formally became the Republic of Ireland on Easter Sunday 1949, on which day it left the Commonwealth. The British government thereupon passed the Ireland Act 1949, which guaranteed Northern Ireland's constitutional position, stating in particular: "It is hereby declared that Northern Ireland remains part of His Majesty's dominions and of the United Kingdom, and it is hereby affirmed that in no event will Northern Ireland or any part thereof cease to be part of His Majesty's dominions and of the United Kingdom without the consent of the Parliament of Northern Ireland".

The conflict over the separation of the six counties from the rest of Ireland has run parallel with the conflict within the six counties themselves, where boundaries have become established (from village to village, or between parts of villages and between one street and another in towns and cities) between Protestants and Roman Catholics. On either side of these boundaries the two communities have for generations lived largely in their own world of beliefs and practices and in ignorance of those followed on the other side, as a result of which the two sides have been referred to as "the two nations" of Northern Ireland.

Northern Ireland has a land area of 5,452

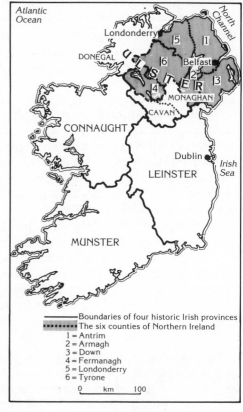

Map 9   Ireland.

square miles (14,121 sq km) and its total population was, as at June 30, 1984, estimated at 1,578,500. The 1971 census showed the population as being 1,519,640, who were, according to their religion, divided as follows: Protestants 811,270 (i.e. Presbyterians 405,717, Church of Ireland members 334,318 and Methodists 71,235), Roman Catholics 477,921, other denominations 87,938, not stated 142,511. The 1981 census showed the total population as being 1,556,039, including about 74,000 in non-enumerated households; of the enumerated population of 1,481,959, the census produced the following breakdown by religion: Protestants 680,021 (Presbyterians 339,818, Church of Ireland 281,472, Methodists 58,731), Roman Catholics 414,532, other churches and no stated denomination 387,406 (over 18 per cent of the enumerated population having declined to answer the voluntary question on religion).

The Irish Republic extends to some 26,600 square miles (68,900 sq km) and according to a census of April 1, 1979, its total population was 3,368,217, of whom almost 95 per cent were Roman Catholics. The total length of the border between Northern Ireland and the Republic is 280 miles (450 km).

Early Historical Background

After the collapse of the Roman empire the inhabitants of Ireland had a common Gaelic language and culture and a common (Brehon) law but no political unity. At the end of the eighth century Norsemen founded settlements which later became the towns of Ireland.

From England Anglo-Normans entered the country in about 1170, and by 1172 the various kings of Ireland were forced to acknowledge the overlordship of King Henry II, who had planned the English conquest of Ireland and who brought the Irish Church, until then independent, into complete union with the Church of Rome. In the following two centuries the Anglo-Normans were more or less absorbed into the Irish population but in 1366 the English forbade intermarriage between English and Irish (in the Statutes of Kilkenny). The Irish were subsequently regarded as enemies by the English, whose overlordship was secure only in a limited area around Dublin known as "The Pale". In the 15th century there was a degree of home rule in Ireland, but this was ended when King Henry VII in 1494 sent Sir Edward Poynings, who (under Poynings' Law) decreed that no Irish parliament should initiate legislation without prior consent of the King and Council in England.

The power of the Norman feudal lords was broken by King Henry VIII, who in 1541 adopted the title of King of Ireland. However, his doctrine of ecclesiastical superiority received little support in Ireland, and the "reformation", although carried out with much bloodshed, was largely ineffective as regards the Irish people, who conformed only outwardly with the reformed doctrines. Under Queen Elizabeth I Roman Catholics in Ireland were persecuted, and Irish nationalism and Catholic religion combined to inspire resistance to English rule. During the counter-reformation insurrections took place (including the Geraldine rebellion of 1579-83 supported by the Spanish and the Italians, and the O'Neill, Earl of Tyrone, rebellion of 1595) but were crushed by the English. Under King James I Irish lands were apportioned to English and Scottish settlers (the latter mainly Presbyterians). After 1649 the recalcitrant Irish were crushed by the troops of Cromwell and Ireton, and land was distributed among Cromwellian soldiers and London merchants; the Catholic religion was suppressed until the Restoration in 1660, when it was given a degree of toleration. However, newly imposed trade restrictions again alienated the Irish people.

The Catholic Irish supported King James II in his fight against William of Orange but were defeated both in the north (at the Battle of the Boyne in 1690) and in the south, where the fighting was concluded by the Treaty of Limerick (1691), which allowed the remnants of the Irish fighting force to go into exile. A new penal code denied the Catholics any rights of citizenship or ownership of property, and the government of Ireland passed into the hands of a Protestant oligarchy, with the Irish peasantry being treated with extreme cruelty. Thousands of Irish people emigrated and many served in the armies of England's enemies.

The American War of Independence caused the British government to make some concessions to the Irish, the principal results being the granting of an independent parliament and the repeal (in 1782) of Poynings' Law. The outbreak of the French revolution brought about the establishment in 1791 of the Society of United Irishmen by Wolfe Tone (a Protestant) as a revolutionary organization (which later became separatist). A planned invasion by a French revolutionary force in support of the United Irishmen failed in 1796, and a subsequent rebellion, aimed at achieving Catholic emancipation, parliamentary reform and separation from Great Britain, was crushed.

A political solution applied by the British Prime Minister, William Pitt the Younger, was the Act of Union (passed in 1800 and in force from 1801), under which the Irish were to be represented in the British Parliament by 28 peers and four bishops (elected to the House of Lords for life by the Irish peerage) and by 100 members in the House of Commons. Pitt had intended the act to be accompanied by a measure of Catholic emancipation but King George II opposed this and Pitt resigned in 1801. Roman Catholics were unable to sit in the House of Commons until 1829, when the Roman Catholic Emancipation Act allowed them to do so.

During the middle of the 19th century the Irish nation suffered the greatest human and economic setback in its history. Failure of the potato crop in 1846, competition from the United States in the grain market and Britain's adoption of free trade (whereby Ireland lost protection for its wheat) brought about famine, a state of general misery and mass emigration, mainly to the Americas. Of Ireland's then total estimated population of 8,000,000, over 1,000,000 died as a direct consequence of the famine and 1,250,000 left the country (250,000 of them for Britain). Between 1864 and 1914 Ireland changed from being a land of tillage to being mainly one of pasturage.

Following the failure of British Liberal governments to secure adoption of Irish Home Rule bills in 1886 and 1893, another Home Rule bill received the royal assent in 1914 but its implementation was suspended owing to the outbreak of World War I.

The Protestant Domination of Northern Ireland

The evolution, in parts of Ulster, of a society different in certain fundamental respects from that in the rest of Ireland received its greatest impetus from what has been called "the plantation of Ulster", i.e. the settlement in northern Ireland, begun in 1607, of some 170,000 people from Britain—150,000 of them Presbyterians from the lowlands of Scotland. This settlement followed the flight of the last of the Irish earls who had been defeated by the English. The plantation was resisted by the original inhabitants, who in 1641 murdered thousands of Protestants and expelled others from their lands but were themselves ultimately put down, in particular by Cromwell's troops. The success of the plantation was finally secured by the Battle of the Boyne in 1690, when Protestant forces of William of Orange defeated Catholics led by James II. (The anniversary of this battle, July 12, is celebrated by Northern Ireland's Protestants to this day.)

By 1703 the remaining Catholics in Ulster owned less than 14 per cent of the land. The Presbyterians were responsible for rapid capital accumulation and the development of industry in Ulster in the 19th century, and this further distinguished Ulster from the rest of Ireland.

Nevertheless, the Catholic and Protestant communities in Northern Ireland were not always in opposite camps. Some Ulster Protestants were hostile to the British government even in the 17th century, and a number of them emigrated to America at the time of the American War of Independence and fought against the Crown's forces. Both Protestants and Catholics had to pay tithes to the established (Episcopalian) Church and were deprived of effective participation in political life in Britain. There was a temporary alliance between them in the United Irishmen formed in Belfast in 1791 (largely by Protestants) with the object of uniting "the whole people of Ireland" and "to abolish the memory of all past dissensions and to substitute the common cause of Irishmen in place of the denominations of Protestant, Catholic and dissenter". Both communities contributed to the passing of the 1793 Catholic Relief Act which gave parliamentary franchise to Catholics on equal terms with Protestants (but without allowing them to sit in Parliament). This alliance was ended in 1798, however, when an Irish rebellion received virtually no support from either community in the north.

By the end of the 19th century, the basis of Belfast's prosperity was (in the estimation of a late 19th-century Unionist, Thomas Sinclair) its "economic link with Britain", for which reason it was "not prepared to come under the rule of a Dublin parliament dominated by impoverished small farmers from Munster and Connaught". Both employers and workers among the Protestants feared that Home Rule for all Ireland (as proposed by the British government) might sever the commercial ties which bound them to Britain; the Protestant tenant farmers had not suffered from extortionate landlords as had the farmers in the south; and they all feared Catholic domination and perhaps oppression.

These arguments were taken up by the Conservatives of Britain, among whom Lord Randolph Churchill in 1886 expressed the view that the British Parliament should not leave the Protestants of Ireland in the lurch and that, if necessary, Ulster should "resort to the supreme arbitrament of force", adding: "Ulster will fight [against Home Rule or separation], Ulster will be right".

In 1912 Sir Edward Carson (later Lord Carson), a Protestant Dublin lawyer who stood for the maintenance of the Union of 1800, read out in Belfast what became known as the Ulster Covenant, which was said to have been signed by 471,414 people who undertook to use "all means which may be found necessary to defeat the present conspiracy to set up a Home Rule parliament in Ireland" and, if it were set up, to "refuse to recognize its authority". Also in 1912 an Ulster Volunteer Force was recruited from among Protestants and was armed with rifles and ammunition smuggled in from the continent of Europe. Its formation was backed by the Ulster Unionist Council (founded in 1905) which regarded itself as a provisional government and was led by Carson. The formation of the Volunteer Force was also encouraged by the Conservatives in Britain, whose leader (Bonar Law) was the son of an Ulster Presbyterian minister and believed that a parliament in Dublin would mean the destruction of the Protestant north. When early in 1914 the authorities took precautionary steps to protect military supplies from possible Volunteer Force raids, some of the officers responsible for such protection were prepared to resign rather than carry out orders. This "Curragh Mutiny" was supported by Sir Henry Wilson, head of military operations at the War Office, with the result that it became clear that the Army could not be relied upon to enforce Home Rule.

For most of the 20th century the political mouthpiece of the Protestant community in Northern Ireland has been the Unionist Party, founded in 1898 and the predominant force in the province's politics until the 1970s, since when it has been challenged by other formations and has itself split into different groupings. The Unionist Party has been permeated by the spirit of the Orange Order, which was founded in 1795 as an Episcopalian peasant self-defence group and did not officially admit Presbyterians until 1834, since when it has served to weaken confessional antagonisms within the Protestant community. In the 19th century one of the Order's leaders defined as its enemy "popery ... a religio-political system for the enslavement of the body and soul of man [which] cannot be met by any mere religious system or by any mere political system" and must be opposed "by such a combination as the Orange Society, based upon religion and carrying over religion into the politics of the day". Every Prime Minister of Northern Ireland and 95 per cent of all elected Unionist representatives in the Westminster Parliament were (in 1973) said to have been Orangemen.

Northern Ireland's major Protestant denominations were united in the Irish Council of Churches (which first met in 1923), all of them being united in their aim to maintain the existing border and to resist "Rome rule". An Ancient Order of Hibernians, which had adopted this title in 1938 and formed a Roman Catholic counterpart to the Orange Order, stood for loyalty to the Pope, the principle of a united Ireland, support for the Irish language, and anti-communism. However, it never attracted more than a small percentage of Northern Ireland's Catholic population into membership.

The Rise of Militant Irish Republican Movements

The famine of 1846 entailed the rise of an Irish nationalist movement, first of all of a Young Ireland movement whose leaders were sentenced to transportation to a penal colony before they could carry out a rebellion planned for 1848. It was followed by the Fenians (named after a legendary band of Irish warriors), the core of whom was constituted by the Irish Republican Brotherhood (IRB), founded in 1858 as a conspiratorial revolutionary organization responsible for many acts of violence both inside and outside Ireland. It carried its "war of independence" to England in 1867 by bombing Clerkenwell prison in London and shooting a police officer in Manchester in attempts to rescue Fenian prisoners. Members of the "Invincibles", an offshoot of the IRB, murdered the (Liberal) Chief Secretary for Ireland (Sir Frederick Cavendish) in Dublin's Phoenix Park in 1882, whereupon the British government introduced a drastic Coercive Act.

The effect of this act was that at the 1885 general elections the Irish nationalists, standing for Home Rule and led by Charles Stewart Parnell, won every seat in the three provinces of Connaught, Leinster and Munster and even a small majority in Ulster, thus gaining the balance of power between Liberals and Conservatives in the House of Commons. However, an attempt by the Liberal Prime Minister (Gladstone) to give Ireland Home Rule was defeated by the defection of a number of Liberals led by Joseph Chamberlain. In a fresh election in 1886 the Conservatives and Chamberlain's Liberal Unionists obtained a majority large enough to make any Home Rule legislation impossible at that stage.

In response to the formation of the (Protestant) Ulster Volunteer Force, a National

Volunteer Force was recruited in the south in 1913 (at the suggestion of Eoin MacNeill) and was soon infiltrated by the IRB. However, when this latter force was, in 1914, called upon (by the Irish Home Rule party) to fight on the side of the Allies in World War I in order to prove Ireland's right to full nationhood, it became divided. A minority, which regarded the proposal as a betrayal of Irish nationalism, was supported by the IRB, *Sinn Féin* (a group founded as a political party in 1905 by Arthur Griffith as a purely nationalist movement) and the infant Irish labour movement. This determined and well-disciplined minority formed, with a Labour Citizen Army, the group which carried out the 1916 Easter Rising in Dublin, which had been prepared by the IRB. The original plans for this rising were not fully implemented, and in the event it was only a relatively small force of 1,500 men who occupied the General Post Office in Dublin, where their leader, Padraic Pearse, proclaimed the Irish Republic. Within less than a week the rising was crushed and some 1,000 people had lost their lives; several of the rebel leaders were executed over a period of days, while others, including Eamonn de Valera, were given life sentences (but were released under a general amnesty in 1917).

The effect of the executions was to strengthen the nationalist movement and in particular *Sinn Féin* which, although most of its leaders were under arrest, gained 73 of the 105 Irish seats in the House of Commons in the 1918 general elections, standing on an outright Republican programme. *Sinn Féin* had campaigned on an abstentionist platform and thus did not take its seats in the British Parliament, forming instead a Constituent Assembly (*Dáil Eireann*) in Dublin. However, when this Assembly met in January 1919, only 28 members attended, the Ulster Unionists staying away and half the *Sinn Féin* members being in prison.

Under the leadership of Michael Collins, *Sinn Féin* embarked on guerrilla warfare against the British government, which decided to reinforce the country's constabulary by an additional security force which became known as the Black and Tans. This force became immensely unpopular because of its indiscriminate raids, which included attacks even on the houses of Unionist families. *Sinn Féin*, however, obtained control of much of the machinery of government, and in 1921 the British Prime Minister (Lloyd George) began negotiations with Eamonn de Valera, the president of *Sinn Féin*, which led to the conclusion of the Anglo-Irish treaty in December of that year.

The 1921 treaty, however, divided *Sinn Féin*. One section led by Arthur Griffith (who died in August 1922) and Michael Collins (who was assassinated, also in August 1922) regarded the treaty as a first step towards independence, but the majority section led by Eamonn de Valera rejected the settlement because it abandoned the principle of an all-Ireland Republic. The settlement was endorsed by a small majority of the Irish Parliament and by a decisive majority at the ensuing general election. The anti-treaty wing of *Sinn Féin* began a civil war which lasted until 1923, and in 1926 de Valera formed the Republican Party (*Fianna Fáil*) and brought his followers into the *Dáil*, agreeing to take the oath of allegiance (by disregarding it as "an empty formula").

During the civil war the Volunteer Force adopted the name of Irish Republican Army (IRA), which at a meeting in Dublin in July 1923 broke with the IRB. It later decided, in April 1924, to support the *Sinn Féin* party, but its influence subsequently declined. In 1936 the Dublin government declared it an illegal organization and its leaders were imprisoned. During World War II some of its members were pro-German and were responsible for bomb explosions in England in 1940. In 1956-62 the IRA emerged in Northern Ireland with a bombing campaign, which the authorities were able to confine to the border areas.

Provisional IRA Campaign in Northern Ireland since 1969

The political scene in Northern Ireland changed with the establishment in Belfast in February 1967 of the Northern Ireland Civil Rights Association by non-political liberals who wished to co-ordinate the activities of local associations aiming at improving the status of Catholics. In the late 1960s the Association came under the influence of members of People's Democracy, a group founded in 1968 by the (Trotskyist) International Socialists at

Queen's University, Belfast, but after People's Democracy had broken away from the Association in 1970 its leadership was gradually taken over by the Official IRA. The latter was the rump of the IRA, from which the Provisional IRA (the "Provos") had broken away in 1969 as a direct-action organization intent upon launching a guerrilla campaign with the aim of making Northern Ireland ungovernable and forcing the British to withdraw their armed forces from the province and to relinquish all responsibility for it.

While both the Official and the Provisional IRA have been declared illegal, their respective political wings have remained legal organizations—(i) the official (Marxist) *Sinn Féin*, which later became the Workers' Party, with the aim of uniting the working class and rejecting sectarianism because it "killed workers", and (ii) the Provisional *Sinn Féin*, which later dropped the description "Provisional" from its title.

An Irish Republican Socialist Party broke away from the Official IRA in December 1974 and became a legal party in the Republic, with the aim of "ending British rule in Ireland" and establishing "a united democratic socialist republic". The military wing of this party, the Irish National Liberation Army (INLA), emerged in 1975 with the object of conducting armed warfare to bring about a British military withdrawal from Northern Ireland, which was to be united with the Republic on the basis of "socialist" principles. The INLA was proscribed in Northern Ireland and in Britain in July 1979.

The sectarian conflict in Northern Ireland took on a violent complexion after the Civil Rights Association had, in a march on Oct. 5, 1968, defied a police ban designed to keep it out of a traditionally Unionist area in Londonderry/Derry, and had thus clashed with the police. William Craig, then Northern Ireland Minister of Home Affairs, said afterwards that the Association was "definitely a Republican front" and "clearly unacceptable to the loyalist community". Further marches and clashes took place in the ensuing months, and early in 1969 the British government agreed to make troops available to protect key installations against attacks, especially by militant Protestants. Disturbances nevertheless spread and reached a climax in Belfast in August 1969, when troops moved in to prevent Protestants from invading the Catholic Falls Road area and to create a "peace line".

In October 1969 the Provisional IRA began a campaign of sniping at soldiers and bombing property; by September 1971 the IRA was using rocket launchers, and in April 1973 letter bombs appeared, to be followed by parcel bombs sent to senior civil servants. In August 1971 the authorities introduced internment without trial of suspects, which remained in force for four years despite a civil disobedience campaign called by the Catholic opposition parties in Northern Ireland. Counter-terrorist action by British troops led to the death of 13 persons in Londonderry/Derry from army gunfire on Jan. 30, 1972, and in a reprisal action for this so-called "Bloody Sunday" the British embassy in Dublin was attacked. The front was now clearly drawn between, on the one hand, the Provisional IRA and, on the other, the British Army, the locally-recruited Ulster Defence Regiment (UDR) and the Royal Ulster Constabulary (RUC, the Northern Ireland police), while members of paramilitary Protestant organizations such as the Ulster Defence Association were held responsible for numerous deaths (not all of them of Catholics).

Throughout most of the 1970s the sequence of violence was unremitting, although from the late 1970s a gradual reduction was apparent, as the security forces succeeded in reducing the effectiveness of the paramilitary groups and the latter themselves concentrated more on specific targets (usually persons regarded as representing the "occupation regime") rather than on indiscriminate attacks. Official British statistics for the period 1971-86 showed that over those 16 years the number of people killed in Northern Ireland as a result of the troubles totalled 2,487, of which 1,711 were civilians (including several hundred suspected members of paramilitary movements), 544 army or UDR personnel and 232 RUC members or reservists. Having averaged around 275 a year in 1971-76, the annual average death toll fell to about 83 over the succeeding decade.

Over the same period (1971-86) the violence resulted in injuries to 19,251 civilians, 3,483 army or UDR personnel and 4,146 RUC members or reservists. The statistics also recorded 29,723 shooting incidents (excluding shots merely heard), 8,151 bomb explosions (estimated to have involved over 270,000 lb of explosive material), 3,754 bombs neutralized (containing some 170,000 lb of explosive material), 12,306 armed robberies by paramilitaries in which about £11,357,000 was stolen, and 7,264 malicious fires. As regards activity by the security forces, during the 16-year period there were a total of 325,137 house searches resulting in the seizure of 9,568 firearms and 1,170,876 rounds of ammunition. There were also a total of 13,085 persons charged with terrorist-type offences, including 968 for murder and 1,074 for attempted murder. As with the number of deaths, most of these indicators of the level of violence showed a gradual reduction from the late 1970s.

The material and spiritual damage caused to the economic and social fabric of Northern Ireland over almost two decades of internal conflict has not been assessed even approximately. At the end of 1986 there were still over 9,000 British troops in Northern Ireland (excluding the UDR), mostly deployed along the border with the Republic.

Within Ireland the most prominent victim of the Provisional IRA (to end-1986) was Earl Mountbatten of Burma, who was killed by a bomb explosion on his fishing boat at Mullaghmore (County Sligo, in the Republic) on Aug. 27, 1979, together with members of his family and a boat boy. Major actions undertaken by the Provisional IRA in Great Britain have included (i) a series of public house bombings in Guildford, Woolwich and Birmingham in November 1974 in which 28 people died; (ii) two bomb attacks on British soldiers on ceremonial duty in central London on July, 20, 1982, in which 11 men and seven horses were fatally injured; and (iii) a bomb explosion on Oct. 12, 1984, at the Brighton hotel where the Prime Minister, Margaret Thatcher, and other government members were staying for the Conservative Party conference, five people being killed. For its part, the INLA was held responsible for the killing of Airey Neave, then Conservative opposition spokesman on Northern Ireland, in a car bomb explosion at the House of Commons on March 30, 1979.

The Provisional IRA has made use of its international contacts to obtain arms supplies or financial support from European countries (some Soviet-bloc weapons having been intercepted) and from radical Arab states, notably Libya. It has also continued to receive substantial financial contributions from members of the large Irish community in the United States (clandestine arms shipments from this country having also been intercepted), despite efforts by both the British and the Irish governments to dissuade Irish Americans from giving such support.

Within Ireland a significant measure of support for the Provisional IRA among Catholics has been reflected not only at public gatherings, in particular at funerals of IRA members, but also in election results, especially in Northern Ireland. In a by-election held in the Fermanagh-South Tyrone constituency of the British House of Commons in April 1981, Robert (Bobby) Sands, an IRA prisoner then on hunger strike in the Maze prison in Belfast in support of demands for political status for Republican prisoners, was elected by a narrow majority; after his death, Owen Carron (*Sinn Féin*) was elected with an increased majority in August of that year. In the Northern Ireland Assembly elections of October 1982 [see below], *Sinn Féin* won 64,191 votes (10.2 per cent) and five of the 78 seats. In the British general elections of June 1983, the *Sinn Féin* leader, Gerry Adams, was elected in the Belfast West constituency previously held by Gerry Fitt (a moderate Catholic socialist). In the May 1985 district council elections *Sinn Féin* (in its first province-wide election contest in recent times) won 12 per cent of the vote.

In the Republic's general elections of June 1981 two Provisional IRA members, both of them also on hunger strike in the Maze, were elected (one of them dying on Aug. 2), as was one candidate of the Workers' Party. No Provisionals were elected in either of the two 1982 general elections or in the 1987 elections (when *Sinn Féin* secured less than 2 per cent of the vote), although the Workers' Party increased its representation from two to four seats in 1987 with 3.8 per cent of the vote. In the 1984 European Parliament elections *Sinn Féin* and the Workers' Party won 4.9 and 4.3 per cent respectively, but no seats. In November 1986 *Sinn Féin* decided to end its ban on its members taking up seats in the Irish Parliament if elected and was officially registered as a political party in the Republic shortly before the 1987 elections.

The Search for a Political Solution, 1965-81

Northern Ireland's relations with the South were in a state of "cold war" during the rule of Eamonn de Valera, who regarded the ending of partition as the over-riding goal of the Irish government. The division between North and South was further exacerbated by provisions of the 1937 constitution of the Republic, which not only (as stated above) implied a territorial claim to the whole of Ireland but also included certain other provisions which reflected Catholic social doctrine. In particular, the constitution made the Irish language the country's first official language, forbade divorce, recognized the family as "a moral institution possessing inalienable and imprescriptible rights antecedent and superior to all positive law" and gave the Roman Catholic Church a "special position" (which was, however, abandoned in 1972).

The situation changed with the advent of Sean Lemass as Prime Minister of the Republic in 1959, when a period of state-aided industrialization began and the Dublin government started to play a role in international affairs (e.g. at the United Nations). In 1965 Lemass went to Belfast to meet the Northern Ireland Prime Minister (Capt. Terence O'Neill), this being the first meeting of the heads of the two Irish governments for 40 years, and a return visit took place a few weeks later. However, these meetings and his attempts to introduce some reforms in favour of the Catholics led to the downfall of Capt. O'Neill, not only owing to loyalist agitation against him led by the Rev. Dr Ian Paisley but also because of opposition from within the Unionist Party led by Brian Faulkner. O'Neill was replaced as Prime Minister on May 1, 1969, by Maj. James Chichester-Clark, who was himself replaced by Faulkner in March 1971.

In the wake of the January 1972 "Bloody Sunday" incident, the Northern Ireland Catholics withdrew all co-operation with the Northern Ireland government, and talks between that administration and the British government broke down on March 23, 1972, over the question of which of the two was to control security. The British government thereupon invoked powers granted under the 1920 act to enact legislation (on March 30, 1972) which prorogued the Northern Ireland Parliament and provided for the assumption of direct rule over the province by the UK Parliament and government for an initial period of one year (which was extended for another year in March 1973). In conjunction with this step a new UK office of Secretary of State for Northern Ireland was created and William Whitelaw appointed as its first incumbent.

A year after the imposition of direct rule, a referendum was held in Northern Ireland on March 8, 1973, to ascertain the views of the population on any possible change in the province's status. However, this so-called "border poll" was boycotted by the Catholic community with the result that only 58.6 per cent of the eligible electorate went to the polls. The results showed that 591,820 people (57.4 per cent of the total electorate of 1,030,084) had voted in favour of Northern Ireland remaining as part of the United Kingdom and 6,463 (0.63 per cent) for Northern Ireland to be joined with the Irish Republic outside the United Kingdom, while 5,973 (0.58 per cent) spoiled their ballot papers.

The British government thereupon enacted the 1973 Northern Ireland Constitution Act, which confirmed the status of Northern Ireland as part of the United Kingdom for as long as a majority wished it to be so, but abolished the Northern Ireland Parliament and put in its place (i) a Northern Ireland Assembly, to be elected by the single transferable vote method of proportional representation (as used in the Republic of Ireland but not in Britain), and (ii) an Executive based on the principle of power-sharing between the Protestant and Catholic communities.

This act, however, led to disagreement within the Unionist movement, where it was opposed by the Orange Order, Dr Paisley's Democratic Unionist Party and the Vanguard Unionist Party (VUP)—the last newly founded in March 1973 by William Craig. In the Assembly elected under the act in June 1973, the 78 seats were distributed as follows: Unionist followers of Brian Faulkner in favour of power-sharing 22, Official Unionists opposed to power-sharing 13, Paisley supporters 8, Craig supporters 7, Social and Democratic Labour Party (SDLP, founded in 1970 as a mainly Roman Catholic party standing for reconciliation and partnership between Catholics and Protestants in Northern Ireland with a view to achieving Irish unity by peaceful means) 19, the Alliance Party (AP, also formed in 1970 "to cross the sectarian divide in Northern Ireland") 8, Northern Ireland Labour Party (NILP) 1.

The principle of power-sharing was endorsed at a conference held in December 1973 at Sunningdale (Berkshire) between members of the British government (led by Edward Heath), of the Irish Cabinet (led by Liam Cosgrave) and of the Northern Ireland Executive-designate (set up by Faulkner with SDLP and AP participation); at the same time agreement was reached on the formation of a Council of Ireland consisting of representatives of Northern Ireland and the Republic to develop North-South relations. At the conference the Irish government "fully accepted and solemnly declared" that there could be no change in Northern Ireland's status until a majority in the province so wished, while the UK government reaffirmed that its policy remained to support the wishes of the majority of the people of Northern Ireland and that if in the future such a majority "should indicate a wish to become part of a united Ireland the British government would support that wish".

Direct rule was ended under a Northern Ireland Constitution (Devolution) Order which (effective Jan. 1, 1974) implemented an amendment to the Northern Ireland Constitution Act by allowing for the appointment of an 11-member Executive and a 15-member Administration in Belfast. However, on Jan. 4, 1974, the Ulster Unionist Council, the policy-making body of Faulkner's party, rejected the Sunningdale proposals by 427 votes to 374, and the first meeting of the Assembly on Jan. 22 had to be suspended when Faulkner's opponents prevented members of the Executive from taking their seats; on the following day the Official Unionists led by Harry West and also the Paisley and Craig parties withdrew from the Assembly. In elections to the British House of Commons on Feb. 28, 1974 (held under the traditional first-past-the-post system), the 12 Northern Ireland constituencies returned 11 candidates opposed to the Sunningdale agreement.

The anti-Faulkner Unionists were supported by two paramilitary organizations, namely (i) the Ulster Volunteer Force (UVF), originally formed in 1912 and reconstituted in 1966, and (ii) the Ulster Defence Association (UDA), formed in 1972 to defend Protestant areas from IRA incursions and estimated to have recruited 50,000 members within three months. These groups in turn supported a general strike called in May 1974 and widely endorsed in the Protestant community. The British (Labour) government declared a state of emergency in the province on May 19 and sent in troops. The Executive resigned on May 28, the Assembly was prorogued on May 29 and the British government again assumed direct authority in Northern Ireland.

On May 1, 1975, elections were held to a Constitutional Convention which was to report on the establishment of a future government of Northern Ireland commanding the support of the whole community. The result of these elections was not very different from that of the elections for the Assembly of June 1973, seats being gained as follows: the anti-power-sharing United Ulster Unionist Council (UUUC) 46, Unionist Party of Northern Ireland (UPNI, supporting Faulkner) 5, SDLP 17, AP 8, NILP 1, Independent Loyalist 1. The UUUC was divided into 19 Official Unionists (led by West), 14 VUP members, 12 Paisley supporters and an independent with UUUC support. However, all UUUC members of the Convention except Craig stated during September 1975 that they were opposed to any coalition with the SDLP, and the Convention ceased to meet on Nov. 7 of that year and was formally dissolved on March 5, 1976, having failed to agree on a government system based on partnership between Protestants and Catholics. The British government admitted in February 1976 that there was "no instant solution to the problems of Northern Ireland".

Also on March 5, 1976, the British and Irish Prime Ministers (respectively Harold Wilson and Liam Cosgrave) met and agreed that "an acceptable form of government for Northern Ireland could be established only by both communities agreeing on a system of government providing for partnership and participation" and that, pending such an agreement, a period of direct rule (by Britain) and stability was necessary.

A call for a general strike made in May 1977 by a United Unionist Action Council, which included the Paisley formation and the UDA, with the aim of forcing the British government to carry out the Unionist demand for a virtual return to the 1920 act, was called off on May 13 for lack of support. It led, however, to the foundation in October 1977 of two new parties—the Irish Independence Party and the Ulster Independence Party—to promote the idea of an ultimate declaration of independence by Northern Ireland from the United Kingdom. (William Craig's VUP was dissolved in February 1978, when he joined the Official Unionist Party.)

In the Republic the Prime Minister (then Jack Lynch, the *Fianna Fáil* leader) on Jan. 8, 1978, called for a British declaration of intent to withdraw from Northern Ireland and stated in particular that he would like to see a start in "bringing Irish people together"; that the British government should indicate "in a general way" that they did "not wish to continue subsidizing a small corner of Ireland to the extent that they have been doing over the past 50 years"; and that the British people themselves had "no stomach for that kind of subsidization which involves taxation on them". He added that "the people of Northern Ireland would be realistic enough to know that there should be, and ought to be, accommodation found between the [Catholic] minority and themselves in the first instance, and between them and us in the long term".

Lynch's successor, Charles Haughey, called on Feb. 16, 1980, for a joint initiative on Northern Ireland by the United Kingdom and Irish governments. He found the picture in Northern Ireland "a depressing one" as its agriculture and industry were producing less than in the early 1970s and the population had remained static. While emphasizing that in the Republic the rule of law would be firmly upheld and democracy defended, he said that for over 60 years the situation in Northern Ireland had been a source of instability because "the very entity [of Northern Ireland] itself is artificial and has been artificially sustained". The reality, he claimed, was that Northern Ireland as a political entity had failed and that a new beginning was needed. He added that it would be his concern to ensure that the place of Protestants in the Ireland of the future would be secure and that their traditions were honoured and respected. He looked forward to "some free and open arrangement in which Irish men and women on their own without a British presence but with active British goodwill will manage the affairs of the whole of Ireland in a constructive partnership with the European Community".

A constitutional conference held in Belfast from Jan. 7 to March 24, 1980, but not attended by the Official Unionist Party, was adjourned after it had failed to reach agreement by the parties represented on the role of the Catholic minority in a devolved government of the province. After the publication in July 1980 of further British proposals on Northern Ireland, Humphrey Atkins, then British Secretary of State for Northern Ireland, announced in the House of Commons on Nov. 27, 1980, that there was not sufficient agreement among the parties to justify bringing forward proposals for setting up a devolved administration at that stage, and that new ways would have to be explored.

On the other hand, Charles Haughey and Margaret Thatcher (the British Prime Minister), meeting in London on May 21, 1980, stated that they agreed that "they wished to develop a new and closer political co-operation between the two governments" and to hold regular meetings. At a further meeting (held in Dublin on Dec. 8, 1980), the two Prime Ministers agreed inter alia that the economic, social and political interests of their peoples were "inextricably linked" but that the full development of these links had been "put under strain by division and dissent in Northern Ireland" and that peace, reconciliation and stability must be achieved there.

The Anglo-Irish meetings at Prime Ministers' level were particularly strongly opposed by Dr Paisley, who on Feb. 19, 1981, signed in Belfast, with other members of his party, a covenant similar to that of 1912 in which the signatories pledged themselves to use all means necessary "to defeat the present conspiracy . . . to edge Northern Ireland out of the United Kingdom and to establish an ongoing process of all-Ireland integration".

Notwithstanding Unionist opposition, a further UK-Irish summit meeting was held in London on Nov. 6, 1981, at which Mrs Thatcher agreed with Dr Garret FitzGerald (who had succeeded Haughey in June 1981 at the head of a *Fine Gael*-Labour coalition) to set up an Anglo-Irish Inter-Governmental Council (AIIC). It was stated that this body would meet regularly at ministerial and official levels to discuss matters of common concern, in which context the London meeting received a report on joint studies (commissioned by the previous session in Dublin) covering possible new institutional structures to link the two countries, citizenship rights, economic co-operation, measures to encourage mutual understanding and co-operation on security matters. A communiqué said that the two Prime Ministers had "agreed on the need for efforts to diminish the divisions between the two sections of the community in Northern Ireland and to reconcile the two major traditions that exist in the two parts of Ireland"; that Dr FitzGerald had "affirmed that it was the wish of the Irish government and, he believed, of the great majority of the people of the island of Ireland to secure the unity of Ireland by agreement and in peace"; and that both Prime Ministers took the view that "any change in the constitutional status of Northern Ireland would require the consent of the majority of the people of Northern Ireland".

Before meeting Mrs Thatcher, Dr FitzGerald had stated in a radio interview on Sept. 27, 1981, that he favoured changes in the Irish constitution to make the reunification of Ireland more attractive to Northern Protestants, including amendments to the definition (in Articles 2 and 3) of the national territory as being the whole of Ireland. Maintaining that the Republic had "slipped into a partitionist attitude with institutions which . . . could never be the basis to enter discussions with Unionists in Northern Ireland", Dr FitzGerald continued: "What I want to do is to lead a crusade—a Republican crusade—to make this a genuine Republic on the principles of Tone and Davis [i.e. Wolfe Tone and Thomas Davis, two early Irish patriots who were both Protestants], and if I can bring the people of this country on that path and get them to agree down here to the type of state that Tone and Davis looked for, I believe we could have the basis then on which many Protestants in Northern Ireland would be willing to consider a relationship with us . . . ."

Dr FitzGerald lost office as a result of the February 1982 Irish elections, however, and was succeeded by Haughey, who had made it clear that his *Fianna Fáil* party was opposed to any piecemeal abandonment of the national ideals and aspirations enshrined in the constitution. There followed a sharp deterioration in UK-Irish relations, notably over the Haughey government's attitude to the UK-Argentinian conflict over the Falklands, which was described in Dublin as being one of neutrality but which was seen in London as leaning towards support for the Argentinian case.

Failure of 1982 Devolution Proposals and Abortive New Northern Ireland Assembly

After consultations with interested parties, the British Conservative government secured the enactment on July 23, 1982, of a new Northern Ireland Bill providing principally for the eventual resumption of legislative and executive functions by an elected Assembly in Northern Ireland, in succession to the Assembly which had been dissolved in 1974 with the reintroduction of direct rule from Westminster [see above].

The legislation specified (i) that a 78-member unicameral Assembly would be elected by the single transferable vote method of proportional representation from multi-member constituencies which would be co-terminous with House of Commons constituencies, then numbering 12 (but increased to 17 for the 1983 UK general elections); (ii) that the Assembly's functions, pending devolution of powers, would be consultative and deliberative, including scrutiny of draft legislation and making reports and recommendations to the Secretary of State for Northern Ireland, who would lay them before Parliament; (iii) that prior to devolution the Assembly would have departmental committees, whose membership, chairmen and vice-chairmen would, in their party affiliation, reflect the distribution of seats in the Assembly (i.e. minority parties would be represented); (iv) that the Assembly could proceed to full devolution of powers either directly or via partial devolution, the essential criterion being that representatives of both communities should agree on how executive powers should be discharged; (v) that the support of at least 70 per cent of the total membership of the Assembly would normally be required for any devolution of powers to be activated (although the Secretary of State could pursue specific proposals to that end if they had the support of a majority of the total membership and if he believed that they were acceptable to both sides of the community); (vi) that under full devolution the Northern Ireland Executive would consist of not more than 13 members, who could be replaced following consultation with the parties; and (vii) that as under the 1973 Northern Ireland Constitution Act certain "excepted" matters (e.g. Crown affairs, foreign policy and defence) would remain the permanent responsibility of Westminster and certain "reserved" matters (principally law and order) could not be devolved immediately, while "transferred" matters (i.e. those which could be devolved) would include responsibility for agriculture, commerce, education, environment, finance and personnel, health and social services, and manpower services.

Adopted with the tacit consent of the opposition Labour Party, the 1982 Northern Ireland Bill was vigorously opposed by the Unionist representatives at Westminster, supported by a small group of Conservative backbench MPs. The main thrust of the Unionist opposition was that, while the prospect of a restored Northern Ireland administration was welcomed, the proposals were unworkable because they would effectively enable a minority of 31 per cent of the new Assembly's members to block progress towards devolution of powers. In their subsequent manifestos for the Assembly elections, both the Official Unionist Party (OUP) and Dr Paisley's Democratic Unionist Party (DUP) pledged themselves to resist any power-sharing in the new body and to seek to change the 70 per cent requirement for the activation of devolution steps.

On the Republican side, both the SDLP and *Sinn Féin* also condemned the new Assembly, the former proposing an alternative plan for a "Council for a New Ireland" to consist of members of the Dublin Parliament and those elected to the Assembly; both formations in addition pledged that their successful candidates would refuse to take their seats in the new body. Only the small Alliance Party (AP) expressed positive support for the Assembly, although with the qualification that it would not enter into any partnership arrangement for devolving power until the Unionist parties agreed in principle that any major party which recognized the present institutions of the state, whatever its ultimate aspirations, had the right to share in that arrangement.

The results of the elections, held on Oct. 20, 1982, gave the OUP 26 seats, the DUP 21, the SDLP 14, the AP 10, *Sinn Féin* five and one seat each to an Independent Unionist and the Ulster Popular Unionist Party (UPUP). There was a valid turnout of 632,664 voters (60.3 per cent) among an electorate of 1,048,807. One of the successful SDLP candidates, Seamus Mallon (the party's deputy leader), was subsequently disqualified because of his membership of the Irish Senate; the SDLP did not contest the consequential by-election on April 20, 1983, which was won by the OUP, whose representation was thus increased to 27.

At the first meeting of the Assembly on Nov. 11, 1982, in the main chamber of Stormont Castle, James Kilfedder (UPUP) was elected presiding officer (combining the functions of Speaker with the task of appointing departmental committee chairmen) by 31 votes (DUP and AP) to 25 (OUP). Both the SDLP and *Sinn Féin* carried out their threat to boycott the Assembly, which was thereby effectively reduced to 59 members (60 after the April 1983 by-election), of which 55 would be required to support any devolution proposal to meet the 70 per cent requirement. The chairmanships of six committees were allocated by Kilfedder on Dec. 8, those covering economic development, finance/personnel and health/social services going to the OUP, agriculture and environment to the DUP and education to the AP; the SDLP would have been allocated health/social services if it had been in attendance.

The Assembly failed to make any substantive progress in the directions envisaged by the British government. The OUP boycotted its proceedings from November 1983 to May 1984 in protest against an attack by the "Catholic Reaction Force" on a Pentecostal gospel hall in Darkley on Nov. 20, 1983, in which three worshippers were killed. Moreover, in November 1985 the OUP and the DUP combined to suspend Assembly business in protest against the signing of the Anglo-Irish Agreement [see below]. Against this background, both Houses of the UK Parliament on June 19, 1986 approved an Order dissolving the Assembly, although this measure did not abolish the legal basis of the Assembly and left open the date for possible new elections (which had been due in October 1986).

Irish-UK Consultations leading to Signature of 1985 Anglo-Irish Agreement on Northern Ireland

Dr FitzGerald's return to office in Dublin in December 1982 brought about an improvement in UK-Irish relations and the resumption of direct ministerial contacts within the framework of the AIIC. Meetings at the level of Prime Ministers were resumed at Chequers on Nov. 7, 1983, and continued with a further session, also at Chequers, on Nov. 18-19, 1984. After the latter meeting some tension developed over Mrs Thatcher's categoric dismissal of all three options for the future of Northern Ireland identified in May 1984 by the New Ireland Forum initiative (set up in early 1983 by the Irish government on the proposal of the SDLP and consisting of representatives of the SDLP and the three main parties in the Republic), namely a unitary Irish state (the Forum's preference), a federal or confederal arrangement between North and South, and joint UK-Irish authority over Northern Ireland—all of which the British Prime Minister said were "out".

However, the next summit, held at Hillsborough Castle (the former residence of Northern Ireland governors) on Nov. 15, 1985, was the occasion of the signature by Mrs Thatcher and Dr FitzGerald of a major new agreement establishing, within the framework of the AIIC, an Inter-Governmental Conference concerned with Northern Ireland and with relations between the two parts of Ireland. This Anglo-Irish Agreement, or Hillsborough Accord, specified in particular that the Conference would deal on a regular basis with political matters, with security and related matters (including the administration of justice) and with the promotion of cross-border co-operation.

Article 1 of the agreement was worded as follows: "The two governments (*a*) affirm that any change in the status of Northern Ireland would only come about with the consent of a majority of the people of Northern Ireland; (*b*) recognize that the present wish of the majority of the people of Northern Ireland is for no change in the status of Northern Ireland; (*c*) declare that, if in the future a majority of the people of Northern Ireland clearly wish for and formally consent to the establishment of a united Ireland, they will introduce and support in the respective parliaments legislation to give effect to that wish". Article 2, after providing for the establishment of the Inter-Government Conference, continued: "The UK government accept that the Irish government will put forward views and proposals on matters relating to Northern Ireland within the field of activity of the Conference in so far as those matters are not the responsibility of a devolved administration in Northern Ireland. ... The Conference will be mainly concerned with Northern Ireland, but some of the matters under consideration will involve co-operative action in both parts of the island of Ireland, and possibly also in Great Britain. Some of the proposals considered in respect of Northern Ireland may also be found to have application by the Irish government. There is no derogation from the sovereignty of either the UK government or the Irish government, and each retains responsibility for the decisions and administration of government within its own jurisdiction."

Article 3 dealt with the structure and modalities of the Conference, specifying that meetings at ministeral level would be chaired jointly by the UK Secretary of State for Northern Ireland and an Irish minister designated as the Permanent Irish Ministeral Representative: Article 4 stated inter alia that the Conference "shall be a framework within which the Irish government may put forward views and proposals on the modalities of bringing about devolution in Northern Ireland, in so far as they relate to the interests of the minority community". Article 5 included a clause that "if it should prove impossible to achieve and sustain devolution on a basis which secures widespread acceptance in Northern Ireland, the Conference shall be a framework within which the Irish government may, where the interests of the minority community are significantly or especially affected, put forward views on proposals for major legislation and on major policy issues which are within the purview of the Northern Ireland departments and which remain the responsibility of the Secretary of State for Northern Ireland".

Article 6 provided that the Irish government "may put forward views and proposals on the role and composition of bodies appointed by the Secretary of State for Northern Ireland or by departments subject to his direction and control, including the Standing Advisory Commission on Human Rights, the Fair Employment Agency, the Equal Opportunities Commission, the Police Authority for Northern Ireland and the Police Complaints Board". Article 7 covered the Conference's consideration of security policy, relations between the security forces and the community, and prisons policy; Article 8 set out how the Conference would deal with legal matters, including the administration of justice; Articles 9 and 10 dealt with cross-border co-operation on security, economic, social and cultural matters; Article 11 specified that the working of the Conference would be reviewed three years from signature of the agreement, or earlier if requested by either government; Article 12 stated that "it will be for parliamentary decision in Westminster and in Dublin whether to establish an Anglo-Irish parliamentary body"; and Article 13 specified that the agreement would enter into force on exchange of notifications of acceptance by the two governments.

The Anglo-Irish Agreement was approved by the *Dáil* on Nov. 21, 1985, by 88 votes to 75 (mainly *Fianna Fáil* deputies) and by the Irish Senate on Nov. 28 by 37 votes to 16. In the UK Parliament it was approved in the House of Lords on Nov. 26 and in the House of Commons on Nov. 27; the Commons vote was 473 in favour (most Conservative and Labour members, Liberals, Social Democratic Party and John Hume, leader of the SDLP) with 47 against (20 Conservatives, 13 Labour members and 14 Ulster Unionists). The agreement came formally into force on Nov. 29 following the exchange of notifications of acceptance in Dublin, and the inaugural meeting of the Inter-Governmental Conference was held in Belfast on Dec. 11, 1985.

In a communiqué issued after the first meeting, the two sides expressed their agreement that the RUC and the British armed forces must "not only discharge their duties even-handedly and with equal respect for the Unionist and nationalist identities and traditions, but be seen by both communities to be doing so". A code of conduct for the RUC was to be introduced in 1986, and it was stipulated that all army and UDR patrols which had contact with the public should, unless the circumstances were exceptional, have a police presence. The Conference also discussed border security co-operation, on which the Irish representatives said that manpower and support resources had been recently been increased on the Irish side of the border. The communiqué added that a working group of officials would be set up to consider the machinery for further discussion of legal matters, including the administration of justice in the North.

Reactions to Anglo-Irish Agreement—Unionist Opposition

In the Republic *Fianna Fáil*'s opposition to the agreement derived principally from the party's view that Article 1 gave a treaty guarantee to the Northern Unionist position, in contravention of the national aspirations enshrined in the Irish constitution. As opposition leader, Charles Haughey in the course of 1986 said that a *Fianna Fáil* government would seek to renegotiate the agreement, which he claimed brought no real benefits to Northern Catholics. However, after regaining the premiership as a result of the February 1987 Irish elections, Haughey said that his government would "fulfil and operate" the agreement and accepted that Article 1 was "an integral part of a biding international agreement" and that the mutual agreement required to change it "would not emerge".

At the same time, the Haughey government indicated that it would review new extradition legislation, associated with the parliamentary ratification in the last days of the FitzGerald government, of the 1976 European Convention on the Suppression of Terrorism (Ireland's early accession to which had been envisaged under the Hillsborough Accord). Adopted against the opposition of *Fianna Fáil*, the legislation was intended to facilitate the extradition of political terrorists and was due to come into force in December 1987, to allow time for the administration of justice in the North to be made more acceptable to the minority community. Particular areas of concern to the Dublin government were the continued use of single-judge, non-jury ("Diplock") courts to try suspected terrorists and also of uncorroborated informer evidence in so-called "super-grass" trials. In addition to sharing these concerns, *Fianna Fáil* had called during the Irish election campaign for the addition to the legislation of a requirement that an authority requesting extradition should make a prima facie case in support of each application.

Within Northern Ireland the Unionist parties declared a policy of categoric opposition to the Anglo-Irish Agreement, which they regarded as giving a foreign government the right to intervene in the sovereign affairs of the United Kingdom. At a special meeting of the Northern Ireland Assembly in Belfast on Nov. 16, 1985, a Unionist resolution calling for a referendum on the agreement in Northern Ireland was carried by 44 votes to 10 (the Alliance Party); following the rejection of this proposal by the UK government, the Unionist majority suspended Assembly business indefinitely (having also announced the withdrawal of Unionists from all government advisory boards and authorities in the province). Moreover, the UK Parliament's approval of the agreement on Nov. 26-27 provoked the resignation from their House of Commons seats of all 15 Unionist MPs (11 OUP, three DUP and one UPUP) and the calling of by-elections, in which the Unionists sought to demonstrate the extent of opposition to the agreement.

In the event, the contests (on Jan. 23, 1986) resulted in the OUP losing one seat to the SDLP and the other 14 Unionists being re-elected. The Unionists candidates increased their aggregate vote slightly as compared with the 1983 general elections, polling 418,230 votes in a lower turnout, but fell short of what was generally considered to be their target of 500,000 votes.

Other actions taken to demonstrate Protestant opposition to the agreement included a one-day "loyalist strike" on March 3, 1986, and an instruction given by Unionist leaders on Nov. 15, 1986 (the first anniversary of the signature of the agreement), that all Unionist local councillors should resign their seats, the aim being to make Northern Ireland ungovernable until the Anglo-Irish Agreement was revoked. The agreement was also denounced by the Provisional IRA as perpetuating the "British occupation" of Northern Ireland.

Further Meetings of Anglo-Irish Inter-Governmental Conference

Further meetings of the Inter-Governmental Conference established under the 1985 Anglo-Irish Agreement were held at regular intervals in 1986 and the first half of 1987. A joint communiqué issued after the third session, held in Belfast on March 11, 1986, recorded that the Chief Constable of the RUC and the Commissioner of the *Garda Siochana* (Irish police) had reported on progress in enhancing cross-border co-operation on security matters, and that information had also been provided on the efforts of the RUC in developing relations with the minority community. Also considered was the development of cross-border co-operation in the economic and social fields and the prospects of international assistance being made available in this field (notably from the United States), while the Irish side put forward views on matters of significant or special interest to the minority community in the areas of education, health and housing. On the present illegality of displaying the Irish tricolour flag in Northern Ireland, the British side said that this question would be addressed in the context of the Public Order Bill currently before the Westminster Parliament.

The fourth and fifth sessions of the Conference were held in Belfast and London respectively in April and May 1986 and did not result in the announcement of any specific measures; neither did the sixth session held in Belfast on June 17, 1986, although significant progress was understood to have been made in the sphere of security co-operation. The seventh meeting, held in Dublin on Oct. 6, 1986, discussed the implementation of cross-border security measures, as well as relations between the security forces and the minority community in Northern Ireland; it also welcomed an agreement between the two governments to set up an Anglo-Irish aid fund. A statement issued after the eighth session, held in Belfast on April 22, 1987, recorded the agreement of the two sides that improvements in security along the Irish border would be sought by a joint group of senior police officers and that a new approach would be made towards the abolition of discrimination in employment in Northern Ireland.

AJD

Italy-Yugoslavia (Trieste)

The dispute over Trieste and its surroundings—which had been part of Italy between 1919 and 1945—arose out of a Yugoslav claim to this area made in 1945, the principal grounds why it should not continue to be part of Italy being (i) that the latter was one of the defeated Axis powers and had been guilty of aggression against Yugoslavia; (ii) that as part of Italy the port of Trieste would be cut off from its natural hinterland; and (iii) that the area was partly inhabited by Slovenes and Croats. Although a final settlement of the dispute was achieved by the two governments under the 1975 Treaty of Osimo, certain aspects of this agreement have continued to be opposed by a substantial minority of the Trieste population.

Trieste between World Wars I and II

Map 10   The position of Trieste.

The Adriatic town of Trieste, which had with its hinterland been under Austrian control during most of the period since the 14th century, had by the outbreak of World War I in 1914 become the principal port of the Austro-Hungarian empire. Of its population at that time about two-thirds were Italian (of either Italian or Austrian nationality), while most of the remainder were Slovenes or Croats. In a then secret Treaty of London, concluded on April 26, 1915, by Britain, France and Russia with Italy, the latter was promised, in return for joining the war on the side of the Allies and against Germany and Austria-Hungary, control of specified territories which were then part of the Austro-Hungarian empire but had been claimed as Italian by an Italian irredentist movement. These territories included Trieste, the counties of Gorizia and Gradisca and all Istria (as well as certain islands in the Adriatic and the province of Dalmatia).

After President Wilson of the United States had insisted on a revision of these promises, the final frontiers of Italy in this region at the end of World War I were fixed under the

73

Treaty of Rapallo concluded between Italy and Yugoslavia in 1920. Under this treaty most of the coast of Dalmatia (except the Zara enclave and the island of Lagosta) was given to Yugoslavia; Fiume (Rijeka), east of Istria, became a Free City until Jan. 27, 1924, when under a new Italo-Yugoslav treaty it was annexed to Italy after it had already been seized by an Italian force led by Gabriele d'Annunzio. For Trieste its transfer to Italy after World War I meant that it was cut off from its natural hinterland (now part of Yugoslavia), and its port activities declined considerably.

The 1945 Attempt by Yugoslavia to seize Trieste

Towards the end of World War II Marshal Tito of Yugoslavia (who had on April 11, 1945, signed a treaty of friendship, mutual assistance and post-war collaboration with the Soviet Union) officially claimed, on April 15, 1945, Trieste and the Istrian peninsula (Venezia Giulia) for Yugoslavia, and his claim was immediately strongly opposed by all political parties in Italy except the Communists (then led by Palmiro Togliatti). On April 30 Marshal Tito announced that his armed forces had entered the area, in particular Rijeka (Fiume), Pula (Pola) and Trst (Trieste), and on May 1 he added that these forces had occupied Trzic (Monfalcone) and Goriza (Gorizia). On May 3, 1945, however, it was announced that a New Zealand division had occupied Trieste and received the surrender of its German garrison. In an official statement by the Allied authorities it was affirmed that all Italo-Yugoslav frontier questions could be settled at a peace conference but that in terms of the armistice concluded between the Allies and Marshal Badoglio (for Italy) the disputed territory was to be entrusted to an Allied military administration.

On May 14 the US government expressed its opposition to "the unilateral action" taken by Marshal Tito in the Trieste area and asserted that the Marshal had himself, in negotiations with Field Marshal Alexander of Britain in February 1945, agreed to Allied military control in Istria and Trieste. In identical British and US notes presented in Belgrade on May 15 it was reported to have been stated (i) that military occupation in the wake of the enemy's surrender could not be allowed to prejudge final decisions; and (ii) that the disposal of disputed territories must form part of the general peace settlement.

In Yugoslavia the territories concerned were on May 14, 1945, described as "our own sovereign land snatched from Yugoslavia in the past". The Italian government, on the other hand, insisted on the same day on a neutral administration of Trieste for the time being by the powers with which Italy had concluded the armistice, although it also declared its readiness to have the pre-war frontiers revised in "a pacific fair compromise carried out in the proper manner at the proper time". At the same time Togliatti stated that Trieste was Italian and its fate should not be compromised by unilateral actions and declarations.

The Yugoslav position was made clear in a reply to the Allied notes (of May 15), issued on May 19, 1945, as follows: "The Yugoslav Army, as one of the Allied armies, has equal rights to remain in the territory it has liberated in the struggle against the common enemy . . . . The fact that the population of these regions has for two years taken part in the war of liberation, that in its overwhelming majority it is Yugoslav, and that it has borne enormous sacrifices in the struggle against Italian and German fascism, cannot be an obstacle to our demand to entrust our army with the organization of military administration and to entrust the People's Committee of Liberation, chosen from the people, with the organization of civil administration. The needs of our Allies concerning ports and communications have been completely safeguarded in the spirit of the talks between Marshal Tito and Field-Marshal Alexander. The honour of our country demands the presence of the Yugoslav Army in Istria, Trieste, and on the Slovene coastline. The decisions of the peace conference, which will be final as regards the apportioning of the regions concerned, are in no way prejudiced. Yugoslavia is opposed to all unilateral declarations".

In Trieste itself the Anglo-American forces which had entered the city did not interfere with the Yugoslav civil authority constituted by an Italo-Slovene executive committee with an Italian chairman and one Italian and one Slovene vice-chairman. This committee was, however, opposed by a Trieste National Committee of Liberation, which had sought refuge in Rome.

Establishment of the Free Territory of Trieste

Subsequent negotiations between the Allied and Yugoslav authorities led to the conclusion of an agreement officially announced on June 9, 1945. This agreement on a temporary military administration of the area laid down (i) that part of Istria, including Trieste, the railways and roads from Trieste towards Gorizia, Caporetto and Tarvisio, as well as Pula and anchorages along the coast, should be under the control of the Supreme Allied Commander; (ii) that Yugoslav troops not exceeding 2,000 could occupy, in this area, a district to be selected by the Supreme Allied Commander but not have access to other areas; (iii) that the Supreme Commander would govern these areas through an Allied military government, while a small Yugoslav military mission might be attached to the Eighth Army headquarters as observers; (iv) that Yugoslav forces would be withdrawn from this area by June 12; (v) that the Yugoslav government would return residents of the area whom it had deported or arrested (except persons possessing Yugoslav nationality in 1939) and make restitution for property confiscated or removed: and (vi) that the agreement was not to prejudice the ultimate disposal of the two zones thus created—Zone A (northern Istria, including the city of Trieste) under Allied military government and Zone B (southern Istria) under Yugoslav administration.

The agreement was implemented accordingly; Yugoslav forces were withdrawn from the western zone within the time-limit set, and an agreement on the demarcation of the boundaries between the two zones was signed in Trieste on June 20, 1945. However, a four-power commission of experts (from Britain, France, the Soviet Union and the United States) appointed in March 1946 to make a final boundary delimitation failed to reach unanimous conclusions in a report published the following month. The Allied Council of Foreign Ministers, after considering the commission's report, approved (on July 12, 1946) an agreement on the constitution of a Free Territory of Trieste, with boundaries (based on a French recommendation) running from north of Duino to south of the port of Cittanuova (Novigrad), and with all territory east of the Free Territory and east of a northward extension of the latter's boundary to a point east of Tarvisio to be ceded to Yugoslavia (but with Monfalcone and Gorizia remaining Italian). Under this agreement the Free Territory was to have a permanent statute subject to the UN Security Council, which was to appoint a governor after consultation with Italy and Yugoslavia, and legislative and executive authorities were to be established in the Free Territory on democratic lines and on the basis of universal suffrage. The agreement was, however, rejected as unacceptable by both Italy and Yugoslavia.

Nevertheless, the UN Security Council took over the administration of the Free Territory on Jan. 10, 1947. In the peace treaty signed in Paris on Feb. 10, 1947, by the Allied powers and Italy, the Free Territory of Trieste was declared demilitarized and neutral, and all its inhabitants were guaranteed equal rights and fundamental freedoms, with Italians resident in it becoming citizens of the Territory unless they opted for Italian citizenship, in which case they could be required to leave the Territory. However, no agreement was subsequently reached on the appointment of a governor, as all candidates, although drawn mainly from neutral powers, proved unacceptable to either the Western powers or the Soviet Union. The treaty also provided for the cession of the Zara (Zadar) enclave, Lagosta (Lastovo) and other Dalmatian coast islands to Yugoslavia.

On March 20, 1948, the British, French and US governments proposed to the Soviet Union and Italy that Trieste should be placed under Italian sovereignty on the grounds that the statute which it had been given under the UN Security Council had proved unworkable, and there had been frequent incidents between Italians and the Slovenes. In the latter context, the British head of the Allied administration reported to the Security Council that the Italians tended "to look to the democratic ideals of the West" while the Slovenes rallied "round the standard of communist totalitarianism". The Western powers' proposal was immediately rejected by Yugoslavia.

On June 25, 1948, the Anglo-American military authorities in Trieste issued a decree on reforms in Zone A of the Free Territory designed to bring its administration into line with Italian practices, and on July 3 they appointed an Italian as Trieste's first Mayor (*Sindaco*). As no agreement had been reached on the appointment of a governor for the Free Territory between the Western powers and the Soviet Union, the UN Security Council shelved the question sine die on Feb. 21, 1949.

The first free elections in Trieste since 1922 were held in Zone A in June 1949. (i) In elections held on June 12 to the 60-member Trieste municipal council, 40 seats were gained by the Italian parties—25 of them by Christian Democrats; of the remaining 20 seats, 13 went to the "Cominform" wing of the Trieste Communist Party and only one to the "Tito" wing (which had been expelled from the party in August 1948, following the break between Tito and the Cominform); a Christian Democrat was thereupon elected Mayor of Trieste. (ii) In elections held on June 19 in five communes in Zone A the "Cominform" Communists polled 51 per cent of the vote, the combined Italian parties 30 per cent, the (anti-communist) Slovene Democrats about 6 per cent and the "Tito" Communists about 4 per cent.

On March 18, 1950, the Yugoslav military government of Zone B announced that the zone had been completely integrated in the Yugoslav economy, with all customs barriers having been abolished and the Yugoslav dinar having replaced the Italian lira as legal currency in July 1949. Elections held on April 16, 1950, for the zonal administrative council of Zone B resulted (according to the State Electoral Commission in Belgrade) in the Italo-Slovene Popular Front (supporting the Yugoslav government) gaining almost 89 per cent of the valid votes cast (with Socialists gaining 1.7 per cent and Christian Socials 1.1 per cent).

Separate Developments in Zones A and B of the Free Territory

Meanwhile Count Carlo Sforza, the Italian Foreign Minister, had on April 8, 1950, offered to enter into direct negotiations with Yugoslavia, but had made this conditional on "substantial acceptance" by Yugoslavia that the whole of the Free Territory would have to be returned to Italy. The Soviet government, on the other hand, on April 20 called for the withdrawal of Anglo-American troops from Trieste and the appointment of a governor of the Free Territory, alleging in particular that the Western powers had unlawfully violated the Italian peace treaty as a governor should have been appointed for the Territory by Sept. 15, 1947, and the troops withdrawn a few months later, and that the United States and Britain had converted Trieste into "an unlawful Anglo-American naval base" which constituted "a threat to the peace and security of Europe". The Soviet demand and allegations were rejected by the three Western powers on June 16.

An indication that Yugoslavia might adopt a compromise solution of the Trieste problem was first given on Sept. 21, 1951, when Edvard Kardelj, the Yugoslav Federal Secretary for Foreign Affairs, said in the National Assembly in Belgrade that, although Yugoslavia could not agree to the tripartite proposal for the reversal of Trieste to Italy, the question could not be solved by the incorporation of the Free Territory in Yugoslavia and that a third solution should therefore be sought. In February 1952 the Yugoslav government submitted its proposals for a direct settlement of the Trieste question between Italy and Yugoslavia to the Italian government. These proposals involved inter alia the integration of Zones A and B in one Free Territory to be placed under a governor to be nominated alternately for three years by the Italian and Yugoslav governments. These proposals were, however, rejected by the Italian government on Feb. 25.

Anti-British and anti-Yugoslav demonstrations, accompanied by disturbances, took place in Trieste on March 20-27, 1952, when Italians, including the mayor of Trieste, called for the return to Italy not only of Trieste but of the whole of Istria. Talks were thereupon held in London between the British Foreign Secretary and the Italian ambassador on Italian proposals for the virtual transfer of Zone A to Italy, with Italian forces joining in its occupation within the framework of the North Atlantic Treaty Organization (NATO).

Under a memorandum of understanding signed in London on May 9, 1952, Italy was more fully associated with the administration of Zone A "in preparation for a final settlement", but the Yugoslav government declared on May 13 that these changes should not have been made without Yugoslav consent and were "an unlawful and unilateral violation" of the international status of the zone. On May 15 the Yugoslav military government of Zone B announced a series of measures designed to link the zone more closely with Yugoslavia (providing inter alia for travel of Zone B residents to and from Yugoslavia without identity documents and for their travelling abroad on Yugoslav passports).

Further municipal elections held in Trieste and five smaller towns in Zone A took place on May 25, 1952, and had the following results:

	Whole of Zone A	Trieste City
Italian parties	116,258	112,616
Yugoslav parties	12,116	8,483
Independent Autonomy parties* ...	27,094	26,907
Cominform Communists and Nenni Socialists	38,348	33,759
Total of valid votes	193,816	181,765

*Standing for the continued status of Trieste as an independent Free Territory.

In the Trieste city council seats were thereupon distributed as follows: Christian Democrats 28, Socialist Party five, Republicans four, (right-wing) Italian Social Movement (MSI) four, Liberals three, Communists six, Independence Party five, others five.

Administrative elections held in Zone B on Dec. 7, 1952, resulted, according to the Yugoslav military government, in 97 per cent of the 42,000 registered voters casting their votes for candidates of the Popular Front, except for 1.2 per cent of the votes declared invalid.

Following further conflicting statements made by Italian and Yugoslav leaders on the future of Trieste and a deterioration in relations between the two countries, the British and US governments announced on Oct. 8, 1953, that they were "no longer prepared to maintain responsibility for the administration of Zone A" and that they had "therefore decided to terminate Allied military government, to withdraw their troops and, having in mind the predominantly Italian character of Zone A, to relinquish the administration of that zone to the Italian government". The Yugoslav government officially protested against the decision on Oct. 9, calling it (i) "a unilateral violation of the Italian peace treaty of 1947 for the benefit of a power which committed aggression against Yugoslavia and waged war on the side of the Axis powers" and (ii) "unjust" because it included the cession of territory inhabited by Slovenes and cut off Trieste from its natural hinterland.

The Anglo-US decision was also followed by anti-British, anti-American and anti-Italian speeches and demonstrations in Yugoslavia. After the (British) Allied zone commander had forbidden the hoisting of the Italian flags on official buildings in Trieste, anti-Allied riots took place in the city, and also anti-British demonstrations in Italy, during November 1953. However, Italian and Yugoslav troops which had been deployed on both sides of the Italian-Yugoslav border since the end of August 1953 were, under an agreement reached on Dec. 5 of that year, withdrawn by Dec. 21.

Four-Party Agreement reached in 1954

Following negotiations between Italy and Yugoslavia (partly sponsored by John Foster Dulles, US Secretary of State under President Eisenhower), a memorandum of understanding between the Italian, Yugoslav, British and US governments was initialled in London on Oct. 5, 1954. Under this memorandum Italy was given control of Zone A of the Free Territory of Trieste—except for a strip of about five square miles (13 sq km) inhabited mainly by Slovenes—while the whole of Zone B and the above strip were entrusted to Yugoslav control; the Italian government undertook to maintain the free port at Trieste (as laid down in the Italian peace treaty); no residents of the Territory would be penalized for past political activities connected with the solution of the Trieste problem; arrangements for border traffic were to be negotiated; provision was made for the protection of persons wishing to move out of or into the area, and for that of their property; and a special statute regulated the rights of the population of the areas to be transferred, including the right to use their own language and the use of bilingual street names and other public inscriptions in districts where the ethnic minority constituted at least one-quarter of the local population.

The memorandum was subject to formal approval of all the signatories of the Italian peace treaty, including the Soviet Union, which officially took cognizance of it in a letter to the president of the UN Security Council on Oct. 14, 1954. Because of Soviet objections, the Security Council had the previous year, during sessions held between Oct. 20 and Dec. 15, failed to reach agreement on the Trieste problem and had postponed any further session after the United States had proposed that the Western powers should be given more time to reach an amicable solution.

The memorandum was implemented on Oct. 26, 1954, when the Allied military government in Zone A was terminated and an Italian military governor entered the zone. Three days later he was replaced by a commissioner-general directly responsible to the Italian Prime Minister. On Oct. 14 the Italian government had approved a comprehensive programme of economic aid and development for Trieste (and in 1963 Trieste became the capital of the newly-created special-statute region of Friuli-Venezia Giulia).

Final Settlement of the Dispute under the 1975 Treaty of Osimo

The London memorandum of 1954 was a de facto settlement of the problem but not a de jure solution, as was emphasized by the Italian government in February 1974, when in protest against Yugoslavia's erection of border markers between the two zones (indicating an international frontier) it pointed out that neither the peace treaty nor the 1954 London memorandum had extended Yugoslav territory "to the Italian territory designated as Zone B". However, on Oct. 1, 1975, the Italian government announced that it had established "the basis for agreement" with Yugoslavia, which would accept the status quo as permanent, with slight alterations to the frontier in favour of Italy near Gorizia, where an area of about $1\frac{1}{4}$ square miles (3.2 sq km) was ceded to Italy. The total area going to Italy of about 90 square miles (233 sq km) had a population of over 302,000 (275,000 of them in Trieste) and that going to Yugoslavia (about 200 square miles) a population of about 73,500. This settlement was formalized in the Treaty of Osimo, which was signed on Nov. 10, 1975, at Osimo (Ancona), together with 10 annexes and an agreement on the development of economic relations between the two countries (with four annexes).

The treaty laid down the new frontiers (in Art. 1) and specified (in Art. 3) that "the nationality of persons who were on June 10, 1940, Italian nationals and permanent residents in the territory ... and that of their descendants born after June 10, 1940" would be regulated by the law of one or the other of the parties to the treaty in accordance with the place of residence of these persons at the moment of the entry into force of the treaty, but that such persons (constituting respectively the Italian or the Yugoslav minority) had the right to move to Yugoslav or Italian territory and would then be regarded as possessing the nationality relating to their new place of residence. The treaty also provided for the conclusion of an agreement on compensation payable to those whose property had been nationalized, expropriated or otherwise subjected to restrictive measures by the Yugoslav military, civil or local authorities since Yugoslav armed forces had entered the territory (Art. 4).

The economic co-operation agreement provided for the creation of an industrial zone, in the region of Sezana-Fernetti, partly on the Italian and partly on the Yugoslav side of the newly-agreed frontier, which covered about 20 square kilometres and would be an extension of the regime for commodities under the free port facilities of Trieste, with imports being duty- and tax-free and labour from both countries being employed. The details for the arrangements concerning this zone were laid down in a protocol valid for 30 years and tacitly renewable for five-year periods. The establishment of the zone had been approved by the European Commission and all the members of the European Communities.

The treaty and the agreement were approved by the two Houses of the Italian Parliament on Oct. 3 and 9, 1975, with only members of the (extreme right-wing) Italian Social Movement (MSI) and a few other parliamentarians from the border areas voting against approval.

In Trieste parts of the settlement were opposed by an autonomist *Per Trieste* movement, whose members objected in particular to the proposed industrial zone and which, in municipal elections held in Trieste in June 1978, gained about one-quarter of the votes and subsequently obtained the post of mayor. However, in an official communiqué issued on Oct. 12, 1979 (at the end of a visit to Belgrade by the Italian President), it was stated that since the conclusion of the Treaty of Osimo there no longer existed any difficulties between the two countries.

HWD

The Macedonian Question

The period since World War II has seen the revival of arguments, which first surfaced in the late 19th century, relating to the sovereignty and the ethnic character of Macedonia, an area lying in the central southern Balkans and centring on southern Yugoslavia and the Greek/Yugoslavian/Bulgarian borders. The Yugoslavian Federation at present includes a federated republic of Macedonia which incorporates part of what was until 1913 the territory of Macedonia; other parts of what was until then Macedonian land have been distributed between Greece (Greek Macedonia) and Bulgaria (Blagoevgrad district). At present none of these countries maintains any formal claim to the Macedonian territory of any other, but the underlying tensions over the sovereignty of the area have repeatedly come to light in the form of claims regarding the cultural and ethnic unity of the area; moreover, Yugoslavia and Bulgaria see in one another's historical attitudes elements of a territorial claim.

Yugoslavia maintains that Macedonians in all three countries have a common cultural and historical identity separate from that of the predominant populations of any of the surrounding republics, and formally recognizes Slav Macedonians as comprising one of its federal nationalities. Bulgaria, however, refuses to recognize the existence of a Macedonian minority within its own borders and regards the Macedonian language as a Bulgarian dialect, giving rise to Yugoslavian complaints that it is suppressing the Macedonian culture. Greece for its part similarly refuses to accept the existence of a true Macedonian minority within its territory, claiming rather that its Slav-speaking minority living in former Macedonian areas is in fact composed of ethnic Greeks who were forced by centuries of Slavic domination to relinquish their original Greek language. Greece, Yugoslavia and Bulgaria all base their cases to some extent on the findings of archaeologists and of art and architectural historians who have, however, to date arrived at no consensus as to the cultural unity of the Macedonian people as propounded by Yugoslavia.

The main developments in the post-war debate on the Macedonian issue have centred on Yugoslavia and Bulgaria, with Greece regarding itself as only peripherally involved. The Yugoslavian/Bulgarian debate has often been highlighted by the continuous and periodically intensifying differences between Yugoslavia and the countries of the Warsaw Pact, to which Bulgaria belongs. It also received a new impetus in the late 1960s when Bulgarian historians began to present Macedonian historical figures as Bulgarians, and to celebrate the short-lived 1878 Treaty of San Stefano (which had created a "Greater Bulgaria" including Macedonia and part of Albania, but which had in the same year been drastically altered at the Congress of Berlin to reduce the area of Bulgarian territory). Yugoslavia sees in this "chauvinist" Bulgarian attitude an implicit territorial claim by Bulgaria to the whole of Macedonia, and the resulting escalation of polemics over the issue has since then been a serious obstacle to international co-operation in the Balkans.

The Treaty of San Stefano and the Congress of Berlin

Macedonia was inhabited from the seventh century BC onwards by Greek, Thracian and Illyrian peoples, achieving its peak under Philip and Alexander of Macedon before its incorporation in the second century BC into the Roman empire. The influx of Turkish, Bulgarian and Slavic peoples began in the sixth century AD, and in the ninth and 10th centuries Macedonia belonged to the Bulgarian empire, although in 1018 it returned to the Byzantine empire. In 1230 the second Bulgarian empire recaptured its southern part (except Salonika); it then passed to the Serbians, but by 1371 the whole of Macedonia had fallen to the Ottoman Turks (who controlled it until 1912). The rest of the Bulgarian empire fell to the Turks in 1396 and for almost 500 years thereafter Bulgaria had no independent political existence.

Amid a general upsurge of nationalism among the declining Ottoman empire's subject peoples in Europe, Bulgarian aspirations to the restoration of the Bulgarian state emerged in the first half of the 19th century. A revolt against the Turkish rulers in May 1876 was put down with much brutality against the Bulgarian population. In the same year (amid general signs of unrest in Macedonia, Serbia and Albania) Serbia and Montenegro, supported by Bulgarian volunteers, declared war on Turkey, as did Russia in 1877. The combined Russian and Slav forces achieved notable victories against the Turks,[1] leading on March 3, 1878, to the signature of the Treaty of San Stefano, which created inter alia the principality of Bulgaria. The new principality, which continued under the suzerainty of the Turkish Porte, was to comprise some three-fifths of the Balkan peninsula and was to include parts of Serbia, almost all of Macedonia with its extensive Aegean coastal territories except for Salonika and Khalkidiki, as well as part of the present Albanian state.

The European powers expressed strong concern that the new greater Bulgarian state, with its population of some 4,000,000, would prove to be dangerously dependent on Russia, and pressed at the Congress of Berlin for a reduction of its size. Consequently the final treaty signed at the congress on July 13, 1878, returned Macedonia to Turkey, limiting Bulgaria to most of the territory between the Danube and the Balkan mountains; the area between the Balkan mountains and the Rhodope mountains became the autonomous province of Eastern Rumelia, subject to the Turks but under a Christian governor-general. Bulgaria annexed Eastern Rumelia in 1885, and in 1909 the powers recognized the independent kingdom of Bulgaria including Eastern Rumelia, which territory currently forms the southern half of Bulgaria.

The Division of Macedonia

The return of Macedonia to Turkey at the Congress of Berlin caused great resentment in

---

[1]See also section on Romania-Soviet Union, pages 85-90.

the Balkans and resulted in widespread unrest in Macedonia which contributed considerably to the eventual overthrow of Turkish rule during the First Balkan War of 1912. Resistance to the Turks was conducted by a wide range of groups pursuing widely varying aims. The first was the pro-Bulgarian "Internal Macedonian Revolutionary Organization" (IMRO), which was formed in 1893 and which campaigned under the slogan "Macedonia for the Macedonians". Two years later the Bulgarians formed a "Supreme Committee for Macedonia and Adrianopolis" (the latter being the present-day Turkish border town of Edirne); known as the "Komitajis", this movement campaigned for the restoration of the Treaty of San Stefano and attempted to persuade Macedonians to declare themselves Bulgarians. Also in the 1890s Serbia sent its "Chety" to Macedonia to instigate pro-Serbian unrest, while the Greeks created a "National Society" whose guerrillas were largely responsible for the outbreak of the Greek-Turkish war in 1897. In 1903 the "Komitajis" instigated an uprising in all parts of Macedonia.

In March 1912 Serbia and Bulgaria reached basic agreement, under Russian auspices, on the eventual division of Macedonia, and thereupon, joined by Greece, formed an alliance which later that year declared war on Turkey. They achieved considerable victories in the First Balkan War, liberating inter alia Serbia, Macedonia and the Aegean islands, and driving the Turks back almost as far as Constantinople (Istanbul), but disagreed almost immediately over the actual division of Macedonia. In June 1913 Bulgaria therefore attacked Greece and Serbia, precipitating the Second Balkan War, but was rapidly defeated; the originally agreed division of Macedonia was restored, although Bulgaria ceded additional territory to Romania (which, seeing Bulgaria's weakness, had simultaneously attacked from the north).

The peace treaty signed in Bucharest on Aug. 10, 1913, established basically the present Macedonian borders of Greece and Bulgaria, while Serbian Macedonia was later to become the Yugoslavian republic of Macedonia. Under the treaty Greece received Aegean

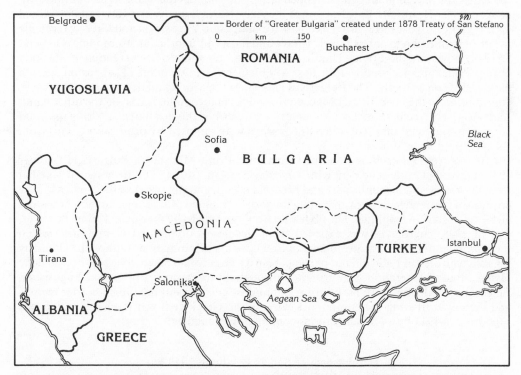

Map 11   Present territorial relationships of Yugoslavia, Albania, Greece and Bulgaria with reference to the Macedonian question. The borders of the Yugoslav republic of Macedonia are shown in map 1 on page 2.

Macedonia, amounting to 34,602 square kilometres and including all of the Aegean coastal area, while Serbia received Vardar Macedonia (northern and central Macedonia, amounting to 25,713 square kilometres) and Bulgaria received Pirin Macedonia, the eastern region amounting to 6,789 square kilometres. (NB. Greece does not recognize the designations "Aegean", "Vardar" or "Pirin" Macedonia, since it regards the political use of the term "Macedonia" as a Yugoslavian/Bulgarian usurpation of a Greek concept, and as suggesting what it claims is a non-existent historical unity; it therefore accepts, as exclusively geographical concepts, the terms "Greek Macedonia", "Yugoslavian Macedonia" and "Bulgarian Macedonia".)

Bulgaria, thus thwarted in its aspirations to direct access to the Aegean, sought redress by joining the Central Powers in World War I, and indeed occupied parts of Aegean (Greek) Macedonia from 1915 to 1918. However, the Paris peace conference of 1919 decided broadly in favour of the 1913 division of Macedonia and thus confirmed what are essentially the present-day borders in the region, while the treaties of Neuilly and Lausanne provided for exchanges of populations between the relevant Balkan states. This exchange resulted in what Greece now describes as a highly homogeneous population in Aegean (Greek) Macedonia, in support of which claim it has quoted figures compiled by the League of Nations showing that between 1912 and 1926 the proportion of Greeks in the area rose from 42.6 per cent to 88.8 per cent; the same figures show that the proportion of Moslems fell from 39.4 per cent to 0.1 per cent, Bulgarians from 9.9 per cent to 5.1 per cent, and miscellaneous others from 8.1 per cent to 6 per cent. A Greek census of 1928 is reported to have found that of a national population of 6,032,761 only 81,984 (1.36 per cent) were Slavophones.

World War II and the Balkan Federation

Although Bulgarian-inspired unrest in non-Bulgarian Macedonia continued throughout the 1920s, the Macedonian issue remained largely dormant in the years before the outbreak of World War II. In 1941 Bulgaria joined the Axis (Nazi Germany and Italy) and permitted German forces to use its territory as a base for attacks on Yugoslavia and Greece, receiving in return permission to annex Greek Thrace and most of Yugoslavian Macedonia. On Sept. 5, 1944, however, the Soviet Union declared war on Bulgaria, whereupon it abruptly changed sides and declared war the next day on Germany. Accounts of the ensuing period have varied considerably. The Bulgarians claim that their forces made a major and decisive contribution to the liberation of Macedonia and Serbia from the Nazis; on the other hand, some relatively recent Yugoslavian sources have described this account as a falsification and have even suggested that Yugoslavian partisans were opposed by pro-fascist troops from Bulgaria until the end of the war.

After Georgi Dimitrov became the Communist Prime Minister of Bulgaria in October 1946, a period of rapprochement with Yugoslavia began. In 1947 Dimitrov visited Marshal Tito, his Yugoslavian counterpart and personal friend, and the two discussed plans for the creation of a Balkan federation including Bulgaria, a reunited Macedonia, Greek Thrace and all the Yugoslavian republics. The plan was strongly opposed by the Soviet Union, however, and in 1948 Yugoslavia was expelled from the Soviet-dominated Cominform, which thereupon commenced a prolonged anti-Yugoslavian campaign (although Dimitrov himself, who died in 1949, did not participate in it). Greece had meanwhile also opposed the planned Balkan federation, and protested throughout the period 1944-47 that Yugoslavia, Bulgaria and Albania were harbouring communist guerrillas in the Greek border regions and thereby furthering the communist cause in the Greek civil war (a charge which was supported in 1947 by a United Nations commission of inquiry).

Development of Balkan Relations, 1949-66

Although in August 1947 Bulgaria and Yugoslavia had signed a treaty of mutual assistance, this was revoked on Oct. 3, 1949, by Bulgaria following the denunciation of

Yugoslavia by all of the other Cominform countries. Yugoslavia responded by accusing Bulgaria of sabotaging the proposed Balkan federation by demanding an excessively large say in it, and of expansionism and provoking border incidents. Bulgaria in 1949-50 tried and executed Traicho Kostov, a former Deputy Prime Minister and secretary of the Bulgarian Communist Party (BCP), for allegedly plotting to overthrow the Bulgarian government with Yugoslavian assistance, to murder Dimitrov and to sabotage Bulgaria's trade links with other Cominform countries, as well as promoting "the absorption of Bulgaria by Yugoslavia". Yugoslavia replied to this and other political trials with similar trials, and although Kostov was subsequently rehabilitated by the BCP in 1956 lasting damage was done to relations between the two countries.

During the next 10 years, however, relations in the Balkans showed signs of relaxation. Greece re-opened full diplomatic relations with Yugoslavia in 1952 and with Bulgaria in 1954. A Treaty of Alliance (Balkan Pact) was signed in August 1954 by Yugoslavia, Greece and Turkey (although it had collapsed by 1960 because differences between Greece and Turkey over Cyprus had effectively paralyzed its Council of Ministers and its Secretariat). Bulgaria agreed with Greece in 1953, 1955 and 1958 on the avoidance and settlement of frontier incidents, although Greek suspicion of its neighbours was reflected in its continued opposition to the holding of various proposed Balkan ministerial conferences.

Bulgaria began a new anti-Yugoslavia campaign in September 1958, when Dimitri Ganev, a leading member of the Bulgarian Politburo, accused the Belgrade government of "denying the national individuality of the Macedonian people" by refusing to accept their alleged communality with the Bulgarians and of forcing upon its own Macedonians an "artificial language" bearing more resemblance to Serbian than to their native tongue. Soviet concern at this deterioration in relations was expressed in May 1962 during a visit to Sofia by Nikita Khrushchev, then Soviet party leader and Prime Minister. Consequently Bulgaria and Yugoslavia adopted more conciliatory paths, signing on June 28, 1964, 12 agreements on war reparations, joint developments and other matters, while Bulgaria also agreed in 1964 with Greece on an arrangement giving it direct access to the Mediterranean via the free port area of Salonika harbour. Yugoslavia received a similar facility at Salonika in 1975.

Deterioration of Bulgarian-Yugoslavian Relations over Macedonian Issue

In December 1967 the BCP approved a speech by Todor Zhivkov, the Bulgarian Prime Minister and First Secretary of the BCP, in which he called for the intensification of "patriotic education" concentrating inter alia "on the golden centuries of Bulgarian national history, their kings and emperors", adding the observation that "we Bulgarians are the descendants of the Thracian culture". During the following months Bulgarian publishers began to produce a number of books referring to allegedly Bulgarian characters who were normally regarded by Yugoslavia as Macedonians. Although Yugoslavia immediately expressed its reservations at this practice, on March 2 and 3, 1968, demonstrations were held in the Bulgarian capital to celebrate the 90th anniversary of the Treaty of San Stefano; in May, moreover, the Bulgarian *Narodna Kultura* was alleged to have carried an article describing the Yugoslavian Macedonians as slaves to the Serbs. Yugoslavian press sources regarded these actions as open provocations and reacted angrily, countering the Bulgarian argument that there were no Macedonians in Bulgaria with the claim that a 1946 census had shown that about 70 per cent of Pirin residents had described themselves as Macedonians. (In the 1956 Bulgarian census only 179,000 or about 10 per cent fewer than in 1946 had so described themselves; the 1965 census had shown only 8,750 Macedonians, while none at all were recorded in 1975. This fall in numbers was attributed to the wording of the census forms and to a general loss of Macedonian identity in Bulgaria, rather than to any major demographic development.)

A visit to Yugoslavia in December 1969 by the Bulgarian Foreign Minister, Ivan Bashev, for discussions on the Macedonian question led to such heated debate that the discussions were broken off without a concluding communiqué being issued. Zhivkov proposed further talks in July 1970, but a proposed discussion with President Tito did not take place because of the Bulgarian insistence during preliminary rounds that Yugoslavian Macedonians were in fact Bulgarians. President Tito, speaking at Skopje (the Macedonian capital) on Nov. 10, 1972, referred to the Bulgarian attitudes as "illusions which are founded on a distant past" and indicated that they still represented a major obstacle to satisfactory relations.

Further bilateral discussions took place in Bulgaria in February 1973 and in Belgrade in November 1975, but led to no progress on the issue. Stane Dolanc, then a secretary of the Yugoslavian League of Communist Youth, referred in a speech on Oct. 1, 1976, to the policies of "countries where not even the fundamental rights of nationalities are respected", adding: "There are countries—unfortunately even among our own neighbours—in which the policy of denationalization of our minorities is even today pursued more or less openly and brutally". Although each side continued to stress that it was making no territorial claims against the other, Yugoslavia was by this time regularly publishing allegations that the Bulgarian government, by intimidation, resettlement and indoctrination, was attempting to eradicate the notion of a Macedonian nationality. A further round of talks in Bulgaria on Sept. 22-28, 1976, had again produced no significant progress on the issue.

Bulgaria took a new initiative on June 15, 1978, when Zhivkov offered in a speech at Blagoevgrad (the administrative capital of Pirin Macedonia) to sign with Yugoslavia a bilateral treaty on the final recognition of the Bulgarian/Yugoslavian border. Furthermore, on July 24 (the day before the opening of a conference of the non-aligned countries in Belgrade) he presented a lengthy memorandum to the Yugoslavian government containing an undertaking to respect the borders and autonomous character of Yugoslavian Macedonia. At the same time, however, he added that Bulgaria could not accept "the formulation of the Macedonian nation on an anti-Bulgarian basis involving the distortion of well-known historical facts", and asserted that the problem of the alleged Macedonian minority in Bulgaria had been solved by the only people with the right to do so, namely the Bulgarians.

President Tito indicated in a speech on Nov. 26, 1978, his intention to avoid further escalation of the dispute, but Bulgarian/Yugoslavian relations suffered another setback in January 1979 with the publication of (i) a 900-page Bulgarian documentation on the "indissoluble links" between the Macedonians and the Bulgarians from 681 AD onwards, and (ii) the memoirs of Mrs Tsola Dragoicheva, a member of the Politburo of the BCP, who claimed that Macedonia had been "snatched" from Bulgaria at the 1878 Congress of Berlin and again in 1945. Later in the year, in response to strong Yugoslavian protests, Mrs Dragoicheva added that Yugoslavia, in the guise of concern for Pirin Macedonians, was encroaching on the territorial and ethnic integrity of Bulgaria.

Konstantinos Karamanlis, then Prime Minister (and later President) of Greece, held talks with Todor Zhivkov in Athens on April 29-30, 1979, during which the former was understood to have expressed concern at the escalation of tensions over the Macedonian issue and to have appealed for the multilateral solution of problems in the Balkans. Bulgaria and Yugoslavia subsequently resumed discussions in Belgrade during June 1979, but failed to reach any resolution of the Macedonian question. On Aug. 2 of that year Bulgaria protested in strong terms at Yugoslavia's decision to celebrate Nicholas Vapsarov as a prominent Macedonian poet, claiming that this writer was in fact Bulgarian.

The two sides have continued to be sharply at odds over their respective historical approaches to the Macedonian question in particular and Bulgarian-Yugoslavian relations in general. Thus on Feb. 11, 1981, the official Yugoslavian news agency Tanjug issued a strong criticism of an extensive article published in the latest issue of *Vekove* (the journal of the Society of Bulgarian Historians) under the title "Yugoslav historiography on Bulgarian-Yugoslavian relations, 1941-44". According to Tanjug, the author of the article claimed that the Yugoslavian press and publishers were continuing "a rabid anti-Bulgarian campaign to falsify the historic past and to appropriate the history and the cultural heritage of the Bulgarian people" with the aim of imposing on Bulgaria the Yugoslavian nationalistic and hegemonistic line on the Macedonian question.

Since 1982 the Macedonian question has continued to arouse controversy in the bilateral relations between Greece and Yugoslavia—although both sides have been at pains to stop it from affecting material issues. Yugoslavia has complained at the Greek authorities' decision to withdraw Greek students from the Yugoslavian university at Skopje, and to change official policy on the repatriation of certain Yugoslavian refugees. Greece for its part has expressed grievances about what it calls Yugoslavian propaganda against Athens's refusal to recognize a Macedonian minority in northern Greece, or the existence of a "Macedonian nation".

The issue surfaced again in April and May 1986, following two public statements by the Greek Prime Minister, Andreas Papandreou, in which he denied the existence of a Slav-Macedonian minority in Greece and in which he averred that Yugoslavian Macedonia was purely a matter for the Yugoslavs. The collective State Presidency of the Yugoslavian Federation responded a few days later with a protest that the Greek position impaired the quality of all-round co-operation between the two countries. An exchange of official statements ensued which confirmed the continuing differences between them on the Macedonian issue.

MW

Romania-Soviet Union (Bessarabia)

The territorial settlement established between Romania and the Soviet Union after World War II was intended to be a definitive and final solution of longstanding Romanian-Russian conflict over the eastern part of Moldavia (Bessarabia) and certain other territories which had been under Romanian sovereignty in the inter-war period but which were now incorporated into the Soviet Union. In the post-war period the Communist government of Romania has consistently stressed that it has no territorial dispute with its fellow Warsaw Pact member, but the "Bessarabian question" has nevertheless remained an important underlying factor in Romanian-Soviet relations. Within what is now the Moldavian Soviet Socialist Republic the predominantly Romanian population has not only resisted Russification but has also shown increasing support for Romanian nationalist and irredentist ideas. Since the late 1960s, moreover, the Romanian government has steadily distanced itself from Soviet authority and a number of Romanian publications have emphasized the historical unity of the Romanian-speaking peoples. (For position of Bessarabia, see map on page 53.)

The present-day Bessarabian question is essentially a continuation of disagreements which arose as far back as the early 18th century, when Tsarist Russia first began to threaten what were then the Turkish-dominated principalities of Moldavia and Walachia. Since 1812 Russia, and subsequently the Soviet Union, have held almost continuous sovereignty over most of Bessarabia—the exceptions being the periods 1918-1940 and 1941-1944, when it was held by Romania. However, the long years of Russian rule have made little impact on the essentially Romanian character of the people, almost two-thirds of whom still speak a Romanian dialect. The result has been prolonged dissension over this densely populated and fertile territory, in the course of which some parts have changed hands up to seven times since 1812 as a result of successive conquests, agreements and ultimatums.

Up to 1812 Moldavia was a Turkish-dominated principality reaching westwards from the right bank of the Dnestr (Dniester) river across the Prut river as far as the Carpathians; in that year, however, Russia annexed the area between the Dnestr and the Prut (i.e. Bessarabia), the rest of Moldavia remaining under Turkish suzerainty until it became part of the independent state of Romania which received international recognition in 1878. Some 40 years later Bessarabia was among the territories acquired by Romania at the end of World War I and was thereupon reintegrated into Romanian Moldavia. The Soviet Union refused to recognize the transfer and was ceded Bessarabia (as well as Northern Bukovina) in mid-1940 after presenting an ultimatum to the Romanian government. Although Romania reconquered Bessarabia and Northern Bukovina in 1941 as Germany's ally in the war against the Soviet Union (and also annexed a large additional tract of Soviet territory), the eventual Soviet victory in eastern Europe again forced Romania to relinquish the disputed territories and to accept the incorporation of Bessarabia into the Moldavian Soviet Socialist Republic (SSR)—the post-war status quo being formally recognized by Romania in 1947. Thus the term Moldavia, as used in the context of Romania, nowadays means the area immediately to the west of the Prut.

Geographical and Demographic Aspects of the Region

The Moldavian SSR (essentially Bessarabia) covers an area of some 33,700 square kilometres to the east of the River Prut. It is bounded in the east by the Dnestr river valley, although its territory does not, as formerly, follow the Dnestr down to the Black Sea but turns south-west before reaching Odessa and joins the Prut at Galati. The area is of particular importance in agricultural terms, producing important tobacco, grape and rose-oil crops, as well as sunflower seeds, maize and wheat, and is also a major producer of wines and of preserved foods.

The January 1979 census showed a population of 3,948,000, of whom the great majority live on the land. Clear cultural, economic and political distinctions must be drawn, however, between the Romanian-speaking Moldavians (who according to a 1970 survey made up 64.6 per cent of the population of the republic), Ukrainians (14.2 per cent in 1970), Russians (11.6 per cent in 1970, but rapidly increasing in numbers), Turkish-speaking Gagauzi (3.5 per cent in 1970), Jews (2.7 per cent in 1970) and Bulgarians (2.1 per cent in 1970). By January 1985 the population of the Moldavian SSR was estimated at 4,100,000.

The Moldavian SSR has a very high birth rate (more than 20 live births per thousand of the population each year) and a low death rate, and the consequent increase in the population has been accentuated since the 1950s by the development of urban centres, in which the great majority of the Russians have come to live. Thus, although Russians accounted for only 11.6 per cent of the population in 1970, 77 per cent of them lived in urban areas (compared with 67 per cent in 1959). On the other hand, only 18 per cent of Moldavians lived in the towns in 1970, compared with 10 per cent in 1959. The growth in the proportion of Russians living in the towns appears to be a continuing development, and has been accompanied inter alia by the appointment of Russians to many, or indeed most, of the key positions in local administration. This latter process has applied particularly to the Moldavian Communist Party, of which 7.3 per cent of all Russians in the Moldavian SSR were members in 1970, compared with 3.8 per cent of all Ukrainians and only 1.3 per cent of the Moldavian majority.

It has been claimed in some Romanian quarters that the growing influence of Russian speakers in the Moldavian SSR has a political character. Whatever the truth of such allegations, it is clear that an attempt has been made to establish a new national culture within the Moldavian SSR which largely overlooks the ever-present Romanian influence in the traditional Bessarabian culture. For example, the Romanian dialect still spoken by much of the population has been renamed "Moldavian" and is listed by the Soviet Union among its national languages; "Moldavian" differs from Romanian only in that it is nowadays written in the Cyrillic alphabet instead of the Roman letters previously used, and Moldavians have no difficulty in understanding Romanian radio or television broadcasts. These factors apart, however, Moldavian links with Romania have been largely suppressed since the Soviet annexation of Bessarabia.

A consequence of this policy has been what some Romanians have described as the cultural isolation of the Soviet Moldavians. More than 55 per cent of the newspapers and periodicals on sale are in Russian, a language which in 1970 only a very small proportion of Moldavians living in the Moldavian SSR gave as their first language and only 33.9 per cent as a fluent second language. In the same census 97.7 per cent of Moldavians living in the Moldavian SSR gave "Moldavian" as their first language, but although illiteracy (formerly widespread) has been virtually eliminated since 1946, the absence of important writers or other artists using the "Moldavian" language has been noticeable.

Historical Background to the Bessarabian Question

Bessarabia was until 1812 part of the autonomous principality of Moldavia under Ottoman suzerainty; in that year it was formally ceded by the Peace of Bucharest to the Russian empire (whose troops had in fact invaded it many times since the early 18th century and which had occupied almost all of Moldavia and Walachia since defeating the Turks in 1806). War broke out again between Russia and Turkey in 1828, whereupon Russian troops again occupied all of Moldavia and Walachia, and remained in a protective capacity until 1834, by which time the Turkish Porte had approved the promulgation of constitutions for the two principalities (the Moldavian territory extending only as far east as the Prut and thus excluding Bessarabia). The Russians returned in 1848 to put down a peasants' rebellion and stayed this time until 1851.

Throughout this period the Russians had retained the sovereignty of Bessarabia itself; however, under the 1856 Treaty of Paris which ended the Crimean War they returned a strip of southern Bessarabia to Moldavia (then still under Turkish suzerainty), and Moldavia and Walachia were placed under a form of international guarantee. The Turkish divans were dissolved in 1858, and in 1859 the state of Romania was created from the two provinces; however, when Romanian independence was formally recognized at the Congress of Berlin in 1878 the whole of Bessarabia was declared Russian territory. Romania protested at this decision, since it had expected to be awarded the Bessarabian territory in return for having joined the recent war against Turkey and for having signed in 1877 a secret pact allowing Russian troops free passage against the Turks. Although Romania received instead the northern Dobruja (whose Romanian population was small), its dissatisfaction with the 1878 settlement gave rise to an irredentist campaign for the return of Bessarabia.

Since 1812 Russia had pursued a policy of Russification of Bessarabia, largely through resettlement; however, by 1917 at least two-thirds of the population were still Romanian, and in December 1917, shortly after the October Revolution, the dominant and anti-Bolshevik political forces in Bessarabia set up a Council whose main purpose was to facilitate the eventual return of Bessarabia to Romania. In November 1918 it voted for unconditional union with Romania, and in December 1918 Romania therefore annexed Bessarabia. The fusion, which was formalized in the Treaty of St Germain, has never been recognized by the Soviet Union, which in October 1924 demonstrated its position by setting aside a narrow strip of Ukrainian land to the east of the Dnestr for the establishment of the "Autonomous Moldavian Soviet Socialist Republic".

The new republic, whose constitution was approved in April 1925, was clearly intended eventually to incorporate Bessarabia and indeed subsequently formed the basis of the Soviet annexation in 1940. This followed the presentation on June 26, 1940, of a direct Soviet ultimatum to King Carol of Romania and his government demanding the cession of Bessarabia and Northern Bukovina and claiming that in 1918 "Romania took advantage of the military weakness of Russia and robbed the USSR by force of part of her territory—namely Bessarabia—and thus broke the century-old unity of Bessarabia". The demand for the cession of Northern Bukovina was based on the Soviet claim that "the predominant majority is connected with the Soviet Ukraine by common historical destinies" and that the two areas were similar in their language and national composition. (Bukovina as a whole had been a Moldavian province until 1777, when the Ottoman empire had ceded it to the Austrians, and had thereafter been administered by the Austro-Hungarian empire until its transfer to Romania in November 1919; Northern Bukovina had a mixed population consisting of Romanian, Jewish, Ukrainian and Russian elements.)

Faced with the June 26 ultimatum Romania was obliged to cede Bessarabia and Northern Bukovina to the Soviet Union, whose troops occupied them within seven days. Most of Bessarabia was thereupon joined to the former Autonomous Moldavian SSR and became the Moldavian SSR, although one southern area of about 1,900 square miles (5,000 sq km) on the Black Sea coast was incorporated into the Ukraine. Romanian nationalists have since claimed that the Soviet annexations of 1940 were carried out in accordance with secret provisions of the non-aggression pact signed in August 1939 between Germany and the Soviet Union. At about the same time Romania was forced to cede Northern Transylvania to Hungary and part of the Dobruja to Bulgaria, losing altogether about one-third of its territory and over 6,000,000 subjects.[1]

The period immediately preceding World War II had been characterized in Romania by considerable political confusion. A succession of short-lived governments, many of them anti-semitic and extreme right-wing in character, culminated on July 4, 1940 (i.e. directly after the cession of Bessarabia and Northern Bukovina), in the formation of a fascist government under Ion Gigurtu, who intensified Romania's links with Nazi Germany. Gigurtu was in turn replaced on Sept. 5, 1940, by Gen. Ion Antonescu (whose similarly fascist government was to remain in power until 1944), whereupon King Carol abdicated and was succeeded by King Michael.

Romania quickly declared its support for Germany and in June 1941 declared war on the Soviet Union. A joint Romanian/German advance swiftly captured Bessarabia and made rapid progress deep into Soviet territory, enabling the Romanians to set up the province of Transdnistria in the land between the Dnestr and the Bug (now mostly in the Ukraine). By 1944, however, the Red Army was advancing into Romania, and on Aug. 23, 1944, the Antonescu government was overthrown. In September 1944, following negotiations with the Allies, Romania signed an armistice with the Soviet Union in which it recognized the legality of the 1940 Soviet annexation of Bessarabia and Northern Bukovina, and the acknowledgement was further confirmed in the 1947 peace treaty between the wartime Allies (including the Soviet Union) and Romania. The consolidation of effective power in the hands of the Soviet-backed Romanian Communists culminated in the abdication of King Michael in December 1947 and the declaration in early 1948 of the Romanian People's (later Socialist) Republic within its present borders.

Post-war Developments and the Resurgence of Moldavian Nationalism

A Treaty of Alliance was signed between Romania and the Soviet Union on Feb. 4, 1948, in which each country undertook to adhere to the principles of mutual respect for the independence and sovereignty of the other, and to refrain from interference in the other's internal affairs. The treaty was valid for 20 years, and on its expiry in 1968 was replaced by a similar 20-year agreement. In 1955 Romania joined Albania, Bulgaria, Czechoslovakia, the German Democratic Republic, Hungary, Poland and the Soviet Union in the inauguration of the Warsaw Pact.

From 1956 onwards, however, Romania began to distance itself from the Soviet conception of the internationalist character of communism, and on numerous occasions expressed clearly nationalistic attitudes. At the time of the Hungarian uprising in October 1956 the Romanian Workers' Party (as the Communist Party was then called) expressed its belief in "differing forms and methods for the construction of socialism", and in December 1964 Romania caused considerable offence to the Soviet Union by its publication of one of

---

[1]For an account of the Northern Transylvania question, see pages 52-56.

the works of Marx, his *Notes on the Romanians*, in which he had strongly condemned Tsarist Russia's annexation of Bessarabia in 1812 and had argued for the indivisibility of the Romanian people. Although the work was not openly circulated in the Moldavian SSR, its content became known there, leading the first secretary of the Moldavian Communist Party, Ivan Bodyul, to make a speech at a 1965 party congress in which he strongly denounced the book as well as all Moldavians who accepted its implicit endorsement of the Romanian claim to Bessarabia. In 1966, moreover, documents were published by the Soviet Union indicating that in 1940 the Romanian Communists had welcomed the Soviet annexation.

By late 1966, however, Soviet concern had clearly increased, and on Dec. 15-17 a "Scientific Conference on Problems of the Development and Reconciliation of Soviet Nations and Peoples" was held at Tiraspol in the Moldavian SSR. In February 1967 Ivan Bodyul toured the republic with Alexander Shelepin, a member of the Politburo of the Soviet Communist Party (CPSU), and subsequently called for "an elucidation in depth of the real history of the Moldavian people" since, he said, "our children and future generations must know that their fathers did not conceive of a life for themselves outside Russia". In an ensuing intensification of historical argument the Soviet Communist side frequently took issue with Romanian portrayals of Moldavian history.

Meanwhile, the Romanian position had become more openly nationalistic with the election of Nicolae Ceausescu as First Secretary of the Romanian Communist Party (as it now became) at the July 1965 party congress. Ceausescu promoted the ideas of increased economic independence, protested at the numbers of Soviet-appointed officials in his administration, and at one point in 1966 proposed that, in view of the reduced danger of international conflict, both the Warsaw Pact and the North Atlantic Treaty Organization should be simultaneously dissolved. At the 1965 party congress he quoted a text of Engels which implied that Romanian communism had already developed by 1888 and that it had thus preceded Russian communism. The revised Romanian constitution of 1965 referred to the "inalienable and indivisible" territory of the Republic and dropped the specific pledge of alliance with the Soviet Union which had featured in the 1952 constitution. Moreover, in 1968 Romania joined with Yugoslavia in strongly denouncing the intervention of Warsaw Pact troops in Czechoslovakia, while Soviet-Romanian relations were further strained as a result of Ceausescu's visit to China.

Following the virtual abolition in March 1974 of preliminary censorship in the Romanian press, a book was published in April 1976 which was widely interpreted as re-opening the Bessarabian question. The book, entitled *Political Life in Romania between 1918 and 1921*, pointed out that a Tsarist census carried out in 1817 had found that 87 per cent of the Bessarabian population were Romanian. Meanwhile, there were continued unofficial reports of nationalist unrest in the Moldavian SSR, where Ivan Bodyul had informed the 24th local party congress (in April 1971) that "harmful phenomena" had recently occurred, instigated by countries promoting "so-called special roads to socialism" (regarded as a clear reference to Romania). *Pravda* had also attacked those who presented what it termed a distorted view of socialist reality through their adherence to outmoded traditions.

On June 4, 1976, Ceausescu asserted that Romania had "no territorial or other problem with the Soviet Union or with the other neighbouring socialist countries", and in a further apparent attempt to pacify the Soviet Union he visited the Moldavian SSR on Aug. 2 before passing on to the Crimea on an official visit. On the Soviet side, Leonid Brezhnev himself stated during a visit to Bucharest on Nov. 22-24, 1976, that there were "no important unsolved problems between our two countries", and on Nov. 24 he signed with Ceausescu a "statement on the further development of co-operation and on fraternal friendship between the Communist Party of the Soviet Union and the Romanian Communist Party, and between the Soviet Union and Romania". Ivan Bodyul also visited Romania in December 1976 and said that the two sides would expand their contacts in all fields.

Nevertheless, notwithstanding the absence of government-level conflict on territorial issues, evidence continued to surface concerning underlying Romanian attitudes to the post-war settlement of boundaries. In mid-1979 two Romanian historians, Stefan Lache and

Gheorghe Tsutsiu, published a controversial book entitled *Romania and the Paris Peace Conference of 1946* in which they sharply attacked the manner in which the Soviet Union had negotiated and carried out the annexation of Bessarabia and Northern Bukovina in 1940. Alleging the "spoliation" of Romania's territory, the book claimed that, in view of the Aug. 23, 1944, overthrow of the Antonescu government, the advancing Soviet troops should have treated Romania as a country which had "freely decided to put an end to the war", instead of which they had treated it as a "conquered country". (Ceausescu himself had also dwelt on this theme as early as 1965.)

Against a background of continued unofficial reports through the 1970s of sporadic unrest in the Moldavian SSR and other Soviet republics, new constitutions were promulgated on April 12-21, 1978, for each of the union republics, it being claimed that the main theme of the new texts was the extension of the rights of national minorities in the Soviet Union. Like those of several other republics, the constitution for the Moldavian SSR, which was promulgated on April 15, included a provision (Article 103), according to which the laws of the republic, decrees and other notices issued by the Supreme Soviet (Parliament) of the Republic, were to be published in both the Russian and (in this case) the "Moldavian" languages.

MW

Spain-United Kingdom (Gibraltar)

British sovereignty over Gibraltar—a strategic naval base on the tip of southern Spain acquired by Britain in 1713—has in the last 30 years been persistently disputed by Spain, which claims it as part of its national territory. In 1969 the land frontier between Spain and Gibraltar was closed and all other communications cut by Gen. Franco in pursuance of the Spanish claim, to which the UK government has consistently responded by upholding the self-proclaimed desire of the Gibraltarian people to retain their British status. Although the basic dispute over Gibraltar remains unresolved, the death of Franco in 1975 and the subsequent decision of the new democratic government in Madrid to seek membership of the European Community and the North Atlantic Treaty Organization brought about an improvement in Spanish-UK relations. This in turn led to the conclusion of an agreement in Lisbon in April 1980 that the Gibraltar border would be reopened and substantive negotiations on the Gibraltar issue initiated. Although it was subsequently agreed that these provisions would be put into effect in April 1982, implementation was postponed because of the development of the Argentinian-UK crisis over the Falkland Islands in that month. The border was not reopened until February 1985, after the UK government had specifically agreed the previous November to discuss the sovereignty of Gibraltar with Spain.

Gibraltar covers an area of only $2\frac{1}{4}$ square miles (5.8 sq km) and has a population of some

30,000. It faces the coast of north Africa, from which it is about 14 miles (22 km) distant. The area around Gibraltar is known as the Campo de Gibraltar and includes the towns of La Linea and San Roque (whose economies were badly affected by the 1969 border closures) as well as Algeciras.

Gibraltar was held by the Moors for many centuries until the Spanish captured it in the 15th century. During the War of the Spanish Succession it was taken by a combined British and Dutch force in 1704, and British possession was confirmed in 1713 under the Treaty of Utrecht. Spanish efforts to regain the Rock included an unsuccessful 3½-year siege from 1779 to 1783 by a combined French and Spanish force; various British proposals in the 18th century to exchange Gibraltar for other pieces of territory came to nothing.

Gibraltar was declared a Crown Colony in 1830. It was granted a greater measure of internal self-government in 1964, and in 1967 a referendum was held in which it voted overwhelmingly to retain links with Britain. In 1969 it received a new constitution giving it a House of Assembly, executive authority being vested in a governor who represents the Queen. Gibraltar has been part of the European Community since 1973 (when the United Kingdom became a member) under Article 227(4) of the Treaty of Rome.

British and Spanish Positions on Gibraltar

The United Kingdom bases its claim to sovereignty over Gibraltar on Article X of the Treaty of Utrecht, which in the translation (from the original Latin) used by the UK government specified that "the Catholic king [of Spain] does hereby, for himself, his heirs and successors, yield to the Crown of Great Britain the full and entire propriety of the town and castle of Gibraltar, together with the port, fortifications and forts thereunto belonging . . . to be held and enjoyed absolutely with all manner of right for ever, without any exception or impediment whatsoever". The same article stated inter alia (i) that, so as to prevent "fraudulent importations of goods" into Spain via Gibraltar, it was understood that "the above-named propriety be yielded to Great Britain without any territorial jurisdiction [over], and without any open communication by land with, the country round about", although it would be "lawful to purchase for ready money, in the neighbouring territories of Spain, provisions and other things necessary for the use of the garrison, the inhabitants and

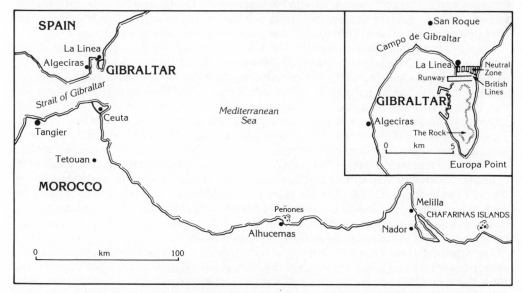

Map 12   Southern Spain and North Africa, showing Gibraltar and the Spanish enclaves on the north Moroccan coast.

the ships which lie in the harbour"; (ii) that at the request of the Spanish king Britain "does consent and agree that no leave shall be given under any pretence whatsoever either to Jews or Moors to reside or have their dwellings" in Gibraltar; and (iii) that "in case it shall hereafter seem meet to the Crown of Great Britain to grant, sell or by any means to alienate therefrom the propriety of the said town of Gibraltar, it is hereby agreed and concluded that the preference of having the same shall always be given to the Crown of Spain before any others". The British title to Gibraltar was subsequently confirmed in the treaties of Paris (1763) and of Versailles (1783).

Spain, however, has described the provisions of the Treaty of Utrecht as anachronistic and has accused Britain of consistently violating them. A contentious visit to Gibraltar in May 1954 by Queen Elizabeth gave rise to protests by Spanish students in Madrid, the closure of the Spanish consulate in Gibraltar and the tightening of border controls by the Spanish authorities on Spanish workers crossing into Gibraltar. Since then the question of the cession of Gibraltar has been brought up at intervals by Spain.

After the introduction in August 1964 of a new constitution granting Gibraltar a greater measure of internal self-government, the Spanish government in October of that year began to enforce restrictions on the transit of people, traffic and goods from Spain into Gibraltar in support of its claim to Gibraltar. The Gibraltar issue had also been considered by the UN Committee of 24 (concerned with decolonization) at the request of Spain in September 1963 (for the first time) and in September-October 1964. On April 5, 1965, the British government published a White Paper dealing with these and other aspects of the Gibraltar issue and reiterating Britain's full support for Gibraltar's wish to remain British. The White Paper made the following points:

Historical Background. The paper noted that "when the British captured Gibraltar in 1704 almost the entire Spanish population left the town and settled in the neighbouring countryside" and that the present population began to establish itself in Gibraltar from 1727 onwards, consisting of "time-expired British soldiers" and "Genoese and other foreign elements". By the time the Napoleonic wars had ended, the population also comprised British, Maltese, Moroccan and Portuguese elements, and "this community has now existed in Gibraltar for over 250 years and, since 1830 when a Charter of Justice was proclaimed, has had legal recognition".

Constitutional Position. The paper said that the institutions of Gibraltar and the arrangements in force corresponded with the wishes of the Gibraltarian people and were "in accordance with modern democratic ideals and the principles of the UN Charter". The Gibraltarian people wished Gibraltar to remain in close association with Britain.

Consideration of Gibraltar at the UN. The White Paper described the proceedings in the UN Committee of 24 in September-October 1964 during which the parties concerned had put forward their positions [namely, the Spanish claim that Gibraltar formed part of Spanish territory notwithstanding the views of its inhabitants; the Gibraltarian wish to remain closely associated with Britain without becoming independent and their opposition to being handed over to Spain; and the British assertion that the grant of Gibraltar to Britain in the Treaty of Utrecht was absolute and that Spain had no right to be consulted on any change in its status or relations with Britain]. The paper noted the UN Committee's conclusion of Oct. 16, 1964, that there was a dispute between Britain and Spain over the status and situation in Gibraltar, its invitation to Britain and Spain to seek a negotiated solution, and its statement that UN Declaration 1514 (XV) on the granting of independence to colonial countries and peoples was fully applicable to Gibraltar. It also noted that Britain had not accepted that there was a dispute over status, nor a conflict between the Treaty of Utrecht's provisions and the application of the principle of self-determination to the Gibraltarians.

The Situation at the Frontier. Describing the situation at the frontier since the Spanish authorities at La Linea began enforcing procedures and regulations more strictly on Oct. 17, 1964, the White Paper said that cars and visitors had been delayed and most exports into Gibraltar stopped. Traffic, including tourist traffic, was almost at a standstill, restrictions were affecting Spanish workers commuting daily to Gibraltar, and the customs were refusing to accept as valid any British passports issued or renewed in Gibraltar, or those issued or renewed "on behalf of the government of Gibraltar".

Conclusion. The White Paper pointed out that the civilian population, who were not Spanish, had "been established there for longer than many immigrant communities in the New World" and concluded: "Great Britain has at no time renounced her title to Gibraltar or failed to defend her position there, and she will not do so now. She has no desire to quarrel with Spain but she will stand by the people of Gibraltar in their present difficulties and take whatever measures may be necessary to defend and sustain them."

In December 1965 the Spanish government in response published a Red Book on the Gibraltar issue, incorporating many maps. This said that the "sole legal basis" for the British presence in Gibraltar was Article X of the Treaty of Utrecht and that legally the cession of Gibraltar to Great Britain was therefore "subject to a series of limitations". In practice, these had been consistently ignored by Britain, it went on, notably in that since 1713 Britain had advanced its sphere of control steadily northwards "in quest of more space for the [Gibraltar] fortress over and above that stipulated at Utrecht". By the end of the 19th century Britain had advanced her frontier half a mile across the neutral zone north of Gibraltar, and as evidence of this "encroachment" the Red Book cited the construction in 1938 (i.e. during the Spanish Civil War) "of a military/civilian aerodrome, in the heart of the neutral zone, that is to say on Spanish sovereign territory". Britain had also erected a wall "which, after the Berlin manner, physically separates from Spain by walls, wire and railings a territory which is Spanish and which the British had been gradually engulfing in their advance through the so-called neutral zone".

The Red Book accused Britain of "passivity or even benevolence" towards smuggling by land and sea from the Rock in contravention of the treaty provision; it described the economic bases of the life of Gibraltar as "artificial" and added that the population of the Rock was also "artificially planned" to the prejudice of the original population, which had been driven out. After referring to the border measures taken by Spain in 1964 as normal police and customs measures, the Red Book said that in strict compliance with the Treaty of Utrecht Spain would be justified in (i) requesting the removal of the wall and fence at Gibraltar 800 metres further south "to evacuate a piece of Spanish sovereign territory which ... was unjustifiably annexed by Britain on the isthmus of Gibraltar and in which the present aerodrome of Gibraltar is situated"; (ii) exercising the right to cut off land communications with Gibraltar, leaving only sea communications open; (iii) abolishing trade with Gibraltar; and (iv) refusing to recognize the political institutions created in Gibraltar since 1950.

Commencement of Anglo-Spanish Talks on Gibraltar

Following the adoption by the UN General Assembly at its 20th session on Dec. 16, 1965, of a resolution (2070) inviting Spain and Britain to enter into negotiations on the Gibraltar issue without delay (both Spain and Britain voting in favour of the resolution), the two countries met for an initial round of talks in London in May 1966. In the course of the talks Spain made a formal claim to sovereignty over Gibraltar in a four-point plan. It proposed (i) that an Anglo-Spanish convention should be signed cancelling Article X of the Treaty of Utrecht and providing for "the restoration of the national unity and territorial integrity of Spain through the reversion of Gibraltar"; (ii) that Spain would accept a British military base at Gibraltar "whose structure, legal situation and co-ordination with the defence organization of Spain or the free world would be the subject of a special agreement" attached to the proposed convention; (iii) that a legal regime protecting the interests of the present citizens of Gibraltar should be the subject of an additional Anglo-Spanish agreement which would be negotiated with the UN and that it should contain, in addition to the appropriate economic and administrative formulae, a personal statute by which fundamental rights including the British nationality of the inhabitants of Gibraltar would be respected and their right of residence guaranteed, as well as the free exercise of their lawful acts and a guarantee of permanence in their place of work; and (iv) that such a convention would take effect after the additional agreements provided for under (ii) and (iii) had been regulated with the United Nations.

At the second round of talks in July 1966 Britain made counter-proposals which inter alia envisaged the exercise of internal self-government by the municipal authorities instead of by legislative and executive councils. However, no progress was made on either set of proposals at this or the next round of talks in September (which was preceded by the introduction in August 1966 of a Spanish ban on British military aircraft overflying Spanish territory).

On Oct. 5, 1966—just before a fourth round was due to commence—the Spanish government issued a decree closing the frontier with Gibraltar to all but pedestrian traffic, with the result that several thousand Spaniards who entered Gibraltar every day to work had to travel on foot. The measure took effect on Oct. 24, and in November the Spanish frontier authorities at La Linea also began to refuse to accept Gibraltarian passports issued by the Governor, thus effectively placing a ban on Gibraltarians entering Spain.

The British delegation proposed at the October 1966 round of talks that the legal issues involved in the Gibraltar dispute should be referred to the International Court of Justice. However, this was rejected by Spain in a note of Dec. 14 on the grounds that it would contradict a UN Committee of 24 resolution adopted on Nov. 17 which (i) recommended that Britain should "expedite, without any hindrance and in consultation with the government of Spain, the decolonization of Gibraltar", (ii) regretted "the delay in the process of decolonization" and (iii) called on Britain and Spain to "continue their negotiations taking into account the interests of the people of the territory". A similar resolution (2231)—which did not, however, contain the latter reference to the interests of the Gibraltarian people—was adopted by the UN General Assembly on Dec. 20, 1966, with both Spain and Britain voting in favour.

The 1967 Referendum in Gibraltar

On June 14, 1967, the British government announced that a referendum would be held in Gibraltar to allow the people to decide whether to "pass under Spanish sovereignty" in accordance with the terms proposed by the Spanish government on May 18, 1966, or "voluntarily to retain their link with Britain with democratic local institutions and with Britain retaining its present responsibilities". If the majority voted in favour of the first option, Britain would, it stated, enter into further negotiations with Spain, but if the majority voted for the second option Britain would regard this choice as constituting "a free and voluntary relationship of the people of Gibraltar with Britain" and would "thereafter discuss with representatives of Gibraltar appropriate constitutional changes which may be desired".

The decision to hold a referendum was regarded by Spain as unilateral and in violation of UN resolutions and the Treaty of Utrecht, and in a note of July 3, 1967, it declined Britain's invitation to send an observer on the grounds that this would imply approval of the measure. After a Spanish complaint to the United Nations was filed on Aug. 18, 1967, the Committee of 24 on Sept. 1 adopted a resolution stating that the holding of the referendum would "contradict" previous UN resolutions. Britain denounced this resolution as "wholly partisan" and in contradiction with the spirit of the UN Charter, Chapter XI of which required the political aspirations of the people to be taken into account; the referendum, it was confirmed, would take place as planned. A similar point was made by Gibraltar's Chief Minister, Sir Joshua Hassan, who said that the resolution appeared to "disregard the interests of a colonial people and would seem to deny them the elementary human right of stating their interests through a referendum".

The referendum took place in Gibraltar on Sept. 10, 1967, and resulted in an overwhelmingly pro-British vote. Out of 12,762 registered voters (all of them normally resident in Gibraltar), 12,138 voted for continued association with Britain and 44 voted for Spanish sovereignty. A Commonwealth observer team which had been present in Gibraltar during the referendum said that it had been conducted in a fair and proper manner with adequate facilities for the free expression of views.

The UN General Assembly on Dec. 19, 1967, adopted a further resolution (2353) which had already been adopted by its Fourth Committee (on decolonization) on Dec. 16 and which (i) described the holding of the referendum as a "contravention" of Resolution 2231 and of the Committee of 24's resolution of Sept. 1, 1967; (ii) regretted the interruption of negotiations; and (iii) urged the resumption of negotiations without delay in order to put an end to the "colonial situation" in Gibraltar and to safeguard the interests of the population "upon the termination of that situation". The Spanish government meanwhile on Dec. 11, 1967, published a second Red Book reiterating its repudiation of the referendum and recapitulating the state of negotiations with Britain since May 1966.

Anglo-Spanish talks resumed on March 18, 1968, but broke down again on March 20. With effect from May 5 of that year Spain began what it described as a progressive implementation of the Treaty of Utrecht by closing the land frontier to all traffic including pedestrians with the exception of those Spaniards holding work permits for Gibraltar and permanent residents of Gibraltar; the others were obliged to use the ferry from Algeciras.

1969 Constitutional Changes leading to Closure of the Border and Severance of Communications

In July 1968 Britain and Gibraltar held talks on proposed constitutional changes at the instigation of Gibraltar, which sought a new political status under the continued, permanent and exclusive sovereignty of Britain. It was agreed that such changes would give Gibraltarians maximum control over their domestic affairs but should not conflict with the Treaty of Utrecht or worsen Anglo-Spanish relations.

At the conclusion of these talks a joint communiqué was issued, which revealed that the British government believed that it could best respond to the wishes of the Gibraltarian people by inserting in the revised Gibraltar constitution a declaration to the effect that Gibraltar was "a part of Her Majesty's dominions and will remain so unless an act of Parliament otherwise provides, and furthermore that HM government has made it clear that it will never hand over the people of Gibraltar to another state against their freely and democratically expressed wishes". Other constitutional changes agreed at the talks covered the replacement of the legislative and city councils of Gibraltar by a House of Assembly and the installation of an executive headed by a governor, a Gibraltar council and a council of ministers. The new constitution for Gibraltar (which was henceforth to be known as the City of Gibraltar) entered into force on May 30, 1969.

In strongly attacking the constitution, the Spanish government accused Britain of disregarding UN General Assembly resolution 2429, adopted on Dec. 18, 1968, which declared that the "colonial situation in Gibraltar" was "incompatible with the UN Charter" and which called upon Britain to "terminate the colonial situation in Gibraltar" not later than Oct. 1, 1969. As a reprisal the Spanish government on June 8, 1969, closed the border and customs post at La Linea "to defend Spanish interests in Gibraltar", with the result that some 5,000 Spanish workers (about one-third of Gibraltar's normal labour force) were prevented from going to their jobs. On June 27 Spain suspended the ferry service from Algeciras to Gibraltar, and on July 4 it announced that Spanish nationality would be offered to all residents of Gibraltar or those born there. Finally, only hours after the expiry of the Oct. 1 deadline contained in the December 1968 UN resolution, Spain on Oct. 1 cut telephone links between the Spanish mainland and Gibraltar. Against a background of the deployment of large Spanish and British naval forces off Gibraltar, the Gibraltar government was obliged to put into effect contingency plans to deal with its new situation in the face of the Spanish restrictions.

Despite the tension which the Spanish measures caused, relations between Britain and Spain had already begun to improve by the end of 1969 and continued on a cordial basis with informal contacts taking place throughout 1970-72, although the Spanish restrictions remained in force. Finally, formal talks resumed on May 30-31, 1974.

Later in 1974 Spanish proposals for a new regime in Gibraltar were published for the first time in Britain, although they had been handed to Sir Joshua Hassan in February 1973 (and he had described them as "utterly unacceptable" in the light of the result of the 1967 referendum). The proposals foresaw (i) that as soon as Spanish sovereignty was recognized over Gibraltar, the Gibraltar area [i.e. the Campo] would become a special territory with legislative, judicial, administrative and financial autonomy; (ii) that Gibraltarians would take Spanish nationality but need not renounce their British nationality; (iii) that the Spanish legal system "as developed by the special legislation of Gibraltar" would apply after the 1969 constitution had been suitably amended, and that Spanish penal and police laws would apply in all areas concerning Spain's internal and external security; (iv) that the senior authority in Gibraltar would be a civil governor appointed by the Spanish head of state; (v) that the most senior members of the executive would be Spaniards or Gibraltarians of Spanish nationality; and (vi) that Spanish would be the official language of Gibraltar, although a wide use of English would be safeguarded.

Developments following Gen. Franco's Death

Following the death of Gen. Franco on Nov. 20, 1975, King Juan Carlos stated on ascending the Spanish throne two days later that Spain's efforts to regain sovereignty over Gibraltar would continue. The following month, however, he restored telephone links between Spain and Gibraltar over the Christmas-New Year period and subsequently in April 1976 for the Easter period, setting a pattern for subsequent years. In July 1977—following Spain's first general elections since 1936—the democratically-elected government headed by Adolfo Suárez González as Prime Minister stated that it would insist on resuming negotiations with Britain "with the aim of restoring Spain's territorial integrity"; and in September 1977 Dr David Owen became the first UK Foreign and Commonwealth Secretary to visit Spain since 1961. During this visit (when Dr Owen met King Juan Carlos, Suárez and the new Spanish Foreign Minister, Marcelino Oreja Aguirre) and in the course of a subsequent brief visit to London in October by Suárez in connexion with Spain's recently-filed application to join the European Community, talks were held on the Gibraltar issue.

Dr Owen told a press conference on Sept. 7, 1977, after the visit that Britain had requested Spain to lift the restrictions on Gibraltar. He also said that Britain's support for Spain's application to join the European Community would not be dependent on the settlement of the Gibraltar issue and that the attitude of the Spanish government contained "a degree of sensitivity and understanding which did not exist before", and which he felt was the best ingredient for a settlement.

The Spanish Prime Minister for his part told a press conference in London on Oct. 19, 1977 (after talks with Dr Owen and James Callaghan, the Prime Minister), that he believed that Spain's political evolution and restructuring on a regional basis could permit a negotiated solution of the Gibraltar issue which would respect the "identity, culture and special characteristics of the Gibraltarian people and eventually can bring about the reintegration of Gibraltar into Spanish territory in conformity with UN resolutions". However, he ruled out the removal of restrictions, which, according to a British communiqué issued after the London talks, would have to be lifted if there was to be progress on the Gibraltar issue.

After routine talks in Madrid in November 1977 between Spanish and British representatives, later that month a meeting took place in Strasbourg between Dr Owen, his Spanish counterpart, Sir Joshua Hassan and Maurice Xibberas (for the Gibraltar opposition). At a subsequent meeting of these four representatives in Paris in March 1978 it was agreed to set up Anglo-Spanish working groups to deal with matters including telephone communications and maritime links, and the working groups held two meetings in 1978, in July and December (a Gibraltarian delegation attending the latter).

1980 Lisbon and 1982 London Agreements on Reopening Border—Postponement of Implementation

After the Conservative election victory in Britain in May 1979 the new government was reported to have indicated to Spain—contrary to Dr Owen's assurance of Sept. 7, 1977—that British support for Spain's entry into the European Community would not be forthcoming as long as restrictions on Gibraltar remained in force. Publicly, it was stated that it was "inconceivable" that the frontier should remain closed when Spain joined the Community. With fresh moves afoot in Spain itself to reopen the frontier and negotiate over Gibraltar, Lord Carrington (the new UK Foreign and Commonwealth Secretary) and Marcelino Oreja Aguirre met in Lisbon on April 9-10, 1980, and agreed in principle that the land frontier would be reopened and that the other restrictions imposed in 1969 would be suspended. A joint communiqué issued on April 10 stated that "the British and Spanish governments, desiring to strengthen their bilateral relations and thus to contribute to European and Western solidarity, intend, in accordance with the relevant UN resolutions, to resolve, in a spirit of friendship, the Gibraltar problem" (Paragraph 1 of the Lisbon agreement), and that they had accordingly agreed to start negotiations (Paragraph 2).

The Lisbon agreement, in its subsequent paragraphs, was worded as follows: "(3) Both governments have reached agreement on the re-establishment of direct communications in the region. The Spanish government has decided to suspend the application of the measures at present in force. Both governments have agreed that future co-operation should be on the basis of reciprocity and full equality of rights. They look forward to the further steps which will be taken on both sides which they believe will open the way to closer understanding between those directly concerned in the area. (4) To this end both governments will be prepared to consider any proposals which the other may wish to make, recognizing the need to develop practical co-operation on a mutually beneficial basis. (5) The Spanish government, in reaffirming its position on the re-establishment of the territorial integrity of Spain, restated its intention that in the outcome of the negotiations the interests of the Gibraltarians should be fully safeguarded. For its part, the British government will fully maintain its commitment to honour the freely and democratically expressed wishes of the people of Gibraltar as set out in the preamble to the Gibraltar constitution. (6) Officials on both sides will meet as soon as possible to prepare the necessary practical steps which will permit the implementation of the proposals agreed to above. It is envisaged that these preparations will be completed not later than June 1."

By the end of 1980, however, the border was still closed and Anglo-Spanish contacts appeared deadlocked, it being reported that Spain was stipulating fresh conditions, among them that Spaniards working in Gibraltar should be granted equal status to Gibraltarians as soon as the border reopened. Gibraltar's response was that the local labour market was too complex and fragile for Spain to be given immediate access to it, and also that there were now several thousand Moroccan workers to be protected. The Gibraltar House of Assembly on Dec. 18, 1980, adopted a resolution stating that "Spanish nationals could not be granted the same rights as European Community nationals in Gibraltar, prior to Spain obtaining full membership of the Community".

In mid-1981 further aggravation in Spanish-UK relations over the Gibraltar issue arose when King Juan Carlos and Queen Sofia of Spain declined an invitation to attend the wedding of Prince Charles and Lady Diana Spencer on July 29 in view of an earlier announcement that the latter couple would embark on the royal yacht *Britannia* at Gibraltar to begin their honeymoon. Relations between the two sides subsequently improved, however, and on Jan. 8, 1982, talks in London between the UK and Spanish Prime Ministers (Margaret Thatcher and Leopoldo Calvo Sotelo) resulted in an agreement that the Gibraltar border would be reopened on April 20, 1982, and that negotiations would begin on that day to resolve the Gibraltar issue in terms of the April 1980 Lisbon agreement. However, in view of the development of a serious crisis between Argentina and Britain in early April 1982 over the Falkland Islands[1], it was agreed between the UK and Spanish governments on June 21 that implementation of the Lisbon agreement should be indefinitely postponed.

During the Falklands crisis the Spanish government consistently supported the Argentinian claim to sovereignty over the islands and abstained in UN votes calling for a cessation of hostilities and the withdrawal of Argentinian forces. In Gibraltar the Argentinian invasion of the Falklands (on April 2, 1982) gave rise to fears that similar action might be taken by Spain to recover the Rock, it being noted that extreme right-wing groups in Spain were demanding such action. However, the Spanish Council of Ministers issued a statement on April 3 giving an assurance that it regarded Gibraltar and the Falklands as separate issues.

Impasse in Negotiations—Decision to close Naval Dockyard at Gibraltar

Despite the indefinite deferment of the Lisbon agreement, the Spanish authorities in July 1982 initiated a slight relaxation of the border restrictions by allowing a small number of daily crossings into Spain for humanitarian reasons. Following the election of a Socialist government in Spain in October 1982, the border was reopened from Dec. 15 for pedestrians (restricted to one crossing a day per person) although not to vehicular and other traffic. Nevertheless, the commitment of the new Spanish government to new initiatives to achieve a settlement of the Gibraltar dispute produced no substantive movement on the diplomatic front through 1983 and most of 1984, notwithstanding the more favourable climate created by Spain's accession to NATO from May 1982 and the progress made in this period in the negotiations for full Spanish membership of the European Community.

Indeed, bilateral Spanish-UK relations deteriorated in April 1983 over a five-day visit to Gibraltar by the Royal Navy aircraft carrier HMS *Invincible* and about a dozen support vessels. The British ambassador in Madrid was twice summoned to the Spanish Foreign Ministry to receive protests against the visit (about which Spain had been notified in advance), and Spanish warships were stationed in Algeciras Bay to observe the British flotilla. While the UK government described the visit as "regular, annual and routine" since the ships were proceeding to NATO exercises in the Atlantic, Spanish spokesmen claimed that it could not be described as routine because of the number of ships involved and the fact that they had participated in the Falklands war. The first Spanish protest note expressed "deep concern and displeasure" over the effect that the visit would have on Spanish public opinion and warned that Spain would take "appropriate diplomatic and political measures" to protect its national waters. During a subsequent visit to Gibraltar by HMS *Invincible* and six other ships in September 1983, however, the Spanish Foreign Minister made no public statements.

In an earlier significant development, the UK Defence Minister had announced on Nov. 22, 1981, that "changed plans for the Royal Navy no longer sustain a need for a naval dockyard in Gibraltar" and that the process of closure would commence in 1983; he had added that consultations would shortly begin with the Gibraltar government on possible economic alternatives, including the commercialization of the dockyard. In these consultations, Sir Joshua Hassan secured the postponement of the closure for one year (from the initially proposed date of Dec. 31, 1983) and the promise of a British grant of £28,000,000 to cover costs and initial losses; moreover, in the three years following the dockyard's transition to a commercial ship repair yard on Jan. 1, 1985, the UK government would pay £14,000,000 for the refitting of tankers and Royal Fleet Auxiliary landing ships and up to a further £1,000,000 for the refitting of other ships.

1984 Brussels Agreement—Reopening of Spain-Gibraltar Border

The impasse in Spanish-UK relations over Gibraltar was eventually unblocked by an

---

[1] For an account of the Falklands/Malvinas dispute, see pages 387-97.

agreement concluded in Brussels on Nov. 27, 1984, under which the 1980 Lisbon agreement was to be reactivated and applied by not later than Feb. 15, 1985, on the basis of a clarification of certain provisions which had been the subject of conflicting interpretations. The new agreement contained, for the first time, a specific British undertaking to discuss the sovereignty of Gibraltar with Spain and was seen as removing a major obstacle to Spain's entry to the European Community (the date of which was subsequently fixed for Jan. 1, 1986).

The Brussels agreement, which was the outcome of some seven months of unpublicized contacts, stated that implementation of the Lisbon agreement would involve the simultaneous application of the following measures: "(1a) The provision of equality and reciprocity of rights for Spaniards in Gibraltar and Gibraltarians in Spain. This will be implemented through the mutual concession of the rights which citizens of European Community countries enjoy, taking into account the transitional periods and derogations agreed between Spain and the Community. The necessary legislative proposals to achieve this will be introduced in Spain and Gibraltar. As concerns paid employment, and recalling the general principle of Community preference, this carries the implication that during the transitional period each side will be favourably disposed to each other's citizens when granting work permits. (1b) The establishment of the free movement of persons, vehicles and goods between Gibraltar and the neighbouring territory. (1c) The establishment of a negotiating process aimed at overcoming all the differences between Spain and the United Kingdom over Gibraltar and at promoting co-operation on a mutually beneficial basis on economic, cultural, touristic, aviation, military and environmental matters. Both sides accept that the issues of sovereignty will be discussed in that process. The British government will fully maintain its commitment to honour the wishes of the people of Gibraltar as set out in the preamble of the 1969 constitution. (2) Insofar as the airspace in the region of Gibraltar is concerned, the Spanish government undertakes to take the early actions necessary to allow safe and effective air communications. (3) There will be meetings of working groups, which will be reviewed periodically in meetings for this purpose between the Spanish and British Foreign Ministers."

In a note accompanying the agreement, the Spanish government clarified the questions which, in its view, Britain had agreed to deal with regarding sovereignty. These included "both the theme of sovereignty of the territory referred to in the Treaty of Utrecht, as well as sovereignty of the isthmus, which was never ceded to Britain". The Spanish Foreign Minister, Fernando Morán, described the Brussels agreement, and particularly its reference to discussions on sovereignty, as "the biggest diplomatic success for Spain over the Rock since 1713", while stressing that Spain had "the greatest respect for the feelings of the Gibraltarians themselves".

In Gibraltar itself, Sir Joshua Hassan said that the Brussels agreement was an "honourable outcome" and a first step towards fruitful co-operation between Gibraltar and its surroundings, but added that many Gibraltarians retained deep reservations about the prospect of discussions on sovereignty. For the opposition Gibraltar Socialist Labour Party (GSLP), which had won seven of the 15 Assembly seats in the January 1984 general elections, Joe Bossano condemned the agreement and said that his party would "disown" it if it came to power. Also leader of the Transport and General Workers' Union in Gibraltar, Bossano added that he would seek to protect the jobs of some 2,000 Moroccans (representing about a third of his union membership) who had taken over from Spanish workers following the closure of the border in 1969.

After it had been announced (on Jan. 3) that the border would be reopened at midnight on Feb. 4-5, 1985, talks on border procedures, passport requirements and customs formalities opened on Jan. 10 in La Linea (the nearest Spanish town to Gibraltar) and continued the following day in Gibraltar, this being the first time since the border closure that Spanish representatives had made the crossing on official business. On Jan. 16 the Gibraltar House of Assembly adopted by eight votes to none a bill bringing forward to Feb. 5 certain of the rights which were due to accrue to Spain on its accession to the European Community, allowing Spaniards entry and residence in Gibraltar, as well as the right to land purchase, establishment of businesses, payment of family allowances and emergency medical treatment. The ruling Gibraltar Labour Party-Association for the Advancement of Civil Rights supported the bill, on the grounds that sovereignty was "a totally unrelated question" and that Gibraltar should accept the advantages of an open border, whereas the GSLP members expressed their opposition by boycotting the vote. For its part, the Spanish Council of Ministers of Jan. 31 formally removed the 1969 border restrictions, to allow the free passage of people, vehicles and merchandise and the resumption of direct passage to Gibraltar by boat (hitherto only possible from countries other than Spain).

The frontier between Gibraltar and Spain was officially reopened as scheduled at midnight on Feb. 4-5, 1985, when the gates closed in June 1969 on the orders of Gen. Franco were ceremonially unlocked by the civil governor of Cadiz, Mariano Baquedano. Later on Feb. 5 the UK Foreign and Commonwealth Secretary, Sir Geoffrey Howe, opened talks with his Spanish counterpart in Geneva, with Sir Joshua Hassan forming part of the UK delegation. As well as signing an agreement on economic and cultural co-operation, the two sides agreed a detailed procedure for discussing issues relating to Gibraltar entailing regular annual meetings of Foreign Ministers to discuss "matters of mutual interest", including sovereignty, on which the Spanish side put forward detailed proposals [see below]. Working parties of British, Spanish and Gibraltarian officials were also to start work immediately with the aim of promoting co-operation in other spheres.

Lack of Substantive Progress in Spanish-UK Negotiations, 1985-87

The second meeting of the Spanish and UK Foreign Ministers took place in Madrid on Dec. 5-6, 1985, with Sir Joshua Hassan in attendance for appropriate parts of the talks. A joint communiqué stated that in their exchanges on Gibraltar Sir Geoffrey Howe and Francisco Fernández Ordóñez (who had become Spanish Foreign Minister in July 1985) had had a full discussion of the issues of sovereignty, in which connexion they had "reviewed the proposals put forward by the Spanish government in February 1985 and agreed that study of the issues of sovereignty should continue through diplomatic channels against the background of their shared aim of overcoming all the differences between the two governments". While not made public, the Spanish proposals were widely reported to include the possibility of a "lease-back" arrangement (under which the sovereignty of Gibraltar would revert to Spain, which would grant Britain a lease on the Rock for an agreed period) or some form of Spanish-UK condominium over Gibraltar.

The communiqué also referred to the "common objective of developing the civilian use of Gibraltar airport on a mutually beneficial basis". Although the Spanish government had on April 1, 1985, partially lifted 18-year-old restrictions of the use of Spanish airspace over the Bay of Algeciras (in partial fulfilment of the 1984 Brussels agreement), major differences remained arising from the fact that Gibraltar's airport (used by both civil and military aircraft) had been constructed during World War II on the isthmus north of the Rock, which according to Spain was "no man's land" not covered by the Treaty of Utrecht but annexed illegally by Britain in 1908-9. Moreover, Spain was understood to be demanding that two terminals should be established at the airport, so that passengers bound for Spain would not have to pass through the UK-Gibraltar customs and immigration control.

Amid reports that the UK government was ready to make concessions on the airport issue, Sir Joshua Hassan and other Gibraltarian leaders sent an open letter to Sir Geoffrey Howe in September 1986 urging that the Spanish demands be rejected and requesting a referendum of the people of Gibraltar if any concessions were being contemplated. (Subsequently, on Dec. 17, 1986, the Gibraltar House of Assembly unanimously adopted a resolution calling for the airport to remain exclusively under the control of the British and Gibraltar authorities.) The open letter also protested against the withdrawal of July 31, 1986, of the ceremonial British military guard at the Spanish-Gibraltar border, to which Sir Geoffrey responded by stressing that he was pressing the Spanish government to reciprocate by withdrawing its own border guards.

Meanwhile, Spanish-UK relations had been subject to new tensions in March-April 1986 following an alleged incursion into Gibraltar's territorial waters by the Spanish aircraft carrier *Dédalo* during the night of March 20-21 and the launching of two helicopters into Gibraltar's airspace. In reply to a UK aide-mémoire dated April 2, the Spanish Foreign Ministry asserted that the Treaty of Utrecht recognized as Gibraltar's territorial waters only the immediate area of the port and that the surrounding waters remained Spanish.

The *Dédalo* incident preceded a state visit to Britain on April 22-25, 1986, by King Juan Carlos and Queen Sofia, the first such visit by a reigning Spanish monarch since 1905. In an address to both Houses of Parliament on April 23, the Spanish King said: "The recently resumed dialogue over Gibraltar is a step forward, but there remains a long way to go. I trust our respective governments may be capable of standing the test of history, and so find the formula that will transform any shadow into an element of harmony for greater co-operation between our countries and the general well-being of the international parties as well as the future of Europe".

Addressing the UN General Assembly in New York on Sept. 22, 1986, King Juan Carlos also made reference to the Gibraltar question, as follows: "Spain maintains, vigorously and with the weight of the reason inherent in its cause, the will to find a rapid solution to the problem of Gibraltar, so that the Rock can be reintegrated into the Spanish national territory. A new chapter has opened since the Brussels declaration of Nov. 27, 1984, and since the governments of the United Kingdom and Spain decided in February 1985 in Geneva to resolve the problem in all its aspects, including that of sovereignty, through negotiation. This new phase is dominated by the hope of putting an end to an unjust situation without harm for the interests of the local population".

A further meeting of the Spanish and UK Foreign Ministers took place in London on Jan. 13-14, 1987, during which Fernández Ordóñez met the UK Prime Minister, Margaret Thatcher. A communiqué issued after the session recorded that the two sides had agreed that co-operation between Gibraltar and Spain "should continue to take place on a fair and balanced basis consistent with their common Community obligations" and had noted that "contacts had developed satisfactorily in a number of fields, including tourism, the environment, culture and sport, public health and education". The statement also recorded that there had been "a full discussion of sovereignty", in which the Spanish Foreign Minister had "underlined the importance of proposals put forward by Spain in February 1985", while Sir Geoffrey Howe had "reaffirmed the British government's commitment to honour the wishes of the people of Gibraltar" and had stressed "the importance of managing any differences between Britain and Spain in a spirit consistent with their links of traditional friendship and their common membership of the European Community and NATO".

After the talks the Spanish Foreign Minister told a news conference on Jan. 14, 1987, that an "abnormal situation" existed when one NATO member country had a colony in another and when one European Community member had a colony in another. He also said that NATO military communications facilities in Gibraltar would have to be removed, on the basis that Gibraltar was part of Spain and that Spanish membership of NATO did not involve participation in its integrated military structure.

JB/AJD

2. AFRICA

Introduction

With regard to the boundaries between African states, the map of Africa today is not very different from the map of 1914, as Prof. Brownlie noted in the introduction to his book *African Boundaries*,[1] although of course there has been a transformation in the *colour* of the map, brought about by the post-1945 decolonization process. "The generalization which certainly holds up under scrutiny", Brownlie comments, "is the statement that African boundaries are those of the colonial period, providing allowance is made for the fact that many of the boundaries are the former *intra*-colonial boundaries of the units of French West Africa and French Equatorial Africa".

Many nationalist leaders, it is true, initially expressed a commitment to pan-Africanism—even to the extent of a fullscale political union of Africa in the post-colonial era. However, as Brownlie describes, this commitment gave way to an acceptance that for the foreseeable future African self-determination and nation-building should be pursued within the framework of numerous independent states defined for the most part by the former colonial boundaries. Thus the Charter of the Organization of African Unity (OAU) set up in 1963 reflects (says Brownlie) "the least dynamic common denominator of pan-African thinking" and places emphasis on "the equality and the sovereignty and territorial integrity of member states".

Moreover, a resolution adopted by the OAU Assembly of Heads of State and Government held in Cairo in July 1964 recorded that "all member states pledge themselves to respect the borders existing on their achievement of national independence", on the grounds inter alia that "border problems constitute a grave and permanent factor of dissension" and that "the borders of African states, on the day of their independence, constitute a tangible reality". The reasoning behind this decision "is clear enough", wrote Brownlie: "If the colonial alignments were discarded, alternative alignments would have to be agreed upon. Such a process of redefinition would create confusion and threats to peace. Even if the principles on which revision was to be based were agreed upon, there would be considerable difficulty in applying the principles to the ethnic and tribal complexities of African states".

The 1964 Cairo resolution has had considerable effect in discouraging the development of territorial disputes between OAU member states, and those which have arisen have often been resolved by negotiation (e.g. the Algerian-Moroccan border dispute, settled in 1972). Nevertheless, as described in the following pages, there do exist between various OAU member states a number of outstanding issues with a territorial dimension of one sort or another, even though it may not be

---

[1]Ian Brownlie, *African Boundaries—A Legal and Diplomatic Encyclopaedia*. The following section draws heavily on this comprehensive work.

appropriate to describe some of them as intergovernmental disputes in the international legal sense.

Certain African border disputes, such as those between Chad and Libya and between Malawi and Tanzania, involve specific territorial claims, often centring on uncertain boundary-drawing during the colonial period. Moreover, notwithstanding the 1964 OAU resolution, ethnic or tribal divisions created by colonial boundary-drawing continue to surface in tensions and rivalries between certain African states, for example in the Horn of Africa.

In addition, there are a number of outstanding territorial issues between ex-colonial powers and their former African dependencies, mostly involving Indian Ocean islands which have remained under the sovereignty of the former but which are claimed by the latter. The position of the one remaining European state which continues to exercise territorial sovereignty on the African continent itself—namely Spain in its enclaves on the north Moroccan coast—is under challenge from Morocco. Moreover, Morocco has asserted a claim to sovereignty over the territory of the former Spanish Sahara—an issue which has taken on the character of a national liberation struggle but which was originally a territorial issue.

The remaining category of disputes dealt with in this section involves South Africa, the only internationally-recognized independent state in Africa which is not a member of the OAU. Territorial claims against South Africa are made by Lesotho, as well as the "independent" black homelands created by the Pretoria government (and not internationally recognized). In addition, South Africa is in dispute with the international community over the status of Walvis Bay on the Atlantic coast of Namibia (South African control over Namibia itself being regarded as illegal by the United Nations).

Burkina Faso-Mali

An area extending along the border between the West African Republics of Burkina Faso (known as Upper Volta until August 1984) and Mali for about 90 miles (145 km) and of a width of between nine and 12 miles has been in dispute between the two states since their achievement of independence in April and July 1960 respectively. At the end of 1985 the two sides fought a brief war over the disputed territory, but subsequently accepted a demarcation judgment of the International Court of Justice which was to come into effect at the end of 1987. (A map illustrating this dispute appears on page 139.)

Geography and Historical Background of the Dispute

The area disputed between Burkina Faso and Mali contains a chain of pools in the Dori district (*cercle*), through which flows the Béli river, the only source of fresh water in the region. It includes pasture and agricultural land and has therefore attracted settlers as well as nomads who have seasonally migrated to the area with their livestock.

The colony of Upper Volta was first created by France under a decree of March 1, 1919, which laid down that seven districts (including that of Dori) which had until then been part of Upper Senegal-Niger (renamed the French Sudan on Dec. 4, 1920) would constitute the new colony. Its creation was officially motivated by the "particularly homogeneous ethnic and linguistic character of the region", which was said to be inhabited by "Mossis, Bobos and other related ethnic groups". However, under a further French decree of Sept. 5, 1932, the Governor-General of French West Africa dissolved the colony of Upper Volta and distributed its territory among the French colonies of Niger, the French Sudan and Côte d'Ivoire, with the Dori district being allocated to Niger (except for one canton which went to the French Sudan).

This 1932 decree was in turn revoked under a French law of Sept. 4, 1947, which restored Upper Volta, laying down that its frontiers should be those which had existed on Sept. 5, 1932, but that adjustments to these frontiers could be made later by consultation among the local assemblies concerned. The frontiers created by France were in principle accepted by both Mali (the former French Sudan) and Upper Volta in their 1960 declarations of independence.

Inconclusive Discussion of the Border Problem, 1961-74

The border problem was first discussed at a bilateral meeting at San (Mali) on Nov. 18-19, 1961, when it was agreed to have the frontier demarcated by a mixed commission of heads of border districts of the two states. This mixed commission agreed on Dec. 7, 1961, at Ansongo (Mali) that the frontier was as shown on a 1925 colonial map (of a 1:500,000 scale), and the Ansongo commander accepted that on all maps the Béli region was shown as being in Upper Volta. The San decision was, however, superseded by the creation of a new bipartisan commission set up in Bamako (the capital of Mali) on Feb. 24, 1964, and charged with proposing the demarcation of the frontier on the basis of the work done by the district heads.

The problem was again discussed at a meeting at Bobo-Diolassou (Upper Volta) in 1966 and at a meeting of the two heads of state at Orodara (Upper Volta) in May 1968, when two bodies were created—a permanent bipartisan commission to study the problems of co-operation between the two states and a mixed technical commission to explore the frontier on the basis of pre-independence documents held by the two states. On Sept 29-30, 1968, it was agreed in Bamako that, if no texts could be found to support the frontier demarcation, then reference should be made to maps to solve the problem. The mixed technical commission was later instructed to explore the situation on the ground in certain areas, but in 1974 Mali declared that the commission had failed to carry out all its instructions fully, and it also rejected a 1926 atlas submitted by Upper Volta as a means of settling the question. All discussion was thereupon broken off.

The Cases of the Two Governments

Mali. As set out in a memorandum of Dec. 11, 1972, the thesis of the Malian government has been that the Béli region had geographically and historically always been part of the French Sudan and hence of Mali, in particular as part of the subdivision of Ansongo. In particular, Mali asserted in its memorandum that the delineation of a frontier on a map must be based on legal documents; that the maps available are often in conflict with existing legal documents and among each other; and that the people who inhabited the disputed area were of Malian origin and had contributed significantly to the development of the area during the colonial era.

The Mali government newspaper *L'Essor* declared at that time that, as the area was inhabited by Malians, the desire to keep the Béli region was "not a territorial claim" but was "simply an historically and geographically incontrovertible fact" and that "the claims of a state can be founded only on those of its population [who] have possessed and inhabited the zone". Radio Mali reiterated the claim to the region of Béli as Malian territory on Dec. 20, 1974, when it declared that Malian people had been settled there for centuries, had been born and had grown up there and had "possessed and inhabited the zone". It also stated that an additional strip extending for 140 kilometres between Coro and Bouanza was similarly in dispute.

Burkina Faso. Burkina Faso/Upper Volta has based its claim on the following principal considerations: (i) the provisions of the French law of Sept. 5, 1947, restoring Upper Volta with its frontiers as at Sept. 5, 1932; (ii) the principles of the Charter of the Organization of African Unity (OAU), which include "respect for the sovereignty and territorial integrity of each member state and for its inalienable right to independent existence" (Article III, Para. 3 of the Charter) and "unreserved condemnation . . . of subversive activities on the part of neighbouring states" (Article II, Para. 5); and (iii) the provisions of a resolution adopted by the OAU Assembly of Heads of State and Government in July 1964, declaring that all member states undertook to respect the frontiers existing at the moment of their achievement of independence. In this context, Upper Volta quoted a speech made at the inaugural OAU Assembly in 1963 by the then President of Mali, endorsing the maintenance of existing frontiers and calling for a multilateral non-aggression pact guaranteed by all states represented at the Assembly.

The Upper Volta point of view was set out in detail in a 58-page memorandum submitted to an OAU mediation commission appointed in December 1974. In this memorandum Upper Volta adduced historical, geographical and demographic arguments in support of its thesis that the disputed area had never been part of Mali (or of the earlier French Sudan). With regard to earlier frontiers, Upper Volta, while not excluding legal texts, considered maps to be the only objective documents because they were drawn on the basis of legal texts and by an official organ (the cartographic service of French West Africa). At the same time, Upper Volta rejected a 1925 map showing part of the Béli pools to be in the French Sudan, on the ground that this map was only provisional and was replaced by later maps showing all Béli pools to be inside Upper Volta.

In connexion with migration, Upper Volta pointed out that, according to official documents, migrants had moved mainly from the north to the south, the majority of these migrants being Tuaregs and Bellahs (population groups also represented in Algeria, Mauritania and Niger); that under conventions concluded between the French Sudan (or Mali) and Upper Volta also after their achievement of independence, to facilitate migration into the Béli region, the latter was recognized as part of Upper Volta and as not having always been inhabited by Malians; and that Mali had no right to use the presence of people of Malian origin as a basis for territorial claims as "to change the frontiers so as to embrace homogeneous groups would inevitably upset the present configuration of all African states".

Upper Volta therefore considered the Malian thesis to be indefensible in law, even if it was conceivable on the strictly human level, and also to be dangerous because other states might claim sovereignty over Malian villages inhabited by Tuaregs. It also rejected Mali's claim based on the achievements of Malians in the region, pointing out that Upper Volta was not making any claims in respect of regions in neighbouring countries where people from Upper Volta had worked.

Border Incidents and Mediation Efforts, 1974-76

Armed clashes which broke out on Nov. 25, 1974, and continued into December of that year were the subject of talks held at the frontier village of Faramana on Dec. 4 by Presidents Moussa Traore of Mali and Lamizana of Upper Volta. These talks did not lead to peace, however, and on Dec. 17, 1974, it was claimed in Bamako that Upper Volta had launched a general offensive against Mali, whereas it was announced in Ouagadougou (the capital of Burkina Faso/Upper Volta) on Dec. 18 that Malian forces had taken up positions in Upper Volta territory along the whole length of the disputed frontier. Mali claimed at the same time that it was merely taking possession of territory which was legally its own.

Following mediation efforts by Presidents Senghor of Senegal and Eyadema of Togo, a meeting was held on Dec. 26, 1974, in Lomé (the capital of Togo), at which a joint communiqué (issued on the following day) was signed by the Presidents of Mali, Niger, Togo and Upper Volta. In this communiqué it was agreed that a mediation commission was to be set up, with Guinea, Niger, Senegal and Togo as members, to guarantee the safety of the two countries' nationals on each other's territories, as well as their property; to supervise the effective withdrawal of troops from the border zone; and to seek a solution to the dispute. At the same time, the Presidents of Mali and Upper Volta agreed to cease their propaganda campaigns against each other.

The mediation commission subsequently carried out this work, under the auspices of the OAU, in two sub-committees—a juridical one examining the arguments on the two sides and a military one which visited the disputed area but was not admitted to Mali. The commission eventually recommended the independent demarcation of the border by a neutral technical commission which would determine sovereignty over certain villages in the disputed area, but as a result of Mali's refusal to admit the OAU's military committee such a commission was never set up.

Fresh border incidents were reported early in June 1975, when Mali alleged that Upper Volta forces had raided two villages and killed two persons on June 3. The government of Guinea appealed to both sides on June 5 to halt hostilities and to evacuate their troops from the contested zone pending a settlement agreement. At a further meeting held in Lomé on June 18 and attended also by the Presidents of Guinea, Niger, Senegal and Togo, the Presidents of Mali and of Upper Volta undertook to "end their dispute on the basis of recommendations of the mediation commission", which was to appoint a neutral committee (including a cartographer and an ethnologist) to determine the position of several villages, while the government of Mali agreed to "restore to Upper Volta the equipment belonging to it and seized during the events of December 1974" and also to release two Upper Volta prisoners held in Mali. This undertaking was honoured on June 24, and on July 5 President Lamizana of Upper Volta announced that he had set free 33 detained Malians.

On July 11, 1975, the two Presidents signed, jointly with President Sekou Touré of Guinea, an agreement in which they undertook "definitely to renounce the use of force" in any dispute between them. The following year, at a meeting of ministers from the two countries held in Upper Volta on March 9, it was agreed that the two Presidents should instruct the joint commission to resume its work with the aim of achieving a final settlement of the problem of the border area between specified villages, and that the administrative officers in the border districts should meet frequently to educate the population.

Agreed Recommendations of 1979

At a meeting between the Upper Volta and Malian Interior Ministers held in Ségou (Mali) on Nov. 21-22, 1979, the two sides agreed on recommendations for continued meetings of the administrative and local authorities in order to settle any border incidents promptly; on empowering a technical joint commission to set up a programme of action and to define its working procedures; and on the adoption of a policy of consultation to find adequate solutions to the problem. The Malian minister was quoted as saying that there was "no point of divergence between Upper Volta and Mali" and that "we could and must settle our problems without any foreign intervention".

Agreement to Submit Dispute to International Court of Justice—Renewed Fighting in December 1985

In a joint communiqué issued on Sept. 16, 1983, the two countries' heads of state agreed to submit the border dispute to the International Court of Justice (ICJ) "while continuing the bilateral dialogue within the existing ad hoc structures". An ICJ chamber to hear the case was formed on April 3, 1985, and by September 1985 the two countries' border commissions had reached agreement on the demarcation of some 1,000 kilometres of the common border. (Meanwhile, on Aug. 4, 1984, Upper Volta had been renamed Burkina Faso, meaning "Democratic Land of Honest Men".)

However, fighting broke out in the border area on Dec. 25, 1985, apparently as the result of an attempt by Burkina Faso to carry out (between Dec. 10 and 20, 1985) a census operation in four villages in the disputed border region. According to Malian reports, villagers who refused to submit to the census had been mistreated, but the Burkinabe authorities claimed that the census operations in the villages (three of which were, according to maps in current usage, in Burkina territory) had been obstructed by Malian troops.

Malian airborne attacks were carried out on Dec. 25, 1985, on various towns far south of the border, and on Dec. 26 Burkina Faso launched an air attack on Sikasso, a Malian town some 700 kilometres south-west of the area of conflict, whereupon Mali retaliated by attacking Koloko in Burkina Faso. The fighting was ended by a truce negotiated by the member governments of the Non-Aggression and Defence Aid Agreement (ANAD), (embracing Burkina Faso, Côte d'Ivoire, Mali, Mauritania, Niger, Senegal and Togo). After being formally endorsed by the two heads of state, the truce came into force on Dec. 31, 1985. In Burkina Faso it was announced in mid-January 1986 that 41 of its nationals had been killed in the fighting, among them 21 civilians. No official casualty figures were given by Mali.

The ICJ chamber dealing with the border dispute held an emergency meeting on Jan. 9, 1986, and called on both parties to observe the truce, to take no action which might aggravate the situation and to effect, within 20 days, a troop withdrawal behind lines to be agreed by both governments. Such an agreement was concluded at an ANAD meeting held in Côte d'Ivoire on Jan. 17-18, 1986, when the heads of state of Burkina Faso and Mali effected a public reconciliation. Exchanges of prisoners took place between the two sides between Jan. 9 and Feb. 27, 1986.

Judgment of the International Court of Justice

On Dec. 22, 1986, the ICJ chamber (consisting of Judge Mohammed Bedjaoui as president and Judges Manfred Lachs and José Maria Ruda, as well as Judges ad hoc François Luchaire and Georges Abi-Saab) unanimously agreed on the frontier line between the two states (although the two ad hoc judges dissociated themselves from some of the reasons and conclusions). The judgment had the effect of that of the full Court and was accepted as binding and to be effected within a year by the two parties. The Court was asked to nominate three experts to assist in the demarcation of the border.

In the judgment the disputed area of some 1,200 square miles was divided into roughly equal parts on both sides of a 124½-mile border line, with Mali obtaining a bigger part of the disputed territory's western zone and Burkina Faso a lesser portion in the eastern zone. In its judgment the ICJ chamber came to the following conclusions:

Historical background. Both states derived their existence from the process of decolonization which had been unfolding in Africa during the past 30 years. Their territories and that of Niger were formerly part of French West Africa. Burkina Faso corresponded to the colony of Upper Volta and Mali to Sudan (formerly French Sudan). Both parties stated that the settlement should be based on respect for the principle of the intangibility of frontiers inherited from colonization.

The principle. In those circumstances, the Court could not disregard the principle of *uti possidetis juris* [i.e. the presumption that post-colonial states possessed sovereignty within antecedent colonial boundaries]. It emphasized the general scope of the principle in matters of decolonization and its exceptional importance for the African continent. Although invoked for the first time in Spanish America, the principle was not a rule pertaining solely to one specific system of international law. It was a general principle logically connected with the phenomenon of the obtaining of independence and its obvious purpose was to prevent the independence and stability of new states being endangered by fratricidal struggles provoked by the challenging of frontiers following the withdrawal of the administering power. The principle accorded pre-eminence to legal title over effective possession as a basis of sovereignty. Its primary aim was to secure respect for the territorial boundaries which existed when independence was achieved. When those boundaries were delimitations between different administrative divisions or colonies subject to the same sovereign, the application of the principle resulted in their being transformed into international boundaries, as in the instant case. The principle appeared in conflict with the right of peoples to self-determination; however, the maintenance of territorial status quo in Africa was often seen as the wisest course. The essential requirement of the stability in order to survive and develop had induced African states to consent to the maintenance of colonial frontiers.

French colonial law. The parties agreed that the delimitation of the frontier had to be appraised in the light of the French colonial law. The line to be determined as that which existed in 1959-60 was originally no more than an administrative boundary dividing two former French overseas territories and as such was defined at that time not according to international law but according to the relevant French legislation. International law, and therefore the principle of *uti possidetis*, applied as from the accession of independence but had no retroactive effect. The principle froze the territorial title; it stopped the clock but it did not put back the hands. International law did not effect any return to the law of the colonizing state, which was but one factual element among others, evidence indicative of the colonial heritage at the critical date.

Administrative heritage. French West Africa was headed by a governor-general and divided into colonies, headed by a lieutenant-governor. Colonies were subdivided into *cercles* headed by a commandant. Mali gained its independence in 1960 succeeding the Sudanese Republic which had emerged from the French Sudan. Upper Volta came into being in 1919, was abolished in 1932 and reconstituted in 1947, with the 1932 boundaries, and gained independence in 1960. The problem for the Court was to ascertain what in the disputed area was the frontier which existed in 1959-60 between Sudan and Upper Volta. Both parties agreed that when they became independent there was a definite frontier and both accepted that no modification had taken place since.

Tripoint problem. The easternmost point of the disputed frontier, the tripoint Niger-Mali-Burkina Faso, gave rise to conflict between the parties. Mali claimed that it could not be determined without Niger's agreement, and Burkina Faso considered that the Court had to reach a decision. The Court held that its jurisdiction was not restricted merely because the end-point of the disputed frontier lay on the frontier of a third state not a party to the proceedings. The rights of Niger were in any event safeguarded by Article 59 of the Statute of the Court which provided that the decision of the Court had no binding force except between the parties and in respect of that particular case. In any event, the Court was not required to fix a tripoint, which would require the consent of all three states, but to ascertain in the light of the evidence which the parties had made available how far the frontier they had inherited from the colonial power extended. Such a finding implied that the territory of a third state lay beyond the end-point and that the parties had exclusive sovereign rights up to that point. However, since the parties had contended that they possessed a common frontier with the other as far as a specific point, neither could change its position to rely on sovereignty of a third state. The Court would merely define the end-point where the frontier ceased to divide the territories of Burkina Faso and Mali but that would not amount to a decision that that was a tripoint which affected Niger.

Evidence. The parties relied on different types of evidence. (1) They referred to legislative and regulative texts or administrative documents. However, as those contained no complete description of the disputed area they were limited in scope and the correct interpretation of them was a matter of dispute between the parties. (2) Both produced an abundant collection of cartographic materials (maps). But the Court noted that in frontier delimitations maps merely constituted information and never constituted territorial titles in themselves. They were merely extrinsic evidence which might be used along with other evidence to establish the real facts. Their value depended on their technical reliability and their neutrality to the parties in the dispute. None of the maps available could provide an official illustration of any of the texts produced although it was clear from their wording that two of the texts were intended to be accompanied by maps. Further, no indisputable boundary line could be discerned from the documents. One map, issued between 1958 and 1960 by the French *Institut géographique national* (IGN), was drawn up by a body neutral towards the parties. Although it did not possess the status of a legal title, it was a visual portrayal both of the available texts and of information available on the ground. Where other evidence was lacking or not sufficient to show an exact line, the probative force of the IGN map had to be viewed as compelling. (3) The parties also invoked the conduct of the administrative authorities as proof of the effective exercise of territorial jurisdiction in the region during the colonial period. The role played by such conduct was complex and the Court had to make a careful evaluation of their legal force in each particular instance.

The Court emphasized that the present case was decidedly unusual as concerned the facts to be proved or the evidence to be produced. Although the parties had produced as complete a case file as possible, the Court could not be certain of deciding the case on a basis of full knowledge of facts. The case file showed inconsistencies and shortcomings. The Court considered what relationship could be established among the pieces of information provided by the various texts of which it had to make use and reached a number of conclusions. In certain points the sources agreed and bore one another out, but in some respects, in view of the shortcomings of some of the older maps, they tended to conflict. The western end-point was already agreed between the parties and the Court drew in a series of straight lines between co-ordinates the boundary from there to the frontier of Niger. At one place, the pool of In Abao, the co-ordinates were not specified but left to the three experts who are to be appointed to be drawn. The Court considered it inappropriate to appoint those experts in the judgment, but said they would be appointed later by an order of the Court.

The Court noted with satisfaction the agreement in January 1986 of the heads of state of Burkina Faso and Mali to withdraw all their armed forces from either side of the disputed area and to effect their return to their respective territories. The Court finally noted that the parties had declared that they would accept the judgment as binding upon them and was happy to record the attachment of both parties to the international judicial process and to the peaceful settlement of disputes.

HWD

Cameroon-Nigeria

Relations between Nigeria and Cameroon were temporarily strained in May-July 1981 by what was in Nigeria officially described as a border dispute, centring on the frontier between the adjoining coastal regions of the two states. (A map of the region appears on page 139.)

Background to Dispute

On the question of two countries' common border President Ahmadou Ahidjo of Cameroon had stated in an interview (published in *Le Monde* on July 18-19, 1976) that, although Cameroon had strongly challenged the correctness of a plebiscite held in 1961 and resulting in the transfer of Northern Cameroon to Nigeria and had unsuccessfully tried to appeal to the United Nations and the International Court of Justice, his government had bowed to the facts and preferred to refrain from making any territorial claims. He added that where Cameroon's boundaries with any of its six neighbours (Nigeria and Chad to the north, the Central African Republic to the east and Congo, Gabon and Equatorial Guinea in the south) were imprecisely delimited the problem would be solved amicably.

It was, however, widely acknowledged that in parts of Western Cameroon (i.e. near the border with Nigeria) there remained a minority of people who were opposed to the incorporation of their area in Cameroon as a result of a plebiscite also held in 1961, when almost 30 per cent of the valid votes were cast against such incorporation. In particular, the Bakassi peninsula, situated on the Cameroon side of the border and to the west of the Rio del Rey river, was largely inhabited by Nigerians who had settled there before this part of the former British Cameroon was united with the former French Cameroon in 1961. Many of these Nigerians were fishermen and some were engaged in smuggling, and they tended to seek protection from the authorities of the Nigerian Cross River State.

A maritime border agreement signed at the northern Cameroon town of Maroua on May 31, 1975, by Gen. Yakubu Gowon (then Nigeria's head of state) and President Ahidjo had left the access channel to the port of Calabar in Nigerian territorial waters and had also provided that the lawful activities of Nigerian fishermen in a two-kilometre-wide strip should not affect the territorial waters issue. However, Gen. Gowon was deposed in July 1975 and the agreement was never ratified by Nigeria on the grounds that it was "defective in parts".

Escalation of Tension in 1981

On May 18, 1981, Prof. Ishaya Audu, the Nigerian Minister of External Affairs, announced that, although the Nigerian President had recently visited Cameroon as "part of the exercise of defusing the tension along this border and generally trying to settle issues by peaceful means", the situation had taken "a different turn". He maintained that at a Nigerian village in Cross River State, well within Nigerian territory and separated from the Cameroon border by the Akpa Yafi river [also referred to as the Ate Akate or Agpa Yafé river] ... on May 15, 1981, "a platoon of Nigerian soldiers and five support boats were fired upon by a Cameroonian support boat" and five Nigerian soldiers had been killed and three others seriously wounded, whereupon the Cameroonians had fled. The minister added that his government had sent the Cameroonian government "a very stern note of protest"; that it reserved the right to take any appropriate action to protect the lives and property of Nigerians; and that it would report the matter to the Organization of African Unity (OAU).

Prof. Audu later contended that there had been "regular harassment" of Nigerians living in the border area and also incursions by Cameroonians into Nigerian villages. The Cameroonians, on the other hand, alleged that the incident of May 15 had taken place on the Rio del Rey river, i.e. in Cameroonian territorial waters 20 miles to the east of the boundary, while on May 22 President Ahidjo was reported to have ordered an inquiry into an earlier exchange of artillery fire on the Rio del Rey river. In a message delivered in Lagos on May 24 by a delegation led by Paul Dontsop (Cameroon's Foreign Minister), President Ahidjo expressed his regrets at the incident of May 15 and made proposals for working out a peaceful solution to the border problem, but the National Security Council of Nigeria found that these proposals did not cover all the issues referred to in Nigeria's protest note.

There followed strong expressions of hostility to Cameroon in the Nigerian press, where it was claimed that Cameroon was massing forces for a military confrontation and was prospecting for oil in Nigerian waters. Alhaji Akanbi Oniyangi (the Minister of Defence) refused to rule out the possibility of war, and demonstrating university students called for war and caused damage to Cameroon's embassy in Lagos. A presidential spokesman admitted in a statement issued on June 2, 1981, that President Shehu Shagari was restraining calls for war (which had also been made by the Speaker of the Federal House of Representatives).

Ayissi Mvodo, Cameroonian Minister of State for Territorial Administration, said in an interview published on June 3 that many other incidents had occurred in the past and had been settled peacefully by the authorities of both countries, and that the position of the Cameroonian government was always to seek such a settlement without recourse to force, in particular because the two "brotherly and neighbouring countries" harboured "huge members of each other's citizens".

With regard to Nigeria's appeal to the OAU, the Secretariat of the OAU declined to place the matter on the agenda of the OAU Assembly of Heads of State and Government held in Nairobi on June 24-28, 1981, and President Shagari thereupon refused to attend the session. However, Edem Kodjo, the OAU Secretary-General, and Dr Robert Ouko, the Foreign Minister of Kenya (whose President was currently President of the OAU), visited Lagos and Yaoundé (the capital of Cameroon) for discussion of the issue during the second week of July 1981.

Lagos radio stated on July 15, 1981, that, while Nigeria wished the OAU Secretary-General success in his "mediation efforts in the Nigeria-Cameroon border dispute", it was necessary to ask why the issue was not placed on the OAU Assembly's agenda; whether the OAU Secretariat was "inadvertently inciting Nigeria into embarking on a military adventure against Cameroon"; or whether "Edem Kodjo and his men" felt that the matter was "not serious enough".

After it had been disclosed that mediation efforts had also been made by Presidents Houphouët-Boigny of Côte d'Ivoire, Seyni Kountché of Niger and Gnassingbe Eyadema of Togo, it was reported on July 15, 1981, that an OAU ministerial committee was to be set up to look into the situation. President Ahidjo had earlier (on July 7) been reported to have emphasized that calm had been restored to the area; that Cameroon would not be the origin of any eventual conflict with its neighbours; and that it was ready to take part in any mediation efforts.

In Lagos it was announced on July 20, 1981, that President Ahidjo had promised that his country would pay compensation to the families of the five Nigerian soldiers killed on May 15, and that he had tendered an unreserved apology. President Shagari, in accepting this offer (as reported on July 24), suggested the establishment of "an arbitration tribunal comprising countries acceptable to both nations to look into the entire boundary question with a view to forestalling further unrest". The details of this plan were to be worked out during a proposed visit to Nigeria by President Ahidjo at the invitation of President Shagari, tendered on July 22.

On August 6, 1981, it was reported from Lagos that the Director of Immigration had told a parliamentary committee that a border fence was to be erected along Nigeria's boundaries with Benin, Cameroon, Chad and Niger, but that this fence would not initially affect the Nigeria-Cameroon border, the main purpose of the fence being to keep out illegal immigrants.

In a joint communiqué issued on Jan. 13, 1982, at the end of President Ahidjo's visit to

Lagos, it was stated inter alia that the two countries' Presidents had expressed their regret at the border clash of May 1981, had resolved not to allow the incident to affect co-operation between them, and had decided to reactive a Nigeria-Cameroon joint commission to strengthen co-operation in all fields.

Although Nigeria had early in 1983 expelled an estimated 120,000 Cameroonians as "illegal aliens", the two countries' Presidents agreed on April 21, 1983, to establish a new Nigeria-Cameroon joint commission and to "pursue, intensify and consolidate" the co-operation between their countries. Nevertheless, further border incidents occurred in May 1987, in what Lagos radio described as "another unprovoked attack on Nigeria".

HWD

Chad-Libya

In 1973 the Libyan government of Col. Moamer al Kadhafi annexed an area south of the existing border between Libya and Chad known as the Aozou strip. Whereas the Libyan action met with no opposition from the then government of Chad led by President Ngarta (François) Tombalbaye nor from other states in the area, objections to the annexation were first raised by Gen. Félix Malloum, who had become President of Chad after the overthrow of President Tombalbaye in April 1975. In 1980, by which time Chad had been devastated by civil war, Libyan forces, invited into the country by a provisional government "of national unity" formed in November 1979 under the presidency of Goukouni Oueddei, temporarily occupied the greater part of Chad. President Oueddei accepted the Libyan annexation of the Aozou strip as "an accomplished fact", whereas rebel groups, especially that led by Hissène Habré, continued to dispute Libya's right to the strip. Thus Hissène Habré's eventual military victory and assumption of power in Chad in June 1982 reopened the dispute over the Aozou strip, which advancing Chadian government forces succeeded in penetrating in early August 1987, when the town of Aozou was captured from the Libyans.

History of Chad's Northern Boundary

The boundary between Libya and Chad was first laid down under a convention signed in Paris by France and the United Kingdom on June 14, 1898 (with ratifications being exchanged in Paris on June 13, 1899), with the object of delimiting the spheres of influence of France and the United Kingdom east of the Niger river. Under an Anglo-French declaration of March 21, 1899, the French zone was delimited to the north-east and east by a line starting "from the point of intersection of the Tropic of Cancer with the 16th degree of longitude east of Greenwich" and running "thence to the north until it meets the 24th degree of longitude east of Greenwich". Italy concurred with the above line in an exchange of notes with France on Nov. 1, 1902. Under a convention of Sept. 8, 1919, France and the United Kingdom determined the line's point of intersection with the 24th meridian (which had not been specified in the 1899 declaration) at 19°30′N.

Whereas the territory to the north of this line had been under Turkish suzereignty as part of the Ottoman empire, Italy occupied the region of Tripoli in September 1911, and in the Treaty of Ouchy of Oct. 18, 1912, the Ottomon empire recognized Italian sovereignty over the territory which became officially known as Libya after 1934. Following Libya's declaration of independence on Dec. 24, 1951, the boundary between Libya and French Equatorial Africa was recognized in a French-Libyan treaty of Aug. 10, 1955, as fixed under

113

AFRICA

the above-mentioned agreements. Chad, which had been part of French Equatorial Africa, became independent on Aug. 11, 1960.

Libya's Annexation of the Aozou Strip

In June 1973 the Libyan government of Col. Kadhafi annexed the Aozou strip, basing its action on the provisions of a Franco-Italian protocol signed in Rome on Jan. 7, 1935. This protocol, dealing with the delimitation of "the frontier between Libya and the French colonies" (and also "between Eritrea and the French coast of Somaliland", i.e. Djibouti), defined the proposed southern frontier of Libya (as described in an official communiqué of Jan. 8, 1935) as follows: "The frontier separating Libya from French West Africa and French Equatorial Africa is determined by the line which runs from Tummo, the terminating point of the line traced in the Italo-French agreement of Sept. 12, 1919, meeting the western frontier of the Anglo-Egyptian Sudan at 24°E, 18°45′N. This line leaves (in Italian territory) Aozou and Guezendi, and in French territory Bardai and Tecro. The size of the territories thus recognized as belonging to Italian Libya is approximately 114,000 square kilometres (43,000 square miles)".

This protocol was agreed to "in application of Article 13 of the Treaty of London"—which had been concluded by France, Italy, Russia and the United Kingdom in 1915 with the object of inducing Italy to join the Allies in World War I. The article in question read as follows: "In the event of France and Great Britain increasing their colonial territories in Africa at the expense of Germany, those two powers agree in principle that Italy may claim some equitable compensation, particularly as regards the settlement in her favour of the questions relative to the frontiers of the Italian colonies of Eritrea, Somaliland and Libya and the neighbouring colonies belonging to France and Great Britain". However, France never ratified the protocol (which was said to have been interpreted by Mussolini as giving him, as far as France was concerned, a free hand in his invasion of Abyssinia in October 1935).

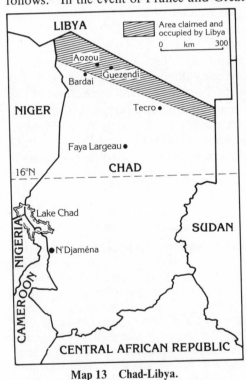

The timing of Libya's annexation of the Aozou strip was widely regarded as being connected with the existence of uranium deposits in the strip (in the same geological formation which included uranium deposits in Gabon). Although consisting (according to the European Nuclear Energy Agency) of low-grade, high-cost ores, the deposits were considered adequate to complete the required basis for the nuclear independence of Libya, which had concluded an agreement with the Soviet Union for the supply of a 10-megawatt nuclear reactor and associated technology to Libya.

Map 13   Chad-Libya.

The annexation of the Aozou strip was not officially announced in Libya until early September 1975 (in the Tripoli newspaper *Al Fateh*).

Reactions in Chad to Annexation

At the time of the annexation of the Aozou strip Chad had close relations with Libya. Following a visit to Tripoli by President Tombalbaye, the Libyan government had, on Dec.

23, 1972, undertaken to "contribute to the strengthening of unity" in Chad, to grant Chad development credits and (reportedly) also to hand over to the government of Chad any members of the rebel *Front de libération nationale* (Frolinat) who might be in Libya. During a visit to Chad by Col. Kadhafi on March 5-6, 1974, the Aozou strip was not officially referred to. However, on April 26, 1976, President Malloum, who accused both Libya and Algeria of supporting the Frolinat rebels, denounced Libya for having illegally occupied the Aozou strip. On Oct. 16 of that year Chad closed its border with Libya, and a few days later President Malloum notified Col. Kadhafi that there could be no talk of co-operation between the two countries until Libya had withdrawn from the Aozou strip.

At a meeting of the Council of Ministers of the Organization of African Unity (OAU) in Libreville (Gabon) in June 1977, the Foreign Minister of Chad accused Libya of arming and aiding rebels in northern Chad, and he asked the OAU to use all its authority "to restore Chad's rights in the Aozou strip". The Libyan representative at the meeting asserted in turn that the strip was in fact "not northern Chad" but "southern Libya". The OAU Assembly of Heads of State and Government, meeting also in Libreville early in July 1977, thereupon set up a commission to deal with the dispute. On Feb. 6, 1978, the government of President Malloum suspended its diplomatic relations with Libya.

At an OAU Assembly of Heads of State and Government, meeting in Khartoum, President Malloum on July 20, 1978, denounced Libya's "expansionist desires" and called on the OAU to demand Libya's withdrawal from Chad and to set up a mission to be sent to northern Chad to ascertain that it had been invaded by Libyan forces. The OAU subsequently established a committee of five African Presidents to investigate Chad's allegations and also Libyan accusations to the effect that Chad had been relying on French "colonial forces" to suppress a popular uprising in Chad by "genocidal methods". Subsequent OAU efforts were directed mainly at the prevention of further escalation of the civil war in Chad and had no bearing on the status of the Aozou strip which remained firmly under Libyan control.

President Malloum resigned on March 23, 1979, and after lengthy negotiations a provisional government "of national unity" was established under the presidency of Goukouni Oueddei on Nov. 10, 1979. On June 15, 1980, this government signed a treaty of friendship with Libya, under which both sides undertook "mutually to defend each other in the event of one of the two parties being threatened by direct or indirect aggression". On Jan. 6, 1981, the two governments announced, at the end of a visit to Tripoli by President Goukouni Oueddei, their intention to work towards "full unity" between the two countries, with Libya sending military personnel to Chad to help preserve security and maintain peace. After it had become apparent that there was widespread opposition to any eventual merger between Libya and Chad (not only outside but also inside Chad), it was stated in Libya and in Chad that no such merger was intended. The Vice-President of Chad, in particular, said in a broadcast on Jan. 11, 1981, that the Tripoli announcement did not represent a treaty with Libya but concerned only "complete unity of the two peoples in historical, ethnical and ideological terms" and not a merger of the two countries.

President Goukouni Oueddei had stated on Dec. 26. 1980, that the Libyan occupation of the Aozou strip had placed him before an "accomplished fact" inherited from the Tombalbaye regime, and he added: "Nobody will be able to intervene to disunite Chad and Libya".

Civil War and Libyan Intervention in Chad

In November 1981 the Libyan troops which had entered Chad at the invitation of President Goukouni Oueddei were withdrawn from the country at his request. This withdrawal was followed by the advance of the *Forces armés du nord* (FAN) led by Hissène Habré, which gradually occupied all major towns in Chad and finally overthrew the Goukouni Oueddei government in June 1982. While the ex-President attempted to regroup his forces in northern Chad, where Libya continued to maintain a military presence, the

Foreign Minister in Hissène Habré's government declared on Sept. 13, 1982, that Chad would seek to expel the Libyans from the Aozou strip by resorting to the United Nations, the Organization of African Unity and, if necessary, the International Court of Justice. The Libyan government, however, denied on Sept. 20 that the Aozou strip was Chadian territory.

Early in October 1982 it was announced in Libya that eight different factions had formed a 15-member "national peace government" under the leadership of Goukouni Oueddei and based in Bardai (northern Chad). There ensued heavy fighting between the two sides' forces. At the request of President Habré, French troops entered Chad and launched, on Aug. 13, 1983, an operation designed to form a defensive line at the southern limit of the range of Libyan aircraft operating from bases in southern Libya and northern Chad, and with French fighter aircraft standing by at a base in the Central African Republic.

In January 1984 the French declared the area of Chad south of the 16th parallel to be an exclusive zone in which no Libyan-backed forces would be tolerated. In April of that year France and Libya began to discuss a mutual withdrawal of forces from Chad. In this context the French Defence Minister (Charles Hernu) issued a warning that France would "not leave Chad as long as there was one Libyan soldier remaining south of the Aozou strip", which President Habré still regarded as part of Chad.

The mutual troop withdrawal was finally agreed on Sept. 17, 1984 (although Hernu stated that the Aozou strip was not included in the withdrawal and that its future sovereignty was a matter for the United Nations). On Nov. 10, 1984, both France and Libya stated that the withdrawal had been completed by both sides; however, by Nov. 16, 1984, it became clear that there still remained strong Libyan forces inside Chad. Subsequent efforts by the opposing Chadian sides to reach an agreement remained fruitless.

After renewed fighting had broken out in northern Chad in February 1986, French fighter bombers from the Central African Republic bombed a northern airbase on Feb. 16, and in response to a Libyan air attack on the airport of N'Djaména (the Chadian capital) the French government announced that it would send "a deterrent force" to Chad. In October 1986, however, Goukouni Oueddei was ousted as leader of the Libyan-backed government and thereupon directed his forces, estimated at 3,000 men, to form an alliance with the government of President Habré. (Goukouni Oueddei himself was later reported to have been placed under house arrest in Tripoli for having advocated a peaceful settlement of the conflict in Chad.) In December 1986 the United States approved an extra US$15,000,000 in military aid to the Habré government, in addition to US$5,000,000 for 1987.

By January 1987 some 1,400 French troops were said to be deployed in Chad south of the 16th parallel. Following a Libyan air raid on government positions south of the line on Jan. 4, 1987, the forces of the Habré government, with French logistical support, launched a major offensive against Libyan positions south of the Aozou strip. Peace talks between Chad and Libya were initiated in Khartoum (Sudan) in early March but failed to make any progress. Later that month Chadian government forces achieved major military successes by recapturing Ouadi-Doum (on March 22) and Faya Largeau (March 27) from the Libyans, taking many prisoners and capturing large quantities of armaments. In consequence of this defeat, Libya became virtually restricted to the Aozou strip.

Renewed Libyan military action south of the Aozou strip in July 1987 was repulsed by Chadian forces, who pressed north to capture the town of Aozou itself on Aug. 8, although they subsequently came under heavy aerial bombardment from Libyan war planes. With most of the Aozou strip now under Chadian control, the OAU appealed for a ceasefire and offered to resume its mediation.

HWD

Chad-Nigeria

A dispute concerning sovereignty over a number of islands in Lake Chad led to a series of clashes between Chadian and Nigerian troops in April-May 1983. (The position of Lake Chad is shown on the map appearing on page 114.)

In addition to Chad to the east and Nigeria to the west, both Cameroon to the south and Niger to the north extend to the shores of Lake Chad, sovereignty over which is thus divided between the four countries.

As a result of the April-May 1983 clashes, the border between Chad and Nigeria was closed for several months. In Nigeria it was claimed on May 16 that over 300 Chadian soldiers had been killed in a Nigerian counter-attack. Although an agreement to end the fighting was signed on May 7, clashes continued, and on May 19 it was reported that Chadian troops supported by French mercenaries had launched a major offensive. Later in May it was claimed by Chad that Nigerian MiG fighter aircraft were bombing Chadian lakeside villages.

On July 11, 1983, the two countries' Presidents agreed to end the fighting and to reopen the border. The border was nevertheless closed again temporarily until the heads of state of the two countries agreed on May 15, 1984, to reopen it and also to set up a joint economic commission.

HWD

Comoros-France (Mayotte)

The dispute between the governments of the Comoros and France over the island of Mayotte in the Indian Ocean arose when the people of Mayotte opted by a large majority in favour of remaining a French dependency rather than joining the other Comoro islands on their assumption of independence in 1975. Since Mayotte had previously been part of the French overseas territory of the Comoro Islands, the Comoro government has consistently asserted that the island is part of its national territory, whereas the French government has upheld the right of its people to determine their own future status.

The Comoro Islands, situated in the Indian Ocean some 300-500 kilometres (200-320 miles) north-west of Madagascar, consist of four main islands—Njazidja, Nzwani, Mwali (until 1980 known respectively as Grand Comoro, Anjouan and Mohéli) and Mayotte (or Mahoré)—as well as numerous smaller islands, covering 2,236 square kilometres (or 833 square miles) and having a population of about 430,000 (while an almost equal number of Comoro islanders have settled in Tanzania and Madagascar).

The islands were an Arab sultanate until the 1840s, when they became a French protectorate, with Mayotte being declared a French colony in 1843, and the three other islands on July 21, 1912. Between 1914 and 1946 the Comoros were attached to the French government-general of Madagascar but on May 9, 1946, they were granted administrative autonomy. Under a French *loi-cadre* of June 26, 1956, the Comoros were given the status of a French overseas territory with its own Council of Government and with wider powers for its Territorial Assembly. Under a French law promulgated on Dec. 29, 1961, the Comoros were granted full internal autonomy, with the existing Territorial Assembly becoming a Chamber of Deputies, which elected the President of the territorial Council of Government, and with France retaining responsibility for foreign affairs, defence, currency and external economic relations—these arrangements coming into effect in April 1962. In January 1968 the islands were given a new statute, extending the powers of the Chamber of Deputies vis-à-vis the government and the local councils, and also in regard to courts administering both Islamic and territorial law, and giving the Prime Minister sole responsibility for internal security.

The Character of Mayotte

The population of Mayotte (which covers about 375 square kilometres or 145 square miles) has a tradition of independence vis-à-vis the other islands of the archipelago. In 1590 the people of Mayotte refused to recognize the authority of the successor of Sultan Mohamed ben Haissa of Anjouan, who had died, and there followed a four-year war between the two islands. Their differences with the other islanders are enhanced by the fact that they are mainly Christians, whereas Islam predominates elsewhere in the archipelago. Living on a subsistence basis and trading by barter until the 1970s, they have enjoyed better basic living standards than the other islanders, although most are illiterate (in 1978 only 45 per cent of children between the ages of six and 11 went to school). The island's total population numbers about 40,000, of whom only 10 per cent speak French, the main language being Swahili.

Politically the people of Mayotte, in their majority, follow the *Mouvement populaire mahorais* (MPM), which was founded in 1958 and which has normally been linked with the centrist current in French metropolitan politics, most recently with the *Union pour la démocratie française* (UDF). The party is well organized, with cells in every village, usually led by women; the fact that its leaders hold not only many key political posts but also the economic power in the island has made it difficult for opposition parties to gain ground. Among such opposition parties is the *Parti pour le rassemblement démocratique des Mahorais* (PRDM), which is led by Ali Said as its secretary-general and which held its first meeting on Jan. 21, 1979. It favours the return of Mayotte to the Comoros, i.e. independence for Mayotte within the framework of the Comoro state, and it holds the view that French departmental status for Mayotte would destroy the island's indigenous culture. Apart from the MPM and the PRDM, the French (neo-Gaullist) *Rassemblement pour la république* (RPR) is represented in Mayotte by the *Rassemblement mahorais pour la république* (RMPR), which was launched in January 1979 by Frédéric Gabriel, a former RPR deputy of St Pierre and Miquelon (the French overseas territory off Newfoundland). About the same time the *Union démocratique des Mahorais* (UDM) was founded by young people who had left Madagascar (from which about 16,000 Comoro islanders were repatriated early in 1977 after serious rioting in which over 100 others had lost their lives).

In 1961 the MPM strongly opposed the Comoro government for moving the islands' capital from Dzaoudzi (Mayotte) to Moroni (Grand Comoro), and from then onwards the movement campaigned for complete integration with France. It held four of 31 seats in the Comoros' Chamber of Deputies until 1972, and five seats in the 39-member Chamber elected thereafter. An MPM leader, Senator Marcel Henry, was quoted in *Le Monde* in June 1975 as saying: "We do not want independence, but even the status quo does not satisfy us at all. Indeed, we have always shown our opposition to the status of internal autonomy because we wish to be administered directly by Paris and reject any form of Comoro administration." As a result of this attitude the MPM was often in conflict with the French-appointed prefect of Mayotte.

The conflict between the government of the Comoros and the majority of the inhabitants of Mayotte came into the open in 1972, when the majority parties in the Chamber of Deputies joined forces, on Sept. 10, 1972, in order to promote independence for the islands "in friendship and co-operation with France", against the votes of the five members from Mayotte. In consequence, the French government soon found itself in the position of a third party to the conflict.

Unilateral Declaration of Independence by Comoro Government

Following negotiations between the Comoro and French governments, a joint declaration was signed in Paris on June 15, 1973, by Ahmed Abdallah, then Prime Minister of the Comoros, and the French Minister of Overseas Departments and Territories, providing for independence for the Comoro Islands within five years, provided approval of independence was obtained "in consultation with the populations of the archipelago". The declaration stated in particular: "The popular consultation summoned to endorse the independence of the territory, in the case of a positive response from the electorate, will have the effect of giving to the Chamber of Deputies of the territory in existence at that date the powers of a Constituent Assembly, and to the Prime Minister the powers of a head of state. ... The Chamber of Deputies will then have to draw up the constitution of a new state, which will preserve the rights and interests of the regional entities and which will be submitted to popular ratification."

The declaration also stated that relations between the French Republic and the Comoros would then be governed by co-operation agreements, and that during the transitional period governmental responsibility in the fields of finance, external trade, utilization of aid, education, justice and the maintenance of order was to be exercised by the Comoro government, which would also gradually take over from the French government responsibility for external relations, defence and civil aviation.

The MPM, however, strongly condemned any moves towards a negotiated independence

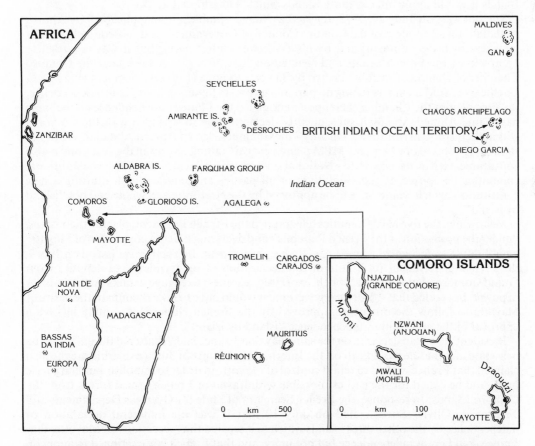

Map 14   The Indian Ocean islands off the eastern coast of Africa, illustrating the residual territorial claims of the Comoros, Madagascar and Mauritius against France and the Mauritius-UK dispute over Diego Garcia.

119

which did not provide for a referendum on an island-by-island basis. Ahmed Abdallah had stated on June 7, 1973, that in the independence referendum the four islands would be consulted collectively, since according to the terms of the law they constituted a single territorial entity. The referendum itself was held on Dec. 22, 1974, when a total of 154,184 votes (or 95.96 per cent of the valid votes) were cast in favour of independence, compared with only 8,854 votes against it. On Mayotte, however, 63 per cent of those who went to the polls were understood to have come out against and about 25 per cent of the 16,000 registered electors did not vote.

After a visit to the Comoros by a French parliamentary mission in March 1975 and the submission of its report, the French National Assembly adopted, on June 26, 1975 (by 291 votes to 184, the latter including the Socialists and Communists), a Comoro Islands Independence Bill. This bill provided for independence for the islands and for the creation, within six months from the promulgation of the act, of a constitutional committee (consisting of representatives of all political groups which had been allowed to take part in the December 1974 referendum campaign, the territory's representatives in the French National Assembly and Senate and the members of the Comoro Chamber of Deputies) to draw up a constitution guaranteeing the democratic freedom of citizens and the political and administrative individuality of the islands comprising the future state. This draft constitution was to be approved "island by island" by a majority of votes cast in a referendum; if one or several of the islands rejected the draft, the committee would have to submit a new text within three months, and if the new draft was not approved by all the islands it would apply only to those islands which had adopted it.

The bill was, on June 27, 1975, rejected as "unacceptable and inapplicable" by Ahmed Abdallah, then President of the Comoro Council of Government, and subsequently also by ministers of his government and by his *Oudzima* (Unity) party, but it was nevertheless approved by the French Senate and enacted on June 30, 1975. A week later the Comoro Chamber of Deputies (on July 6) voted by 33 votes to none (with one member being absent and the five MPM members taking no part in the vote) in favour of immediate independence; the President of the Chamber thereupon announced the islands' independence on the same day, while Ahmed Abdallah subsequently declared "the independence of the Comoros within their colonial frontiers". On July 7 the Chamber elected Ahmed Abdallah as head of state by 32 votes to one (with the MPM members again taking no part in the vote), and it also constituted itself as the new state's National Assembly and decided to set up a constitutional committee composed of representatives of all parties and charged with drafting a new constitution, which would have to be approved by the electorate as a whole and not "island by island".

Meanwhile, the five MPM deputies telegraphed the French President, placing their island "under the protection of the French Republic" and declaring that the population of Mayotte would refuse to recognize Ahmed Abdallah's government. In a statement issued on July 9, the French government took note of the declaration of independence of deputies from Grand Comoro, Anjouan and Mohéli, expressed readiness to engage in talks on the transfer of power, but added that the French government would have to take account of the desire of Mayotte to follow the procedure approved by the French National Assembly involving approval of the accession to independence "island by island".

President Abdallah declared on the same day that France had "shattered the unity" of the new state and that he would call on the International Court of Justice to arbitrate; he also claimed that France wished to retain control of Mayotte in order to establish a military base on it, and he called for the earliest possible withdrawal of French armed forces from the Comoro Islands. In response, the French Secretary of State for Overseas Departments and Territories (Olivier Stirn) stated on July 10 that it was the unilateral declaration of independence by the other three islands which had created the "secession" of Mayotte; that France could grant independence but not unity; and that French law continued to apply on Mayotte.

On July 22, 1975, the French government announced that it had decided to withdraw from

Grand Comoro the last remaining military detachment of 26 men. However, some 200 soldiers of the French Foreign Legion remained stationed on Mayotte, to which the French government had appointed a representative on July 14. On Aug. 1 pro-French demonstrators entered the French administration offices on Mayotte, asked officials of the newly-established independence government to leave and installed members of the local council in these offices and also appointed Younoussa Bamana (one of the MPM leaders) as prefect.

Developments following Deposition of President Abdallah

On Aug. 3, 1975, the government of President Abdallah was overthrown by armed supporters of the *Front uni national*, which combined four (pro-independence) opposition parties under the leadership of Ali Soilih. The latter declared on Aug. 3 that he wished to preserve the territorial integrity of the archipelago and to "maintain the ties of friendship and co-operation with France which have been broken by President Abdallah", whom he also accused of having "provoked" the break-up of the Comoros. On Aug. 10 the Revolutionary Council formed by Ali Soilih handed over its powers to a 12-member National Executive Council which included two members from Mayotte, one being a member of the MPM.

On Oct. 27, 1975, the National Executive Council claimed that 2,000 people, who had many years earlier moved from Anjouan to Mayotte, had been expelled from the latter island by the MPM. According to reports from Mayotte itself, at least 200 people had been forcibly expelled by the MPM which had threatened to use the French troops stationed on the island against them. The French authorities declared on Oct. 28 that no ships leaving Mayotte would be allowed to carry passengers and that earlier deportations would be the subject of an inquiry.

The following month, on Nov. 21, 1975, a total of 160 men led by Ali Soilih flew from Grand Comoro to Mayotte in an attempt to persuade the inhabitants of Mayotte to end their "secession", but they were met by a hostile crowd and withdrew from Mayotte after a few hours. At the same time, the National Executive Council decided to launch a "general mobilization for the cause of national liberation", and on Nov. 26 the Council declared that all property of the French administration on the Comoro Islands was the property of the new state (including a radio station and civil aviation equipment). Two days later, the Comoro authorities announced that all French nationals would be repatriated; accordingly, the teachers at the 1,000-pupil lycée in Moroni left and the school was closed on Dec. 2; the last of some 400 French nationals to leave was the French delegate-general (Henri Beaux) on Dec. 14.

A bill approved by the French government on Oct. 29, 1975, recognized the independence of Grand Comoro, Anjouan and Mohéli and provided for a referendum to be held on Mayotte within two months from the promulgation of the act in order to determine that island's future. If the decision was in favour of its remaining part of the French Republic, a second referendum to be held within another two months was to decide whether Mayotte was to be a French overseas department or an overseas territory. The bill was approved by the National Assembly (in amended form) on Dec. 10, 1975, by 300 votes to 179, and by the Senate on Dec. 31 by 198 votes to 78, and it was enacted on Dec. 31, 1975, when the three islands ceased to be part of the French Republic. During the proceedings, the then left-wing opposition claimed that the bill did not confirm to the French constitution and violated the UN Charter, and pointed out that the new state "of four islands" had been admitted to the United Nations [see below].

Comoro-French Relations following Ahmed Abdallah's Return to Power

On the three islands of the independent Comoro state, the Ali Soilih regime attempted to introduce a radical socialist system on the Chinese model, involving the suppression of traditional Islamic practices. However, the regime was overthrown on May 12-13 1978, in a coup organized with the help of Col. Robert Denard, a French mercenary. A new government of the state, henceforth to be known as the Federal and Islamic Republic of the Comoros, was set up by May 24 with the participation of ex-President Ahmed Abdallah as one of two co-presidents of a Political-Military Directory. Later that year, on Oct. 22, Ahmed Abdallah was, as the sole candidate, elected head of state with 99.95 per cent of the votes cast.

In a referendum held on the three islands on Oct. 1, 1978, a new constitution was approved by 99.31 per cent of the 187,124 voters. With regard to the situation of Mayotte, the constitution stated (in Article 44) that "where the regular functioning of the constitutional institutions is interrupted by force the present constitution's provisions relating to these institutions are suspended and the island [concerned] will provisionally exercise on its territory all powers previously held by the Federal Republic". In an order of Sept. 16 it had been stated that the constitution, when approved in the referendum, would be applied to Mayotte "as soon as the administration of Mayotte returns to the Comoro community".

Between the new government and France a treaty of friendship and co-operation and four co-operation agreements, including a military one, were signed on Nov. 10, 1978. Under the military agreement France was to supply aid in the event of external aggression against the Federal and Islamic Republic of the Comoros and to provide technical assistance in the training of the Comoro Army.

French Government's Position in the Dispute

The French government's attitude to the MPM's demand for continued close links between Mayotte and France was, generally speaking, that France was not opposed to such links but did not consider the granting of the status of a French department to Mayotte as appropriate. Pierre Messmer, then French Minister of State for Overseas Departments and Territories, declared during a visit to Mayotte in January 1972: "Mayotte, which has been French for 130 years, can remain French for as many years as it wishes. The population will be consulted to this end, and on that occasion a referendum will be held island by island."

In the event, however, the proposals approved by the government on Oct. 2, 1974, were for a global referendum on all four islands as one entity, although the government accepted amendments to its proposals, moved in the National Assembly and the Senate in November 1974, to the effect, inter alia, that parliamentary ratification of independence should not be sought until Mayotte had received a measure of regional autonomy as proposed by the Comoro Chamber of Deputies in January 1974.

President Giscard d'Estaing made a strong case for the unity of the Comoros at a press conference on Oct. 24, 1974, as follows: "The population of the Comoros is homogeneous, with a virtualy non-existent or very limited element of French descent. Was it reasonable, confronted with the request for independence presented by the government of the islands, to imagine part of the archipelago becoming independent and one island, however much one may sympathize with its inhabitants, retaining a different status? I think we have to accept contemporary realities. The Comoros are and always have been an entity, and it is natural for them to share a common destiny, even though some of them might have wanted a different solution, a fact that naturally touches us although we were not to act in consequence. It is not for us, on the occasion of a territory's independence, to propose to break up the unity of what has always been one Comoro archipelago."

During a visit to all four islands of the Comoros on Feb. 24-26, 1975, Olivier Stirn, then French Secretary of State for Overseas Departments and Territories, described the question of Mayotte as "an internal problem of the Comoros" which could be "settled within the framework of an agreement between the different parties on a draft constitution" which would embody "the maximum respect for a very broad autonomy of the islands". Subsequently, during the debate on the 1975 bill, Olivier Stirn denied that there was any link between the government's position and the maintenance of a naval base on Mayotte. (The island's large lagoon offers exceptionally good shelter to ships and, situated at the northern entrance to the Mozambique Channel, serves as base for a French fast patrol boat and as a staging post for French naval units in the Indian Ocean.)

The French government's objectives in Mayotte were redefined during a visit to the island on Sept. 10-11, 1980, by Paul Dijoud, who had been appointed Secretary of State for Overseas Departments and Territories on April 6, 1978. He said at public meetings and also before the island's mayors and members of its *conseil-général* (who were all members of the MPM) that the inhabitants of Mayotte should not be afraid of talking about their future; that public debates should be organized with all representatives of political life; and that all political parties should be enabled to express their views on the radio. He also said that Mayotte should make progress "within reason"; that the "irreversible" status of a department was not suitable for the conditions of the island; and that it ought to improve its relations with the rest of the archipelago. Before the elected representatives of the island he declared that France wished to raise the standard of living of the whole population, and not just that of a few to a great extent. (Since August 1975 Mayotte's development under French administration had been concentrated on the provision of roads, water and schools; electricity was first introduced in 1977, and the number of motor vehicles rose from 30 in 1971 to 800 in 1979.)

French Legislation and Administrative Measures concerning Mayotte

On Mayotte the first referendum provided for under the French act of Dec. 31, 1975, was held on Feb. 8, 1976, and (according to official results published on March 13) 18,061 voters or 83.3 per cent of the registered electorate of 21,671 took part in it; there were 17,949 valid votes, of which 17,845 (or 99.4 per cent of the votes cast) were for remaining with France and only 104 for union with the other Comoro islands.

In a second referendum held on April 11, 1976, Mayotte's voters were asked whether they wished the island "to retain its status as an overseas territory" or to abandon that status. As the voters were not expressly asked whether they favoured the status of an overseas department for Mayotte, the MPM had a third ballot paper printed (in addition to the two official ones, one for each alternative) containing the demand for overseas departmental status. The MPM realized that these additional ballot papers would be declared invalid, and it therefore instructed voters in certain areas to use the official ballot paper rejecting territorial status (to ensure the defeat of those who favoured maintenance of the existing territorial status), while massive casting of the unofficial ballot paper would make it clear that there was a majority in favour of departmental status.

In the event, the official result (announced on April 2) showed that of 21,659 registered voters 17,384 had taken part in the poll; 13,837 papers (or 79.59 per cent) had been blank or invalid; 3,547 (or 20.4 per cent) had been valid; and of those 3,457 (or 97.46 per cent of the valid votes) had been in favour of abandoning the overseas territory status and only 90 (or 2.53 per cent) in favour of maintaining it. Olivier Stirn commented afterwards that the result had shown that Mayotte wished to be given departmental status "now".

Following the introduction of the French franc as legal tender in Mayotte in February 1976, under a bill approved by the French government on Dec. 1, 1976, and passed, with amendments, by the National Assembly on Dec. 14 and by the Senate on Dec. 18, Mayotte was given a special status as a *"collectivité territoriale"*. According to this new status Mayotte was administered by a 17-member *conseil-général* elected by direct universal suffrage; a representative of the French government with the rank of prefect was in charge of national interests (including defence), administrative control and respect for the law; and laws which had applied in the Comoros before their independence remained valid on Mayotte. After at least three years from the date of the bill's promulgation of the people of Mayotte would, if the *conseil-général* demanded it by a two-thirds majority, be consulted on the statute which they wished to adopt. Under another bill passed at the same time a senator from Mayotte was to be elected to the French Senate in 1977.

After the opposition PRDM had, on the French administration's insistence, been allowed to broadcast its views, the MPM temporarily boycotted all prefectural activities and also instructed its followers to vote against the centrist UDF list in the elections to the European Parliament held on June 10, 1979. The result was that out of a total of 15,249 valid votes 13,826 were cast for the list headed by Jacques Chirac, i.e. the *Défense des intérêts de la France en Europe* (DIFE), opposed to the "Giscardian" UDF, with which the MPM had traditionally been associated.

In the general elections to the French National Assembly, held on March 16, 1986, the candidate of the *Union pour la démocatie française-Centre des démocrates sociaux* (UDF-CDS), i.e. of the MPM, was elected on the first round.

Hostile Attitude of United Nations and Organization of African Unity to French Status of Mayotte

The continued adherence of Mayotte to the French Republic was strongly opposed by a majority of the member states of the United Nations and by the Organization of African Unity (OAU). Thus the UN General Assembly unanimously decided on Nov. 12, 1974, with France not taking part in the vote, to approve a recommendation by the UN Security Council to accept the Comoros as a whole as a member of the United Nations. The French permanent representative at the United Nations explained that France did not wish to oppose the Comoros' admission but had to reconcile the need to facilitate the creation of the new state with the procedure required by the French constitution.

Upon an urgent call by Ali Soilih (then head of state of the Comoros) the UN Security Council met on Feb. 4-6, 1976, and eventually formulated a draft resolution declaring the proposed referendum on Mayotte to constitute interference in the Comoros' internal affairs, and calling on France to abandon the referendum and to hold immediate talks with the Comoro government on safeguarding that country's unity and territorial integrity. However, the draft resolution was vetoed by France, which had argued that the principle of self-determination would override that of territorial integrity, while Italy, the United Kingdom and the United States abstained from voting on the resolution.

A commission of inquiry sent to the Comoros in June 1976 by the UN General Assembly reported that the "French occupation" of Mayotte involved "atrocities", including the enforced marriage of women to French soldiers ("to make the island white") and the expulsion of Comoro citizens opposed to Mayotte's "illegal occupation", and that there existed a French military base on the island. The French Ministry of Defence stated, however, that it had no intention of establishing such a base on Mayotte.

On Oct. 21. 1976, the UN General Assembly called, by 102 votes to one (France) with 28 abstentions, on France to withdraw from Mayotte. The resolution condemned the Mayotte referendums as "null and void" and asked France to negotiate with the Comoro government on the integration of Mayotte in the independent Republic of the Comoros. The French permanent representative at the United Nations, however, declared that Mayotte was an integral part of France, that its inhabitants had freely chosen to remain so, and that France had no strategic ambitions on Mayotte, did not wish to recolonize it and would give it an "evolutionary" status.

On Dec. 6, 1979, the UN General Assembly adopted, by 112 votes to one (France) with 23 abstentions, a further resolution reaffirming the sovereignty of the Comoro Islands over Mayotte and calling on the French government to enter into early negotiations with the Comoro government in order to comply with UN resolutions in this matter, but the French permanent representative rejected the resolution as "impermissible interference in the internal affairs" of his country. On Nov. 28, 1980, the UN General Assembly reaffirmed "the sovereignty of the Islamic Federal Republic of the Comoros over the island of Mayotte" in a resolution adopted by 100 votes to one (France) with 26 abstentions. Virtually identical resolutions were adopted at subsequent Assembly sessions.

After the Comoros had, early in July 1975, been admitted as a member of the OAU, the latter also repeatedly condemned France for its continued "occupation" of Mayotte. On Dec. 15, 1976, the OAU rejected the bill passed by the French National Assembly on Dec. 14, granting Mayotte a special status within the French Republic. On July 8, 1978, however, the OAU Council of Ministers excluded the new Comoro government from current OAU sessions on the grounds that it had been installed with the help of a white mercenary. Nevertheless, the subsequent Assembly of Heads of State and Government of the OAU, held on July 18-22, 1978, again condemned the continuing presence of France on Mayotte.

At its session held in Freetown (Sierra Leone) on July 1-4, 1980, the OAU Assembly of Heads of State and Government decided to send to Moroni a committee of seven members to discuss with the Comorian government "appropriate means likely to speed up the settlement of the question". At its Assembly of Heads of State and Government held on July 28-30, 1986, the OAU again called for Mayotte's return to the Comoros.

December 1979 French Law on Status of Mayotte

In a further law, approved by the French Senate and the National Assembly and promulgated on Dec. 22, 1979, it was laid down that the island of Mayotte was "part of the French Republic and cannot cease to belong to it without the consent of its population"; and that within five years the people of Mayotte would be consulted, following the opinion of their *conseil-général*, as to whether the statute defined in the law of Dec. 26, 1976, should be maintained, or Mayotte should be made a department, or possibly a different statue should be adopted. Meanwhile, the government was authorized to extend by order, before Sept. 30, 1982, existing laws on internal affairs with amendments as deemed necessary. While the then left-wing opposition in the National Assembly abstained from voting on the legislation, the then deputy for Mayotte (Younoussa Bamana) voted against it and again called for departmental status for Mayotte.

Before the Assembly's law commission Paul Dijoud, Secretary of State for Overseas Departments and Territories, had earlier stated that the obstacles to giving departmental status to an island of whose population only 10 per cent spoke French were the lack of sanitary, social, economic and cultural structures, illiteracy, the specific character of its Moslem culture and customs, and underdevelopment.

French Reaffirmations of Status of Mayotte

On the relations between France and Mayotte the French Minister for External Relations stated in the French National Assembly on April 4, 1983, that the French government's objectives were to promote balanced and harmonious economic development in the Comoro archipelago while taking account of the specific needs of each island, and envisaged the implentation of co-operation projects corresponding to the aspirations of the whole population of the Comoros.

The French Prime Minister, Jacques Chirac, visited Mayotte on Oct. 1, 1986, when he reaffirmed his government's decision to maintain Mayotte's status as a French territory as long as the island's population wished it; he added that he would make this clear to the President of the Comoros in talks with him the same day. Chirac also undertook to carry out in Mayotte a five-year programme to bring the island to the level of development necessary for the status of an overseas department.

HWD

Ethiopia-Somalia

The status of the Ogaden area, regarded by the Ethiopian government as belonging to the country's eastern provinces of Hararghe, Bale and Sidamo, has been called into dispute by the successive governments of Somalia since that country's independence in 1960. The Somalis refer to the area as Western Somalia, and regard it as a Somali-inhabited region under foreign (Ethiopian) domination, for which they assert that the principle of self-determination should be applied. (For Somalia's related dispute with Kenya, see pages 144-50.)

Properly speaking, the name "Ogaden" refers to a geographical area defined by its physical characteristics as the Ogaden desert rather than by clearly demarcated political boundaries. A sub-area known as the Haud or Reserve, lying on the southern side of the border of former British Somaliland, is generally also included when reference is made to the "Ogaden dispute". Insofar as the disputed area can be defined precisely, it is that area inhabited by nomadic pastoral peoples belonging ethnically to the Somali nation, their numbers being variously estimated at between one and three million. Somali irredentist claims have also a historical dimension, that the Somali tribes of the Horn of Africa constituted one political system prior to the colonial divisions of territory in the late 19th century. Prior to 1886, according to the Somali view, effective Ethiopian sovereignty extended no further eastward than the line of the Awash river, i.e. excluding the towns of Diredawa, Harar and Jijiga and the whole of the now-disputed area, and it was only in the last part of the 19th century, as the European powers were establishing their authority over what became British and Italian Somaliland, that the Ethiopian empire extended its control eastwards, to the limits set in subsequent agreements with the British and Italians [see below].

A brief summary is given below of historical developments affecting the disputed area up to the establishment of an independent Somali Republic in former British and Italian Somaliland in 1960. This is followed by an account of the nature of the conflicting arguments put forward by the parties to the dispute, and an indication of the extent to which such arguments have found international acceptance. The chapter concludes with a review of the manner in which the dispute has been pursued since 1960.

Historical Developments up to 1960

The British protectorate on the northern Somali coast, which was to become British Somaliland, was established in a series of treaties concluded with local tribes in 1884-86. Its extent was to be limited both by competing Italian ambitions (resulting in the establishment of Italian Somaliland) and, to the west, by the consolidation of authority in 1886-92 by the Ethiopian Emperor Menelek II.

Ethiopian successes included the capture in 1887 of the independent Moslem citadel of Harar and the installation of Ras Makunan (father of the late Emperor Haile Selassie of Ethiopia) as governor of Harar and its dependencies. The Ethiopian Emperor, in his circular letter to the European powers in 1891, declared that Ethiopia "has been for centuries a Christian island in a sea of pagans". The letter went on to state that "if powers at a distance come forward to partition Africa between them, I do not intend to be an independent spectator". In a military campaign culminating in the Battle of Adowa in 1896, the Ethiopian empire successfully defended its independence vis-à-vis Italian imperialist aspirations. The borders between Ethiopia and the British and Italian protectorates in Somaliland were the subject of treaties in the ensuing period which left the Somali-inhabited Ogaden area under Ethiopian jurisdiction.

The treaty between Ethiopia and Britain, signed on May 14, 1897, established a boundary between Ethiopia and British Somaliland which was subsequently demarcated by an Anglo-Ethiopian boundary commission in 1932-35 (an agreed report being signed in Addis Ababa on March 28, 1935). This boundary was that existing at the time of Somalia's independence in 1960. Its alignment explicitly accepted that certain Somali tribespeople would come under Ethiopian jurisdiction; thus in Annex 1 to the 1897 treaty the British envoy required and obtained of the Ethiopian Emperor an assurance that "in the event of a possible occupation by Ethiopia of territories inhabited by tribes who have formerly accepted and enjoyed British protection in the districts excluded from the British protectorate ... it will be your special care that these tribes receive equitable treatment and are thus no losers by this transfer of suzerainty". In Annex 3, agreed on June 4, 1897, the representatives of both sides agreed that "the tribes occupying either side of the line shall have the right to use the grazing grounds on the other side, but during their migrations it is understood that they shall be subject to the jurisdiction of the territorial authority". These treaty-based grazing rights were in existence until Somalia's independence in 1960, at which time the Ethiopian government took the position that they would cease to exist.

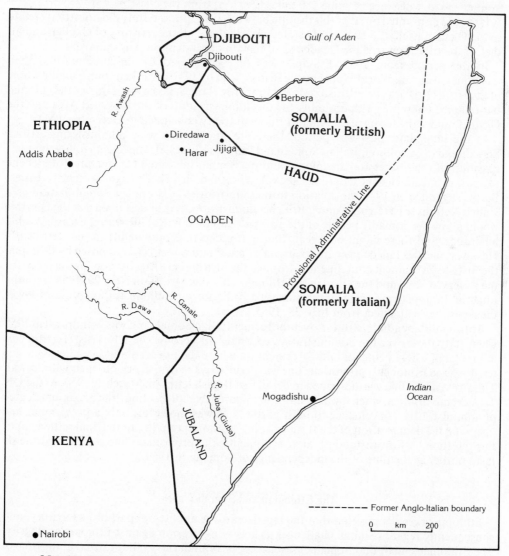

Map 15   Present territorial relationship of Somalia with Djibouti, Ethiopia and Kenya.

127

The boundary between Ethiopia and Italian Somaliland was rather more complex. The 1896 peace treaty signed on Oct. 26 stated that the frontier should be settled within one year, but this was not done until 1908, when a further treaty was concluded (on May 16). The fact that the two sides gave different interpretations to this agreement, as to the line of the frontier, made it impossible for a joint boundary commission to complete its work of delimitation and demarcation, and the precise alignment intended by the 1908 treaty was still in dispute at the time of Somali independence in 1960. Essentially, the Ethiopians maintained that a frontier line agreed in negotiations in 1897 between Emperor Menelek and the Italian representative, Maj. Nerazzini, ran more or less parallel with the coast and 140 miles (225 km) from it, to a tripoint with British Somaliland. The Ethiopian contention was that the southern part of this frontier (from Dolo to the Uebi Scebeli river) was then pushed northward in favour of Italy in return for the payment of 3,000,000 lire, as stipulated in an Additional Act to the 1908 treaty. The Italian interpretation was that the Menelek-Nerazzini agreement in 1897 (to which the 1908 treaty refers only as "the line accepted by the Italian government in 1897") covered only the frontier north of the Uebi Scebeli river and that this frontier ran at a distance of some 180 miles (290 km) from the coast.

It should be pointed out that this dispute between Ethiopia and Italy did not strictly relate to the Ogaden itself; the 1908 treaty stated clearly that "all the territory of Ogaden and all that of the tribes towards the Ogaden shall remain dependent on Abyssinia".

In the period from 1935, Ethiopia was first conquered by the Italians, and then reconquered during World War II by the British, who by 1941 had taken control of the whole of the Horn of Africa. The British restored Emperor Haile Selassie to his throne in Ethiopia, but retained temporary responsibility for the administration of the Reserved Area and the Ogaden, under the terms of an Anglo-Ethiopian treaty concluded in December 1944.

In the immediate post-war period, therefore, the British were administering British Somaliland (as a colony), Italian Somaliland (under military arrangements following their conquest of the former Italian colony) and the Somali-inhabited Ogaden area (under the temporary arrangements described above). The then British Foreign Secretary, Ernest Bevin, suggested in 1948 the creation in these territories of a unified Somali nation as a United Nations trust territory under British administration. As he described it at the UN, this would allow the nomadic people of the area to "lead their frugal life with the least possible hindrance, and there might be a real chance of a decent economic life in that territory". However, the idea failed to win international support and was strongly opposed by Ethiopia; the British government consequently dropped the idea and made provision for the return of the Reserved Area and the Ogaden to Ethiopia. This was agreed on Nov. 29, 1954, with the Imperial Ethiopian government reassuming jurisdiction and administration of, in and over the territories with effect from Feb. 28, 1955.

British military administration over the former Italian Somaliland was withdrawn in 1950 when Italy took over the administration of what had become the UN Trust Territory of Somaliland. There being still no agreement on where the border should run between this territory and Ethiopia, a provisional line was defined by the British prior to their withdrawal. This provisional line was described in detail in a British letter on March 1, 1950, to the UN Trusteeship Council, when it was justified as apparently representing "the maximum degree of administrative convenience to both parties". It was, however, only a provisional line "pending the demarcation of the frontier" and "without prejudice to the final settlement of this question". Notwithstanding these sentiments, the provisional line represented the de facto border at the time of the independence of Somalia in 1960.

The Ethiopian and Somali Cases

Ethiopia takes the position that the Ogaden area is an integral part of its territory, and consequently regards Somali challenges as acts of aggression against Ethiopia's integrity. The Ethiopians insist that Somalia must accept its boundaries as they existed at the time of independence, i.e. in 1960. They consider that the northern sector of the boundary was defined beyond any possibility of subsequent argument by the Anglo-Ethiopian treaty of 1897, substantiated by the demarcation of the boundary in 1932-35. (However, the Ethiopian government took the position in 1960 that trans-border grazing rights as provided by their agreements with the British would cease to apply after Somalia became independent.) With regard to the southern sector of the boundary, the Ethiopians base their position on the existence of the 1908 treaty between Ethiopia and Italy. Their contention is that a dispute with Somalia could only properly exist within the framework of the known Ethiopian-Italian disagreement over interpretation of that 1908 treaty. Such a dispute, it is argued, would be susceptible to resolution by careful inquiry into the treaty, and possibly by arbitration over its meaning.

The Somali argument is that the Ogaden area, to which they refer as Western Somalia, is inhabited by ethnic Somalis and belonged to the historic Somali nation, before undergoing foreign conquest during the colonial period. According to the Somali position, the area should be viewed as a case for decolonization; the fact that the colonial conquest was not by a European power but by an African one (the "Black Abyssinian imperialists", as the Ethiopians are frequently termed in Somali propaganda) should not affect this principle, in the Somali view. The government of Somalia accordingly presents itself in the role of supporter of an indigenous liberation struggle for the right to self-determination of the people of so-called Western Somalia.

The objective of Somali nationalism and irredentism has been to secure the independence of each of the five parts into which the Somali nation was divided in the colonial period. It was assumed that a unified Somali state would then be formed by the voluntary merger of these five parts. Independent Somalia as established in 1960 consisted of two of these units (former British and Italian Somaliland); the new country's constitution included a commitment to furthering the process, and the ideal of unity is symbolized by the five-pointed star on Somalia's flag. "Western Somalia", with its estimated one to three million inhabitants, is the most populous of the three Somali-inhabited areas remaining outside the Somali state (the other two being what is now Djibouti and the north-eastern part of Kenya).

The Organization of African Unity (OAU), when it was set up in 1963, was immediately faced with the existence of this dispute between two of its member countries. The Somali government sought to involve the OAU in the matter by calling for a plebiscite to establish the wishes of the inhabitants of the Ogaden. The Ethiopians meanwhile condemned as an act of aggression the support given by Somalia to ethnic Somali guerrilla forces in the area. Somalia referred to Article III of the OAU Charter, setting out the organization's principles including the inalienable right of each state to independent existence, and (in 1964 and 1965 respectively) called for an OAU fact-finding mission and for direct discussions to be held with Ethiopian leaders in Khartoum. These proposals came to nothing, in the face of (i) Ethiopia's insistence that its territorial integrity was not open to any discussion, and (ii) the great reluctance of African leaders in general to encourage any variation in the African state boundaries inherited from the colonial period. It should be noted, however, that the key resolution on the latter theme—adopted by the OAU Assembly of Heads of State and Government in Cairo in July 1964 and solemnly declaring "that all member states pledge themselves to respect the borders existing on their achievment of national independence"— was not accepted by Somalia.

Conflict in the Disputed Area, 1964-80

Relations between Ethiopia and Somalia deteriorated as far as a brief direct military conflict in 1964 over the question of Somali government support for guerrillas in the Ogaden. Somali irredentist feeling was held more strictly in check after 1967 by the government of Mohammed Ibrahim Egal, who favoured a policy of dialogue with Somalia's neighbours. According to a communiqué published simultaneously in Addis Ababa and Mogadishu on Sept. 22, 1967, Ethiopia and Somalia agreed to "eliminate all forms of tension" between themselves, to establish a joint military commission to examine complaints by either side, and to "perfect co-operation" by means of quarterly meetings of their administrative authorities.

After the military takeover in Somalia in 1969 and the military overthrow of the Ethiopian Emperor in 1974, the Somali government led by Gen. Siyad Barreh sought to re-open the Ogaden question in a diplomatic initiative towards Ethiopia. However, the new Ethiopian regime showed itself no less intent than its imperial predecessor on retaining possession of the Ogaden. Under these circumstances, the government of Somalia in 1977 ceased its attempt to restrain the militant irredentism of Ogaden Somali groups, principal of which was the Western Somalia Liberation Front (WSLF), together with the Somali Abo Liberation Front (SALF).

Guerrilla violence in the Ogaden escalated in mid-1977 to the point of full-scale direct warfare, with heavy casualties on both sides. An initial phase of the war was characterized by Somali successes, including notably the capture of the town of Jijiga in September 1977 and an advance as far as Harar by November. A successful Ethiopian counter-offensive was launched in January 1978 with the backing of Soviet and Cuban forces (the Soviet Union having in 1977 reversed its former policy of providing military aid to the Somali government). Ethiopian forces recaptured Jijiga in early March 1978 and regained control of strategic points in the region. However, despite the maintenance of Ethiopian garrisons in a network of towns and villages in the Ogaden, Somali-backed guerrilla forces remained active in the countryside and continued to broadcast (by radio from Mogadishu) claims of heavy casualties inflicted against Ethiopian and Cuban troops.

It was not until Feb. 21, 1978, that the Somali government had acknowledged the presence of its troops in the Ogaden area alongside WSLF forces. Prior to this acknowledgement, the Somali government had alleged that the Ethiopians were not fighting only in the Ogaden as they claimed, but that they were also launching air attacks on towns over the border in Somalia. A general mobilization was declared in Somalia on Feb. 9, 1978, and on the following day Cyrus Vance, the US Secretary of State, declared that the US would supply arms to Somalia in the event of Ethiopian aggression. Responding to a ceasefire proposal made by the US, the Somali government announced on March 8 that all Somali regular troops would be withdrawn from the Ogaden area. The following day a further announcement appealed to the great powers to ensure "the withdrawal of all foreign forces present in the Horn of Africa", called for "recognition by the interested parties of the right to self-determination" of the Ogaden people, and looked for the initiation of a process which would lead to "a negotiated, peaceful, just and durable settlement". The Ethiopian government responded on March 11, 1978, and has subsequently repeatedly reiterated, that one requirement for a just and durable peace would be unconditional abandonment by Somalia of all claims to territory in Ethiopia, Kenya and Djibouti, and the abrogation of all juridical bases for such claims.

The Ogaden dispute continued after the 1977-78 war, with guerrilla warfare and heavy casualties, and the Somali government giving its backing to the guerrillas while denying Ethiopian allegations that its regular troops were involved. Somalia also made repeated complaints of Ethiopian air raids on its territory, while in human terms the conflict led to many hundreds of thousands of displaced persons pouring into refugee camps in both Somalia and Ethiopia, with a resultant heavy burden being placed on both the Ethiopian and Somali economies and on international relief organizations.

There was an apparent increase in tension between Ethiopia and Somalia in 1980, with reciprocal allegations of attempted invasions. By the end of that year Ethiopian forces had reoccupied almost all the territory of the Ogaden up to the Somali border, having expelled from it most of the WSLF guerrilla forces.

A restatement of the Ethiopian position was contained in a joint Ethiopian-Kenyan communiqué issued in Nairobi on Dec. 4, 1980, following a visit there by Lt.-Col. Mengistu Haile Mariam, the Ethiopian head of state. The communiqué emphasized co-operation against what was described as Somali expansionism and called on Somalia to "renounce publicly and unconditionally all claims to the territories of Ethiopia, Kenya and Djibouti".

Referring to international principles of the inviolability of frontiers and non-interference in internal affairs, it called on Somalia to withdraw its reservation (entered on July 23, 1964) whereby Somalia had refused to be bound by the 1964 OAU resolution on the acceptance of frontiers existing at independence. The communiqué referred to the intention of the Kenyan and Ethiopian governments of eliminating "the root cause of tension and insecurity in the region" and called on all countries to cease military assistance to Somalia.

In the latter context, the United States and Somalia had negotiated an agreement in August 1980 allowing US use of Somali base facilities. The implementation of this agreement, which provided for US military assistance to Somalia for the purchase of large quantities of "defensive weapons and equipment", was delayed until January 1981, the US Congress having insisted that the State Department should first provide "verified assurances" that there were no Somali troops in the Ogaden area.

The Somali government responded to the Ethiopian-Kenyan communiqué, which it described as provocative and threatening, by urging "the Somali people whereever they are" to be ready to defend their national sovereignty and their motherland. A statement issued by the Somali government on Dec. 7, 1980, commented inter alia that the Kenyan government had been ensnared in an Ethiopian trap, and called on both countries to withdraw their communiqué, which it described as tantamount to a declaration of war.

1981 OAU Resolution adopted against Somali Objections

The apparently intractable nature of the Ethiopia-Somalia dispute has meant that there has been little prospect of successful mediation during the period since Somalia attained independence. An eight-member OAU "good offices" committee was set up in 1973, at a time when the dispute was in a less acute phase, and the OAU committee held a meeting in Lagos on Aug. 18-20, 1980, which ended with the reaffirmation of the OAU's principles for the resolution of disputes. Although both Ethiopia and Somalia claimed this to be a vindication of their own position, it was generally seen as underlining, by one more instance, the failure of Somalia to win support for changing the status of the Ogaden area. The OAU 18th Assembly of Heads of State and Government, held in Nairobi on June 24-28, 1981, adopted against Somali objections a resolution reaffirming that the Ogaden was "an integral part of Ethiopia", condeming all subversion and use of force against Ethiopia, but also calling for efforts to bring together the Ethiopians and the Somalis for a round-table summit conference to work out a lasting solution to the problems in the Horn of Africa.

The Somali government, claiming that continuing Ethiopian air raids and artillery attacks against Somali territory had caused nearly 200 deaths between November 1979 and June 1981, asserted that Somalia was indeed willing to co-operate in finding a peaceful solution, but that Ethiopia was unwilling to respond. President Barreh said on June 29, 1981, that he was prepared for talks immediately over the disputed Ogaden territory, that Somalia did not seek territorial expansion, and that he would try to persuade WSLF guerrillas to cease hostilities. Lt.-Col. Mengistu for his part said in Addis Ababa on June 18, 1982, that Ethiopia was prepared to forget the past and hold peaceful talks with Somalia; each side, however, accused the other of insincerity.

Intensified Border Fighting in 1982—Continuing Sporadic Hostilities—Barreh-Mengistu Meeting in January 1986 and Creation of Joint Ministerial Committee

A year of only occasional WSLF activities in the Ogaden was followed by an apparent increase in actions in mid-1982, and then by a marked intensification in border fighting in late June 1982. President Barreh claimed in a message on July 12 to President Moi of Kenya (current OAU President) that Ethiopia was preparing for full-scale war. President Moi on July 14 called for an immediate ceasefire and appealed to Ethiopia to desist from any action which could plunge the entire region into war. On July 24 a US State Department spokesman confirmed that the USA had begun airlifting military equipment to Somalia (as also had

Italy) "in connexion with the recent incursion by Ethiopia and Ethiopian-backed forces". By early August it appeared that Ethiopian-backed forces were holding positions some 20 miles inside Somalia. Over subsequent years (for instance on Feb. 20, 1985) Somalia repeatedly complained that parts of central Somalia along the border had been under Ethiopian occupation since July 1982, the village of Gholdogob being cited frequently in this connexion.

The Arab League at its summit meeting in Fez on Sept. 6-9, 1982, declared its full backing for Somali efforts to "drive out the Ethiopian forces from Somali territory", after which the League would support the sovereignty and independence of each state.

The Ethiopian government claimed, in relation to the mid-1982 border fighting and all subsequent allegations of Ethiopian involvement, that its forces were not involved in any violation of Somali territory. Ethiopia characterized the fighting inside Somalia as purely an internal Somali affair, ascribing it to opponents of the Barreh regime (three anti-Barreh groups having come together in October 1981 to form a Somali Democratic Salvation Front, while a fourth such group remained active as the Somali National Movement). The fighting apparently entered a more intense phase once again inside Somalia in June and July 1983. WSLF spokesmen also claimed that Ethiopian forces had massacred civilians in the Ogaden in September 1982 and September 1983 in retaliation after guerrilla attacks.

As a result of lengthy Italian mediation efforts, the two sides were eventually brought together for a meeting in Djibouti on Jan. 17-18, 1986, between President Barreh and Lt.-Col. Mengistu, following a summit meeting of members of the Permanent Inter-Governmental Authority on Drought and Development. The meeting was the first between the two leaders since a Cuban-sponsored meeting in March 1977 before the outbreak of the Ogaden war. It resulted in the creation of a joint committee to improve relations, and this committee met for the first time at the level of Foreign Ministers in Addis Ababa on May 7-9, 1986, when the Ethiopian Foreign Minister, Lt.-Col. Goshu Wolde, declared that Ethiopia maintained its demand that the Somali government should recognize existing territorial boundaries. Further meetings of the committee took place in Mogadishu in August 1986 and in Addis Ababa on April 1-3, 1987, although this most recent meeting was preceded by renewed fighting in February 1987, described by Somalia as an Ethiopian attack and by Ethiopia as an anti-Barreh offensive by the Somali National Movement.

RE

France-Madagascar

There exists a dispute between the governments of France and of Madagascar concerning sovereignty over a number of small islands, originally uninhabited, off the coast of Madagascar, and having a total area of 28 square kilometres (about 11 square miles). These islands are the Glorioso Islands (Iles Glorieuses) to the north of Madagascar, as well as Juan de Nova, Bassas da India and Europa, situated in the Mozambique Channel. (For map illustrating this dispute, see page 119.)

The islands in question have been under French sovereignty since 1896 and are administered by the prefect of the French overseas department of Réunion (east of Madagascar and south-west of Mauritius) through the intermediary of Réunion's Director of Meteorological Services, who has stationed personnel on them for weather observation (except on Bassas da India, which is almost totally submerged at high tide). Since December 1973 the French government has had small "symbolic" contingents drawn from a parachute regiment (itself stationed on Réunion) on each of these islands (again except Bassas da India), and an airstrip on Juan de Nova has been enlarged so as to enable Transall transport aircraft to use it. The government of Madagascar, however, has forbidden such aircraft to overfly Malagasy territory, and all supplies flown in from Réunion to the islands in the Mozambique Channel are therefore flown round the northern end of Madagascar.

The government of Madagascar has persisted in claiming sovereignty over the islands. During negotiations conducted on new co-operation agreements between France and Madagascar, President Didier Ratsiraka of Madagascar stated on May 22, 1973, that the problem of these islands had been raised by his government in the talks; that the French government had, however, replied that the question would be settled later between the two governments; that no agreement or consensus had been reached on the question and that it had therefore not been dealt with within the framework of the co-operation agreements; and that the dispute might eventually be placed before the International Court of Justice.

In September 1973 the government of Madagascar announced that it had extended its territorial waters limit to 90 kilometres (56 miles) and that of its continental shelf to 180 kilometres (112 miles) from its coasts so as to include the above-mentioned islands, and it accordingly informed the United nations in 1976. In an interview given in June 1976 President Ratsiraka said: "We are not giving up hope that one day these islands will revert to us. I do not see why France should not surrender them seeing that it has granted independence to all its former colonies in Asia and Africa". The French government, on the other hand, under a decree of Feb. 3, 1978, declared exclusive 200-mile (320-km) economic zones around its dependencies in the Indian Ocean, expressly including the above-mentioned islands.

On March 21 of that year the government of Madagascar officially protested against the French decision to include the islands in France's exclusive economic zone and affirmed that the Iles Glorieuses, Juan de Nova, Bassas da India and Europa were "an integral part of Madagascar's territory". In this protest no mention was made of the island of Tromelin, about 560 kilometres, or 350 miles, north of Réunion, also included in the French government decree of Feb. 3, 1978; the government of Madagascar had in fact ceded its claim for this island to Mauritius, which had claimed it for itself.[1]

Madagascar's claim was, however, not raised by President Ratsiraka when he visited Paris on Sept. 24-27, 1978, and had discussions with President Giscard d'Estaing, with the result of which he afterwards declared himself to be "fairly satisfied". A statement made in May 1979 by Rear-Admiral Jean-Paul Orosco, then commander of French naval forces in the Indian Ocean, reiterated that the disputed islands formed part of the French dependencies in the Indian Ocean, the defence of which would have to be conducted from the French base in Djibouti.

Endorsement of Madagascar's Claim by the UN General Assembly

At the request of Madagascar the United Nations General Assembly took up the question of the sovereignty over these islands in 1979 and 1980. The UN General Assembly, in a resolution (34/91) adopted on Dec. 12, 1979, noted Madagascar's claim for the reintegration in its territory of the Iles Glorieuses, Juan de Nova, Bassas da India and Europa; requested the government of France to repeal measures which "infringe the sovereignty and territorial integrity of Madagascar"; and called on the French government to initiate negotiations with Madagascar on the reintegration of these islands in Madagascar. The resolution was approved by 93 votes to seven (Belgium, France, Italy, Luxembourg, Senegal, the United Kingdom and the United States) with 36 abstentions (including other Western countries).

The Special Political Committee of the UN General Assembly (which has the same composition as the Assembly) adopted, on Nov. 25, 1980, a resolution demanding that the islands, which, the committee claimed, had been "arbitrarily separated" from Madagascar,

---

[1] For an account of the Tromelin Island dispute, see pages 136-37.

should be returned to that country. The resolution was passed by 83 votes to 13 (Belgium, France, the Federal Republic of Germany, Greece, Guatemala, Honduras, Italy, Luxembourg, Morocco, the Netherlands, Senegal, the United Kingdom and the United States) with 32 abstentions.

In a further resolution (35/123), adopted on Dec. 11, 1980, by 81 votes to 13 with 37 abstentions, the UN General Assembly expressed regret that the negotiations envisaged in its previous resolution had not been initiated; took note of a report of the UN Secretary-General on the subject; and again invited France urgently to initiate negotiations with Madagascar in order to settle the question "in accordance with the purposes and principles of the United Nations". Those voting against this resolution included the member states of the European Community except Denmark and Ireland (which both abstained) and also the United States. Thereafter the question of the disputed islands remained on the Assembly's agenda, although since 1981 active consideration of the issue has been repeatedly deferred with the consent of Madagascar.

Madagascar's Appeals to the OAU and the Non-Aligned Movement

In an explanatory statement deposited with the Organization of African Unity (OAU) the government of the Democratic Republic of Madagascar declared inter alia that on April 1, 1960 (on the eve of Madagascar's achievement of independence), France had presented Madagascar with a *fait accompli* by the arbitrary detachment of the islands from Madagascar and their transfer to the direct control of the French Ministry of Overseas Departments and Territories; that under a decree of Sept. 19, 1960 (confirmed on March 11, 1972, and April 17, 1973), the French government had entrusted the administration of the islands to the prefect of Réunion; but that until 1960 France had consistently confirmed the "organic unity" of Madagascar and the islands; that under international law a state had "a natural right of sovereignty" over nearby small islands; that the government of Madagascar therefore intended to denounce all measures taken by France in relation to the disputed islands, to ask for the opening of significant negotiations on the subject, and to inform regional and national organizations accordingly.

The government of Madagascar also stated that it had denounced the progressive militarization of the islands and their inclusion in a strategy which was incompatible with the demands of national and regional security and with the creation of a zone of peace in the Indian Ocean; had protested against the French declaration of 200-mile economic zones round the islands; had taken part in the work of a joint Franco-Malagasy commission from March to June 1979, without result; had placed the question before the OAU in July 1979 and before the Non-Aligned Movement in September 1979, with the result that (i) the 16th OAU Assembly of Heads of State and Government (in Monrovia on July 12-17, 1979) had approved a resolution stating that the islands were an integral part of the territory of the Democratic Republic of Madagascar and inviting the French government to restore them to Madagascar, and (ii) the sixth conference of heads of state and government of Non-Aligned countries (in Havana on Sept. 3-9, 1979) had similarly demanded the restoration of the islands to Madagascar.

French Rejection of UN Resolutions

In a statement made in reply to claims made by the permanent representative of Madagascar at the UN General Assembly, Jacques Leprette, the French permanent representative at the United Nations, said before the vote of Dec. 11, 1980, inter alia: "The territories concerned have been part of the French Republic since the last century. These small islands, with a total area of about 11 square miles, were 'vacant lands without owner' and without any population. They were taken possession of under international law within the legal forms required and without any protest from the international community. These territories were [on April 1, 1960] placed under the authority of the [French] Minister of

Overseas Departments and Territories. The government of Madagascar took note of this situation on April 2, 1960, when the first series of co-operation agreements with France was concluded. On the legal level ... French sovereignty, which had been uncontested until recent years, has never been interrupted since its inception. It has been expressed by the effective and continued exercise of state functions".

Stating that Madagascar's claim to the islands was in conflict with Article 2, Paragraph 7, of the UN Charter (laying down that "nothing in the Charter shall authorize the United Nations to intervene in matters which are essentially within the domestic jurisdiction of any state"), the French representative also rejected the argument of "contiguity" (advanced by the representative of Madagascar) as not recognized in international law and as inapplicable to territories at a distance of 150 to 380 kilometres (about 90 to 240 miles). The delimitation of such territories, he said, must be effected in agreement between neighbouring states, and he continued: "If any coastal state were able to claim all the islands situated at less than 200 miles off its coasts the world's political map would be overturned and world peace would be threatened".

The French representative also rejected the Malagasy argument that the islands were part of the continental shelf of Madagascar, stating that in fact they were separated from Madagascar by ocean depths of more than 3,000 metres. In this context he referred to a decision by the International Court of Justice laying down that parts of the continental shelf situated at about 100 miles (160 km) from a coast, or separated from these coasts by a trench, could not be regarded as lying adjacent to the coast.

On the constitutional aspect he said that the decision of Oct. 15, 1958 (when Madagascar became an autonomous republic within the French Community), which rendered void the law on the annexation of Madagascar, contained no mention of the islands in question; that they had not been annexed at the same time as Madagascar but had been the object of a direct occupation; and that they could therefore not be regarded as dependencies of Madagascar. He also emphasized that the question was not one of decolonization, as these islands lacked all resources, even drinking water, and had never been able to sustain any living soul.

Following Madagascar's achievement of full independence on June 26, 1960, the property records of the Iles Glorieuses and of Juan de Nova (there being none for Bassas da India, Europa or Tromelin), which had been held by the French authorities in Madagascar, were transferred to the French ambassador to Madagascar; the French government regarded this fact as implying recognition of French sovereignty over the islands by Madagascar.

French Statements of Intent, 1981 and 1984

On Oct. 1, 1981, it was reported that President Ratsiraka had stated that France was ready to negotiate on the question of the disputed islands in the Indian Ocean and that his government was "satisfied with this promise". The French Minister for External Relations thereupon declared in the French Senate on Nov. 4, 1981, that the Malagasy position on the islands was "essentially based on an argument not recognized in international law", i.e. that of proximity; that the French government "must look after France's interests in that region of the world and the development of her relations of co-operation and friendship both with Madagascar and with the region's other states"; and that France would "be committed only by her own official statements on this subject".

On June 11, 1984, the minister declared in the French National Assembly: "The government is intent on conducting in the Indian Ocean an active policy both as regards development aid and increasing France's influence in the cultural and other fields in that region, particularly as a result of the spread of francophony. To this end, it is according priority to giving greater substance to its relations with the various partners in the area, which are currently developing in a climate of restored trust. It is in that spirit that it is looking at the question of the scattered islands and it does not intend refusing a dialogue, once our partners have expressed a desire to start discussions on that issue. The fact that, since 1981, the Malagasy authorities have agreed to postpone the debate on that question at every session of the United Nations General Assembly, bears witness to the spirit in which they now intend to see that aspect of our friendly relations evolve. The government considers that the conditions appear right for finding a solution to the question of the scattered islands that can take into account all the legitimate interests of the partners involved, particularly those which France regards as fundamental."

In January 1986, the government of Madagascar decreed the extension of its exclusive economic zone to 200 nautical miles from the shore and a reduction in its territorial waters limit from 56 to 12 miles "in accordance with the new International Law of the Sea". The decree was intended in part to reassert Madagascar's claim to the disputed islands.

HWD

France-Mauritius (Tromelin Island)

The government of Mauritius formally claimed sovereignty, with retroactive effect from 1814, over the island of Tromelin in a document presented to the French ambassador to Mauritius by the latter's Prime Minister on April 2, 1976, and the French government officially rejected this claim on Dec. 17, 1976. (For map illustrating this dispute, see page 119.)

The island of Tromelin, situated about 450 kilometres (280 miles) east of Madagascar and 550 kilometres (340 miles) north of Mauritius and the island of Réunion (a French overseas department), consists of a volcano which is crowned by a coral plateau and the ocean floor around which is about 4,000 metres deep. Its total area is only about one square kilometre, and its highest point rises to only seven metres above sea-level. The island has no economic importance (except for the export of turtles), there is no fresh water and no agriculture is possible. It is difficult of access by sea but has a landing strip suitable for light aircraft only.

Tromelin was discovered by French seafarers in 1722 and was named after a Frenchman who landed there in 1776. There is no evidence that the French government ever announced its occupation or notified foreign powers of such occupation, but the island's status was not in dispute until the middle of the 20th century.

At the first session of the regional association of the World Meteorological Organization (WMO) held in Antananarivo (Madagascar) in January 1953 France was asked to examine the possibility of setting up a weather observation station on Tromelin. According to some sources, the British government acceded to a request by the French meteorological services in Madagascar to be allowed to set up such a station on Tromelin. A permanent observation station was eventually set up on the island by France on May 7, 1954, which thus constituted a date of effective French occupation of Tromelin. At a further WMO congress held in 1959, however, Mauritius declared that it considered Tromelin to be part of its territory. The French delegation stated in reply that France had always considered the island to be French and that the French title to it dated back to the island's discovery by a Frenchman in 1722. Since 1961 the weather station on Tromelin has been attached to the French meteorological service in St Denis (Réunion), although it has functioned in liaison with Madagascar's service, which has, however, made no financial contribution to the cost of its operation.

Until 1960 Tromelin was administered from Madagascar, which after its achievement of independence had also laid claim to the island. After 1976, however, this claim was waived in favour of Mauritius, as confirmed by President Didier Ratsiraka during a visit to Madagascar by Paul Bérenger, a leader of the left-wing Mauritian Militant Movement, which had emerged as the strongest political party in general elections held in Mauritius in 1976.

The government of Mauritius—since its achievement of independence on March 12, 1968, the legal successor of Britain in matters concerning Mauritius—based its claim to Tromelin on its own interpretation of the first Treaty of Paris of May 30, 1814, under which Britain restored to France certain Indian Ocean islands which it had taken in 1810, "except the Isle of France (i.e. Mauritius) and its dependencies, especially Rodrigues and the Seychelles" (over which France ceded sovereignty to Britain). In its claim of April 2, 1976, the Mauritian government interpreted the word "especially" as meaning "in particular, among others or notably" and asserted that in addition to Rodrigues and the Seychelles the exception included also "minor dependencies" (among them Tromelin) such as the Chagos Archipelago, Agalega and the Cargados-Carajos (St Brandon) islands, which have in fact, with French acquiescence, remained under British sovereignty. The Mauritian government also referred to certain administrative acts carried out by the Port Louis authorities after 1814, in particular to leases issued between 1901 and 1956 to Mauritian nationals for the exploitation of guano. According to French sources, however, there was no guano on Tromelin and the leases had never been taken up.

The French government's interpretation of the 1814 Treaty of Paris is based on the treaty's French text, which it considers as authentic (French having then been the accepted language of diplomacy) and in which the word "especially" is rendered as "nommément" (i.e. namely). In the French view Tromelin, which had never been occupied by Britain, therefore again became a French territory in 1814; this had never been contested by any of the signatories to the treaty; and the question of Tromelin's status had not been affected by juridical or political changes in the south-western Indian Ocean area. In addition, the British Foreign and Commonwealth Office had stated on April 2, 1973, that there had never been, and was not, any Franco-British dispute over Tromelin.

The government of Mauritius reiterated its claim during an international conference on radio diffusion by satellite in Geneva in February 1977, when it called for individual receiving installations to be erected on Tromelin. The French delegation at the conference insisted on the inclusion in the final protocol of the conference of an express restatement of the French position in regard to continued sovereignty over the island. The Mauritian government's claim was also reaffirmed on June 20, 1980, when it was announced that the constitution of Mauritius would be amended so as to include Tromelin in a list of dependencies.

The French Minister for External Relations stated in the French National Assembly on April 4, 1983, that the question of French sovereignty over Tromelin was to be reviewed in the context of France's global policy in the region of the south-western Indian Ocean; that "an important financial effort" begun in 1983 would be continued in favour of Mauritius; and that a constructive dialogue had begun "on the different aspects of our presence in the region".

The minister also said that the government's plans implied an active policy of aid for the economic development of the countries concerned, and that a climate of dialogue and co-operation between France and the states in the south-western region of the Indian Ocean was essential for the success of the policy, which would contribute to the perpetuity of the French presence in the region.

HWD

Ghana-Togo

Relations between the neighbouring West African Republics of Ghana and Togo have been impaired, especially between 1957 and 1962 and again in 1974-78, by a dispute which has its origins in the colonial era. The dispute has centred on (i) the division of the former German colony of Togoland under a 1920 League of Nations mandate into French-administered and British-administered territories, the former eventually becoming present-day Togo and the latter being now part of Ghana, and (ii) the separation of the Ewe tribe between the two countries, about four-fifths of this tribe forming the majority of the population of Togo and the remainder living in Ghana (although not all in the area which was once part of German Togoland). Although not much publicized since 1978, the dispute has remained unresolved, especially in the view of some Ewes living on both sides of the border. The government of Ghana has, however, made it clear on many occasions that it will not agree to any request for the surrender to Togo of the former British-administered Togoland, while the Togolese government has for its part consistently rejected Ghanaian aspirations towards the integration of Togo with Ghana to achieve Ewe reunification.

Origins of the Dispute

At the beginning of World War I Togo, which had been a German colony since 1884 (formally since Dec. 24, 1885), was occupied by both British and French forces, and on July 10, 1919, Britain and France divided the territory between them, with France obtaining two-thirds of it, including the entire coast line and the railways, and with Britain obtaining the remainder which was contiguous with the (British) Gold Coast Colony. This division was confirmed in 1920, when the League of Nations granted Britain and France mandates for the administration of their respective parts of Togo. Greatly affected by the division was the Ewe tribe, which had first been divided between British and German colonial territories (in 1884) and of which the section previously resident in Togo was now divided further between British and French administration.

According to J. R. V. Prescott,[1] the Ewe tribe had, before European intervention, been divided politically into about 120 sub-tribes, lying between the centralized military kingdoms of Abomey and Ashanti; during periods of war the Ewe groups had formed temporary alliances, but these had been dissolved in times of peace, and no complaints had been recorded from the various Ewe groups when they were first divided in 1884. Opposition to the division after World War I among some Ewes in the Lomé area was unsuccessful. The Ewes in French Togoland were encouraged to assume French culture, were conscripted (for local defence) and were ruled by a centralized government. In British Togoland, however, and later in Ghana, the Ewes were taught in their own language, were encouraged to maintain their Ewe traditions, were not conscripted and had representatives on government councils at all levels.

At the end of World War II the two Togoland territories became UN trust territories and remained respectively under French and British administration, with unchanged boundaries. At this stage, a revived pan-Ewe movement made new demands for Ewe reunification but did not agree on the methods of union. A UN commission stated in 1950 inter alia: "The problem has attained the force and dimensions of a nationalistic movement and a solution should be sought with urgency in the interests of peace and stability in that part of the world". In 1952 the Ewe area in the British-administered Togoland was constituted into a Trans Volta-Togoland region, so that the western section of the Ewes was administered as a single group.

---

[1]*The Geography of Frontiers and Boundaries*, London, 1965.

The British government announced in 1955 that British Togoland would cease to be a UN trust territory when the Gold Coast attained independence, for which preparations were then being made. Upon a recommendation made by a United Nations mission which had visited Togoland and submitted its report on Oct. 30, 1955, a plebiscite was held in British Togoland on May 9, 1956, on the question whether the territory should be integrated with the Gold Coast on the latter's achievement of independence or whether it should remain a UN trust territory under British administration. The plebiscite resulted in 93,365 votes being cast for integration with the Gold Coast and 67,422 for continued British administration (with 161,687 voters having cast valid votes out of a total of 194,613 electors). However, of the territory's six districts only four showed majorities for integration, whereas in the other two districts—Ho and Kpandu (inhabited by Ewes of whom many wished for eventual unification of their territory with the French-administered Togoland)—there was a majority of 35,940 votes in favour of continued British trusteeship (as against only 16,068 votes for integration with the Gold Coast).

The United Nations General Assembly, in a resolution approved on Dec. 13, 1956, noted

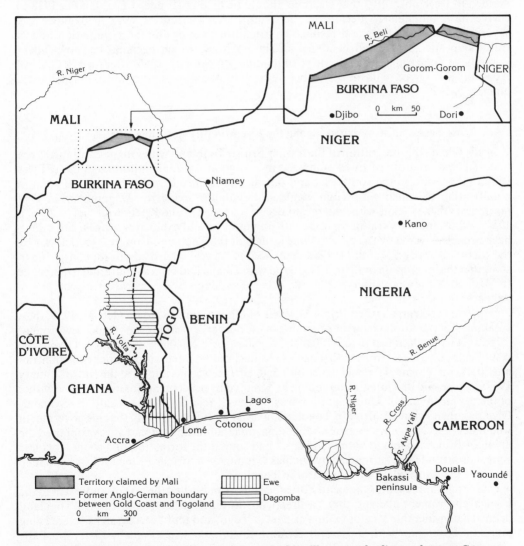

Map 16   The above map of part of West and Central Africa illustrates the disputes between Cameroon and Nigeria and between Mali and Upper Volta as well as that between Ghana and Togo.

the result of the plebiscite and also the proposed granting of independence to the Gold Coast by Britain with effect from March 6, 1957, and declared that as from that date the UN trusteeship over British Togoland would cease and the territory would be united with the Gold Coast (which upon independence would become Ghana).

In the French-administered Togoland, on the other hand, the Territorial Assembly approved, on Aug. 14, 1956, a new statute published by the French government early in August and conferring self-government on the territory within the French Union. This new statute and the consequent abolition of the territory's trusteeship status were approved in a referendum held on Oct. 28, 1956, by a total of 313,458 of the territory's 438,175 registered voters (this majority varying from about 62 per cent in the south to 80 per cent in the north), with the principal opposition to the new statute coming from those Ewes who favoured union of both British- and French-administered Togoland. The UN General Assembly, however, declined to recognize the referendum and to comply with a French request for the ending of the trusteeship over the territory and instead appointed, on Dec. 13, 1956, a commission to examine the situation. As a result of this commission's report the Assembly decided in December 1957 that elections should be held in (French) Togoland in 1958 to enable its inhabitants to decide on their future. Such elections were held under UN supervision in April 1958 and resulted in a majority voting for the termination of UN trusteeship and for the independence of the territory, which became the independent Republic of Togo (outside the French Community) on April 27, 1960, after the UN General Assembly had agreed to its independence on Nov. 14, 1958, and to the date of independence on Dec. 5, 1959.

Secessionist Activities among the Ewe Minority in Ghana, 1957-63

Inside Ghana the integration of the former British Togoland with Ghana continued to be opposed by a minority of Ewes organized in a Togoland Congress (although many Ewes within Ghana live in the south-east and outside the former British-administered area—a reunification of which with Togo would, incidentally, divide the Dagomba people of north-east Ghana). Riots with fatal results occurred in the Ho and Kpandu districts in March 1957, and two military training camps with ammunition and explosives were earlier said to have been discovered by the police. Four leaders of the Togoland Congress (which was by then defunct) were on March 11, 1958, sentenced to six years' hard labour for conspiring to show that the integration of British Togoland with Ghana had been a failure and to persuade the United Nations to intervene; three other defendants were given three-year prison sentences at the same time.

Dr Kwame Nkrumah, then Prime Minister of Ghana, said at Ho on Oct. 28, 1959, that, speaking "for our kinsmen on the other side of the border" (meaning the 700,000 Ewes out of Togo's total population of then 1,100,000, as against some 200,000 Ewes living in Ghana), he would enter into discussions with Togolese leaders on the integration of the two countries after the achievement of independence by Togo. He renewed his appeal at the end of January 1960 when he said that integration should be achieved by peaceful means based on the wishes of the people involved. The suggestion was, however, rejected as "an insult" by Sylvanus Olympio, then Prime Minister of Togoland, who said on Feb. 4, 1960, that his government would never accept a unitary state with Ghana, and that he himself had always opposed the union of British Togoland with Ghana and had sought the formation of a single Togolese state. His attitude was supported by Nicolas Grunitzky, a former Prime Minister and then leader of the principal opposition party in Togoland.

On March 15, 1960, the Ghanaian Foreign Ministry published the text of a note sent to the French government alleging that "a draft constitution" circulated in French Togoland defined a considerable area of Ghana as part of Togo, and that "certain steps" were being taken in Togoland "with a view to creating disturbances in Ghana". In the note the Ghanaian government requested France to take steps to prevent the territory from being used as "a base for an armed attack on Ghana". These allegations were wholly rejected by the Togoland government on March 16, and the French government categorically denied on March 25 that there existed any Togolese "draft constitution". While 14 persons were detained in Ghana in connexion with charges that they were "planning violence in conjunction with persons in French Togoland", it was announced in Lomé (the capital of French Togoland) on March 19 that 12 persons who had fled from Ghana had been granted political asylum. By 1961 several thousand refugees were said to have fled from Ghana to Togo for fear of being detained (under Ghana's Preventine Detention Act) because of their membership of the (opposition) United Party or of being opposed to the incorporation of the former British Togoland in Ghana.

The attitude of the government of the Republic of Ghana—of which Dr Nkrumah had become President upon its proclamation on July 1, 1960—towards the Republic of Togo was set out in a White Paper published on Dec. 11, 1961. In this White Paper it was stated that the partition of the former German colony of Togo after World War I had produced "a continuing source of trouble", leading inter alia to an unsuccessful "revolt" in the Ghanaian part of Togoland on the eve of Ghana's independence in 1957. It was alleged that a current "plot" consisted in part of "an attempt to repeat what was unsuccessfully tried in 1957, this time with the support of the Republic of Togo", which was described as "one of the countries on the African continent where neocolonialism has its strongest hold". The White Paper implicitly reiterated Ghanaian territorial claims to the Republic of Togo and stated that a plebiscite on the issue of union with Ghana was desirable in Togo. The White Paper also accused Dr Kofi A. Busia, the leader of Ghana's United Party, then in exile, of planning to set up a government-in-exile in Lomé.

During 1962 the Ghanaian government made further accusations against Togo, alleging in particular that Togo had given asylum to persons responsible for attempts to assassinate President Nkrumah, and that it tolerated the existence of a "subversive organization" among Ghanaian refugees in Togo. The Togolese government, however, stated on Dec. 19, 1962, that Ghanaian exiles were allowed to remain in Togo only on condition of taking no part in political activities.

On Jan. 6, 1963, the government of Ghana demanded the extradition by Togo of Dr Busia and of other Ghanaian exiles. On Jan. 13, however, President Olympio (an Ewe) was killed in a military coup, and upon a request by the newly-appointed President Grunitzky the Ghanaian government recognized the new regime in Togo on Jan. 21 and reopened the border between the two countries which had been virtually closed to road traffic for about a year. The frontier was, however, subsequently closed again by Togo and was not officially reopened until April 23, 1966 (i.e. after the overthrow of President Nkrumah on Feb. 24 of that year).

Ghanaian Measures against pro-Togolese Secessionists, 1973-76

No further political activities in favour of secession of the former British Togoland from Ghana were officially reported from that country until 1973, by which time the country was under a military regime with Col. Ignatius Kutu Acheampong as head of state. In July 1973 the government of Ghana disclosed that there had been a secessionist conspiracy among chiefs of the Ewe tribe and that all those concerned had been temporarily arrested.

On Feb. 21, 1975, a delegation of chiefs from the Volta region of Ghana and former nationals of British Togoland, who had become Ghana nationals in 1957, reported to Col. Acheampong that a resolution had been adopted by chiefs in the region on Dec. 28, 1974, calling for negotiations between the government of Ghana and the National Liberation Movement of Western Togoland (NLMWT or Tolimo), a clandestine organization said to be active on both sides of the border and agitating for the secession from Ghana of the former British Togoland. Early in 1975 the government offered an amnesty to all NLMWT members who ended their secessionist activities by Dec. 1, 1975, stating that they would not be punished and that those in voluntary exile could return to Ghana and live there as law-abiding citizens. On Dec. 23, 1975, Col. Acheampong declared before a delegation of chiefs

141

from the Volta region that the deadline of the amnesty had been extended to the end of January 1976; he also stated that the authorities had recently uncovered a plot to overthrow the government and that the persons involved, whom he described as "a small group of political agitators in the Volta Region" who wished part of that region to be joined to the neighbouring Togo, would be prosecuted.

While many NLMWT members were reported to have taken advantage of the amnesty, some 22 leading members of the movement (some of them being employees of the Togolese government) remained in Togo. The NLMWT had responded to the amnesty in an open letter to Col. Acheampong, asking for negotiations "directly or through the Organization of African Unity in order that permanent peace should exist in the territory, if necessary by handing over this problem, which cannot be done away with by the mere granting of an amnesty, to an arbitration which shall find a means by which it can be solved permanently". On Jan. 13, 1976, it was reported that the Ewe people of Ghana had "reacted strongly" to a government reorganization which had reduced their representation in the Cabinet and thus ended "the ethnic neutrality of the regime".

The government of Togo, in a statement as an advertisement in *The Times* (of London) on Jan. 13, 1976, called upon Col. Acheampong to "show his statesmanship and restore Togo as she was before the Europeans got to work" and asserted that "no one could call the 'plebiscite' of 1956 fair or a thoughtful reflexion of the aspirations of the local inhabitants". The Ghanaian authorities, however, officially terminated the amnesty on March 3, 1976, under a decree (amended on March 18) which banned "any organization whose objects include advocating and promoting the secession from Ghana of the former British-mandated territory of Togoland or any part of it, or the integration of this territory with any foreign territory", and specifically the NLMWT, "variously known as the Togoland Liberation Movement and Tolimo", under pain of a fine up to 5,000 cedis (£2,000) or imprisonment for up to five years, or both, for any activities on behalf of the movement.

During a treason trial held in Accra between May 19 and July 28, 1976, the chief accused, Capt. (retd.) Kojo Tsikata, was reported to have said that the Acheampong government had "a psychosis of an Ewe plot against it" which, he claimed, was being played out at this trial. The eight defendants in the trial, all members of the Ewe tribe, pleaded not guilty, but seven of them were sentenced (five to death and two to 20 and 15 years' imprisonment respectively).

Official Togolese Statement of January 1977 and Renewed Ghanaian Accusations against Togo

The government of Togo took up the border issue once again by issuing a statement, published as an advertisement in *The Times* of Jan. 28, 1977, by the Togolese Ministry of Information. In this statement it was claimed that the plebiscite of "May 9, 1957" (which in fact took place a year earlier and, as stated above, showed a majority in favour of integration of the British-administered Togoland with the Gold Coast, later Ghana), had "not completely resolved" the problem and that "the question of reunification" had "never ceased to affect relations between Ghana and independent Togo", although "this thorny problem" was "rarely mentioned elsewhere". While Togo did not wish to quarrel with her neighbours, the statement asserted: "One thing is certain: sooner or later a peaceful solution will be found to this problem".

The January 1977 Togolese statement continued: "Border problems are common in Africa, of course. Throughout the world, except in a few privileged nations, there are no natural frontiers to separate nations, large or small. Borders have always been created by men. It is hardly surprising, but in Togo men have flouted principles which have been defended at such high cost elsewhere. ... The Togo drama in fact began with World War I. In 1884 colonization by the Germans was a matter of negotiation between the traditional leaders and representatives of the people and the German authorities. From August 1914, however, the allied forces set about breaking up the inherent unity of Togo (political,

142

economic, social and cultural), sharing the occupation of the colony between themselves. Following the Franco-British agreement of July 10, 1919, confirming this act of demolition, a senior official on the spot in Togo declared: 'As it is traced today, the Franco-British border has many political drawbacks and places us at such economic disadvantage that it would be impossible not to grasp any opportunity of abolishing it, especially as the two parties will suffer from it one day. Whole peoples have been split by the new frontier: the Kondombas, the Adeles, the Akpossos, the Ewes. It should be borne in mind that the divided region is particularly fertile and that cocoa is a crop that is widely grown in it'.

"Many arguments are advanced in favour of maintaining the status quo, both in the Organization of African Unity and at the international level. The principle that the frontiers inherited from colonialism are sacrosanct undoubtedly prevents Africa from tearing itself apart, but general principles have never ruled out consideration of individual cases. Togo existed as an entity before and during colonization. In view of the reunification of British and French Cameroons, the Togolese wonder why there should be one law for one nation and another for the other. They are inclined to place the responsibility for dismemberment upon the British, who were confident of the results of the 1957 [sic] plebiscite in advance. The Gold Coast of the time—now Ghana—never formulated territorial claims against its neighbour; it was merely caught up in the manoeuvres of the European nations.

"It is not hard to understand why the peoples concerned were not able to express themselves freely at the time of the plebiscite. A period should have been allowed during which they would have been able to free themselves of the pressure in fact exerted by Great Britain and Ghana. Peoples who are administered by a foreign power and who are economically linked with that power cannot be said to have a free choice. The United Nations Organization was not wrong in applying the universal principle of self-determination, but it should first have created the conditions in which a full and free decision could have been reached.

"In the capital of Togo it is generally emphasized that Ghana has never been looked on as an enemy, despite the expansionist goals nurtured by the former President, Nkrumah, against Togo. Notwithstanding statements by the current Ghana Minister of Foreign Affairs, Togolese officials point out that a hostile climate cannot exist while the two countries are brought together by objective ties. The Ghana-Togo Grand Commission meets twice a year, meetings are arranged fairly frequently between the two Presidents, and Togo uses power supplied by the Akomsombe dam in Ghana; finally both countries are members of the ODEAC [which should presumably have read CEDEAO, as referring to the *Communauté Economique des Etats de l'Afrique de l'Ouest*, or Economic Community of West African States, ECOWAS].

"Nevertheless, the 1957 [sic] plebiscite has not really solved the problem of unification of the Togolese people . . . . Many of them believe that the day will come when all its people will be united in peace, stability and progress, and can direct all its efforts to the objective of development".

This statement was followed by further accusations against Togo made by the Ghanaian government during 1977. Ghana's head of state (the former Col. Acheampong, promoted general on March 7, 1976) said on Aug. 27, 1977, that Ghana had "no territorial ambitions on any country" but would "never permit an inch of its territory to be encroached upon by any country."

The Ghanaian Chief of Defence Staff alleged in September of that year that Togo was harbouring certain subversive elements and in complicity with another member state of the Organization of African Unity was giving military training to those elements in order to subvert Ghana. Moreover, on Oct. 10, 1977, the commander of Ghana's border guard (Maj.-Gen. Emmanuel K. Utuka) said that since the formation of the NLMWT in 1972 there had been "ample evidence of the complicity of the Togolese authorities" in its activities, and that an unnamed North African country was reliably known to have voted a considerable amount of money in support of secessionist movements operating against the Volta region.

It was generally assumed that the unnamed North African country referred to by Maj.-Gen. Utuka was Col. Moamer el Kadhafi's Libya.

In November 1977 Gen. Acheampong issued a further warning against the activities of secessionists in the border region and stated that his country was "prepared to shed blood to the last drop to defend the territorial integrity of the nation". In February 1978 he declared that his government would "foster closer relations with Togo" once that country stopped "supporting the so-called reunification of parts of Ghana with Togo". However, on July 5, 1978, Gen. Acheampong was removed from office, and since then the issue of the border with Togo has not been officially raised again. On May 18, 1979, the commander of the Ghanaian border guard said that relations between the two countries were "very cordial" and that there was nothing that the two countries could not agree on.

Border Developments in the 1980s

As a result of the military coup in Ghana on Dec. 31, 1981, all Ghana's borders with neighbouring countries, including Togo, were temporarily closed; although Ghana reopened its borders on Jan. 8, 1982, the Togolese government closed its side of the Ghana-Togo border the following day without official explanation.

A further difference over the border situation arose in March 1987. The Ghanaian Ministry of Foreign Affairs was, on March 18, reported to have made strong representations to the Togolese government over (i) alleged border incidents during the previous six months, (ii) reports of Togo's intention to build a concrete wall along parts of the border and to erect a barbed wire fence along another part and (iii) arrests of Ghanaians in border villages by Togolese soldiers and officials crossing into Ghana. These allegations were categorically denied by the Togolese Foreign Ministry (as reported on the same day), which stated that Togo had merely taken measures to ensure its security and had no intention of building a wall along part of the border. The ministry's spokesman also said that Togo would be quite happy to discuss the border issue peacefully within the framework of the two countries' existing joint commission. On March 19, however, the Togolese Ministry of Foreign Affairs confirmed that a barbed wire fence had been erected along a section of the border and added that the Ghanaian authorities had been informed of this beforehand.

HWD

Kenya-Somalia

The boundaries of the former British colony of Kenya at independence on Dec. 12, 1963, encompassed an area of approximately 50,000 square miles or 130,000 sq km (defined as the country's North-Eastern province) whose population was predominantly Somali-speaking (the number of ethnic Somalis being estimated at approximately 200,000). Somalis have regarded this population as one of the five elements of the historic Somali nation, and from 1960, when the Republic of Somalia became independent, its successive governments espoused the goal of unification of the Somali nation, of which the Republic comprises only two of the five elements, namely the former British Somaliland Protectorate and Italian-administered Somalia (which had latterly been a United Nations trust territory). Somali irredentism was expressed as a demand for the right of self-determination for the three categories of Somali-speaking peoples under foreign administration. The dispute with Kenya is detailed below. (For that with Ethiopia, see pages 126-32, with a map of the region appearing on page 127. The third dispute related to the fifth element of the "historic Somali people", the Issa, who form the largest population group in Djibouti. Djibouti was known for most of the colonial period as French Somaliland, before being renamed in 1967 as the French Territory of the Afars and Issas. Somali demands for its self-determination were effectively ended after Djibouti gained independence from France on June 26, 1977, with a governing coalition in which the Issas were in a majority. Somalia recognized and established diplomatic relations with the new Republic of Djibouti. The Ethiopian and Kenyan governments, in calling for the explicit renunciation by Somalia of all territorial claims against its neighbours, continued to refer to the existence of a Somali territorial claim on Djibouti, although Somalia has not actually done anything to pursue such a claim.)

The demand for self-determination for Somalis within Kenya, as expressed by leaders of the local population and supported by the government of Somalia, was addressed in the first instance to Britain as the colonial authority prior to Kenyan independence, and was subsequently pursued in the form of a dispute between Somalia and Kenya. The position adopted by the government of Somalia has been that this does not constitute a territorial dispute as such since Somalia did not desire to annex the territory in question, although if the population should desire union with Somalia, having once achieved self-determination, such a union would be encouraged by Somalia.

Historical Background

The situation in Kenya prior to independence was that ethnic Somalis formed approximately half the population of the Northern Frontier District (NFD), an area of 150,000 square miles (388.000 sq km) which in fact comprised six administrative districts, the eastern three of which (Garissa, Wajir and Mandera) were inhabited almost entirely by Somali-speaking people. The border demarcation between Kenya (specifically the NFD) and Somalia was not recognized by the latter, its alignment having been determined by a commission in 1930 on the basis of a treaty of July 15, 1924, between Britain and Italy whereby the territory known as Jubaland was detached from the British Kenya Colony and incorporated within Italian Somaliland. The NFD was administered by the British as a "closed district", entry from and exit to the rest of Kenya being subject to permit, and Somali nationalist aspirations as expressed notably by the Somali Youth League (SYL—formed in 1943) were affected by a ban on all political activity in the NFD from 1948 to 1960.

Harold Macmillan, speaking as British Prime Minister, said in the House of Commons on April 11, 1960, that "Her Majesty's government does not and will not encourage or support any claim affecting the territorial integrity of French Somaliland, Kenya or Ethiopia; this is a matter which could only be considered if that were the wishes of the governments and peoples concerned". This was apparently interpreted by Somali leaders to mean that a claim for self-determination for the NFD would indeed be considered if that were the wish of the British government (then responsible for governing Kenya) and the Somali people.

Local Somali chiefs made clear their demand for secession from Kenya at a meeting on November 1961 with Reginald Maudling, the then British Colonial Secretary, and further representations to the same effect were made by an NFD delegation to the Kenya Constitutional Conference held in London in February-April 1962. This delegation met with a special representative group of the conference, its direct participation having been strongly opposed by Kenyan nationalist leaders.

Without acceding to Somali demands for a referendum on the NFD, the British government proposed instead the establishment of an independent fact-finding commission, which was subsequently set up in September-October 1962 with the brief that it should ascertain and report on public opinion in the NFD "regarding arrangements to be made for the future of the area". The commission visited the NFD in October-November 1962 and reported in December that the population was divided but vigorous and determined in its opinions, with the largest areas (in both population and size) seeking secession when Kenya became independent, and ultimate union with the Republic of Somalia.

Duncan Sandys, Reginald Maudling's successor as the British Colonial Secretary, issued a statement on March 8, 1963, at a session of the Kenyan Council of Ministers in Nairobi, containing the British government's decision on the NFD. While the Somali-populated areas would not be allowed to secede, he said, they were to be formed into a separate, seventh (North-Eastern) province of Kenya; this decision was incorporated into the Kenyan constitution, which was laid before Parliament in London in the form of an Order in Council on April 18, 1963. Although the decision was represented by the British government as an interim rather than a final one, there seemed little prospect in the foreseeable future of a Kenyan government allowing the Somali-speaking area to secede. Kenyan leaders had already made clear their opposition to any such secession, during visits which they made to Somalia in the latter part of 1962, and Jomo Kenyatta (subsequently the first Prime Minister and later President of Kenya) reiterated on March 14, 1963, that Kenya would not entertain "any secession or handing over of one inch of our territory" to Somalia or to any other country. Talks between Kenyan and Somali government representatives, held in Rome on Aug. 25-28, 1963, did nothing to alter this position. Britain made it known during this meeting that it would not take responsibility for a final decision, although legally Britain remained the responsible authority until Kenyan independence.

Meanwhile the Republic of Somalia had on March 12, 1963, broken off diplomatic relations with Britain in view of what it described as the British failure "to recognize the wishes expressed by the overwhelming majority of the peoples inhabiting the NFD of Kenya". This marked the end of Somali attempts to obtain from Britain the satisfaction of their demands for the self-determination of the NFD. The issue thereafter became one between Somalia and Kenya, in the context of relations between independent African states in the post-colonial period.

The definition of the precise area in dispute was complicated by the Kenyan regional administrative reorganization implemented during the transition to independence. The NFD, to which Somalia continued to refer, officially ceased to exist, being subdivided in such a way that ethnic Somali peoples within Kenya were for the most part incorporated within the new North-Eastern province.

In the period immediately following the independence of Kenya, the Kenyan government held the Somali government responsible for rebel activity in the North-Eastern province, as a consequence of which activity a state of emergency was declared in the region on Dec. 25, 1963. In the same month a defence pact was ratified between Kenya and Ethiopia, the pact having been concluded in July 1963 with a view to safeguarding the integrity of the existing borders between the two countries and Somalia. Kenyan-Somali border hostilities continued sporadically until 1967, when (in September of that year) a degree of reconciliation was achieved following prolonged attempts at mediation by other African states.

Kenya-Somali Dispute and the OAU

From its foundation in 1963, and indeed from its antecedents in the pan-African movement, the Organization of African Unity has generally been associated with the doctrine that independent African states should ahere to the boundaries existing at the time of their independence. The principle of mutual respect for the territorial integrity of African states was expressly reaffirmed by a resolution adopted in Cairo on July 21, 1964, at the first ordinary session of the OAU Assembly of Heads of State or Government. The resolution included a solemn declaration that all member states pledged themselves "to respect the borders existing on their achievement of national independence". The representative of Somalia had been absent for the vote on this resolution, however, and he made it clear in a statement on July 23 that his government did not consider itself bound by its terms. Moreover, he said, Somalia opposed the perpetuation in independent Africa of what he described as "the uncorrected mistakes which still existed" with regard to state borders inherited from the colonial era.

The substantive issue of Kenya-Somali border hostilities was removed from the agenda of the OAU's 1964 Cairo summit meeting and referred to bilateral talks. Such attempts as were made at mediation (notably talks arranged in Tanzania in December 1965) failed to resolve the matter, and violent border incidents continued, accompanied by a further deterioration in relations between the two countries and the imposition of restrictions on trade between them in July 1966. Kenyan government sources in late 1966 estimated that 1,650 Somali "shifta" (bandits) had been killed in the border area in clashes over a three-year period, during which time it was said that 69 Kenyan forces personnel, police and administrators had also died along with over 500 Kenyan civilians.

A list of "prerequisites for normalizing relations", which the Kenyans put forward in December 1965 and subsequently reiterated, stipulated in particular that Somalia should recognize the former NFD area as an integral part of Kenya and cease all material and propaganda support for ethnic Somali "shifta" insurgents in the area. Rather to the contrary, however, a new Somali government established in July 1967 issued an explicit statement of its position in the form of a speech by Mohammed Ibrahim Egal, the new Prime Minister and Minister of Foreign Affairs. While stating that "we in the Somali Republic make no claims on the territory of any of our neighbours", the new Prime Minister went on to say that "what we are after is simply independence through the proper process of self-determination for our brothers" and that "we do intend to champion the cause of Somali territories under foreign domination, in order that they may attain sovereign independent status through the process of self-determination". After such independence it was envisaged that unions would be arranged "out of discussion and mutual agreement between independent Somali states".

Notwithstanding these divergent positions, however, on Sept. 13, 1967 (i.e. only two months after the change of government in Somalia), the Kenyan and Somali governments issued a joint declaration at the OAU Assembly in Kinshasa, undertaking to end the violent clashes and expressing the desire to respect each other's sovereignty and territorial integrity and to resolve their outstanding differences.

The following month a further Memorandum of Agreement was signed by President Kenyatta of Kenya and Prime Minister Egal of Somalia. Known as the Arusha Agreement, this was concluded at a meeting held in Arusha (Tanzania) on Oct. 8, 1967, under OAU auspices with the mediation of President Kaunda of Zambia. It called for the ending of clashes, the resumption of normal relations, the gradual suspension of emergency measures on both sides, the ending of hostile propaganda, and the formation of a joint committee (with Zambian mediation) to supervise the implementation of these processes and to seek solutions to outstanding differences. The agreement formed the basis for the establishment of diplomatic relations between Somalia and Kenya in January 1968, when trade restrictions were also lifted. In the same month Somalia re-established diplomatic relations with Britain, broken off over the NFD issue at the time of Kenyan independence. Continuing Kenyan-Somali bilateral contacts led to the lifting by Kenya on March 15, 1969, of the state of emergency in the North-Eastern province, and it was also agreed that restrictions on the movement of livestock across the border (i.e. by nomadic herdsmen) would be relaxed.

The essence of the Kenyan-Somali accommodation was not that their disagreement had moved towards being resolved, but rather that it had been allowed to become dormant under the mutually convenient ambiguity of the Arusha formula. The Somalis could interpret the call for a working committee "to examine ways and means of bringing about a satisfactory solution to major and minor differences between Kenya and Somalia" as an acceptance that what they continued to call "the NFD question" remained on the agenda to be settled in future negotiations. The Kenyans, meanwhile, interpreted the commitment at Arusha to respect each other's territorial integrity "in the spirit of paragraph 3 of Article III of the OAU

Charter" to mean that Kenya's borders at independence, encompassing the North-Eastern province with its majority ethnic Somali population, would no longer be called into question. There was thus no further need, according to this interpretation, for Kenya to insist as a precondition for any negotiation that Somalia explicitly declare its recognition of the North-Eastern province as an integral and de jure part of the Kenya Republic.

Course of Kenyan-Somali Relations, 1967-79

The Somali government's acceptance of the Arusha formula has not passed entirely without domestic criticism; indeed, hostile demonstrations had met Prime Minister Egal on his return to Mogadishu, and former Prime Minister Abdirizak Hadji Hussein had denounced the agreements. The government had responded by closing down the Mogadishu branch of the Somali Youth League, of which Abdirizak Hussein was the secretary-general, and Egal (although the SYL central committee voted to expel him from the party) had won the support of Parliament in a vote on Nov. 23, 1967, endorsing his efforts to settle outstanding differences between Somalia and her neighbours.

This policy approach continued essentially unchanged under the military government of Gen. Siyad Barreh, installed after a coup in Somalia in October 1969. Although a Revolutionary Charter, promulgated following the suspension of the 1960 constitution, reaffirmed a commitment to "the fight for the unity of the Somali nation", assurances were given to Kenya that the new regime would continue its predecessor's policy of seeking co-operation to solve outstanding differences.

Report of incidents in the area in 1977 and early 1978 were accompanied by renewed Kenyan pressure for the Somali government to make a formal renunciation of any territorial claims against its neighbours. The first of the new series of incidents occurred on June 27, 1977, when (according to the Kenyan government announcement) Somali troops believed to be passing through on their way into Ethiopia were involved in clashes at the Ramu border post in northern Kenya in which six Kenyan police and seven Somalis were reportedly killed. Kenyan complaints over this incident at the OAU ministerial meeting in Gabon on June 30 were met by Somali denials; the Somalis insisted that Somalia had no intention of attacking Kenya and that there had been no clashes in the area since the 1967 agreement. A Somali assertion, that the attack had in fact come from Ethiopia, was in turn denied by the Ethiopians.

A meeting was held on July 19, 1977, between Daniel arap Moi, then Kenyan Vice-President, and his Somali counterpart, Hussein Kulmia Afrah, following which a joint communiqué was issued stating that both sides had pledged to maintain the peace and to set up a border commission to "normalize and restore tranquillity" in the region. However, according to President Kenyatta of Kenya in a speech in Nairobi on Oct. 20, 1977, official Somali maps "still lay false claim on Kenyan territory", and it was reported at this time that the Kenyan government had conveyed to the Somalis by way of the Egyptian government as intermediary a renewed demand for the public renunciation of any Somali territorial claims against Kenya. It was further reported that the governments of the United Kingdom and the United States were unwilling to provide military assistance sought by Somalia, unless and until Somalia formally declared that it had no territorial claims against Ethiopia, Kenya and Djibouti.

Meanwhile, Vice-President Moi of Kenya had announced on Oct. 15, 1977, his government's intention of carrying out a census to establish the number of Kenyans of Somali origin, any of whom regarded as "favourable to Somalia" would be expelled from Kenyan territory. On the same day the Somali ambassador to Kenya replied to allegations that Somali travel documents had been furnished to Kenyans of Somali origin, and that the recipients of such documents had then gone abroad for military training. The issue of travel documents, he said, had occurred only for humanitarian reasons when individuals without Kenyan papers had wanted to travel abroad, and he stated that this would not happen again. In an announcement on Dec. 12, 1978, on the occasion of the release of 26 political detainees by the new Kenyan government (now under President Moi following President Kenyatta's death), it was stated that the majority of those released were ethnic Somalis arrested in the border area for alleged subversive activities.

On Sept. 10, 1979, the first ever meeting between a Kenyan and a Somali head of state (Presidents Moi and Barreh) was arranged in the Saudi Arabian city of Taif. At this meeting the Kenyans reportedly unsuccessfully pressed their demand for a public Somali renunciation of support for the self-determination of ethnic Somalis in Kenya. Shortly after returning from this meeting, President Barreh gave on Sept. 23 his assent to the new Somali constitution, as drawn up by the ruling Somali Revolutionary Socialist Party in January 1979, and approved in a national referendum on Aug. 25. Article 15 stated that "the Somali Democratic Republic shall firmly uphold the principle of self-determination of peoples and fully support the national liberation movements and all peoples fighting for their freedom and independence", while Article 16 stipulated that the Republic "adopting peaceful and legal means shall support the liberation of Somali territories under colonial occupation and shall encourage the unity of the Somali people through their own free will".

Further Incidents Near Border in late 1980—Somali Denial of Territorial Aspirations

In November 1980 further violent incidents were reported near the Kenyan-Somali border, and the provincial commissioner of the North-Eastern province of Kenya announced on Nov. 10 that a curfew would be imposed throughout the province and all Kenyan citizens of Somali origin would be confined in security villages. The following day the Somali government denied any involvement in the disturbances (in which six Kenyan officials were reportedly killed). On Nov. 13, according to Kenyan radio, President Moi sent a message to President Barreh welcoming "assurances given yesterday by the Somali ambassador to Kenya that Somalia had no territorial claim in Kenya whatever", and President Barreh said on Nov. 30 in a speech in Mogadishu (as reported on Somali radio) that Somalia was not seeking any Kenyan territory and that it would be to the mutual benefit of both countries if Kenya understood Somalia's desire for a peaceful relationship. He stated that Kenya was responsible for the future and the rights of the people of Kenya's North-Eastern province, but that Somalia in turn "would not tolerate the killing and the denial to these people of their rights". He repeated also the Somali claim that it was the Ethiopians who were responsible for creating disturbances in the area, with the intention of marring relations between Kenya and Somalia.

Somali Response to December 1980 Ethiopian-Kenyan Joint Communiqué

The Kenyan-Somali dispute, being one facet of the wider issue of Somali nationalist aspirations, was intimately connected with the most salient issue for irredentist Somali policy, namely the territorial dispute with Ethiopia over the Ogaden region (see pages 126-132). Since January 1979 Ethiopia and Kenya had had a 10-year treaty of friendship and co-operation (concluded on Jan. 31 during an official visit to Addis Ababa by President Moi) which included a pledge to maintain the inviolability of their frontiers and to mutual defence to resist "the expansionist policies of any country or group of countries". Lt.-Col. Mengistu Haile Mariam, the Ethiopian head of state, made an official visit to Nairobi in December 1980, during which (on Dec. 1) he described Somalia's policies as "a thorn in the flesh of both Ethiopia and Kenya". An Ethiopian-Kenyan joint communiqué issued on Dec. 4 called on Somalia "to renounce publicly and unconditionally all claim to the territories of Ethiopia, Kenya and Djibouti". According to Addis Ababa radio the communiqué set out a series of conditions which Somalia must fulfil, including (besides the payment of reparations for war damages to Ethiopia) the renunciation of territorial claims, the acceptance of the inviolability of existing state frontiers and the withdrawal of Somalia's reservation entered when this principle had been reiterated at the OAU in 1964. The two leaders reportedly agreed that "non-acceptance of these conditions by Somalia would mean the perpetuation of the existing tension and insecurity in the area", and that active Kenyan-Ethiopian collaboration should be intensified, and they called for an end to all international military aid to Somalia.

The Somali government responded vehemently to this communiqué, calling an emergency joint meeting on Dec. 7 of the Supreme Revolutionary Council, the SRSP central committee, the People's Assembly and the Council of Ministers. This meeting condemned the communiqué as provocative and threatening and tantamount to a declaration of war, and urged "the Somali people wherever they are to be ready to defend their motherland and national sovereignty". The President's Office issued a statement on Dec. 8 (which was substantially reiterated in a speech by President Barreh the next day) warning that the Abyssinians (i.e. Ethiopians) planned a systematic liquidation of Somalis under their rule. With Kenyan collaboration, it was alleged, Ethiopia intended to declare war on Somalia. The statement distinguished between "Abyssinian colonialism" and the Somali-Kenya issue, which it described as "a colonial legacy needing a just and responsible solution, in accordance with the OAU Charter". With regard to former colonial boundaries, Somalia "continued to uphold its 1964 principle" and to oppose "the uncorrected mistakes which still existed".

Improvement in Relations following Moi-Barreh Meeting in June 1981—Signature of 1984 Border Security Agreement

Bilateral talks on June 29, 1981, between Presidents Moi and Barreh after an OAU Assembly meeting in Nairobi, led to an improvement in Kenyan-Somali relations; a joint communiqué referred to a "commitment to promote better understanding and collaboration in the interest and welfare of the two nations". Subsequent meetings included discussions in August 1981 of a Somali offer to assist Kenya in controlling border violence. The Nairobi *Standard* newspaper on Sept. 8, 1981, quoted President Barreh as stating: "We in Somalia have no claim whatsoever on any part of Kenya's territory .... It is of course a historical fact that there are people of Somali origin in Kenya. But we regard them as Kenyans."

The continuing problem of violent incidents involving ethnic Somalis in northern Kenya nevertheless remained a potential source of friction. In the Wajir area in early 1984, many members of the Somali-speaking Degodia tribe were killed as Kenyan forces moved in to disarm them after they had been involved in clashes with another local Somali-speaking group. However, the absence of Somali government support for local irredentism was illustrated in mid-September 1984 by the announcement of the closure of the headquarters in Somalia of the Northern Frontier District Liberation Front (NFDLF, a group whose existence had first been reported in April 1981) and the return to Kenya of 331 NFDLF members under the terms of an amnesty announced by the Kenyan authorities in December 1983.

Meanwhile, President Moi had visited Somalia in July 1984 (appealing on July 24 for peace between Somalia and Ethiopia), and later that year a Somali delegation visited Nairobi, where on Dec. 2 it was announced that a border security agreement had been signed. Under this agreement, both countries would grant entry visas to the nationals of the other, thereby facilitating the free movement of peoples across their common border.

The Kenyan government, particularly in the context of meetings with Ethiopian delegations, continued to make reference on occasion to the importance of all African states accepting formally their boundaries as at independence. Thus for example on March 5, 1987, a joint communiqué issued after an Ethiopian-Kenyan ministerial committee meeting (and coinciding with heightened Ethiopian-Somali tensions) praised the Ethiopian-Somali dialogue of the past year but said that the acceptance of boundaries established at independence was "a fundamental principle for the promotion of mutual trust and co-operation" and "the foundation of lasting peace among states".

RE

Lesotho-South Africa

The Kingdom of Lesotho, an enclave of territory completely surrounded by the territory of the Republic of South Africa (the length of the border being in all some 565 miles or 900 km), attained independence on Oct. 4, 1966. The validity of the country's existing borders, as inherited from the colonial era, has been called into question by the country's rulers on the grounds that these borders perpetuate an unjust arrangement imposed on the Basuto or South Sotho people in the 19th century. The following article gives an account of the historical background to Lesotho's territorial claims, which relate to substantial if imprecisely-defined areas generally described as "the conquered territories". (For a map illustrating this dispute, see page 185.)

Lesotho's Existing Boundaries

Lesotho's boundaries today are essentially as defined in the Second Convention of Aliwal North, which was concluded on Feb. 12, 1869, and which brought to an end a series of wars between the Basuto and neighbouring Boer settlers. This treaty, although it was signed by the Basuto ruler King Moshoeshoe, had actually been negotiated between the British governor of the Cape of Good Hope (to whom Moshoeshoe had successfully appealed for protection) and the (Boer) authorities of the Orange Free State. The new boundary was adjusted the following year to include in Basutoland a parcel of territory (Chief Molapo's territory) in the north-west around Butha Buthe. The revised border ran from the confluence of the Caledon and Putisani (or Phuthiatsana) rivers eastwards to the Drakensberg following the centre of the Caledon river rather than the centre of the more southerly Putisani.

The British high commissioner's Notice of May 13, 1870, as amended by Government Notice No. 74 of Nov. 6, 1871, defines the borders of Basutoland (now Lesotho) as follows: "From the junction of the Cornetspruit [Makhaleng] with the Orange river, along the centre of the former to the point nearest to Olifantsbeen; from that point, by Olifantsbeen, to the southern point of Langeberg to its north-western extremity; from thence to the eastern point of Jammerberg; along the top of Jammerberg to its north-western extremity; from thence by a prolongation of the same, to the Caledon river; along the centre of the Caledon river to the heads of the Orange river at the Mount aux Sources; thence westward [in fact first south-eastward and then south-westward—ed.] along the Drakensberg, between the watersheds of the Orange river and the St John's river [Umzimvubu] to the source of the Tees [Telle]; down the centre of the river to its junction with the Orange river, and down the centre of the latter river to its junction with the Cornetspruit".

Extent of Earlier Basuto Settlement and Authority

Moshoeshoe I had succeeded, in the period to 1835, in establishing his authority as king over the Basuto people, whose area of settlement extended into areas to the north and west of the Caledon river as well as to the south-west of Lesotho's modern boundaries. Other tribes migrating into the northern part of the Basuto-dominated area were brought into a vassal relationship as tributaries of King Moshoeshoe. (See below, however, for dispute over the status of the Barolong tribe in the Thaba Nchu area.)

From the late 1830s the position of the Basuto was affected by the migration into this area of Afrikaner or Boer farmers from the south, notably in the Boer treks which began on a large scale in 1836. By these treks the Boers aimed to remove themselves from British colonial rule (the colony of the Cape of Good Hope having been ceded by the Netherlands to Britain in 1814) and to establish themselves anew in what are now the South African territories of the Orange Free State, Transvaal and parts of Natal.

King Moshoeshoe signed a treaty with the British governor of Cape Colony on Oct. 5,

1843, in which the extent of Moshoeshoe's territory was described in Article III. According to this description (known as the Napier line) the territory extended westward to the junction of the Caledon and Orange rivers, south to the Orange river, east to the Drakensberg and north to "a line extending from about 25 to 30 miles north of the Caledon river, excepting near its source and at its junction with the Gariep [Orange]". However, neither this description, nor a series of disputed attempts to give greater precision to the boundary definition (including the so-called Maitland, Southey and Warden lines), prevented continual cross-border conflict, cattle raiding and similar disturbances between Basuto and Boers.

First, Second and Third Basuto Wars with Orange Free State

Soon after the formal establishment of the independent Boer republic of the Orange Free State (the British having proclaimed their sovereignty over the new Boer settlements in 1848 but established a separate administration for the Orange River Territory in 1851 and allowed independence on Feb. 23, 1854), a conflict known as the First Basuto War or Senekal's War began in 1856 between Basutoland and the Orange Free State. This war was officially concluded by the First Treaty (or Convention) of Aliwal North on Sept. 29, 1858.

As shown on the map on page 185, the territorial limits of Basutoland as defined in this treaty were based on the Warden line proposals of 1849. Although the territory thus defined does not include the full extent of all areas of Basuto settlement (and notably omits an area in the south-west which had been described as part of King Moshoeshoe's territory in his 1843 treaty with the Cape Colony—see above), it is to this territory, substantially larger than modern Lesotho, that the claims expressed by Lesotho's leaders generally relate.

A subsequent Second Basuto War (Sequiti War) from 1865 to 1866 ended with the Basuto becoming subject to the Orange Free State as well as ceding part of their territory. The terms of the peace were accepted by Moshoeshoe's son Molapo in the Imperani Treaty, which was confirmed a month later by the Treaty of Thaba Bosiu, concluded between King Moshoeshoe and the Orange Free State authorities on April 3, 1866.

The Basuto, who had already sought British protection against the Boers in 1861 but without success, renewed their appeal after the outbreak of the Third Basuto War in 1867. As a result of a petition from King Moshoeshoe in January 1868, the British governor of the Cape on March 12, 1868, proclaimed the Basuto to be British subjects and their land to be British territory. The governor subsequently concluded a treaty with the Orange Free State (the Second Treaty or Convention of Aliwal North of Feb. 12, 1869), by which a new boundary was delimited (the agreement also being accepted by King Moshoeshoe on behalf of his people—see above).

Complexities affecting Lesotho's Territorial Claims

Although, as already indicated, the principal basis for Lesotho's territorial claims is that the Basuto lands were unjustly taken from them by force, a more general claim to lands south and east of the Drakensberg has also been expressed. The areas in question, currently lying within Griqualand East and Transkei, in particular the districts of North and South Maluti, were settled by 19th-century Basuto migrants, with the support of the British authorities in the 1880s.

A different complication affects the Thaba Nchu area in the north-west, where an enclave within the Orange Free State has been apportioned by South Africa as part of the so-called Bophuthatswana "independent" homeland. The area was inhabited by the Barolong tribe migrating southward in 1833, and it has been disputed whether the tribal chief did or did not become a vassal or King Moshoeshoe at this time, as did other tribal chiefs. The claim that he did not do so would affect Lesotho's historical claim to that particular enclave, which falls geographically within the area regarded by Lesotho as "the conquered territories".

Lesotho's Claims following Achievement of Independence

Basutoland, transferred to be part of the Cape Colony from 1871 to 1884 and thereafter administered as a British High Commission Territory, attained independence as Lesotho on Oct. 4, 1966, as already noted above. Prior to independence, certain members of the Legislative Assembly had demanded (on Nov. 2, 1965) that the British should secure the return to Basutoland of areas of South Africa in Orange Free State, Natal and eastern Cape Province, this demand reportedly being generally supported by all political parties in the country.

Although reference to seeking the return of the "conquered territories" was included in the programme of the ruling Basuto National Party (BNP) as well as the opposition Basuto Congress Party, the BNP adopted an attitude of restraint on the issue, at least until 1973. In June of that year the Lesotho government requested United Nations legal advice to prepare for negotiations which it was seeking with South Africa, and in January 1975 Chief Jonathan, the Prime Minister, declared that he would press his country's claims at the United Nations and, if necessary, at the International Court of Justice. The then Foreign Minister, Kebby Kotsokoane, said at the UN in November 1975 that there could soon be a confrontation with South Africa over the border issue, and his successor, Charles Molapo, told the UN General Assembly in October 1976 that the South African government should open talks on the return of land which he said had been "illegally ceded" during the colonial era.

From late 1976 the position was complicated by a dispute which arose from the Lesotho government's refusal to recognize the sovereignty or the existence of the so-called tribal homeland of the Transkei, bordering on southern Lesotho and including areas claimed by Lesotho. In a move which received no international recognition, South Africa on Oct. 26, 1976, granted "independence" to the Transkei, which consisted of territory formerly administered as a tribal homeland within South Africa (see pages 184-88). Transkei authorities thereupon assumed jurisdiction over the territory's borders and border crossing points, which included three crossing points into Lesotho.

The Lesotho government refused to comply with Transkeian border formalities, since this might imply recognition of Transkeian sovereignty (Lesotho allegedly being the target of South African pressure to this end). Lesotho successfully appealed at the United Nations for international assistance to compensate for what was described as the effective closure of the border crossings in question. A total of 33 other border crossings between Lesotho and South Africa, lying along the remaining sections of the border between the two countries, were apparently not affected directly; the three affected crossing points were reopened in 1980.

In the wake of the dispute over the Transkei issue and its border implications for Lesotho, Chief Jonathan in February 1977 asserted his country's territorial claims in very broad terms, apparently encompassing much of the Orange Free State and other lands "fraudulently taken during the wars". It was reported in *The Times* on June 2, 1977, that Chief Jonathan had again reiterated his country's claims and expressed once again his intention of bringing the matter before the International Court of Justice. South Africa responded by reiterating a proposal first made in 1968 for the appointment of a joint border commission. In the 10 years since mid-1977 there have, however, been no significant developments with regard to this territorial claim. (Lesotho in 1979 reiterated its demand for restitution of the "conquered territories" whereas South Africa continued to regard these areas as an integral part of its own territory, on which no negotiation would be conducted.) The issues of border security and border controls, on the other hand, have continued to feature in recurrent friction between Lesotho and South Africa, primarily over security issues.

Lesotho has repeatedly alleged that the South African government was assisting guerrillas of the Lesotho Liberation Army (LLA), and South African forces have carried out actions (including a commando raid on Maseru in December 1982) against alleged bases in Lesotho of the African National Congress (ANC). Chief Jonathan's government in 1983-84 resisted

South African demands for a non-aggression pact, despite South African pressure in the form of non-payment of customs dues and holding up of imports of weapons and equipment. A Lesotho government announcement of Oct. 1, 1984, that the ANC had agreed to withdraw completely from Lesotho, led to better relations and a resumption of feasibility studies for the Highlands development scheme, which would provide water to South Africa and hydroelectric power for Lesotho. However, in late 1985 there was again an increase in South African "warnings" about the presence of ANC guerrillas. Raids on Maseru on Dec. 20, 1985, claimed by the LLA, were followed on Jan. 1, 1986, by the imposition of a de facto South African blockade, by means of strict controls and checks at border crossing points.

Following the deposition of Chief Jonathan in a bloodless coup on Jan. 20, 1986, the new regime of Maj.-Gen. Lekhanya established good relations with South Africa, marked by the lifting of the South African border controls, an agreement on mutual security, and the signature on Oct. 24, 1986, of a treaty on commencement of work on the Highlands water project.

RE

Malawi-Tanzania

In 1967 the government of Tanzania formally stated that in its view Tanzania's border with Malawi lay not along the eastern shore of Lake Nyasa (or Lake Malawi), as shown on current maps, but along the median line of the lake. This assertion implied the right of Tanzanians to enjoy access to the waters of the lake and the use of its resources.

Origins of the Dispute over the Lake Nyasa/Malawi Border

In Article I of an agreement concluded in 1890 between Britain and Germany the alignment of the western border of what had, in 1885, become German East Africa was described as running along the (eastern) shore of Lake Nyasa and to be subject to modification by agreement and demarcation (as provided for in Article VI of the 1890 agreement). In 1891 the British government proclaimed a protectorate over the Nyasaland region (later known as the British Central African Protectorate and renamed, in 1907, the Nyasaland Protectorate). A second Anglo-German agreement (of 1901) merely gave formal approval to the conclusions of a joint boundary commission which had been surveying the frontiers of the two territories for the purpose of demarcation.

In practice, however, German sovereignty extended to the median line of Lake Nyasa until 1922, when most of German East Africa became the Mandated Territory of Tanganyika administered by Britain under the League of Nations. Official British sources for the period 1916-34 showed the western border of the territory as being the median line through Lake Nyasa (e.g. in a map attached to Britain's report for 1923 to the Council of the League of Nations, and in subsequent reports for 1924 to 1939, which referred to the western extent of the Tanganyika Territory as "the centre line of Lake Nyasa to a point due west of the Rovuma river", which constitutes the border between Tanzania and Mozambique).

After World War II Tanganyika was declared a United Nations trust territory, with the British government being answerable for its administration to the UN Trusteeship Council, and with Britain being responsible for bringing the territory intact to independence. However, British reports issued between 1947 and 1961 for Tanganyika and Nyasaland generally abandoned the median-line alignment and showed the boundary between the two territories as being the eastern shore of Lake Nyasa in accordance with the 1890 Anglo-

154

German agreement. This change was apparently reaffirmed with the proclamation of the Central African Federation of Rhodesia and Nyasaland in 1953.

The government of Tanzania—since 1961 the successor to British authority in what is now mainland Tanzania—has rejected this change on the ground that no arbitrary change of boundaries by the administering authority of a UN trust territory could have any legal justification in view of the territory's UN trust status. In addition it has declared itself bound by the July 1964 resolution of the Assembly of Heads of State and Government of the Organization of African Unity which stated that the borders of African states, as on the day of their independence, constituted "a tangible reality" and that all member states pledged themselves "to respect the borders existing on their achievement of independence".

Tanzanian Initiative of January 1967 and President Banda's Territorial Claims of 1968

The Tanzanian government raised the question of this border in a note to the government of Malawi in January 1967, stating inter alia: "The government of Tanzania has noted that maps produced in recent years give the impression that the international boundary between Malawi and Tanzania follows the eastern and northern shore of Lake Nyasa. It has also noted that certain actions of the Malawi government appear to give [support to this impression]. The government of Tanzania does not want an international issue to arise between countries sharing the waters of Lake Nyasa. Accordingly it wishes to inform the government of Malawi that Tanzania has no claim over the waters of Lake Nyasa beyond a median line running through the lake and that it is this line alone which is recognized by the government of Tanzania as both the legal and the just delineation between Malawi and Tanzania". The Malawi government, in replying to this note, stated that the matter would receive consideration. At a Malawi Congress Party meeting in September 1968 President

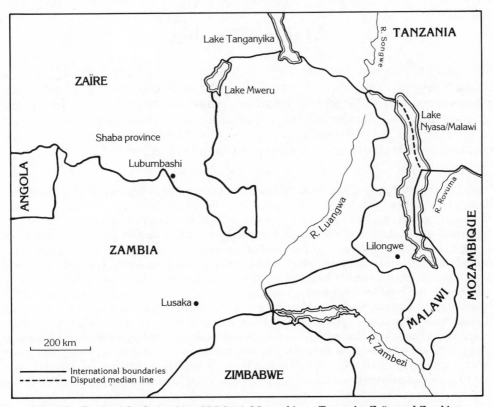

Map 17   Territorial relationship of Malawi, Mozambique, Tanzania, Zaïre and Zambia.

155

Banda of Malawi declared in regard to what he considered to be Malawi's territory: "The real boundaries [of Malawi] are 100 miles [160 km] north of the Songwe river [Malawi's present northern boundary with Tanzania]. To the south it is the Zambezi river [in Mozambique]. To the west it is the Luangwa river [in Zambia], and to the east it is the Indian Ocean". He based these claims on the ancient Maravi empire shown on early Portuguese maps. In his speech he also stated that Lake Nyasa had always belonged to Malawi and that he had every right to change its name to Lake Malawi.

At a meeting at Mbeya (Tanzania) on Sept. 27, 1968, Presidents Nyerere of Tanzania and Kaunda of Zambia discussed inter alia a common stand against President Banda's claims. The government of Tanzania subsequently dismissed them as having "absolutely no substance whatever" and not deserving any reply.

Establishment of Diplomatic Relations

No further exchanges on the Lake Nyasa/Malawi dispute have been reported since 1968, although the border delineation question has remained an unresolved, albeit dormant, issue between the two countries. Not until May 1985 were diplomatic relations established between Malawi and Tanzania, who the following April signed an agreement designed to give the former improved access to the Tanzanian port of Dar es Salaam via a road link through northern Malawi to the Tazara railway running from Zambia to the Tanzanian coast.

HWD

Malawi-Zambia

Relations between Malawi and Zambia were strained in the early 1980s by a declared dispute over a border area claimed by both countries. Since achieving independence in 1964, Malawi has from time to time asserted a claim to a substantial area of present-day Zambia (and also of other neighbouring states), basing its case on the extent of the pre-colonial Maravi empire. (A map showing the territorial relationship of Malawi and Zambia appears on page 155.)

Addressing a meeting of the ruling Malawi Congress Party in September 1968, President Hastings Banda declared that Malawi's "real" boundary in the west (i.e. with Zambia) was at the Luangwa river, which runs from north to south about 100 miles (160 km) to the west of the present-day Malawi-Zambia border. He based this assertion on the presumed territory of the ancient Maravi empire as shown on early Portuguese maps (which were also adduced as grounds for claims on substantial areas of Mozambique and Tanzania[1]). However, Malawi's claim was not taken seriously by Zambia, which declined to make any official response.

Although the broader Malawian claim has not been reasserted in recent years, a more limited dispute arose in August 1981 over an area on Zambia's Eastern province border with Malawi. In a statement to the Zambian Parliament on Aug. 11, 1981, Minister of State Fitzpatrick Chuula said that an official dispute had been declared over the area, adding that discussions were in progress between the two sides with a view to resolving the issue. Subsequently, a spokesman for the Zambian Foreign Ministry confirmed on Jan. 11, 1982, that 10 Zambian nationals were being held in Malawi for allegedly straying into Malawi and

---

[1]For an account of Malawi-Tanzanian territorial issues, see pages 154-56.

that a protest had been lodged with the Malawi high commissioner in Lusaka in an effort to secure their release.

In February 1982 President Kaunda of Zambia paid his first official visit to Malawi since the two former British colonies became independent in 1964 and received a warm welcome in Lilongwe. Nevertheless, a year later Lusaka radio reported (on Feb. 7, 1983) that villagers at the Kanyara border post, some 50 miles east of Nakonde, had complained of harassment by Malawian police and young pioneers, it being alleged that some Malawians had started cultivating crops on Zambian territory. A joint commission was subsequently established to resolve the dispute, and in August 1986 a Zambian government minister informed Parliament in Lusaka that the commission had recommended that the Zambian government should withdraw its claim to the disputed land.

AJD

Mauritius-United Kingdom (Diego Garcia)

A dispute concerning the island of Diego Garcia—the principal island of the Chagos Archipelago, situated in the Indian Ocean some 1,200 miles (1,900 km) to the north-east of Mauritius and forming part of the British Indian Ocean Territory—came into the open in 1980 when the government of Mauritius demanded that the island should revert to Mauritius, of which it had been a dependency until 1965 (when Mauritius was still a British Crown Colony). The grounds for the claim were in part that, in the view of the government of Mauritius, the British government had violated an undertaking allegedly given in 1967 to the effect that the island of Diego Garcia would not be used as a base for military purposes. However, the UK government has repeatedly denied having given such an undertaking. (A map illustrating this dispute appears on page 119.)

Historical and Geographical Background

During the 18th century the Indian Ocean and its African, Arabian and Indian coasts became an area of rivalry between British, French and Dutch companies seeking dominance over the spice trade and routes to India and the Far East. Having colonized Réunion in the mid-17th century, France claimed Mauritius in 1715 and subsequently took possession of the Seychelles island group and the Chagos Archipelago (the latter having strategic rather than commercial importance). During the Napoleonic Wars Britain captured Mauritius and Réunion from the French, who under the 1814 Treaty of Paris recovered Réunion but were obliged to cede Mauritius and its dependencies (the Seychelles and various other islands, including the Chagos Archipelago) to Britain. All these dependencies were administered from Mauritius until in 1903 the Seychelles group was detached to form a separate Crown Colony, the Chagos Archipelago continuing to be administered from the Crown Colony of Mauritius.

British official sources describe the connexion between Mauritius and the Chagos islands (and the Seychelles until 1903) as one of administrative convenience, following pre-1814 French practice, in that (i) there was little actual contact between them and Mauritius given the great distance between the two territories, and (ii) the islands had no economic relevance to Mauritius other than as a supplier of copra oil and as an employer of contract labour for the copra plantations.

The British Indian Ocean Territory (BIOT) was established under an Order in Council of

Nov. 8, 1965, and originally consisted of (i) the Chagos Archipelago and (ii) the islands of Aldabra, Farquhar and Des Roches (until then administered from the Seychelles, then still a Crown Colony): however, the latter islands were eventually returned to the Seychelles on their achievement of independence in June 1976. Thereafter the BIOT covered some 21,000 square miles (54,400 sq km) of ocean, the Chagos islands themselves (an archipelago of six main island groups on the Great Chagos Bank) having a land area of only 23 square miles (60 sq km). Diego Garcia, the most southerly of the Chagos islands, has a land area of about 17 square miles (44 sq km) and consists of a V-shaped sand cay almost enclosing a large deep-water lagoon.

Anglo-US Co-operation in the Development of a Communications Centre on Diego Garcia, 1965-76

When the creation of the BIOT was announced in the UK House of Commons on Nov. 10, 1965, it was explained that the arrangement had been made in agreement with the Mauritian and Seychelles governments; that the BIOT would be "available for the construction of defence facilities by the British and US governments"; and that "appropriate compensation" would be paid to the Mauritian and Seychelles governments, the amount involved being mentioned as £3,000,000, partly for the resettlement of some 1,000 people from the Chagos Archipelago in Mauritius.

In Mauritius the transfer of the islands to Britain was opposed by the *Parti mauricien social-démocrate*, then the second largest political party, which withdrew from the existing government coalition and whose leader, Gaëtan Duval, said on Nov. 7, 1965, that the party would not accept an Anglo-American base on Diego Garcia or the other islands unless Britain and the United States agreed "to buy all our sugar at a preferential price and to accept Mauritian immigrants".

An agreement concluded between the United Kingdom and the United States on Dec. 30, 1966, provided that the BIOT should remain under British sovereignty but be available to meet the defence needs of both countries. On Dec. 15, 1970, it was jointly announced in London and Washington that work planned under the 1966 agreement would begin in March 1971 on the construction of an Anglo-US naval communications facility consisting of "communications and minimum necessary support facilities, including an airstrip", on Diego Garcia.

On March 23, 1971, the United States opened a military communications station on Diego Garcia for the purpose of controlling the movements of US submarines, surface vessels and aircraft in the area, the station becoming fully operational in 1973. On Jan. 21, 1974, US Defence Department officials were reported to have confirmed plans for the expansion of the naval station into a base for the support of naval operations, as the reopening of the Suez Canal was expected to lead to increased Soviet naval activity in the Indian Ocean. The UK Foreign and Commonwealth Office disclosed on Feb. 5, 1974, that "in response to a US proposal and in accordance with the 1966 Anglo-American agreement" the UK government had agreed in principle to the expansion of the facilities on Diego Garcia (which would accommodate aircraft carriers and also KC-135 tanker planes used to refuel B-52 strategic bombers). This agreement was formalized in an exchange of notes on June 22 and 25, 1976, which amended the 1966 agreement.

The high commissioner of Mauritius in New Delhi (India) stated on April 7, 1974, that if the United States were allowed a base on Diego Garcia, Britain would be violating an undertaking given in 1967. The British government, however, denied having given any such undertaking. In a statement made on Dec. 3, 1974, by the UK (Labour) government's Secretary of State for Defence it was confirmed that the British government had agreed to US proposals "for a relatively modest expansion of the facilities on the island of Diego Garcia", but it was added that the US use of the facilities other than for routine purposes would be a matter for joint decision of the two governments. The proposed expansion of the US naval facilities on the island was finally approved by the US Congress on July 28, 1975, and as a result the US Navy was enabled to proceed with the construction on Diego Garcia of a 12,000-foot runway and refuelling facilities for a carrier task force, involving an increase in US military personnel from 430 to about 600 men.

The matter was apparently not raised in talks which Sir Seewoosagur Ramgoolam, then Prime Minister of Mauritius, had in London with the UK Minister of State for Foreign and Commonwealth Affairs on Sept. 24, 1975, when a Mauritian request for British assistance towards an acceptable resettlement scheme was discussed. It emerged that the British government had paid £650,000 to Mauritius for the purpose of resettling 434 families consisting of 1,151 people (according to Mauritian government records) who had been transferred from the entire Chagos Archipelago between 1965 and 1973, including 359 taken from Diego Garcia when the copra plantations on that island were closed down in 1971. It was later reported that the money had not been paid to these people until 1978, when most of them were living in destitution in Mauritius. In that year the British government offered a further £500,000 but this offer was rejected by a representative committee of the islanders. In mid-1979 a new British offer was made, amounting to £1,250,000 of about £1,000 per person payable on condition that the islanders undertook that neither they nor their children would ever return to the Chagos Archipelago. By January 1980 it appeared that this offer had been widely accepted by the evacuees.

On Oct. 13, 1975, the UK Secretary of State for Defence confirmed that under the 1966 agreement with the United States the latter had agreed to contribute half the total cost of setting up the BIOT (up to a limit of £5,000,000) by an offset arrangement against surcharges arising out of the British purchase of the US Polaris missile system.

Establishment of US Naval Base on Diego Garcia

It was announced in Washington on Jan. 4, 1980, that as a result of the crises in Afghanistan and Iran the US government had decided to maintain a permanent US naval presence on Diego Garcia, and on Jan. 12 the US government accordingly informed the British government of its intention to reinforce its military facilities on the island. In a summary of the US military position at the end of March 1980, submitted to the House of Representatives foreign affairs committee on April 2, 1980, the US Under-Secretary of Defence for Policy stated inter alia: "The network which we have developed for the region (of the Arabian Sea) is centred around Diego Garcia, where we expect to expand our facilities greatly in consultation with the United Kingdom".

The British Foreign and Commonwealth Office stated on May 29, 1980, that six or seven US cargo ships would be sent to Diego Garcia, and the UK Foreign and Commonwealth Secretary said on June 16 that the United States had a long-term programme for strengthening its military capability in the Indian Ocean. He said in particular: "This programme includes the pre-positioning of equipment to be available for use by forces deployed rapidly to the region in an emergency. At Diego Garcia such equipment will be held in converted merchant ships which will periodically be rotated within the Indian Ocean area. They do not constitute a naval task force. HM government were fully consulted over the proposal to send these ships to Diego Garcia in accordance with the provisions of the 1976 exchange of notes". It has been reported on May 11 that, as soon as adequate facilities were built, up to 4,500 US and other military personnel would be permanently established on Diego Garcia.

Opposition to the Militarization of Diego Garcia

Opposition to the establishment of US military facilities in the Indian Ocean area was registered by many of the states bordering the Indian Ocean (and also by the Soviet Union) and was expressed in repeated international calls for declaring the Indian Ocean a zone of peace.

On a proposal by Sri Lanka (then Ceylon), the General Assembly of the United Nations adopted, on Dec. 16, 1971 (in Resolution 2832/XXVI), a Declaration of the Indian Ocean as a Zone of Peace—the voting being 61 in favour to none against with 55 abstentions (which included those of all major powers except China and Japan, which voted in favour). In this resolution it was solemnly declared that "the Indian Ocean, within limits to be determined, together with the airspace above and all the ocean floor subjacent thereto, is hereby designated for all time as a zone of peace"; the great powers were called upon "to enter into immediate consultations with the littoral states of the Indian Ocean with a view to (*a*) halting the further escalation and expansion of their military presence in the Indian Ocean [and] (*b*) eliminating from the Indian Ocean all bases, military installations, logistical supply facilities, the disposition of nuclear weapons and weapons of mass destruction and any manifestation of great power military presence in the Indian Ocean conceived in the context of great power rivalry".

The declaration also called on the littoral and hinterland states of the Indian Ocean, the permanent members of the UN Security Council and other maritime users of the Indian Ocean to enter into consultations with a view to implementing the declaration. They were asked specifically to ensure that warships and military aircraft should not use the Indian Ocean for any threat or use of force against the sovereignty, territorial integrity and independence of any littoral or hinterland state; that the right to free and unimpeded use of the zone by vessels of all nations was unaffected; and that arrangements should be made to give effect to any international agreement which might ultimately be reached for the maintenance of the Indian Ocean as a zone of peace.

The Declaration of the Indian Ocean as a Zone of Peace subsequently was the subject of supporting resolutions adopted at every regular session of the UN General Assembly, and also at its first and second special sessions on disarmament (held in May-July 1978 and June-July 1982 respectively). However, various initiatives to achieve the implementation of its provisions have made no substantive progress to date.

The Mauritian Claim to Diego Garcia

In Mauritius the claim to sovereignty over Diego Garcia was officially made with greater emphasis during 1980. Thus Sir Satcam Boolell, the Mauritian Minister of Agriculture, Natural Resources and the Environment, said in January 1980 that the US plans to improve the naval base on Diego Garcia might "increase tension in this part of the world and constitute a potential danger to Indian Ocean countries and to Mauritius in particular".

By early June 1980 the return of Diego Garcia to Mauritius was called for by leaders of all political parties of Mauritius. Sir Seewoosagur Ramgoolam (then Prime Minister and leader of the Labour Party) was quoted on June 17 as saying that he had originally been forced to cede Diego Garcia because Britain "would have been able to take it anyway"; that he had understood that Britain would use the island as a communications centre; that he had not been told of plans to let it be used by the United States; and that, as Britain was not using the island for the purpose for which it was ceded, he had let it be known that Mauritius wanted it to be returned.

Paul Bérenger, the founder of the (leftist) Mauritian Militant Movement (the largest party in Parliament from 1976 to 1983) said at the same time that his party's fight was "political and diplomatic" for the return of Diego Garcia, which he called "part and parcel of Mauritian territory".

The British Foreign and Commonwealth Office, however, stated on June 24, 1980, that Mauritius had "at no stage" demanded the return of the island and that the matter had not been raised during a recent visit to Mauritius by the UK Minister of State at the Foreign and Commonwealth Office (Richard Luce).

On June 26, 1980, a bipartisan majority (of 48 out of the 70 members) of the Mauritian Parliament formally urged the government to demand the return of Diego Garcia to Mauritius, and Sir Seewoosagur stated on the following day that he would make the claim in London in 10 days' time; at the same time he did not rule out the possibility of taking the matter to the International Court of Justice in The Hague. The Mauritian Parliament subsequently passed an all-party motion calling for the return of Diego Garcia, and Sir Seewoosagur formally lodged the claim in talks which he had with the British Prime Minister in London on July 7, 1980.

Following his return to Mauritius, he said on July 16, 1980, that he had pointed out to the British Prime Minister that it had been agreed that Diego Garcia would be returned to Mauritius without compensation when it was no longer needed; he denied that he had received "a polite refusal"; and he added that he would rally world opinion around Mauritius's claim. Earlier, the Assembly of Heads of State and Government of the Organization of African Unity had on July 4, 1980, called for the demilitarization of Diego Garcia and for its unconditional return to Mauritius.

Under an agreement signed on July 7, 1982, the United Kingdom undertook to pay Mauritius £4,000,000 in resettlement assistance for families moved in 1965-73 from the Chagos Archipelago (i.e. the British Indian Ocean Territory). The Mauritian government, however, continued to claim that the Diego Garcia atoll had been wrongfully detached from the territory in 1965.

HWD

Morocco-Spain

Since achieving independence in 1956 Morocco has actively pursued a claim to four small enclaves of land and three small islands on the north Moroccan coast, all under Spanish sovereignty and comprising the only remaining European possessions on the African continent. The enclaves, over which Spanish rule dates from the 15th and 16th centuries, are the towns of Ceuta and Melilla and the Peñones (Rocks) of Alhucemas and Vélez de la Gomera; the islands, which were acquired by Spain in the 19th century, are the nearby Chafarinas. Of Spain's former colonial possessions in north-west Africa, the enclave of Ifni on the south-west Moroccan coast was returned to Morocco in 1969 and Spanish (Western) Sahara was effectively ceded to Morocco and Mauritania in 1979.[1] The Moroccan government has demanded that this decolonization process should be completed by the cession of the northern coast enclaves, but Spain has continued to insist that for historical and demographic reasons they are part of Spanish territory rather than colonial possessions. (For map showing the enclaves see page 91.)

Ceuta, situated near Tangier and opposite Gibraltar, has a land area of 19 square kilometres, 20 kilometres of sea coast and eight kilometres of land boundaries; it has a predominantly Spanish population of about 67,000. Melilla, situated to the east of Ceuta, close to the town of Nador, has a land area of 12 square kilometres, 3.9 kilometres of sea coast and 10 kilometres of land boundaries; its population, also predominantly Spanish, numbers 65,000. There are currently some 15,000 Spanish troops stationed in Ceuta and Melilla.

The Peñones de Alhucemas are made up of three small islands facing Alhucemas (near Ajdir) and, like Peñones de Vélez de la Gomera, are situated between Ceuta and Melilla. The Chafarinas Islands, 27 sea miles east of Melilla, face Kebdana cape. The Peñones have a

---

[1]For an account of the Western Sahara question, see pages 172-83.

civilian-military population of less than 100 each, and the Chafarinas of about 200.

Of the five territories, only Ceuta and Melilla are of economic importance, Ceuta being mainly a port for petroleum products and passenger traffic and Melilla a port for the export of iron ore as well as a fishing port. Ceuta, Melilla and the Chafarinas became free port areas in 1863, while the Peñones achieved this status in 1872. Their economic progress proved harmful to traditional Moroccan ports such as Tetouan, particularly when the Rif tribes abandoned the latter in favour of contraband trade with the free ports.

Spain bases its claim to continued possession of the enclaves (known as the Presidios, or penal colonies, because of their use as such up to the early 20th century) on its conquest of them in the past, on its lengthy occupation of the areas over several centuries, on bilateral treaties concluded with the sultans of Morocco, and on their largely Spanish population. It also points out that the enclaves were acquired before Morocco became an independent nation. The new Spanish constitution which entered into force on Dec. 29, 1978, described Ceuta and Melilla as Spanish cities and provided for them to be represented in the Spanish *Cortes* by one deputy and two senators each.

Morocco, on the other hand, has consistently claimed the territories as being within the "natural boundaries" of its kindgom, together with the former Spanish Sahara. It adds that, because it has no access to Ceuta and Melilla, it has had to equip ports such as Nador and Tangier for passenger traffic and trade; that the territorial waters around the enclaves interfere with fishing rights; and that Spain has used the same arguments in favour of retaining the enclaves as Britain has used in defence of its possession of Gibraltar against Spain's wishes.[2]

Historical Background to the Dispute

Ceuta was conquered by the Portuguese in 1415 and became an important town with a military and economic role. When Portugal became attached to Spain in 1580 after the death of King Sebastian of Portugal without an heir, all Portuguese settlements on the north Moroccan coast—Ceuta, Tangier and Mazagan—became Spanish possessions. The union of Spain and Portugal ended in 1640 (when Lisbon rose against Philip IV), and Portugal claimed back its territories; however, Ceuta proclaimed its allegiance to Spain and was later definitely reincorporated into the kingdom of Castille in 1668.

Of the other enclaves, Melilla was taken by the Spanish in 1497; Peñon de Vélez de la Gomera was occupied in 1508, Spanish sovereignty being confirmed in 1509 by the Treaty of Sintra (although the Spanish lost control of the Peñon from 1522 to 1564); and the Peñones de Alhucemas were occupied in 1673 and then ceded to Charles II by the Sultan of Morocco on condition that Spain prevented the Turks from seizing strongholds on the Mediterranean coast. The Chafarinas Islands were occupied by Spain in 1848, allegedly to forestall a French occupation of the area; Spain named them Congress, Isabella II and King's Island, although a French study team had previously named them Buckland, Busch and Brongniart.

In the 17th and 18th centuries there were repeated Moroccan attempts to oust the Spanish from the enclaves. Ceuta in particular came under persistent siege from 1694 to 1720, in 1727-28, in 1732 and again in 1790-91 for a 14-month period. Melilla was besieged in 1694-96 and for 100 days in 1774-75. The Peñon de Vélez de la Gomera was besieged in 1687 and its fort was razed to the ground in 1702, although Peñon itself remained in Spanish hands and was besieged again in 1774 at the same time as Melilla. However, although such attacks (mounted largely by undisciplined tribesmen) continued into the 19th century, the sultans of Morocco meanwhile entered into a series of treaties recognizing the sovereignty of Spain over the Presidios and also dealing with their borders.

In May 1767 a peace and trade treaty was concluded between Charles III of Spain and Sidi Mohamed ben Abdallah (Mohammed III) guaranteeing the safety of any "Christian or renegade" who took refuge in the Presidios and rejecting any request by Spain for an

---

[2]For an account of the Gibraltar dispute, see pages 90-101.

extension of the limits of the Presidios. It stated that "ever since these places have been occupied by Spain, their Imperial Majesties have set their limits according to the opinion of their tolbas and ulemas and have promised not to change anything".

In March 1799, following a siege of Melilla by the same Sidi Mohamed ben Abdallah, a treaty of peace, friendship, navigation, trade and fishing was signed between Charles IV and Moulay Slimane. It renewed the 1767 treaty, confirmed a 1782 agreement on "the boundaries of the camp of Ceuta", and gave Spain the authority to use heavy guns against the Moors of Melilla, Alhucemas and Peñon de Vélez if they continued to cause trouble. This treaty was confirmed by the May 1845 Larache Convention (signed after further tribal incidents) which dealt with the boundaries of Ceuta. Melilla's boundaries were laid down in an August 1859 agreement and were confirmed in an 1862 boundary convention.

In August 1859 the Convention of Tetouan was signed between representatives of Isabella II and Moulay Abderrahman, allowing an extension of Melilla's borders to facilitate its defence. The convention agreed to "cede to her Catholic Majesty the possession and full jurisdiction over territory near the Spanish place known as Melilla as far as necessary for the defence and tranquillity of this Presidio". The limits of the Presidio were to be established as being equivalent to "the range of an old-model 24 cannon shot", and the demarcation took place later the same year when a cannon ball was fired from the top of Melilla's fortress and landed on a southern beach of the town 2,900 metres away, the boundary being then traced in detail from that point. An act delimiting the territory of Melilla was signed in Tangier in June 1862.

Under the Convention of Tetouan the Sultan also promised to place soldiers at Melilla's frontier to suppress any unrest among the Rif tribesmen which might compromise good relations, and troops were also to be placed in the vicinity of the Peñones "to enforce respect for Spain's rights and effectively to ensure free entry into these towns of the necessary foodstuffs and supplies for its garrisons". A neutral area was designated between Spanish and Moroccan territory.

In the meantime hostilities took place between Spain and Morocco in 1859-60 (over reparations for damage caused when tribesmen laid siege to Ceuta). A peace and friendship treaty signed in April 1860 (also in Tetouan) ended the war and prescribed the extent of Ceuta's territory "as far as necessary for the safety and complete defence of the garrison"; it also set out full details of reference points necessary to define a zone "ceded in full possession and sovereignty" to Spain in conformity with the results of a study which had been agreed in detail by Spanish and Moroccan commissioners in April 1860. A neutral areas was declared around Ceuta as in the case of Melilla. Other agreements specifying the status of the Presidios were signed up to 1911, all of which confirmed the existing frontiers as well as dealing with the day-to-day aspects of life in the enclaves. The only Spanish "jurisdictional territory" in North Africa which did not have a status decreed by convention between Spain and Morocco was the Chafarinas Islands.

Agreements among the great powers of the day recognizing Spain's presence in the Presidios were also signed in the early 20th century, although the major content of the treaties dealt with the delimitation of the borders of Spanish Sahara. Among these, the Franco-British Declaration of April 1904 affirmed Britain's freedom of action in Egypt in return for a British guarantee of France's freedom of action in Morocco, while at the same time it took into consideration "the interests of [Spain] by reason of its possessions on the Moroccan coast of the Mediterranean". Moreover, the Franco-Spanish Convention of October 1904, which was designed to secure Spanish co-operation regarding the April 1904 agreement, recognized the "extent of Spain's rights to guarantee its interest . . . as the result of having these possessions on the Moroccan coast".

The Franco-Moroccan Treaty of Fez of March 1912 established the French Protectorate in Morocco but specified also that the French government should "come to agreement with the Spanish government with respect to the interest that the latter has as a result of its geographical position and its territorial possessions on the Moroccan coast". The Franco-Spanish Agreement of November 1912 was drawn up "to clarify the respective situations of the two countries with respect to the cherifien empire" and was largely concerned with Spanish Sahara and Ifni.

After Spain had extended its presence around Melilla in 1908, hostilities broke out in July 1909 when Rif tribesmen hostile to the idea of Spanish mineral prospecting in the region attacked the site of a proposed railway connecting the mines with Melilla. Violent battles that month marked the beginning of years of hostilities between Spain and the Rifs, and by 1920 Spain retained only its enclaves. Larache and Tetouan on the north African coast. The last major battle of the war was at Alhucemas in 1925, which was decisive for the Spaniards and put an end to all but isolated skirmishes.

Moroccan Claims to Enclaves since Independence

Since its independence in 1956 Morocco has strongly reaffirmed its claims to the Presidios before international organizations and in Non-Aligned and Arab forums. In 1961 Morocco called on the UN General Assembly to recognize its rights over the enclaves and began a diplomatic offensive, whereupon Spain reinforced the borders of the enclaves and Morocco imposed transit restrictions. On June 29, 1962, Morocco reasserted its claim to Ceuta and Melilla and on the following day extended its territorial waters from six to 12 miles; this affected the operations of Spanish fishing boats in the waters off the enclaves and resulted in Spain sending warships to escort its fishing vessels in the area, and also in the reinforcement of the military garrisons in the enclaves. Over the next few years, however, the attention of Spain and Morocco was diverted to other questions such as the status of Gibraltar, Spanish Sahara and Ifni. A meeting in July 1963 between Gen. Franco and King Hassan at Madrid airport marked the beginning of a rapprochement between the two countries, and King Hassan visited Spain in 1965.

In the mid-1970s, as trouble blew up over the question of Spanish Sahara, Morocco again began to press its claims to the enclaves. On Jan. 27, 1975, it formally requested the UN Decolonization Committee to place on its agenda the question of the remaining Spanish enclaves on or close to the Moroccan coast and alluded to UN Resolution 1514/XV of Dec. 14, 1960, condemning colonialism. Spain, however, condemned the Moroccan move as a "threat to Spain's national unity and territorial integrity" and warned that it would use all necessary legitimate means to defend the enclaves, communicating these views to the United Nations on Feb. 12, 1975. The Spanish government maintained that although the Presidios were "geographically separate" from Spain they were not "ethnically or culturally distinct" since their "true indigenous population was of Spanish origin, nationality and language as are their feelings, customs and culture"; it added that this was what differentiated them from Gibraltar, whose population had been driven out when the British entered. Spain also claimed that since the enclaves were "sovereign territories", and not "non-autonomous territories", they did not come within the competence of the Decolonization Committee.

Later the same year three people were killed in bomb explosions in Ceuta and Melilla in June, and about 400 Moroccans were subsequently reported to have been arrested in Ceuta. Spanish and Moroccan troops later confronted each other on the borders of Melilla. These incidents led Morocco to protest in a letter to the UN Secretary-General on June 30, 1975, at the "violations of human rights committed by the Spanish authorities" in Ceuta and to warn that, "if such practices continue, the Moroccan government will be constrained to take the measures necessary to protect the rights and interests of its nationals".

Attention was diverted from the question of the enclaves to the Spanish Sahara with the signature of the Madrid agreement in November 1975 under which Spain withdrew from the latter territory. However, after King Juan Carlos ascended the Spanish throne on the death of Gen. Franco in November 1975 and reaffirmed Spain's aim of re-establishing sovereignty over Gibraltar, King Hassan asserted at a press conference the same month that if Spain came into possession of Gibraltar, Morocco would retrieve Ceuta and Melilla because "no power can permit Spain to possess both keys to the same straits".

Development of the Dispute in the 1980s—Tensions arising from 1985 Spanish Aliens Law

Following the conclusion in August 1984 of a Moroccan-Libyan treaty of federation, Spanish officials privately expressed fears that this could lead to active Libyan support for Morocco's claims. The matter was raised in talks between Col. Moamer al-Kadhafi, the Libyan leader, and Felipe González, the Spanish Prime Minister, in December of that year. Some tension between the two countries ensued from a statement made by Kadhafi at a press conference after the talks when he referred to Ceuta and Melilla as "Arab cities". In an interview on Spanish television on Feb. 8, 1985, King Hassan again argued that the enclaves could not remain in Spanish possession following the return of Gibraltar to Spanish sovereignty. In subsequent months, Moroccan officials frequently portrayed the issues as linked, suggesting that both were anachronistic anomalies of colonialism.

The enclaves question came to a head in July 1985 with the passage in Spain of the Organic Law on the Rights and Liberties of Foreigners, under which all foreigners residing in Spain were required to reapply for residence permits and those whose documents were not in order would face expulsion. The law caused particular resentment among the Moslem residents of Ceuta and Melilla, who (in contrast to certain other longstanding minority groups in Spain) were not granted special status excepting them from the law's provisions. According to Spanish government figures, less than 3,000 of Melilla's 17,000 Moslems currently held Spanish nationality.

Moslem opposition in Melilla crystallized around the "Terra Omnium" organization, led by Aomar Mohamedi Dudu, which organized a mass demonstration in November 1985. The Spanish government subsquently promised that the law would be interpreted "generously" with regard to the enclaves, and that virtually all Moslems who applied could count on obtaining legal residence permits guaranteeing them Spanish citizenship within 10 years if all conditions were fulfilled. This assurance was rejected as inadequate by Dudu and his supporters, who continued to press for a moratorium on the application of the law to the enclaves. Further demonstrations, some of them violent, occurred in Melilla over the next two months, and there were also demonstrations in support of the legislation by European residents.

Growing tension between the European and Moslem communities in Melilla was reflected in the return to the Spanish Parliament in the June 1986 general election of three Coalicíon Popular (conservative) deputies, the enclave having previously returned Socialist representatives. A "parallel election" for the majority of Moslems who did not enjoy Spanish nationality (and were thus deprived of the right to vote) was organized by Dudu. A number of violent communal clashes broke out around the time of the election, and included fighting between European demonstrators and Spanish riot police, after which one of the newly-elected deputies was arrested. In an effort to defuse the tension, the government agreed to an 18-month schedule for the granting of residence permits, and in September 1986 appointed Dudu as special adviser to the Minister of the Interior to represent Moslem communities in Spain. Soon after taking up the post, however, Dudu antagonized the government by visiting Morocco for talks with Driss Basri, the Interior Minister, with whom he agreed on the "Arab and Moslem" character of the enclaves. At the inter-governmental level, the issue remained unresolved throughout 1986, despite being discussed during a visit to Morocco in March by King Juan Carlos, and by the Moroccan Foreign Minister, Abdel Latif Filali, when he met Spanish leaders in Madrid in October.

In November 1986, the Moslem community in Melilla staged a four-day general strike in support of demands for the immediate granting cf Spanish citizenship, and violent clashes between Europeans and Moslems erupted at the end of January 1987, in which one Moslem died of gunshot wounds. Arrest warrants were issued for a number of leading Moslems, including Dudu, who had fled into Morocco, on charges of inciting subversive movements. A planned rally by European residents requesting assistance from the United Kingdom, in the absence of sufficient support for their cause from the Spanish government, was banned by security police at the beginning of February.

In a move to defuse the inter-communal tension, Felipe González confirmed in a state of the nation address to the Spanish Parliament on Feb. 24, 1987, that Spanish nationality would normally be granted to Moslem residents of the enclaves. On the other hand, the Spanish government had meanwhile rejected a Moroccan proposal made in January that a joint commission should be set up to discuss the enclaves question at inter-governmental level.

JB/MWr

Namibia-South Africa

The southern border between Namibia (which as South West Africa has been administered by South Africa since 1920) and South Africa itself runs for a continuous length of 600 miles (965 km). The border itself has not been the subject of dispute, the alignment having been agreed in 1890 by the then relevant colonial authorities, Britain and Germany. Questions that have been disputed, however, concern the proper status of the port of Walvis Bay, which constitutes an enclave within the territory of Namibia and which since 1977 has been administered by South Africa as an integral part of its territory. A number of small islands off the Namibian coast, known collectively as the Penguin Islands, are also regarded by South Africa as forming an integral part of its own territory.

The South African position is that Walvis Bay and the Penguin Islands became British possessions during the colonial period in the latter half of the 19th century, and were annexed by Britain to the British Cape Colony. The whole of Cape Colony became part of the Union of South Africa, established in 1910. What is now Namibia, on the other hand, had come under German colonial rule in 1884 with the establishment of the German protectorate of South West Africa. The historical details are set out below.

The South African view has in practice prevailed hitherto, since the South Africans have controlled not only the areas in question, but the whole territory of Namibia. This situation arose after the former German colony became a League of Nations mandated territory and was entrusted by the League to South African administration in 1920. After the League was dissolved, the United Nations as its post-war successor organization took over responsibility for the mandated territories (redesignating them as UN trust territories), but the South Africans refused to conclude a UN trusteeship agreement and continued to administer the territory, even framing their own abortive constitutional and independence initiative in the mid-1970s. Meanwhile, the UN General Assembly in 1966 declared the South African mandate terminated and in 1967 set up a UN Council to administer the territory, which it resolved in 1968 should be known as Namibia. The illegality of the South African presence in Namibia was confirmed by the UN Security Council in 1969 and in an advisory opinion of the International Court of Justice in 1971.

Since 1978, protracted negotiations have been under way to arrange for a transition to independence in Namibia, in a form which would be accepted by the people of the territory as well as by the UN and South Africa. The nationalist South West Africa People's Organization (SWAPO) has been recognized by the UN General Assembly since 1973 as the authentic representative, and since 1976 as the sole and authentic representative, of the Namibian people.

It is in the context of moves towards a future independent Namibia that the territorial status of Walvis Bay has become an active dispute. Having found it convenient from 1920 to 1977 to administer Walvis Bay as if it were part of the territory of South West Africa under their administration, the South Africans in 1977 announced that Walvis Bay would henceforth be administered as an integral part of Cape Province, to which it had technically belonged all the time. This was declared by SWAPO to be an act of illegal annexation, the contention that Walvis Bay is an integral part of Namibia being endorsed by the UN General Assembly and the UN Council for Namibia. The details of the recent emergence of this dispute are also set out below.

Walvis Bay is the only deep-water port along the Namibian coast, and the enclave has a total area of some 350 square miles (900 sq km). The port handles cargo including uranium from the Rio Tinto-Zinc mine at Rössing (about 40 miles inland) and has a significant fishing, canning and fishmeal industry. South Africa ranks Walvis Bay as its fifth largest port.

Territorial Divisions by the Colonial Powers

British annexation of the Penguin Islands. The Penguin Islands are situated a few miles off the Namibian coast in a line running from Hollandsbird or Hallamsbird island (about 100 miles south of Walvis Bay) southward over a distance of some 250 miles (400 km), the most southerly being Roastbeef Island. The group includes the islands called Mercury, Ichaboe, Seal, Penguin, Halifax, Long, Possession, Albatross Rock, Panama and Plumpudding.

A short-lived Dutch occupation of Halifax Island in 1793 was followed by the visit of a British ship in 1795 to a number of bays which were declared British possessions. However, it was not until the 1860s that clear action was taken by the British with regard to the islands, which had become valuable as sources of guano (the guano deposits having been declared by the British governor of Cape Colony in 1845 to be the property of Her Majesty). In 1861 the British took formal possession of Ichaboe Island, and on August 12 of that year the governor of Cape Colony declared British sovereignty over all 12 islands and rocks. This proclamation was disallowed in 1864 but restored in 1866, when on May 5 the captain of a British ship took possession of Penguin Island and declared British sovereignty and dominion over the others. On July 16, 1866, the governor of Cape Colony proclaimed the islands annexed to and part of the colony, this action being authorized in the Royal Letters Patent of February 1867.

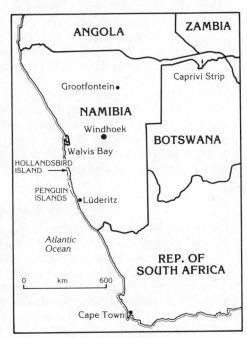

Map 18   Namibia-South Africa.

The British claim to the islands was recognized by the German colonial authorities in 1886 and 1890 (i.e. after the establishment of the German mainland protectorate), and the islands continued to be regarded as part of the Cape Colony, passing as such from British rule in 1910 and coming thereafter under the administration of the Union (later the Republic) of South Africa.

British annexation of Walvis Bay. Walvis Bay, where a small whaling settlement was established in the 18th century, was one of the bays claimed first by the Dutch in 1793 and then by the British two years later. However, it was not until the 1870s that the British took formal steps towards the annexation of Walvis Bay, after perceiving a possible threat to their interests in south-west Africa if Boer trekkers were to establish themselves north of the Orange river.

The government of the British Cape Colony appointed in March 1876 a commissioner extraordinary for Namaland and Damaraland (the Nama and Damara being tribes indigenous to what is now Namibia), whose report in 1877 recommended the annexation of Walvis Bay (then known as Walfish Bay) and surrounding territory. The captain of a British ship accordingly landed at Walvis Bay and marked out an area which was annexed as British territory on March 12, 1878. His proclamation was ratified by Letters Patent of Dec. 14, 1878, in which it was provided that Walvis Bay and adjacent territory could be annexed to the Cape Colony if the Cape government were to enact legislation to that effect. This was done on July 25, 1884, in the Walfish Bay and St John's River Territories Annexation Act, and the annexation was formalized by the Cape governor's proclamation published on Aug. 8, 1884. The proclamation set out what were the limits of "the port or settlement of Walfish Bay and certain territory surrounding the same" which with effect from Aug. 7, 1884 "shall under the name, designation and title of Walfish Bay become and be part of the Colony of the Cape of Good Hope, and subject to the laws in force therein".

German annexation of South West Africa. The establishment of the German protectorate followed purchases of land along the coast by a German merchant, F. Luederitz, beginning on May 1, 1883, with the bay of Angra Pequena (renamed Luederitzbucht). British and German naval vessels were sent to the area to protect their respective trading interests, and on April 24, 1884, the German consul at the Cape informed the British that Luderitz's possessions along the coast would henceforward come under German protection. A formal declaration of the German protectorate was proclaimed on Aug. 16, 1884, covering the area north of the Orange River as far as the 26th parallel, and extending some 20 miles inland. On Sept. 8, 1884, the German protectorate was extended northward to Cape Fria with the exception of Walvis Bay.

The protectorate's expansion westward was accomplished in the succeeding years by land acquisitions from the tribes of the interior, while its northern border with Portuguese possessions was settled in 1886. The British recognized South West Africa as a German sphere of influence in an agreement of July 1, 1890, in which the Germans also recognized the British title to Walvis Bay subject to the delimitation of the enclave's southern boundary, which was then in some dispute.

Early Dispute over Boundaries of Walvis Bay

The Walvis Bay territory as annexed to the Cape Colony in 1884 was defined in the original description of 1878 as bounded "on the south by a line from a point on the coast 15 miles [24 km] south of Pelican Point to Scheppmansdorf; on the east a line from Scheppmansdorf to the Rooibank, including the plateau, and thence to 10 miles inland from the mouth of the Swakop river; on the north by the last 10 miles of the course of the said Swakop river". However, when this definition was considered by an Anglo-German joint commission in 1885 it was found to contain certain ambiguities with regard to the southern sector, and a degree of vagueness as to what was the "plateau" and whether the distance southward from Pelican Point should be measured in statute or nautical miles.

A unilateral survey by a surveyor from Cape Town, Philip Wrey, was conducted for the Cape government in 1885, in which the southern limit of Walvis Bay was taken as running from 15 nautical miles south of Pelican Point, and the eastern boundary was extended past Scheppmansdorf to Ururas, taking in an area regarded by Wrey as corresponding to the "plateau" of the 1878 description. Wrey's demarcation was disputed by the Germans (with respect only to the southern sector), a second joint commission failing to resolve the dispute in 1888. Under a provision for the matter to be taken to arbitration, set out in Article III of the 1890 Anglo-German agreement, the King of Spain was asked to appoint an arbitrator in 1909, after a third Anglo-German joint commission in 1904 had been unable to reach agreement. The Spanish arbitrator studied the issue and reported in May 1911, his award following Wrey's demarcation. This settled in international law the boundaries of Walvis Bay as an enclave territory.

Contemporary Dispute over Status of Walvis Bay and Penguin Islands

The contemporary dispute turns on the contention that, if Namibia is to attain and retain independence, its aspiration for territorial integrity requires the inclusion in Namibia of Walvis Bay and the Penguin Islands. The historical developments as set out above are not themselves disputed, but rather their relevance is contested. Two factors have contributed to the recent emergence of an active dispute over Walvis Bay: the prospect of Namibian independence in the foreseeable future, and the South African decision in 1977 to resume direct administration of the enclave as part of Cape Province.

The second factor was clearly related to the first. In 1922 South Africa had found it convenient for obvious geographical reasons to commence administering Walvis Bay as if it were part of the mandated territory of South West Africa. The South African government made applicable to Walvis Bay as well as to the mandated territory the terms of its South West Africa Affairs Act of 1922, validated by Proclamation No. 145 of the governor-general, dated Sept. 11, 1922. Section I of the act provided that acts of the South African Parliament or proclamations by the governor-general relating to South West Africa would also apply to Walvis Bay unless otherwise stipulated, and that the port and settlement would be regarded as part of South West Africa for judicial purposes. However, the proclamation of the administrator of Walvis Bay (No. 30 of Oct. 1, 1922) confirming this measure referred explicitly to "the port and settlement of Walvis Bay, which forms part of the province of the Cape of Good Hope" being henceforth administered "as if it were" part of the mandated territory.

The convenience of this arrangement, from the South African point of view, ceased to apply when administrative provision in Namibia had to take into account the prospect of the territory's eventual transition to independent status. Unless Walvis Bay were to be part of an independent Namibia, there was little alternative but to resume administering it as part of Cape Province, and it was this latter course that the South African government decided to pursue. The then Prime Minister, B. J. Vorster, declared in the House of Assembly in Cape Town on April 23, 1976, that there should be no misunderstanding about the status of the port of Walvis Bay, which formed part of the Republic of South Africa. In August 1977 (two months after the passing of the South Africa Constitution Amendment Act), two separate South African government proclamations were issued, providing respectively for the administration of South West Africa (Namibia) and Walvis Bay. The Walvis Bay Administrative Proclamation (No. R202 of Aug. 31, 1977, taking effect from Sept. 1) stated that "Walvis Bay shall cease to be administered as if it were part of the territory [Namibia] and as if inhabitants thereof were inhabitants of the territory and shall again be administered as part of the [Cape] province". In terms of Section 5 of the proclamation, Walvis Bay ceased to be part of the electoral division of Omaruru (a division of Namibia) and later became part of the electoral division of Green Point, Cape Province. South African Defence Headquarters announced on Oct. 27 that the "dormant naval command and control facilities which already exist at Walvis Bay" would be reactivated as from Nov. 1, 1977.

Reactions from the five Western nations party to the Namibia independence negotiations (the United States, Canada, Britain, France and West Germany) reflected the perception that this development was likely to make the negotiations more difficult. A UN spokesman speaking on Sept. 1, 1977, on behalf of Dr. Kurt Waldheim, then UN Secretary-General, also described the move as "unfortunate" and as a "unilateral act" at a time when concerted efforts were being made "to find a peaceful solution to the whole problem of Namibia". Although the question of Walvis Bay had not hitherto been prominent, the possibility that South Africa would press its territorial claim had already resulted in explicit references by Namibian nationalists to the territorial integrity of Namibia *including* Walvis Bay. SWAPO's draft constitutional proposals for the territory, published in 1976, had emphasized this point, and in May 1977, at the International Conference in Support of the Peoples of Zimbabwe and Namibia, held in Maputo, Mozambique, the conference declaration referred to Walvis Bay as an integral part of Namibia and the conference programme of action called upon governments to reject all attempts by South Africa to

169

dismember the territory of Namibia and especially its design to annex Walvis Bay.

It was in similar terms that SWAPO spokesmen, and the UN Council for Namibia, denounced what they described as South Africa's annexation of Walvis Bay in statements issued in September 1977. Daniel Tjongarero, the SWAPO deputy chairman, said on Sept. 1 that Namibians could not be bound by colonial treaties of the 1880s and that South Africa's claim to Walvis Bay was "an expansionist venture and it could be used for possible aggression against Namibia" in the future. Moses Garoeb, the SWAPO administrative secretary, said in Lusaka on Sept. 8 that South Africa's claims to Walvis Bay were wild and baseless, and that he was not aware of any "colonial arrangements" which would give South Africa title over the port, which he described as "part of our country". Peter Katjavivi, the SWAPO information secretary, said in London that South Africa's historical claim to Walvis Bay was legally invalid and that "Walvis Bay is an integral part of Namibia and as our only port it will be of crucial importance to an independent Namibia". South African moves to hold on to the port were described by Katjavivi as an attempt to sabotage the economic future of Namibia. SWAPO later announced (on Oct. 15) that it would not accept any settlement plan for Namibia which did not include the retention of Walvis Bay as part of its territory.

Dirk Mudge, who was then the chairman of the Turnhalle Constitution Committee (and who was emerging as the most prominent politician working within the framework of the South African administration in Namibia), did not challenge South Africa's claim to Walvis Bay in legal terms, but he did express the hope on Sept. 9, 1977, that South Africa might at some later date feel in a position to hand Walvis Bay over to an independent Namibia.

A statement issued on Sept. 7, 1977, by the UN Council for Namibia, condemned "in the strongest possible terms this unilateral attempt by South Africa to destroy the territorial integrity and unity of Namibia". The Council stated that Walvis Bay had always been an integral part of Namibia and that South Africa had no right to change its status, and described as illegal the South African appropriation of the port as part of its territory. Walvis Bay, the statement said, was "inextricably linked by geographical, historical, cultural, and ethnic bonds" to Namibia, and without the port the independence of Namibia could not be complete. The Council called on the UN Security Council to take measures to maintain the status of Walvis Bay as part of the international territory of Namibia. The UN General Assembly, in its Resolution 32/9D of Nov. 4, 1977, also condemned South Africa's decision to annex Walvis Bay as illegal, null and void and an act of colonial expansion in violation of the Charter of the UN and of the UN Declaration on Decolonization. (The United States, Canada, Britain, France and West Germany, i.e. the five Western nations then party to the Namibia independence negotiations, abstained on Resolution 32/9D, having expressed their view that "all aspects of the question of Walvis Bay" should be discussed between South Africa and an elected government in Namibia.)

The UN Council for Namibia reaffirmed its position in the Lusaka Declaration adopted on March 23, 1978, in which it was stated that "Walvis Bay is not a question of territorial claims; it is an inviolable and non-negotiable part of Namibia". The UN General Assembly has also reiterated on a number of occasions that Walvis Bay is an integral part of Namibia and that South African annexation was illegal, null and void.

Without explicitly endorsing the General Assembly's assertion that South Africa has no legal claim to Walvis Bay, the UN Security Council has nevertheless accepted the contention that Nambia's integrity, unity and economic viability requires that Walvis Bay be part of its territory. In its resolution No. 432 of 1978, adopted unanimously, the UN Security Council declared that Namibia's territorial integrity and unity must be assured by the reintegration of Walvis Bay within its territory and that, pending attainment of this objective, South Africa must not use Walvis Bay in any manner prejudicial to the independence of Namibia or the viability of its economy. It decided to lend its full support to the initiation of steps necessary to ensure early reintegration of Walvis Bay into Namibia.

In the Algiers Declaration and Programme of Action on Namibia, adopted by the UN Council for Namibia on June 1, 1980, there was a recognition of the uncertainty involved in deferring the question of Walvis Bay for settlement only after Namibian independence. The Council declared that Namibia should accede to independence with its territorial integrity intact and that Walvis Bay was an integral part of Namibia, and added that "any further steps which South Africa may take in the future to undermine the unity and integrity of Namibia are illegal, null and void". The Algiers Programme of Action called upon the UN Security Council to declare categorically that Walvis Bay is an integral part of Namibia and that the question should not be left as a matter for negotiation between an independent Namibia and South Africa. The UN Council for Namibia also decided to take "all necessary action to ensure that South Africa's false claims with respect to the Penguin and other islands along the coast of Namibia are declared illegal, null and void by the relevant organs of the United Nations".

The continuing negotiations over Namibian independence have, however, left open the question of the future of Walvis Bay. South African policy has remained that the status of the enclave cannot be discussed in the context of Namibian independence talks. In the latter part of 1981 a new diplomatic initiative was undertaken by the US government with a view to resolving the deadlock in the Namibia peace talks, and this US initiative included inter alia a proposal for the parties to hold separate negotiations on Walvis Bay after Namibia had attained independence. This has remained unacceptable to SWAPO, and to the UN General Assembly, as has been made clear in resolutions passed by the Assembly each year on Namibia. Thus for instance its Resolution 41/39A of Nov. 20, 1986, adopted by 130 votes to none with 26 recorded abstentions (mainly by Western developed countries), "solemnly reaffirms that Namibia's accession to independence must be with its territorial integrity intact, including Walvis Bay, the Penguin Islands and other offshore islands, and reiterates that ... any attempt by South Africa to annex them is therefore illegal, null and void" and "calls upon the Security Council to declare categorically that Walvis Bay is an integral part of Namibia and that the question should not be left as a matter for negotiation between an independent Namibia and South Africa". Similarly a UN-sponsored International Conference for the Immediate Independence of Namibia, held in Vienna on July 9-11, 1986, and attended by representatives of 120 countries (but with the USA, UK and Canada sending only observers) included in its Declaration the explicit demand "that South Africa withdraw immediately and unconditionally from the entire territory of Namibia, including Walvis Bay and the Penguins and other offshore islands".

South Africa, meanwhile, pursuing its own arrangements for Namibia's future (with the international peace talks deadlocked), has transferred various services in the territory from South African control to the transitional government which it set up by proclamation on June 17, 1985. In doing so, however, it has excluded those services covering Walvis Bay. This applied notably to railway lines and harbour and other facilities in Walvis Bay, when the financial and operational control of the railways in Namibia was transferred from the South African Transport Services in May 1985 (i.e. just before the transitional government was brought into being). Assets and control of the South West African Water and Electricity Corporation were transferred to the transitional government from the Industrial Development Corporation of South Africa, hitherto the sole shareholder, in October 1986.

RE

171

The Western Sahara Question

Since Morocco became independent in 1956 it has strongly pressed a claim to sovereignty over the large expanse of desert to its south known as Western Sahara. Controlled by Spain since the 19th century, Western Sahara was divided up between Morocco and Mauritania under a tripartite agreement of November 1975 when Spain decided to withdraw from the territory. However, the occupation of Western Sahara by Morocco and Mauritania was opposed by the region's main guerilla organization, and Algerian-backed Polisario Front, which in 1976 proclaimed an independent Saharan Arab Democratic Republic (SADR) and intensified hostilities against both countries. This led to a large-scale military conflict which placed a heavy burden on the Moroccan and Mauritanian economies; in 1979 Mauritania concluded a peace agreement with Polisario, declared its neutrality in the conflict and withdrew from the southern sector. Morocco immediately occupied the area and has since been harassed by Polisario guerrillas on a broad front in Western Sahara and also inside Morocco proper.

The Western Sahara covers an area of approximately 125,000 square miles (325,000 sq km) within boundaries defined by the colonial powers. Since the colonial era its northern section had been named after the Saguia el Hamra river and its southern section after the Rio de Oro; however, on occupation by Mauritania Rio de Oro was renamed Tiris el Gharbia and later, under Morocco, Oued Eddahab (the Arabic for Rio de Oro).

The Sahrawis of Western Sahara are nomadic livestock-herding Moors (*beidan*) of Berber stock whose migratory area extended from the Oued Draa in southern Morocco to the Senegal river valley in southern Mauritania. They became arabicized after invasions by the (Bedouin) Maqil from the 13th century onwards and came to speak the Hassaniya Arab dialect instead of Berber. They remained largely autonomous within the Western Sahara area and ruled themselves by councils known as *yemaâ*. The major Sahrawi tribes are the Reguibat (the largest), Izarguien, Oulad Delim, Ait Lahsen, Oulad Tidrarin and Arosien.

The Polisario Front (*Frente Popular para la Liberación de Saguia el Hamra y Rio de Oro*, or Popular Front for the Liberation of Saguia el Hamra and Rio de Oro) is believed to have drawn many of its recruits from the Sahrawi population outside Western Sahara—in Morocco, Mauritania and Algeria—where their numbers are estimated to be as great as the numbers in Western Sahara itself; many Sahrawis fled to Morocco in 1958 after a joint Franco-Spanish operation crushed the Army of Liberation which fought against Spanish rule in the region and others were forced into exile in neighbouring countries after the Movement for the Liberation of Saguia el Hamra and Oued Eddahab (MLS)—Polisario's forerunner in Western Sahara—was crushed in 1970. In addition, many Sahrawis have in recent years become sedentary, due to factors such as the rural exodus and droughts which have reduced herds, and have settled all over the region. These factors are thought to be the basis for Polisario's consistent claim that the population of Western Sahara is far greater than the 74,000 accounted for in the Spanish census of 1974.

History of the Dispute

Morocco's ties with the region south of the Oued Draa (including Western Sahara) and also to other areas in north-west Africa including present-day Mauritania (to whose territory Morocco harboured claims as part of a proposed "Greater Morocco" until 1969) date back centuries. However, the pattern of nomadic life in the desert regions meant that Moroccan rulers in the north enjoyed only limited polical control over the tribes whose leaders swore allegiance to them, since the area occupied by specific tribes was constantly changing. For this reason also no reliable maps showing the territorial limits of Morocco's old empire existed prior to the 19th century.

Spain, which claimed "historic rights" in southern Morocco because of its early presence north of Cape Yubi (in what later became the Spanish enclave of Ifni) from 1476 to 1524, was drawn to the Western Sahara region by a trading centre at Cape Yubi and established claims to areas south of the Cape, opposite the (Spanish) Canary Islands. It concluded treaties of protection with tribal leaders south of the Cape, and in 1884 it took possession of Rio de Oro—the area of Western Sahara between Cape Bojador and Cape Blanc, then arbitrarily considered to stretch 150 miles (240 km) inland—as the "Spanish Protectorate of the African Coast". It confirmed its rights to Rio de Oro in 1886 under the Treaty of Idjil, concluded with the Emir of Adrar, and the territory was attached to the General Office of the Captain of the Canary Islands by a royal decree of April 1887; Sultan Moulay Hassan, however, refused to confirm Spanish rights there.

By the late 19th century, with Spain in control of Rio de Oro, Morocco in the eyes of the colonial powers was exercising control only as far south as the Draa region, along the coastal strip as far as Cape Yubi and, inland, around Tindouf (now in Algeria). Moulay Hassan, however, regarded his empire as extending to the Senegal river and, inland, up to Timbuktu (Mali) and southern Algeria. Morocco later consolidated its influence over tribes south of the Oued Draa (in what became Saguia el Hamra), and in 1895 Moroccan rights to the area between the Oued Draa and Cape Bojador, including Saguia el Hamra and Cape Yubi, were established under an Anglo-Moroccan agreement. However, Saguia el Hamra was subsequently allocated to Spain under a Franco-Spanish convention of 1904, title to the territory being confirmed in an agreement of November 1912. Spain was at the same time granted a protectorate in the Tarfaya region from the northern border of Saguia el Hamra to

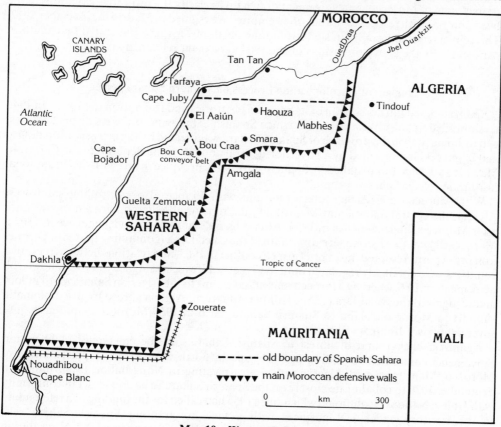

Map 19   Western Sahara.

the Oued Draa, and this zone (Spanish Southern Morocco) was not transferred back to Morocco until 1958.

At the beginning of the 20th century France defined in conjunction with Spain (but without the collaboration of Morocoo) the borders of its influence in north-west Africa and the respective zones of influence of the two countries in Morocco. In June 1900 an "agreement on the delimitation of French and Spanish possessions on the coast of the Sahara and on the coast of the Gulf of Guinea" was signed in Paris, establishing the southern and eastern (but not the northern) borders of the Spanish Sahara [see map]. The agreement specified that France should be allocated the salt mines of the Idjil region (this accounting for the curve along part of Rio de Oro's eastern border) and demarcated the frontier on Cape Blanc "in such a way that the western portion of the peninsula including the western bay be given to Spain, and Cape Blanc proper plus the eastern portion of the same peninsula remain in France's possession".

The main purpose of the Franco-Spanish Convention of October 1904 was to secure Spanish co-operation regarding the April 1904 Franco-British declaration (affirming British and French freedom of action in Egypt and Morocco respectively) in return for recognition of a Spanish zone of influence in northern Morocco. At the same time, the convention completed the delimitation of the French and Spanish zones of influence, taking the eastern border of Western Sahara up as far as the Oued Draa. Article 6 of the agreement stated that Spain had "complete freedom of action over the region (i.e. Saguia et Hamra) included between 26° and 27°40' latitude north and the meridian 11°, which is outside Moroccan territory", but recognized as Moroccan territory everything north of the present-day border between Saguia el Hamra and Morocco.

Consequent upon the Franco-Moroccan agreement of March 1912 setting up a French protectorate of Morocco, an "agreement drawn up to clarify the respective situations of the two countries with respect to the cherifien empire" was signed in Madrid in November 1912. This agreement reduced Spain's control in the north of Morocco but stated that south of parallel 27°40' the above provisions of the 1904 agreement remained applicable.

Impact of Decolonization Process on Western Sahara Issue

Spain assumed full possession of its Saharan territories and Ifni only in the 1930s. In 1946 it established Spanish West Africa, in which Spanish Sahara and Ifni were distinct entities, and in January 1958 the province of Spanish Sahara was created by the merger of Rio de Oro and Saguia el Hamra, ruled by a governor-general and returning deputies to the *Cortes*. In May 1967 a *Yemaâ* was installed by Spain to govern the province in line with the "traditional institutions of the Sahrawi people".

With Morocco a French protectorate and with France also controlling south-west Algeria, the central Sahara and Mauritania, the territorial issue remained dormant until after Morocco's independence in 1956. After Algeria's subsequent independence in 1962 a Moroccan claim to Algerian territory south of the Oued Draa (containing the Gara Djebilet iron ore deposits) erupted into a brief armed conflict in 1963, and relations between these two countries were not finally regulated until the Treaty of Ifrane was signed in 1969, followed by agreements in 1972 whereby Morocco renounced claims to the Algerian Sahara and Tindouf and recognized the Oued Draa as the frontier. In return, Algeria agreed to give diplomatic support to Morocco's claim to Spanish Sahara. Also in 1969 Morocco acquired de jure sovereignty over Ifni from Spain.

Against a background of unrest in Spanish Sahara and the emergence of liberation movements committed to ending Spanish rule in north-west Africa, representatives of Morocco, Mauritania and Algeria agreed at a meeting in Nouadhibou (Mauritania) in September 1970 to collaborate closely on the Spanish Sahara issue and to act in conformity with United Nations resolutions (which since 1965 had called for the holding of a referendum in the territory under UN auspices with a view to granting Spanish Sahara self-determination). The three countries themselves also in 1970 sponsored a UN resolution inviting Spain to organize a referendum among the Sahrawis to determine the territory's future. However, relations subsequently deteriorated between Morocco and Algeria, and in July 1974 King Hassan of Morocco began a diplomatic campaign to assert the Moroccan claim to the Sahara.

In line with a number of UN resolutions—including 2983/XXVII of Dec. 14, 1972, which called for the independence of Spanish Sahara and urged the Spanish government to consult with the Moroccan and Mauritanian governments to organize a referendum in the territory to this end—Spain finally announced on Aug. 21, 1974, that a referendum was to be held in Spanish Sahara in the first half of 1975 to determine the future status of the territory. This followed (i) the announcement by Gen. Franco in September 1973 of a programme of "progressive participation" by the Sahrawis in preparation for their eventual self-determination; and (ii) his announcement in July 1974 that Spanish Sahara would soon be granted internal autonomy (this being opposed by King Hassan, who warned Franco against unilateral action regarding Spanish Sahara).

The announcement of the proposed referendum was also followed by a deterioration in relations between Mauritania and Morocco, the latter accusing the former of making trouble by maintaining its own claim to Spanish Sahara (in support of which Mauritania mounted its own diplomatic campaign in August 1974).

Submission of Dispute to ICJ for Advisory Ruling

The UN General Assembly on Dec. 13, 1974, approved a resolution (3292/XXIX) sponsored by Morocco and Mauritania urging that an advisory opinion should be sought from the International Court of Justice (ICJ) on two questions, namely (i) whether the Spanish Sahara was a territory belonging to no one (*res nullius*) at the time of its colonization by Spain, and (ii) if it was not, what "legal ties" existed between the territory and the Kingdom of Morocco and the "Mauritanian entity". The UN transmitted the request to the ICJ on Dec. 21, and the proposed referendum in Spanish Sahara was postponed while the ICJ considered the issue.

In the ensuing period, before the ICJ published its ruling on Oct. 16, 1975, there were a series of major developments concerning the Spanish Sahara. Against a background of diplomatic and military tension as Morocco pressed its claim to Spain's African possessions, violent guerrilla activity and disturbances erupted both in Spanish Sahara and the enclaves. Amid UN efforts to find a solution to the Spanish Sahara problem Spain announced on May 23, 1975, that it was ready to grant independence to the territory "in the shortest period possible" and made moves to open negotiations with Morocco, Mauritania and Algeria as well as with Polisario, which had by now emerged as the main guerrilla front.

Before the emergence in 1975 of Polisario as the main formation opposing the Spanish presence in the territory, several other liberation movements had also been prominent. They included the Moroccan-backed Liberation and Unity Front (FLU); the Sahrawi National Union Party (PUNS), a moderate indigenous autonomist movement sponsored by Spain in order to secure an orderly transfer of sovereignty in which its own interests would be protected; and Morehob (the *Mouvement de résistance des hommes bleus*—referring to the Reguibat or "blue people" of Spanish Sahara), which, however, had little influence.

The Polisario Front itself emerged from among Sahrawi students at Rabat University in Morocco. Its original aim was to reorganize the opposition to Spanish rule and drive the Spaniards out of Western Sahara; it adopted the aim of independence for the territory only later after it had failed to receive practical assistance from Morocco. Polisario at first based itself in Mauritania but subsequently moved to Algeria, where it received support from the Algerian government.

At the time of the violent upsurge of guerrilla activity, a fact-finding mission of the UN Decolonization Committee visited Spanish Sahara in May 1975 and also held talks with Spain, Morocco and Mauritania. It found evidence of widespread support for Polisario among the people but little following for the Spanish-backed PUNS, and stated that almost all the people it had met in the territory were "categorically for independence and against the territorial claims of Morocco and Mauritania". In its report, published on Oct. 14, 1975, it recommended that the people of Spanish Sahara should be enabled to determine their own future "in complete freedom and in an atmosphere of peace and security".

Spanish Decision to grant Independence

After a meeting of the Spanish Council of Ministers presided over by Franco on May 23, 1975, the government announced that due to the "progressive deterioration" of the situation and the clear desire for independence in the territory, it was ready to "transfer the sovereignty of the Spanish Sahara in the shortest period possible" after the ICJ had delivered its opinion and the United Nations had taken an appropriate decision. It subsequently announced that it would seek to convene a duadripartite conference with Morocco, Mauritania and Algeria to discuss the future of the territory.

Morocco strongly opposed the Spanish decision, accusing Spain of creating an "equivocal situation and a climate of confusion". Mauritania for its part expressed satisfaction at the Spanish intention and recorded its wish that the decolonization should take place within a UN framework; however, at the same time President Ould Daddah of Mauritania said in an interview that Mauritania would take "all appropriate measures to preserve its legitimate rights over the Sahara, which it considers as forming part of its territory".

It became known at this stage (in mid-1975) that Morocco and Mauritania had reached a secret agreement at the end of the previous year on a plan to partition Spanish Sahara between them after the withdrawal of Spain, whereby Morocco would obtain the northern Saguia et Hamra sector and Mauritania the southern Rio de Oro sector, while the phosphate deposits at Bou Craa would be jointly exploited.

Publication of ICJ Advisory Opinion

On Oct. 16, 1975, the ICJ published the advisory opinion that while certain "legal ties of allegiance" existed between Western Sahara and both the Kingdom of Morocco and the "Mauritanian entity" at the time of colonization by Spain in 1884, these did not in either case support a claim of territorial sovereignty, nor did they affect the application of the principle of "self-determination through the free and genuine expression of the will of the peoples of the territory", as enunciated in the 1960 UN declaration on the granting of independence to colonial countries and peoples.

It went on: "The materials and information presented to the Court show the existence at the time of Spanish colonization of legal ties of allegiance between the Sultan of Morocco and some of the tribes living in the territory of Western Sahara. They equally show the existence of rights, including some rights relating to the land, which constituted legal ties between the Mauritanian entity ... and the territory of Western Sahara. On the other hand, the Court's conclusion is that the materials and information presented to it do not establish any tie of territorial sovereignty between the territory of Western Sahara and the Kingdom of Morocco or the Mauritanian entity ...".

The first question. The Court ruled that, according to state practice at the time of Spain's colonization of Western Sahara in 1884, territories inhabited by tribes or peoples having a social and political organization were not regarded as *terrae nullius*; in their case, sovereignty was not generally considered as effected through simple occupation but through agreements concluded with local rulers. Information furnished to the court showed that at the time of colonization Western Sahara was inhabited by peoples which, although nomadic, were socially and politically organized in tribes and under chiefs competent to represent them. Furthermore, it showed that Spain did not proceed upon the basis that it was establishing its sovereignty over *terrae nullius* (the King of Spain having proclaimed in his royal decree of 1884 that he was taking Rio de Oro under his protection on the basis of agreements entered into with the chiefs of local tribes).

Legal ties. The Court ruled that "legal ties" must be understood as referring to such legal ties as might affect the policy to be followed in the decolonization of Western Sahara and rejected the view that the ties in question could be limited to ties established directly with the territory and without reference to the people in it. The Court found that at the time of its colonization the territory had a sparse population consisting for the most part of nomadic tribes of the Islamic faith, whose members traversed the desert on more or less regular routes, sometimes reaching as far as southern Morocco or regions of present-day Mauritania, Algeria or other states.

Moroccan claims. Morocco had claimed "ties of sovereignty" over Western Sahara on the grounds of "alleged immemorial possession" of the territory. It had cited in support of its claim (i) the special historical structure of the Moroccan state, namely that it was founded on the common religious bond of Islam and on the allegiance of various tribes to the Sultan through their caids or sheikhs rather than on the notion of territory; (ii) evidence said to show the allegiance of Saharan caids to the Sultan; and (iii) certain treaties dating from the 18th to the early 20th century said to constitute recognition by other states of Moroccan sovereignty over the whole or part of Western Sahara.

The Court found that none of the internal or international acts relied upon by Morocco indicated the existence at the relevant period of either the existence or the international recognition of legal ties of territorial sovereignty between the Wester Sahara and the Moroccan state. They did, however, provide indications that a legal tie of allegiance existed between the Sultan and some of the nomadic peoples of the territory and that the Sultan was recognized by other states to possess some authority or influence with respect to these tribes.

Claims of "Mauritanian entity". The court noted that the term "Mauritanian entity" had been used to denote the cultural, geographical and social entity within which the Islamic Republic of Mauritania was later to be created. According to Mauritania, at the relevant period that entity—the Bilad Shinguitti or Shinguitti country—was a distinct human unit, characterized by a common language, way of life, religion and system of laws, with political authority emanating from emirates and tribal groups. While recognizing that the latter did not constitute a state, Mauritania had suggested that the concepts of "nation" and "people" would be most appropriate to explain the position of the Shinguitti people at the time of colonization. At that period, Mauritania said, the Mauritanian entity extended from the Senegal river to the Oued Saguia et Hamra, so that the territory at present under Spanish administration and the Islamic Republic of Mauritania together constituted indissoluble parts of a single entity and had legal ties with one another.

The Court found, however, that while these various links existed, the emirates and many of the tribes in the entity were independent in relation to one another and had no common institution or organs; the entity therefore did not have the character of a personality or corporate entity distinct from the several emirates or tribes which comprised it. On the other hand, the nomadic peoples of the Shinguitti possessed rights, including rights to the lands through which they migrated; these rights constituted legal ties between Western Sahara and the Mauritanian entity which knew no frontier between the territories and were vital to the maintenance of life in the region.

Overlapping Moroccan and Mauritanian claims. The Court noted (i) that Morocco and Mauritania had both laid stress on the overlapping character of the respective legal ties which they claimed Western Sahara had had with them at the time of colonization; and (ii) that, although their views appeared to have evolved considerably in that respect, they both asserted at the end of the proceedings that there was a north appertaining to Morocco and a south appertaining to Mauritania without any geographical void in between, but with some overlapping as the result of the intersection of nomadic routes.

On this aspect the Court confined itself to noting that this geographical overlapping indicated the difficulty of disentangling the various relationships existing in the Western Sahara at the time of colonization.

177

Moroccan "Green March" and November 1975 Tripartite Agreement

Immediately upon the delivery of the ICJ ruling, King Hassan on Oct. 16, 1975, declared his intention to stage a "green [i.e. peaceful] march" of 350,000 unarmed Moroccans into Spanish Sahara to claim the territory symbolically for Morocco. Despite Spanish and Algerian warnings to Morocco and the convening of the UN Security Council by Spain (which itself was experiencing a political crisis with Franco in the last stages of a fatal illness), the march went ahead on Nov. 6. The marchers penetrated about six miles (10 km) into the north of Western Sahara, kneeling to pray as they crossed the border for the return of "the land of our forefathers, after 90 years of separation". All Spanish troops in Western Sahara had withdrawn behind a mined "dissuasion line" about seven miles inside the Western Sahara frontier on the Tarfaya-El Aaiún road, and the area in between this line and the frontier formed a no-man's-land into which the marchers were allowed to penetrate without reprisals; however, Spanish destroyers, aircraft and troops waited on the alert in the Canary Islands, and Moroccan and Algerian troops were reported to be facing each other within striking distance near their borders. Finally, at the instigation of the United Nations, King Hassan on Nov. 9 ordered the marchers to withdraw to Tarfaya.

Shortly after the march ended it was announced from Madrid on Nov. 14, 1975, that Spain, Morocco and Mauritania had reached an agreement satisfactory to all three parties on the withdrawal of Spain from Western Sahara. After the publication in Spain of a decolonization bill, the terms of the agreement were revealed on Nov. 21. They provided for the immediate establishment by Spain of a provisional administration in the territory "with the participation of Morocco and Mauritania and with the co-operation of the *Yemaâ* [the Spanish Sahara General Assembly]" and for Spain to hand over to it "the responsibilities and powers which it has discharged in the territory in its capacity as administering power". Two assistant governors would be appointed respectively by Morocco and Mauritania to assist the governor-general of the territory in his duties, and the Spanish presence would come to an end in Spanish Sahara on Feb. 28, 1976.

The agreement was strongly opposed by Algeria and by Polisario, which said that the implementation of the tripartite agreement would open the way for "a bloody war with disastrous consequences for the entire region".

Moroccan and Mauritanian Occupation of Western Sahara

Although according to the agreement a Spanish presence was to be maintained in Western Sahara until Feb. 28, 1976, Morocco rapidly asserted its influence over the territory and during December 1975 and January 1976 occupied the main towns of northern Spanish Sahara, incuding the capital, El Aaiún. In the meantime, the UN General Assembly on Dec. 10, 1975, adopted two contrasting resolutions on the future of Western Sahara. The first (3458A/XXX), known as the "Algerian resolution", made no mention of the tripartite agreement, requested Spain to take immediate steps to enable "all Saharans originating in the territory" to exercise their "inalienable rights to self-determination" under UN supervision, and appealed to all parties to refrain from unilateral or other action. The second (3485B/XXX), known as the "Moroccan resolution", noted the tripartite agreement and requested the interim administration to take all necessary steps to ensure that "all the Saharan populations originating in the territory" were able to exercise their "inalienable right to self-determination" through free consultations organized with the help of a UN representative.

The last Spanish troops left Western Sahara on Jan. 12, 1976, and the Spanish presence in the territory terminated on Feb. 26, two days before the date laid down in the agreement. On the same day the *Yemaâ* (meeting in El Aaiún with only two-thirds of its full contingent) unanimously voted to ratify the Madrid agreement. The Polisario Front thereupon on Feb. 27-28 proclaimed the Western Sahara as a free, independent and sovereign state known as the Saharan Arab Democratic Republic (SADR), and formed a government which was recognized by Algeria (causing Morocco and Mauritania to break off diplomatic relations with the latter).

Under a convention signed in Rabat on April 14, 1976, Morocco and Mauritania agreed on the delimitation of their border in Western Sahara. This was to run eastwards from a point on the Atlantic coast, north of Dakhla (formerly Villa Cisneros), leaving Bir Enzaran in the Moroccan sector as a border post, and then south-east in the direction of Zouerate (Mauritania). Mauritania received less than one-third of the territory, which became known as Tiris el Gharbia. The Moroccan sector was divided into the administrative provinces of El Aaiún, Smara and Bojador, and the Bou Craâ phosphate mines remained in this sector, a majority share in the Spanish Sahara phosphate company, Fosbucraâ, being in February 1976 transferred to Morocco.

Mauritanian Withdrawal from Conflict

Over the ensuing years the Polisario Front intensified its hostilities in Western Sahara against both Morocco and Mauritania. Mauritania's involvement in the conflict resulted in over 9,000 Mauritanian troops being stationed in the country itself, particularly after Polisario attacks on Nouakchott (the capital) in 1976 and 1977, and Mauritania was forced to expand its own Army to 12,000 men and to devote 60 per cent of its budget to defence, with disastrous effects on the economy and on development projects.

In July 1978, however, the government of President Ould Daddah was overthrown by the armed forces, which said that they had seized power because the country was on the verge of bankruptcy and which vowed to co-operate with Morocco in seeking a solution to the war. The Polisario Front immediately ordered a ceasefire in Mauritania and the Mauritanian government began diplomatic initiatives to bring about peace in Western Sahara; later in 1978 Mauritania commenced negotiations with Polisario, which in September extended its ceasefire indefinitely and concentrated its hostilities against the Moroccan sector of Western Sahara. Mauritania also sought closer relations with Algeria following the death in December 1978 of President Houari Boumedienne of Algeria.

In May 1979 there were further changes of orientation in the Mauritanian leadership, the outcome being the recognition by Mauritania on July 17, 1979, of the right to self-determination of the Tiris el Gharbia sector; the conclusion by Mauritania and Polisario of a peace agreement on Aug. 5, 1979; and the withdrawal of Mauritania from Tiris el Gharbia during that month.

The first section of the August 1979 agreement stated that "considering the urgent need to find a definitive global solution to the conflict between the two parties which will guarantee the Sahrawi people their full national rights, and the region peace and stability", Mauritania relinquished all present and future claims to Western Sahara and resolved to "extricate itself definitively from the unjust war over Western Sahara"; Polisario declared that "it neither has nor will make any territorial claims on Mauritania" and resolved, in the name of the Sahrawi people, to sign a definitive peace agreement with Mauritania. A second section of the agreement, apparently referring to the application of "agreed principles", remained secret.

The Mauritanian Prime Minister, Lt.-Col. Haydalla, visited Morocco for talks on Aug. 10, 1979, and, before leaving later that day, he read out a statement to the press which said (i) that Mauritania had "renounced all claims to Tiris el Gharbia and considers itself definitively disengaged from this conflict", (ii) that Morocco, "noting this new situation, intends to ensure the defence of its rights, its territorial integrity, its security and the stability of the region", and (iii) that Morocco and Mauritania had undertaken not to do "anything which might damage the reciprocal security of the two countries".

Morocco immediately afterwards took control of the Mauritanian sector of Western Sahara, renamed it Oued Eddahab and allocated seats in the Moroccan Parliament to the new "province". Lt.-Col. Haydalla described the occupation as an aggression against Mauritania, but he received no response to his demand for the withdrawal of Morocco's troops. Mauritania and Algeria on Aug. 13, 1979, re-established diplomatic relations, and later in August, after the withdrawal of its own troops, Mauritania declared its "total neutrality" in the Western Sahara conflict.

Military and Diplomatic Developments, 1979-87

During the remainder of 1979 and throughout 1980 the Polisario Front concentrated its hostilities in southern Morocco proper as well as continuing to attack positions mainly in the north of Western Sahara. The Front became increasingly better armed and organized, and proved a strong adversary for the Moroccan Army, which now had a land border with Algeria and Mauritania of some 2,000 miles (3,200 km) to defend and which was obliged to spend one quarter of its annual budget on the war.

Over this period a "committee of wise men", which had been established at the 1978 OAU summit to mediate in the conflict and which comprised a number of African heads of state, held meetings and the OAU itself passed a number of resolutions on the Western Sahara issue. At the organization's Council of Ministers' meeting in Freetown (Sierra Leone) in June 1980 the SADR submitted an application for OAU membership. In the event 26 of the 50 OAU members favoured the admission of the SADR, but Morocco (supported by a number of other states) claimed that the SADR was not a sovereign state, maintained that according to some interpretations the OAU Charter required a two-thirds majority for the admission of new members, and threatened to leave the OAU if the SADR was admitted.

The matter of admittance was put in abeyance and a compromise was eventually reached whereby the committee of wise men was charged with organizing a meeting of all interested parties within three months. This accordingly took place in Freetown in September 1980, attended by the Presidents of Guinea, Mali and Nigeria; representatives of Sudan and Tanzania; and, as "interested parties", the Presidents of Algeria and Mauritania and delegations from Morocco, Polisario and other guerrilla organizations such as the FLS, the FLU, PUNS and Morehob. The meeting formulated a six-point plan for a UN-supervised ceasefire and an OAU-organized referendum, which it said should be implemented from December 1980. The plan was reportedly welcomed by Mauritania and Polisario but was described by Morocco as "nothing new".

In the first half of 1981 Morocco consolidated its position in Western Sahara by completing the first stage of what was to become, with later extensions [see below], a comprehensive line of fortifications across the desert; this defensive wall was intended to protect important towns and installations to its west and became a major target of Polisario attacks. During this period Morocco continued to receive moral and material support from the conservative Arab states and also, following the inauguration of President Reagan in January 1981, from the United States. The SADR, on the other hand, had by mid-1981 been recognized by at least 50 states, in eight of which it had ambassadors and three of which (Mexico, Cuba and Nicaragua) had in March 1981 become the first countries to accredit ambassadors to the SADR.

In a speech on March 3, 1981, on the 20th anniversary of his accession to the throne, King Hassan called on Algeria to hold a summit meeting to "end the spilling of blood in the region"; at the same time he asserted that any agreement to end the conflict should not be "detrimental to an integral part of our national territory". Amid a renewed Moroccan diplomatic offensive in May 1981 directed in particular against Libya for its suport of Polisario, the latter accused Morocco of using Libya as a scapegoat for its own failure to end the war and of refusing to submit to the decisions of international bodies.

However, when the Western Sahara issue was discussed at the 18th annual summit of the OAU held in Nairobi on June 24-28, 1981, proceedings were dominated by a rapprochement between Morocco and Libya and by a proposal by King Hassan that a referendum should be held in the territory. Addressing the assembled heads of state and government, King Hassan said that to avoid the OAU being "torn apart" on the Western Sahara issue, Morocco envisaged a procedure for a 'controlled referendum" which would "simultaneously respect" the objectives of the latest recommendations of the committee of wise men and "the conviction which Morocco has of its legitimate rights". Earlier, at a press conference in Rabat on June 1, 1981, King Hassan had asserted that the OAU Charter was clear and free of ambiguity in stating that "only countries legally and intentionally recognized within recognized frontiers established on the human and geophysical foundation necessary for entering into a regional grouping" could be members of the OAU. He had also warned that Morocco and other states would leave the OAU if the SADR were admitted to membership.

A resolution adopted by the Nairobi OAU summit recorded its decision to set up an implementation committee in respect of the Moroccan referendum proposal, it being specified that the committee would have full powers and would consist of Guinea, Kenya, Mali, Nigeria, Sierra Leone, Sudan and Tanzania. The same resolution (i) invited the parties to the conflict to observe an immediate ceasefire; (ii) it requested the implementation committee to meet before the end of August 1981 to work out, in collaboration with the parties to the conflict, the modalities and all the details relating to the establishment of a ceasefire as well as to the organization and the holding of a referendum; (iii) requested the United Nations to furnish, in collaboration with the OAU, a peacekeeping force to be stationed in Western Sahara to maintain peace and security during the referendum and subsequent elections; and (iv) instructed the implementation committee to take, with the participation of the United Nations, all necessary measures to guarantee the holding of a general and regular referendum on self-determination for the people of Western Sahara.

The resolution contained no reference to the Polisario Front or to its demand for the withdrawal of Moroccan forces and administration from the territory, even though such a concession had been urged on Morocco by a number of OAU member states and was included in a series of conditions laid down in July by Polisario for the holding of a referendum. The other major conditions were (i) that direct negotiations should be held between Morocco and Polisario to agree on steps to bring about a ceasefire and create favourable conditions for the referendum; (ii) that a provisional international administration of the United Nations and the OAU should be established in co-ordination with the SADR to ensure the necessary conditions and security; and (iii) that all Sahrawis should return to their towns and villages.

Little progress was subsequently made towards holding a referendum in Western Sahara, the major problem facing the OAU implementation committee being the refusal of Morocco to engage in direct negotiations with the Polisario Front. Moreover, the military conflict acquired a new dimension in late 1981 when Polisario began to deploy sophisticated new weaponry, including tanks and anti-aircraft missiles, in its operations against Moroccan forces. Within the OAU, a deep rift developed after the SADR was given an OAU seat for the first time at the 38th regular session of the Council of Ministers held in Addis Ababa on Feb. 22-28, 1982. In protest against this step—which was taken at the instigation of the OAU Secretary-General, Edem Kodjo, on the grounds that 26 of the 50 member states had recognized the SADR—the representatives of a third of OAU members (including Morocco) walked out of the conference. Subsequently, another OAU conference (of Information Ministers) was indefinitely adjourned in Dakar (Senegal) on March 15 after 14 of the 27 participating countries withdrew in protest against Senegal's refusal to admit SADR delegates.

Polisario's military operations were hampered during 1982 by the extension of the Moroccan defensive wall as far as Bojador on the Western Sahara coast. The wall, constructed of sand and stone, was between three and four meters high, and had command posts every four kilometers, equipped with US-supplied electronic monitoring equipment, reportedly capable of detecting movement up to 20 km distant. The phosphate mines at Bou Craa, which had previously been the target of Polisario attacks, re-opened in July 1982.

In the diplomatic sphere, Polisario continued to demand direct negotiations as a basis for any settlement, claiming that clandestine contacts had already taken place. The guerrillas continued to receive financial and logistical support from Algeria and Libya; Mauritania denied Moroccan accusations that it was allowing arms supplies for the Polisario to pass through its territory. The first "President of the Saharan Republic" was named as

Mohammed Abdelazziz, the Polisario secretary-general, at the movement's fifth congress in October 1982.

At the 19th Assembly of Heads of State and Government of the OAU in June 1983, the SADR agreed "voluntarily and temporarily" to refrain from taking its seat, so as to allow the summit to take place. After a report by the implementation committee, the Assembly adopted by consensus a resolution calling for "direct talks" (without specifying the parties to be involved) as a precursor to a referendum to be held in December 1983 under UN and OAU auspices. The resolution also called for the installation of an international peacekeeping force in the Western Sahara. Despite Morocco's repeated undertakings that it would be bound by the result of a referendum, King Hassan warned on July 8, 1983, that whatever the outcome he would not "hand the Sahara on a silver platter to a rabble of mercenaries".

A series of Polisario attacks in July 1983 marked the end of a one-year unilateral ceasefire, adopted by the Front in an effort to encourage a peaceful solution. The guerrillas' freedom of movement was limited by the extension of the defensive perimeter from Zag (in Morocco proper), past Mabhès and Farsia, to Amgala, in June 1984. In the same month, Moroccan officials took journalists on a tour of Haouza, which had formerly been claimed by Polisario to be "the capital of the liberated territories".

Despite these military reverses, the SADR received diplomatic support from a growing number of states. Ecuador, Venezuela and Upper Volta (Burkina Faso) were among those announcing official recognition in late 1983 and early 1984. In February 1984 Mauritania carried out its threat to recognize the SADR if Morocco failed to take steps towards implementing relevant OAU resolutions. Chad, Yugoslavia and Nigeria announced their recognition of the SADR later in the year.

At the 20th OAU summit, held in November 1984, both Morocco and Zaïre withdrew from the organization after the SADR delegation was allowed to take its seats. Three days before the summit opened, Dr Abdel Latif Filali (the Moroccan Foreign Minister) had expressed a willingness "to sit at the same conference table as the so-called Polisario", adding that Morocco was ready to participate in a referendum in the territory, to be held under the auspices of the UN and OAU.

Libyan support for Polisario was withdrawn following the conclusion of a treaty of federation with Morocco in August 1984. In December the same year, a military coup in Mauritania resulted in a new government headed by President Taya, who criticized the Haydalla regime for allegedly supporting Polisario. President Taya undertook to maintain strict neutrality in the conflict. Diplomatic relations with Morocco, which had been severed in 1981, were restored.

Polisario continued to claim significant military victories against Morocco, although independent observers treated these claims with considerable scepticism, bearing in mind the logistical and numerical superiority of the Moroccan forces. An important factor was the apparent effectiveness of the defensive wall, which largely prevented major incursions by Polisario into the populated areas of the territory, although the guerrillas were able to stage harassing attacks along much of the perimeter and to penetrate the wall in small numbers on foot. Many of the more successful Polisario attacks were carried out in the vicinity of Zag (i.e. inside Morocco proper).

During early 1985, Morocco repeatedly denied Polisario claims that there had been direct contacts between the two sides. In particular, Polisario asserted that talks had been held in Madrid in January 1985 with the then Moroccan Interior Minister, Driss Basri, who had rejected an Algerian suggestion that the Western Sahara be granted autonomy, under Polisario control, within the framework of a Moroccan dominion arrangement. King Hassan confirmed in March 1985, however, that there had recently been a series of talks on the Western Sahara question between Moroccan and Algerian officials. The King repeated that Morocco was ready to participate in a referendum, which he said should be conducted by the UN, "without, of course, discarding the OAU from the process". A resolution supporting the referendum proposal was passed unanimously by the Moroccan National Assembly later the same month. (The government's policy on the Western Sahara was endorsed by all legal political parties in Morocco.)

There was some speculation at this time that Morocco would propose ceding to the Polisario the southern, relatively unpopulated and inhospitable portion of the territory, known as the Tiris el Gharbia (Oued Eddahab, or Rio de Oro). In January 1985, the government had announced plans for the creation of a new province of the Moroccan Sahara, which would encapsulate all of the Western Sahara as well as some of southern Morocco, with its capital at Goulimine (inside Morocco itself).

On the ground, Morocco succeeded in completing further extensions to the defensive perimeter. The first, completed in January 1985, took the wall south from the Ouarkziz Hills, tracing a line to the east of Mabhès and the 1984 extension before joining up with the existing fortifications at Amgala. A second extension, completed in 1985, ran west from Amgala along the Mauritanian frontier before turning south through Guelta Zemmour and thence running south-west to the coast of Dakhla. Moreover, the completion in April 1987 of a further extension running due south to the Mauritanian border and then westward to the coast meant that fortifications now extended the length of the Western Sahara frontier, added to which the walls completed earlier to the north and west of the frontier defenses provided additional internal security capability. The number of Moroccan forces permanently stationed in Western Sahara was put at some 100,000 in May 1987, the annual cost being estimated at about US$1,000 million. Polisario, meanwhile, made increasing use of SAM-missiles to bring down foreign light aircraft flying over its declared "war zone", while ships in Saharan "territorial waters" also came under guerrilla attack. After a Spanish trawler had been sunk in September 1985, Polisario information offices in Spain were closed and its representatives expelled.

The UN Decolonization Committee in November 1985 voted by 91 to six, with 43 abstentions (including most Western countries), in favour of "direct negotiations" between Morocco and the Polisario. In response, Dr Filali declared that the situation was now one of "total impasse", and that Morocco would no longer regard itself as bound by UN Resolutions or participate in UN discussions on the issue. He added, however, that Morocco would remain open to personal initiatives from the UN Secretary-General, Javier Pérez de Cuellar. A series of "proximity talks", arranged by Pérez de Cuellar, were held in April 1986, but failed to make any progress.

Towards the end of 1986, however, some diplomatic movement became apparent when on Dec. 2, 1986, the UN General Assembly's customary resolution reaffirming that Western Sahara was "a question of decolonization which remains to be completed on the basis of the exercise by the people of Western Sahara of their inalienable right to self-determination and independence" was not, as in previous years, specifically opposed by Morocco (which was absent from the vote) and was thus adopted by 98 votes to none with 44 abstentions. Subsequently, on the initiative of King Fahd of Saudi Arabia, King Hassan had talks with President Chadli of Algeria on May 4, 1987—the meeting taking place in the border town of Akid Lufti. A joint communiqué gave no details of their discussions on the Western Sahara question, but recorded that they had agreed to "continue meetings between the two brother countries to resolve outstanding problems". By May 1987 the SADR had secured diplomatic recognition from over 70 countries.

JB/MWr

South Africa-Black Homelands

The emergence in South Africa of homelands for blacks—either as territories with varying degrees of internal autonomy or as "independent" states (none of which have been recognized by the international community)—has created what are now territorial disputes, arising out of the division of land between blacks and whites during the 19th and the early part of the 20th century.[1]

Historical Background

The clash between blacks (successively referred to as natives, Bantu or Africans) on the one hand and whites on the other over the right to land has at its roots two entirely different concepts: (i) the African tribal concept based on occupation rights, which might refer to land of three different types—communal grazing areas, residential sites and small areas for the growing of crops—all based on occupation but not ownership of land; and (ii) the European concept of private ownership of land, which could involve the possible renting, sale, subdivision or other disposal, even for speculative purposes.

During more than 100 years tribally-owned land in southern Africa gradually passed into white ownership until a first effort to halt this process was made by the (South African) Bantu Land Act, No. 27 of 1913, which fixed the boundaries of the tribally-occupied land, or "native reserves".

Until 1913 Africans had been legally entitled to acquire land from whites in parts of the country which were outside the native reserves (which later became the homelands), but the 1913 act prohibited such purchases unless they were in areas which various commissions had recommended for "release" to Africans. Gen. J. B. M. Hertzog, then Minister of Native Affairs, said at the introduction of the 1913 bill that in their own areas the natives were free to live as they liked and added that if possible they should govern themselves, perhaps "in an autonomous way".

No further action was taken until the Bantu Trust and Land Act, No. 18 of 1936, which tried to reverse the process of further reduction and fragmentation of the tribally-occupied land by encouraging the "release" from white ownership of certain lands which were to be added to and consolidated with the reserves. Whereas the courts had found that the 1913 prohibition of land purchases from whites by blacks unless the land had been recommended for release could not be applied in the Cape Province, the 1936 act extended the prohibition to the whole country, while it upheld the right of Africans to purchase land in "released" areas. The 1936 act also enabled the government to eliminate so-called "black spots", i.e. tribal land wholly surrounded by white-owned land. The act provided that a quota of 6,209,857 hectares (over 7,250,000 morgen) should gradually be added to the scheduled reserves. However, the total land area to be assigned to Africans, who constituted 70 per cent of the country's population, was only 13 per cent of South Africa's total area.

The government subsequently proceeded with its policy of apartheid, later called "separate development" or "plural democracy", establishing from 1957 onwards Bantu Territorial Authorities under a Bantu Authorities Act and "Bantu national units" or Bantu homelands under the Promotion of Bantu Self-Government Act of 1959, with the object (as explained in a White Paper in the same year) of, inter alia, uniting "the members of each Bantu national group in one national unit concentrated in one coherent homeland where possible".

Consolidation of the homelands was continued in the following years, and on Sept. 13, 1977, Dr F. Hartzenberg, then South African Deputy Minister of Bantu Development, stated that since the 1950s the homelands had been consolidated from 264 separate areas to 24, but that total consolidation was neither possible nor necessary for economic development.

---

[1]For related South African-Swaziland territorial issues, see pages 191-93.

P.W. Botha, then South African Prime Minister, conceded at a Transvaal National Party congress on Sept. 1, 1980, that the homelands could not be consolidated sufficiently to meet their economic and material aspirations, as in most homelands less than 20 per cent of their people's income was generated in their own geographical area and "of course we cannot give away the whole of South Africa merely to create economically viable states". The government was therefore, he said, as part of its "constellation of southern African states programme", to launch an offensive to promote regional economic co-operation, to which he added: "In developing such co-operation projects we must be willing to transcend the

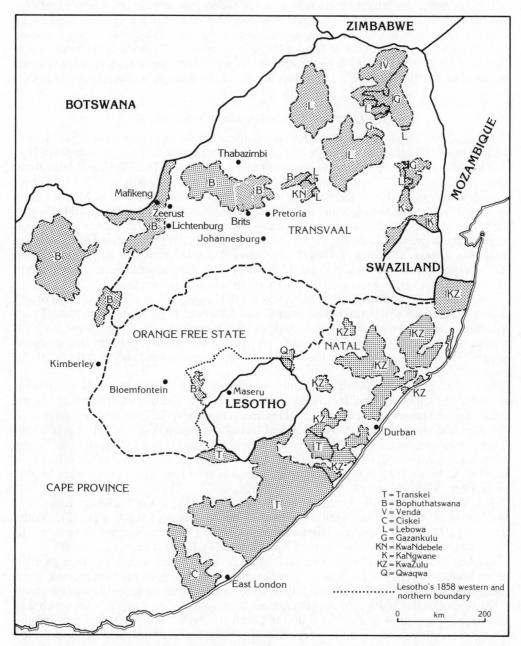

Map 20   The South African Black homelands, also showing the disputed Lesotho-South Africa border and Swaziland.

boundaries of the traditional areas in South Africa and to extend a hand of co-operation over the borders of states".

In new guidelines for the consolidation of black homelands—now referred to as black national states—agreed upon by the South African Cabinet on Oct. 28, 1980, it was proposed eventually to transfer land to these states to "satisfy their most important development requirements and to end South Africa's responsibility for land through negotiation with the national states individually but with Parliament having to give its final approval to any decisions.

Land demands made by the various homelands leaders from time to time included calls for the general enlargement of their territories and also demands for specific areas to be transferred to them. In a joint statement on constitutional changes in South Africa, issued on Feb. 18, 1980, by the leaders of seven (not yet "independent") black homelands, it was demanded as a "non-negotiable prerequisite for blacks" that "the allocation of land cannot be based on the 1913 and 1936 Land Acts but should be done on a more equitable basis.

Territorial Demands made by Transkei

Among the demands for additional land, those made by Paramount Chief Kaiser Matanzima of Transkei, both before and after the latter's achievement of "independence" on Oct. 26, 1976, were particularly persistent and far-reaching. In 1968 Chief Matanzima, then Chief Minister of Transkei, asked for the incorporation in his territory of Port St Johns, the white districts of Elliot and Maclear (eastern Cape Province) as well as Mount Currie (Kokstad) and the adjoining white parts of the districts of Matatiele and Umzimkulu (the three last-named districts being known as East Griqualand). The South African government rejected this request in 1969, but Port St Johns was eventually incorporated in Transkei in 1976. On June 4, 1968, the Transkei Legislative Assembly passed a motion giving the Transkei government a mandate to ask the South African government for the amalgamation of Transkei and Ciskei into one Xhosa state under a united government.

On April 13, 1971, Chief Matanzima described the land question as "the most important aspect of the policy of separate development" and declared: "Most white South Africans are ashamed that seven-eighths of South African land is occupied by them. Unless the land question is settled fairly early there can be no really good relations between the two racial groups. We shall negotiate with the Republican government until they accede to all our requests".

M.C. Botha, then South African Minister of Bantu Administration and Development, replied to the Chief on April 16, saying that there was "no land dispute between the South African government and the Bantu"; that the areas claimed by the Chief had become part of the Republic "by tradition, convention and legislation and not as a result of war"; that Transkei was not overcrowded but parts of it were not properly occupied; and that according to the late Dr Verwoerd (who as Minister of Native Affairs and later Prime Minister had been the chief architect of separate development) Transkei would, with proper planning, be able to support 50,000,000 people.

B.J. Vorster, then South Africa's Prime Minister, referring to the Transkei's requests in the House of Assembly on April 21, admitted that of the 53,400,000 acres (21,600,000 hectares) of land to be transferred to the Bantu under the 1936 act a balance still remained to be transferred—64,682 hectares in the Cape Province and 67,372 hectares in Natal.

On Aug. 14, 1971, Chief Matanzima said that, if Africans from South Africa were resettled in the homelands (as was the policy of the South African government), "we must be given more land". The following year, on April 11, he declared with reference to the land question: "The refusal of the South African government to release that part of Transkei which was unilaterally expropriated after the Union of South Africa Act was passed has now put the Transkei people politically, in their relations with white South Africa, back to the pre-1963 days" (i.e. before Transkei was given internal self-government).

Vorster in turn stated in the House of Assembly on April 19, 1972, that his government would fulfil its obligations under the 1936 Act but would reject any demand for land beyond that envisaged in the act. However, Chief Matanzima again emphasized on May 10 that the land claim would not have arisen if it were not for the migratory labour policy of South Africa under which thousands of Africans were "repatriated" to their "homelands" every year.

On Aug. 7, 1972, the Chief stated that he envisaged a black-controlled multi-racial Xhosaland consisting of Transkei, Ciskei, East Griqualand and white-owned land between the Fish and Kei rivers and in which blacks and whites would have equal rights. In reply, A.J. Raubenheimer, then South African Deputy Minister of Bantu Development, said on Aug. 9 that the South African government would not oppose a union of Transkei and Ciskei but that it could not be a wholly contiguous territory incorporating white-owned land.

After Transkei had been granted "independence", Chief Matanzima said at a press conference on Oct. 27, 1976, that the South African government had "no right to give the Ciskei self-government" (as had been done in 1972) and that he would "just take this land", as it belonged "to the Xhosa nation". However, a secretary in his department said on Oct. 29 that the Prime Minister had merely said that areas of the Ciskei where the people themselves wished to be governed by Transkei should be allowed to become part of Transkei.

On March 8, 1977, Chief Matanzima again named the South African districts of Elliot and Maclear and added farms in Cedarville, Matatiele, Mount Currie, Harding and part of Port Shepstone west of the Umzimkulu river (forming part of the Transkei border with Natal) as being areas which should be "added as soon as possible to our small state under Section 1 of our Constitution Act". M.C. Botha retorted on March 9, however, that the South African government did not agree that the Chief had "historical claims to all the areas mentioned", and emphasized that any land still to be acquired by Transkei had been scheduled in a 1976 agreement.

On March 30, 1977, Chief Matanzima claimed that East Griqualand (situated between Transkei and the Province of Natal as well as the Transkeian district of Umzimkulu physically separated from the main part of Transkei) was historically part of Transkei. This claim was, however, rejected by a committee of inquiry appointed by the Administrators of Natal and the Cape Province, which found that East Griqualand had never been a black tribal territory but had for 115 years been an area of Griqua, coloured (mixed-race) and white settlement.

Under a bill passed on March 9, 1978, the South African government transferred, with effect from April 1, 1978, control of East Griqualand from the Cape Province, with which it had had no common border since Transkei's achievement of "independence", to the province of Natal. The Transkei government thereupon decided on April 10 to sever its diplomatic relations with South Africa.

Chief Matanzima stated on the same day that before the formation of the Union of South Africa (in 1910) the British government had declared the East Griqualand area to be "part of Kaffraria proper, belonging to the aborigines of Transkei", and that the (white) South African Parliament of 1913 had had no right to annex the area. He claimed that Britain was "under an obligation to render all the necessary assistance to us, their former colony and subjects", but added: "Knowing the strength of the Republic of South Africa militarily, Transkei will bide its time before taking up arms to recover the land that has been cynically raped from it".

On Feb. 13, 1979, the Transkei government made further representations to the South African government regarding East Griqualand, and it was stated in the South African House of Assembly on Feb. 23 that the documents concerned would be studied without prejudice. On Oct. 27, 1979, Chief George Matanzima, who had earlier become Prime Minister of Transkei, was quoted as having emphasized that Kokstad and other areas in East Griqualand should be "returned" to Transkei, and that the land question was crucial to a resumption of diplomatic relations between South Africa and Transkei.

Under a Borders of Particular States Extension Bill, which passed its second reading in the South African House of Assembly on Feb. 11, 1980, with the support of the Opposition, provision was made for the transfer of land, most of which had already been set aside under the 1936 act, to the "independent" black states (then Transkei, Bophuthatswana and Venda). The bill in particular enabled the South African State President to transfer land or portions from the districts of Mount Currie, Maclear, Elliot, Indwe and Queenstown to Transkei. In reference to this bill, Chief George Matanzima was on Feb. 7 reported to have said: "We claim all the land that historically belonged to us." He also disclosed that negotiations were being carried out between land commissions of both the Transkei and the South African governments. In these circumstances diplomatic relations between the two sides were resumed on March 30, 1980.

After P.W. Botha (then South African Prime Minister) had announced on Feb. 20, 1981, that Ciskei would become fully "independent" on Dec. 4, 1981, the National Assembly of Transkei passed, on April 8, 1981, a motion resolving that political delegates from South Africa, Transkei and Ciskei should have discussions on the proposed splitting of the Xhosa nation through the granting of independence to Ciskei. In July 1981 it was reported that the Transkei government was financing a legal action to prevent Ciskei from becoming South Africa's fourth independent homeland—but the action was not successful.

On May 5, 1982, Chief George Matanzima (the Prime Minister of Transkei) challenged Ciskei's jurisdiction over Fort Hare University which, he claimed, belonged to the Xhosa nation as a whole. He also accused the Ciskei police of brutality against students who had, on May 1, demonstrated against a rumoured proposal to rename Fort Hare as the University of Ciskei, with President Lennox Sebe of Ciskei as its first chancellor.

Claims made by Other Homelands Leaders

General or specific claims for more land have also been made by leaders of other homelands from time to time, as described below.

Bophuthatswana. Chief Lucas Mangope, the Chief Councillor of Bophuthatswana (which was then not yet "independent"), proposed on Jan. 23, 1973, that all areas predominantly occupied by Tswanas should be handed over to his government, with whites owning property in these areas being free to remain there. Consolidation proposals made by the South African government on April 9, 1973 were unanimously rejected by the territory's Legislative Assembly, which produced its own plan designed to double the size of the homeland and to take in the white towns of Kuruman, Taung, Warrenton, Vryburg, Delareyville, Lichtenburg, Mafeking, Koster, Zeerust, Rustenburg, Brits and Swartruggens.

The South African government's plan was thereupon revised so as to give Bophuthatswana 605,000 hectares of previously White-owned land while excising from the Territory 352,000 hectares. None of the above-mentioned towns were to be handed over to Bophuthatswana except Taung and later Mafeking (which was ceded on Sept. 19, 1980, when it reverted to its original African name of Mafikeng).

When Bophuthatswana was granted "independence" on Dec. 6, 1977, it consisted of six separate areas. Under a Bophuthatswana Border Extension Bill, which passed all its stages in the South African Parliament on Feb. 22, 1978, parts of five districts of the Transvaal and northern Cape Province were transferred to the "independent" Bophuthatswana, and it was officially stated at the same time that further consolidation could follow if both parties agreed to it. On Sept. 6, 1978, it was announced that 25,000 hectares of Bophuthatswana's territory would be exchanged against 25,000 hectares of white territory adjoining Thaba Nchu.

At the beginning of January 1987 the South African Minister of Lands and Rural Development announced that the territory of Bophuthatswana had been extended by over 25,000 hectares as as result of (i) the cession of former white-owned farmland north of Brits and south of Thabazimbi (this land having previously formed a corridor between two districts of the homeland), and (ii) the cession of other farms to the west of Lichtenburg and Zeerust. Asked about the possibility of the town of Zeerust being consolidated into Bophuthatswana, the minister cited the precedent of Mafeking/Mafikeng and said that it would depend on the views of the government and of the local residents.

Venda. Chief Patrick Mphephu, the President of the Republic of Venda (which had become "independent" on Sept. 13, 1979), announced on Sept. 13, 1980, that his government had asked South Africa to incorporate into Venda the Northern Transvaal towns of Louis Trichardt, Messina, Soekmekaar, Tshipise and Levumbu, as they would be "growth points acting as springboards for the economic development of Venda". He added that whites who wished to keep their land and property should be allowed to do so, as was the case in Swaziland and Bostwana.

Ciskei. Chief Justice Mabandla, who was then Chief Minister of Ciskei, said on Aug. 2, 1972, that all white-owned land between the Kei and Fish Rivers and north from the coast to the Orange River—which would include the port of East London—should form part of Ciskei.

Chief Lennox Sebe, having become Chief Minister of Ciskei, stated on May 21, 1973, that his government would work within the framework of South Africa's separate development policy provided that the entire Ciskei was consolidated into a single territory stretching from the Kei River in the east to the Fish River in the west and from the Indian Ocean to the Stormberg Mountains in the north, and incorporating all white-owned land in this region, probably even the towns of East London, Queenstown and King William's Town. This claim thus included what became known as the "white corridor" between Transkei and Ciskei.

After the Ciskei government, Legislative Assembly and other leaders had on Sept. 30, 1980, accepted "independence" for Ciskei "in principle", Chief Sebe disclosed on Oct. 5 that details for the independence plan to be worked out included Ciskei's demands for more land, and on Feb. 20, 1981, he stated that negotiations over the land question would continue after "independence" (which was subsequently achieved on Dec. 4, 1981).

The South African government, however, did not approve all of the recommendations made by its own consolidation commission for the transfer of certain towns to Ciskei. This applied in particular to King William's Town, where the white voters overwhelmingly rejected the proposed transfer in January 1981, whereupon the government declared in April that the town would not become part of Ciskei.

Gazankulu. Prof. Hudson W.S. Ntsanwisi, the Chief Councillor of the Machangana Territorial Authority (which changed its name to Gazankulu as from April 1, 1972), declared on July 28, 1971, that more land would be needed if the 736,000 Shangaan people then in South Africa were to be resettled in the territory. On May 30, 1973, the Gazankulu Legislative Assembly rejected the South African government's consolidation proposals and demanded the incorporation in its territory of the white Transvaal towns of Tzaneen, Phalaborwa, Mica, Hoedspruit, Komatipoort and White River, as well as large tracts of white-owned agricultural land and parts of the neighbouring homelands of Venda and Lebowa.

KwaZulu. Chief Gatsha Buthelezi, the Chief Executive Officer of the newly established Zululand Territorial Authority, said at the inauguration of the new Authority on June 11, 1970, that he expected the South African government, if they meant what they were saying, "to provide us with more land and to consolidate it", as this was "the only way in which a meaningful state can be created".

After B.J. Vorster, then South Africa's Prime Minister, had in April 1972 stated that he was not prepared to make more land available to homelands than had been promised under the 1936 act, Chief Buthelezi retorted that the Zulus were "not so naive as to participate in a scheme to defraud us by asking for so-called independence before land consolidation and without the purchase of foreign territories within our boundaries". He also urged that Richards Bay (then a new port being built on the Natal coast) should be developed as a seaport for KwaZulu (Zululand's new name as from April 1, 1972) instead of as an overflow port for Durban, but the South African government made it clear, on April 27, 1972, that the new port of Richards Bay would be controlled by white South Africa. On the other hand, KwaZulu gained control, as from April 1, 1977, of the black township of KwaMashu (of some 150,000 inhabitants), previously controlled by the Durban city council.

The (Zulu) *Inkatha* movement (officially described as a cultural movement), which had gained all 55 elective seats in the KwaZulu Legislative Assembly in elections completed on Feb. 24, 1978, had rejected early independence for KwaZulu on the grounds that the Zulus, as the largest ethnic group in South Africa, would not accept "independence of separate pieces of inadequate territory" without any share in the South African economy which they had helped to develop.

Lebowa. Chief M. Matlala, then Chief Councillor of the Lebowa Territorial Authority, called, in April and again in June 1971, for more land to be transferred to his territory to accommodate former squatters and tenants evicted from white-owned farms.

KwaNdebele. Simon Skhosana, the Chief Minister of the KwaNdebele homeland, was in May 1981 reported to have stated that he had asked the South African government for more land and to have added: "When they give it to you, you say 'thank you' and ask again."

By 1983 the KwaNdebele homeland covered about 200 square miles (518 sq km), but under consolidation proposals this area was to be increased to 1,320 square miles (3,419 sq km). The KwaNdebele Minister of Agriculture declared on Feb. 21, 1983, that the proposals, although increasing the homeland's size more than sixfold, did not fully meet KwaNdebele's land demands, and that representations for more land would be made to the consolidation committee.

A South African proposal to transfer the Moutse area (with some 120,000 residents) from the Lebowa homeland to the KwaNdebele homeland with effect from Jan. 1, 1986, was opposed by the Lebowa homeland authority. The deputy for the Moutse area in the Lebowa Legislative Assembly was quoted as saying that only about 10 per cent of the people of Moutse were Ndebele-speaking, with the majority being Sotho-speaking; that the area had potential resources of coal and asbestos and some social amenities which KwaNdebele did not have; and that the proposed transfer was intended to enhance KwaNdebele's image as a potential independent state.

Although the formal transfer of the area to KwaNdebele had not yet been gazetted, an armed Ndebele vigilante force entered the Moutse area on Jan. 1 in order to claim it and to attack villagers in the area; the resultant fighting caused the death of at least 21 persons, including two black policemen.

It was subsequently reported that in protest against the proposed transfer of Moutse, the Lebowa homeland authority had, on Feb. 14, 1986, severed its ties with South Africa. By that time the transfer had not yet been ratified by the South African Parliament.

The KwaNdebele Legislative Assembly, on Aug. 12, 1986, rejected a South African proposal for complete independence for the KwaNdebele homeland. However, on May 5, 1987, the Assembly voted unanimously to reverse this decision and thus to become South Africa's fifth "independent" black homeland.

Conclusion

The South African government does not appear to regard the process of consolidation of the black homelands as having been completed and seems ready to transfer to them certain areas of agricultural land of limited extent. However, it is fair to conclude that, despite the exceptional case of the transfer of Mafeking/Mafikeng to Bophuthatswana, the government does not wish to alienate white voters by ceding further white towns to black homelands.

HWD

South Africa-Swaziland

In 1982 the South African government made proposals to accede to territorial aspirations harboured by Swaziland by transferring to the latter the KaNgwane black homeland and also the Ingwavuma district of the KwaZulu homeland—both areas being predominantly inhabited by Swazis. However, both homeland governments strongly resisted the proposals, which were subsequently shelved in 1984 pending future agreement on the transfers between Swaziland and the two homelands concerned. (For a map showing Swaziland, KaNgwane and KwaZulu, see page 185.)

Negotiations between the governments of South Africa and of Swaziland on the cession to Swaziland of the (South African) black homeland of KaNgwane and the KwaZulu homeland's Ingwavuma district (bordering on Swaziland) were begun in 1981. The Chief Minister of KaNgwane, Enos Mabuza, claimed on Dec. 16, 1981, that in these negotiations the South African government's real aim was to deprive South Africa's 750,000 Swazis (of whom some 220,000 lived in KaNgwane) of their South African citizenship and to deny them access to South Africa's wealth.

As a first step towards the proposed cession, the South African government issued, on June 18, 1982, a proclamation dissolving the KaNgwane Legislative Assembly and placing that homeland, together with the Ingwavuma district, under the direct control of the (South African) Department of Co-operation and Development. The proposed border adjustment was defended by Dr Piet Koornhof (then South African Minister for Co-operation and Development) as a step towards the fulfilment of the "long-cherished ideal of the Swazi people, who have for long been deprived of Swazi citizenship by an accident of history, to be united under one king in one country".

However, Western commentators suggested that the South African government was seeking to use Swaziland's territorial aspirations as a lever to persuade its government to adopt a firmer attitude towards African National Congress (ANC) guerrillas, who in some instances operated from or through Swaziland. It was subsequently disclosed (in March 1984) that South Africa and Swaziland had signed a non-aggression pact in February 1982, under which each side undertook to combat terrorism, to respect the other's sovereignty and territorial integrity, and to prevent any activity within its boundaries which might threaten the integrity of the other.

The proclamation was opposed by the great majority of the members of the KaNgwane Legislative Assembly and of KaNgwane's Swazi chiefs. It was also opposed by most members of the Organization of African Unity (OAU) on the grounds that it violated the OAU principles on the maintenance of existing boundaries in Africa and that it was based on citizenship principles which had accompanied the birth of South Africa's "independent" homelands.

The proposed cession of South African territory was also opposed by the ANC (banned in South Africa) which, on July 16, 1982, sent a memorandum to the Swaziland government declaring that the land deal, if implemented, would "seriously complicate and impede the struggle for the liberation of South Africa and transform Swaziland into an ally of the apartheid regime".

The Swaziland government, on the other hand, claimed on July 12, 1982, that there had been a favourable response from OAU members to a Swaziland mission sent to explain the border negotiations. It also argued that its territorial claims preceded the establishment of black homelands and that it was merely seeking to correct an historical injustice at the expense of South Africa. (It was reported in the Western press that most Swaziland ministers had been opposed to the deal but had been overruled by two strongly royalist ministers.)

Inside South Africa, the Natal Provincial Council (dominated by the opposition New

Republic Party) on June 30, 1982, passed a motion calling on the government to hold a referendum among those affected by the proposed land deal. However, P.W. Botha, then South African Prime Minister, claimed in late June that most South African-born Swazis supported the move, declaring that the government had evidence, "obtained from petitions and reports by different experts", that the people of Swazi origin in South Africa "would generally welcome a border adjustment if their resident rights, work opportunities and general living standards are not prejudiced".

Court Actions taken by KwaZulu Authorities—Establishment of Rumpff Commission

Dr Oscar Dhlomo, the KwaZulu Minister of Education and Culture, on June 23, 1982, filed an application that the proclamation be set aside, and on June 25 Justice D.L. Shearer of the Natal Supreme Court ruled that the Ingwavuma district should revert to KwaZulu control since consultation had not taken place, pending a court action challenging the South African government's decision to take over the administration of the area. However, the government on June 28 issued a retroactive proclamation (this time under the 1927 Administration Act, which empowered the State President to alter the borders of South Africa's native areas without consultation), repealing the original proclamation but again removing the Ingwavuma district from KwaZulu control. The new proclamation further stated that the chiefs appointed by the Ingwavuma regional authority should cease to be members of the KwaZulu Legislative Assembly and that no members of the Assembly should be elected from those areas concerned.

Nevertheless the Natal Supreme Court in Pietermaritzburg on June 30, 1982, nullified the government's second proclamation and again returned control of the Ingwavuma district to KwaZulu. Government lawyers lodged an appeal with the Appeal Court in Bloemfontein and contended on July 1 that the latter proclamation remained valid until the appeal was heard, arguing that the government's administration of Ingwavuma was therefore legal. Christopher Albertyn, representing the KwaZulu Executive Council, maintained on the other hand that the Supreme Court's decision meant that the Department of Co-operation and Development must relinquish administrative control over Ingwavuma, as Justice Shearer had originally ruled. On July 2, 1982, the KwaZulu magistrate in Ingwavuma refused to hand over the administration of the district to the commissioner for black affairs in Nelspruit (Transvaal), who had been appointed by the South African government to administer both KaNgwane and the Ingwavuma district.

The Natal Supreme Court, sitting in Pietermaritzburg on July 5, 1982, allowed an interdict ordering the government and the Department of Co-operation and Development and their officials not to interfere in the administration of the Ingwavuma district until the case had been finally decided by the Appeal Court. The state counsel immediately gave notice of intention to appeal against the interdiction, but leave to appeal was refused and the government was ordered to pay costs.

The Appeal Court in Bloemfontein ruled on Sept. 30, 1982, that the presidential proclamation issued in June purporting to restore Ingwavuma to South African jurisdiction was null and void since the State President had acted ultra vires. The Appeal Court's decision rested on two factors: (i) the right of KwaZulu to seek legal redress against the state, and (ii) the failure of the State President to consult the KwaZulu government as required under the 1971 National States Constitution Act.

It was also announced on the same day that a commission under the chairmanship of Frans Rumpff, a former South African Chief Justice, would be appointed to investigate and report on the conflicting claims between KaNgwane, KwaZulu and Swaziland.

Further Opposition from KaNgwane Authorities—Subsequent Out-of-Court Settlement

Enos Mabuza declared on June 22, 1982, that the KaNgwane Legislative Assembly would defy the June 18 proclamation. The KaNgwane authorities' opposition to the proposed border adjustment was backed by popular demonstrations of support, including a strike by black civil servants in late June and a number of rallies in July; at one of these rallies Mabuza declared on July 25 that his people "would rather the ground opened up and swallowed us than be ruled by Swaziland".

An application brought on behalf of the KaNgwane Executive Council contesting the validity of the proclamation dissolving the KaNgwane Legislative Assembly—on the grounds (i) that the South African government had not consulted the Assembly and (ii) that it had dissolved the Assembly by proclamation, not by statute as required by law—was on July 22, 1982, referred to the full bench of the Transvaal Supreme Court.

However, Dr Koornhof subsequently announced on Nov. 25, 1982, that the South African government had agreed to withdraw the proclamation dissolving the KaNgwane Legislative Assembly within 14 days or at a mutually agreed date. Consequently, Mabuza withdrew the application to the Supreme Court in Pretoria, which was due to be heard that day, for the return of the administration of KaNgwane to the tribal authorities (it being subsequently decided that the KaNgwane government would be re-established on Dec. 9). In addition, costs were awarded against the South African government. Both parties agreed that the issue of whether KaNgwane should be included in the border adjustment should be referred to the Rumpff Commission, to which the KaNgwane government was allowed to appoint three members (the South African government having already appointed five and the KwaZulu authorities three). Mabuza declared on Nov. 27 that the agreement represented a "positive basis for future co-operation" and that the most important outcome was that "the people of KaNgwane would not be incorporated into Swaziland against their will".

Shelving of Territorial Transfer Proposals

The South African government on June 19, 1984, announced the dissolution of the Rumpff Commission and stated that there would be no unilateral incorporation of KaNgwane and Ingwavuma into Swaziland. In its report the commission had recommended that the territorial transfers should not go ahead without the majority support of the people involved, but the South African government took the view that the threat of intimidation made it impossible to hold plebiscites to determine the wishes of the homeland residents.

In dissolving the commission, the South African government recommended that the leaders of Swaziland and the two homelands concerned "should deliberate amongst themselves" on the matter, adding that any proposals made jointly and unanimously would be considered sympathetically. Subsequently, in August 1984, "self-government" status was restored to KaNgwane, while in March 1987 an agreement was reached between the two sides under which the KaNgwane government was to assume responsibility for economic development, administration and township management as soon as possible after April 1, 1987.

HWD

Zaïre-Zambia

Relations between Zaïre and Zambia have been troubled in the 1980s by a continuing border dispute centring principally on the area around Lake Mweru on Zambia's northern border with Zaïre. (A map showing the Zaïre-Zambia border is published on page 155.)

Although Presidents Mobutu of Zaïre and Kaunda of Zambia joined with President dos

Santos of Angola in October 1979 in signing a tripartite non-aggression pact, bilateral relations between Zaïre and Zambia became strained in August 1980 over Zambian claims that Zaïre had set up border posts some 30 kilometres inside Zambian territory in the Kaputa district of Zambia's Northern province. In June 1981 the Zambian Prime Minister announced that the Kaputa border dispute, which also involved the nearby Lake Mweru border area, might be referred to the Organization of African Unity (OAU) and that Zambia was confident of the OAU finding in its favour on the basis of the OAU's 1964 declaration that boundaries drawn up by the former colonial powers should be respected.

Tensions escalated in 1982 amid a series of incidents and skirmishes in various sections of the border area. Thousands of Zambians were reported to have fled from villages along the border near Mufulira (in Zambia's Copperbelt province), following an exchange of fire on Feb. 28, 1982, and the alleged seizure by Zaïreans of Zambian soldiers, two buses and a lorry. The Zaïrean authorities on March 2 closed the border between the two countries in the Sakania area (in southern Shaba province) and claimed that three of their soldiers had been killed by Zambian forces on Zaïrean territory the previous month. Diplomatic sources in Lusaka (the Zambian capital) attributed much of the tension to shortages of food and other essentials in Zaïre's Shaba province and to a recent tightening of customs and immigration regulations in an effort to halt smuggling.

A meeting of the Zaïre-Zambia permanent regional joint commission in April 1982 agreed on a reciprocal release of prisoners (involving 55 Zaïreans held by Zambia and 25 Zambians held by Zaïre). However, in June 1982 Lusaka radio claimed that Zaïre had established border posts at Mutambala and Musasa, some 18 and 12 miles respectively inside Zambian territory.

After three days of talks in Zaïre, Presidents Mobutu and Kaunda on Aug. 30, 1982, issued a communiqué which pledged the two countries to continue negotiations to find a permanent solution to the border dispute. Nevertheless, Lusaka radio subsequently claimed that three Zambians and two tourists on a hunting safari had been abducted in the Kaputa area on Sept. 5. An emergency meeting of the Zaïre-Zambia joint commission on Sept. 16, 1982, in the Zaïrean border town of the Kasumbalesa considered Zambian accusation of Zaïrean violations of its territory and resulted in Zaïre agreeing to remove its soldiers from a border village in Luapula province some 10 miles inside Zambia.

In September 1983 Zambian troops were deployed along the border with Zaïre following an incident on Sept. 21 in which two Zambian workers were killed and two wounded in an ambush by Zaïreans near the border town of Mufulira. In announcing the move, President Kaunda said that, in view of an escalation of crimes of banditry and smuggling by Zaïrean nationals in the border area, troops and increased police resources were needed to bring the situation under control. Further strain was caused by a Zambian decision of July 17, 1984, to deport over 2,500 Zaïrean and other African nationals, whereupon Zaïre the following month said that a similar number of illegal residents were to be expelled from Shaba province, most of them Zambians; although the order against the Zambians was later revoked, some 2,000 Zambian workers had by that time fled from the country.

Relations between Zaïre and Zambia continued to be strained in 1985 and were aggravated by an influx into Zambia of Zaïrean refugees from disturbances in Shaba province in November 1984. On Oct. 4-5, 1986, Presidents Mobutu and Kaunda met for talks at Gbadolite (northern Zaïre) and succeeded in bringing about an improvement in their countries' relations, although the causes of the border tensions of recent years remained unresolved. On June 26, 1987, however, President Kaunda announced that a formula for resolving the Kaputa dispute had been worked out by the two governments and that accordingly the issue would be settled by the end of the year.

AJD

3. THE MIDDLE EAST

Introduction

Most of the present-day borders between states of the Middle East region have their origins in the territorial arrangements arising from the dismemberment of the Ottoman Turkish empire at the end of World War I. At that time the emergence of the Arab peoples from centuries of Ottoman overlordship was accompanied by aspirations to Arab unity among their leaders, many of whom subscribed to the aim of creating a single Arab independent state, or at least a federation of states. Such aspirations were not fulfilled, however, partly because large areas of the Middle East came under the direct or indirect control of Britain and France, whose influence served to strengthen traditional rivalries between the different centres of Arab power. Although the concept of Arab unity remained a potent force, the result was that the eventual independence of the peoples of the region came about largely on the basis of the post-1918 territorial dispositions of the European powers. However, because borders across much of the vast desert tracts of the Arabian peninsula and western Asia had never been clearly demarcated, the inevitable consequence has been a substantial degree of border and territorial dispute between the successor states.

Since its creation in 1945 the Arab League has, as the major organ of inter-Arab co-operation, sought to act as a channel for the peaceful resolution of border and territorial disputes between its member states. It has achieved some successes in this respect, notably in that few such inter-Arab disputes have been allowed to escalate into open hostilities and others have in fact been brought to a negotiated settlement under Arab League auspices. However, as detailed in the following section, there exist a number of instances where territorial uncertainties have not been finally resolved, or where dormant claims may possibly become active disputes given the relative political instability of the Middle East region.

It should also be noted that the territorial relationships between the longer-established major Arab states and several of the newer and smaller states on the littoral of the Arabian sub-continent constitute a particular category of existing or potential disputes. Given that most of the littoral states came to independence relatively recently after being actual or effective British protectorates, claims have been made that they are artificial creations of the former colonial power in territories which historically owed allegiance to other centres of Arab power. Thus Iraq has in the past laid claim to the whole of Kuwait, while Saudi Arabia's relations with southern and eastern neighbours are coloured by the suspicions of the latter concerning Saudi territorial aspirations.

The Middle East region is also affected by territorial disputes between Arab and non-Arab states, in which the added ingredient of racial or religious difference has tended to make such antagonisms considerably more violent and protracted than those between Arab countries. Iran's longstanding dispute with Iraq over the Shatt al-Arab waterway and over Iraqi claims to Arab-populated areas of western Iran escalated into a major war in 1980. Moreover, in the Arab-Israeli conflict over the land of Palestine the Middle East region has the dubious distinction of containing the world's most bitter and apparently irreconcilable territorial dispute, which the two sides have failed to resolve despite four major wars (six if the 1978 and 1982 Israeli incursions into Lebanon are counted) in the space of four decades.

The Arab-Israeli Conflict

The longstanding and still unresolved conflict between Israel and the Arab world has two main territorial dimensions. At a fundamental level, many Arabs do not accept the existence of a Jewish state within any borders and assert that the Palestinian Arabs are the rightful heirs to predominant political authority in the former British mandated territory of Palestine. On another level, the outcome of the 1967 Arab-Israeli war, which left Israel in control of large tracts of territory beyond the de facto borders resulting from the 1948-49 war, brought Israel into direct territorial dispute with Egypt, Jordan and Syria, each of which demanded the return of their Israeli-occupied territories as well as a settlement of the basic Palestinian question. In March 1979 an historic breakthrough was achieved with the signature of an Egyptian-Israeli peace treaty, the first between Israel and an Arab state; under this treaty the whole of Sinai (but not the formerly Egyptian-controlled Gaza Strip) was restored to Egyptian rule over the following three years and relations between the two countries were normalized.[1] But Israel has remained in deadlock with Jordan over its continued occupation of the West Bank and with Syria over its retention (and effective annexation in December 1981) of the Golan Heights, while sporadic post-1979 negotiations on the establishment of some form of Palestinian "autonomy" in the West Bank and Gaza Strip had made no substantive progress by mid-1987.

Historical Background

The Zionist[2] case for the creation of a modern Jewish state in Palestine was based pre-eminently on the historical connexion between the Jewish people and the region in question; but the extent to which Palestine can be regarded as the historic homeland of the Jewish people is a subject of considerable dispute in which both sides have their distinguished supporters. Zionist historians contend that throughout most of the last 1,200 years of the pre-Christian era Jews constituted the main settled population of what in Roman times became known as Palestine, enjoying long periods of independence in states which included coastal cities and plains (notably under the reigns of Kings David and Solomon). In contrast, Arab historians maintain that the Jews were only one of many Semitic tribes which penetrated the region in ancient times and that Jewish states were relatively short-lived and never at any time extended to the coastal plains (which were inhabited by Philistines, from whom the name "Palestine" is itself derived). What is not in dispute is that Palestine came under effective Roman control in the first century BC; that in 70 AD the (Roman puppet) Jewish state of Judaea was overthrown by the Roman Emperor Titus, who captured Jerusalem, destroyed the Jewish Temple and took many Jews as captives to Rome; and that after repeated rebellions by the Jews against their Roman overlords Jerusalem was finally razed to the ground in 135 AD and most of the surviving Jewish inhabitants of Palestine were expelled. This was the beginning of the diaspora (dispersion) of the Jewish people, who in the succeeding centuries became scattered throughout Europe and eventually the world in a complex sequence of large and small migrations from one country to another.

In the Arab view, the dispersion of the Jews in the second century AD marked the effective termination of the Jewish connexion with Palestine; moreover, according to this viewpoint, the conquest of Jerusalem by Moslem Arabs in 636 AD and the subsequent conversion and

---

[1]For the unresolved Egyptian-Israeli dispute over the Taba strip, see pages 232-34.

[2]Zionism, the movement promoting Jewish settlement of Palestine, takes its name from the hill in Jerusalem on which the ancient palace of King David, and later the Temple, were built.

Arabization of the Semitic inhabitants of Palestine irreversibly established the identity of the region as part of the Arab world. Against this, Zionists point out that the dispersed Jewish people never abandoned the hope—however metaphysically expressed through the centuries—of returning to the land from which their forbears had been expelled. They also cite historical evidence showing that Jews continued to live in Palestine in sizeable numbers after 135 AD—although the continuity and extent of this presence after the fifth century AD is again a matter of dispute. Certainly in the crusading era of the 11th, 12th and 13th centuries there were significant Jewish communities in several cities of the "Holy Land" and Jews are known to have fought alongside Arabs against the warriors of the cross in full awareness that, in victory, the Christian crusaders made no distinction in their treatment of Moslem and Jew.

Historians are also agreed that the Moslem reconquest of Palestine in 1291 and the relative tolerance shown thereafter to Jews stimulated a degree of Jewish migration to Palestine from European countries where anti-Jewish persecution was becoming endemic. The expulsion of the Jews from Spain in 1492 accentuated this migratory trend, which continued following the establishment of Ottoman Turkish rule over Palestine from 1517. In the early 16th century there were, for example, an estimated 10,000 Jews living in the region of Safed (north-west of the Sea of Galilee and one of the four "holy cities" of Judaism together with Jerusalem, Hebron and Tiberias) and the importance of Safed as a centre of Jewish learning is indicated by the fact that a Hebrew printing press set up there in 1563 was the first press of any language to be installed in the Asian continent. Nevertheless, as a proportion of the total population, the Jews of Palestine remained a tiny minority and formed only one non-Moslem community among the several which enjoyed a relatively tranquil existence under Turkish rule.

In 1880 there were still only 25,000 Jews in Palestine, as against an Arab population which has been variously estimated at between 150,000 and 450,000; however, over the next three decades there occurred a dramatic upsurge of Jewish immigration. Between 1880 and the outbreak of World War I in 1914 Jewish settlement of Palestine almost quadrupled to some 90,000, as over 60,000 Jews entered the country, mainly from Russia and Poland. And these new arrivals were of a different type and with a different motivation than previous Jewish migrants. Inspired by the Zionist ideals of Theodor Herzl (1860-1904), the new wave of Jews came as farmers and artisans, seeking to build a new Jewish society based on the land and thus to recreate a national identity for the dispersed Jewish people. As propounded by Herzl in his celebrated pamphlet *Der Judenstaat* published in 1896 and by the first Zionist congress in 1897, Zionism called for the preservation of the Jewish people by national reunion, which was to be achieved by "establishing for the Jewish people a publicly and legally assured home in Palestine". Such ideas became particularly influential in the ghettos and Jewish villages of Eastern Europe, where millions of Jews were living in poverty and facing a mounting threat from the growth of virulent anti-semitism in the host societies.

Although efforts by Zionist leaders to secure the agreement of the Turkish Sultan to the establishment of a Jewish homeland in Palestine proved inconclusive, the piecemeal purchase of land for Jewish settlers proceeded apace, the finance being provided by wealthy Jews of Western Europe (and later the United States). Such purchases were made mainly from Arab landlords (although land owned by Europeans and Turks was also sold to Jews) and often at inflated prices, considering that the tracts acquired were usually desert wasteland or malarial marsh, which were then drained, irrigated and cultivated by Jewish settlers. In 1909 the first entirely Jewish town in modern Palestine was founded on the sandhills north of the Arab Mediterranean port of Jaffa and given the name Tel Aviv.

The new wave of Jewish immigration into Palestine met with an immediate hostile response from the Arab population. Although major Arab opposition developed only after World War I, as early as 1882 the Turkish authorities responded to Arab disquiet at Zionist plans by seeking to prevent the entry of Jews through the Mediterranean ports and the first Arab attacks on Jewish agricultural settlements took place in the mid-1880s. In 1891 leaders of the Arab community in Jerusalem sent a petition to Constantinople demanding the prohibition of Jewish immigration and land purchase, and in the early years of the 20th century anti-Zionist newspapers and societies were founded by Arabs in several cities of Palestine and also further afield. The scene was thus set for the fundamental confrontation of national aspirations which is still with us today. In the words of the Arab writer Neguib Azoury set down in 1905: "These two movements [i.e. Zionism and Arab nationalism] are destined to fight each other continually, until one of them triumphs over the other".[1]

The Balfour Declaration, Arab-British Undertakings and the Sykes-Picot Agreement

Having failed to make any real progress with the Ottoman authorities, Zionist leaders concentrated their efforts on persuading European governments of the validity and desirability of establishing a Jewish homeland in Palestine. An important consideration in this respect was the realization that the days of the Ottoman empire were numbered. Ultimately, the decision of Turkey to ally itself with the central powers in World War I created a constellation of forces in which this aim became a practical proposition, given that Britain and France saw themselves as the joint post-Ottoman powers in the Middle East. In what was widely construed as a move to ensure international Jewish support for the allied war effort, the then British Foreign Secretary, Arthur Balfour, sent a letter to Lord Rothschild (a prominent British Jewish Zionist) dated Nov. 2, 1917, and worded as follows:

"I have much pleasure in conveying to you, on behalf of His Majesty's government, the following declaration of sympathy with Jewish Zionist aspirations which has been submitted to, and approved by, the Cabinet. His Majesty's government view with favour the establishment in Palestine of a national home for the Jewish people, and will use their best endeavours to facilitate the achievement of this object, it being clearly understood that nothing shall be done which may prejudice the civil and religious rights of existing non-Jewish communities in Palestine, or the rights and political status enjoyed by Jews in any other country. I should be grateful if you would bring this declaration to the knowledge of the Zionist Federation."

The Balfour declaration, which was approved by the French government and published immediately (and subsequently reflected in the Palestine mandate given to Britain by the League of Nations—see below), is seen by Jews as a cornerstone of the legitimacy of the eventual establishment of a Jewish state in Palestine. But it was rejected then and subsequently by the Palestinian Arabs as a colonialist instrument which, by failing to take account of the wishes of the majority population, contravened the fundamental principle on which the allied powers claimed to be fighting the 1914-18 war, namely the right of self-determination of peoples. It is also claimed by the Arab side that the Balfour declaration and other allied agreements of the time ran counter to undertakings given by Britain to its wartime Arab allies that Britain would support the independence of the Arabs once the Turks had been defeated. In the latter respect the crucial documents are the correspondence in 1915-16 between Sir Henry McMahon (the British high commissioner in Cairo) and Sharif Hussain of Mecca (head of the Hashemite dynasty of Hejaz and the father of the subsequent King of Iraq, Faisal) and also the agreement between Sir Mark Sykes of Britain and Georges Picot of France concluded in May 1916. Over both these sets of undertakings considerable controversy still flourishes.

In his first note to Sir Henry McMahon (dated July 14, 1915), Sharif Hussain requested that Britain should recognize "the independence of the Arab countries" bounded (i) in the north by a line drawn from Mersin (on the northern Mediterranean coast of Turkey) running north-east through Adana to the 37°N parallel and thence eastward to the Persian frontier, (ii) on the east by the Persian frontier down to the Persian Gulf, (iii) on the south by the Indian Ocean (with the exception of Aden) and (iv) on the west "by the Red Sea and the

---

[1]Quoted by Martin Gilbert in *The Arab-Israeli Conflict—Its History in Maps* (London, 1974). p. 6, from *Le Reveil de la Nation Arabe* (Paris, 1905).

Mediterranean Sea back to Mersin". In his reply (dated Oct. 24, 1915), Sir Henry declared on behalf of the British government that "the districts of Mersin and Alexandretta[2] [the present Turkish port of Iskenderun], and portions of Syria lying to the west of the districts of Damascus, Homs, Hama and Aleppo, cannot be said to be purely Arab, and must on that account be excepted from the proposed delimitation"; subject to that modification and to the proviso that nothing should be done to the detriment of the interests of France, Great Britain was "prepared to recognize and uphold the independence of the Arabs in all the regions lying within the frontiers proposed by the Sharif of Mecca". Subsequent exchanges between the two correspondents achieved no clear reconciliation of these contrasting delimitations of the future independent Arab state or states, although Britain achieved its object of securing active Arab assistance in the war against Turkey.

At no point in the Hussain-McMahon correspondence was mention made of Palestine or of the Ottoman administrative unit centred on Jerusalem. Since this area was not one of potential French interest, the Arabs took the view that it had been promised as part of the territory of Arab independence, whereas the British government consistently maintained that McMahon's reservations were intended to exclude the whole of the eastern Mediterranean littoral from Turkey down to Sinai. At the centre of this particular controversy is the meaning in the correspondence of the term "district", for which both men used the Arabic word *wilaya*, and whether the term was intended to refer precisely or at all to the *vilayet*, the largest unit of Ottoman local administration. In support of the British interpretation, it is pointed out that the Ottoman *vilayet* containing the city of Damascus stretched right down to the Gulf of Aqaba in the south, on the strength of which it is argued that all the territory to the west of this *vilayet* was excluded in the undertakings given to the Arabs. On the other hand, Arab analysts have pointed out that the "districts" referred to in the correspondence did not correspond with Ottoman *vilayets* (either in intention or in fact) and signified only geographical areas relating to the cities mentioned. On this basis, they contend that the littoral excluded from future Arab rule was that to the north of the approximate level of the city of Damascus, and also note that even this exclusion was contested by Sharif Hussain in the course of the correspondence.

The uncertainties arising from the Hussain-McMahon correspondence will probably never be resolved to universal satisfaction. There is, however, general agreement that Britain's promises to the Arabs in 1915-16 were in conflict in certain important respects with the terms of the almost concurrent Sykes-Picot agreement under which Britain and France (with Russian concurrence) drew up a plan for the post-war dismemberment of the Ottoman empire in the Middle East. This secret agreement (which was eventually disclosed to the Arabs by the Russian Bolsheviks) divided the region into French and British spheres of influence to the north and south respectively of a line roughly corresponding with the present-day Syrian border with Jordan and Iraq (except in the east, where the Mosul region was included in the French sphere). It further specified that in these spheres the two powers would recognize and uphold "an independent Arab state or a confederation of Arab states ... under the suzerainty of an Arab chief". But it also stipulated (i) that France and Britain would be allowed to establish "direct or indirect administration or control" in certain designated areas, France being allocated the eastern Mediterranean littoral north of a line just south of Safed, and Britain the Tigris-Euphrates basin (Mesopotamia); (ii) that Palestine from just south of Safed down to a line just south of Gaza (and bounded in the east by the Dead Sea and the Jordan river) would be under "an international administration, the form of which is to be decided upon after consultation with Russia, and subsequently in consultation with the other allies and the representatives of the Sharif of Mecca"; (iii) that within this international zone Britain would be "accorded" the ports of Haifa and Acre and a surrounding enclave of territory.

---

[2]For an account of the later dispute between Syria and Turkey over the Sanjak of Alexandretta (now the Turkish province of Hatay), see pages 256-59.

Establishment of British Palestine Mandate

In the event, the post-1918 disposition of former Ottoman territories showed significant variations from both the Hussain-McMahon undertakings (such as they were) and the Sykes-Picot agreement, although it was closer to the latter than to the former. After protracted and complex negotiations accompanied by confrontations and some actual military conflict between various of the interested parties, the shape of the post-war map of the Near East was not finally determined until the signature of the Treaty of Lausanne on July 24, 1923. But already, at the San Remo conference of April 1920, Britain and France had reached agreement on the establishment of British and French mandates (as opposed to spheres of influence) over territories which extended well into the area previously designated as part of an independent Arab entity.

As eventually agreed by the new League of Nations (established in January 1920), France obtained a mandate over an area almost corresponding with the present territory of Lebanon and Syria—i.e. extending substantially to the east of the littoral designated for "direct or indirect" French rule by Sykes-Picot. Moreover, the two British mandates encompassed not only Palestine (defined as including Transjordan and the Negev desert down to the port of Eilat on the Gulf of Aqaba) but also the whole of present-day Iraq. As for the rest of the Arabian peninsula to the south, this area was recognized as independent Arab territory, but through a system of protectorates, treaties and financial subsidies it became effectively a British sphere of influence.

The mandatory instrument for Palestine differed significantly from the others in that it committed Britain to securing the establishment of a Jewish national home in the mandated territory (and also in that it contained no specific provision for the constitutional development of the inhabitants towards eventual independence). As approved by the Council of the League of Nations in 1922, the instrument said in its preamble that the principal allied powers had agreed "that the mandatory should be responsible for putting into effect the declaration originally made on Nov. 2, 1917, by the government of His Britannic Majesty, and adopted by the said powers, in favour of the establishment in Palestine of a national home for the Jewish people, it being clearly understood that nothing should be done which might prejudice the civil and religious rights of existing non-Jewish communities in Palestine, or the rights and political status enjoyed by Jews in any other country". The preamble then recorded that "recognition has thereby been given to the historical connexion of the Jewish people with Palestine and to the grounds for reconstituting their national home in that country".

In its detailed provisions the instrument specified inter alia that the mandatory "shall be responsible for placing the country under such political, administrative and economic conditions as will secure the establishment of the Jewish national home ... and the development of self-governing institutions, and also for safeguarding the civil and religious rights of all the inhabitants of Palestine, irrespective of race and religion" (Article 2); that "an appropriate Jewish Agency shall be recognized as a public body for the purpose of advising and co-operating with the Administration of Palestine in such economic, social and other matters as may affect the establishment of the Jewish national home and the interests of the Jewish population in Palestine, and subject always to the control of the Administration, to assist and take part in the development of the country" (Article 4); that "the Administration of Palestine, while ensuring that the rights and position of other sections of the population are not prejudiced, shall facilitate Jewish immigration under suitable conditions and shall encourage, in co-operation with the Jewish Agency referred to in Article 4, close settlement by Jews on the land, including state lands and waste lands not required for public purposes" (Art. 6); and that a nationality law would be framed for Palestine "so as to facilitate the acquisition of Palestine citizenship by Jews who take up their permanent residence in Palestine" (Article 7). (The Jewish Agency referred to in the mandatory instrument was eventually set up in 1929 and recognized by Britain for the purposes of the instrument.)

The importance of the mandate's terms from a Zionist point of view was that for the first time the commitment to a Jewish national home in Palestine was enshrined within an internationally recognized instrument which superseded the ambiguous and conflicting undertakings entered into previously. For the Arabs, however, the system of British and French mandates represented a betrayal of wartime promises of independence, the Palestine mandate in particular being regarded as a device to facilitate the settlement of Arab territory by an alien people, i.e. the Jews. The regime imposed was therefore seen not only as a denial of the right of self-determination proclaimed by the allies during the war but also as a direct contravention of Article 22 of the Covenant of the League of Nations, which in its rationale of the mandatory system specifically excluded "certain communities formerly belonging to the Turkish empire" from those former colonies and territories defined as "inhabited by peoples not yet able to stand by themselves under the strenuous conditions of the modern world" and therefore as appropriate for the mandatory system.

Then and subsequently Zionists pointed out that the area allotted for the establishment of a Jewish national home amounted to only a tiny fraction of the Middle East territories taken from the Turks; mandated Palestine west of the River Jordan, it was noted, covered less than 11,000 square miles (28,500 sq km), whereas the total area of Arab lands (including mandated territories) stretched to nearly 1,200,000 square miles (3,000,000 sq km). But this argument was not appreciated by Palestinian Arabs in the actual circumstances of the Palestine mandate, where a post-war new wave of Jewish immigration, mainly from Russia and Poland, was seen as a direct threat to their way of life and political future. In the latter context, the Arabs laid particular stress on the "European" character of the Jewish immigrants who were arriving under the impulse of Zionism, maintaining that the Ashkenazic Jews of Europe were not Semitic like the Sephardic Jews of the Arab world and had no historical connexion with Palestine because they were descended from the Khazar tribes of south-east Russia who embraced Judaism in the eighth century and later spread through eastern and central Europe.

Attacks by Arabs on Jewish settlements in Palestine began in earnest in early 1920, and after one such incident at Kinneret on the Sea of Galilee the Jews decided (in June 1920) to set up their own defence force, the *Haganah*. Later in the year the first Arab riots under British rule led to a decision by the British authorities in September (but later rescinded) that Jewish immigration to Palestine should not exceed 16,500 people a year; moreover, from 1921 the area east of the River Jordan was entirely closed to Jewish settlement (whereas Zionist plans of the period envisaged a Jewish national home stretching well across the Jordan, and also into southern Lebanon and south-west Syria). The latter measure was taken in the context of the separation of Transjordan from the rest of the mandate and its establishment as an autonomous state under Emir Abdullah, this process leading to semi-independence in 1928 (although Transjordan did not become fully independent until 1946). The other British mandated territory became the fully independent state of Iraq in 1932 under King Faisal, whereas Lebanon and Syria remained under French mandate until being declared independent by the Free French during World War II, at the end of which they both became founder members of the United Nations. From 1923 mandated Syria included the Golan Heights, which were ceded by Britain in that year after originally forming part of the Palestine mandate.

Development of Arab-Jewish Conflict under British Mandate

The disturbances of 1920 set the pattern of the history of the British mandate west of the Jordan, where opposing Arab and Jewish national aims not only precluded any agreement on the constitutional future of Palestine but also generated increasingly violent inter-communal conflict. As early as May 1921 the British authorities reacted to Arab rioting by placing a temporary ban on all Jewish immigration, and although this was quickly lifted the official British position became that immigration should not exceed "the economic capacity of Palestine to absorb new immigrants". In September 1921 Britain promulgated a constitution for Palestine, but it was never implemented because the Arabs were unwilling to accept its provisions relating to the Jewish national home. Thereafter, all attempts to secure

Arab-Jewish political co-operation foundered against the rocks of diametrically opposed and increasingly entrenched Jewish and Arab positions.

By 1928 the Jewish population of Palestine had reached 150,000 (and the Arab population 600,000), and increasing Arab disquiet resulted in the first large-scale Arab-Jewish clashes in 1928-29. Further serious violence occurred in 1933, when Hitler's advent to power in Germany heralded a sharp increase in Jewish immigration from Europe, taking the Jewish population of Palestine to 400,000 by 1936 and close to 30 per cent of the total. In that year Palestinian Arabs set up an Arab High Committee to organize opposition to Jewish settlement and the situation quickly deteriorated into one of widespread inter-communal clashes accompanied by an Arab general strike. With increasing numbers of British soldiers being killed (almost all at this stage in clashes with armed Arab bands), the British government responded (in April 1936) by setting up a royal commission under Lord Peel charged with recommending means of implementing the Palestine mandate in such a manner as to lessen Jewish-Arab friction. In its report, published on July 7, 1937, and accepted by the British government, the Peel Commission found that "the hope of harmony between the races has proved untenable" and recommended the partition of Palestine into separate Arab and Jewish states, with Britain retaining a permanent mandate over two enclaves containing Jerusalem, Bethlehem and Nazareth. Particular features of the Peel proposals were that the Arab state would consist of Transjordan (still legally part of the mandate) united with that part of Palestine allotted to the Arabs and that there should be treaty provision for the exchange of land holdings and population between the two new states.

The Peel Commission report summarized the advantages of partition to the Arabs as follows: "(i) They obtain their national independence and can co-operate on an equal footing with the Arabs of the neighbouring countries in the cause of Arab unity and progress. (ii) They are finally delivered from the fear of being 'swamped' by the Jews and from the possibility of ultimate subjection to Jewish rule. (iii) In particular, the final limitation of the Jewish national home within a fixed frontier and the enactment of a new mandate for the protection of the Holy Places, solemnly guaranteed by the League of Nations, removes all anxiety lest the Holy Places should ever come under Jewish control. (iv) As a set-off to the loss of territory the Arabs regard as theirs, the Arab state will receive a subvention from the Jewish state [and] also, in view of the backwardness of Transjordan, obtain a grant of £2,000,000 from the British Treasury [as well as a further grant for the conversion of uncultivable land in the Arab state into productive use]".

As regards the Jews, the advantages of the Peel proposals were also summarized: "(i) Partition secures the establishment of the Jewish national home and relieves it from the possibility of its being subjected in the future to Arab rule. (ii) Partition enables the Jews in the fullest sense to call their national home their own: for it converts it into a Jewish state. Its citizens will be able to admit as many Jews into it as they themselves believe can be absorbed. They will attain the primary objective of Zionism—a Jewish nation, planted in Palestine, giving its nationals the same status in the world as other nations give theirs. They will cease at last to live a 'minority life'."

The concept of partition was reluctantly accepted by the Jews as the best solution that could be hoped for in the circumstances; but it was totally rejected by the Arabs, who in 1937 launched a general revolt not only against the Zionists but also against the British authorities endeavouring to keep the peace between the two sides. A feature of the escalating violence from 1937 was the increasing incidence of Jewish retaliation against Arab attacks, despite reiterations by the Jewish National Council (the representative body of Jews in mandated Palestine) of the need for continued restraint in the face of Arab provocation. Various alternative partition plans were put forward over the next two years—notably those of the Woodhead Commission of 1938—but none overcame the fundamental opposition of the Arabs to any legitimization of a Jewish entity in the territory of Palestine.

As organized guerrilla warfare by both communities developed during 1938, the British government abandoned partition as a possible solution and in May 1939 published a White Paper asserting that it was not British policy that Palestine should become either a Jewish state or an Arab state; that an independent Palestinian state should be set up within 10 years; that meanwhile Jews and Arabs should be asked to take an increasing share in the country's administration; and that Jewish immigration into Palestine should be limited to 75,000 people over the next five years (after which such entry would require Arab consent). In pursuance of this new policy, the British government on Feb. 28, 1940, published regulations banning further land purchases by Jews in about two-thirds of the territory of Palestine, restricting such purchases in most of the remaining third and leaving only the narrow coastal plain from Haifa southward to beyond Tel Aviv as a free zone for further acquisitions.

Like earlier blueprints for the future, the 1939 White Paper failed to obtain any positive response from either community. The Arabs rejected it as failing to meet their longstanding demand for the termination of the mandate and the creation of an independent Palestinian state based on majority rule. For the Jews it represented a betrayal by Britain of its commitment under the mandate to promote the establishment of a Jewish national home in Palestine. And throughout the late 1930s the increasingly perilous position of Jewish communities in Europe gave particular urgency to the Zionist demand that Palestine should be open to unrestricted Jewish immigration (especially since most countries of the world were either wholly or partially closed to Jewish refugees). By 1939 the Jewish population of Palestine had risen to 445,000 (about 30 per cent of the total), but whereas over 30,000 Jews entered the country in 1939 the British authorities allowed in only 10,000 in 1940, 4,500 in 1941 and 4,200 in 1942. In this situation the Zionists sought to step up illegal immigration, but the war conditions prevailing from 1939, combined with British counter-measures, seriously hampered such activities, at the very time when millions of Jews in Europe were being liquidated by the Nazis.

Termination of the British Mandate—Establishment of the State of Israel and the 1948-49 Arab-Israeli War

The constitutional position of Palestine was frozen by the British government for the duration of World War II, during which civil strife between Arab and Jew remained largely in abeyance. But the end of the war in 1945 signalled a resurgence of the political and inter-communal struggle in Palestine in ever greater intensity than before, particularly since the cause of the Palestinian Arabs now took on concrete pan-Arab dimensions. In March 1945 the independent Arab states formed the Arab League, proclaiming their intention to give active support to Palestinian Arab aspirations and asserting that, while the League "sympathizes as deeply as anyone with the Jews for the horrors and sufferings they have endured in Europe", it nevertheless believed that "nothing would be more arbitrary or unjust than to wish to resolve the question of the Jews of Europe by another injustice of which the Arabs of Palestine ... would be the victims". On the Jewish side, the traumatic experience of Nazi persecution massively reinforced the Zionists' determination to secure a Jewish political entity in Palestine, to which end they obtained the active support of the United States.

Despite pressure from the US government for a relaxation of immigration restrictions, the British authorities maintained the 1939 White Paper policy, at a time when settlement in Palestine was the goal of tens of thousands of survivors of the European holocaust. The Jews responded by organizing large-scale illegal immigration and also by bringing in arms supplies (notably from the Soviet-bloc countries) for use in the increasingly ferocious struggle with the Arabs, whose armed groups were now often supplemented by units from the surrounding Arab countries. British soldiers and policemen attempting to control the rapidly deteriorating situation were frequently the target of extremists of both sides. Eventually, after various new partition-type proposals had again failed to move the Arabs from their demand for a unitary Palestinian state based on majority rule, the British government decided in February 1947 to refer the Palestine question to the United Nations (as the successor to the League of Nations for the purposes of the mandate).

Following the British referral, a Special Committee on Palestine (UNSCOP) was established by the UN General Assembly in May 1947 and this committee subsequently submitted a majority recommendation that Palestine should be partitioned into Arab and Jewish states (three of the 11 members favouring a federal state and one abstaining). With some frontier adjustments, the UNSCOP recommendation was eventually adopted by the UN General Assembly in an historic vote on Nov. 29, 1947, in which the required two-thirds majority was surpassed with 33 states voting in favour, 13 against, 10 abstaining and one absent. Those in favour of partition (and thus in favour of the creation of a Jewish state) included the Soviet Union and its satellites (then anxious to assist the British retreat from empire) as well as most Western and Latin American nations; those against were Afghanistan, Cuba, Egypt, Greece, India, Iraq, Lebanon, Pakistan, Persia (Iran), Saudi Arabia, Syria, Turkey and Yemen; those abstaining were Argentina, Chile, China, Colombia, El Salvador, Ethiopia, Great Britain, Honduras, Mexico and Yugoslavia; and the absent country was Siam (Thailand).

The UN partition plan (the territorial aspects of which are shown in map 21 on page 213) provided for (i) the creation of a Jewish state in three linking segments, made up of eastern Galilee in the north, the coastal plain from Haifa south to the Rehovoth area (except Jaffa) and most of the Negev desert in the south; (ii) the creation of an Arab state in three linking areas of western Galilee, central Palestine and the southern littoral extending inland along the Egyptian border into the western Negev, with Jaffa as a coastal Arab enclave; (iii) the establishment of Jerusalem and Bethlehem as an international zone to be administered by the United Nations; and (iv) the creation of an economic union between all three parts. The General Assembly resolution specified inter alia that the British mandate should be terminated (and the withdrawal of British forces completed) as soon as possible and not later than Aug. 1, 1948; that the independent Arab and Jewish states and the special international regime for Jerusalem should come into existence two months after the British evacuation and not later than Oct. 1, 1948; and that "the period between the adoption by the General Assembly of its recommendation on the question of Palestine and the establishment of the independence of the Arab and Jewish states shall be a transitional period". The General Assembly also appointed a five-nation UN commission (Bolivia, Czechoslovakia, Denmark, Panama and the Philippines) which was to proceed to Palestine under the aegis of the UN Security Council to take over the country's administration when the British withdrew and then to transfer power to Arab and Jewish provisional governments.

The General Assembly's decision was immediately rejected by the Arab states and the Palestinian Arabs as contrary to the principles of the UN Charter and to the terms of the original League of Nations mandate, on which grounds the six Arab governments voting against partition declared that they did not consider themselves bound by the decision and reserved full liberty of action. In contrast, although it gave them less than half of the Palestinian territory, the partition plan was immediately accepted by the Jews as the means of achieving internationally-recognized statehood. After the British government had announced in December 1947 that it would relinquish the Palestine mandate on May 15, 1948, it was announced from Jerusalem on Jan. 12, 1948, that the Jewish Agency and the Jewish National Council had completed plans for a provisional government of the proposed Jewish state after the termination of the mandate. As Jewish units fought for control of the area designated for the Jews and organized warfare with Arab forces developed, President Truman of the United States proposed on March 25, 1948, that since it had "become clear that partition cannot be carried out at this time by peaceful means" the partition plan should be shelved in favour of a temporary UN trusteeship of the whole territory. This suggestion was categorically rejected by the Jews, however, and on May 14, a few hours before the termination of the British mandate at midnight, the establishment of the state of Israel was officially proclaimed in Tel Aviv by the Jewish National Council.

After recalling the origins and aims of Zionism in its preamble, the proclamation declared that the state of Israel "will be open to the immigration of Jews from all countries of their dispersion; ... will uphold the full social and political equality of all its citizens, without distinction of religion, conscience, education and culture; will safeguard the Holy Places of all religions; and will loyally uphold the principles of the United Nations Charter". It would also be "ready to co-operate with the organs and representatives of the United Nations in the implementation of the resolution of the Assembly on Nov. 29, 1947, and will take steps to bring about the economic union over the whole of Palestine". It concluded: "In the midst of wanton aggression, we yet call upon the Arab inhabitants of the state of Israel to preserve the ways of peace and play their part in the development of the state, on the basis of full and equal citizenship and due representation in all its bodies and institutions—provisional and permanent. We extent our hand in peace and neighbourliness to all the neighbouring states and their people, and invite them to co-operate with the independent Jewish nation for the common good of all. The state of Israel is prepared to make its contribution to the progress of the Middle East as a whole. Our call goes out to the Jewish people all over the world to rally to our side in the task of immigration and development and to stand by us in the great struggle for the fulfilment of the dream of generations for the redemption of Israel."

Simultaneously with the birth of the state of Israel at midnight on May 14-15, 1948, Palestine was invaded by the unco-ordinated forces of Egypt from the south, Transjordan and Iraq (backed by Saudi Arabian units) from the east and Syria and Lebanon from the north. The aims of these Arab armies, as proclaimed in a statement issued by the Arab League countries on May 15, was to establish the independence of Palestine for its lawful inhabitants on the basis of majority rule, which clearly implied the destruction of the new Jewish state. The Arab invasion was immediately condemned as an act of aggression by the UN Security Council, forceful statements being made to this effect by both the US and the Soviet representatives, respectively Warren Austin and Andrei Gromyko.

The Arab League statement, after a forceful recapitulation of the alleged infringement of Arabs' rights and interests during the mandate and a reiteration of the Arabs' rejection of the UN partition plan, concluded as follows: "The governments of the Arab states recognize that the independence of Palestine, which has so far been suppressed by the British mandate, has become an accomplished fact for the lawful inhabitants of Palestine. They alone, by virtue of their absolute sovereignty, have the right to provide their country with laws and governmental institutions. They alone should exercise the attributes of their independence, through their own means and without any kind of foreign interference, immediately after peace, security and the rule of law have been restored to the country. At that time the intervention of the Arab states will cease, and the independent state of Palestine will co-operate with the states of the Arab League in order to bring peace, security and prosperity to this part of the world. The governments of the Arab states emphasize ... that the only just solution of the Palestine problem is the establishment of a unitary Palestine state, in accordance with democratic principles, whereby its inhabitants will enjoy complete equality before the law, [and whereby] minorities will be assured of all the guarantees recognized in democratic constitutional countries, and [whereby] the Holy Places will be preserved and the right of access thereto guaranteed. The Arab states most emphatically declare that [their] intervention in Palestine is due only to these considerations and objectives and that they aim at nothing more than to put an end to the prevailing conditions in [Palestine]. For this reason they have great confidence that their action will have the support of the United Nations [and that it will be] considered as an action aiming at the realization of its aims and at promoting its principles, as provided for in its Charter".

In the first Arab-Israeli war initial Arab advances were quickly stemmed by Israeli forces, who subsequently mounted a successful counter-attack and not only secured virtually all of the territory allotted to the Jews under the UN partition plan but also took control of substantial additional areas (see map 22 on page 213). When the fighting finally ended in early 1949 on the basis of a UN-sponsored ceasefire declared on Dec. 29, 1948, the territory controlled by Israel extended to the whole of Galilee in the north and to the whole of the Negev in the south, where only a narrow coastal strip around Gaza remained in Arab hands; the proposed Arab enclave of Jaffa was also taken by the Jews. Moreover, although the Jordanian Arab Legion held much of the area of central Palestine designated for the Arabs (and also expelled the Jews from the Old City of Jerusalem), Israeli forces succeeded in establishing control over a wedge of territory connecting the coastal plain with Jerusalem. Armistices were signed by Israel with Egypt on Feb. 24, 1949, with Lebanon on March 23, with Transjordan on April 3 and with Syria on July 20 (but not with Iraq), under which Israel surrendered areas of captured territory in southern Lebanon, northern Sinai and the Gaza Strip but was left in control of over two-thirds of the territory of Palestine. Over the next decade these boundaries were to gain widespread international acceptance (outside the Arab world) as the frontiers of the state of Israel. Official Israeli figures showed that during the fighting from November 1947 to January 1949 over 4,000 Jewish soldiers and some 2,000 Jewish civilians were killed; no official Arab casualty figures were released.

An important aspect of the 1948-49 war was the massive displacement of Arab Palestinians from their homes and land, although the circumstances of this displacement and the numbers involved are both matters of considerable dispute. Arab accounts insist that the Arab Palestinians were driven out by Israelis seeking to acquire their land to ensure that the new state had a Jewish majority; but the Israelis have always maintained that most Arab refugees simply fled to escape the fighting and were in some cases ordered to leave by Arab leaders confident of a speedy return following the destruction of the Jewish state. As regards numbers, by June 1950 the total number of refugees registered with the newly-established UN Relief and Works Agency for Palestine Refugees (UNRWA) was 960,021 (a figure itself regarded as inflated by Israeli and some independent sources). The two biggest concentrations were located in the West Bank and the Gaza Strip. Only some 150,000 Arabs remained within the new borders of the Jewish state (concentrated in Galilee in the north), the Jewish population of which at the end of the war was about 660,000.

Unsuccessful Efforts to achieve Peace leading to the 1956 Arab-Israeli War

In the immediate aftermath of the 1948-49 Arab-Israeli war UN-sponsored attempts to bring about a peace settlement between the two sides made some initial progress, the two central issues being the refugee question and the position of the borders between Israel and the neighbouring Arab states. As early as Dec. 11, 1948, the UN General Assembly established a Palestine Conciliation Commission charged with assisting the governments and authorities concerned to achieve a final settlement of all outstanding questions. The relevant resolution asserted inter alia that "refugees wishing to return to their homes and live in peace with their neighbours should be permitted to do so at the earliest practicable moment and that compensation should be paid for the property of those choosing not to return and for loss of or damage to property"; it also called for peace negotiations between Israel and the Arab states. Then and subsequently, Israel expressed its readiness to deal with the refugee problem within the framework of peace talks, but this offer was persistently rejected by the Arab side.

Under the auspices of the commission, representatives of Israel, Egypt, Transjordan, Lebanon and Syria began indirect negotiations in Lausanne in April 1949 and the following month signed a protocol under which they agreed that "a basis for discussions" on the refugee and border issues should be the November 1947 UN partition plan. It has since been claimed by the Arab side that Israel's signature of this protocol amounted to acceptance of the UN partition borders, whereas Israel has pointed out that the latter were to be "a" basis for discussions rather than "the" basis. In any event, the initial progress represented by the protocol quickly encountered the fundamental difficulty that Israel insisted that the Arab refugee problem should be dealt with in the context of a general peace settlement, whereas the Arab states demanded that the refugee problem should be dealt with prior to any general settlement. Under pressure from the US government, the Israeli side eventually made certain proposals on the refugee question—firstly the "Gaza plan" under which 500,000 Arab refugees would be resettled in the Gaza Strip provided that Egypt transferred this area to Israel, and then a proposal that 100,000 refugees should be repatriated to Israeli territory. However, these were rejected by the Arab side, which demanded in the first instance the immediate return of all refugees originating from areas designated for the Arabs under the

UN partition plan and the establishment of an Arab state. With neither side prepared to make further concessions, the Lausanne talks ended in deadlock. (Meanwhile, Israel was absorbing hundreds of thousands of Sephardic Jewish immigrants and refugees from Arab countries, where their position had become actually or potentially endangered by the late 1940s.)

Notwithstanding continuous efforts by the United Nations to salvage its partition plan, the attitudes of the two sides on both the refugee question and the border issue quickly hardened into diametrically opposed positions. All of the Arab states which had signed armistice agreements with Israel maintained that they nevertheless remained in a state of war with the Jewish state and refused to integrate refugees under their jurisdiction on the grounds that their rightful homes were in Palestinian territory now held by the Jews. When on April 24, 1950, the Jordanian Parliament adopted a resolution formally incorporating into the Hashemite Kingdom of Jordan (as Transjordan had been renamed in June 1949) those areas of Arab Palestine held by the Arab Legion at the armistice (i.e. the West Bank and the Old City of Jerusalem), this step was strongly opposed by the other Arab League states as undermining the objective of creating an independent Palestinian state. Earlier in the year the Israeli *Knesset* (Parliament) had, despite UN protests, adopted (on Jan. 23, 1950) a government resolution declaring that Jerusalem had resumed the status of the capital of the Jewish state (but had rejected an opposition amendment designed to make the resolution applicable to the Jordanian-held sector as well as to the Jewish-held New City of Jerusalem). In a parliamentary debate on the question the previous month, Israel's first Prime Minister, David Ben-Gurion, had stated that Israel regarded the November 1947 UN resolution in favour of the partition of Palestine and the internationalization of Jerusalem as no longer possessing any moral force, since the United Nations had failed to implement it.

For their part, the Western powers quickly sought to bring about a measure of stability in the post-armistice realities in Palestine. Under a tripartite declaration issued on May 25, 1950, Britain, France and the United States affirmed "their deep interest in and their desire to promote the establishment and maintenance of peace and stability in the area and their unalterable opposition to the use of force or threat of force between any of the states in that area", and pledged that "should they find that any of these states was preparing to violate frontiers or armistice lines" they would "immediately take action, both within and outside the United Nations, to prevent such violation". The same declaration also committed the three powers to preventing an arms race between the Arab states and Israel by laying down procedures under which the supply of arms to these countries would be restricted to those deemed to be required "to maintain a certain level of armed forces for the purposes of assuring their internal security and their legitimate self-defence and to permit them to play their part in the defence of the area as a whole". In the event, France saw no contradiction between this declaration and its arms supply agreement with Israel of 1952 (albeit secret at the time and principally a response to Egyptian support for the rebels then seeking to overthrow French rule in Algeria), while British attempts to construct an alliance with Iraq and Jordan in the early 1950s also involved the supply of arms.

Israel's interest in obtaining arms reflected the fact that from the territorial point of view the 1949 armistice agreements left the Jewish state with a serious security problem. In the north-east border area Israeli settlements were continually bombarded from positions on the Syrian Golan Heights; in the central coastal plain Israel was only nine miles wide at its narrowest point between the Jordanian West Bank and the sea; and in the south Palestinian *fedayeen* (guerrillas) based in the Egyptian-administered Gaza Strip mounted an increasing number of attacks on Jewish targets across the armistice line. Israel responded to *fedayeen* attacks by carrying out retaliatory actions against guerrilla bases, one such Israeli raid on Gaza in February 1955 causing particularly strong Arab outrage and also provoking general international condemnation. Such raids convinced the Arabs in turn of their need for a modern weapons capability, this objective being a particular preoccupation of the new Egyptian regime of Abdel Gamal Nasser which had come to power in 1954 imbued with a novel mixture of pan-Arab nationalism and revolutionary socialism. In an historic development in September 1955, Nasser concluded a major arms deal with Czechoslovakia, which marked not only the start of increased Soviet influence in the Arab world but also the final breakdown of the Western powers' attempts to prevent an arms race in the Middle East.

Soon after the 1949 armistice Egypt had sought to impose an economic blockade on Israel by denying it the use of the Suez Canal—an action denounced as illegal by Israel but justified by Egypt on the grounds that a state of war still existed between the two countries—and from 1953 Egypt also began restricting Israeli sea-borne trade through the Straits of Tiran at the entrance to the Gulf of Aqaba. Stepped up in 1955, this Egyptian blockade of the southern Israeli port of Eilat combined with increasing Israeli disquiet over Egypt's promotion of *fedayeen* activities in the Gaza Strip contributed substantially to Israel's decision to launch an attack on Egypt in October 1956—in collusion (it later transpired) with Britain and France. For the two Western powers, the key motivation was Nasser's decision of July 1956—taken partly in retaliation for the UK-US decision to withdraw financial aid from the Aswan Dam project—to nationalize the (Anglo-French) Suez Canal Company, in contravention of assurances given in the 1954 Anglo-Egyptian treaty under which British forces had been withdrawn from the Canal Zone. They therefore entered into an agreement with Israel—secret at the time—that an attack by the latter on Egyptian positions in Sinai would be followed by an Anglo-French occupation of the Canal Zone, to be justified in terms of the need to protect the waterway from the warring parties.

The sequence of events was as follows. On Oct. 29, 1956, the Israeli Army attacked Egyptian positions in the Gaza Strip and Sinai, with the declared purpose of destroying *fedayeen* bases. On the next day the British and French governments issued 12-hour ultimatums to both Israel and Egypt, under which they demanded that the two sides should cease warlike actions and withdraw their troops from the immediate vicinity of the Suez Canal, and also requested Egypt to allow Anglo-French forces to be stationed temporarily on the canal to separate the belligerents and safeguard shipping. The rejection of the ultimatum by Egypt was followed by a British and French air offensive on Egyptian airfields and other military targets from Oct. 31 to Nov. 4 and then, on Nov. 5, by Anglo-French paratroop and commando landings in the Canal Zone. Meanwhile, Israeli forces overran the Gaza Strip and most of Sinai, including Sharm el Sheikh and the island of Tiran at the entrance to the Gulf of Aqaba.

The combined opposition of the United States and the Soviet Union brought a quick end to the 1956 Anglo-French-Israeli enterprise, principally because of the political and economic pressure which the US government was able to exert on Britain. Sir Anthony Eden (UK Prime Minister) announced acceptance of a ceasefire on Nov. 6 and a general cessation of hostilities came into effect at midnight on Nov. 6-7, following which the Anglo-French forces were quickly withdrawn. They were replaced by a UN Emergency Force (UNEF) established by the UN General Assembly on Nov. 5, the first contingents of which arrived in Egypt on Nov. 15 and whose presence was agreed to by the Egyptian government under certain conditions. In response to UN and US pressure, Israel quickly evacuated most of its conquests in Sinai but kept its forces in the Gaza Strip and in the coastal strip from Eilat down to Sharm el Sheikh until March 1957. Its eventual withdrawal from these areas was carried out on the assumption that the UNEF units in Gaza would prevent *fedayeen* incursions into Israeli territory and on the basis of assurances from the leading maritime powers that they would support freedom of navigation in the Gulf of Aqaba.

The main beneficiary of the eclipse of Anglo-French influence in the Middle East caused by the Suez episode was the Soviet Union, which in the succeeding years consolidated its relations with the radical Arab states such as Egypt, Syria and Iraq by means of arms supply and economic aid agreements. To counter this development, the United States became increasingly drawn into the power politics of the region, principally as a supporter of Israel but also as the dominant external power on the Gulf and the ally of the conservative Arab states such as Saudi Arabia. The basic Arab-Israel conflict thus became interwoven with great-power rivalries and ambitions which increasingly threatened to transform Middle East instabilities into a wider conflict.

Arab-Israeli Relations from 1957 to 1967 leading to the June 1967 War

With Israel restored to the borders established under the 1949 armistices, armed clashes between Arabs and Israelis continued to occur in the decade following the 1956 Suez war. There were a number of incidents on the Israel-Gaza border in May-June 1957, but by December of that year the area was comparatively peaceful, mainly because of the presence of UNEF. Israeli and Jordanian troops clashed in the Mount Scopus demilitarized zone of Jerusalem in August 1957 and May 1958, each side accusing the other of violation of the armistice agreement in the Jerusalem area. The main trouble area in this period, however, was the Israeli-Syrian border in the demilitarized zone south-east of the Sea of Galilee, which the Israelis claimed to be under their jurisdiction. The most serious incidents in this region took place in March 1962 and August 1963, although clashes were of frequent occurrence from 1957. In August 1963 Syria alleged that there were Israeli troop concentrations on the Syrian border, but an investigation by the UN Truce Supervision Organization (UNTSO) revealed no evidence of a military build-up.

In 1959 Egypt began a new blockade of Israeli trade through the Suez Canal, after having refrained, between 1956 and 1959, from interfering with the passage of Israeli goods when such cargoes were carried in vessels not flying the Israeli flag. During 1959 Egypt detained a number of ships of various nationalities carrying exports from Israel and impounded their cargoes. Egyptian sources justified their action on the ground that there was still a state of war between Israel and the Arab countries, and that Israel therefore had no right to ship goods through the Suez Canal.

A further cause of Arab-Israeli friction was the longstanding dispute over the waters of the River Jordan. A number of plans for an equitable division of the waters between Palestine/Israel and the riparian Arab states (Jordan, Syria, and Lebanon) were proposed between 1944 and 1955, the last of which was agreed at technical level by Israel and the Arab states under US auspices, but broke down at political level, largely because of Syrian opposition. Israel and Jordan subsequently went ahead with separate schemes, Israel pumping water from the Sea of Galilee to be carried by pipeline to the Negev in the south, and Jordan tapping the waters of the two tributaries, the Yarmuk and the Zarqa. Israel's action aroused the anger of the Arabs, whose heads of state, meeting in Cairo in January 1964, decided on a plan to reduce the flow of the northern tributaries of the Jordan, thus reducing the quantity of water Israel would be able to divert. It was some time before work could begin on this scheme, however, as Lebanon and Syria required assurances of their security from Israeli attack during implementation of the diversion projects.

The January 1964 Arab summit also adopted important resolutions endorsing the creation of Palestinian Arab representative bodies, on the basis of which the inaugural meeting of the Palestine National Council (PNC)—a Palestinian parliament-in-exile—was held in the Jordanian sector of Jerusalem in May-June 1964. This first session of the PNC took the decision to establish the Palestine Liberation Organization (PLO) as the armed wing of the Palestinian struggle and also adopted (on June 2) the Palestine National Charter (or "Covenant") as the basic statement of Palestinian Arab aims, which it remains today. Regarded by the Israelis as enshrining the Arab objective of destroying the Jewish state, the 33-article charter states inter alia that "Palestine is the homeland of the Palestinian Arab people ... [and] is an indivisible part of the Arab homeland" (Article 1); that "Palestine, within the boundaries it had during the British mandate, is an indivisible territorial unit" (Article 2); that "the Palestinian Arab people possess the legal right to their homeland and have the right to determine their destiny after achieving the liberation of their country in accordance with their wishes and entirely of their own accord and will" (Article 3); that "the Palestinians are those Arab nationals who, until 1947, normally resided in Palestine regardless of whether they were evicted from it or have stayed there" and also all those born after that date of a Palestinian father "whether inside Palestine or outside it" (Article 5); that "the Jews who had normally resided in Palestine until the beginning of the Zionist invasion will be considered Palestinians" (Article 6).

The charter also declares that "armed struggle is the only way to liberate Palestine" (Article 9); that "the liberation of Palestine, from a spiritual point of view, will provide the Holy Land with an atmosphere of safety and tranquillity, which in turn will safeguard the country's religious sanctuaries and guarantee freedom of worship and of visit to all, without discrimination of race, colour, language or religion" (Article 16); that "the partition of Palestine in 1947 and the establishment of the state of Israel are entirely illegal, regardless of the passage of time, because they were contrary to the will of the Palestinian people and to their natural right in their homeland, and inconsistent with the principles embodied in the Charter of the United Nations, particularly the right to self-determination" (Article 19); that "the Balfour declaration, the mandate for Palestine and everything which has been based on them are deemed null and void" on the grounds that "claims of historical or religious ties of Jews with Palestine are incompatible with the facts of history and the true conception of what constitutes statehood" (Article 20); that "the Palestinian Arab people ... reject all solutions which are substitutes for the total liberation of Palestine and reject all proposals aiming at the liquidation of the Palestinian problem or its internationalization" (Article 21); that "Zionism is a political movement originally associated with international imperialism and antagonistic to all action for liberation and to progressive movements in the world [and] is racist and fanatic in its nature, aggressive, expansionist and colonial in its aims and fascist in its methods" (Article 22); and that "the Palestine Liberation Organization ... is responsible for the Palestinian Arab people's movement in its struggle—to retrieve its homeland, liberate and return to it and exercise the right of self-determination in it—in all military, political and financial fields and also for whatever may be required by the Palestine case on the inter-Arab and international levels".

As the principal guerrilla arm of the PLO, the *Al Fatah* ("Conquest") group led by Yassir Arafat mounted numerous incursions into Israel, initially mainly from Jordan and increasingly during 1965 from Syrian territory. An intensification of such attacks in October and November 1966 gave rise to a serious political crisis which led directly to the third Arab-Israeli war. After a resolution calling on Syria to strengthen its measures against guerrilla activities had been vetoed in the UN Security Council by the Soviet Union on Nov. 4, Israeli forces carried out a reprisal raid on a Jordanian village on Nov. 13, which was condemned by the Security Council on Nov. 25. In late November and early December 1966 violent rioting occurred in the principal towns of the Jordanian West Bank, where the population demanded arms to defend themselves against further Israeli attacks. By the end of 1966 both Israel and Jordan had taken military steps suggesting an anticipation of possible war, while from January 1967 tension between Israel and Syria increased sharply amid repeated armed clashes on the ground and in the air. During Israel's independence day celebrations on May 14, 1967, the Israeli Prime Minister, Levi Eshkol, warned that a serious confrontation with Syria was inevitable if Syrian-backed guerrilla activities continued.

The sequence of events immediately prior to the June 1967 war unfolded as follows. *May 15*: Egyptian troops and tanks began moving across Sinai towards the Israeli border. *May 16*: The Egyptian government declared a state of emergency throughout the country and announced that its forces were "in a complete state of preparedness for war". *May 17*: Syria and Jordan similarly announced that their forces were being mobilized. *May 18*: Egypt made an official request to the UN Secretary-General, U Thant, that UNEF forces should be withdrawn from Egyptian territory and the Gaza Strip (recalling that their presence was subject to Egyptian approval) and Iraq and Kuwait announced the mobilization of their forces. *May 19*: The UNEF was officially withdrawn, with U Thant explaining that "there seemed to me to be no alternative course of action which could be taken by the Secretary-General without putting into question the sovereign authority of the [Egyptian government] within its own territory". *May 21*: Both Egypt and Israel announced the call-up of reservists, and the PLO announced that its forces had been placed under the military commands of Egypt, Syria and Iraq. *May 22*: It was announced in Cairo that President Nasser had accepted an offer of Iraqi army and air force units to assist Egypt in the event of an outbreak of hostilities. *May 23*: Nasser announced the closing of the Straits of Tiran to ships flying the

Israeli flag and to any other vessel carrying strategic goods to Israel (including oil), this action being described by Eshkol as an act of aggression against Israel and as a violation of the freedom of navigation assurances given when Israel withdrew from Sharm el Sheikh in 1957. *May 24*: Egypt announced that the Gulf of Aqaba had been effectively sealed off, while contingents of Saudi Arabian troops were reported to have arrived in Jordan. *May 26*: Following a visit by Abba Eban (Israel's Foreign Minister) to Paris, London and Washington (May 24-25), Israel warned that it had the right to break the blockade of the Gulf of Aqaba if the United Nations or the maritime powers failed to act. *May 27*: U Thant reported to the UN Security Council that Egypt had assured him that it would "not initiate offensive action against Israel" but that Israeli shipping would not be allowed to pass through the Straits of Tiran. *May 28-29*: General mobilization was proclaimed in Sudan (May 28) and Algeria announced that military units were being sent to assist Egypt (May 29). *May 30*: King Hussein of Jordan visited Cairo and signed a defence pact with Egypt under which each country would consider an attack on either as an attack on both, while Abba Eban warned that if the Gulf blockade was not lifted soon Israel would "act alone if we must . . . but with others if we can". *May 31*: Iraqi troops and armoured units were reported to be moving into Jordan towards the Israeli border, while several Arab countries threatened to take action against the oil interests of Western states who aided Israel. *June 2-3*: More than 20 maritime nations were presented with a UK-US draft declaration affirming the right of free and innocent passage through the Gulf of Aqaba but containing no provision for any enforcement action. *June 4*: Nasser said that any such declaration would be regarded as a transgression of Egyptian sovereignty and "a preliminary to an act of war", while Iraq joined the Egypt-Jordan defence pact and Libya pledged troops to assist Egypt in the event of war. *June 5*: Early in the morning the Israeli Air Force launched a pre-emptive strike against Egyptian airfields, while later in the day, after Jordanian forces had moved against Israeli positions on the 1948 armistice line, Israel also attacked airfields in Jordan, Syria and Iraq, destroying virtually all the air capability of these four countries on the first day of what subsequently became known as the Six-Day War.

With the benefit of complete air supremacy, Israeli forces achieved a rapid and complete victory in the June 1967 war. By the time hostilities ended in a ceasefire on June 10 Israel had (i) captured the Gaza Strip and overrun the entire Sinai peninsula up to the Suez Canal, including Sharm el Sheikh; (ii) gained control of the Old City of Jerusalem and overrun all of Jordanian territory west of the Jordan; and (iii) captured the Golan Heights from Syria and penetrated some 12 miles into Syrian territory (this advance being achieved in the final stages of the fighting after both Israel and Syria had signified acceptance of a ceasefire). By the end of the war the Israeli armed forces were in occupation of an area more than three times greater than the territory of Israel at the outbreak of hostilities (see map 23 on page 213), the newly occupied territories extending to some 27,000 square miles (70,000 sq km) as compared with the 8,000 square miles (20,000 sq km) of the Jewish state within the 1949 armistice lines. Israeli soldiers killed in the fighting totalled 766 while Arab losses (never definitively announced) were thought to include about 10,000 Egyptian and 6,000 Jordanian dead.

An important result of the 1967 war was a four-fold increase in the number of Palestinian Arabs under Jewish rule, from a pre-war total of some 300,000 to about 1,200,000 (as against a mid-1967 Jewish population of some 2,500,000). Although up to 200,000 Palestinians fled from the West Bank during the war, about 600,000 remained under the new Israeli administration, as did approximately 300,000 in the Gaza Strip. Virtually the entire population of the Syrian territory captured by Israel—about 60,000—fled eastwards during the fighting, leaving the Golan Heights practically uninhabited in the immediate post-war period.

Map 21   The UN partition plan, 1947.

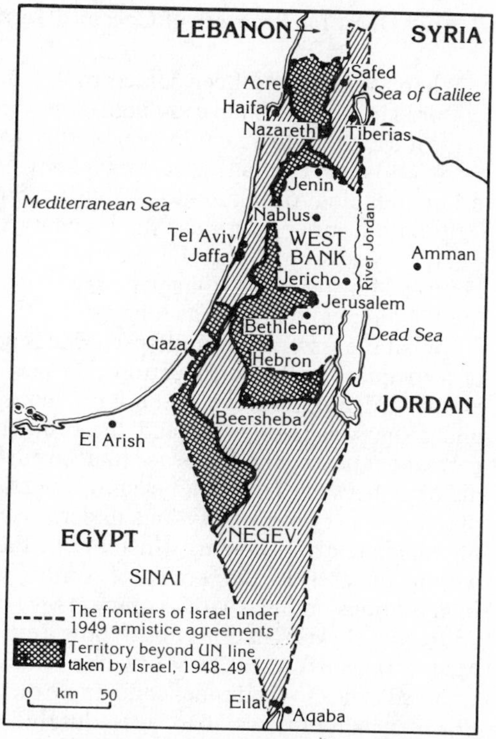

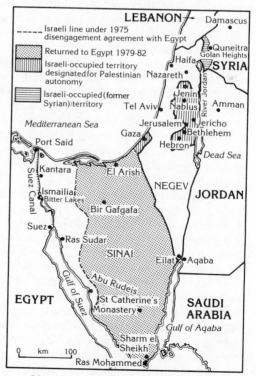

Map 22   Armistice boundaries, 1949.

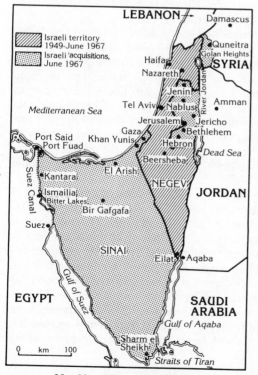

Map 23   1967 Arab-Israeli War.

Map 24   Arab-Israeli boundaries, 1975-87.

Maps 21-24   Israel, Palestine and the Arabs, 1947-87.

213

Arab Quest for Recovery of Occupied Territories leading to the 1973 Arab-Israeli War

Whereas Israel had been forced by US pressure to withdraw from the territory it had captured in the 1956 Sinai campaign, after the June 1967 war Israeli spokesmen immediately made it clear that there could be no return to the 1949 armistice lines. A final settlement of the Arab-Israeli conflict, it was stressed by Israel, was dependent on direct peace talks with the surrounding Arab states to establish definitive boundaries which took account of Israel's legitimate security interests. An eloquent exposition of the Israeli case was put during an emergency session of the UN General Assembly held from June 19 to July 21, 1967, by Foreign Minister Abba Eban, who rejected a Soviet demand that Israel should withdraw to the 1949 lines and argued as follows:

"What the Assembly should prescribe is not a formula for renewed hostilities but a series of principles for the construction of a new future in the Middle East. With the ceasefire established, our progress must not be backward to an armistice regime which has collapsed under the weight of years and the brunt of hostility. History summons us forward to permanent peace, and the peace that we envisage can only be elaborated in frank and lucid dialogue between Israel and each of the states which have participated in the attempt to overthrow her sovereignty and undermine her existence. We dare not be satisfied with intermediate arrangements which are neither war nor peace. Such patchwork ideas carry within themselves the seeds of future tragedy. Free from external pressures and interventions, imbued with a common love for a region which they are destined to share, the Arab and Jewish nations must now transcend their conflicts in dedication to a new Mediterranean future in concert with a renaissant Europe and an Africa and Asia which have emerged at last to their independent role on the stage of history. In free negotation with each of our neighbours we shall offer durable and just solutions redounding to our mutual advantage and honour. The Arab states can no longer be permitted to recognize Israel's existence only for the purpose of plotting its elimination. They have come face to face with us in conflict. Let them now come face to face with us in peace . . . ."

In a speech to the *Knesset* on Oct. 30, 1967, Prime Minister Eshkol reiterated that Israel would not allow the situation which prevailed before June 5 to be restored and stated that in the face of the Arab position of non-recognition of Israel his government would "maintain in full the situation as it was established in the ceasefire arrangements". In a further speech on Dec. 1 Eshkol enumerated five points on which Israel's policy was based: (i) permanent peace between Israel and her Arab neighbours; (ii) the achievement of peace by direct negotiations and conclusion of peace treaties between Israel and its neighbours; (iii) free passage for Israeli ships through the Suez Canal and the Straits of Tiran; (iv) agreed and secure borders between Israel and its neighbours; and (v) a settlement of the refugee problem "within a regional and international context" following the establishment of peace in the Middle East.

The Arab states, however, immediately adopted a policy of continued non-recognition of Israel and refusal to consider any form of peace negotiations. Speaking at the UN General Assembly session on June 26, 1967, King Hussein of Jordan accused Israel of having planned aggression against the Arab countries for many years and of initiating hostilities on June 5. Calling on the United Nations to condemn Israel and to enforce the return of Israeli troops to the pre-war lines, he warned that if this did not happen the Arab nation would rise again and that "the battle which began on June 5 will . . . become only a battle in what will be a long war". At a summit conference of Arab nations held in Khartoum in late August 1967 it was decided inter alia that "any necessary steps" would be taken towards consolidating Arab military strength and that the Arab states would enforce "the principles of non-recognition and non-negotiation" and would "make no peace with Israel, for the sake of the rights of the Palestinian people in their homeland".

Lengthy deliberations at the United Nations eventually resulted in the unanimous adoption by the Security Council on Nov. 22, 1967, of a resolution (242) proposed by Britain which emphasized "the inadmissibility of the acquisition of territory by war and the need to work for a just and lasting peace in which every state in the area can live in security". In its substantive passages this resolution affirmed that "the fulfilment of [UN] Charter principles requires the establishment of a just and lasting peace in the Middle East which should include the application of both the following principles: (i) withdrawal of Israeli armed forces from territories occupied in the recent conflict; (ii) termination of all claims or states of belligerency and respect for and acknowledgement of the sovereignty, territorial integrity and political independence of every state in the area and their right to live in peace within secure and recognized boundaries free from threats or acts of force". It further affirmed "the necessity (i) for guaranteeing freedom of navigation through international waterways in the area; (ii) for achieving a just settlement of the refugee problem; (iii) for guaranteeing the territorial inviolability and political independence of every state in the area through measures including the establishment of demilitarized zones".

Resolution 242 was accepted both by Israel and by the front-line Arab states except Syria, although on the basis of differing interpreations of the key phrase calling for an Israeli withdrawal "from territories occupied in the recent conflict". Israel cited the absence of the definite article before the word "territories" to mean that it was not bound to carry out a complete withdrawal, particularly since the resolution also referred to the right to "secure and recognized boundaries". The Arab states, on the other hand, claimed that the resolution called for a complete Israeli withdrawal and cited the equally authentic French text, where the key phrase is rendered *"retrait des forces armées israéliennes des territoires occupés"*. It should be noted, incidentally, that such semantic arguments were of no interest to the PLO, which has always refused to accept Resolution 242 because it made no reference to the rights of the Palestinian people.

The outcome of the 1967 war and the terms of Resolution 242 set a new tone for the Arab-Israeli conflict, which thereafter revolved less around the fundamental Palestinian Arab challenge to the legitimacy of the state of Israel and more around the quest of Egypt, Syria and Jordan for the recovery of their lost territories. The Israelis made no immediate move to annex their conquests, which were placed under military administration pending a negotiated peace settlement with the interested Arab governments under which definitive boundaries would be agreed. But they did very quickly—by legislation adopted in the *Knesset* on June 28, 1967, empowering the government to apply the law, jurisdiction and administration of the state to any part of *Eretz Israel* ("Land of Israel", effectively signifying the whole territory of Palestine)—merge the Israeli New City of Jerusalem with the Old City, agreeing in July 1967 that Jerusalem was henceforth "one city indivisible, the capital of the state of Israel". This step was condemned not only by the Arabs but also by the UN General Assembly on July 4, by 99 votes to none with 20 abstentions. The Israelis also began a controversial programme of establishing Jewish settlements in the occupied territories, which although limited in the early years and officially related to security requirements was strongly criticized by the international community, including the United States. In this situation the PLO and its various member organizations increasingly resorted to extreme methods, which included a growing number of attacks on Israel targets outside Palestine, notably the El Al airline.

After six years of uneasy truce, the fourth Arab-Israeli war broke out on Oct. 6 1973, when Egyptian and Syrian forces launched major offensives across the Suez Canal and on the Golan front respectively, choosing the Day of Atonement (*Yom Kippur*), the holiest day in the Jewish year, to do so and thereby apparently taking the Israeli armed forces by surprise. Although Jordan did not open a third military front against Israel, units of the Jordanian Army were sent to the Syrian front, as were strong Iraqi armoured contingents and relatively token Saudi Arabian and Kuwaiti units. On the Suez front Egypt received active military assistance from Morocco and Algeria and also from the Iraqi Air Force. The declared war aims of Egypt and Syria were to recover the Arab territories lost to Israel in 1967.

After some of the bitterest and most bloody fighting since World War II, marked by great tank battles and heavy losses of men and material on both sides, a binding ceasefire came into effect on Oct. 24 in response to two successive UN Security Council resolutions. By that time the Egyptian Army had established itself along much of the eastern bank of the Suez Canal north of Ismailia and held a narrow strip of Sinai varying from three to 10 miles in width in different sectors and amounting to some 500 square miles of territory. For their part, the Israeli forces, in addition to having contained an attempted Egyptian thrust deeper into Sinai, had consolidated a successful counter-offensive across the Suez Canal in the southern sector, giving them control of about 500 square miles of Egyptian territory west of the Great Bitter Lake and the town of Suez.

On the northern front the Syrians also achieved initial successes, recapturing much of the Golan Heights lost in the 1967 war and advancing almost to the edge of Galilee plain. However, they were eventually checked and driven back in a powerful Israeli counter-offensive, so that when a ceasefire came into effect on Oct. 24 the Syrians had not only surrendered all their initial gains but had also lost an additional 300 square miles of territory to the Israelis, who had advanced to within 20 miles of Damascus.

Total Israeli casualties in the 1973 Arab-Israeli war included 2,400 soldiers killed. As in previous wars, the casualties of the Arab side were never officially released.

1974 and 1975 Disengagement Agreements

The UN Security Council's first 1973 ceasefire resolution (338), which was adopted on Oct. 22 but not observed until a further resolution had been passed late the following day, was proposed jointly by the United States and the Soviet Union and received the support of 14 of the 15 Security Council member states, with China refraining from voting. In addition to calling for a ceasefire, it urged the parties concerned "to start immediately ... the implementation of Resolution 242 [of November 1967] in all of its parts" and decided that immediate negotiations should be initiated "aimed at establishing a just and durable peace in the Middle East".

The co-operation of the two super-powers in securing the passage of Resolution 338 reflected their joint concern that the Middle East conflict might escalate into a broader confrontation, although the situation remained tense for several days. President Nixon disclosed on Oct. 26, 1973, that he had ordered a precautionary alert of US military forces throughout the world early the previous day after receiving information which had "led us to believe that the Soviet Union was planning to send a very substantial force" into the Middle East. In the event, the threat of a US-Soviet confrontation had been dissipated by the adoption during the night of Oct. 25-26 of a Security Council resolution providing for the creation of a UN peace-keeping force for the Middle East, the personnel of which would not be drawn from any of the five permanent members of the Security Council (i.e. the USA, the Soviet Union, Britain, France and China). On the basis of this resolution a new UN Emergency Force (UNEF) was deployed on the Suez front by early November 1973 and on Nov. 11 Egypt and Israel formally signed a ceasefire agreement at the "Kilometre 101" checkpoint on the Cairo-Suez road at the edge of the Israeli-occupied enclave west of the Suez Canal. This was the first major agreement between Israel and an Arab country since the signature of the 1949 armistice agreements.

A feature of the complex negotiations which led over the next two years to the conclusion of military disengagement agreements between Israel on the one hand and Egypt and Syria on the other was the key diplomatic role played by the United States and in particular by the US Secretary of State, Dr Henry Kissinger. Another important and related factor was the emergence from the 1973 war onwards of the "oil weapon" as a potent means by which the Arab states, taking advantage of the near-monopoly position which they then enjoyed as oil exporters, could exert pressure on Western states with a view to securing support for Arab conceptions of a just Middle East settlement, i.e. one which involved major concessions by Israel. At the time of the 1973 war use of this weapon took the form of an embargo on supplies to the United States and the Netherlands (because of their open support for Israel) and restrictions on supplies to other developed countries; subsequently it took the form of massive price increases which not only threw the economies of the industrialized states into recession but also had serious consequences for the existing international monetary system. Against this background (and with the ever-present threat of further total embargoes on Arab oil supplies), the quest for a resolution of the Arab-Israeli conflict took on added urgency for the industrialized countries, beyond their fundamental concern that Middle East instabilities represented a threat to world peace.

In December 1973 the United States and the Soviet Union made a joint effort to bring about meaningful Arab-Israeli negotiations by inviting Egypt, Jordan, Syria and Israel to a peace conference in Geneva on the basis of the UN Security Council's call for a "just and durable peace"; however, Syria refused to attend (and the PLO was not invited) and the conference was adjourned inconclusively on Jan. 9, 1974. Thereafter, the Soviet Union was able to play little direct part in the overall Middle East negotiating process, particularly since President Sadat of Egypt had already reversed Nasser's policy of close alignment with the Soviet Union—a reveral culminating in his unilateral abrogation in March 1976 of the 1971 Egyptian-Soviet Treaty of Friendship and Co-operation.

With Egypt now accepting that the road to progress ran through Washington, Dr Kissinger was able to mount a direct diplomatic effort with the Middle East parties, the first fruit of which was the signature by Egypt and Israel on Jan. 18, 1974, of an initial military disengagement agreement. Under its terms Israel withdrew its forces from the areas west of the Suez Canal held since the October 1973 ceasefire and also pulled back several miles on the Sinai front east of the canal, where three roughly parallel zones were created, each about six miles wide. The first of these, immediately to the east of the canal, became an Egyptian limited-forces zone, the second a central buffer zone in which UNEF contingents were stationed and the third an Israeli limited-force zone. For Egypt the general effect of the agreement was that it regained control of all Egyptian territory west of the canal and also the whole of the eastern bank; Israel, although withdrawing 12-13 miles east of the canal, was left in control of the rest of Sinai, including the strategically important Mitla and Giddi passes in Sinai and the Bir Gafgafa defence zone behind them, as well as Sharm el Sheikh commanding the Straits of Tiran.

Further intense "shuttle" diplomacy by Dr Kissinger resulted in the signature on May 31, 1974, of a similar military disengagement agreement by Syria and Israel covering the Golan front, where the two sides had continued to engage in regular hostilities notwithstanding the official existence of a ceasefire. The general effect of the agreement was that Israel withdrew from all the territory it had captured in the October 1973 war as well as from some areas occupied since the 1967 war, including the town of Quneitra. Limited-force zones were established on either side of a central buffer zone in which contingents of a newly-created UN Disengagement Observer Force (UNDOF) were stationed. The agreement also provided that Syrian civilians who had fled during the hostilities would be able to return to the areas vacated by Israel and Syrian administration restored. Since the May 1974 Syrian-Israeli disengagement agreement, no further changes have been negotiated as regards the territorial position on the Golan Heights.

As regards the Sinai front, however, a second Egyptian-Israeli disengagement agreement was signed on Sept. 4, 1975, again after protracted diplomatic efforts by Dr Kissinger. Under this agreement Israel withdrew its forces by a further 12 to 26 miles and the vacated area became the new UN buffer zone, with the old buffer zone being added to the existing Egyptian limited-forces zone. As part of this general withdrawal Israeli forces moved back to the eastern end of the Mitla and Giddi passes and a new Israeli limited-forces zone was established adjacent to the vacated area on the eastern side. Israel also vacated the Abu Rudeis and Ras Sudar oilfields on the Gulf of Suez (by February 1976), together with a narrow coastal strip running northwards to Egyptian-controlled territory south of Suez (this strip being demilitarized and placed under joint UN-Egyptian administration).

Other features of the Egyptian-Israeli agreement were that each side undertook to refrain from the use or threat of force or military blockade, to observe the ceasefire scrupulously and to renew the UNEF mandate annually; that non-military cargoes moving to and from Israel in non-Israeli vessels would be allowed to pass through the Suez Canal; and that the United

States would provide up to 200 civilian technicians to man electronic early-warning stations in the area of the Mitla and Giddi passes.

In conjunction with the second Egyptian-Israeli disengagement agreement, the United States made a number of important commitments to Israel, namely (i) to be "fully responsive" to Israel's defence, energy and economic needs; (ii) to hold consultations with Israel in the event of a "world power" (i.e. the Soviet Union) interfering militarily in the Middle East; (iii) to accept the Israeli view that a further Egyptian-Israeli agreement and any negotiations with Jordan should take place within the context of an overall Middle East peace settlement; (iv) to consult and "concert" policy with Israel on the timing and procedure of a reconvened Geneva peace conference; and (v) not to recognize or negotiate with the PLO under its present orientation.

Egypt was able to comply with the provision concerning Israel's right of passage through the Suez Canal because on June 5, 1974, President Sadat had reopened the waterway on the eighth anniversary of its forcible closure by Egypt at the start of the 1967 war. On Nov. 2, 1975, the Greek freighter *Olympus* made a north-south passage of the canal bound for the Israeli port of Eilat with a cargo of cement, which thus became the first Israeli cargo shipped through the canal with the official approval of the Egyptian government since the establishment of the state of Israel in 1948.

For Egypt the 1974 and 1975 disengagement agreements were psychologically important because they confirmed and consolidated the limited territorial gains made in the 1973 war, in which the Egyptian armed forces had for the first time performed creditably against those of Israel. The attempted invasion of the new Jewish state in 1948 had ended in a debacle; in both the 1956 and the 1967 wars Nasser's forces had been comprehensively defeated; but in 1973 President Sadat became the "hero of the crossing" of the Suez Canal. Although many military analysts of the time took the view that if the fighting had continued Egypt would have been defeated for a fourth time, the ceasefire left Egyptian forces in control of the first stretch of territory wrested from Israel by military force since the creation of the latter in 1948. With Arab military honour thus restored—at least in Egyptian eyes—it became easier for Egypt to move towards its historic rapprochement with Israel.

Egyptian-Israeli Rapprochement, the 1978 Camp David Agreements and the 1979 Egypt-Israel Peace Treaty

Completion of the implementation of the second Egyptian-Israeli disengagement agreement in February 1976 was followed by protracted international negotiations aimed at reconvening the Geneva peace conference as the appropriate forum for the negotiation of an overall Middle East settlement. However, these efforts repeatedly came up against the stumbling block of Israel's refusal to accept the PLO as a participant at a reconvened conference, whereas Egypt, Jordan and Syria insisted on some form of PLO participation in accordance with a decision taken by the October 1974 Arab League summit conference held in Rabat (Morocco) to recognize the PLO as the sole legitimate representative of the Palestinian people. Moreover, the Arab states continued to insist that a settlement must not only satisfy the legitimate rights of the Palestinians but also involve an Israeli withdrawal from all the territories conquered in 1967, including the former Jordanian sector of Jerusalem. (Israel's refusal to recognize or negotiate with the PLO stems from its view, as formulated by its Foreign Ministry, that "the very existence of the PLO is predicated on the total denial of Israel's inherent right to national self-expression and statehood" and that "there can be no point or utility in negotiations . . . when one side *a priori* negates the other's very right to exist".)

The prospects of further accommodation appeared to recede even further when the Israeli general election of May 1977 resulted in Menachem Begin becoming Prime Minister at the head of a government dominated by his own right-wing nationalist *Likud* front. A major plank of the *Likud* programme was an assertion of inalienable Israel sovereignty over all the land between the Mediterranean Sea and the Jordan river, in which context *Likud* opposed "any plan envisaging a renunciation of the smallest piece" of the West Bank on the grounds that any such renunciation "will lead inevitably to the creation of a Palestinian state which will be a threat to the security of the civil population, will place the existence of Israel in danger and will endanger any chance of peace". The *Likud* platform also called for unrestricted Jewish settlement throughout the historic "Land of Israel" (*Eretz Israel*), including the Arab-populated West Bank. It therefore marked a significant departure from the approach pursued by the hitherto dominant Israel Labour Party, which had been prepared in principle to make territorial concessions on the West Bank as well as in Sinai and on the Golan Heights and had insisted that Jewish settlements in the occupied territories should only be authorized where security factors rendered them desirable. Yet it was to be Begin's government, apparently much less prepared to compromise than its Labour-led predecessors (but nevertheless as ready as the latter to have direct peace talks), which took Israel into a reconciliation with Egypt involving large territorial concessions (albeit not affecting the new Israeli government's conception of Jewish rights in the "Land of Israel").

In a speech to the Egyptian People's Assembly on Nov. 9, 1977, President Sadat urged other Arab states to unite in an all-out drive to reconvene the Geneva peace conference and declared that he was "ready to go to the *Knesset* itself" to unblock the peace-making process. Begin responded positively two days later, with the result that on Nov. 19-20, 1977, President Sadat undertook the first official visit ever made to Israel by an Arab leader and was received with the ceremonial appropriate to a head of state despite the existence of a technical state of war between the two countries. The centre-piece of the visit was an address by the Egyptian President to the *Knesset* in Jerusalem on Nov. 20 in which he explicitly accepted the existence of Israel as a Middle East state but reiterated his belief that a just and lasting peace depended on an Israeli withdrawal from all occupied Arab territory and on recognition of the rights of the Palestinians. The following month Menachem Begin became the first Israeli Prime Minister to be officially received in an Arab country when he had two days of talks with President Sadat in Ismailia on Dec. 25-26, 1977.

At the Ismailia meeting Begin presented Israel's proposals for "self-rule" for the Palestinian Arab residents of Judea, Samaria and Gaza, involving the election of an Administrative Council responsible for economic and social affairs, but with security and public order remaining the responsibility of the Israeli authorities. Under the proposals, which envisaged the abolition of the Israeli military administration, residents of these areas would have the option of choosing either Israeli or Jordanian citizenship, and those who chose the former would be entitled to acquire land and to settle in Israel; at the same time, residents of Israel would be entitled to acquire land and to settle in Judea, Samaria and Gaza. A tripartite committe of Israel, Jordan and the Administrative Council would determine, by unanimous decision, "the norms whereby Arab refugees residing outside Judea, Samaria and the Gaza district will be permitted to immigrate to these areas in reasonable numbers". The proposals also included the following assertion: "Israel stands by its right and its claim of sovereignty to Judea, Samaria and the Gaza district. In the knowledge that other claims exist, it proposes, for the sake of the agreement and the peace, that the question of sovereignty in these areas be left open."

In most other Arab states the reaction to the radically new departure represented by Sadat's visit to Israel was one of hostility, which mounted as it became clear that Egypt was serious about achieving a rapprochement with Israel. Particularly vociferous in its condemnation was the PLO, which saw the new policy as a means by which Egypt would seek to recover its own lost territory in desertion not only of the agreed principles of Arab solidarity but also of the interests of the dispossessed Palestinian people.

The impetus towards a peace settlement created by Sadat's initiative was checked by a serious deterioration in the general Middle East situation from March 1978, when major Palestinian guerrilla raid on Israel was immediately followed by a large-scale Israeli invasion of southern Lebanon designed to secure Israel's northern border against Palestinian incursions. However, the deployment of a UN peace-keeping force (UNIFIL) in southern Lebanon from late March 1978 and the subsequent withdrawl of Israeli forces by mid-June facilitated efforts by the United States to bring about a resumption of direct Egyptian-Israeli negotiations, culminating in talks between Sadat and Begin at Camp David (near Washington) in September 1978, with President Carter acting as intermediary. These talks resulted in the signature in Washington on Sept. 17 of two framework agreements, one on an overall Middle East settlement and the other specifically on the conclusion of a peace treaty between Egypt and Israel within three months.

The first of the Camp David agreements dealt in particular with the granting of what was termed "full autonomy" to the Palestinian Arab inhabitants of the West Bank and Gaza Strip, the following main stages being envisaged: (i) the inhabitants of the West Bank and Gaza would elect a "self-governing authority" whose powers would be defined in negotiations between Israel, Egypt and Jordan in which the delegations of Egypt and Jordan would be open to "Palestinians from the West Bank and Gaza and other Palestinians as mutually agreed"; (ii) the self-governing authority would replace the existing Israeli administration in these areas; (iii) a five-year transitional period would begin when the self-governing authority had been established and would be marked by the withdrawal of Israeli forces or their redeployment into "specified security locations"; (iv) not later than the third year of the transitional period negotiations would take place between Israel, Jordan, Egypt and the elected representatives of the West Bank and Gaza inhabitants "to determine the final status of the West Bank and Gaza" by the end of the transitional period. In an undertaking separate from the actual agreement, President Sadat stated that Egypt was prepared to assume "the Arab role" in these negotiations on Palestinian autonomy "following consultations with Jordan and the representatives of the Palestinian people" (i.e. if these two parties refused to participate directly—as in fact turned out to be the case).

On the broader aspects of the Middle East conflict, the first framework agreement specified inter alia (i) that parallel negotiations would take place between Israel, Jordan and elected Palestinian representatives to conclude a peace treaty between Israel and Jordan by the end of the transitional period; (ii) that Egypt and Israel would seek to conclude within three months a full peace treaty on the basis of detailed specifications set out in the second Camp David framework agreement "while inviting the other parties to the conflict to proceed simultaneously to negotiate and conclude similar peace treaties with a view to achieving a comprehensive peace in the area"; and (iii) that peace treaties between Israel and each of its neighbours (i.e. Egypt, Jordan, Syria and Lebanon) should be based on principles establishing "relationships normal to states at peace with one another".

Contentious issues which remained unresolved under the Camp David agreements included the future of Jewish settlements in the Israeli-occupied territories and the status of east Jerusalem (it being placed on record by Begin in the latter connexion that in July 1967 the Israeli government had decreed "that Jerusalem is one city indivisible, the capital of the state of Israel"). These and other difficulties meant that the Dec. 17, 1978, target date for an Egyptian peace treaty could not be met (even though Sadat and Begin were jointly awarded the 1978 Nobel Peace Prize for their efforts at Camp David and earlier). However, further US mediation efforts culminating in some personal Middle East shuttle diplomacy by President Carter on March 8-13, 1979, resulted in President Sadat and Prime Minister Begin signing the first-ever Arab-Israel peace treaty in Washington on March 26, 1979.

The draft treaty and its associated documents had been approved by the *Knesset* on March 22 by 95 votes to 11 (with two abstentions, three deputies not participating in the vote and two absent) and the signed text was subsequently ratified by the Israeli Cabinet on April 1 (with one minister abstaining). In Egypt the draft treaty received unanimous approval from the Cabinet on March 15 and its definitive text was ratified by the People's Assembly on April 10 by 328 votes to 15 (with one abstention and 16 members absent) and also by the electorate as a whole in a national referendum on April 19 (by 99.5 per cent of the valid votes cast). Instruments of ratification were exchanged at the US surveillance post at Um-Khashiba in Sinai on April 25, 1979—at which point the 31-year-old state of war between Egypt and Israel was officially terminated.

The main provisions of the Egyptian-Israeli peace treaty and the various documents associated with it were as follows: (i) Israel would evacuate its military forces and civilians from the whole of the Sinai peninsula in a phased withdrawal over a three-year period, as part of which some two-thirds of Sinai, comprising the area west of a line from El Arish in the north to Ras Mohammed in the south, would be returned to Egypt in five subphases within nine months of the treaty being ratified (see map 24 on page 213); (ii) agreed security arrangements would be instituted involving the establishment of limited-force zones and the stationing of UN forces in key border areas, while the US Air Force would continue its surveillance flights over the area to verify compliance with the treaty's terms; (iii) after the completion of the Israeli withdrawal to the El Arish-Ras Mohammed line within nine months, normal diplomatic and other relations would be established between the two countries, including an exchange of ambassadors within 10 months of ratification; (iv) Israeli ships and cargoes would be granted the same right of passage in the Suez Canal and its approaches as the vessels of other countries; (v) both countries recognized the Straits of Tiran and the Gulf of Aqaba as international waterways; (vi) Egypt undertook to end its economic boycott of Israel and to sell oil from the Sinai oilfields to Israel on a non-discriminatory basis; (vii) within a month of the exchange of ratification instruments Egypt and Israel would begin negotiations with a view to implementing the provisions of the first Camp David framework agreement concerning the granting of "full autonomy" to the Palestinian Arab inhabitants of the West Bank and the Gaza Strip and the establishment of a "self-governing authority".

In letters addressed to Egypt and Israel, the US government confirmed that in the event of actual or threatened violation of the treaty the United States would, on request of one or both of the parties, consult with them and "take such other action as it may deem appropriate and helpful to achieve compliance with the treaty"; and that if the UN Security Council failed to establish and maintain the peace-keeping arrangements called for in the treaty, the US President would be "prepared to take those steps necessary to ensure the establishment and maintenance of an acceptable alternative multinational force".

In an Israeli-US memorandum of understanding signed on March 26, 1979, the United States undertook to give strong support to Israel in certain circumstances, stating in particular: "The United States will provide support it deems appropriate for proper actions taken by Israel in response to ... demonstrated violations of the treaty of peace. In particular, if a violation of the treaty of peace is deemed to threaten the security of Israel, including inter alia a blockade of Israel's use of international waterways, a violation of the provisions of the treaty of peace concerning limitation of forces or an armed attack against Israel, the United States will be prepared to consider, on an urgent basis, such measures as the strengthening of the US presence in the area, the providing of emergency supplies to Israel, and the exercise of maritime rights in order to put an end to the violation." The Egyptian government stated subsequently, however, that it would not recognize the legality of this memorandum and considered it null and void. Among 16 reasons listed by Egypt for rejecting the memorandum were that it had never been mentioned to or negotiated with Egypt; that it could be "construed as an eventual alliance between the United States and Israel against Egypt"; and that it gave the United States "the right to impose a military presence in the region for reasons agreed between Israel and the United States".

In the Arab world the price paid by Egypt for its signature of the peace treaty with Israel was virtually total political and economic isolation. Acting on preliminary decisions taken following the signature of the Camp David agreements, the Foreign and Economy Ministers of all Arab League member states except Egypt, Oman and Sudan, meeting in Baghdad on March 27-31, 1979, imposed a wide-ranging political and economic boycott on Egypt, including an embargo on oil supplies. The measures agreed to by the conference included the withdrawal of all remaining Arab ambassadors from Cairo, the suspension of Egypt from Arab League membership as well as from a large number of joint Arab organizations and projects, and the transfer of the Arab League's headquarters from Cairo to Tunis. Other international groupings which suspended Egypt's membership over the peace treaty with Israel included the Islamic Conference Organization, the Organization of

African Unity, the Non-Aligned Movement and the Organization of Arab Petroleum Exporting Countries.

Implementation of Egyptian-Israeli Peace Treaty—Israeli Invasion of Lebanon

Notwithstanding some last-minute uncertainty engendered by the Israeli bombing of Iraq's (French-supplied) Osirak nuclear reactor near Baghdad (on June 7, 1981) and by assassination of President Sadat (on Oct. 6, 1981), the Israeli withdrawal from Sinai was carried out in accordance with the timetable laid down in the 1979 peace treaty. Completion of the fifth subphase on Jan. 26, 1980, took Israeli forces back to the El Arish-Ras Mohammed line, at which point the Egyptian-Israeli border was officially declared open. A month later, on Feb. 26, Israel and Egypt exchanged ambassadors—the Egyptian envoy taking up residence in Tel Aviv to signify Egypt's non-recognition of unified Jerusalem as the capital of Israel. Finally, on the third anniversary of the ratificiation of the 1979 treaty, Israel completed its withdrawal from the remainder of Sinai on April 25, 1982, after a core of hard-line Jewish settlers in the Yamit area of northern Sinai had been forcibly removed by the Israeli Army.

Concurrently with the final hand-over in Sinai, troops of an international peace-keeping force were deployed along the reinstated international border between Egypt and Israel. In accordance with the 1979 treaty, this force had been assembled at the instigation of the US government outside the UN framework, it having become clear that the Soviet Union would veto any move in the Security Council to designate a UN force for the purpose. Countries which had declared their willingness to contribute troops to the Sinai force included (in addition to the United States itself) Britain, France, Italy, the Netherlands, Australia, Canada and New Zealand. As agreed by Egypt and Israel on April 26, 1982, the first duties of the new force included taking control of certain sections of the international frontier where precise demarcation remained in dispute, notably a stretch of about 750 metres at Taba (to the west of Eilat on the Gulf of Aqaba).[1]

Against a backcloth of considerable unease within Israel over the Sinai withdrawal, Israeli ministers of the *Likud*-dominated government stressed that no further territorial concessions would be made to the Arabs. Indeed, in the period since the signature of the 1979 treaty Israel had taken several important steps to give internal legal substance to this attitude. On July 30, 1980, the *Knesset* had adopted legislation strengthening the status of Jerusaelm as the "indivisible" capital of Israel, while on Dec. 14, 1981, the Golan Heights were effectively annexed under a government decree which extended Israeli "law, jurisdiction and administration" to that area of former Syrian territory. Both of these moves were strongly condemned by the United Nations (which had repeatedly called upon Israel to refrain from altering the status of the occupied territories), as was the Begin government's acceleration of Jewish settlement of the West Bank.

For its part, the Israeli government of that period repeatedly asserted its historic right to sovereignty over the "Land of Israel" and declared its aim of annexing the West Bank and the Gaza Strip at the end of the five-year transitional period laid down in the first Camp David framework agreement. At the time of the final Sinai withdrawal, however, this aim remained somewhat academic because the transitional period had not yet started and Israeli military administration remained in place. Despite constant efforts by the US government to bring about progress in the Palestinian "autonomy" negotiations, Egypt and Israel remained deadlocked on the nature of the Palestinian "self-governing authority", the installation of which was to initiate the five-year transitional period. Various difficulties had prevented progress being made in these negotiations (not least the refusal to participate of two directly interested parties, namely the Palestinians themselves and Jordan), but the

---

[1] See pages 232-34.

major underlying obstacle was the Israeli government's insistence that "full autonomy" could imply no element of Palestinian sovereignty.

The April 1982 Sinai withdrawal therefore left Israel in control of the whole of the territory of the former British Palestine mandate west of the River Jordan (plus the Golan Heights, which as explained above formed part of the original mandate) and with an estimated Arab population of some 1,700,000 (including 500,000 in Israel proper) as against a Jewish population of about 3,400,000. While Israel continued to insist that Palestinian Arab political aspirations could be reconciled with its own territorial position, this view was clearly not shared by the Palestinians themselves, among whom increasingly violent opposition to Israeli rule was accompanied by widespread open support for the PLO. Against this background, the Arab-Israeli territorial conflict continued to have important external dimensions arising from Israel's occupation of territory captured from Syria and Jordan in 1967 and from its determination to eradicate the PLO presence in Lebanon—this latter factor becoming the most critical aspect of the Arab-Israeli conflict after the Sinai withdrawal.

Although the international border between Israel and Lebanon has never itself been in dispute, the transplantation to Lebanon of the main bulk of Palestinian activists after their forcible expulsion from Jordan in September 1970 had led to increasing Israeli concern over the security of northern Galilee in the face of guerrilla attacks mounted from southern Lebanon. This concern had increased when Palestinian movements obtained substantial scope for autonomous action amid the collapse of central government authority which accompanied the 1975-76 civil war in Lebanon. Thereafter Israel had responded by making frequent direct attacks on Palestinian guerrilla bases in southern Lebanon and by promoting the establishment of a buffer zone under the control of anti-PLO Lebanese Christian forces immediately to the north of the border. At the same time Israel had repeatedly warned that it would not tolerate any move into southern Lebanon by the Syrian-dominated "Arab deterrent force" which had been stationed in Lebanon since the end of the civil war.

Nevertheless, from the Israeli point of view, the Lebanese border situation remained a serious security threat, with the result that in early June 1982—less than two months after the Sinai withdrawal—the Israel Defence Forces launched a fullscale invasion of Lebanon. Israel's main aims in this operation, called "Peace for Galilee", were widely seen as the elimination of the PLO as a military and political force and also the creation of conditions for a restoration of a sovereign and effective government of Lebanon by the Lebanese. Although the latter aim remained a distant prospect, then and in subsequent years, some progress was made by Israel towards the former when, after a two-month siege of Palestinian positions in west Beirut, an agreement was finalized on Aug. 19, 1982, under which PLO units withdrew from the Lebanese capital by early September (together with regular Syrian troops of the Arab deterrent force) and were dispersed in various Arab countries.

The Lebanese security situation then deteriorated with the assassination of President-elect Bashir Gemayel on Sept. 14, 1982, shortly after which several hundred Palestinian inhabitants of the Chatila and Sabra refugee camps in Beirut were massacred on Sept. 16-18 by Phalangist Christian militia. In the face of widespread accusations that Israeli forces stationed around the camps had colluded in the massacre, the Israeli government instituted an independent judicial inquiry, whose report (published in February 1983) found that, although the actual killings had been carried out by Lebanese Phalangists, various Israeli political and military leaders bore varying degrees of indirect responsibility. Particular criticism was directed at the Israeli Defence Minister, Ariel Sharon, for having taken the decision to allow the Phalangists to enter the camps unsupervised, in the light of which Sharon was obliged to relinquish the Defence portfolio (although he remained a member of the Cabinet).

Following the PLO evacuation of Beirut, and in the face of growing international and internal criticism of the Lebanese operation, the Begin government repeatedly stated that Israeli forces would be withdrawn from southern Lebanon only in the context of an overall peace agreement with a Lebanese government restored to proper authority. Particular Israeli objectives at this time included the withdrawal of all non-Lebanese Arab forces from Lebanon and the establishment of a "PLO-free" demilitarized zone on Israel's northern border. Against this background, talks opened in Khaldé (south of Beirut) on Dec. 28, 1982, between Israeli and Lebanese officials (with the United States also represented)—these being the first official direct negotiations between the two countries since the conclusion of their March 1949 armistice. The talks eventually resulted in the signature of an agreement on May 17, 1983, providing for (i) the withdrawal of Israeli forces from Lebanon; (ii) the ending of the state of war between Israel and Lebanon; and (iii) the establishment of a security region in southern Lebanon, to prevent the reinfiltration of Palestinian guerrillas into the area.

Internal security and political conditions continued to deteriorate in Lebanon, however, and on March 5, 1984, the Lebanese government, under pressure from Syria, unilaterally abrogated the (as yet unratified) agreement with Israel. Accordingly, the Israeli government decided in January 1985 on a unilateral three-stage withdrawal from Lebanon, the first two stages of which were completed by mid-April 1985, while the last Israeli troops left Lebanon on June 6, 1985 (exactly three years after the 1982 invasion). As the Israelis withdrew, it became clear that they intended to reserve the right of re-entry into a "security zone" extending up to six miles from the border, to be patrolled by units of the Israeli-backed, and mainly Christian, South Lebanon Army (SLA) militia. Over the next two years, Israeli forces frequently exercised this right, to assist the SLA in resisting what appeared to be an attempt by Palestinian guerrilla units to resume anti-Israeli operations from southern Lebanon. Moreover, Israeli aircraft and naval vessels have continued to make strikes against Palestinian bases elsewhere in Lebanon, to which many of the Palestinians dispersed in 1982 have gradually returned.

Diplomatic Efforts to unblock Negotiating Process

In an attempt to unblock the peace negotiating process, President Reagan of the United States on Sept. 1, 1982, announced important new US proposals for the achievement of an overall settlement, envisaging in particular the granting of self-determination to the West Bank and Gaza Palestinians within a political entity linked to Jordan. The new US proposals received a cautiously positive response from some Arab leaders, notably King Hussein of Jordan, but were immediately rejected by the Israeli government as a deviation from the 1978 Camp David framework agreement. Also rejected by Israel was a new peace plan drawn up by a summit conference of the Arab League held in Fez (Morocco) on Sept. 6-9, 1982, which appeared to hold out the prospect of Israel securing recognition in return for a withdrawal from all territories captured in 1967 (although the categoric refusal of the Arab side to negotiate directly with Israel was maintained).

The 1982 Fez summit plan (which remains the League's official stance on how to resolve the Arab-Israeli conflict) was based substantially on earlier Saudi Arabian proposals (published on Aug. 8, 1981) but with certain modifications designed to meet the demands of the hard-line Arab states. The plan had the following eight points: (i) the withdrawal of Israel from all Arab territories occupied in 1967 including "Arab Jerusalem"; (ii) the dismantling of Israeli settlements established in the occupied territories since 1967; (iii) the guarantee of freedom of worship and practice of religious rites for all religions in the Holy Places; (iv) the reaffirmation of the Palestinian people's right to self-determination and "the exercise of its imprescriptible and inalienable rights under the leadership of the PLO, its sole legitimate representative, and the indemnification of all those who do not wish to return"; (v) placing the West Bank and Gaza under UN control for a transitional period not exceeding a few months; (vi) the establishment of an independent Palestinian state with Jerusalem as its capital; (vii) UN Security Council guarantees of "peace among all states of the region, including the independent Palestinian state"; and (viii) UN Security Council guarantees for the principles of the foregoing. (The Saudi Arabian plan had made no specific mention of the PLO and had envisaged an affirmation of "the right of all countries of the region to live in peace", i.e. implicitly including Israel.)

Major diplomatic and political developments arising from the formulation of the respective Reagan and Arab League peace plans included (i) an exploration of the federation concept at a series of meetings between King Hussein and Yassir Arafat (the PLO leader); (ii) talks between President Reagan and a League delegation in Washington on Oct. 22, 1982, to evaluate the common and disparate elements in the two plans; (iii) an official visit to Washington by King Hussein on Dec. 21-23, 1982, during which he discussed with President Reagan the obstacles to future Jordanian participation in the peace negotiation process; and (iv) growing opposition within the PLO to any settlement involving an accommodation with Israel. In this process, the role of King Hussein became pivotal, in that the only realistic way forward, given Israel's determination to adhere to the Camp David agreement and its insistence of direct peace negotiations, lay in Jordan being persuaded to come to the negotiating table to discuss the future of the West Bank and Gaza. However, at his Washington talks and subsequently, King Hussein continued to reiterate his unwillingness to join in the Palestinian "autonomy" negotiations without the full backing of the PLO and the Arab League.

During 1983-85 the prospects for the Camp David peace process appeared to be improved by (i) a visit to Cairo by Arafat on Dec. 22, 1983, for talks with President Hosni Mubarak; (ii) Jordan's decision on Sept. 25, 1984, to resume full diplomatic relations with Egypt (whose gradual rehabilitation in the Arab and Islamic worlds subsequently continued with its resumption of full participation in the Islamic Conference Organization in December 1984 and the resumption of Djibouti-Egypt diplomatic relations on Sept. 30, 1986); and (iii) an announcement on Feb. 11, 1985, that King Hussein and Arafat had reached agreement on a joint approach to peace negotiations based on the concept of a future confederal relationship between a Palestinian entity and Jordan. As regards this last development, however, seriously conflicting interpretations quickly emerged between the two sides as to what exactly had been agreed, notably whether or not the PLO had implicitly accepted UN Resolution 242 (and thus Israel's right to exist) as a basis for negotiations.

At the same time, Arafat's position came under increasing challenge from hard-line PLO elements (mostly backed by Syria), who formed a Palestinian National Salvation Front, based in Damascus, in opposition to Arafat's leadership and his alleged willingness to compromise on established PLO policy principles. These and other complications resulted in King Hussein announcing on Feb. 19, 1986, that Jordan was "unable to continue to co-ordinate politically with the PLO leadership until their words become bonds, characterized by commitment, credibility and consistency". Thereafter, Jordan consolidated a rapprochement with Syria which had been underway for some months, a realignment which indirectly assisted Arafat in reasserting his authority over Syrian-backed PLO dissidents by early 1987. Nevertheless, there seemed to be no immediate prospect of a new Jordanian-PLO joint approach to peace negotiations.

Meanwhile, the Israeli general elections of July 1984 had resulted in the Labour Alignment returning to government in a national unity coalition with the *Likud* front and with the Labour Party leader, Shimon Peres, becoming Prime Minister for the first two years of the government's four-year term. In its policy platform, the Alignment had proposed that Israel should be prepared to make territorial concessions, consistent with its security requirements, in return for a peace treaty with Jordan, and had also advocated a complete freeze on all settlement activity in occupied areas of dense Palestinian population (while promising that no existing settlements would be dismantled). In contrast, *Likud* had rejected any "territorial compromise" (thus effectively reaffirming its goal of establishing full Israeli sovereignty over all the remaining occupied territories) and had urged continuing Jewish settlement throughout the West Bank and Gaza.

Against this policy background, Peres concentrated during his premiership on establishing a framework which would enable the Jordanian government to enter into some form of direct negotiations with Israel. To this end, he advanced the idea that such direct negotiations could be initiated within the framework of a wider international conference, to which the permanent members of the UN Security Council might be invited provided they had diplomatic relations with both sides of the conflict. In a surprise development, Peres had talks in Morocco on July 22-23, 1986, with King Hassan, resulting in a joint communiqué stating that they had been "essentially" concerned with the Arab League's 1982 Fez peace plan and of "a purely exploratory nature". After the meeting, the Moroccan King claimed that he had broken off the talks once it had become clear that Israel would not recognize the PLO or agree to a complete withdrawal from the occupied territories; he nevertheless added that "Arab leaders must meet directly with the leaders of Israel to know exactly what they want".

The concept of an international conference on the Arab-Israeli dispute featured prominently in talks between Peres and President Muburak of Egypt held in Alexandria on Sept. 10-12, 1986, when both leaders agreed to make 1987 "a year of negotiations for peace". However, after Peres had vacated the Israeli premiership the following month in favour of Itzhak Shamir (*Likud*) and succeeded the latter as Foreign Minister, the proposal for an international conference, as currently formulated, failed to command majority support in the Israeli Cabinet.

AJD

Bahrain-Iran

A longstanding dispute arising from an Iranian (Persian) claim to sovereignty over the island of Bahrain—which appeared to have been settled in December 1970 when the government of the Shah of Iran endorsed a UN Security Council resolution affirming the complete independence of the state of Bahrain—was revived by Iran in September 1979 in the wake of the Iranian revolution. The Iranian claim was strongly repudiated in Bahrain (and also in Iraqi official circles) and has not been reasserted by Iran since 1979. (For a map of the Gulf region, see page 231.)

History of the Dispute

The island of Bahrain was part of the Islamic empire between the seventh and 11th centuries and was thereafter ruled by various Arab dynasties until it was occupied by the Portuguese in 1522; it was under Persian domination from 1602 until 1783, this domination being interrupted by short periods of rule by Arab shaikhs and ended by the island's conquest by the rulers of Zubarah (Qatar), whose descendants have ruled Bahrain to the present day. Between 1861 and 1971 Bahrain was under British protection, with defence and external affairs being the responsibility of the United Kingdom.

An agreement concluded on Aug. 30, 1822, by the British Political Resident in the Gulf with the Persian authorities in Shiraz—which provided that Bahrain should be regarded as "subordinate to the [Persian] province of Fars" and that the British government would supply Persia with war vessels to conquer Bahrain—was disowned as "unauthorized" by the British Governor of Bombay, who denounced the admission of the King of Persia's title to Bahrain as being without "the least proof". The agreement was also denounced by the Shah of Persia, who declared that it had been made "without his knowledge or injunction".

In 1844, however, the Persian Prime Minister submitted a claim to Bahrain in a note to the British government, after the Ruler of Bahrain had been expelled by his nephew and had asked the British, the Persians and the Sultan of Muscat for help to enable him to regain Bahrain. When it became known that Persia was preparing military action in support of the expelled Shaikh, the British government informed Persia that it would actively oppose any action against the lawful government of Bahrain.

The Persian Prime Minister (Haji Meerza Aghassi), in a statement of March 15, 1844, listed the following arguments in favour of Persia's claim to Bahrain: (i) "The Persian Gulf from the commencement of the Shatt al-Arab to Muscat belongs to Persia and ... all islands of that sea, without exception and without participation of any other government, belong entirely to Persia" (as was supported by the English usage of referring to the "Persian" Gulf); (ii) "Bahrain has always been under the authority of the Governor of Fars from 1300 AD"; (iii) "all European and Turkish books of geography as well as the books of travellers considered Bahrain as Persian"; and (iv) the 1822 agreement [see above] recognized Persia's ownership of Bahrain.

These arguments were refuted by the (British) East India Company, whose Secret Committee stated on July 31, 1845, inter alia (i) that the British government had treated the Shaikhs of Bahrain as independent authorities since their occupation of the island in 1783; (ii) that Bahrain might have been a dependency of Fars while the Persians were in actual possession of the island but that to allege that the Persians had possessed it since 1300 AD was "contrary to the best evidence" that could be produced on the subject; and (iii) that the 1822 treaty had no legal significance as it had been "expressly disavowed". The committee therefore concluded that Persia had no legitimate claim to sovereignty over Bahrain.

In subsequent years the British government ignored Persia's claim to the island, but in a note dated April 29, 1869, the British government conceded that it would inform the Persian government beforehand "of any measures of coercion against himself which the conduct of the Shaikh of Bahrain may have rendered necessary" (the Shaikh having solicited military aid from Persia and Turkey and having attacked Qatar). The Persian government considered this concession as involving British recognition of Persia's claim to Bahrain.

Persia did not raise the matter again until Nov. 22, 1927, when it protested to Britain against the conclusion of a treaty (on May 27, 1927) with Saudi Arabia, in which reference was made to the maintenance of "friendly and peaceful relations with the territories of Kuwait and Bahrain, who are in special treaty relations with [the British] government". The Persian government regarded this clause, "so far as it concerns Bahrain", as "an infringement of the territorial integrity of Persia". The British Foreign Secretary (Sir Austen Chamberlain), replying to the protest on Jan. 18, 1928, denied categorically that there were "any valid grounds upon which the claim of the Persian government to the sovereignty over Bahrain is or can be based". This exchange was followed by further notes sent respectively on Aug. 2, 1928, and Feb. 18, 1929, when the British government stated inter alia: "It would be necessary for Persia to prove that she is, or ever has been, the lawful owner of Bahrain, and that such rights as she may have acquired in former ages by conquest and the exercise of force outweigh those not only of the Portuguese but of the Arab inhabitants themselves."

Persia also protested unsuccessfully against the granting of oil concessions by the Shaikh of Bahrain (in a note to the British government on July 23, 1930, and in another note, to the United States, on May 22, 1934).

In reply to a British statement of April 5, 1956, to the effect that Bahrain was an independent shaikhdom, the Persian Foreign Minister contended on April 8 that Bahrain was "an inseparable part of Persia"; that Persia would not recognize it as a British-protected shaikhdom; that during the 19th century Britain had several times recognized Persian sovereignty over the island; and that its ruling dynasty had on several occasions sworn fealty and paid taxes to Persia.

Following the passing of a bill by the Persian Parliament declaring Bahrain the 14th Persian province, the British position of not recognizing Persian sovereignty over Bahrain was reaffirmed on Nov. 27, 1957, by the then British Foreign Secretary (Ormsby Gore), who declared that the British government would continue to fulfil its obligation to safeguard the independence of Bahrain, and that the Ruler of Bahrain had received an assurance to this effect.

Persia's claim was also rejected by the Arab League, which reaffirmed on Nov. 15, 1957, that Bahrain was "Arab territory". This was underlined by the fact that its population was overwhelmingly Arab, it being estimated in 1965 that the naturalized Iranian population of Bahrain was less than 7 per cent of the total Arab population. Nevertheless, the Shah of Iran restated his claim on Nov. 22, 1958, when he said at a press conference in Tehran: "We consider Bahrain an integral part of Persia." He added that he would gladly accept the allegiance of its Ruler "in the capacity of the first Iranian governor-general of Bahrain."

Developments leading to 1970 Settlement

In the late 1960s the Iranian attitude towards the Bahrain question became more conciliatory. On Jan. 5, 1969, the Shah declared that Bahrain's inhabitants (numbering some 200,000 people) were welcome to decide their own fate, although Iran would not want the island to be made over to anyone else without Iranian consent. At the request of both Iran and Britain, the United Nations Secretary-General (U Thant) agreed on March 28, 1970, to appoint a special representative to visit Bahrain in order to ascertain the wishes of its population in regard to its future status. This UN representative, Vittorio Winspeare Guicciardi (Italy), visited the island between March 30 and April 18, 1970, and in his report, issued on May 2, he declared: "My conclusions have convinced me that the overwhelming majority of the people of Bahrain wish to gain recognition of their identity in a fully independent and sovereign state free to decide for itself its relations with other states."

In this connexion the Ruler of Bahrain had on March 29, 1970, declared inter alia: "The question of Bahrain's relations with Iran is a matter which needs to be tackled at its very roots, not only because it concerns these two countries, but because it has a direct bearing upon the future stability of the whole area [after the withdrawal of Britain from the Gulf at the end of 1971]. ... Our belief is that Bahrain is an Arab country [and] has its own independent personality and existence. We believe these to be facts which reflect the deepest feelings of the people of Bahrain, and that they should be acknowledged by all. We believe, too, that these facts are supported both in history and in the reality of the present situation; and that they allow of no doubt or of any contrary claim, which we never recognize nor admit in any way."

Meeting on May 11, 1970, at the request of Iran and the United Kingdom, the UN Security Council unanimously endorsed the report of the Secretary-General's special representative, and this endorsement was ratified by the Iranian *Majlis* (Lower House of Parliament) by 186 votes to four on May 14, and unanimously by Iran's Senate on May 18. This apparent settlement of the dispute was followed by visits to Tehran by the Prime Minister of Bahrain on May 24, 1975, and to Bahrain by the then Iranian Prime Minister (Abbas Hoveyda) on Nov. 29, 1975, when the latter stated that there were no difficulties in relations between Iran and Bahrain and that co-operation between them was being fostered by a joint ministerial commission.

Revival of Iranian Claim

The 1970 settlement of the dispute was in line with the Shah's endeavours to improve Iran's relations with Arab countries, in which connexion he concluded a "treaty of reconciliation" with Iraq in 1975. With the advent to power of the Shah's successors and the establishment of the Islamic Republic of Iran in early 1979, the latter regime's relations with most Arab countries deteriorated, in particular those with Iraq, and the revival of Iran's claim to Bahrain underlined this development. The renewed Iranian claim to Bahrain was announced in September 1979 by Ayatollah Ruhani, a leading figure in the Iranian Islamic revolution; however, it was strongly rejected by the Bahrain government on Sept. 22, 1979, and also denounced in Baghdad on Sept. 24 by *Al-Thawra*, the official organ of the ruling Baath party.

The Bahraini Ministry of the Interior announced on Dec. 13, 1981, that it had foiled an attempted coup by members of an Islamic Front for the Liberation of Bahrain said to have been trained in Iran. Of 73 persons charged in this connexion, inter alia with possession of arms supplied from Iran, three were on May 23, 1982, sentenced to death, 60 to 15 years in prison each and 10 to seven years each. The Iranian government denied any implication in the alleged plot.

While Iran has not formally renounced the revived claim to Bahrain made in 1979, it has not been publicly reasserted since, and in the 1980s Bahrain has maintained normal diplomatic relations with Iran. At the same time, Bahrain has sought to enhance the security of the smaller Gulf states within the framework of the Gulf Co-operation Council (GCC), whose declared support for Iraq in its war with Iran[1] has from time to time provoked Iranian threats against the independence of GCC member states.

HWD

Bahrain-Qatar (Hawar Islands)

The question of the Hawar (Huwar) Islands, situated about $1\frac{1}{2}$ miles (2.4 km) off the east coast of Qatar but under the sovereignty of Bahrain, has been the subject of exchanges between the two countries since 1967 and also of unsuccessful mediation efforts by Saudi Arabia. Following the adhesion of both countries to the Gulf Co-operation Council established in February 1981, efforts to resolve the dispute were pursued within that framework. However, in 1986 the two sides came into direct military confrontation over the issue.

Historical Origins of the Dispute

The dispute first became apparent in 1938 when the Ruler of Bahrain claimed the Hawar Islands purely for the purposes of oil exploration and this claim was immediately rejected by the Ruler of Qatar.

The Qatari position has been that the Hawar Islands are situated within the geographical boundaries of Qatar and are an extension of Qatar's territory within its territorial waters. Qatar has also pointed out that the narrow channel between the islands and Qatar is covered by Qatar's territorial waters only during a tidal period and that at low tide it is possible to walk from the coast to the islands; that Bahrain, on the other hand, is separated from the islands by an 18-mile wide waterway used for international navigation in its various forms; and that Qatar's claim is supported by international judgments to the effect that "islands situated in the territorial waters of any state are subject by law to the sovereignty of that state ... even if that state does not actually occupy these islands".

Bahrain's 1938 claim was supported by the United Kingdom (then responsible for the foreign policy of the two countries under treaty obligations). The British Political Agent in Bahrain informed the two countries' Rulers on July 11, 1939, that "having considered the claim ... the British government has decided that the Hawar Islands belong to Bahrain and not to Qatar". This decision has been consistently contested by the Ruler of Qatar. In 1947 the British government also endorsed a claim by Bahrain to the shoals of Al-Dibal and Jarada, situated north-east of Qatar and considered by Qatar, on geological and geographical grounds, to be part of the Qatari peninsula.

In 1965 Bahrain requested that the median line drawn by Britain as the boundary between the two countries should be changed, to which request Qatar responded by proposing that the issue should be submitted to arbitration along with the territorial dispute. The

---

[1] For an account of the Iran-Iraq dispute, see pages 234-41.

governments of both Bahrain and the United Kingdom agreed to this proposal, but by March 1966 the government of Bahrain appeared to take the view that arbitration was not the best method of settling the issue.

During a visit to Qatar by the Ruler of Bahrain in March 1967, the Ruler of Qatar raised the question of the sovereignty over the Hawar Islands. The subject was later discussed within the framework of an offshore boundary settlement between the two countries, with Qatar insisting on obtaining ownership of the islands before agreeing to a settlement satisfactory to Bahrain, but the latter did not agree to this demand.

Post-Independence Acceptance of Saudi Mediation

Following the attainment of independence by both Bahrain and Qatar in 1971, the two sides agreed to accept mediation by Saudi Arabia, and in 1978 they both agreed to a set of principles proposed by Saudi Arabia to guide relations between the two countries until a final solution was found. Both sides undertook (i) to refrain from any action which would strengthen their respective legal positions, weaken the position of the other party or change the status quo in the disputed area; and (ii) to refrain from any action which would block negotiations between them or harm the brotherly atmosphere necessary to achieve the aim of the negotiations.

On March 1, 1980, Yusuf as-Shawari, Bahrain's Minister of Industry and Development, stated that the Hawar Islands were governed by a concession agreed between the government of Bahrain and a group of US companies which were planning to drill a new experimental well in search of oil (following the failure of two earlier drilling attempts).

Shaikh Abdel Aziz bin Khalifa, the Qatar Minister of Finance and Petroleum, thereupon replied on March 4 that "all geographical, historial, legal and logical indications" categorically proved that "these islands constitute an indivisible part of Qatar, since they are situated within its territorial waters". The minister added that Bahrain had nothing to support its claim of sovereignty over these islands except the British decision made in 1939, which Qatar considered "null and void" since it contradicted "the basic norms of international law governing such matters" and also "the established geographical, material and historical facts". The minister also accused Yusuf as-Shawari of disregarding the fact that there was "an agreed mediation being conducted by a big sister state (i.e. Saudi Arabia) for solving the dispute", and he declared that Qatar was "keen" to safeguard its close fraternal relations with Bahrain and that he hoped that the two countries would settle the dispute "in a manner that would restore right in accordance with the principles of justice and law".

On March 7, 1980, diplomatic sources in Kuwait were quoted as saying that Saudi Arabia was again to mediate between Bahrain and Qatar in order to prevent the dispute from worsening and had asked officials in the two countries not to allow the media to exacerbate the situation.

The issue was complicated by a claim by the Shaikh of Bahrain relating to rights in Zubarah, on the northern coast of Qatar, on the grounds that it was his ancestral home and was inhabited by a tribe owing him allegiance. This is not regarded as a territorial claim but as one for jurisdiction over the subjects of a state in another territory; it has not been pursued in recent years, but in the view of the Shaikh of Bahrain it remains unsettled in the absence of any written agreement on the frontiers between the two states.

In February 1981 both Bahrain and Qatar—together with Kuwait, Oman, Saudi Arabia and the United Arab Emirates—became members of the newly-established Gulf Co-operation Council (GCC) of Arab states, one of the professed functions of which was to resolve territorial disputes between member states. After the Qatar government had protested in early March 1982 against the Bahrain government's decision to name a new warship the *Hawar*, the GCC ministerial council, meeting in Riyadh on March 7-9, 1982, requested Saudi Arabia to continue its efforts to resolve the dispute. According to a statement issued at the conclusion of the meeting, both sides had agreed "to freeze the situation and not to cause an escalation of the dispute", to halt "information campaigns exchanged between the two countries" and to continue their fraternal relations on the basis of "a return to the status quo ante". However, no progress was made in subsequent discussions.

1986 Confrontation over Al-Dibal

Late in 1985 Bahrain began to construct a man-made island on the shoal of Al-Dibal, while it continued to erect military and other installations on the Hawar Islands. Qatar protested, but Bahrain pursued its intention of building a coastguard station on Al-Dibal. On April 26, 1986, a small contingent of Qatari troops landed on Al-Dibal in order to halt Bahrain's operations. On April 30 Bahrain denounced this occupation of the shoal as "a violation of good-neighbourliness". Following efforts at mediation by the leaders of Oman, Saudi Arabia and the United Arab Emirates, agreement was reached in May 1986 on the withdrawal of Qatari forces from Al-Dibal and the removal of dredging and construction works under the supervision of a team of military officers sent by the GCC ministerial council.

Thereafter Saudi Arabia proposed the creation of a joint committee to study all matters relating to the dispute. This proposal, accepted by both Bahrain and Qatar, envisaged that, if it was found impossible to reach a solution acceptable to both parties, the dispute should be referred to an international arbitration commission which should settle the dispute on the basis of the principles of international law and whose judgment would be final and binding on both parties.

HWD

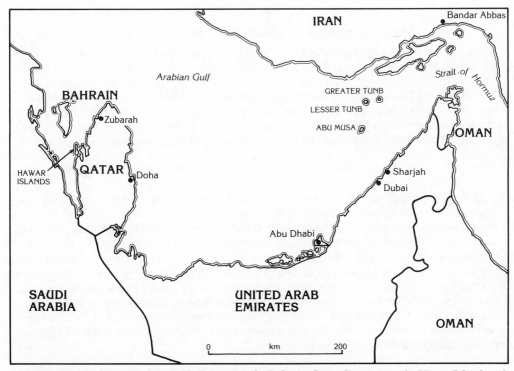

Map 25   The Arabian (Persian) Gulf, illustrating the Bahrain-Qatar dispute over the Hawar Islands and also showing Abu Musa and the Tunbs, which are disputed by Iran and the United Arab Emirates.

231

Egypt-Israel (Taba Strip)

A dispute between Egypt and Israel over the ownership of a strip of land at Taba, on the shore of the Gulf of Aqaba, arose during the Israeli withdrawal from Sinai, as agreed in the 1979 peace treaty, which was completed in April 1982.[1] Substantial progress towards solving the dispute was made during 1986, when both sides agreed to accept binding arbitration by an international tribunal.

Origins of the Dispute

The dispute had its origins in 1906, when Turkish forces occupied the coastal settlement of Taba, but were subsequently forced to withdraw under British pressure. After negotiations between Anglo-Egyptian and Turkish representatives, an agreement was reached by which the border was fixed as running through Taba itself. In 1915, however, a British military survey produced a map in which the border was shown as running along a line some three-quarters of a mile to the north-east. The head of the team which produced the survey, Col. T.E. Lawrence ("Lawrence of Arabia"), admitted later that, acting under instructions, he had "invented" certain details of the map. The discrepancy resulted in an undefined area of roughly triangular shape, its southern edge extending about three-quarters of a mile eastwards along the coast from Taba, with the remaining two sides converging at a point about a mile inland.

The 1915 line became the boundary with Egypt under the British Palestine Mandate (established in 1920 and formally approved by the League of Nations in 1922) and remained as such on the establishment of the state of Israel in May 1948. In the June 1967 Arab-Israeli war Israel's capture of the Sinai peninsula from Egypt brought the Taba strip under Israeli control.

Negotiations following Israel's Withdrawal from Sinai

The question of the ownership of the Taba strip was reopened after the signature of the Egyptian-Israeli peace treaty of March 1979, under the terms of which Israel agreed to withdraw its forces from the Sinai over a three-year period. A series of negotiations held in early 1982 to resolve outstanding border questions failed to produce an agreement on Taba before the completion of the Israeli withdrawal to the pre-1967 border. Pending a final agreement being reached through further negotiations, the two sides agreed that the area would be placed under the control of the incoming Multi-National Force and Observers (MFO).

During the talks, the Israeli side had insisted that the 1906 agreement had provided the only valid demarcation, while the Egyptians demanded that the 1915 map should be regarded as the definitive version. Over the ensuing years, much of the coastal strip was developed as a tourist resort by Israeli businessmen.

Tripartite talks involving negotiators from Israel, Egypt and the United States were held in Ismailia (Egypt) in March 1983 but failed to result in any significant progress. The matter was next raised in November 1983 during talks in Cairo between Dr Boutros Boutros-Ghali (then Egyptian Foreign Minister) and David Kimche (then director-general of the Israeli Foreign Ministry). The lack of agreement on the issue was cited by President Mubarak of Egypt in September 1984 as the reason for his refusal to hold a summit meeting with Shimon Peres, then Israeli Prime Minister. A meeting the same month between Itzhak Shamir, then Israeli Foreign Minister, and his Egyptian counterpart, Dr Ahmed Esmat Abdel Meguid, similarly failed to produce an agreement.

---

[1]For an account of the broader Arab-Israeli conflict, see pages 197-226.

Position papers on the Taba dispute and an outstanding problem concerning the divided town of Rafah, on the border of Egyptian Sinai and the Israeli-occupied Gaza Strip, were exchanged at negotiations held in January 1985 (at which US observers were also present). In further talks in Cairo in May (also in the presence of US observers), the Israeli side rejected Egypt's request that the matter be referred to arbitration. (These talks did, however, produce an agreement on the Rafah question, under which residents living in the Egyptian half of the town would be allowed to cross into the Israeli zone if they wished).

Submission of Dispute to International Arbitration Panel

From early 1985 onwards, efforts to resolve the Taba dispute were complicated by conflicting opinions within the Israeli coalition Cabinet. Members of the Labour Alignment faction, led by Peres, expressed a willingness to agree to some form of arbitration; this was, however, strongly resisted by the *Likud* front, led by Shamir. These internal divisions within the Israeli government hampered further bilateral talks on the dispute which took place in September, October and December of 1985.

In January 1986, however, the Israeli Cabinet decided to accept binding international arbitration on the issue, this concession being welcomed as a positive step by President Mubarak. Talks concerning the details of the arbitration took place on several occasions over the ensuing months, culminating in an arbitration agreement which was endorsed by the Israeli Cabinet on Aug. 13, 1986, and by the Egyptian Cabinet on Sept. 10. The agreement provided for the establishment of a five-member arbitration tribunal, of whom three members would have to be mutually acceptable to Egypt and Israel, while each country would have the exclusive right to appoint one member.

The agreement cleared the way for a summit meeting between President Mubarak and Peres, which was held in Alexandria (Egypt) on Sept. 11-12, 1986. The Egyptians had

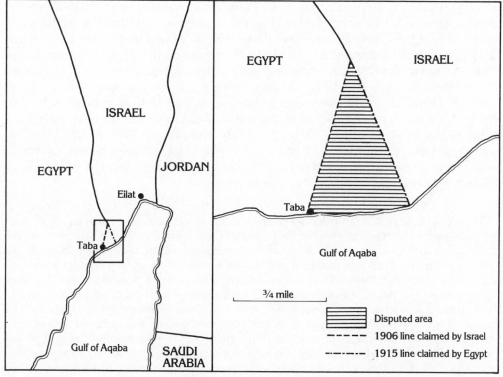

Map 26 The Taba strip dispute between Egypt and Israel.

233

maintained their refusal to agree to a summit until all arrangements relating to the dispute had been approved by both sides. Richard Murphy, the US special presidential envoy to the Middle East, had travelled regularly between Cairo and Jerusalem during late August and early September, in an effort to resolve the remaining differences, which in particular concerned the questions of mapping the disputed area and the composition of the arbitration tribunal. As eventually agreed, the tribunal was composed of an Israeli, an Egyptian, an American, a Swiss and a Swede (who was appointed as its president).

The first meeting of the arbitration tribunal took place in Geneva on Dec. 8, 1986, while on Jan. 7, 1987, a team of US soldiers from the MFO opened an observation post in Taba to ensure that neither side introduced troops into the area during the arbitration process, which was expected to last about two years.

MWr

Iran-Iraq

A major source of strain in relations between Iran and Iraq has been the longstanding dispute over the Shatt al-Arab waterway, which runs into the Arabian (Persian) Gulf in the southern border area between the two countries. Whereas Iraq has traditionally claimed to have succeeded to the Ottoman empire's jurisdiction over the whole waterway and that therefore the border between the two countries in this area runs along the eastern (i.e. Iranian) bank, Iran has consistently maintained that such a delimitation is not only unjust but also contrary to the Thalweg line principle (whereby riverine frontiers are defined as following the median line in the deepest channel). Under early partial agreements, Iran succeeded in securing the application of the Thalweg principle to the vicinity of Mohammerah (Khorramshahr) in 1914 and to the waters off Abadan in 1937; moreover, in return for a cessation of Iranian support for Kurdish rebels in Iraqi Kurdistan, Iraq agreed in 1975 that the entire Shatt al-Arab should be delimited along the median line of the deepest channel. However, the Shia Moslem revolution in Iran in 1979 not only served to revive Arab Iraq's traditional suspicion of its non-Arab neighbour but also led to a reactivation of the Iraqi claim to the Shatt al-Arab. In September 1980 Iraq unilaterally abrogated the 1975 agreement, declared its sovereignty over the whole of the Shatt al-Arab and moved to assert its claim by force of arms. Seven years later the war between Iran and Iraq was still in progress.

The Shatt al-Arab ("Arab river")—given on some modern Iranian maps as the Arvand river—is formed by the confluence of the Euphrates and Tigris rivers and flows for some 160 miles (255 km) through a swampy delta before opening out into the Gulf. From the north the land boundary between Iran and Iraq reaches the waterway about 60 miles (100 km) from the coast and about 10 miles (16 km) upstream from the town of Khorramshahr. The area where the Shatt al-Arab flows into the sea has acquired major importance for both Iran and Iraq, in particular since the development of their respective oil industries. Iran has built its major oil refinery at Abadan (its principal oil terminal being on Kharg island in the Gulf), while Iraq's main terminal is at Fao at the southern end of the waterway and its main port at Basra upstream from Khorramshahr. This development of the Shatt al-Arab has served to accentuate what Iran regards as the anomaly of its ports being enclosed by territorial waters claimed by Iraq, whereas Iraq has attached increasing importance to the waterway as its main outlet to the sea and has also pointed out that Iran in any case possesses a substantial coastline further round the Gulf.

Early Historical Background

The border between Iraq (Persia) and the Turkish Ottoman empire was first defined in a treaty signed at Zuhab in 1639, although this document left the boundary line extremely vague in that the allocation of territory between the Zagros mountains to the east of the Shatt al-Arab and the Tigris to the west was based largely on tribal loyalties. Following the conclusion in 1724 of a Russo-Turkish agreement providing for the partition of Iran, the Turks invaded Iran and under the 1727 Treaty of Hamadan were ceded that country's western provinces. Although further hostilities in the 1740s resulted in a reaffirmation of the 1639 agreement in the Treaty of Kherden of 1746, the latter treaty was itself declared invalid under the first Treaty of Ezerum signed in 1823 after renewed warfare betwen the Turks and Iran in 1821-22.

Following the signature of the first Treaty of Ezerum in 1823, Britain and Russia exerted pressure on Turkey and Iran to achieve a resolution of their border difficulties, to which end a boundary commission was formed in 1843 comprising representatives of the four powers. As a result of the commission's work a second Treaty of Ezerum was signed in May 1847 which delimited a boundary in the Shatt al-Arab for the first time. Iran received the town and port of Mohammerah (Khorramshahr), the island of Abadan and its anchorage and the eastern bank of the river, but Turkey retained sovereignty over the waterway. (Mohammerah had been founded in 1812 by the Muhaisin tribe and had been claimed by both Iran and Turkey. The Shaikh of Mohammerah had maintained his independence, however, and controlled southern Arabistan, east of the Shatt al-Arab, where the Turks had also sought to enforce their suzerainty.) In the middle of the 19th century the Shatt al-Arab was of only minor importance to Iran as a trade channel, and the second Treaty of Ezerum in any case provided that "Persian vessels have the right to navigate freely without let or hindrance on the Shatt al-Arab from the mouth of the same to the point of contact of the frontiers of the two parties".

Under the 1847 treaty (which also settled certain other territorial issues between Iran and Turkey), the quadripartite boundary commission undertook to continue its work to delimit the entire frontier. However, the boundary line recommended by the commission in 1850 was rejected by both Iran and Turkey and further efforts to draw up a satisfactory border were halted by the Crimean War (1853-56). Several years after the war had ended, Britain and Russian drafted separate maps of the Iran-Turkey border revealing a number of discrepancies, and in a joint map (known as the *Carte identique*) produced in 1869 stretches of the border were again left vague. Inhabitants of the southern border region were, however, understood to have reached an informal agreement under which the boundary was regarded as running down the centre of the Shatt al-Arab, with both sides controlling navigation.

20th-Century Developments prior to 1975 Agreement

In the early 20th century, sovereignty over the Shatt al-Arab became an important issue for Iran with the growth of the port of Mohammerah and the discovery of oil at Masjed Sulaiman in 1908 (the latter necessitating the construction of an oil terminal). Iran was now particularly concerned that vessels carrying oil-drilling equipment and other cargo into new berths at Mohammerah had to anchor in Turkish waters and were obliged to pay Turkish import duties. In this situation Britain and Russia (which in 1907 had made a de facto division of Iran into Russian and British spheres of influence) again put pressure on Iran and Turkey to settle their differences and renewed efforts were made to work out a detailed delimitation of their boundary. In Constantinople on Nov. 17, 1913, a protocol was signed by representatives of the boundary commission which reaffirmed Turkish sovereignty over the Shatt al-Arab and again called for the boundary to be demarcated. In 1914, however, the commission reached a verbal agreement which recognized the changed importance of

Mohammerah by moving the boundary opposite the port to the Thalweg line from about a mile below to a mile above the mouth of the Karun river, although the rest of the water remained under Turkish control. (The commission also demarcated the land boundary to the north where Iran, in return for Turkish concessions over the river boundary, ceded larger areas of territory to the Ottoman government.)

From the late 19th century Britain had exercised effective control of the Shatt al-Arab, and at the end of World War I (which marked the dissolution of the Ottoman empire) British forces, now occupying Iraq, set up a Basra port authority to supervise navigation of the estuary and to maintain essential services (lighting, dredging, buoying, pilotage, etc.), such work being financed largely by levies on commercial shipping. The Iranians were thus unable to carry out informal policing and patrolling of the river as they had done previously, even though the growth of the oil port of Abadan was rapidly increasing its strategic importance for Iran. Accordingly, the new Iranian ruler, Reza Shah, repudiated Iraq's claim to the Shatt al-Arab as successor to Ottoman sovereignty and urged a complete revision of the river boundary. Iran also protested (i) that Iraq (which had become a British mandated territory in 1920) was using the bulk of revenues collected from ships using the waterway for its own benefit rather than for maintaining services on the river, and (ii) that riverine boundaries were normally determined by the Thalweg line. Iraq, for its part, argued that the Shatt al-Arab was the only exit to the sea from its major port of Basra while Iran had the potential of developing ports on the Gulf.

In 1934 the League of Nations (of which Iraq had been accepted as a member on Oct. 3, 1932, upon becoming an independent sovereign state) was brought into the dispute on an Iraqi initiative and urged Iran and Iraq to negotiate directly. However, little progress was made on reaching an agreement on the Shatt al-Arab until in 1936 the attitude of Iran and Iraq to one another changed following the Italian attack on Abyssinia. In mid-1937 Iran and Iraq signed an agreement on their border problems, paving the way for the signing, on July 8 of that year, of the Saadabad Pact which brought Iran, Iraq, Turkey and Afghanistan together in a treaty of friendship and non-aggression.

In the border agreement (signed in Baghdad on June 29, 1937, and in Tehran on July 5) the two countries reached a compromise on the Shatt al-Arab, over which Iran had become more amenable in view of its development of a new port (Bandar Shahpur) on the Gulf. The agreement reaffirmed the boundary established by the four-party commission in 1913-14 but also applied the "Mohammerah principle" to Abadan, the border thus following the Thalweg line for some four miles (6.4 km) in the immediate vicinity of and downstream from the port. The treaty also provided for both countries to reach an agreement on matters concerning navigation, pilotage and collection of dues in the river, and furthermore laid down that ships using the river should fly the Iraqi flag except in the vicinity of Mohammerah and Abadan.

In the late 1950s improved technology enabled Iran to develop oil fields in the Gulf (a large oil terminal being built at Kharg island some 30 miles from the mainland), with the result that Iran became less dependent on Abadan (which had the disadvantage of having a shallow approach channel under Iraqi control). Nevertheless, Iran's other imports and exports still depended on Mohammerah and the Shatt al-Arab thus remained vital to Iran. In the mid-1960s the Shah of Iran (Mohammed Reza) reiterated his father's earlier claims that ships using Iranian ports in the Shatt al-Arab contributed the preponderant part of revenues from the waterway, but that Iraq used none of these funds to benefit the river's facilities and moreover did not give a share to Iran as had been stipulated under the 1937 agreement. On April 19, 1969, Iran declared (i) that it no longer considered the 1937 treaty valid and (ii) that Iranian vessels would henceforth neither pay Iraqi tolls nor fly the Iraqi flag in the waterway. Iran alleged at the same time that the provisions of the 1937 treaty had been formulated to benefit British naval vessels using the Shatt al-Arab at that time, although this was no longer relevant, and again pointed out that international river boundaries normally followed the Thalweg line.

Iraq responded to Iran's abrogation of the 1937 treaty by declaring that the Shatt al-Arab was Iraqi territory and by threatening to take action against any Iranian vessels contravening the terms of the treaty. Despite these warnings no action was taken against an Iranian flagship which on April 22, 1969, sailed down the Shatt al-Arab to the Gulf with Iranian pilots and an Iranian escort and refused to pay dues to the Iraqi authorities. Iranian ships taking similar action were similarly unmolested, although in an apparent act of retaliation several thousand Iranians resident in Iraq were forcibly expelled.

1975 Reconciliation and Border Agreement

Strained relations between Iran and Iraq following Iran's abrogation of the 1937 treaty were exacerbated by (i) Iran's support for Kurdish rebels fighting against the Iraqi regime, and (ii) Iran's occupation in 1971 of three disputed islands in the Strait of Hormuz (Abu Musa and the Greater and Lesser Tunbs[1]), over which Iraq broke off diplomatic relations with Iran until 1973. Moreover, in the early 1970s there was a series of border incidents between the two countries. At a meeting of the UN Security Council in February 1974 both the Iranian and Iraqi governments expressed their desire to settle their border dispute peacefully and through direct negotiations, although the main obstacle to a speedy resolution of the problem remained Iran's objections to the provisions of the 1937 agreement and Iraq's insistence that Iran fulfil its obligations.

The failure of Iran and Iraq to resolve their dispute through direct talks was of concern to other oil-exporting countries, certain of whom attempted to mediate. Eventually, in the course of a conference of the heads of state of members of the Organization of the Petroleum

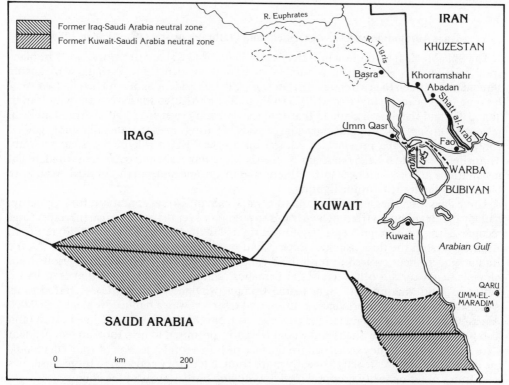

Map 27   Territorial relationships of Iran, Iraq, Kuwait and Saudi Arabia.

---

[1]For the dispute between Iran and the United Arab Emirates over these islands, see pages 242-44.

Exporting Countries (OPEC) held in Algiers on March 4-6, 1975, Iran and Iraq, on the initiative of the Algerian President, reached an agreement which they claimed "completely eliminated the conflict between the two brotherly countries". In a joint communiqué issued on the final day of the OPEC meeting Iran and Iraq agreed inter alia (i) to demarcate their land boundaries on the basis of the Protocol of Constantinople of 1913 and the detailed records (*procès-verbaux*) of the boundary commission of 1914 and (ii) to delimit the river frontier according to the Thalweg line. In return for Iraqi concessions on the Shatt al-Arab Iran ceased its support for Iraq's Kurdish guerrillas (whose rebellion collapsed).

During a meeting of their Foreign Ministers in Tehran on March 15-17, 1975, Iran and Iraq signed a protocol providing for the establishment of committees to (i) demarcate their land boundary; (ii) delimit the river boundary and (iii) prevent any violations of the border. Under a subsequent *procès-verbal* of May 20 the two sides agreed to draw up a final treaty on the boundary, and on June 13 the governments of Iran and Iraq accordingly signed in Baghdad a Treaty Relating to the State Boundary and Good Neighbourliness. Under three protocols to this agreement the two sides (i) established that the border between the two countries in the disputed Shatt al-Arab waterway should be drawn according to the Thalweg line principle; (ii) delineated some 670 positions on the land border between the two countries on the basis of the Protocol of Constantinople of 1913; and (iii) provided for the establishment of border security arrangements to prevent the infiltration of undesirable elements in either direction.

With regard to the river frontier the relevant protocol provided for the boundary line to follow the Thalweg line in the event of a "shift in the bed of the Shatt al-Arab or its mouth caused by natural phenomena" and also stipulated that a survey of the river was to be conducted jointly at least every 10 years.

Iraqi Abrogation of 1975 Agreement and Outbreak of Iran-Iraq War in 1980

The Shia Moslem revolution in Iran of early 1979 led to a sharp deterioration of Iranian-Iraqi relations, as reflected in a number of border incidents and exchanges of hostile statements between the two states. On Sept. 17, 1980, President Saddam Hussein (who had become Iraqi head of state in mid-1979) unilaterally abrogated the agreement with Iran of June 1975 and thereupon claimed that Iraq's sovereignty over the Shatt al-Arab had been restored. On Sept. 21 Iraq launched a large-scale offensive against Iran and rapidly gained control of part of the province of Khuzestan on the eastern side of the Shatt al-Arab, capturing the town of Khorramshahr (formerly Mohammerah) and encircling Abadan. Oil installations in both countries suffered serious damage and ships in the Shatt al-Arab were blocked by the ferocity of the fighting.

Three days after the outbreak of the war Iraq (on Sept. 24) set conditions for a ceasefire, namely that Iran should (i) recognize Iraq's sovereignty over the border area; (ii) respect and recognize Iraq's sovereignty and "legitimate rights" in the Shatt al-Arab; and (iii) return to Arab ownership the three islands which it had occupied in the Strait of Hormuz. As the Iranian government refused to fulfil these conditions, fighting persisted and various Iraqi officials made certain other territorial demands, claiming in particular that Iraq had a "historic" and "nationalist" right to the Iranian province of Khuzestan (referred to as Arabistan by Iraq). This province, with vast oil reserves, was inhabited by some 2,000,000 Arabs who had already agitated for concessions from the new Islamic regime in Iran (and also previously from the Shah) and whom Iraq now promised to help form an independent state in Khuzestan if they so wished. In the face of Iran's total rejection of Iraq's demands, the latter country threatened to occupy more Iranian territory and also to forge closer ties with Iran's other minority groups, largely occupying border areas of the country.

Mediation efforts were undertaken by the United Nations, the Islamic Conference and Organization and the Non-Aligned Movement, but both Iran and Iraq remained intractable, the latter insisting on Iranian territorial concessions and the former refusing to accept a settlement outside the 1975 agreement. With regard to this latter agreement, Iraq maintained that Iran had invalidated it by violating at least two of its terms by (i) refusing to restore to Iraq the areas of Zein al-Kaous and Seif-Saad (comprising some 400 square miles or 1,000 sq km) near Qasr-e-Shirin, which had allegedly been "usurped" some 10 years earlier but which Iran claimed it had returned in accordance with the agreement; and (ii) permitting a Kurdish leader to return to Iran for the presumed purpose of rekindling the Kurdish rebellion.

The Iran-Iraq war continued sporadically throughout 1981, with the military position changing little from that reached in the early stages of the fighting. Although Iranian forces succeeded in September 1981 in lifting the Iraqi siege of Abadan, a situation of military stalemate appeared to have been reached by early 1982, with Iraq still in control of substantial stretches of the eastern bank of the Shatt al-Arab waterway and also pockets of Iranian territory further north. However, from mid-March 1982 the situation changed dramatically when the Iranians launched a major counter-offensive in the southern war zone, driving the Iraqi forces back to the border by mid-May and recapturing Khorramshahr on May 24. With its forces having thus achieved what appeared to be a major military victory, the Iranian government stressed that it had no territorial ambitions against Iraq but insisted that the latter should pay war reparations to Iran and that the Saddam Hussein government should be removed from power.

Henceforward there was considerable speculation, fuelled by official Iranian statements, that Iran would shortly launch a "final offensive" to end the war. No operation on such a scale materialized over the following five years, however, as Iraq continued to benefit from diplomatic and financial support from many Arab states, and from increasingly sophisticated weapons supplies from the Soviet Union, France and other sources. Although there was no active intervention by other Arab armies, both Jordanian and Sudanese "volunteers" took part in the fighting in limited numbers, while talks were reportedly held with Egyptian officials in December 1982 on the possibility of several Egyptian armoured divisions joining the Iraqi forces. For its part, Iran enjoyed some diplomatic support from Libya and several radical third-world governments, but was restricted to the international and clandestine markets for its arms supplies. A report commissioned by the US Senate foreign relations committee, which was published in August 1984, asserted that both the United States and the Soviet Union had gradually shifted from their original stance of professed neutrality to one which overtly favoured Iraq.

Evidence of the Arab world's support for Iraq was apparent in the declaration of the September 1982 Fez summit of Arab League leaders, which praised Iraq's "withdrawal" from Iranian territory, warned that "any aggression against an Arab country" would be considered an aggression "against all Arab countries", and called on all League members to "abstain from taking any measure to encourage either directly or indirectly" the prolongation of the conflict. Despite earlier support for Iran, the Syrian President, Hafez el-Assad, supported the resolution. Earlier in the year, the war had led to the postponement of the seventh summit of Non-Aligned leaders, which was scheduled to be held in Baghdad.

From mid-1983 onwards, Iraqi aircraft flew repeated missions against Iranian oil installations, notably the Kharg island terminal, while the loan of French Super-Etendard fighter aircraft equipped with Exocet anti-ship missiles enabled them to carry out accurate attacks on oil tankers travelling to and from Iranian terminals. In response, Iran threatened to "close the Gulf" to international shipping by using its naval power to prevent safe passage of ships through the narrow Strait of Hormuz at the southern end of the Gulf. The US government responded in early 1984 by warning that there should be "absolutely no doubt" that it would take steps to ensure that the Gulf remained open, to which end a US naval task force was stationed in the vicinity of the Strait.

In May 1984 Iran began attacking Kuwaiti and Saudi tankers by way of retaliation. This "Iranian aggression" on non-belligerents was condemned by meetings of the Foreign Ministers of the Arab League (not including Syrian and Libyan representatives) and the six-member Gulf Co-operation Council (GCC) grouping Kuwait, Oman, Bahrain, Saudi Arabia, the United Arab Emirates and Qatar. The following month, the UN Security

Council passed a resolution condemning the latest attacks (although it failed to condemn Iran by name, as requested by the GCC) and demanding respect for the principle of freedom of navigation in the Gulf. Commenting on the resolution, the Iranian permanent representative at the UN said: "We strongly support freedom of navigation; the Gulf should remain a zone of peace and security for all. But we cannot permit anyone to use the Gulf against us; it will either remain free and open to all of us, or nobody will be allowed to use it."

In the land war, Iran launched a major offensive, code-named "Al-Fajr" (Dawn) in February 1983, directed at the strategic town of Al Amarah, which lay on the road from Basra, Iraq's second city, to the capital. Described by Iranian spokesmen as "the final military operation which will determine the destiny of the region", the attack was beaten back by the Iraqis, who used armour and airstrikes to break the "human waves" of lightly-armed Iranian soldiers. In subsequent diplomatic developments, the UN Security Council again appealed for an "immediate ceasefire" following the attack, while in June 1983 President Hussein similarly called for an end to hostilities. Iranian leaders, however, continued to insist that peace would only come after Hussein had been overthrown.

Iran gained some ground in October 1983 in the border regions of north-eastern Iraq, when its troops seized several mountains in the Penjwin area, thereby cutting communications between Iraqi units and Iranian Kurdish fighters who had been assisting them as part of their own long-running guerrilla war against the Tehran government. At the end of 1983, Iran staged a successful operation in the Majnoon oil fields, just inside the border in southern Iraq. During late 1983, evidence began emerging of Iraqi use of chemical weapons, mostly forms of mustard gas similar to that used in Europe in World War I. Examination of wounded Iranian soldiers by international medical experts confirmed the fact that such weapons were being employed, and Iraq's use of them was specifically condemned in a resolution of the UN Security Council in March 1986.

Air attacks on civilian targets, which had become a regular feature of the war, were suspended by both sides in June 1984 as a result of a moratorium agreement arranged by the UN Secretary-General, Javier Pérez de Cuellar. Iraq resumed bombing of Iranian cities in December of that year, however, leading to retaliatory missile strikes on Iraqi towns. (Throughout the war, the superiority of the Iraqi Air Force enabled it to carry out frequent raids deep into Iran.)

Continuation of Hostilities, 1985-87

In an attempt to achieve a decisive breakthrough against Iraq, the Iranians launched a major offensive in the central sector in March 1985, but their forces were repulsed with heavy casualties. This apparent failure of the "human wave" tactics reportedly fuelled increasing differences within the Iranian political and military leadership over the wisdom of attempting such costly operations and over the viability of any "final offensive". Some officials started to speak of the overriding strategy as being that of a "defensive *jihad* (holy war)".

Mediation efforts were pursued without success during 1985 by the Algerian government and the Islamic Conference Organization, and also by the Indian Prime Minister, Rajiv Gandhi, on behalf of the Non-Aligned Movement. In November the Iranian Foreign Minister, Dr Ali Akbar Vellayati, held talks on possible peaceful solutions to the conflict with King Fahd of Saudi Arabia (one of Iraq's closest allies). In what was seen as an attempt to go some way towards meeting Iran's demand that the Iraqi regime should be condemned and punished as the "aggressor", the UN Security Council passed a resolution in February 1986 which "deplored the initial acts which gave rise to the conflict". In May of that year, the Iranian permanent representative at the UN suggested that negotiations could begin if Saddam Hussein was replaced as President by Ali Saleh, a former Iraqi ambassador to the UN.

In the sea war, both sides escalated attacks on oil tankers and merchant shipping; 46 tankers were attacked in 1985, while approximately double this amount were fired on the following year. In September 1985 Iran began to stop and search vessels suspected of supplying Iraq with military equipment. US and Soviet ships were among those boarded and searched in this manner in 1986. In response to the increase in attacks and interceptions, naval patrols in the southern Gulf by French, British and US ships were stepped up. Iraq's attacks on enemy oil installations became increasingly effective during 1986 and early 1987, as their pilots adopted low-level bombing tactics, which, while increasing the risk of the aircraft being struck by ground fire, also heightened the chances of scoring accurate hits against the target. By the latter half of 1986, Western oil experts were estimating that Iran's refined oil exports had been cut by half as a result of Iraqi air strikes. The Kharg island terminal was seriously damaged, while Iran's coastal shuttle tanker fleet, together with its terminals at Sirri and Larak, in the southern Gulf, were also attacked.

Iranian ground forces gained a significant victory early in 1986 when they overwhelmed Iraqi defences at the deserted port of Fao, on the outlet of the Shatt al-Arab. Repeated Iraqi counter-attacks failed to recapture the town. Further Iranian gains resulted from a major offensive mounted in January and February 1987, when they seized several islands in the Shatt al-Arab opposite Basra; for a time, it appeared possible that they might succeed in capturing the city, but the attack was halted after Iranian leaders had declared that the purpose of the "Karbala-5" offensive was to "destroy the Iraqi war machine", rather than achieve territorial gains. Much of Iraq's defensive strategy in the region relied on the flooding of marshlands to impede the progress of the Iranian infantry. Following the latest attack, it was reported that Iranian engineers were constructing a system of drainage channels in an attempt to draw off the waters which fed Iraq's own complex of artificial lakes.

An element of Iran's success in the Karbala-5 operation was attributed to the arrival of US weapons and spare parts, delivered as part of the secret "arms-for-hostages" arrangement, details of which emerged during late 1986. In particular, the availability of sophisticated anti-tank missiles was thought to have hampered counter-attacks by Iraqi armoured units. Iranian forces also scored limited successes in the central and northern sectors during the opening months of 1987. Iraq responded by increasing the frequency and severity of air attacks on Iranian cities. On Feb. 19, however, the two sides agreed to a further moratorium.

In a renewed effort to satisfy Iranian diplomatic demands, Pérez de Cuellar used the occasion of an address to the Islamic Conference Organization's summit meeting in Kuwait in January 1987 to propose the establishment of an international panel to determine the blame for the war. President Hussein issued an appeal the following month for a complete and unconditional ceasefire, to be followed by a mutual withdrawal to "the internationally-recognized borders", an exchange of prisoners and an agreement by both parties to respect the political and social system of the other. The Iranian government failed to respond to the calls, however, and in April 1987 launched new attacks on the southern front.

The following month international concern over the continuing Iran-Iraq war intensified when on May 17 the US frigate *Stark*, on patrol in the Gulf north of Qatar, was hit by two Exocet missiles fired by an Iraqi Mirage warplane; one missile exploded, causing the deaths of 37 US sailors. (The previous day a Soviet tanker on lease to Kuwait struck a mine at the northern end of the Gulf and was severely disabled.) The USA subsequently accepted Iraqi assurances that the attack on the USS *Stark* had been a case of mistaken identity; at the same time, it said that the US naval presence in the Gulf would be strengthened and that plans would proceed to allow Kuwaiti tankers to fly the US flag so that they could be afforded full protection from potential Iranian attacks.

GG/MWr

Iran-United Arab Emirates

A dispute has existed since the early 1970s between Iran and the United Arab Emirates over the islands of Abu Musa, Greater Tunb and Lesser Tunb, which are strategically situated at the entrance to the Persian (or Arabian) Gulf, opposite the Strait of Hormuz. The Tunb Islands are respectively known to the Arabs as Tunb as-Sughra and Tunb al-Kubra, and to the Iranians as Tunb-e Bozorg and Bani Tanb. (For position of the three islands, see map on page 231.)

On Nov. 30, 1971—two days before the proclamation of the United Arab Emirates (UAE) as a new state, consisting of the Emirates of Abu Dhabi, Dubai, Sharjah, Ras al-Khaimah, Fujairah, Ajman and Umm al-Quwain—Iranian troops occupied the three islands of Abu Musa, Greater Tunb and Lesser Tunb. Abu Musa was occupied by Iran under an agreement reached by the government of Iran and the Ruler of Sharjah, who had held sovereignty over the island, whereas the other two islands were occupied by force after an attempt at negotiating their peaceful transfer from the Ruler of Ras al-Khaimah, under whose jurisdiction they fell, had failed.

The agreement on Abu Musa, announced on Nov. 29, 1971, contained the following provisions: (i) Iranian troops would be stationed on part of Abu Musa, and in this area the Iranian flag would be flown and Iran would exercise full jurisdiction; (ii) Sharjah would retain jurisdiction over the rest of the island, including the existing Sharjah police post on it; (iii) both Iran and Sharjah recognized a 12-mile territorial waters limit around the island, and both agreed to the eixsting concessionaire—the (US) Buttes Gas and Oil Company—continuing oil exploration both on the island and offshore; (iv) revenues accruing from oil exploration would be shared equally between Iran and Sharjah; (v) Iran would give Sharjah £1,500,000 a year in aid until Sharjah's annual revenue from oil deposits reached £3,000,000; and (vi) Iranian and Sharjah nationals would have equal fishing rights in the island's territorial waters.

Notwithstanding this agreement, the UAE Council of Ministers stated on Dec. 2, 1971, that the UAE "repudiates the principle of the use of force, rejects Iran's recent occupation of a part of the cherished Arab homeland and advocates the need to respect legitimate rights and discuss any differences that may occur among states through internationally agreed methods".

Conflicting Arab, Iranian and British Views

Iran's action against the three islands was condemned by all Arab states as an act of aggression against Arab territories, and at the request of Algeria, Iraq, Libya and the People's Democratic Republic of Yemen (South Yemen) the United Nations Security Council met on Dec. 9, 1971, to discuss the situation.

The representative of Iraq claimed during the debate that the islands had been "under Arab jurisdiction for centuries", and he rejected as "invalid" three reasons given by Iran for its action—alleged historical rights, filling a presumed "power vacuum" in the area, and finally the strategic value to Iran of the islands. He also criticized Britain for not honouring its obligation to defend the islands although Britain's special treaty relations with the Arab rulers who held sovereignty over the island had "not terminated at the time of Iran's occupation of the islands". The representative of South Yemen stated that Iran had never "presented any convincing evidence of its claim to the islands" and had refused to negotiate the matter with the UAE but had chosen to use force.

On the other hand, the representative of Iran, invited to take part in the debate, declared that the Iranian title to the islands was long-standing and substantial, that both maps, hundreds of years old and modern, and a highly authoritative encyclopaedia treated the territories as belonging to Iran; that in line with its policy of settling disputes by peaceful means Iran had tried to settle the problem through negotiation; but that these efforts had failed and Iran had been left with no alternative but to exercise its sovereign right.

The British representative explained that his government was satisfied with the agreement reached on Abu Musa between the Ruler of Sharjah and Iran, and that it had declared that it could not protect the Tunb Islands if agreement on their future was not reached before Britain's withdrawal from them (by Dec. 1, 1971). The UN Security Council subsequently decided to defer consideration of the question "in order to allow sufficient time for third-party efforts to work".

Iran's intention to occupy the islands had been stated by the Shah of Iran, who had been reported on Feb. 16, 1971, to have stressed that he would act "by force if necessary" if no peaceful agreements for the islands' transfer was reached before Britain's withdrawal from the Gulf before the end of 1971. The intention was subsequently reaffirmed by Iranian ministers, and on Nov. 10, 1971, Abbas Khalatbari, then Iran's Foreign Minister, was quoted as saying that Iran's sovereignty over the islands was "not negotiable" and that Iran had rejected Arab suggestions that they should be leased to Iran when Britain left the area.

Arguments used by Iran were (i) that the islands had been owned by Iran before they were occupied by Britain 150 years earlier "on the assumption that they were essential to combat piracy" in the Gulf; (ii) that Britain had "in pursuit of its imperial interests" considered the islands as belonging to the Arab Shaikhs of the Trucial States and had transferred them to the de facto administration of Sharjah and Ras al-Khaimah when Iran was "politically weak"; and (iii) that the islands had been shown in Iranian colours on a map which had been issued by the British Intelligence Section of the Ministry of Defence in 1886 and a copy of which had been presented to the Shah in 1888.

In the British view, however, Iran had no title to the islands which, Britain argued, had reverted to the administration of the Trucial coast of Qawasim by the early part of the second half of the 19th century, and the Rulers of Sharjah and Ras al-Khaimah had disclosed documentary evidence based on official British records, supporting their respective "prescriptive title" to the islands since 1872. On instructions from the Ruler of Sharjah on the question of Abu Musa, a firm of British counsels completed (in July 1971) a report based on the examination of "thousands of documents and hundreds of maps and charts" and concluding that Abu Musa had "from the earliest recorded date belonged to the Rulers of Sharjah". The report rebutted in particular the British map of 1886 [see above], stating that the colouring showing Abu Musa as Iranian was "in error" and had not had the consent of the Trucial Rulers.

The Iranian landing on Abu Musa was also criticized by the Arab League, which questioned the validity of the agreement between Iran and Sharjah on the grounds that the latter's Ruler had signed it under duress, i.e. under Iranian pressure and threat to take over the island by force if no solution satisfactory to Iran was reached. In this context it should be noted that Article 52 of the Convention on the Law of Treaties of May 23, 1969, states: "A treaty is void if its conclusion has been produced by the threat of use of force in violation of the principles of international law embodied in the Charter of the United Nations". It is, however, also important to note that the agreement had been concluded with the British Foreign Secretary acting as the channel of communication between Iran and Sharjah.

The government of Iraq broke off its diplomatic relations with Iran and with Britain on Nov. 30, 1971 (i.e. after Iran's occupation of the islands), and described Iran's action as a "flagrant aggression in collusion with Britain". Iraq also warned Britain that it had "the obligation to preserve the Arab character of the islands". The Arab League, in reports published on Dec. 2, 1971, similarly declared that Britain's failure to act was contrary to its treaty obligations towards the Trucial Rulers. The British Foreign Office, however, argued that it was impossible to stop the Iranian action just one day before the treaty relations were terminated on Dec. 1, 1971—an attitude which was criticized as "hypocrisy" in *The Times* on Dec. 2 on the grounds that a treaty was "as valid on the last day as on the first".

Reaffirmation of Arab Claim to the Islands by Iraq

The question of sovereignty over the islands was again raised on Oct. 31, 1979, when the Iraqi ambassador in Beirut (Lebanon) issued a declaration containing far-reaching political demands to be fulfilled by the government of the Islamic Republic of Iran—among them a demand for the evacuation of the three islands by Iran. All these demands were, however, rejected by Iran on Nov. 1 of that year.

On April 6, 1980, the Iraqi Foreign Minister was reported to have called, in a message to the UN Secretary-General, for the immediate withdrawal of Iranian troops from the islands and to have accused Iran of pursuing "an aggressive and expansionist policy in the Gulf region". The Iranian Foreign Minister, however, stated on the same day that Iran's differences with Iraq went beyond the disputed islands and that the Iraqi government was "under the control of Zionists and imperialists" while "pretending that it wants to preserve Arab interests in the region". Following the outbreak of full-scale war between Iraq and Iran, the Iraqi government on Sept. 24, 1980, reiterated its call for the return to Arab sovereignty of the three Gulf islands.

The UAE government, in a message to the United Nations reported on Dec. 11, 1980, stated that while it desired to maintain good-neighbourly relations and co-operation to maintain security and stability in the Gulf area, it insisted on the restoration of its full sovereignty over the three islands and declared that it was ready to negotiate with the Iranian government to reach a solution which would fully recognize the UAE's sovereignty over the islands in accordance with the UN Charter and principles. At the same time the UAE's representative at the United Nations asked for the distribution of this message as an official document of the UN General Assembly.

In a statement published on March 28, 1982, Shaikh Saqr bin Muhammed Al-Qasimi, the ruler of Ras al-Khaimah and a member of the UAE Supreme Council, said that his country would not compromise or change its position on the issue of the three islands, adding: "The three islands are an Arab right about which there can be no discussion. Iran's rulers know this better than others; however, no contact on this issue has been made between them and us."

HWD

Iraq-Kuwait

On June 25, 1961—just six days after Kuwait had gained independence—the Iraqi Prime Minister, Gen. Kassem, laid claim to all of Kuwait, arguing that the latter had been an "integral part" of Basra province under Ottoman rule and that Iraq had succeeded to Turkish territorial sovereignty over Basra with the dissolution of the Ottoman empire after World War I. Gen. Kassem was unsuccessful in winning international recognition for the validity of his claim to Kuwait (one of the world's leading petroleum producers) and in 1963, after his overthrow and the accession of President Aref, Iraq relinquished its claim and recognized Kuwait as a sovereign state. However, the otherwise good relations between these neighbouring countries over the following 10 years were marred by a long-standing dispute centring principally on Iraq's interest in two islands owned by Kuwait, namely Warba and Bubiyan. Iraqi possession of these islands, situated just south of the Iraq-Kuwait border in the north-east Arabian (Persian) Gulf, would give that country greatly improved access to the Gulf. In 1973 Iraqi troops moved towards this part of the frontier and occupied a border post, from which they were, however, rapidly forced to withdraw in the face of general Arab opposition. Iraq and Kuwait then began a series of negotiations—at times with external mediation—with a view to settling the border question but, despite frequently optimistic reports, agreement on the demarcation of their common border was not accomplished. Having in September 1980 reasserted its territorial claims on Iran by force of arms,[1] Iraq the following year also revived its claim to Warba and Bubiyan. However, the prolongation of the Iran-Iraq war and Kuwait's support for Iraq in that conflict had the effect of defusing Iraq-Kuwait territorial issues, at least for the time being. (For a map showing Warba and Bubiyan, see page 237.)

Historical Background

In the 19th century Kuwait had been administered as part of the Ottoman province of Basra, although the Turks had never occupied or gained full sovereignty over it. In 1896 Shaikh Mubarak the Great seized power in Kuwait after murdering his pro-Turkish half brother, Shaikh Mohammed, and asserted Kuwait's independence from the Ottoman empire, saying that his people owed no allegiance to the Turks. To this end Shaikh Mubarak sought protection from Britain and in 1899, without the approval of the Ottoman Sultan, an agreement was signed under which Britain undertook to give Kuwait protection in return for control over its foreign affairs. Under an Anglo-Turkish convention of July 29, 1913, Britain secured Turkish recognition of Kuwait's autonomy within an area formed by a 40-mile (64-km) radius around the town of Kuwait; however, the outbreak of World War I in 1914 prevented ratification of this agreement. On Nov. 3, 1914, Shaikh Mubarak was promised British recognition as an "independent government under British protection" in return for his co-operation in the capture of Basra from the Turks. Kuwait retained this status until June 19, 1961, when an exchange of notes was signed between Britain and Kuwait which terminated the 1899 agreement between the two countries and provided for British recognition of Kuwait as a sovereign and independent state (although a military assistance agreement remained in force).

Iraq had formerly comprised three Mesopotamian provinces (*vilayet*) of Baghdad, Mosul and Basra and was administered by the Ottoman empire through appointed governors (pashas) answerable to the Sultan-Caliph in Constantinople. After the dissolution of the Ottoman empire in 1918 it was agreed that Mesopotamia should form a self-governing state and on Oct. 20, 1920, Britain accepted a League of Nations mandate for Iraq until it was ready for independence. Under the Treaty of Lausanne of July 24, 1923, Turkey renounced all the territory it had previously possessed outside the borders of present-day Turkey, this renunciation applying also to Kuwait as a part of the former Ottoman province of Basra. After Britain had on Jan. 28, 1932, given up its mandate over Iraq, on Oct. 3 of that year Iraq became an independent sovereign state and was admitted to the League of Nations.

The border between Iraq and Kuwait had first been defined in an exchange of letters, dated April 4 and April 19, 1923, between Shaikh Ahmad al Sabah of Kuwait and Maj.-Gen. Sir Percy Cox, then British high commissioner for Iraq. In a subsequent exchange of letters, dated July 21 and Aug. 10, 1932, Shaikh Ahmad and the then Iraqi Prime Minister, Nuri al Said, reaffirmed the "existing frontier between Iraq and Kuwait" on the basis of the 1923 letters as follows: "From the intersection of the Wadi al-Audja with the Batin and thence northwards along the Batin to a point just south of the latitude of Safwan; thence eastwards passing south of Safwan Wells, Jebel Sanam and Umm Qasr leaving them to Iraq and so on to the junction of the Khor Zobeir with the Khor Abdulla. The islands of Warba, Bubiyan, Maskan (or Mashjan), Failakah, Auhan, Kubbar, Qaru and Umm el-Maradim appertain to

---

[1]For an account of the Iran-Iraq territorial dispute, see pages 234-41.

Kuwait." However, this early border demarcation was later regarded as invalid by Iraq on the grounds that Iraq had not been an independent state on the date of Nuri al Said's letter of July 21, 1932.

The Iraqi Claim to Kuwait

On June 25, 1961, Gen. Kassem made a claim of Iraqi sovereignty over Kuwait, which he described as an "integral part of Iraq". Gen. Kassem's claim was based on the Iraqi argument that (i) Kuwait had been part of Basra province in the Ottoman empire, and (ii) that Britain and other powers had recognized Ottoman sovereignty over Kuwait both before and after the signature of the 1899 agreement under which Kuwait became a British protectorate. In addition, Gen. Kassem said that he had issued a decree appointing the Shaikh of Kuwait as *Qaim Maqaam* (prefect) of Kuwait.

Elaborating on Gen. Kassem's assertions, the Iraqi Foreign Ministry in a statement issued on June 26, 1961, said that it recognized neither the "secret agreement" of 1899, as it had been concluded without the authority of the Ottoman Sultan, nor the agreement of 1961, as it aimed "under the new cloak of national independence . . . to maintain imperialist influence and to keep Kuwait separate from Iraq". The statement added that formerly the Ottoman Sultan had appointed the Shaikh of Kuwait "by a decree conferring on him the title of *Qaim Maqaam* and making him representative of the governor of Basra in Kuwait", and that the Shaikhs of Kuwait had thus "continued to derive their administrative powers from the Ottoman Sultan until 1914".

Kuwait rejected the Iraqi arguments, asserting that it had never been subject to Turkish sovereignty, that Kuwait had been governed "without direct Turkish interference" by the same dynasty since 1756 and that the title of *Qaim Maqaam* was never used in Kuwait and "never influenced the course of life or the independence of Kuwait from the Turkish empire". (It should be noted in this context, however, that historians of the area have generally taken the view that Shaikh Mubarak—in 1896—was the first Kuwaiti ruler to refuse this title.)

In response to a Kuwaiti request for military assistance, prompted by rumours that Iraq was moving troops southwards in the Basra area (which Iraq denied), forces from Britain and also Saudi Arabia arrived in Kuwait by early July 1961, and Kuwait's own forces were mobilized. Efforts by the UN Security Council in early July to defuse the crisis were unsuccessful and mediation was taken over by the Arab League (which on July 20 admitted Kuwait as a member despite Iraqi opposition). On Aug. 12 the Arab League countries, Iraq alone dissenting, signed an agreement with Kuwait under which British forces were to be replaced by a force from the League itself and under which they also pledged (i) to preserve Kuwait's integrity and independence under her present regime; (ii) to regard any aggression against the shaikhdom as aggression against the League's members; and (iii) in the event of any such aggression, to render Kuwait immediate assistance and, if necessary, repel it with armed force. Notwithstanding this agreement Iraq reiterated its claim to Kuwait and withdrew its representatives from all countries which had recognized that country.

Developments following Iraqi Recognition of Kuwait in 1963

The overthrow of Gen. Kassem on Feb. 3, 1963, led to an easing of the friction between Iraq and Kuwait. Under President Aref, the new Iraqi regime on Oct. 4, 1963 (in the course of a visit to Baghdad by an invited Kuwaiti delegation), entered into an agreement with Kuwait under which Iraq inter alia "recognized the independence and complete sovereignty of the state of Kuwait with its boundaries as specified in the letter of the Prime Minister of Iraq dated 21.7.1932 and which was accepted by the ruler of Kuwait in his letter dated 10.8.1932". In addition, the two countries agreed to work towards improving relations and establishing co-operation at all levels and to this end decided to establish immediately diplomatic relations at ambassadorial level.

Nevertheless, it became apparent that Iraqi recognition of Kuwait did not involve acceptance of the latter's frontiers, and in succeeding years longstanding Iraqi claims to certain parts of Kuwait's border territory were revived. Iraq's interest lay particularly in improving its access to the Gulf through the acquisition of the islands of Warba and Bubiyan, the importance of which had increased considerably in view of Iraq's development of the north Rumaila oilfield and the expansion of its port of Umm Qasr. In March 1973, with a view to forcing the issue, Iraqi forces occupied a border post in the disputed area but were forced to withdraw when Iraq was confronted with Arab disapproval of its action. Subsequently, talks between Iraq and Kuwait on the border issue were stepped up, with other Arab countries offering their assistance in mediation, and in May 1975 Iraqi officials announced that they had made concrete proposals to settle the dispute. These involved essentially the leasing by Kuwait to Iraq of half of Bubiyan for 99 years and the ceding of Kuwaiti sovereignty over Warba in return for Iraqi recognition of Kuwait's land borders. The following month Saudi Arabian sources, quoting Kuwaiti news reports, said that the two countries had finally established the basis for an agreement on the territorial issues in dispute.

However, on July 12, 1975, negotiations reached an impasse when the Kuwaiti National Assembly, while expressing support for the efforts latterly made to come to an agreement with Iraq, stressed "Kuwait's sovereignty over all its territory within the borders which have been approved in accordance with international and bilateral agreements between Kuwait and its neighbours". On Dec. 13, 1976, Kuwait's acting Minister of Information, Shaikh Jabir al-Ali, stressed that Warba and Bubiyan belonged to Kuwait as defined in the 1932 exchange of letters and the 1963 agreement between Iraq and Kuwait; he also complained that, in addition to the "previous Iraqi military presence in Kuwait territory" south of the Umm Qasr area, there were now "regular crossings by Iraqi forces all along the border between the two countries at varying depths".

Talks on the delimitation of the Iraq-Kuwait border made little progress over the following years, despite the formation in 1978 of a joint committee headed by the Interior Ministers of the two countries to work towards resolving outstanding issues. The outbreak of war between Iraq and Iran in September 1980 led to a revival of the Iraqi claim to Warba and Bubiyan in July 1981, when President Hussein of Iraq repeated the Iraqi proposals of 1975 and in particular the demand that Kuwait should grant Iraq a 99-year lease of half of Bubiyan. However, the Kuwait government continued to assert its sovereignty over both islands, and in December 1981 a Kuwaiti spokesman said that no agreed date existed for a resumption of talks between the two sides.

Having become a member of the Gulf Co-operation Council (GCC) on its formation in May 1981 (together with Bahrain, Oman, Qatar, Saudi Arabia and the United Arab Emirates), Kuwait followed the GCC's policy of supporting Arab Iraq's cause against Iran, a non-Arab country which was seen as having expansionist ambitions in the Gulf area. In consequence, relations with Iraq improved in the 1980s, as the Gulf war dragged on and as Kuwaiti installations and ships themselves became the targets of Iranian air attacks. Moreover, with the Iraqi port of Basra on the Shatt al-Arab waterway closed, Iraq became increasingly dependent on Kuwaiti transit facilities for access to the sea.

On the occasion of an official visit to Baghdad by Shaikh Saad as Sabah of Kuwait in mid-November 1984, Iranian radio claimed (on Nov. 16) that Kuwait had reached an agreement with Iraq under which the latter obtained use of Bubiyan and two other islands in the Gulf. The broadcast also quoted a speech by the Speaker of the Iranian Parliament, Hojatolislam Hashemi Rafsanjani, warning Kuwait "not to play with fire" and to take notice that, if Iran were to capture Bubiyan, Kuwait would have no territorial claim to the island. The Kuwaiti Defence Minister responded on Dec. 2, 1984, that in view of recent threats Kuwaiti troops and air defences had been deployed on Bubiyan.

GG/HWD

Iraq-Saudi Arabia

Following the collapse of Ottoman power in Arabia during World War I, the emergence of what were to become the independent state of Iraq and Saudi Arabia was accompanied by bitter territorial rivalry between the two centres of power, exacerbated by the general absence of defined borders in the vast desert territories of the region. Under the aegis of Britain as the dominant post-Ottoman external power, the boundary between present-day Iraq and Saudi Arabia was first defined under agreements signed in 1922, which also created a neutral zone in the contentious eastern border area between the two sides. Although the status quo established by the 1922 agreements prevailed over the next 60 years, the question of the delimitation of the neutral zone remained a potential source of dispute between the two states, especially after the 1958 revolution in Iraq and that country's gravitation to the radical Arab camp opposed to the conservative line of the Saudi leadership. However, the new constellation of interests created by the 1979 revolution in Iran and the outbreak of the Iran-Iraq war the following year led Iraq and Saudi Arabia to sign an agreement in December 1981 defining their common border and also providing for the division of the neutral zone between the two countries. (For a map showing the Iraq-Saudi neutral zone, see page 237.)

Historical Background

By the early 19th century much of Arabia was under the control of the powerful Wahhabi army associated with the al-Saud family (ancestors of the present-day ruling family in Saudi Arabia), which had risen to power in the sultanate of Najd centred on Riyadh in central Arabia. Following a period of suppression by Ottoman forces in 1811-18 the Wahhabi movement enjoyed a revival in the 1820s but suffered a further decline in the latter part of the 19th century coincidentally with the rising power of the al-Rashid family of Hail in the Jabal Shammar area of northern Najd. In 1891 the al-Rashids inflicted a crushing defeat on the rival al-Sauds, occupying Riyadh and forcing the head of the al-Saud family, Abd ar-Rahman, to flee to Kuwait with his young son, Abd al-Azis (Ibn Saud). By 1902 Ibn Saud had recaptured Riyadh and prior to the outbreak of World War I he had consolidated his authority in Najd and Hasa further south. Under the 1915 Treaty of Qatif, moreover, Britain recognized the independence and territorial integrity of Najd and acknowledged Ibn Saud as ruler of both Najd and Hasa, granting him a monthly subsidy.

After World War I territorial problems and tribal rivalries re-emerged and Ibn Saud sought to take control of Hail, in particular since Faisal, the son of the King of Hejaz (Sharif Hussain), had become King of Iraq. In 1921-22 Ibn Saud, his tribesmen now organized in Akhwan brotherhoods, defeated the al-Rashids in Jabal Shammar and spread his sphere of control up to the borders of Transjordan and Iraq, surrounding the kingdom of Hejaz, where the al-Hashimi tribe had latterly become serious rivals to the al-Sauds. Ibn Saud now posed a threat not only to Hejaz but also to Iraq (for which country Britain had accepted a League of Nations mandate in 1920) and also Kuwait, a British protectorate.

British interest in eliminating the potential for conflict in Arabia gave rise to the signing of the Treaty of Mohammerah (Khorramshahr) on May 5, 1922, between Ibn Saud and the British high commissioner for Iraq, Maj.-Gen. Sir Percy Cox. This treaty did not define a boundary between Iraq and Najd (Ibn Saud having objected to the "attempt to curb, by an imaginary line in the open desert, the movement of tribes who are accustomed to roam widely in search of pasturage and water"), but agreement was reached on the assignment of the Muntafiq, Dhafir and Amarat tribes to Iraq and the Shammar Najd tribe to Najd. Both sides undertook to prevent mutual aggression by the tribes, whose traditional wells and lands were allocated relative to the respective host government. It was further agreed that in order

248

to "determine the location of these lands and wells and to fix a boundary line in accordance with this principle, a committee shall be formed of two persons with local knowledge from each government and presided over by a British official selected by the high commissioner".

Later in 1922 Ibn Saud finally agreed to the delimitation of the border between Najd and Iraq on condition that wells and watering places near the frontier would not be used for military purposes and that Najd tribes would not be refused access to watering places on the Iraqi side of the border. The agreement between Ibn Saud and King Faisal was incorporated into two protocols to the Uqair Convention of Dec. 2, 1922, which in addition to defining the boundary also established a neutral zone in which Iraq and Najd would enjoy equal rights. This diamond-shaped zone began at the extremity of Kuwait's western frontier at the junction of the Wadi al-Audja and the Wadi al-Batin, its northern border with Iraq running for some 119 miles (190 km) and its southern border with Saudi Arabia some 125 miles (200 km); at its widest north-south point, the zone measured about 40 miles (65 km) and had a total area of some 2,500 square miles (6,500 sq km).

Article I of the first protocol set out the precise boundaries of the neutral zone, which "will remain neutral and common to the two governments of Iraq and Najd who will enjoy equal rights to it for all purposes". Article II stated: "Whereas many of the wells fall within the Iraq boundaries and the Najd side is deprived of them the Iraq government pledges itself not to interfere with those Najd tribes living in the vicinity of the border should it be necessary for them to resort to the neighbouring Iraq wells for water, provided that these wells are nearer to them than those within the Najd boundaries." Article III stated: "The two governments mutually agreed not to use the watering places and wells situated in the vicinity of the border for any military purpose, such as building forts on them, and not to concentrate troops in their vicinity." Moreover, under the second protocol both sides agreed that if "any tribe or section of a tribe which is outside the boundaries of, and not subject to either government, desires its allegiance to one of them, they will not prevent it from doing so."

Further Agreements between Ibn Saud and King Faisal

The conclusion of the agreements of 1922 did not put an end to the deep-seated rivalry between Ibn Saud and King Faisal or to tribal conflicts. In 1924-25 Ibn Saud succeeded in annexing Hejaz, which had previously been ruled by King Faisal's father, Sharif Hussain, while Najd's expansionist policies also threatened Transjordan, ruled by Faisal's brother, Abdullah. On Jan. 8, 1926, Ibn Saud was proclaimed King of Hejaz—Soviet recognition of his new position being accorded a month later and that of Britain on May 20, 1927, under the Treaty of Jeddah.

Following their conquest of Hejaz, the Akhwan forces made a series of raids on Iraqi tribes inside Iraqi territory and also during their customary migration into Kuwait and Najd, and Iraq's use of aircraft to ward off such attacks was strongly opposed by Ibn Saud. However, in 1929 the latter was himself threatened by rebellious Najd tribes, with the result that he took steps to reach an understanding with King Faisal. In February 1930 the two leaders met on board a ship at the mouth of the Shatt al-Arab waterway and as a result of their discussions a Treaty of Friendship and Good Neighbourliness was signed the following year. Under this treaty both parties undertook to take steps to prevent tribal raiding and agreed at the same time that tribes of either ocuntry were to be permitted free movement within the territory of the other for pasturage or for purchasing provisions; a permanent frontier committee was established to oversee these matters.

There were no further serious incidents of raiding after the 1931 treaty and generally friendly relations prevailed between the two powers, assisted by the growth of the oil industry in both countries and consequent economic advances and by the gradual extension of administrative control throughout their respective territories. In 1932 the dual kingdom of Hejaz and Najd became the kingdom of Saudi Arabia and in the same year Iraq was admitted to the League of Nations as an independent state. Four years later the two countries concluded a Treaty of Arab Brotherhood and Alliance.

Recent Developments leading to 1981 Border Agreement

An agreement concerning the administration of the neutral zone was signed between Iraq and Saudi Arabia in May 1938 but there were no further important developments relating to the zone for many years. In July 1975 it was reported in Saudi Arabia that the two countries had agreed to divide the zone equally by a line drawn as straight as possible which would necessitate modifying the existing border, but the agreement apparently remained unratified. However, the potential threat to the stability of the Gulf area posed by the Shia Moslem revolution in Iran in 1979 and the outbreak of war between Iran and Iraq in September 1980 impelled Saudi Arabia and Iraq to seek closer relations and in particular to achieve a settlement of their common border and the neutral zone question.

Talks on these matters reached a positive outcome on Dec. 26, 1981, when the Saudi Interior Minister, Prince Nayef ibn Abdul Aziz, signed an agreement in Baghdad with his Iraqi counterpart, Sa'adoun Shaker, which the former subsequently described as a treaty ("because the previous agreement was the Mohammerah Treaty with the Uqair protocols"). According to Prince Nayef, the new agreement "defined and fixed" the border between Iraq and Saudi Arabia and also provided for the division of the neutral zone", with the result that the frontier between the two states had been "stabilized".

GG

Kuwait-Saudi Arabia

The Uqair Convention, signed on Dec. 2, 1922, between Kuwait, then a British protectorate, and the sultanate of Najd (which together with the kingdom of Hejaz formed the kingdom of Saudi Arabia in 1932), defined and delimited the boundary between the two states and provided for the establishment of a neutral coastal zone immediately to the south of Kuwait over which both sides would have joint sovereignty pending a final settlement. Although in the 1960s Kuwait and Saudi Arabia reached agreement on the partitioning of the zone (and a new international land boundary came into effect), the area's huge oil reserves constitute a possible source of future territorial dispute between the two countries. Moreover, the agreements signed in the 1960s apply only to the land boundaries of the zone: difficulties still exist relating to offshore boundaries and also to the sovereignty of the Gulf islands of Qaru and Umm el-Maradim. (For a map showing the territorial relationship of Kuwait and Saudi Arabia, see page 237.)

The neutral zone consisted of some 2,500 square miles (6,500 sq km) of desert with a coastline about 40 miles (64 km) long on the Persian (Arabian) Gulf. Little interest was shown in reaching a final agreement on the area until the discovery of oil in southern Kuwait in the late 1930s. The changed importance of the zone and the consequent influx of workers and oil company personnel increased the problems involved in jointly administering the area; accordingly, following lengthy negotiations, Kuwait and Saudi Arabia agreed in principle in 1960 to divide the territory equally. In 1965 the two countries signed an agreement on the partitioning of the zone, the new international land boundary coming into effect following the exchange of instruments of ratification in 1966 and the signing of subsequent demarcation accord at the end of 1967. By 1970 Kuwait and Saudi Arabia had, as agreed, completed the allocation of properties and facilities in the zone.

Historical Background

During the centuries of Ottoman rule over Arabia, the present-day border region of Kuwait and Saudi Arabia was virtually uninhabited desert, although as a historic route for tribes moving northwards to the more fertile areas of the Tigris and Euphrates rivers it was the scene of frequent tribal rivalry. Prominent among the tribes in the 19th century was the Wahhabi movement, which attacked northwards from Najd and which, following a defeat at the hands of Ottoman forces, later revived as the powerful Ikhwan force. In the early 1900s this tribe gave its support to Abd al-Azis (Ibn Saud) of the al-Saud family in Najd in his long dispute over border territories with Shaikh Salim of Kuwait (who was ruler in 1917-21).

Under an Anglo-Turkish convention of July 1913 Kuwaiti autonomy had been recognized up to a 40-mile (64-km) radius of the town of Kuwait; but this agreement was never ratified, and the final eclipse of Ottoman authority during World War I gave rise to a fluid situation in which Ibn Saud's forces engaged in armed hostilities with Shaikh Salim. Following a particularly serious raid by Ibn Saud on the Kuwaiti oasis area of Jahra in October 1920, Maj.-Gen. Sir Percy Cox, then British high commissioner in Iraq (which became a British mandate in 1920), decided that issues concerning tribal loyalties and rights would have to be resolved before permanent and peaceful boundaries could be established in Arabia.

Upon the death of Shaikh Salim in 1921 and the accession of his nephew, Shaikh Ahmad (who ruled until 1950), Ibn Saud declared that he had no further dispute with Kuwait and that there was thus no need to determine a boundary. The British nonetheless proceeded with their efforts to define lasting borders in the area and, after lengthy deliberations between the parties concerned, a conference at Al Uqair reached boundary agreements on Dec. 2, 1922, under which neutral zones were established between Kuwait and Najd on the one hand and between Iraq and Najd on the other.[1]

The Uqair Convention defined the territory of the neutral zone between Najd and Kuwait as follows: "The portion of territory bounded on the north by this line [i.e. the "indisputable southern frontier of Kuwait"] and which is bounded on the west by a low mountainous ridge called Ash Shaq and on the east by the sea and on the south by a line passing from west to east from Ash Shaq to Ayn al-Abd and thence to the coast north of Ras al Mish'ab—in this territory the government of Najd and Kuwait will share equal rights until through the good offices of the government of Great Britain a further agreement is made between Najd and Kuwait concerning it."

Of the two principal parties to the Uqair Convention, Najd subsequently became part of the larger kingdom of Saudi Arabia established by Ibn Saud in 1932, while Kuwait continued as a British protectorate until achieving full independence in 1961.

Agreement to partition the Neutral Zone

The granting of joint sovereignty to both parties in the neutral zone meant that they were able to exploit any natural resources there on an equal basis. After the discovery of oil in Kuwait's southern Burgan fields in 1938, attention was given to oil exploration in the neutral zone itself and towards the end of the following decade Kuwait and Saudi Arabia granted exploration rights in the territory to two private companies which later exploited the oil under a joint agreement. In 1948 Kuwait signed a contract with the American Oil Company (Aminoil) and the following year Saudi Arabia reached a similar agreement with the Pacific Western Oil Company (later renamed Getty Oil Company), both these agreements applying to the land area of the neutral zone. Moreover, in 1957-58 both Kuwait and Saudi Arabia granted the Japanese Oil Company separate concessions for offshore territories.

In view of the administrative problems caused by the construction of oil installations and the increased number of workers in the zone, Saudi Arabia and Kuwait began discussions in the late 1950s on the legal status of the zone and its offshore area. By the end of 1960 both parties had agreed (i) that the land area of the neutral territory should, in principle, be divided into two geographical parts, one to be annexed by Kuwait and the other by Saudi

---

[1]For the Iraq-Najd agreement, incorporating provisions of the earlier Treaty of Mohammerah of May 1922, see pages 248-49.

Arabia; and (ii) that each country should form a committee of experts to draft boundary lines for the partitioned zone. Although talks were hampered over the following year in view of Kuwaiti protests that Saudi Arabia was exerting an unfair amount of control over the zone, further deliberations finally led to an exchange of notes between the two countries on Aug. 5, 1963. In this exchange Saudi Arabia and Kuwait reaffirmed their agreement in principle to divide the zone and, on the basis of a Kuwaiti proposal, decided furthermore that each separate part of the divided zone would be administered by one government (Kuwait having rejected an earlier suggestion by Saudi Arabia that a system of joint administration be introduced on a condominium basis).

Following the initialling of a further bilateral agreement on March 8, 1964, Kuwait and Saudi Arabia on July 7, 1965, signed an agreement at Jeddah (Saudi Arabia) to divide the neutral zone geographically with the proviso that the "equal rights of the two parties shall be preserved in full in the whole partitioned zone as this had originally been decided by the convention made at Al Uqair ... and shall be safeguarded by the provisions of international responsibility". Under Article I of the agreement the boundary line between the two sections of the zone was to be "the line which divides them equally into two parts and which begins from a point at the mid-eastern shore on the low-tide line and ends at the western boundary line of the zone"; the part to the north of the dividing line would be annexed to Kuwait and the area lying to the south to Saudi Arabia (Article II). Both Kuwait and Saudi Arabia would "exercise the rights of administration, legislation and defence" over their own part of the zone "in the same manner exercised in his territory of origin, while observing other provisions of the agreement, and without prejudice to the rights of the contracting parties to natural resources in the whole of the partitioned zone" (Article III). Saudi Arabia and Kuwait undertook to respect the rights of the other to the "shared natural resources" which exist, or might exist, in its own annexed part (Article IV).

With regard to territorial waters adjoining both parts of the zone, each country would have the same rights as it had over the land areas of the zone annexed to them, while "for the purpose of exploiting natural resources" in the partitioned zone, it was agreed that "not more than six marine miles of the seabed and subsoil adjoining the partitioned zone shall be annexed to the principal land of that partitioned zone" (Article VII). The northern boundary of the submerged zone adjoining the partitioned territory would be "delineated as if the zone has not been partitioned and without regard to the provisions of this agreement", and if both sides agreed they would "exercise their equal rights" in this submerged zone beyond the six-mile limit by means of "shared exploitation" (Article VIII).

The agreement did not alter or affect the existing oil concessions in the zone (Article IX), and "without prejudice to the concessionary oil agreements" each country guaranteed freedom of work to citizens of the other in its own annexed part "and the right to practise any profession or occupation on equal levels with its citizens, concerning oil resources granted in the present concessions or in what may supersede them in future" (Article XV). With a view to safeguarding the continued efforts of both parties in exploiting natural resources in the zone it was agreed that a joint permanent committee would be established composed of an equal number of representatives from both sides, among them the two ministers responsible for natural resources (Article XVII), who would jointly decide on matters concerning the amendment or granting of new oil concessions in the zone (Article XX).

Instruments of ratification of the July 1965 agreement were exchanged in Jeddah on July 25, 1966. A demarcation agreement on the dividing line through the zone was formally concluded on Dec. 18, 1968, and became effective almost immediately.

Talks between Kuwait and Saudi Arabia in the 1960s on the onshore and offshore boundaries of the neutral zone had also covered the islands of Qaru and Umm el-Maradim, situated respectively some 23 miles (37 km) and 16 miles (26 km) off the coast of the northern part of the zone. On the basis of an exchange of letters between Iraq and Kuwait in 1923 and 1932 both these islands belonged to Kuwait, but Saudi Arabia had contested their sovereignty. In 1961 Kuwait had offered to share with Saudi Arabia any oil proceeds which might accrue from the islands in return for Saudi Arabia's acknowledgement of Kuwait's sovereignty over them. Saudi Arabia declined this offer, however, preferring to delay a decision on the islands until the boundaries of the neutral zone had been settled. At the present time, the islands remain under Kuwaiti control, but Saudi Arabia has never formally abandoned its claim to sovereignty over them.

GG

Other Arabian Peninsula Border Relationships

Saudi Arabia's southern and eastern borders—i.e. with the present states of the Yemen Arab Republic (North Yemen), the People's Democratic Republic of Yemen (South Yemen), Oman, the United Arab Emirates and Qatar—have not been finally determined by definitive agreements, nor have those of certain of the smaller Arabian peninsula states one with another. Generally speaking none of these situations appears to constitute an actual dispute at the present time, and indeed various initiatives have been taken in recent years to resolve outstanding border issues. Nevertheless, some of the relevant territorial relationships should be noted for the potential which they may contain for future dissension between the states concerned.

Saudi Arabia and the Yemens

The largely undemarcated border between Saudi Arabia and North Yemen was reported to have been the scene of armed confrontations in early 1980, in which five North Yemeni soldiers were said to have been killed. Western press reports suggested that the clashes were related to the Saudis' construction of a new road in the Boa district and may also have reflected their desire to exert pressure against North Yemen's proposed merger with South Yemen [see below] and gravitation towards closer relations with the Soviet Union. A Saudi airliner was hijacked to Tehran (Iran) in November 1984 by North Yemeni nationals protesting at what they alleged was Saudi "interference" in the internal affairs of North Yemen.

As regards Saudi Arabia's relations with South Yemen, the former had opposed the latter following its creation in 1967 and had made frequent attempts to disrupt it either by encouraging northern tribes to make raids or by giving refuge and support to South Yemeni exiles opposed to the Marxist regime in Aden. However, although the Saudi-South Yemen border is also undemarcated, no actual territorial claims appear to have been made by either side, and since mid-1980 the two countries have expressed a mutual desire for improved relations.

There were unconfirmed reports during December 1983 and January 1984 of border clashes between Saudi and South Yemeni troops. The Lebanese newspaper, *As-Safir*, alleged on Jan. 17, 1984, that "many soldiers on both sides" had been killed or wounded in clashes on Dec. 28. Tehran (i.e. official Iranian) radio claimed that further fighting had taken place on Jan. 16. Neither the Saudi nor South Yemeni governments commented on these reports. After the South Yemeni civil war of January 1986, there were unconfirmed reports that Saudi Arabia was supplying arms and equipment to rebel forces loyal to ex-President Mohammed based in North Yemen. Reports in March 1987 that Saudi and North Yemeni troops had recently clashed on the border between the two states were strongly denied by the Saudi authorities.

Saudi Arabia and the United Arab Emirates

A longstanding dispute between Saudi Arabia and Abu Dhabi (one of the United Arab Emirates) over the oil-rich Buraimi oasis was settled by an agreement signed by the respective heads of state in Jeddah in August 1974. Although no details were published, it was understood that under this agreement Saudi Arabia ceded six of the nine villages of the oasis to the United Arab Emirates in exchange for a triangular strip of land on Abu Dhabi's eastern border and also for a land corridor to the Gulf coast. (Saudi Arabia had ceded the three other Buraimi villages to Oman in 1971.)

North and South Yemen

Although it appears that the border between these two countries is not fully demarcated, the two sides do not consider their common frontier to be in dispute. During the 1970s border clashes were reported from time to time involving both countries' armed forces as well as North Yemeni rebels backed by South Yemen. However, from March 1979 the two sides initiated serious negotiations with a view to eventual unification; despite Saudi Arabia's opposition to the proposed merger, agreement was reached in late 1981 on the creation of a "Yemen Council" and other joint bodies which were to prepare for the establishment of a unified state to be known as the Yemeni Republic (although no substantive progress was subsequently made towards this goal).

Some renewed tension between the two countries arose at the end of 1986 as a result of the build-up of forces loyal to ex-President Mohammed of South Yemen in the border areas of the North.

Oman and the United Arab Emirates

A territorial dispute between Oman and the United Arab Emirates surfaced in December 1977 when the former laid claim to a northern portion of Ras al-Khaimah (the most northerly of the seven emirates) where offshore oil deposits had been found. However, it was announced in Abu Dhabi on Sep. 18, 1979, that full agreement had been reached on the border dispute between the two countries and that in the Omani view "all principles and

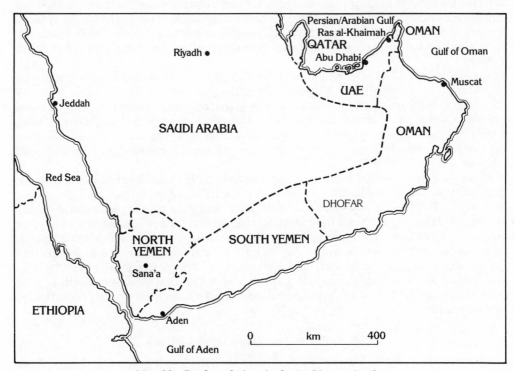

Map 28   Border relations in the Arabian peninsula.

bases pertaining to the ending of all border problems had been adopted within a framework of full understanding in the interest of the area and in the joint interest of the two countries". Subsequently, the UAE government announced on April 7, 1981, that the two sides had "agreed on specific bases for the redemarcation of the border" between Oman and Ras al-Khaimah; this agreement, said the statement, would "finally resolve the issues which have recently been raised" and would preserve "the historic ties between the two fraternal countries".

Oman and South Yemen

Relations between Oman and South Yemen have been seriously strained in recent years by the support given by the latter to the military activities of the Popular Front of the Liberation of Oman (PFLO) in the Dhofar region of Oman, to which South Yemen has itself laid claim from time to time. The dispute has been an additional source of strain in relations between South Yemen and Saudi Arabia, the latter having repeatedly pressed the former to cease supporting the PFLO rebels. Efforts by Kuwait to mediate in the Oman-South Yemen dispute collapsed in mid-1980 after the Omani government had agreed to make military facilities available to the United States.

Oman reported a number of border incidents in 1981, leading to renewed mediation efforts by Kuwait. In December of that year, South Yemen claimed that Oman had conducted a helicopter-borne raid on border village, involving the "abduction" of some South Yemeni citizens.

The Foreign Ministers of Kuwait and the United Arab Emirates (UAE) were entrusted in 1981 with the task of "exerting efforts to ease tension" between the two states by the Supreme Council of the Gulf Co-operation Council (formed earlier in the year by Bahrain, Kuwait, Oman, Qatar, Saudi Arabia and the UAE). The Ministers arranged a series of meetings with Omani and South Yemeni officials, culminating in direct talks between the two sides in July 1982. After further discussions, a four-point agreement on normalizing relations was concluded in November 1982.

Its principal components consisted of (i) a commitment to "establish normal relations" and to form a "technical committee", including Kuwaiti and UAE representatives, to discuss outstanding border problems; (ii) an undertaking not to allow "any foreign forces to use their territories for aggression or provocation against the other country"; (iii) a promise to stop hostile media campaigns; and (iv) an agreement to "exchange diplomatic representation" after further bilateral contacts.

South Yemen's official media portrayed the agreement as falling within the framework of its "intensive efforts to stave off the threat of US military presence in the region". Oman's subsequent participation in joint exercises with US forces the following month was strongly criticized by South Yemen. The PFLO's "Voice of the Oman Revolution" continued to broadcast material denouncing the Omani regime after the signing of the accord. In early January 1983, Oman proclaimed an amnesty for former rebels who had fled to South Yemen, allowing them a four-month period of grace during which they could return to Oman, where "all measures would be taken to receive and resettle them".

The border committee held two meetings during 1983, in the UAE and Kuwait respectively, and in a joint statement issued in late October of that year the Omani and South Yemeni governments declared that they had agreed to establish diplomatic relations and would shortly exchange ambassadors. Members of the South Yemeni delegation who travelled to Muscat for the third meeting of the border committee, in January 1985, were the first official South Yemen visitors to Oman since relations between the two countries began to deteriorate in the late 1960s.

Aircraft which bombed Aden airport in support of forces loyal to President Mohammed during the South Yemeni civil war in January 1986 were reported to have been identified as belonging to the Omani Air Force, although this was never officially confirmed by either government. A further agreement provided for the exchange of ambassadors, which had still not taken place, was reached during a visit to Oman by the South Yemeni Foreign Minister in January 1987.

The fourth meeting of the border committee took place in Aden on Feb. 28-March 2, 1987, at the end of which a press statement recorded that "discussions on the question of the borders between the two countries continued in a cordial and fraternal atmosphere, reflecting a sense of responsibility and common desire for greater efforts to hasten the achievement of positive results which will serve the interests of the two fraternal countries".

HWD/MWr

Syria-Turkey (Hatay)

The separation of the Sanjak of Alexandretta from the French mandated territory of Syria and its incorporation into Turkey in 1939 has never been formally accepted by Syria and has caused periodic tensions between the two countries. The Sanjak became the Turkish province of Hatay, its principal towns being the Mediterranean port of Iskenderun (formerly Alexandretta) and Antakya (formerly Antioch). In March 1987 a Turkish government minister described Syria's claim to Hatay as "one of the negative factors" in current Turkish-Syrian relations.

Historical Background—Establishment of Autonomous State of Hatay

The Sanjak of Alexandretta (including Antioch) was a province of the Ottoman empire from 1516 until the empire's demise at the end of World War I. Occupied by French forces in 1918, the Sanjak was subsequently, under the 1921 Franklin-Bouillon agreement, incorporated into the territory of greater Syria which had been mandated to France by the newly-established League of Nations in 1920.[1] It thereafter formed one of the five "natural anthropo-geographical regions" into which the French divided the mandated territory, the others being (i) Arab Syria, (ii) the coastal territory of Latakia (present-day Al Ladhiqiyah), (iii) Christian Lebanon and (iv) the region further south inhabited by the semi-nomadic Jebel Druse. Of these components, areas (i) and (ii) subsequently became the independent state of Syria and areas (iii) and (iv) the independent state of Lebanon. The Sanjak of Alexandretta, however, was regarded by the French as a special case because of its substantial Turkish population.

Although Turkey formally renounced its former possessions under the 1923 Treaty of Lausanne, the conclusion in September 1936 of a treaty between France and Syrian representatives providing for Syria to become independent after a transitional period led the Turkish government of Kemal Atatürk to raise the question of the Sanjak of Alexandretta at the League of Nations. Whereas France envisaged at that stage that the Sanjak would be under the sovereignty of an independent Syria, the Turkish government claimed that a majority of its population were Turks and that it should therefore be administered completely separately from Syria. At a meeting of the League's Council in December 1936, the French representative stated that when Syria became independent (the date of which had not yet been determined) the existing special administration of the Sanjak would be observed, with the rights of Turks in the region being guaranteed; he also rejected Turkish demands for the Sanjak to be granted separate independence, maintaining that such a course would be contrary to the terms of the French mandate. The meeting concluded with Turkey

---

[1]See also pages 201-2.

and France reaching a provisional agreement that ratification of the Franco-Syrian independence treaty would be postponed to allow time for a League committee to investigate and report on the situation in the Sanjak.

The report of the League's investigating committee (which included French and Turkish members) was presented on May 24, 1937, and contained a draft statute for an autonomous Sanjak of Alexandretta which was endorsed in all essentials by France and Turkey on May 28. Under the statute, (i) the Sanjak would have full control over its internal affairs; (ii) Syria would have responsibility for foreign, diplomatic and consular affairs; (iii) the Sanjak and Syria would have the same customs and monetary administrations; (iv) the Sanjak and Syria would each accredit a commissioner to the other in order to maintain liaison; (v) the Sanjak would be completely demilitarized and compulsory military conscription prohibited, with public order being maintained by a gendarmerie of 1,500 men; (vi) the rights of minorities would be guaranteed without distinction as to birth, nationality, language, race or religion; (vii) Turkey would be guaranteed full use of the port of Alexandretta and leased an area for its customs administration; (viii) a unicameral Assembly of 40 members would be elected in the Sanjak, which would have an Executive consisting of a President and a four-member executive council; (ix) Turkish and Arabic would have equal status as the Sanjak's official languages; and (x) elementary education would be compulsory and freedom of the press would be guaranteed.

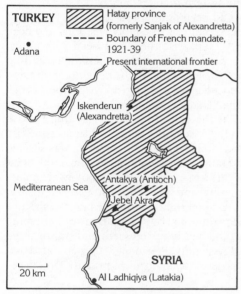

Map 29   The province of Hatay.

The adoption of the statute provoked serious inter-communal violence in the Sanjak, where martial law was declared on June 6, 1937, in response to a general strike by Arabs (both Moslem and Christian) and Armenians in protest in particular against the acceptance of Turkish as an official language. Disturbances continued over the following year and intensified in the early months of 1938 as the authorities attempted to accomplish the registration of voters for elections to the new Assembly. During this period there were several reports of Turkish troop concentrations on the northern border and the Turkish government repeatedly protested against the alleged mistreatment of Turks in the Sanjak. On Dec. 7, 1937, Turkey unilaterally abrogated its treaty of friendship and non-aggression with Syria (originally concluded on May 30, 1926, for five years and subsequently renewed annually).

A central issue at this time was whether, as claimed by the Turkish government, Turks constituted a majority of the Sanjak's population, or whether, as claimed by Syrian nationalists, there were over 100,000 Moslem Arabs, about 25,000 Christian Arabs and Armenians and only 85,000 Turks. A census conducted by the French authorities early in 1938 (on a system advocated by the Turkish government) found that Turks constituted 46 per cent of the population, a finding subsequently disputed both by Turkey and by the Syrians (the latter because it gave the Turks as being the largest single population group in the Sanjak). Syrian and internal Arab protests mounted when it became known in June 1938 that France and Turkey had agreed, on the basis of the "preponderance" of the Turkish population, that Turks would have 22 of the 40 Assembly seats and also that Turkish army officers had arrived in the Sanjak to co-operate with French forces in the maintenance of order. Actions taken by deputies in the Syrian Parliament in Damascus included the sending of telegrams to independent Arab rulers urging them to intervene to preserve the Sanjak as part of the Arab world.

Notwithstanding Syrian Arab opposition, France proceeded to sign a series of four agreements with Turkey on July 3-4, 1938, effectively recognizing Turkish predominance in the Sanjak as well as Turkey's special interest in the province. The first of these agreements was a military convention (signed in Antioch on July 3) providing that, pending the normal functioning of the Sanjak's new statute, the province would be garrisoned by 2,500 French troops, 2,500 Turkish troops and 1,000 men raised locally; it was specified that the Turkish forces (which entered the Sanjak on July 5) would be stationed in the predominantly Turkish parts of the province. The other three agreements (all signed in Ankara on July 4) were (i) a declaration that France and Turkey would apply the new statute on the basis of the preponderance of the Turkish element of the Sanjak, but on the understanding that Turkey had no territorial claim; (ii) a protocol concerning the rights and interests of persons of Turkish, Syrian or Lebanese origin residing in the territory of the other party and wishing to adopt the nationality of their country of residence; and (iii) a treaty of friendship affirming the desire of both parties to maintain peace in the eastern Mediterranean.

Prior to the signature of these agreements, it had been announced from the League of Nations headquarters in Geneva on June 24, 1938, that the Assembly elections had been postponed and that a League commission sent to supervise them had been withdrawn, principally because the Turkish government opposed its presence in the Sanjak and no longer recognized its status. On June 13, 1938, the British member of the League commission had resigned, reportedly because he disapproved of actions being taken by the French authorities against the non-Turkish sections of the Sanjak's population.

The Assembly elections were eventually held at the end of August 1938 and Turkish representatives duly obtained 22 of the 40 seats. At the Assembly's inaugural session on Sept. 5 a former deputy in the Turkish National Assembly, Tayfour Seukmen, was elected President and the Sanjak was officially renamed Hatay. The same session declared (i) that Hatay was "a republican state upheld by a Turkish majority and enjoying absolute independence in its internal affairs"; (ii) that the capital and seat of government would be at Antakya (Antioch); (iii) that all citizens would have equal rights before the law, irrespective of race or religion; (iv) that public order would be maintained by a gendarmerie of not more than 1,500 men; and (v) that the flag of Hatay would be a white crescent and star on a red background. In a message to the Turkish National Assembly, President Seukmen stated that the political principles of the new state would be those of "Kemalism" as practised in Turkey itself.

Incorporation of Hatay into Turkey

In terms of sovereignty, the autonomous state of Hatay remained part of French mandated Syria, the proposed independence of which under the 1936 Franco-Syrian treaty was repeatedly postponed by France in view of the worsening international situation. On the basis of the July 1938 agreements, France subsequently developed its relations with Turkey, principally with the aim of ensuring that in the event of another European war Turkey would not follow the example of the Ottoman empire (in World War I) by taking the side of Germany. This process culminated in the signature in Paris on June 23, 1939, of a Franco-Turkish declaration of mutual assistance "in the event of an act of aggression leading to war in the Mediterranean" (a similar UK-Turkish agreement having been signed on May 12). On the same day, a separate Franco-Turkish agreement was concluded in Ankara providing for the cession of Hatay to Turkey.

Ratified by the Turkish National Assembly on June 30, 1939, the Hatay agreement contained the following main provisions: (i) Turkish sovereignty over Hatay would be unconditional; (ii) Turkey recognized the inviolable character of the newly-drawn Syrian frontiers and undertook to refrain from any form of activity likely to compromise either the territorial integrity of Syria or peace within its borders; (iii) non-Turkish elements who did not wish to become naturalized Turkish citizens would have the right to opt for Syrian or Lebanese nationality within the space of six months, those so opting being obliged to leave

Hatay within 18 months (and being entitled to take their moveable property with them); and (iv) the strategically important heights of Jebel Akra to the south of Antakya would remain within the Syrian borders.

In accordance with the agreement, the evacuation of the French administration from Hatay was completed on July 23, 1939, and a new Turkish governor formally assumed control the same day. Celebrations were held throughout Turkey to mark the completion of the transfer. Among Syrian Arab nationalists, however, the cession was vigorously condemned as an ilegal act, protest demonstrations being held in Damascus and other Syrian cities. When Syria finally achieved independence during World War II, the cession continued to be regarded as illegal by the Syrian government, although it received no support from governments outside the Arab world. In the event, the frontier established between Syria and Turkey in the west followed the old boundary of the Sanjak of Alexandretta, so that the Jebel Akra heights formed part of Turkish territory.

Syrian-Turkish Relations since 1945—Maintenance of Syrian Claim to Hatay

The Turkish government announced its recognition of the independence of Syria (and of Lebanon) on March 6, 1946, but in subsequent years Syrian-Turkish relations underwent periods of severe strain, particularly after Turkey became a member of the North Atlantic Treaty Organization (NATO) in 1952. The conclusion by Turkey and Iraq in February 1954 of a defence co-operation treaty (the Baghdad Pact) was denounced by Syria (and by Egypt and Saudi Arabia) as a threat to the security and cohesion of the Arab world. Moreover, in September 1957 a major crisis developed over Syrian (and Soviet) allegations that Turkish forces were massing on the Syrian border with the intention of invading Syria and overthrowing its (pro-Soviet) government at the behest of the United States. In more recent years, Turkey has periodically complained that Kurdish separatists were being allowed unhindered passage through Syrian territory, while Syria has expressed concern over the effect on water flows in the Euphrates river caused by new Turkish hydroelectric power and irrigation schemes in south-east Anatolia.

Relations between the two countries improved in March 1985 with the signature of a border security agreement, which was followed in October of that year by a protocol on economic, scientific, technical and commercial co-operation. Moreover, in March 1986 the Syrian Prime Minister paid a four-day official visit to Turkey during which further economic co-operation agreements were signed. Nevertheless, the Hatay question has remained a source of friction between the two countries, in that Syria, while not actively prosecuting any territorial claim, has not formally renounced its view that the 1939 cession by France was illegal and has from time to time published official maps showing the province as part of Syria.

After one such map had been published by Syria in a brochure for the 1987 Mediterranean Games, Hasan Celal Guzel (Turkish Minister of State and Government Spokesman) said in answer to a parliamentary question on March 19, 1987, that Syria's claim on Hatay constituted "one of the negative factors in Turkish-Syrian relations" and continued: "We, on every occasion, remind Syria that Hatay is an inseparable part of Turkey and that claims on this province damage Turkish-Syrian relations, which both countries wish to develop." He added that in response to Turkey's protest the offending brochure had been withdrawn and a new version issued with a map showing Hatay as part of Turkey.

AJD

4. ASIA, THE FAR EAST AND THE PACIFIC

Introduction

Current territorial disputes in the Asia-Pacific area fall into several different categories, reflecting the huge geographical extent of the region and its considerable political complexities. As detailed in the following section, there exist longstanding geopolitical rivalries between major Asian powers (e.g. between China and the Soviet Union) as well as traditional territorial tensions arising from ethnic factors. There are also disputes which have their origins in the ambiguities of colonial boundary-drawing or in dissatisfaction with territorial arrangements inherited from the colonial powers. Other unresolved issues exist where the post-war advance of communism has resulted in the territorial division of countries; yet others centre on conflicting claims to various islands, mainly in south-east Asian waters, over which sovereignty has not yet been established to universal agreement.

Over the last two decades several longstanding disputes over residual colonial territories in the Asian region have been resolved in one way or another. Thus for example the dispute between Indonesia and the Netherlands over West Irian (Dutch New Guinea), which developed into open military hostilities in early 1962, was settled by an agreement signed in August 1962 under which the territory became part of Indonesia in 1963, and was finally resolved in 1969 when the local Papuan population expressed their wish to remain in Indonesia. Moreover, in 1974 the new Portuguese government recognized Indian sovereignty over the former enclaves of Goa, Daman, Diu, Dadra and Nagar Haveli, which had been occupied by Indian troops in December 1961 and incorporated into India the following year. On the other hand, neither Portugal nor a majority of the international community has recognized Indonesia's forcible incorporation of Portuguese East Timor into its territory in 1975-76, since when the demand has persistently been made that the people of the territory should have the right to self-determination.

As regards the two remaining colonial outposts on the Asian continent, namely the British colony of Hong Kong and the nearby Portuguese colony of Macao, agreements have been concluded under which they will both revert to Chinese sovereignty before the end of the present century. The 1984 Sino-UK agreement on Hong Kong is described in this section in the context of the China-Taiwan political and territorial relationship.

One factor which has an important bearing on the incidence of territorial dispute between Asian countries is the absence of an all-embracing regional organization through which such disputes might be resolved by diplomatic means. Although the sub-regional Association of South-East Asian Nations (linking Brunei, Indonesia, Malaysia, the Philippines, Singapore and Thailand) has played a local role in this respect, Asia does not have its own equivalent of the Organization of African Unity or the Organization of American States, with their channels for peaceful settlement of disputes between member states. The United Nations Organization itself has on occasion successfully filled this void, but in other instances disputes have been aggravated by the lack of any regional forum to which interested parties can refer their claims, given the sharp, political and ideological divisions which exist in the region.

Afghanistan-Pakistan

An unresolved dispute exists between Afghanistan and Pakistan over areas on the eastern side of their common border inhabited by Pathan (or Pushtu, or Pakhtoon) tribes, whose members are partly settled and partly nomads (i.e. seasonal migrants and also raiders or refugees crossing the border). The dispute has come into the open through Afghanistan's refusal to accept the internationally recognized border between the two countries and Afghan demands for integration of all Pathans either in Afghanistan or in an autonomous or perhaps independent Pakhtoonistan. In some instances Afghan claims have included the transfer to Afghanistan of the Pakistani province of Baluchistan (which would give Afghanistan access to the Indian Ocean).

The Pathan tribes are broadly of the same culture—Sunni Moslem in religion, Pushtu or Pakhtoon in speech—but they are politically divided into the settled tribes of the administered districts of Pakistan's North-West Frontier Province (NWFP), those of tribal agencies in that province and those of Afghanistan.

The border between the two countries was delimited, by means of a map, under an agreement between Afghanistan and British India in 1893 after the so-called Second Afghan War (of 1878-80) and became known as the Durand line. Both sides recognized the area between this line and British India as "free tribal territory"; although under British sovereignty, the inhabitants of this territory were not British subjects and retained their tribal autonomy. The agreement was confirmed by further treaties concluded in 1905, 1921 and 1930, and its effect was to divide the Pathans in such a way that some 2,400,000 remained in British territory.

The Afghan Claim

It was the partition of India in 1947, when a weak Pakistan replaced the British Raj as a sovereign neighbour of Afghanistan, which induced the latter to declare its claim. Arguments adduced by Afghanistan for its claim were legal, historical and ethnic.

It was asserted in Afghanistan that the 1893 agreement was not legally binding because Afghanistan had signed it under duress; that in any case the tribal territories between Afghanistan and the administered areas of the British sphere formed independent territories; and that Pakistan could not inherit the rights of an "extinguished person" (i.e. the British in India).[1] It was also argued that historically Afghanistan had controlled much of India, and certainly the area of what was currently western Pakistan.[2] Finally it was pointed out that the Pathans in Afghanistan and Pakistan formed a single ethnic unit which should be united in one state.

On the other hand, it has been argued that the eastern Pathans had enjoyed close economic and political ties with the major states of the Indus valley and had developed linguistic differences with the western Pathans.[3] Moreover, in its widest extent the area claimed for Pakhtoonistan, stretching from the Pamir to the Arabic Sea and bounded in the west by Afghanistan and Iran and in the east by the Indus river, included large areas where there were few Pathans—such as Chitral, Gilgit, Baltistan and Baluchistan.

---

[1] See Sir W. K. Fraser-Tyler, *Afghanistan*, London, 1953.

[2] In fact, following its formation in 1747 the state of Afghanistan had at its maximum extent as the Durrani empire controlled (in 1797) an area reaching eastwards to Delhi and Lahore; the latter was ceded to the Mughal empire in 1798 and Peshawar was lost in 1923 (see Taussig, "Afghanistan's Big Step", in *The Eastern World*, October 1961).

[3] See Sir O. Caroe, "Pathans at the Crossroads", in *The Eastern World*, No. 15, 1961.

Pathan Aspirations before the Achievement of Independence by Pakistan

In 1946 a British proposal that under the constitution of an independent India the North-West Frontier Province should, for the purpose of drafting provincial constitutions, be grouped with the Punjab, met with strong objections from NWFP political leaders. Khan Abdul Ghaffar Khan (a member of the Indian Congress working committee and leader of the autonomist Redshirt movement) said on Dec. 6, 1946, that the question of whether or not the province should join any group should be left to the free will of the province itself. Dr Khan Saheb, the Premier of the NWFP, said on Dec. 20: "The Frontier people do not bother themselves about sections or groups. They will have their independence and nobody can force them to join anybody else." Nawabzada Allah Nawaz Khan, the Speaker of the NWFP Legislative Assembly, stated on Dec. 16: "The Pathans and the Punjabis are two major nations by any definition or test of nationality, and the very thought of grouping the NWFP with the Punjab is revolting to the Pathan mind. We frontier Pathans are a nation of 3,000,000, with our own distinctive culture, civilization, language, literature, names and nomenclature, legal codes, customs and calendar, history and traditions, aptitudes and ambitions. By all canons of international law, a Pathan is quite a separate entity from a Punjabi."

On the other hand, Mohammed Ali Jinnah (leader of the Moslem League) declared on April 30, 1947: "The question of a division of India, as proposed by the Moslem League, is based on the fundamental fact that there are two nations—Hindus and Moslems. We want a national state in our homelands which are predominantly Moslem and comprise six units— the Punjab, the NWFP, Sind, Baluchistan, Bengal and Assam."

Under a British plan announced on June 3, 1947, for the immediate transfer of British power to India, it was laid down that a referendum was to be held in the NWFP to choose between joining the Pakistan or the Hindustan Constituent Assembly. Khan Abdul Ghaffar Khan, however, urged that the electorate of the NWFP should be given the opportunity of voting for an independent state in the province under the name of Pathanistan. Both the Indian Congress and the Moslem League nevertheless accepted the British plan and its proposal to confine the vote in the NWFP to a straight decision on the issue of union with Pakistan or otherwise. Khan Ghaffar Khan reiterated his demand on June 24 (while admitting that Jinnah was opposed to the idea of a separate Pathan state) and declared on June 25 that the Redshirt movement would boycott the referendum.

On July 3, 1947, it was announced in London and New Delhi that the government of Afghanistan had presented notes to the British and Indian governments concerning the future of the tribal areas of the NWFP and drawing attention to an alleged desire of the tribesmen in these areas to dissociate themselves from India. The Afghan notes were said to have asked that the inhabitants of the NWFP and also of Baluchistan should have the right to decide whether their future should lie with Afghanistan or India or be based on complete independence. However, the British governor of the NWFP (Sir George Cunningham) subsequently toured the tribal territories and heard all the *jirgas* (tribal assemblies) of the leading tribes stating that they were part of Pakistan and wished to retain the same relations with Pakistan as they had with the British.

The referendum, held from July 6, 1947, onwards (after many Hindus and Sikhs had left the NWFP during June), resulted, as announced on July 20, in 289,244 votes for union with Pakistan and only 2,874 for union with India (in a 50.99 per cent poll).

The 1949-50 Afghan Campaign for an Independent Pakhtoonistan

In March 1949 the Kabul press and radio launched a campaign against Pakistan, demanding that the area between the Durand line and the Indus, comprising the NWFP and the tribal territory, should be recognized as an independent Pakhtoonistan and given the right of self-determination.

Afghan spokesmen claimed that the 1893 agreement establishing the Durand line had been "brought about by economic force" because the tribesmen drew from the British, and continued to draw from Pakistan, subsidies amounting to over £3,750,000 a year. They also claimed that the referendum by which the NWFP had entered Pakistan was unsatisfactory because it did not offer the Pathans (whom the Afghans considered as racially akin to themselves) the alternative of joining Afghanistan (where there were an estimated 3,000,000 Pathans out of a total population of 11,000,000, while there were 2,500,000 Pathans in the tribal territory and 3,000,000 in the NWFP).

A statement made by Khwaja Nazimuddin, then governor-general of Pakistan, to the effect that the tribal territory formed an integral part of Pakistan, was strongly criticized by the Afghan government in a communiqué issued on March 24, 1949, describing that statement as contrary to pledges allegedly given by Jinnah in 1948. Moreover, addressing a demonstration in Kabul on April 27, Shah Mahmud Khan, then Prime Minister of Afghanistan, said that his government would "rescue our brother Afghans" from alleged atrocities by Pakistani forces, if possible by negotiation but if not "by other means". In Pakistan, however, Sir Muhammad Zafrulla Khan (then Foreign Minister) stated on July 11, 1949, that neither the Durand line agreement nor any subsequent treaty relating to the frontier was open to question but that Pakistan would welcome discussions with Afghanistan on matters of economic co-operation.

The newly-established government of Pakistan assured the Wazir and Mahsud tribal *jirgas* in the NWFP that it desired to eliminate all suspicion among Moslems and to abandon the military control of their areas established by the British India government. The *jirgas* thereupon made pledges of full loyalty to Pakistan, and between Dec. 6 and 27, 1947, all Pakistan troops were withdrawn from Waziristan (in the NWFP), important frontier posts were abandoned and control of the areas reverted to civil armed forces recruited from the local tribesmen.

Nevertheless, there remained in the NWFP autonomist movements led by Khan Abdul Ghaffar Khan and the Fakir of Ipi, a rebellious tribal leader in Waziristan. On March 8, 1948, the former issued a manifesto announcing the formation of a Pakistan People's Party aspiring to autonomy for "cultural and linguistic units" in Pakistan and to the establishment of a "union of free socialist republics" in Pakistan. However, on June 15 he was arrested on suspicion of complicity with the Fakir of Ipi in the planning of disturbances, and on June 16 he was sentenced to three years' rigorous imprisonment. There followed arrests of some of his followers (including Dr Khan Saheb) and also of adherents of the Fakir of Ipi between June 28 and July 6, 1948, following which the Redshirt organization was banned on Sept. 16.

During June 1949 Afghan territory was, apparently inadvertently, bombed by a Pakistani aircraft which was said to have been fired upon by followers of the Fakir of Ipi and by Afghans. At the same time Afghanistan accused Pakistan of having assisted Agha Amin Jan (half-brother of ex-King Amanullah of Afghanistan, who had abdicated in January 1929) in an unsuccessful attempt to seize the throne of Afghanistan (after he had for some months been living among the Mahsud tribe of Waziristan), but this was strongly denied by Pakistan, which claimed that the authorities of the tribal territories had dispersed Amin Jan's forces and had informed the Afghan government of his activities. Pakistan in turn alleged that Afghan officials had welcomed the Fakir of Ipi when he had entered Afghanistan in June and were planning to proclaim him King of "Pathanistan".

In Britain the Secretary for Commonwealth Relations (then Philip Noel-Baker) said in the House of Commons on June 30, 1949, that Pakistan was in international law the inheritor of the rights and duties of the former government of India and of the UK government in the territories on the North-West Frontier, and that the Durand line was the international frontier. He added that the British government had been in continuous consultation with Pakistan, was convinced that there was no outstanding question between Pakistan and Afghanistan that could not be settled by peaceful means, and was confident that there could be no question of armed aggression by Afghanistan.

The Afghan ambassador in London, however, stated on Aug. 4, 1949, that his government could not accept the British view that Pakistan had inherited the rights and duties of the former government of India in the tribal areas and that, if negotiations with Pakistan for a settlement failed, Afghanistan would appeal to the United Nations.

As part of an intensified Afghan campaign against Pakistan from December 1949, the Afghan ambassador to India alleged on Dec. 20 that the government of Pakistan was refusing to "apply the UN Charter to an oppressed nation" and expressed regret that attempts which had been made by the Afghan government to settle the matter with the governments of Pakistan and Britain had achieved no result. He said in particular that the arrangements whereby the "Pakhtoons" (Pathans) had "found themselves debited to Pakistan's account as a mute transferable commodity" had aroused resentment among "the whole Pakhtoon nation" and that only the influence of the Afghan government had restrained them from taking up arms. He further alleged that the flag of "Pakhtoonistan" had been hoisted throughout the tribal territory; that "national assemblies" had been set up in Tirah and the Khyber; and that the Pakistan government had sent troops against the tribesmen, causing "immense loss of life", had bombed the Waziristan areas from the air, had enforced an economic blockade of the tribal territory and had imprisoned popular leaders from all over the NWFP and Baluchistan.

A number of border incidents which occurred in 1950 included, according to a Pakistan government statement of Oct. 4 of that year, an invasion of Pakistan on Sept. 30 by "a large body of Afghan tribesmen and regular troops" commanded by a brigadier of the Afghan Army, who were driven back on Oct. 5 by Pakistani troops supported by aircraft. The Afghan government, however, denied that any Afghan troops had been involved in the clashes and claimed that the detachment concerned had consisted entirely of tribesmen from the Pakistani side of the border who supported the "Pakhtoonistan" movement.

Period of Dormancy following 1951 NWFP Elections

In elections held in the NWFP between Nov. 26 and Dec. 12, 1951 (the first to be held on an adult franchise, including that of women), the banned pro-Pakhtoonistan Redshirt movement nominated a number of candidates standing as independents; however, after the election all elected independent Moslems applied for Moslem League membership (as a result of which the Moslem League eventually held 80 of the 85 seats in the NWFP Legislative Assembly). The provincial Minister of Education observed that the result had "buried the myth of Pathanistan for all time" and that the fact that the Moslem League had captured all seven seats in the Charsadda sub-division (a former stronghold of the Redshirts) was significant of the scant "respect" which Pathans had for those hostile to Pakistan or to the existing government. During the next few years the Pakhtoonistan issue remained dormant.

On Jan. 5, 1954, it was announced that Khan Abdul Ghaffar Khan, the former Redshirt leader who, after serving his three-year sentence, had been detained under security regulations, would be released. At the same time 45 other detainees were released unconditionally under a general amnesty, with their confiscated property being restored to them, and restrictions imposed on Dr Khan Saheb were lifted.

Afghanistan's Foreign Minister (then Sardar Mohammed Naim) asserted in a press statement during a visit to Karachi on Nov. 7, 1954, that the basic differences between Pakistan and Afghanistan did not involve any territorial adjustment, but he also said that the people of "Pushtoonistan" should be given opportunities to express themselves on "their status and their way of living". He emphasized that the two countries' national interests were similar and that there were good possibilities of close economic co-operation.

Revival of the Dispute after the Integration of West Pakistan in One Administrative Unit

On Nov. 25, 1954, the NWFP Legislative Assembly unanimously approved a government proposal for the integration of West Pakistan into a single administrative unit. A subsequent proposal by the government of Pakistan to incorporate the tribal territory of the NWFP in the unified Province of West Pakistan was met by protests (on March 29, 1955) by Sardar

Mohammed Daud Khan, who had become Prime Minister and Minister of the Interior of Afghanistan on Sept. 7, 1953, and who was known to be a strong advocate of Afghan support for the tribal elements in the NWFP. On March 30, 1954, a formal Afghan note was presented in Karachi, protesting against the proposed merger of territory of "occupied and free Pakhtoonistan" in the new province—but the protest was rejected by the Pakistan government on the ground that the unification of West Pakistan was a purely internal matter.

There followed large-scale demonstrations, leading to riots, before the Pakistan embassy in Kabul and also at Pakistan consulates elsewhere in Afghanistan. These incidents led to counter-demonstrations in Pakistan and to mutual recriminations, and on May 4, 1954, to the proclamation of a state of emergency in Afghanistan and a call-up of men between 25 and 32 years of age who had performed military service. The Pakistan Minister for States and Frontier Regions (Maj.-Gen. Iskander Mirza) said after a tour of the North-West Frontier areas on May 11: "We regard the Afghan government's claim to sponsor the 'Pakhtoonistan' stunt as an interference in Pakistan's internal affairs, and we shall fight for the maintenance of the Durand line as our national boundary with Afghanistan. There can be no compromise on this issue."

Eventually the Afghan government agreed on Sept. 9, 1955, to make amends for insults to the Pakistani flag during the Kabul riots earlier in the year, and both governments undertook not to conduct propaganda calculated to arouse hatred and to incite violence against each other. A proposed meeting between the prime ministers of the two countries was, however, put off by the Afghan government after it had been advised on Oct. 12, 1955, that Pakistan would not accede to Afghanistan's request for a postponement of the One-Unit Act setting up a unitary West Pakistan.

On Oct. 13, 1955, the Afghan government, in a further note to the government of Pakistan, expressed its concern at the incorporation of "Pushtunistan" in the new province of West Pakistan and asserted that this was against the wishes of the Pathans (Pushtus), but it still proposed a high-level meeting to settle "all outstanding differences". This proposal was

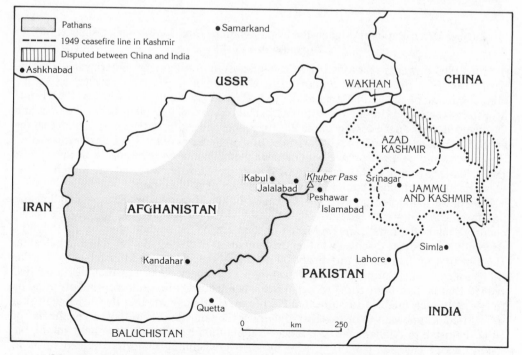

Map 30 Territorial relationship of Afghanistan and Pakistan, also showing Kashmir.

rejected by Pakistan, which reiterated that all territories lying to the east of the Durand line were an integral part of Pakistan and completely outside the jurisdiction of the Afghan government. Nevertheless, the Pakistan government still expressed its willingness to have a meeting of ministers provided that matters purely of Pakistan's own concern were excluded from the discussions. The Afghan minister in Karachi and the Pakistan ambassador in Kabul were recalled in October 1955, as a result of which diplomatic relations between the two countries were in fact suspended.

After the Soviet Union had indicated that it supported Afghanistan in this dispute, the Council of the South-East Asia Treaty Organization (SEATO)—consisting of the foreign ministers of the organization's then eight member countries (Australia, France, New Zealand, Pakistan, the Philippines, Thailand, the United Kingdom and the United States)—declared on March 8, 1956, inter alia: "Insofar as those [Soviet] statements referred to 'Pushtunistan', the members of the Council severally declared that their governments recognized that the sovereignty of Pakistan extends up to the Durand line, the international boundary between Pakistan and Afghanistan."

A marked improvement in relations between the two countries from August 1956 (when the then President of Pakistan, Gen. Mirza, paid a state visit to Afghanistan) culminated in an agreement on June 10, 1957 (during a visit to Kabul by Hussein Shaheed Suhrawardy, then Prime Minister of Pakistan), to restore full diplomatic relations between the two countries, to co-operate in international affairs, to resolve their differences through friendly negotiations and to consolidate the existing basis for permanent friendship. However, the contentious Pathan issue came to the fore again after the proclamation of martial law and the abrogation of the constitution of 1956 in Pakistan in October 1958.

Under martial law the leaders of the left-wing National Awami Party (NAP) were arrested, among them Khan Abdul Ghaffar Khan (who, after all remaining restrictions on his movements had been lifted in July 1955, had reportedly opposed the one-unit plan for West Pakistan and proposed a referendum to be held on this issue) and Abdus Samad Khan Achakzai (known as "the Baluchi Gandhi") as leaders of the movement for an autonomous Pathan province of "Pakhtoonistan" inside West Pakistan.

Further Deterioration in Afghan-Pakistani Relations from 1960—Soviet Support for Afghanistan's Position

From 1960 onwards relations between Afghanistan and Pakistan deteriorated rapidly, partly because of strong Soviet support for Afghanistan on the "Pakhtoonistan" issue. In a joint communiqué issued in Kabul at the end of a visit by Nikita Khrushchev, then Prime Minister of the Soviet Union, it was stated inter alia on March 4, 1960, that the two sides had "exchanged views on the destiny of the Pushtu people and expressed their agreement that the application of the principle of self-determination on the basis of the UN Charter for settling this issue would be a reasonable way of easing tension and ensuring peace in the Middle East". On his return to Moscow the Soviet Prime Minister asserted on March 5 that "historically" Pakhtoonistan had "always been part of Afghanistan".

In response to this development the Pakistan Foreign Minister (then Manzoor Qadir) said on March 6 that it was "regrettable that the Soviet Union deemed it fit to interfere in this country's internal affairs", and on March 7 he challenged the Afghan government to hold a referendum in order to discover whether the Pathans of Afghanistan wished to join Pakistan. He said that he had made this proposal to the Afghan Foreign Minister (then Sardar Mohammed Naim) during talks in Rawalpindi in January 1960, but that the latter had replied that he had "not come to negotiate". Manzoor Qadir explained his proposal as follows: "It is reasonable to assume that Pakhtoons (Pathans), whether they live in Pakistan or in Afghanistan, want to be together and under the same flag. That flag can be the flag of either Pakistan or Afghanistan .... Since a referendum has already been held among the Pakhtoons of Pakistan [in 1947], who by an overwhelming majority decided to be in Pakistan, it is only logical that we should now ask the Pakhtoons in Afghanistan what their wishes are. In all probability their verdict will be in favour of Pakistan. In the unlikely event of Pakhtoons in Afghanistan choosing freely not to join Pakistan, any further steps to be taken can be considered."

The Pakistani suggestion of a referendum was, however, rejected by the Afghan Foreign Minister, and the Afghan government subsequently refused to renew visas for Pakistanis living in Afghanistan. The Pakistan Foreign Minister stated on Aug. 4, 1960, that Pakistan had sent a number of notes protesting against alleged maltreatment of Pakistanis in Afghanistan, and in September 1960 and March 1961 mutual accusations were made about fighting in the border area.

On the latter occasion (i.e. in March 1961) it was alleged in Afghanistan that Pakistani forces were carrying out repressive measures against the Pathans, while *Pravda* (the official organ of the Soviet Communist Party) asserted on April 3, 1961, that eight Pakistani divisions supported by tanks and aircraft were active in the Pathan areas, bombing villages and causing substantial casualties; the paper reaffirmed Soviet support for the Afghan demand for Pathan self-determination and declared: "The situation emerging in the direct proximity of our frontier is not a matter of indifference to us." The government of Pakistan admitted on April 6 that bombing operations had taken place in the Bajaur area early in March when, it claimed, a house had been used as headquarters and an ammunition dump by an Afghan agent for the distribution of arms, ammunition and money among the tribesmen of Bajaur.

Further fighting in the Bajaur area was reported in May 1961, when the Pakistan Minister for States and Frontier Regions stated that Afghan forces had attacked Pakistani border posts and had infiltrated the Bajaur area but had been repulsed, and that 20 Afghan agents had been arrested and had confessed that they had been commissioned by the Afghan government to start terrorist activities in Pakistan. President Ayub Khan of Pakistan said on May 21 that, whereas in the past there had been raids by irregulars from Afghanistan, the Afghan government had now for the first time used army troops in a border incident, and on May 23 he said that Afghanistan had recently received large quantities of Soviet arms; that the border situation was becoming serious as the great powers were showing interest; and that the people of the areas concerned did not want the setting-up of any "Pakhtoonistan"; but he admitted that trouble was being fomented among "the disgruntled and the poor".

Temporary Severance of Diplomatic and Trade Relations ended by Tehran Agreement of 1963

Further concentrations of Afghan troops along the Durand line were reported by Pakistan military sources in June 1961, and in September of that year diplomatic and trade relations between the two countries were broken off, and the common border was closed (although as an exceptional measure the frontier was temporarily reopened on Jan. 29, 1962, to allow for the delivery of goods destined for Afghanistan under US aid schemes). The closure of the border also resulted in the exclusion from Pakistan of large numbers of Pathan tribal nomads (*powindahs*, who were Afghan nationals) who had normally crossed the border for winter employment in Pakistan.

Various mediation efforts failed to result in the reopening of the border until, after a change of government in Afghanistan, agreement was reached in Tehran (Iran) on May 23, 1963, when the governments of Afghanistan and Pakistan agreed (i) to restore diplomatic, consular and trade relations with each other; (ii) to see to it that the duties and conduct of their representatives would be in accordance with the recognized principles of international law, usage and practice, and would be confined to the discharge of their official functions; and (iii) to endeavour to create an atmosphere of goodwill, friendship and mutual trust.

However, the leader of the Afghan delegation (Sayyid Qasim Rashtiya, the Afghan Minister of Information and Broadcasting) was said to have stated in Tehran on May 29, 1963, that Afghanistan had never recognized the Durand line as his country's international boundary with Pakistan and that "Pakhtoonistan" continued to be the main issue dividing the two countries. Zulfiqar Ali Bhutto, then Pakistan's Prime Minister, however, said on the same day that "Pakhtoonistan" was "a closed issue" and that his government would continue to refuse Afghan nomads access to Pakistan.

The Tehran agreement was implemented on July 20, 1963 when the border between Afghanistan and Pakistan was reopened.

The "Pakhtoonistan" issue was again raised in Afghanistan on Sept. 19, 1964, when the *Loe Jirga* (Grand Assembly of Afghanistan, a body which had been summoned only five times during 40 years to consider major questions of policy and which had in 1955 supported the Afghan government's commitment to "Pakhtoonistan") approved, after adopting a new constitution, a government-sponsored resolution referring to "the religious, national and historical duty" of the Afghans to support the rights of the Pathan people of Pakistan to self-determination and stating that Afghanistan was "waiting for the day when the issue of Pakhtoonistan will be settled on the basis of the true aspirations of the people and leaders of Pakhtoonistan".

Constitutional Changes in Pakistan, 1970-73

In Pakistan new constitutional proposals published on March 29, 1970, and a presidential order issued in April of that year provided that the one-unit structure in West Pakistan was to be dissolved and the four former provinces restored—among them the NWFP and Baluchistan (including Las Bela).

After the Supreme Court of Pakistan had, on April 20, 1972, declared illegal the proclamation of martial law (on March 25, 1969), martial law was ended and Zulfiqar Ali Bhutto (who had become President of Pakistan on Dec. 20, 1971) was sworn in as President under the new constitution on April 21, 1972. New provincial governments were thereupon formed, those of the NWFP (under Maulana Mufti Mahmood) and in Baluchistan (under Sardar Ataullah Mengal) being both based on coalitions of the (pro-Soviet) NAP and the *Jamiat-i-Ulema-i-Pakistan* (of left-wing mullahs).

In the new constitution adopted by the Pakistan National Assembly on April 9, 1973, the territory of the Islamic Republic of Pakistan was defined as consisting of Baluchistan, the NWFP, the Punjab, Sind, the federally-administered tribal areas and such states or territories as were or might be included in Pakistan, whether by accession or otherwise.

Revival of the Pakhtoonistan Issue by the Republican Regime in Afghanistan

Afghanistan's claim to the areas of Pakistan inhabited by Pathans was revived by the republican regime which came to power in Afghanistan on July 17, 1973, under Lt.-Gen. Sardar Mohammed Daud Khan, who had, as Prime Minister in 1953-63, expressed his support for the cause of "Pakhtoonistan". After a public rally in support of Afghanistan's claim had been held in Kabul on July 21, President Bhutto declared on July 26 that his country would scrupulously adhere to the good relations which it had enjoyed with Afghanistan, but he added that Pakistan was "quite capable" of defending itself against possible Afghan claims to the NWFP.

In an interview published in *Le Monde* on Feb. 3-4, 1974, President Daud said: "We support in every way the right of our brothers in Pakhtoonistan to self-determination". He added: "When bombs are falling on our brothers, when they are being murdered, if they ask for our aid we shall not remain indifferent." Although expressing the hope that the problem would be solved "in a friendly and peaceful way", he claimed that the NWFP and Baluchistan had "always formed an integral part of Afghanistan", from which they had been separated by "unequal and unjust treaties".

Earlier Developments in the Pakistani Province of Baluchistan

In the Pakistani province of Baluchistan it appeared that the overwhelming majority of the population had endorsed the province's adherence to Pakistan, but from 1963 onwards there was widespread unrest and armed opposition to the federal government, which sent in troops to restore order. At a *jirga* held on June 29, 1947, all the tribal chiefs of what was then British Baluchistan had decided by a unanimous vote to join Pakistan (although Kalat, the largest Indian state in Baluchistan, was not represented at the *jirga*, which was attended only by representatives of the British part of the territory).

On April 12, 1952, the government of Pakistan announced that, on the basis of a recommendation by a committee on constitutional and administrative reforms in Baluchistan, the rulers of the Baluchistan states of Kalat, Las Bela, Makran and Kharan had agreed to integrate their territories in a single Union with a common executive, legislative and judiciary. On June 16, 1954, the Pakistan government decided to merge the resultant Baluchistan States Union with the rest of Baluchistan under one central administration. Moreover, the *Shahi Jirga* of Baluchistan approved, on Nov. 29, 1954, the government proposal for the integration of West Pakistan in a single administrative unit [see above], and an agreement was signed on Jan. 3, 1955, by the rulers of the states forming the Baluchistan States Union for the merger of all these states in a unified West Pakistan.

In provincial elections held on Dec. 17, 1970, one seat in the Provincial Assembly was gained by a Pakhtoonkwa National Awami Party (PNAP), which had been formed by Abdus Samad Khan Achakzai (who had been a close associate of Mahatma Gandhi in the Indian independence movement, had opposed the formation of Pakistan, had after partition been imprisoned for many years for advocating the creation of an independent Pakhtoonistan, had later joined the NAP but had broken with it to form his own party, and had then been regarded as a supporter of Zulfiqar Ali Bhutto). The PNAP leader was assassinated in Quetta (the capital of Baluchistan) on Dec. 3, 1973, however, and his death was followed by riots which were subdued with the aid of troops.

The existence of a Baluchistan Liberation Front (BLF) had been reported in February 1973. It was said to have an office in Iraq and a clandestine radio operating from that country, and to be supplied with finance and guerrilla training for separatist activities in Baluchistan. On Feb. 10, 1973, the Pakistani authorities seized some 300 submachine-guns, 60,000 rounds of ammunition, 40 incendiary grenades and other military equipment at the Iraq embassy in Islamabad, but it was not clear whether these arms were intended for the BLF or for a similar movement in the south-east of Iran. The government of Iraq subsequently emphasized its respect for Pakistan's sovereignty and territorial integrity.

In connexion with this arms find at the Iraq embassy, Sardar Akbar Bugti (leader of the Bugti tribe) alleged on Feb. 10, 1973, that NAP leaders had plotted the secession of Baluchistan with the help of foreign weapons. (Sardar Bugti had himself led a tribal rising in 1963, had been condemned to death and later pardoned by President Ayub Khan, had become the treasurer of the NAP but has resigned from it after the appointment of Ghaus Bakhsh Bizenjo as governor of Baluchistan as the nominee of the NAP on Aril 29, 1972). Although G. B. Bizenjo had on Feb. 13 categorically denied that the arms were meant for use in Baluchistan and had demanded a judicial inquiry, he was dismissed as governor by President Bhutto on Feb. 15 and replaced by Sardar Bugti, while the government of Sardar Ataullah Mengal was also dismissed for failing to check "large-scale disturbances" and President's rule was imposed in Baluchistan.

Khan Abdul Wali Khan, the president of the NAP, and G. B. Bizenjo alleged on Feb. 20, 1973, that Sardar Bugti had, while abroad, sought foreign assistance (in Moscow, Baghdad, Kabul and London) for a plan for an independent Baluchistan, and they suggested that he was connected with the arms seized at the Iraq embassy.

A new provincial government, of which Jam Ghulam Qadir of the Qayyum Moslem League was sworn in as Chief Minister on April 27, 1973, was opposed as illegal by Sardar Mengal, who declared on the same day that he and his followers in the NAP would "defeat it in the Assembly or if necessary in the streets". There followed widespread unrest and G. B. Bizenjo said on Aug. 13 that unless the government's military intervention were ended quickly the situation in Baluchistan would become uncontrollable and sections of the NAP might be tempted to seek aid from abroad. He was thereupon arrested on Aug. 15, together with Sardar Mengal as well as the president of the Baluchistan NAP and the commander of the party's militia.

Sardar Bugti tendered his resignation as governor on Oct. 13, 1973, because he disagreed with the federal government's handling of affairs in Baluchistan. (He was said to have advised the Prime Minister to restore the NAP government and to withdraw the troops from Baluchistan.) He was on Jan. 3, 1974, replaced as governor by the Khan of Kalat (the overlord of the Baluchi sardars or tribal chieftains). On April 14 Bhutto announced that military operations in Baluchistan would cease from May 15 and that an amnesty would be granted to all persons detained in the province except those accused of serious criminal offences. Guerrilla warfare nevertheless continued and the opposition leaders alleged in the National Assembly on June 24 that 800 people had been killed by Air Force bombing a week earlier (but this was denied by the Federal Minister of Law).

Mutual Accusations made in 1974

The government of Pakistan repeatedly accused the Afghan government of supporting the uprising in Baluchistan and of being responsible for bomb explosions in other provinces and alleged that the NAP connived with the Kabul regime. On June 19, 1974, it was asserted by Bhutto (who had ceased to be President and had become Prime Minister again on Aug. 13, 1973) that a professional assassin had been hired in Afghanistan to kill him in February 1973, and that a former general secretary of the NAP (Ajmal Khattak), who had lived in exile in Kabul since March 1973, had been involved in the plot. On Aug. 12 Radio Pakistan referred to another attempt by three Afghan guerrillas to kill Bhutto during a recent tour of Baluchistan.

On Oct. 1, 1974, the Pakistan Prime Minister stated in a note to the UN Secretary-General (Dr Kurt Waldheim) that he possessed "irrefutable evidence that the present Afghan government is systematically organizing, aiding and abetting the commission of acts of sabotage and terrorism through hired elements within our territory". The Afghan Deputy Foreign Minister (Waheed Abdullah) thereupon declared in the UN General Assembly on Oct. 7 that "the use of force, oppression and imprisonment of those who demand their human rights" in Pakistan would "adversely affect the maintenance of peace and stability in our region", and he proposed that Pakistan and Afghanistan should negotiate a peaceful solution of the Pathan and Baluchi questions.

At the end of an official visit to Moscow by Bhutto in October 1974, it was stated in a joint communiqué that the two sides had "expressed the hope that differences between Pakistan and Afghanistan will be settled by peaceful means through negotiations on the basis of the principles of peaceful coexistence". There followed a brief period of improvement in relations between the two countries.

However, after two Pakistani military posts had been temporarily overrun by Pathan tribesmen near the Khyber Pass and hundreds of refugees from Baluchistan had fled to Afghanistan, Bhutto sent a second note to the UN Secretary-General which as published on Jan. 24, 1975, again accused Afghanistan of "actively encouraging and assisting subversive activities and acts of terrorism and sabotage within Pakistan".

Pakistan Government Measures to curb Unrest in the North-West Frontier Province

On Feb. 8, 1975, Hayat Mohammad Khan Sherpao, Home Minister of the NWFP (and previously a member of the federal government), was killed by a bomb at Peshawar. Over 60 leading members of the NAP were thereupon arrested in the NWFP, the Punjab and Sind; the NAP was banned on Feb. 10 and its property and funds were confiscated; and over 300 more party members were arrested during the next three days. On Feb. 10 the National Assembly granted the government full powers, in particular to extend the state of emergency beyond six months without parliamentary approval. The NWFP government was dissolved on Feb. 17 and the province was for three months placed under the rule of the governor because "a neighbouring foreign power is actively involved in disturbing normal life in the province and there can be no doubt that this is a situation which is beyond the power of the provincial government to control". Numerous bomb explosions took place in Peshawar during the next two months, and a new NWFP government (under a Chief Minister from the ruling Pakistan People's Party) was sworn in on May 3, 1975.

The ban on the NAP was on Oct. 30, 1975, upheld by the Pakistan Supreme Court, which ruled that the party had never reconciled itself to the existence and ideology of Pakistan; had attempted to bring about the secession of the NWFP and Baluchistan through insurrection, terrorism and sabotage; had, in order to destroy the idea of a single Moslem nation, promoted the concept that the Punjabis, Pathans, Baluchis and Sindhis constituted separate nations, each of which had the right of self-determination; and had attempted to propagate hatred of the Punjab in the other provinces.

Abdul Wali Khan and 30 other NAP officials were on April 21, 1975, charged with sabotage and causing bomb explosions. Isfayandar Wali (the son of the party's president) and two other men were on Aug. 2 sentenced to 10 years' rigorous imprisonment after having allegedly confessed to causing the explosion which killed H.M. Khan Sherpao, while Isfayandar Wali was sentenced to a further seven years under the Defence of Pakistan rules.

Renewed Tension between Afghanistan and Pakistan, 1975-76

President Daud of Afghanistan renewed his government's campaign against Pakistan on March 2, 1975, when he declared in a letter to the UN Secretary-General: "Afghanistan has, since the time the British divided our land by force of arms and annexed part of our territory to their empire, supported the lawful rights of these people [i.e. the Pathans and the Baluchis] and will continue to do so until they are fully restored." He protested against the dissolution of the NAP and the detention of its leaders in Pakistan; suggested that a UN fact-finding mission should investigate the situation in Baluchistan; and appealed for UN aid to refugees who had entered Afghanistan from Baluchistan and the NWFP.

On the other hand, for the Pakistan government Prime Minister Bhutto stated in a letter to the UN Secretary-General published on April 12, 1975, that President Daud's letter betrayed "Afghanistan's expansionist design", and he reiterated that the frontier of Afghanistan had been delimited almost 100 years earlier by agreement between the Afghan and British Indian governments, and that the areas inhabited by Pathan and Baluchi tribes on the Pakistani side of the frontier constituted integral parts of Pakistan's national territory. He denied that there had been an influx of refugees from Pakistan into Afghanistan and declared: "The Afghan agents provocateurs and a handful of sympathizers who, because of their commission or instigation of unlawful acts, have become unwelcome among the tribal people of Baluchistan have made their way into Afghanistan as fugitives from justice." Some of the so-called refugees, he stated, wished to return but had been forcibly detained in Afghanistan, and thousands of Afghans who traditionally migrated to Pakistan in the winter months were refusing to return to Afghanistan because of the "terror and oppression" which awaited them. He described President Daud's suggestion for a UN fact-finding mission as "a clear attempt to secure UN cover for [Afghanistan's] interference in Pakistan's internal affairs" and he asserted that Afghanistan's "provocative and aggressive posture, accompanied by continuous exhortations from Radio Kabul to its agents to commit acts of murder, sabotage and destruction in Pakistan" had been responsible for the assassination of H.M. Khan Sherpao. The Pakistan Prime Minister nevertheless repeated that Pakistan remained ready to enter into a dialogue with Afghanistan and was committed to a peaceful settlement of the differences between them in conformity with the principles of respect for territorial integrity and sovereignty, and non-interference in each other's domestic affairs.

The Pakistan Minister of State for Defence and Foreign Affairs (Aziz Ahmed) protested in a separate letter to the UN Secretary-General against steps taken by the latter to ascertain what could be done to help Pakistani refugees in Afghanistan and alleged that as a result of the "reign of terror" in Afghanistan over 170,000 refugees had entered Pakistan.

President Daud, in a further letter to the UN Secretary-General on Oct. 10, 1975, denied that Afghanistan entertained expansionist designs against Pakistan; stated that many of the Baluchis entering Afghanistan were women, children and elderly men; and repeated his request for a UN fact-finding mission as "the only way by which the international community could be informed correctly about the truth of the matter and about the real identity of the Baluchi refugees". In an interview with an Indian newspaper (*Blitz*) on March 8, 1975, the Afghan President had stated that Pakistan was directly involved in espionage, arms smuggling and other incidents inside Afghanistan and was strengthening its fortifications on the frontier.

With reference to an incident in the Panjshir district of Afghanistan on July 22, 1975, Kabul radio alleged that "reactionary troublemakers" had engaged in robbery and subversion and had confessed after their arrest that they had been armed and incited by the Pakistan government. Pakistan radio, on the other hand, asserted that a revolt by some 700 tribesmen had been crushed by the Afghan Army, with over 600 people being killed.

There followed, during the next six months, further Pakistan radio allegations about revolts, riots, acts of sabotage and "barbaric repression" by the police in Afghanistan.

1975 Renewal of Afghan-Soviet Treaty—Contacts between Afghan and Pakistani Leaders

Following the renewal for a further 10 years of a 1931 Soviet-Afghan treaty on neutrality and mutual non-aggression (which had been extended for a further 10 years in 1965) during a state visit to Kabul by President Podgorny of the Soviet Union on Dec. 9-10, 1975, the tension betwen Afghanistan and Pakistan abated during 1976. In a joint communiqué issued at the end of the Soviet President's visit it was stated that the two sides were "firmly convinced that the outstanding problems that exist in the South Asian sub-continent should be resolved through talks without any interference from outside" and "expressed the hope that political discord between Afghanistan and Pakistan will be settled by peaceful means by way of talks".

At the invitation of President Daud, Prime Minister Bhutto visited Kabul on June 7-11, 1976, when the two leaders "exchanged views with the aim of solving their political and other differences on the basis of the five principles of peaceful coexistence" and agreed to refrain for the time being from hostile press and radio propaganda against each other. Moreover, a visit to Pakistan by President Daud took place on Aug. 20-24, 1976, as part of "a continuing dialogue" to find an honourable solution to the political and other differences between the two countries. Nevertheless a "Pakhtoonistan national day" was celebrated in Afghanistan on Aug. 31, with members of the Cabinet taking part in the ceremonies.

Continued Unrest in Baluchistan

Although large numbers of rebels surrendered to government forces during the first half of 1975, guerrilla activities continued in Baluchistan in that year. The Chief Minister (Jam Ghulam Qadir) stated on March 4, 1975, that 44 people arrested had confessed that they had been given training in guerrilla warfare by Afghan army officers, and on May 19 it was officially announced that a store of light machine-guns with Afghan markings had been discovered, together with an instruction manual issued by the Afghan War Ministry—but Kabul radio described the announcement as "a blatant lie".

On Dec. 31, 1975, the federal government suspended the Baluchistan administration and Provincial Assembly and placed the province under governor's rule, inter alia because the provincial government had "failed to make good use of the sizeable allocations made by the federal government for the development of Baluchistan".

On April 8, 1976, the Pakistan Prime Minister announced that the sardari system in Baluchistan and the NWFP had been abolished with immediate effect. Under this system the sardars (tribal chieftains) had held great power in the two provinces, had controlled private armies, administered justice, and collected taxes and other dues, including one-sixth of their tribesmen's crops. On April 10 the Prime Minister said that the former sardars must release all prisoners in their private jails, failing which the jail buildings would be demolished.

In the Iranian province of Baluchistan and Sistan (contiguous with the Baluchistan province in Pakistan), where about 550,000 Baluchis constitute the majority of the population and are predominantly Sunni Moslems (whereas the majority of Iranians are Shia Moslems), there exists a Baluchi movement campaigning for autonomy within Iran, economic assistance and cultural equality with the (Shi'ite) Sistans of the province, but this movement has not advocated union with Baluchis outside Iran.

Clemency Measures taken by the Government of Gen. Zia ul-Haq

A change in the situation inside Pakistan took place with the assumption of power by Gen. Mohammed Zia ul-Haq on July 5, 1977, after protest demonstrations, strikes and riots had followed general elections held on March 7, 1977, and had led to the death of about 350 people. The change of regime involved the dissolution of the National Assembly and of all Provincial Assemblies, and it was followed by clemency measures affecting political opponents of the former government of Zulfiqar Ali Bhutto.

On Aug. 15, 1977, it was announced that Gen. Zia ul-Haq had appealed to the Marri tribesmen who had fled Baluchistan in 1973-74 to return to their homes, promising that no action would be taken against them and they would be rehabilitated. Sardar Mengal, the former Chief Minister of Baluchistan (who had been on trial with other former NAP leaders), was released on bail on Aug. 19. On Dec. 9 Abdul Wali Khan and 15 other men, all facing trial on conspiracy charges, were also released on bail, and on Jan. 1, 1978, Gen. Zia announced that the charges against them had been withdrawn and that the special court set up to try them had been dissolved as the charges were "99 per cent politically motivated"— but that the ban on the NAP would remain in force. He claimed at the same time that 11,109 political prisoners had been released since July 1977 and that there were no political prisoners left in Pakistan except "a few" arrested under martial law. It was officially announced in Quetta on March 21 that over 900 people detained during the rebellion in Baluchistan had been released.

The Issue of Afghan Moslem Rebel Refugees in Pakistan

The (Communist) Revolutionary Council which took power in Afghanistan in April 1978 appeared to maintain the previous Afghan governments' attitude on the issue of "Pakhtoonistan", but a new factor affecting relations between Afghanistan and Pakistan was the massive influx of Afghan Moslem rebels who fled Afghanistan, more especially after the Soviet intervention in that country which began in December 1979.

On July 27, 1978, the Deputy Prime Minister and Minister of Foreign Affairs of Afghanistan (then Hafizullah Amin) expressed the hope that "the only political difference between Afghanistan and Pakistan regarding self-determination for the Pushtu [or Pathan] and Baluchi people" would be "solved through cordial and realistic talks". The government of Pakistan stated in response on July 30: "The national destiny of the Pushtu and Baluchi population of Pakistan as of the rest of the people was determined by them freely and jointly when they decided to establish the sovereign state of Pakistan. The Afghan statement, by calling into question Pakistan's territorial integrity, constituted a serious violation of the principles of the UN Charter, of peaceful coexistence and of the Non-Aligned Movement."

During 1978-79 various Moslem organizations waging guerrilla war against the pro-Soviet Afghan government set up headquarters in Peshawar (NWFP). The number of Afghan Moslem refugees in Pakistan reached about 30,000 by Jan. 16, 1979, but rose to over 1,000,000 in 1980. The Pakistan government stated officially on Jan. 31, 1979, that it had accepted the Afghan refugees on purely humanitarian grounds; that it did not allow them to train as guerrillas near Peshawar; and that its policy towards Afghanistan was one of "good-neighbourliness and respect for the principles of non-interference in its internal affairs". According to an estimate made on June 22, 1981, by the UN High Commissioner for Refugees the number of Afghan refugees in Pakistan had by then reached more than 2,000,000.

The Moscow *Pravda*, however, stated on March 19, 1979, that "Afghan reactionaries" were "relying on support from certain circles in Pakistan, China and some Western countries" and continued: "Everything indicates that it was not without the knowledge of the official Pakistan authorities that the activities of the rebels developed." One June 1, 1979, it was stated in *Pravda*: "The attacks on the sovereignty of the young democratic republic [of Afghanistan], the intrusion of armed gangs on its territory from Pakistan and the attempts to create a crisis in the region cannot leave the USSR indifferent." In response to such assertions, the Pakistan government repeatedly denied that it was backing the rebel Moslems in Afghanistan and that its army was planning to conduct raids into that country.

In Baluchistan more than 100,000 Pushtu refugees from Afghanistan were on Sept. 1, 1980, reported to have set up camps near Pishan (with more than 700,000 head of livestock brought in by them competing with the Baluchis' sheep for scarce grazing land).

On March 21, 1982, it was claimed by the *Hizbi-i-Islami* (Moslem rebel organization) in Quetta (Pakistan) that groups of Baluchis in Afghanistan who rejected the 1947 incorporation of much of Baluchistan in Pakistan [see page 271] were betraying the whereabouts of Moslem rebels to the Soviet and Afghan authorities.

Proposals for a peace settlement, made by the Afghan government on May 14, 1980, called for "a guaranteed ending of incursions into Afghanistan by bandit detachments from the territories of the neighbouring states, in the first place Pakistan". The proposals were, however, rejected by Pakistan on June 11 on the ground that they did "not offer an acceptable basis for a settlement of the crisis".

The years since 1980 have continued to be dominated by the armed conflict between the Moslem rebels (*mujaheddin*) on the one hand and the Afghan and Soviet government forces on the other. The Afghan territorial claim against Pakistan has not been officially raised again, but the fighting has involved numerous border violations. These have included Afghan and Soviet air attacks on targets in Pakistan from which the *mujaheddin* received arms and supplies. On the Pakistan side it was stated that such attacks were directed against villages and refugee camps whereas the Afghan and Soviet side described the targets as rebel bases or supply routes.

In March 1984 the Soviet media accused the United States of attempting to set up a "liberated zone" with an autonomous government in eastern Pakistan.

The main object of the government of Pakistan has been to achieve a solution of the conflict in Afghanistan which would enable the millions of Afghan refugees in Pakistan to return to their homes.

By the end of 1986 official Pakistani figures suggested that over 3,000,000 Afghans had sought refuge in Pakistan, and that more than a quarter of Afghanistan's population had fled their country since the 1979 Soviet invasion. They included up to 50,000 Pushtu-speaking people (as were the bulk of the inhabitants of Pakistan's North-West Frontier Province). In Peshawar, the province's capital, there were half-a-million refugees, practically the same number as the population of the city, and this had led to frequent strife and acts of violence directed against refugees.

The government of Pakistan refused to enter into direct negotiations with the Afghan government, but from June 1982 "proximity talks" have been held by Diego Cordóvez, special envoy of the UN Secretary-General, respectively with the Foreign Ministers of Afghanistan and Pakistan. Following such talks held on June 20-24 and Aug. 29-30, 1985, Cordóvez announced that Afghanistan and Pakistan had agreed to invite the Soviet Union and the United States to act as guarantors of a future agreement. Further proximity talks were held on Dec. 16-19, 1985, and on May 5-23, 1986, but no agreement was reached on a timetable for the withdrawal of Soviet troops from Afghanistan. Further inconclusive talks took place between July 31 and Aug. 8, 1986, and from Feb. 11, 1987.

The newly appointed Afghan President, Dr Muhammad Najib, had on Jan. 2, 1987, announced a ceasefire, to become effective on Jan. 15. The ceasefire was designed to pave the way for the return of the refugees and for the creation of a government of national reconciliation. However, it was rejected by the seven major *mujaheddin* organizations, and fighting continued.

HWD

Bangladesh-India

A dispute developed between India and Bangladesh in 1979 over a new island in the Bay of Bengal, which is called New Moore Island by India and South Talpatty Island by Bangladesh and which both governments claim as part of their national territory. (For territorial relationship of Bangladesh and India, see map on page 279.)

The island lies in the estuary of the River Hariabhanga, the mid-stream of the main channel of which forms the western border between Bangladesh and India, and of the Raimangal, an internal river of Bangladesh. Indian official statements maintain that it is 5.2 km from the Indian coast and 7.2 km from the nearest point in Bangladesh, and that the main channel of the Hariabhanga flows to the east of it, whereas Bangladesh claims that the main channel flows to the west. Its area varies between 12 sq km at low tide and 2 sq km at high tide.

The island, which is believed to have been formed after a cyclone and tidal wave in 1970, was discovered in the following year by India, which laid claim to it, named it New Moore Island and notified the British Admiralty of its location. The Bangladesh government first laid claim to it at the end of 1978, and subsequently maintained that during a visit to Dakha in April 1979 Morarji Desai (then the Indian Prime Minister) had agreed to a joint survey to determine its location and ownership. A joint statement issued on Aug. 18, 1980, after a visit to Dakha by the Indian External Affairs Minister, P. V. Narasimha Rao, merely said that "the two sides agreed that after study of the additional information exchanged between the two governments further discussion would take place with a view to settling it peacefully at an early date", no reference being made to a joint survey.

In May 1981, after an Indian naval survey ship had anchored off the island and landed personnel, Bangladesh gunboats entered the area, whereupon an Indian frigate came to the survey ship's assistance. In a subsequent exchange of notes each government accused the other of acting in a provocative manner and of sending warships into its territorial waters. Bangladesh again proposed a joint survey in a note of May 18, but India rejected the proposal two days later.

A joint statement issued on Sept. 13, 1981, after talks in New Delhi between P. V. Narasimha Rao and the Bangladesh Foreign Minister, Prof. Mohammad Shamsul Huq, said that they had agreed to seek an early and peaceful resolution of all unresolved problems, and that the two countries' foreign secretaries would hold early talks to examine all available data on the New Moore-South Talpatty Island dispute. The Bangladesh Foreign Ministry stated on Oct. 6, 1981, that India had withdrawn her presence from the island, and had removed the remaining Indian ships from the area.

Eric Gonsalves and Humayun Rasheed Choudhury, Foreign Secretaries of India and Bangladesh respectively, met in New Delhi on Jan. 13-15, 1982, for discussions on the island. A joint communiqué issued on Oct. 7, 1982, after discussions in New Delhi between Lt.-Gen.

277

Hossain Mohammad Ershad, then Chief Martial Law Administrator of Bangladesh, and Mrs. Indira Gandhi, then the Indian Prime Minister, said that talks at Foreign Secretary level on the status of the disputed island would continue.

After an Indian minister of state had told the Indian Parliament in early April 1987 that the island was "essentially part of India", a spokesman of the Bangladesh Foreign Ministry on April 12 expressed surprise over this assertion and disclosed that his country's high commissioner in New Delhi had been instructed to take the matter up with the Indian government. He added that the ownership of the island had been under discussion between the two countries for several years, and that it had been agreed that the matter would be settled amicably through exchange of data and, if necessary, a joint survey.

CH

Bhutan-China

The boundary between the Kingdom of Bhutan and Tibet (now incorporated in the People's Republic of China), which has a total length of about 300 miles (500 km), has never been formally delimited, but a traditional customary boundary has long marked the extent of each government's jurisdiction. Bhutan maintains that it has no dispute with China, as the border is well defined by geographical features, and that the question at issue relates merely to demarcation of the boundary. China holds, however, that there are discrepancies in the delineation of certain small areas on the two countries' maps on which agreement needs to be reached. (For the territorial relationship of Bhutan and China, see map on page 279.)

A treaty between Bhutan and the Dominion of India signed in 1949, which replaced a treaty of 1910 between Bhutan and the government of British India, provided that Bhutan would seek the advice of the government of India on its external relations, but remained free to decide whether or not to accept it. In a letter of Dec. 14, 1958, to Zhou Enlai (then Prime Minister of China), Jawaharlal Nehru (then Prime Minister of India) alleged that "a considerable region" of Bhutan was shown on Chinese maps as Chinese territory, thereby asserting India's claim to speak for Bhutan on the question of its border with China—a claim which China did not recognize. Following the rebellion in Tibet against Chinese rule in March 1959, Jigme Dorje (then Prime Minister of Bhutan) visited New Delhi in August 1959, when he declared that nearly 400 square miles (about 1,000 sq km) of Bhutanese territory were shown on Chinese maps as belonging to China, and received an assurance from Nehru that India would defend Bhutan against any intrusion by a foreign power.

Since 1971, when Bhutan was admitted to the United Nations, it has increasingly asserted its status as an independent sovereign state. When India protested to China in 1979 against alleged Chinese incursions into Bhutan, China ignored the protest, but informed the Bhutanese government that it was always ready to discuss the demarcation of the border. Bhutan thereupon decided to enter into direct negotiations with China without Indian participation, and India tacitly accepted the decision. Discussions between Bhutanese and Chinese officials opened in Beijing in April 1984, and were followed by further rounds of talks in Thimphu (the capital of Bhutan) in April 1985 and in Beijing in June 1986. Although no final agreement was reached, both sides affirmed their desire to maintain "a peaceful and friendly border" while seeking an early settlement. Further talks were held in Thimphu in June 1987.

CH

China-India

The Sino-Indian frontier, which is some 2,500 miles (4,000 km) long, falls into three sections: (i) the eastern section, about 700 miles long, where Tibet borders on Arunachal Pradesh (formerly the North-East Frontier Agency); (ii) the central section, where Tibet borders on the independent kingdom of Bhutan, Sikkim (since 1975 a state of the Indian Union), the kingdom of Nepal and the Indian states of Uttar Pradesh and Himachal Pradesh; and (iii) the western section (including the Ladakh frontier), where Kashmir borders on Tibet and Xinjiang (Sinkiang) to the east and Xinjiang to the north. Since 1959 the eastern and western sections of the frontier have been the subject of major territorial disputes between India and China.

The Eastern Section

The frontier problem in the eastern section arises from the mountainous terrain and the limited control formerly exercised by the British over the tribal peoples living in the foothills of the Himalayas and by the Chinese over Tibet. Chinese suzerainty over Tibet was nominally established in 1720, but in practice Tibet continued to be ruled by the priestly caste headed by the Dalai Lama. After the annexation of Assam by the British in 1838, British

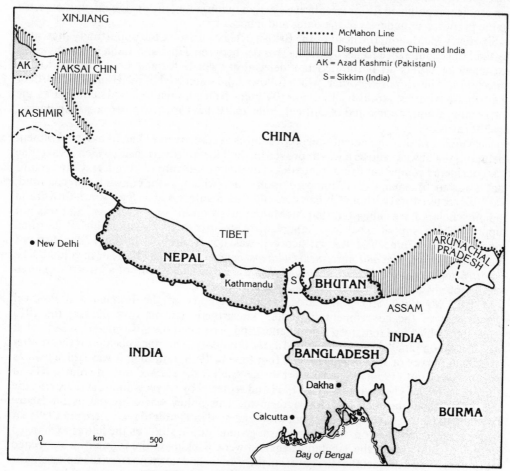

Map 31   The disputed Chinese-Indian border.

279

control was gradually extended into the tribal areas, which were placed under the jurisdiction either of political agents or of the deputy commissioners of the adjoining districts of Assam. To regulate the entry of lowlanders into the tribal areas an "inner line" running along the foot of the hills was defined in 1873; this was purely an administrative device, however, the international boundary remaining undefined. During the same period Nepal, Sikkim and Bhutan increasingly fell within the British rather than the Chinese sphere of influence.

Following violations of the Sikkim border by the Tibetans, a British expeditionary force invaded Tibet in 1903-04, and in 1906 an Anglo-Chinese convention recognized Chinese suzerainty over Tibet. Chinese troops invaded the country in 1910, deposed the Dalai Lama, who fled to India, and proclaimed Chinese sovereignty (as opposed to suzerainty) over Tibet. After the Chinese revolution of 1911, however, the Chinese garrison in Tibet mutinied, and in the following year the Dalai Lama returned and declared Tibet independent.

To achieve a settlement of the controversy over Tibet's status a conference was held at Simla in 1913-14 at which Britain, China and Tibet were represented. A convention which was initialled by representatives of all three countries recognized that Tibet formed part of Chinese territory, whilst China undertook not to convert it into a Chinese province. Tibet was divided into an inner zone under direct Chinese control and an autonomous outer zone; the Chinese government would not interfere in the administration of the latter, send troops into it or provide for its representation in any future Chinese parliament. The convention was subsequently signed by the British and Tibetan representatives, but the Chinese government repudiated its representative's action in initialling the document, as it objected to the proposed boundaries of the outer and inner zones.

Sir Henry McMahon, the head of the British delegation, took the opportunity presented by the Simla conference to negotiate the frontier between Tibet and India by means of an exchange of letters with the Tibetan delegation, which formed an appendix to the convention. The proposed border, which followed the watershed of the Himalayas north of the tribal territories, stood back about 100 miles from the plains of Assam, and as the intervening country consisted of difficult hills and valleys it constituted a strong barrier against invasion.

The validity of this agreement remains a subject of controversy. The Indian government maintains that it was valid as it was approved by the Tibetan government, which at that time was considered competent to enter into direct dealings concerning its borders. China claims that it was an "unequal treaty" imposed upon Tibet (which, as the convention recognized, was Chinese territory) without China's consent, and therefore had no legal force. British and Indian scholars have suggested that McMahon acted on his own initiative, and was not supported by his superiors because the agreement was in breach of treaties which Britain had concluded with China and Russia; hence it was not mentioned in John MacMurray's standard work *Treaties and Agreements with and concerning China* (1921) or in volume XIV of *Aitchison's Treaties, Engagements and Sanads*, the official record of all treaties entered into by the government of India, which appeared in 1929.

In 1935 Mr (later Sir) Olaf Caroe, deputy secretary of the Foreign and Political Department of the government of India, "unearthed" (in his own phrase) the 1914 agreement, which had remained a dead letter, and persuaded the government of India that the "McMahon Line" should be regarded as the boundary. This line appeared as the frontier on official Survey of India maps for the first time in 1938, although it was still shown as undemarcated until 1954, and to support the new policy the 1929 edition of volume XIV of *Aitchison's Treaties* was withdrawn in 1938 and replaced by a new volume, still bearing the date 1929, which included the 1914 agreement. This policy was criticized by Sir Henry Twynam, the acting governor of Assam, who suggested in a letter to the Viceroy in 1939 that the government was not on "absolutely firm ground juridically", as the letters exchanged between McMahon and the Tibetan delegation were "lacking in the formalities associated with a treaty", and the fact that the government of India had taken no steps to implement the agreement from 1914 to 1938 must adversely affect its position in international law.

From 1944 onwards British control over the tribal territories was extended up to the McMahon line, and it was then discovered that some areas south of the line were still under Tibetan administration and the population were paying taxes to the Tibetan authorities. After India became independent in 1947 the new government brought the tribal areas of the North-East Frontier Agency under the direct administrative control of the governor of Assam, and in 1972 they became a union territory separate from Assam under the name of Arunachal Pradesh.

Although successive Chinese governments continued to assert their claim to sovereignty over Tibet, internal strife and the war with Japan prevented them from enforcing it until after the Communist victory in the civil war. In 1950 Chinese troops occupied Tibet, and in the following year an agreement was signed whereby the Dalai Lama accepted Chinese suzerainty and China guaranteed Tibet's internal autonomy. This change in Tibet's status did not immediately affect relations between India and China, which remained friendly. Under an agreement signed in 1954 the two countries agreed to base their relations on the five principles of respect for each other's territorial integrity and sovereignty, non-aggression, non-interference in each other's internal affairs, equality and mutual benefit, and peaceful coexistence, whilst India renounced all extra-territorial rights in Tibet in return for concessions for Indians visiting trade centres and places of pilgrimage.

When his attention was drawn in 1950 to Chinese maps showing Tibet's southern boundary as extending to the Brahmaputra River in Assam, Jawaharlal Nehru, then the Indian Prime Minister, declared that the McMahon line "is our frontier, and we will not allow anyone to cross it". The reference in the 1954 agreement to mutual respect for territorial integrity was interpreted in India as an implicit guarantee that China would accept the existing frontier. During a visit to India in 1956 Zhou Enlai (then the Chinese Premier) told Nehru that although the Chinese government thought the McMahon line unfair, because it was an accomplished fact and because of their friendly relations with India they were of the opinion that they should recognize it, but that they must consult the Tibetan authorities first. Chinese maps continued to show a frontier far south of the McMahon line, however, and a number of minor border incidents occurred in the next three years, none of which involved any clashes between Chinese and India troops.

Relations seriously deteriorated after the Tibetan uprising of March 1959 and the flight of the Dalai Lama to India, which gave rise to Chinese allegations of Indian interference in Chinese affairs. In August 1959 a Chinese force occupied the Indian frontier post of Longju after expelling the small garrison. In a letter to Nehru published on Sept. 8 of that year Zhou Enlai stated that "the Chinese government absolutely does not recognize the so-called McMahon line", and maintained that Indian troops had unlawfully occupied Longju, which he claimed was north of the McMahon line and in Chinese territory. The Indian government declared in a note of Sept. 10 that it "stands firmly" on the McMahon line, though it was prepared to "discuss the exact alignment of the line at places where it departs from the geographical features marking the international boundary". Two days later Nehru told the Indian Parliament that the government was prepared to consider minor rectifications of "a mile here or a mile there", but not "to hand over the Himalayas". A map depicting China's territorial claims, compiled from official Chinese maps, which was published by the Indian External Affairs Ministry showed that China claimed about 32,000 square miles (83,000 sq. km) of territory south of the McMahon line, including three of the four political divisions of the North-East Frontier Agency (Kameng, Subansiri and Siang) and part of the fourth (Lohit).

Zhou Enlai visited New Delhi in April 1960 for talks with Nehru, at the conclusion of which they announced that as they had not succeeded in resolving the differences that had arisen officials of the two governments would meet to examine all relevant documents. At a press conference on April 25, 1960, Zhou suggested that the following six points could form the basis for a settlement: "(i) There exist disputes with regard to the boundary between the two sides. (ii) There exists between the two countries a line of actual control up to which each side exercises administrative jurisdiction. (iii) In determining the boundary between the two countries, certain geographical principles, such as watersheds, river valleys and mountain passes, should be equally applicable to all sectors of the boundary. (iv) A settlement of the boundary question between the two countries should take into account the national feelings of the two peoples towards the Himalayas and the Karakoram mountains. (v) Pending a solution of the boundary question through discussions, both sides should keep to the line of actual control and should not put forward territorial claims as preconditions, but individual adjustments may be made. (vi) In order to ensure tranquillity on the border and thereby facilitate discussions, both sides should continue to refrain from patrolling along all sectors of the boundary." Points (iii) and (iv) were interpreted as a suggestion that China was prepared to accept the McMahon line as the border in the eastern section if India accepted the Chinese claim that the watershed of the Karakoram mountains formed the border in the western section (see below). The proposed talks between officials produced no result.

The eastern section of the border remained quiet for three years after the Longju incident, but on Sept. 20 and Oct. 10, 1962, two clashes occurred in the area of the trijunction of the Bhutanese, Indian and Tibetan borders, with some loss of life on both sides. In a subsequent exchange of notes each side claimed to have acted in self-defence and accused the other of crossing the McMahon line.

On Oct. 20, 1962, the Chinese army launched an offensive at the western end of the McMahon line, which was followed by a similar offensive at the eastern end. During the next month the Chinese troops advanced over 100 miles south of the McMahon line at the western end and 25 to 30 miles south at the eastern end, threatening the plains of Assam. On Nov. 21, however, the Chinese government announced that its troops would observe a ceasefire and would withdraw to positions 20 kilometres (12 miles) north of the McMahon line, and that it would set up checkpoints on its side of the line of actual control existing on Nov. 7, 1959. The Chinese subsequently withdrew, but established checkpoints at Dhola and Longju, at the western end and in the central sector of the McMahon line respectively.

At the proposal of Mrs Sirimavo Bandaranaike, then Prime Minister of Ceylon (Sri Lanka), representatives of six Asian and African non-aligned countries—Burma, Ceylon, Ghana, Indonesia, Cambodia (Kampuchea) and the United Arab Republic (Egypt)—met in Colombo on Dec. 10-12, 1962, to discuss means of bringing India and China together. The following proposals were put forward: (i) In the western section the Chinese should withdraw their military posts by 20 kilometres, as they had proposed on Nov. 21, and the Indian forces should keep their existing positions. The area vacated by the Chinese would be a demilitarized zone, to be administered by civilian posts of both sides. (ii) In the eastern section the line of actual control should serve as a ceasefire line. (iii) These proposals once implemented should pave the way for discussions on solving problems entailed in the ceasefire position. Although both India and China announced their acceptance of the proposals, they differed in their interpretation of them, and in consequence they remained ineffective.

Occasional border incidents have since occurred in the eastern section, in the most serious of which four Indian soldiers were killed in October 1975. The Indian government alleged in a note of July 6, 1986, that about 40 Chinese personnel had intruded into the Sumdorong Chu valley on June 16 to a point seven kilometres south of the McMahon line. A Chinese Foreign Ministry spokesman said on July 16 that they had been north of the line of actual control and hence in Chinese territory. K. R. Narayanan, the Indian Minister of State for External Affairs, said on Aug. 6 that information had been received suggesting that Chinese personnel had constructed a helicopter landing area in the Sumdorong Chu valley. The official New China News Agency accused Indian military personnel and aircraft on Aug. 22 of persistently crossing the line of control in the eastern border region in an attempt to "nibble further at Chinese territory and to create more disputed territory".

The legal status of Arunachal Pradesh has caused controversy on a number of occasions. An Indian parliamentary delegation cancelled a proposed visit to China in October 1981 after the Chinese authorities refused to issue a visa to a delegate from Arunachal Pradesh; a compromise was reached, however, whereby all the delegates were given visas, not on their

Indian passports, but on separate sheets of paper. The participation of dancers from Arunachal Pradesh in the closing ceremony of the ninth Asian Games in New Delhi in December 1982 was strongly criticized by the New China News Agency, which described it as "a deliberate step to propagate India's sovereignty over the state and legalize it".

The constitutional status of the union territory of Arunachal Pradesh was raised to that of a state of the Indian Union under a bill passed by the Indian Parliament on Dec. 9, 1986. A Chinese Foreign Ministry spokesman said on Dec. 11 that this measure had "seriously violated China's territorial integrity and sovereignty"; an Indian official spokesman subsequently described the Chinese protest as "clear interference" in Indian affairs.

The Central Section

Only minor disagreements have arisen concerning the status of a number of mountain passes and other relatively small areas in this sector, and no serious border incidents have occurred. When in 1954 an agreement on trade and travel between India and Tibet was being negotiated the Chinese draft stated that the Chinese government agreed to open six mountain passes. This wording was challenged by the Indian delegation, which maintained that the passes were Indian. In its final form the agreement referred to them as border passes open to nationals of both countries.

A Chinese note of Dec. 26, 1959, stated that "according to Indian maps ... the boundary line in the middle sector is relatively close to the delineation on the Chinese maps, but still a number of areas which have always belonged to China are included in India". The note based the Chinese claims to these areas on the fact that their population was of Tibetan origin. In reply, an Indian note of Feb. 12, 1960, recalled that Zhou Enlai had said in 1957 that the Sino-Burmese boundary line "is often found dividing into two parts a nationality living in compact communities on the borders" and had continued: "This is the result of historical development. ...When we solve the question of the undefined boundary line between China and Burma, we must realize beforehand that it will be hard to avoid separating the nationalities concerned."

The Ladakh Frontier

Ladakh, formerly an independent state, came under the suzerainty of the Moghul Emperors in 1664. When the Tibetans invaded Ladakh in 1681-83 the Ladakhis defeated them with Moghul assistance, and a peace treaty signed in 1684 stated that "the boundaries fixed in the beginning ... shall still be maintained". After the decline of the Moghul empire, Ladakh was conquered in 1834 by the Raja of Jammu, who in 1846 received the title of Maharaja of Jammu and Kashmir. A new war with Tibet in 1841-42 was concluded by a peace treaty signed by representatives of the Raja of Jammu, the Dalai Lama and the Chinese Emperor. Under this agreement Tibet recognized the Raja as the political overlord of Ladakh, although the Ladakhi Buddhists continued to regard the Dalai Lama as their spiritual overlord, and each side undertook to respect "the old-established frontiers". The accession of Jammu and Kashmir to the Indian Union in 1947 and the Chinese occupation of Tibet in 1950 brought the governments in New Delhi and Peking into direct contact in this area.

The border area was described by Nehru in 1959 as "a barren and uninhabited region, 17,000 feet high and without a vestige of grass", and by Sir H. A. F. Rumbold (a former senior India Office official) in 1977 as a "frozen, uninhabitable wilderness". Neither the treaty of 1684 nor that of 1842 defined where the boundary was, and the region was not even surveyed until 1864. Although the British authorities in India proposed on a number of occasions down to 1899 that the boundary should be delimited, they received no response from the Chinese government, and the official *Aitchison's Treaties*, volume XII (1931), described the northern and eastern frontier of Jammu and Kashmir as "undefined". Many British official maps, including that attached to the Simon Commission's report of 1930 and that submitted by the general staff of the Indian Army to the British Cabinet Mission in 1946, showed the boundary as following approximately the crest of the Karakoram mountains, although other British maps showed either a firm line or a colour wash right up to the Kuenlun mountains, about 80 miles (200 km) to the north-east. Suggestions which were put forward by Sir John Ardagh in 1897 that the boundary should be extended to the crest of the Kuenlun range were rejected by the general staff, on the ground that the new frontier would be difficult to defend and strategically useless, and were never officially accepted. In July 1954, however, the Indian government published a new official map which showed a boundary line following the crest of the Kuenlun mountains, and for the first time included the whole of the Aksai Chin plateau (an area of about 14,000 square miles or 36,000 sq km) within Indian territory, although since 1950 this area had been under Chinese control.

Strategically the Aksai Chin is of great importance to China, as it forms the link between Tibet and Xinjiang (Sinkiang), and in 1956-57 the Chinese built a road across it connecting the two regions. As India asserted its claim to sovereignty over the area only by sending occasional patrols, the Indian government remained unaware of the road's existence until its attention was drawn to a Chinese press report. Two reconnaissance parties were sent in 1958 to investigate, one of which was captured by Chinese troops, whilst the other confirmed that the road ran through territory claimed by India. In response to Indian representations the Chinese government released the arrested men, but maintained that the road ran only through Chinese territory.

In a letter of March 22, 1959, to Zhou Enlai, Nehru based India's claim to the Aksai Chin partly on the treaty of 1842 and partly on evidence of actual occupation and administration, such as detailed surveys, explorations, hunting rights, travellers' accounts, use of pastures, collection of salt, construction of trade routes and sending of patrols. In his reply, published on Sept. 8, 1959, Zhou Enlai pointed out that the 1842 treaty "only mentioned in general terms that Ladakh and Tibet would each abide by their borders, and did not contain any specific provisions regarding the location of this section of the boundary", and continued: "This section of the boundary has never been delimited. Between China and Ladakh there does, however, exist a customary line derived from historical traditions, and Chinese maps have always drawn the boundary between China and Ladakh in accordance with this line."

A clash between an Indian police patrol and Chinese troops, in which nine of the former were killed, occurred on Oct. 21, 1959, in the Chang Chenmo valley, west of the Lanak La Pass, which lies on the borderline claimed by India. In a subsequent exchange of notes each government alleged that the incident had taken place on its own territory and had been caused by an intrusion by the other's forces. According to an Indian External Affairs Ministry statement of Nov. 27, 1962, Chinese troops occupied 6,000 square miles (15,000 sq km) of territory in the disputed area during 1959-62, establishing checkposts and constructing roads connecting them with their bases.

Three encounters between Chinese and Indian troops occurred in July 1962 in the Galwan river valley, near Pangong lake and in the Chip Chap valley, the only casualties being two Indian soldiers wounded in the last incident. On Oct. 20, 1962, the Chinese Army opened an offensive in the Aksai Chin at the same time as that on the McMahon line. Fighting took place in three areas: immediately south of the Karakoram Pass, around Pangong lake, 100 miles to the south-east, and around Damchok, in the extreme south-east of the disputed territory. During the fighting the Chinese occupied all the Indian outposts east of the boundary claimed by China, but made no attempt to occupy an Indian post two miles west of this line, which had been evacuated by its garrison. As on the eastern front, China declared a cease-fire on Nov. 21, and announced that its troops would withdraw to positions 20 kilometres behind the line of actual control existing on Nov. 7, 1959. Since 1962 the situation in the Aksai Chin has generally remained peaceful, apart from an incident in September 1965 (when India was at war with Pakistan) in which three Indian policemen were killed.

Demarcation of China-Pakistan Border

Pakistan and China announced on May 3, 1962, that they had agreed to demarcate their common border, i.e. the border of Xinjiang and the area of Kashmir under Pakistani control. An Indian note to Pakistan of May 10 of that year contended that Pakistan and China had no common boundary, as Kashmir formed "an integral part of the Indian Union"; that India would not be bound by the results of any bilateral discussions between Pakistan and China; and that the border of Kashmir west of the Karakoram Pass followed well-known natural features and did not require fresh delimitation. An agreement delimiting the boundary was signed in Beijing on March 2, 1963. A Pakistani Foreign Ministry spokesman stated that out of 3,400 square miles (8,800sq km) in dispute Pakistan had obtained 1,350 square miles under the agreement, including 750 square miles which were actually in Chinese possession, and China had obtained 2,050 square miles. Pakistan also abandoned her claim to over 13,000 square miles of Xinjiang territory, which had previously been shown as part of Kashmir on Pakistani but not on Indian maps.

After the delimitation of the border China and Pakistan co-operated in the construction of two all-weather highways linking the Pakistani-controlled area of Kashmir with Xinjiang, one of which, running through the Mintaka Pass, was opened in 1968, whilst the other (the Karakoram highway), running through the Khunjerab Pass, was opened in 1978. Strong protests against both projects were lodged by India.

Sino-Indian Negotiations on Border Dispute

A goodwill mission led by Wang Bingnan, president of the Chinese People's Association for Friendship with Foreign Countries, which visited India on March 7-23, 1978, met Morarji Desai and A. B. Vajpayee (Prime Minister and External Affairs Minister respectively in the Janata Party government then in power), and on behalf of the Chinese government extended an invitation to Vajpayee to visit China, which was accepted. Desai told Parliament on March 16, however, that he had made it clear to the Chinese mission that "full normalization of relations, of course, cannot be attained till the main outstanding issue—the border question—is resolved to our mutual satisfaction by negotiations".

Vajpayee arrived in Beijing on Feb. 12, 1979, for his visit, the first by an Indian minister for over 20 years, and had talks with Huang Hua (then the Chinese Foreign Minister), whom he invited to visit India to continue the dialogue, before returning to New Delhi on Feb. 18. Reporting to Parliament on Feb. 21, he said that he had emphasized the fundamental importance of the boundary question, which "must be satisfactorily settled if relations of mutual confidence are to be established". He had also informed the Chinese leaders that the attitude towards the Kashmir question adopted by China in the past 15 years had been "an additional and unnecessary complication to the prospects of Sino-Indian relations", and reiterated India's concern at the construction of the Karakoram highway across territory forming part of the state of Jammu and Kashmir.

Eric Gonsalves, the Indian External Affairs Secretary, visited Beijing for discussions on June 20-23, 1980, and delivered a new invitation to Huang Hua to visit India. In an interview with an Indian journalist on June 21, Deng Xiaoping (then the senior Chinese Deputy Premier) said: "So long as both sides are sincere, respect the present state of the border and are tolerant towards each other, the Sino-Indian boundary question can be solved through peaceful negotiations. As a matter of fact, ever since negotiations on boundary questions began China has never asked for the return of all the territory illegally incorporated into India by the old colonialists. Instead, China suggested that both countries should make concessions, China in the eastern sector and India in the western sector, on the basis of the actually controlled border line so as to solve the Sino-Indian boundary question in a package plan, thus fully demonstrating the spirit of mutual understanding and concessions". Indian sources pointed out that this proposal, which was repeated in a New China News Agency commentary on June 25, 1980, was merely a "feeler" which had not been officially put forward during the talks with Gonsalves. Commenting on Deng's proposal, P. V. Narasimha Rao (External Affairs Minister in the Congress government which had held office since the previous January) said on July 2: "The government of India has never accepted the premise on which it is based, namely, that the Chinese side is making a concession in the eastern section by the giving up of territory which they allege is illegally incorporated into India. Nevertheless, we welcome the prospect of the eastern sector being settled without any particular difficulty."

Huang Hua paid a visit to New Delhi (the first by a Chinese minister since Zhou Enlai's visit in 1960) on June 26-29, 1981, and after he had met the Prime Minister, Mrs Indira Gandhi, she announced that it had been agreed to hold talks to resolve the border issue. The first round of talks was held in Beijing on Dec. 10-14, 1981, the Indian delegation being led by Gonsalves and the Chinese delegation by Han Nianlong, a Deputy Foreign Minister. At the second round, held in New Delhi on May 17-20, 1982, the Chinese delegation was headed by Fu Hao, a Foreign Ministry adviser, and at the third, held in Beijing on Jan. 29-Feb. 2, 1983, K. S. Bajpai (Secretary in the Ministry of External Affairs and a former ambassador to China) led the Indian delegation.

Although no details of the negotiations were published officially, China was reported to favour a package deal along the lines suggested by Zhou Enlai in 1960 and by Deng Xiaoping in 1980, i.e. a border settlement along the existing lines of control, whereby China would accept the McMahon line as the frontier in the eastern section and India would accept China's claim to the Aksai Chin. The Indian delegation, on the other hand, proposed at the first round (i) that the two sides should accept the proposal of the Colombo Conference for demilitarization of the territory occupied by China in 1962, and (ii) that they should hold separate and simultaneous discussions on each section of the border, as a prelude to a comprehensive settlement. The next two rounds were devoted to debate on which approach should be adopted.

An advance was achieved at the fourth round, held in New Delhi on Oct. 25-30, 1983, when the Chinese accepted the Indian proposal for a sector-by-sector review of the border, and both sides agreed to take into account the relevance of historical evidence, custom and tradition to the position in each sector. After the fifth round, held in Beijing on Sept. 17-22, 1984, Indian officials said that principles had been formulated upon which the dispute would be negotiated sector by sector, and the New China News Agency reported that the two sides had "made efforts to narrow differences and expand common points". The sixth round, held in New Delhi on Nov. 9-11, 1985, was devoted to matters relating to the eastern sector of the border. At the seventh, held in Beijing on July 21-24, 1986, no substantial progress was made.

In the absence of further negotiations, Sino-Indian tensions increased in mid-April 1987 when the Chinese Foreign Ministry claimed that its Indian counterpart had "totally confounded black and white" in its latest report on alleged Chinese territorial violations. Later the same month Deng Xiaoping told a visiting Indian Communist Party leader (on April 20) that the Sino-Indian border dispute should be settled in a spirit of mutual understanding and accommodation. However, tension again flared in early May 1987 when the Chinese claimed that Indian troops had encroached on Chinese territory and also attributed airspace violations and troop concentrations to the Indians. The Indian Foreign Ministry responded that India did not want a confrontation with China and expressed a willingness to resume talks at any time.

The Indian Foreign Minister, Narain Dutt Tiwari, had talks on the latest crisis in Beijing on June 15-16, 1987, during which he agreed with Chinese leaders that "peace and stability" should be maintained, and "provocations" avoided, along the Sino-Indian border, pending a negotiated settlement of the dispute. It was envisaged that further talks would take place in New Delhi at official level in the second half of 1987.

CH

China-Japan-Taiwan (Senkaku Islands)

The uninhabited Senkaku Islands, known to the Chinese as the Diaoyu and Other Islands, are situated about 200 miles (320 km) west of Okinawa (in the Ryukyu Islands) and about 100 miles (160 km) north-east of Taiwan. They became the subject of a dispute between the People's Republic of China, Taiwan and Japan following the signing of the San Francisco peace treaty between the Western Allies and Japan in September 1951.

The disputed islands were, together with Taiwan and the Pescadores Islands, ceded to Japan by Imperial China under the 1895 Treaty of Shimonoseki signed after China's defeat in the 1894-95 Sino-Japanese war. Under the 1951 San Francisco peace treaty, the Senkaku Islands were included in the Ryukyu Islands and accordingly placed under US administration. Having already denounced the 1951 treaty as "illegal" and its provisions as "null and void", the Beijing government also protested when, in terms of a US-Japan treaty of June 17, 1971, all the islands reverted to Japan on May 14, 1972. In a statement issued on Dec. 30, 1971, China declared that the islands appertained to the island of Taiwan and had, like the latter, been "an inalienable part of Chinese territory since ancient times".[1]

Having also laid claim to the Senkaku Islands on June 11, 1971, the Taiwan government in February 1972 announced their incorporation into Taiwan. The Japanese government protested on Feb. 17, 1972, and later issued a document maintaining that the Senkaku (together with Taiwan and the Pescadores) had only been incorporated into Japan in 1895 after it had been established that the rule of the Chinese empire had not extended to them.

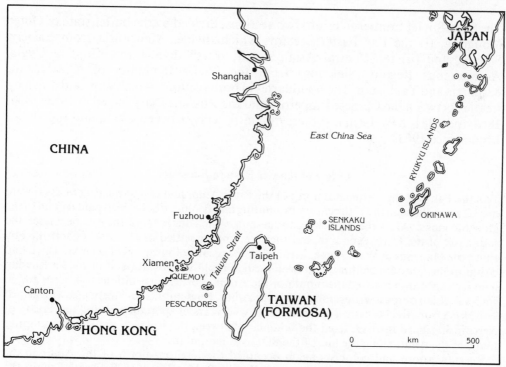

Map 32   The location of the Senkaku Islands.

---

[1]For an account of China-Taiwan territorial issues, see pages 300-9.

During negotiations in February 1975 on a possible treaty of peace and friendship between China and Japan (which was eventually signed on Aug. 12, 1978), it was believed in Japan that China would shelve the issue of these islands. This was corroborated by the Chinese government's attitude to an incident which occurred in April 1978, when a fleet of Chinese fishing vessels began to operate in the territorial waters of the Senkaku Islands, which the fishermen claimed to be in Chinese waters. Following Japanese representations to the Chinese government, a Chinese Deputy Premier stated on April 15 that the incident was not intentional but "an accidental affair", and on the following day the Chinese vessels withdrew from the vicinity of the islands. Liao Cheng-chi, then a vice-chairman of the Standing Committee of the National People's Congress of China, said on April 27 that the government would make all-out efforts to avoid any conflicts over the Senkaku Islands.

After the signing of the treaty between China and Japan, it was stated by a spokesman of Japan's ruling Liberal-Democratic Party on Aug. 13, 1978, that China had effectively recognized Japan's control over the islands, and that Deng Xiaoping (then a Chinese Deputy Premier) had emphasized that no further incidents would take place in the area. Nevertheless, the Beijing government has maintained its claim that legally the islands are part of Chinese territory.

HWD

China-Soviet Union

The Sino-Soviet frontier falls into two sections, divided by the buffer state of Outer Mongolia: (i) the Far Eastern sector, which divides Manchuria from Eastern Siberia, and (ii) the Central Asian sector, which divides the Xinjiang Uygur Autonomous Region (Sinkiang) from the Soviet Republics of Kazakhstan, Kirghizia and Tajikistan. The boundaries in both sections, which were laid down by treaties between the Chinese Emperors and the Russian Tsars signed in 1858, 1860, 1864 and 1881, have been a subject of controversy between China and the Soviet Union since 1963.

Origin of the Far Eastern Boundary

In the Far East the wastelands north of the River Amur and east of the River Ussuri were sparsely populated in the 17th century by hunting and fishing tribes, which paid tribute to the Manchu kings. After the Manchu conquest of China in 1644-62 they came under the suzerainty of the Chinese empire, but they were never settled or effectively controlled by either the Manchus or the Chinese. Meanwhile, Russian colonization of Siberia, which had begun in the late 16th century, had been pushed rapidly eastward, and in 1644 a Russian military expedition reached the mouth of the Amur. Further expeditions followed, and in 1665 a Russian outpost was established on the Amur. Russian encroachment met with armed resistance from the Manchus, and after nearly 40 years of sporadic fighting the Treaty of Nerchinsk, signed in 1689, fixed the boundary between the Russian and Chinese empires north of the Amur along the line of the Stanovoi mountains.

Russian troops and colonists again occupied the territory north of the Amur in the mid-19th century, when China was weakened by the Opium War of 1839-42 with Britain, the Taiping Rebellion of 1850-64 and the Second Opium War of 1858-60 with Britain and France. The Chinese commander on the Amur was forced in 1858 to sign the Treaty of Aigun, which gave Russia sovereignty over 185,000 square miles (480,000 sq km) of territory north of the Amur and placed 130,000 square miles between the Ussuri (the Amur's principal tributary) and the Pacific under joint Sino-Russian sovereignty pending a future decision on the matter. This agreement was confirmed later in the same year by the Treaty of Tianjin (Tientsin), and in subsequent negotiations in 1860 the Tsar demanded the area east of the Ussuri (the Maritime Territory) as his reward for remaining neutral in the Second Opium War and using his good offices to negotiate a peace settlement. The Chinese granted his claim by the Treaty of Beijing (Peking), which also defined the Sino-Russian border in Central Asia. In their newly-acquired territories the Russians founded the city of Khabarovsk on the Amur in 1858, and the port and naval base of Vladivostok in the Maritime Territory in 1860.

Origin of the Central Asian Boundary

Although earlier dynasties had temporarily imposed their suzerainty upon Xinjiang ("New Frontier"), Chinese supremacy was not finally established there until the late 17th century. The population consisted of Kazakhs, Tajiks, Kirghiz, Uighurs and Uzbeks, Turkish in race and Moslem in religion, and there was little Chinese settlement, apart from the military garrisons (soldiers being encouraged to settle there with their families) and political exiles. The garrisons consisted of "permanent pickets" close to the towns and "movable pickets" set up in the frontier areas to prevent the nomadic population from driving their flocks and herds into Chinese territory. Although Chinese rule was exercised indirectly through local chieftains, it was bitterly resented by the native population, and armed uprisings occurred in 1825-26, 1827, 1830 and 1857.

From about 1840 onwards the Russians gradually extended their control of Central Asia into the Kazakh and Kirghiz steppes, which were nominally under Chinese suzerainty. The Treaty of Beijing in 1860 fixed the boundary between the Chinese and Russian empires as "following the mountains, great rivers and the present line of Chinese permanent pickets", and provided for a joint survey of the areas in dispute from the foothills of the Altai in the north to the Pamirs in the south. The survey was protracted for four years, as the Russians contended that under the treaty the boundary should follow the hills where the Chinese maintained permanent pickets, whilst the Chinese also claimed the territory farther west

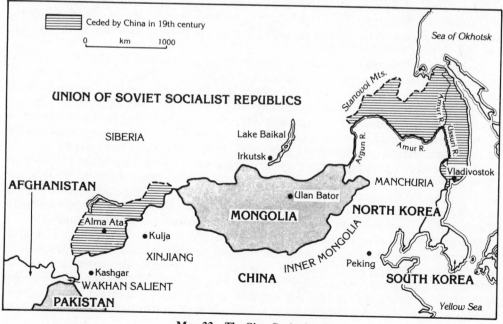

Map 33   The Sino-Soviet border.

occupied by their movable pickets. The Treaty of Chuguchak (or Tarbagatai), signed in 1864, accepted the Russian claim to 350,000 square miles (900,000 sq km) of territory which had not been under effective Chinese control, but in which Chinese movable pickets had operated.

In the same year (1864) the whole of Xinjiang revolted against Chinese rule and established its independence under the leadership of a local chieftain, Yakub Beg. To prevent the revolt from spreading into his own Central Asian territories the Tsar sent troops in 1871 which occupied the Ili river valley as far as the town of Kulja. Although the Chinese reconquered Xinjiang with Russian assistance in 1877, the Russians continued to occupy Kulja and the Upper Ili valley until 1881, when by the Treaty of St Petersburg or of Ili they agreed to evacuate the area.

The Russian Revolution and the "Unequal Treaties"

After the overthrow of the Chinese empire in 1911 the new republican regime headed by Dr Sun Yat-sen demanded the abrogation of all "unequal treaties" and the restoration of China's "traditional" frontiers, the term "unequal treaties" being applied to all agreements by which in the 19th and early 20th centuries China had been compelled to surrender territory or to grant extra-territorial rights to the Western powers, Russia and Japan. This concept met with considerable sympathy from the Bolsheviks after their seizure of power in 1917. By the Karakhan Declaration of July 25, 1919, the Soviet government stated that it "declares null and void all the treaties concluded with China by the former governments of Russia, renounces all seizure of Chinese territory and all Russian concessions in China, and restores to China, without any compensation and for ever, all that has been predatorily seized from her by the Tsar's government and the Russian bourgeoisie".

The declaration specifically mentioned as annulled treaties dealing with spheres of influence in China, with rights of extra-territoriality and consular jurisdiction, concessions on Chinese territory, and the Russian share of the indemnities imposed on China after the suppression of the Boxer Rising of 1900. It did not mention the treaties of Aigun, Beijing and Chuguchak, however, and on territorial questions it stated: "The Soviet government has renounced the conquests made by the Tsarist government which deprived China of Manchuria and other areas. Let the people living in those areas themselves decide within the frontiers of which state they may wish to dwell, and what form of government they wish to establish in their own countries."

An agreement between China and the Soviet Union signed on May 31, 1924, provided that at a future conference they were to "annul all conventions, treaties, agreements, protocols, contracts, etc., concluded between the government of China and the Tsarist government and to replace them with new treaties, agreements, etc., on the basis of equality, reciprocity and justice, ... to re-demarcate their national boundaries ... and pending such re-demarcation to maintain the present boundaries". Talks were held in 1926 to discuss the re-demarcation of the border and the conclusion of a new treaty, but no agreement was reached.

Thereafter the border question remained in abeyance, as China was preoccupied for over 20 years with the civil war between the Kuomintang and the Communists, the Japanese invasion and the renewed civil war which followed the defeat of the Japanese. It was still regarded as unsettled by the Chinese, however, and maps of Central Asia published by the Kuomintang government laid claim to large areas of territory under Soviet control.

During this period of confusion Xinjiang remained virtually independent of central government control, and the Soviet Union was able to bring Xinjiang within its sphere of influence by supplying military aid to the provincial governors, who controlled both its internal and its external policies. A governor who adopted an anti-Soviet policy was expelled in 1944 by a Soviet-inspired Moslem uprising, and an "East Turkestan Republic" was established in the Ili Valley with its capital at Kulja, in the region occupied by the Russians in 1871-81.

Communist China and the Soviet Union, 1949-60

For some years after the victory of the Chinese Communists in 1949, relations between China and the Soviet Union remained apparently friendly. The East Turkestan Republic was reintegrated into China. The Common Programme summarizing the new government's policies said that it would examine all treaties and agreements with foreign powers concluded by the Kuomintang government and either recognize, abrogate, revise or renegotiate them, but did not mention treaties concluded by earlier Chinese governments. Chairman Mao Zedong, the new head of state, said on Dec. 16, 1949, that "the Soviet Union was the first to denounce unequal treaties and concluded with China new equal agreements", suggesting that China did not regard the boundary treaties as "unequal". The 30-year treaty of friendship, alliance and mutual assistance between China and the Soviet Union signed in 1950 contained no reference to boundary questions, apart from an undertaking by each side to respect the other's territorial integrity. As late as April 28, 1960, Zhou Enlai, the Chinese Prime Minister, described the differences on border questions between China and the Soviet Union as "insignificant divergencies on the maps" which could "easily be peacefully resolved".

There were nevertheless indications that China did not regard the boundary question as settled. Up to 1953 official Chinese maps showed the boundary between Xinjiang and Soviet Tajikistan in the Pamirs plateau several hundred miles to the west of its present position, and later maps marked the frontier in this area, as "undefined". A map in *A Short History of Modern China*, published in Beijing in 1954, included among "Chinese territories taken by imperialism" the Far Eastern territories ceded in 1858 and 1860 and parts of Soviet Kazakhstan, Kirghizia and Tajikistan as far west as Lake Balkhash, as well as Nepal, Sikkim, Bhutan, Assam, Burma, Malaya, Thailand, Kampuchea, Vietnam, Laos, Korea and Sakhalin, and showed Outer Mongolia as an integral part of China.

Deterioration of Sino-Soviet Relations, 1960-63

The boundary question again came to the fore as relations between China and the Soviet Union deteriorated from 1960 onwards. Later statements from both Soviet and Chinese sources revealed that border incidents began in July of that year, although at the time no publicity was given to such incidents by either side, and a Soviet statement alleged that the Chinese had violated the Soviet border over 5,000 times during 1960.

Defending Soviet policy during the Cuban missile crisis of October 1962, which had been criticized by China, Nikita Khrushchev (then the Soviet Prime Minister and Communist Party leader) in a speech of Dec. 12, 1962, contrasted the expulsion of the Portuguese from Goa by India with the Chinese government's omission to take similar action against Macao and Hong Kong. In reply, the Beijing *People's Daily* mentioned on March 8, 1963, nine treaties which former Chinese governments had been forced to sign, including the Treaties of Aigun, Tianjin, Beijing and Ili, and enquired: "In raising questions of this kind do you intend to raise all the questions of unequal treaties and invite a general settlement?" This comment—the first in which China had referred to the possibility of a revision of the frontiers—was interpreted as a suggestion that China reserved the right to demand the return of the territories ceded under the treaties named at some future date.

Chinese and Soviet statements issued in September 1964 indicated that a tense situation existed on the Xinjiang border. The *People's Daily* alleged on Sept. 6 that Soviet agencies and personnel had carried out "large-scale subversive activities in the Ili region of Xinjiang and incited and coerced several tens of thousands of Chinese citizens into going to the Soviet Union". This statement appeared to confirm reports from Moscow that riots had occurred in Xinjiang among the Moslem Kazakhs, Uighurs and other nationalities, who resented mass Chinese settlement in the region and attempts to suppress their religion and languages, and that between the middle of 1962 and September 1963 about 50,000 Kazakhs and other tribesmen had fled into the Soviet Union.

A Soviet statement issued on Sept. 21, 1964, declared that "since 1960 Chinese servicemen and civilians have been systematically violating the Soviet border. ...Attempts are also being made to 'develop' some parts of Soviet territory without permission". After quoting a document alleged to have been issued by the Chinese administration in Manchuria, instructing fishermen to ignore orders by Soviet border guards to keep off disputed islands in the Amur and the Ussuri, the statement continued: "The Soviet government has invited the Chinese government a number of times to hold consultations on the question of ascertaining separate sections of the border line, to exclude any possibility of misunderstanding. The Chinese side, however, evades such consultations while continuing to violate the border. This cannot but make us wary, especially in view of the fact that Chinese propaganda is making definite hints at the 'unjust demarcation' of some sections of the Soviet-Chinese border allegedly made in the past. However, the artificial creation of any territorial problems in our times, especially between socialist countries, would be tantamount to embarking on a very dangerous path."

Boundary Negotiations, 1964

Boundary negotiations began in Beijing on Feb. 25, 1964, but were suspended in the following May without any progress having been achieved. According to Soviet sources, the Soviet delegation put forward proposals for the "clarification" of certain sections of the border, but the Chinese delegation laid claim to over 1,500,000 sq km (580,000 square miles) of Soviet territory, while stating that China would not press her claims for the present. According to the Chinese version, the Chinese delegation, while regarding the Treaties of Aigun and Beijing as "unequal treaties", offered to take them as a basis for determining the entire alignment of the boundary, subject to "necessary readjustments" at individual places on the boundary by both sides, but the Soviet delegation refused to accept these proposals. Although it was agreed in principle to resume the talks in Moscow at a later date, no further negotiations took place until 1969.

The controversy was revived by an interview given by Chairman Mao on July 10, 1964, to a group of Japanese Socialists, at which he said: "China has not yet asked the Soviet Union for an account about Vladivostok, Khabarovsk, Kamchatka and other towns and regions east of Lake Baikal, which became Russian territory about 100 years ago". (Kamchatka was colonized by the Russians in the early 18th century, and never formed part of the Chinese empire). *Pravda* printed the interview on Sept. 2, together with a long editorial which accused China of "an openly expansionist programme with far-reaching pretensions", citing the *Short History of Modern China* published in 1954 as evidence, and gave warning that "any attempt to recarve the map of the world" could lead to "the most dangerous consequences".

In an interview with a Japanese delegation on Sept. 15, 1964, Khrushchev pointed out that the Chinese Emperors had acquired Inner Mongolia, Manchuria, Tibet and Xinjiang, with their non-Chinese populations, by conquest, and suggested that if "Mao Zedong wishes to settle political questions not on a political but on an ethnographical basis" China should grant her non-Chinese people the right of self-determination.

Border Tensions, 1966-67

In a letter sent to the other Communist parties of Eastern Europe early in 1966 the Soviet party accused China of provoking border conflicts, which, it stated, had increased in recent months, and of spreading allegations that "the Soviet Union unlawfully holds Chinese territory in the Far East". In reply the Chinese Foreign Minister, Marshal Chen Yi, accused the Soviet Union on May 20 of provoking over 5,000 incidents between 1960 and the end of 1965, and of concentrating troops on the Chinese frontier. He also alleged that the Soviet Union had rejected a Chinese proposal to settle frontier disputes on the basis of the treaties concluded between China and the Tsars, and had "insisted on going beyond these unjust treaties".

The tension on the borders greatly increased with the beginning of the Cultural Revolution in China in the summer of 1966. It was reported from Moscow on Oct. 2, 1966, that an estimated 2,000,000 Chinese had taken part in mass demonstrations on the Soviet frontier, especially in the Far Eastern sector, in support of China's territorial claims, and that Chinese troops had opened fire several times on Soviet ships plying on the Amur. The situation became particularly tense in January and February 1967, when for over a fortnight the Soviet embassy in Beijing was besieged by howling mobs. Beijing radio asserted on Feb. 2 that a plot by the "Soviet revisionists and US and Japanese imperialists" to attack China through Manchuria had been smashed, and on Feb. 11 all Chinese frontier troops were placed on the alert. Western sources estimated the number of troops on the frontier at this time at nearly 40 Soviet divisions, many of which had recently been transferred there from Eastern Europe, and between 50 and 60 Chinese divisions, or more than 600,000 men. The tension relaxed after Feb. 12, 1967, when the siege of the Soviet embassy was lifted, and on Feb. 21 it was reported from Moscow that except for frontier guards all Chinese troops had been withdrawn about 100 miles from the Soviet and Mongolian borders.

The Fighting on Damansky Island

Many minor border incidents were believed to have taken place in the later months of 1967 and in 1968, but neither side gave them any publicity at the time. According to later Chinese and Soviet statements, fighting took place on several occasions around a small uninhabited island in the Ussuri, known to the Russians as Damansky Island and to the Chinese as Zhenbao Island, lying about 110 miles south of Khabarovsk and 250 miles north of Vladivostok.

The status of the island under the Treaties of Aigun and Beijing is disputed. The Soviet Union maintained that a map approved by both governments in 1861 showed the Chinese bank of the Ussuri as the boundary line in this area. The Chinese Foreign Ministry, on the other hand, contended that the map had been drawn unilaterally by the Russian authorities; that the island was situated on the Chinese side of the central line of the river's main channel, which under international law formed the boundary line; and that it had formed part of the bank on the Chinese side until eroded by the river, had always been under Chinese jurisdiction and had been admitted to be Chinese by the Soviet delegation at the 1964 boundary negotiations. The problem was complicated by the fact that after the breaking up of the ice in spring the Ussuri regularly floods its banks and frequently shifts its channel.

Armed clashes between Soviet and Chinese frontier guards, of which the two sides gave contradictory accounts, occurred on the island in March 1969, causing considerable loss of life. According to the Soviet version, about 300 Chinese soldiers crossed the frozen river to the island during the night of March 1-2, opened fire in the morning on Soviet frontier guards, and were expelled only after a two-hour battle in which the Soviet troops lost 31 killed. Chinese official statements, however, declared that a large Soviet force had opened fire on Chinese frontier guards on normal patrol duty, killing and wounding many of them.

Fighting on a much larger scale broke out on March 15, 1969, and continued for several hours, causing heavy casualties; Soviet press reports mentioned by name 12 officers and NCOs, including a colonel, who had been killed, suggesting that a full regiment of frontier guards and reserves had been engaged on the Soviet side. Sporadic incidents continued on the islands in the Ussuri and the Amur throughout the spring and summer, and caused a few casualties on each side.

Proposals for New Negotiations

A Soviet note of March 29, 1969, after reaffirming the Soviet claim to Damansky Island, urged the Chinese government "to refrain from any actions on the frontier that may cause complications and to solve any differences that may arise in a calm atmosphere", and proposed that the consultations started in 1964 should be resumed as soon as possible. At the suggestion of the Soviet chairman of the joint Sino-Soviet commission on navigation on the Far Eastern frontier rivers, the commission met in Khabarovsk from June 18 to Aug. 8, 1969, when an agreement was reached on measures for ensuring normal conditions for shipping on the Amur and Ussuri. The situation subsequently remained peaceful on this section of the frontier.

A long Chinese statement issued on May 24, 1969, after summarizing the Chinese case on the Damansky Island question, declared that "there exists a boundary question between China and the Soviet Union not only because Tsarist Russia annexed more than 1,500,000 sq km (580,000 square miles) of Chinese territory by the unequal treaties it imposed on China but also because it crossed in many places the boundary line stipulated by the unequal treaties and further occupied vast expanses of Chinese territory", and continued: "In the sector of the Wusuli (Ussuri) and Heilung (Amur) rivers the Soviet government, in violation of the Treaty of Aigun, the Treaty of Beijing and the established principles of international law, had gone so far as to draw the boundary line almost entirely along the Chinese bank, and in some places even on China's inland rivers and islands, marking as Soviet territory over 600 of the 700 and more Chinese islands on the Chinese side of the central line of the main channel, which cover an area of more than 1,000 sq km."

After contending that the treaties relating to the present Sino-Soviet boundary were all "unequal treaties", that they should all be annulled and that the boundary question remained an outstanding issue, the statement concluded: "Taking into consideration the fact that it was Tsarist Russian imperialism which compelled China to sign these treaties ... and that large numbers of Soviet working people have lived on the land over a long period of time, the Chinese government, out of the desire to safeguard the revolutionary friendship between the Chinese and Soviet peoples, is still ready to take these unequal treaties as the basis for determining the entire alignment of the boundary line between the two countries and for settling all existing questions relating to the boundary. Any side which occupies the territory of the other side in violation of the treaties must, in principle, return it wholly and unconditionally to the other side, and this brooks no ambiguity. ...The Chinese government maintains that what should be done is to hold negotiations for the overall settlement of the Sino-Soviet boundary question and the conclusion of a new equal treaty to replace the old unequal ones."

The Soviet government's reply, issued on June 13, 1969, commented on the question of "unequal treaties": "Neither the appeal of 1919 nor the agreement between the Soviet Union and the Chinese Republic of 1924 contained, or could contain, indications that the treaties laying down the present Soviet-Chinese borders were regarded as unequal or secret. Naturally there was no question of annulling or revising them, Until recently the leaders of the People's Republic of China had themselves stressed that the Soviet state had abolished unequal treaties with China." Its proposals for future negotiations were as follows: "The Soviet Union proposes that the unanimity of the two sides on the undisputed stretches of the frontier be recorded; that an understanding be reached on individual disputed stretches of the frontier through mutual consultations on the basis of treaty documents; that the two sides should proceed on the basis of the treaties in force, observing the principle of mutual concessions and the economic interests of the local population when delimiting the frontier line on stretches which have undergone natural changes; and that the agreement reached should be recorded by the two sides signing appropriate documents." In conclusion, it suggested that the consultations broken off in 1964 should be resumed in Moscow within the next two or three months.

Agreement between Alexei Kosygin and Zhou Enlai

Meanwhile a series of incidents on the Central Asian border, for which each side held the other responsible, had begun in April 1969 and continued throughout the next three months, culminating in fighting on Aug. 13 which resulted in casualties on both sides. Tension reached such a height that on Aug. 23 the Chinese Communist Party issued a statement declaring that war might break out at any time. The situation was transformed, however, by the death on Sept. 3, 1969, of President Ho Chi Minh of North Vietnam and by the publication of his political testament, in which he appealed for "the restoration of unity among the fraternal parties". After attending his funeral the Soviet Prime Minister, Alexei Kosygin, flew to Beijing on Sept. 11, where he met Zhou Enlai. As a result of this meeting the two sides agreed to reopen border talks.

The exact terms of the agreement reached between them subsequently became a subject of controversy. According to Soviet sources, it was agreed to take measures to avoid armed conflicts on the border, to settle border questions through negotiations, and to take steps to normalize relations between them, such as the restoration of diplomatic relations at ambassadorial level and the expansion of trade. According to the Chinese version, the two prime ministers compared Soviet and Chinese maps, established which parts of the frontier were in dispute, and agreed to withdraw their armed forces from these areas and to conclude an agreement on the preservation of the status quo on the border.

A Chinese statement of Oct. 7, 1969, announcing that it had been agreed to hold talks on the border question said: "The responsibility for the development of the Sino-Soviet boundary question to such an acute state does not all rest with the Chinese side. The Chinese government has never demanded the return of the territory Tsarist Russia had annexed by means of the unequal treaties. On the contrary, it is the Soviet government that has persisted in occupying still more Chinese territory in violation of the stipulations of these treaties and, moreover, peremptorily demanded that the Chinese government recognize such occupation as legal. Precisely because of the Soviet government's persistence in its expansionist stand, many disputed areas have been created along the Sino-Soviet border, and this has become the root cause of tension on the border."

Further Boundary Negotiations, 1969-78

Negotiations on the border opened at Deputy Foreign Minister level in Beijing on Oct. 20, 1969, and continued with a number of breaks until June 1978. No progress was made, as the Soviet delegation rejected the Chinese demand for the withdrawal of troops from disputed areas, on the ground that the border line shown on Chinese maps did not coincide with that defined by the treaty documents. The Soviet delegation proposed in 1971 and again in 1973 that the two countries should sign a non-aggression pact; this was rejected as unnecessary by the Chinese side, which pointed out that the treaty of 1950 still remained in force, and demanded that the Soviet side should carry out the alleged agreement to withdraw its forces from the disputed areas.

In support of their claim that disputed areas existed, Chinese officials in Xinjiang told Western journalists that 20 areas along the Xinjiang border, varying in size from 390 to 11,600 square miles (1,000 to 30,000 sq km), were in dispute, and that Soviet troops had gradually occupied 185 square miles of Chinese territory during 1960-69 and another 1,080 square miles between 1972 and July 1977. The areas in question are largely desert, and are uninhabited or sparsely inhabited.

In the Far Eastern sector of the border, territorial disputes concerned mainly islands in the Ussuri and the Amur. Agreement on one disputed point was reached at a session of the Sino-Soviet joint commission for navigation on the frontier rivers in 1977. The Treaty of Beijing defines the boundary as following the Amur to its junction with the Ussuri and then turning south along the Ussuri. At the junction of the two rivers there is a triangular island with an area of 128 square miles, which is bounded by the Amur to the north, a narrow watercourse to the south-west and a broader one to the south-east. The ownership of the island is disputed, as the Soviet Union holds that the confluence lies west of the island and that the two watercourses are arms of the Amur, whereas the Chinese maintain that the confluence is east of the island, at Khabarovsk, and that the watercourses are arms of the Ussuri. The agreement, which did not deal with the question of ownership of the island, provided that Chinese shipping might use the eastern watercourse when the water in the other was too low for navigation.

Three comparatively minor frontier incidents occurred during 1978-80. In the first, Soviet border guards crossed to the Chinese bank of the Ussuri on May 9, 1978; according to the official Soviet apology, they had mistaken the Chinese bank for a Soviet island while pursuing an armed criminal by night, and withdrew on realizing their mistake. In the second, a Chinese was shot dead and another wounded and taken prisoner by Soviet frontier troops on the Xinjiang border on July 16, 1979; the two governments disagreed on whether the incident occurred on Soviet or Chinese territory and whether the two Chinese were soldiers or civilians. In the third, a Chinese and a Soviet citizen were killed in a clash on the Argun river, which forms the border between Siberia and western Manchuria, on Oct. 5, 1980; the two governments issued contradictory accounts of the incident, which disagreed on which side had opened fire.

Inconclusive 1979 Talks in Moscow and Subsequent Developments

In accordance with the terms of the Sino-Soviet treaty of alliance of 1950, China gave notice on April 3, 1979, of its intention not to extend the treaty when it expired a year later, but proposed that negotiations should be held for the solution of outstanding issues and the improvement of relations between the two countries. After an exchange of notes and five preliminary meetings, talks formally opened in Moscow on Oct. 17, 1979, and continued until Nov. 30. According to unofficial reports, the Chinese delegation repeated its demand for the withdrawal of troops from disputed areas, and also called for the reduction of the strength of the Soviet troops on the frontier and their withdrawal from Outer Mongolia. Following the Soviet intervention in Afghanistan, the Chinese government stated on Jan. 19, 1980, that it would be "inappropriate" to hold the second round of talks at present.

Further proposals for a settlement of the border question were put forward in an article by Li Huichuan, deputy leader of the Chinese delegation to the 1979 Moscow talks, which appeared in *The People's Daily* on June 17, 1981. The article was published on the day that Alexander Haig, then US Secretary of State, left Beijing after talks at which no agreement was reached on the question of US sales of weapons to Taiwan, and was widely regarded as a warning to the United States that China might seek to improve her relations with the Soviet Union. A few days later Li Xiannian (a Vice-Chairman of the Communist Party) told a West German delegation that China wanted to resume negotiations on the normalization of relations, but that the talks must deal with the withdrawal of Soviet troops from the Chinese border and from Afghanistan.

In his article, Li Huichuan stated that the Chinese government was prepared to take the existing treaties, "unequal" though they were, as the basis for determining the border line. Articles in the Soviet press, however, maintained that the present border had not only been delimited by the treaties, but had been "formed historically" and was "actually guarded" by Soviet troops, and the Soviet government demanded that the "historically formed" and "actually defended" boundary line, which went far beyond that delimited by the treaties, should be taken as the basis for solving all boundary questions. In conclusion, Li Huichuan laid down the following conditions for a settlement: (i) the "unequal" nature of the treaties should be recognized; (ii) the boundary question should be settled through peaceful negotiations on the basis of the treaties; (iii) any territory occupied by either side in violation of the treaties must be returned, although adjustments might be made in these areas in the interests of the local inhabitants; (iv) a new treaty should be signed and the boundary line surveyed and demarcated; and (v) pending the reaching of a settlement the status quo should be maintained, armed conflicts should be avoided, the two countries' forces should withdraw from or refrain from entering all disputed areas (i.e. those at which the boundary line was drawn in a different way on the maps exchanged during the boundary negotiations in 1964), and an agreement on the maintenance of the status quo should be signed.

Chinese Condemnation of 1981 Soviet-Afghan Border Treaty

A new source of friction in Sino-Soviet relations arose in June 1981 when the Soviet Union signed a border treaty with Afghanistan which recognized as Soviet territory an area to the north-east of Afghanistan to which China laid claim. The signature of the treaty, on June 16, 1981, coincided with Soviet military occupation of the strategically important Wakhan salient (the narrow strip of Afghan territory running eastwards to the Chinese border between Soviet territory to the north and Pakistan to the south) and gave rise to suspicions in China and the West that the treaty provided for Soviet annexation of the salient.

Although no exact details of the treaty were published either by the Soviet Union or Afghanistan, official comments from both sides indicated that it provided only for the legal delimitation and affirmation of the existing boundary between the two countries. Nevertheless, the Chinese Foreign Ministry on July 22 declared the treaty "illegal and invalid", arguing that the Soviet Union had no right to conclude a border treaty with a third country involving this line, since the territory immediately to the north had been in dispute between Beijing and Moscow for some 90 years. At the same time China stressed that it had no outstanding territorial disputes with Afghanistan itself, with which it had signed an agreement in November 1963 regulating the 43-mile (70-km) Chinese-Afghan border at the eastern end of the Wakhan salient.

China's case against the Soviet Union rested on an 1884 protocol "concerning the Chinese-Russian border in the region of Kashgar" (officially described by China as the "Sino-Russian Kashgar boundary treaty"). This agreement, which had been reached after a long period of Russian penetration into central Asia, had specified that from the Uz-Bel mountain pass in the Pamirs "the Russian boundary turns to the south-west and the Chinese boundary runs due south". According to Chinese accounts, the Russians had nevertheless in the 1890s proceeded to occupy some 20,000 square kilometres of Chinese territory by armed force and had subsequently attempted to legitimize this encroachment by describing a Chinese-Soviet exchange of notes in 1894 as a border treaty regulating the issue. According to China, however, the 1894 exchange of notes showed that the two sides had agreed to differ over the sovereignty of the area in question and had decided to maintain the status quo pending a permanent settlement.

The Soviet news agency Tass responded to the Chinese assertions on Aug. 11, 1981, by stating that the new Soviet-Afghan border treaty was a bilateral matter involving no third countries and by accusing China of "falsifying history" in order to invent a dispute over a question which had been finally settled in 1894. There was "no other line" than that determined in 1894, continued Tass, as demonstrated by the fact that the border in question was shown on Chinese maps exactly as on Soviet maps. This claim was in turn rejected by China on Aug. 31 as a "deliberate misrepresentation", in that the Chinese government had consistently made known its view that the frontier in the Pamirs was not finally delineated and that a dispute existed which had yet to be settled.

Talks on Normalization of Relations

In a note of Sept. 25, 1981, the Soviet government proposed that border negotiations should be resumed in Moscow. A Chinese official spokesman said on Dec. 29 that China had recently replied to the proposal, emphasizing that as previous negotiations had been unsuccessful adequate preparations should be made before they could be resumed. Subsequently, Sergei Tikhvinsky, deputy leader of the Soviet delegation to the Moscow talks, was reported to have arrived in Beijing on Jan. 14, 1982, for 10 days of secret talks with Chinese Foreign Ministry officials. The Soviet government again proposed on Feb. 3, 1982, that the border talks should be resumed, although a Foreign Ministry spokesman said on Feb. 23 that the Soviet Union did not intend to discuss "territorial questions". However, the Soviet approaches apparently met with a cold reception, as demonstrated when Wang Bingnan, president of the Chinese Association for Friendship with Foreign Countries, said on Feb. 23 that relations could not be improved unless the Soviet Union renounced its "policy of hegemonism and expansionism" and withdrew its troops from Afghanistan.

Leonid Brezhnev, then the Soviet President and Communist Party General Secretary, repeated the Soviet offer to reopen border talks in a speech in Tashkent on March 24, 1982, in which he also made a strong appeal for the normalization of relations between the two countries. "There has not been and there is no threat to the PRC [People's Republic of China] from the Soviet Union", he said. "We have not had and do not have any territorial claims on the PRC, and we are ready at any time to continue talks on existing border questions for the purpose of reaching mutually acceptable decisions. We are also ready to discuss the matter of possible measures to strengthen mutual trust in the Soviet-Chinese border area."

Chinese spokesmen during this period repeatedly identified the three major obstacles to improved Sino-Soviet relations as (i) the deployment of large numbers of Soviet troops on the Chinese border and in Mongolia, (ii) the Soviet intervention in Afghanistan and (iii) Soviet support for the Vietnamese occupation of Kampuchea (Cambodia). Chinese statements alleged that 1,000,000 Soviet troops were stationed on or near the border; Japanese military sources, however, estimated the strength of the two countries' forces in the frontier areas as 450,000 Soviet and 1,500,000 Chinese troops. An article published in *Pravda* on May 20, 1982, criticized Chinese demands for "renunciation of support and assistance to the Mongolian People's Republic, the countries of Indo-China and Afghanistan, unilateral withdrawal of the armed forces of the Soviet Union from the border with the People's Republic of China and recognition of China's 'rights' to vast areas of the USSR", and commented that "the piling up of all sorts of preliminary conditions bordering on ultimatums in no way testifies to a desire on the part of the Chinese side to find a way out of the blind alley in which Soviet-Chinese relations are at the moment".

Talks at Deputy Foreign Minister level on normalization of relations took place in Beijing on Oct. 5-21, 1982, the Soviet delegation being led by Leonid Ilyichev, who had headed the Soviet delegation at the Beijing talks of 1970-78 and the Moscow talks of 1979, and the Chinese delegation by Qian Qichen. Although no official communiqué was issued, China was reported to have demanded the withdrawal of 600,000 troops from the border and to have raised the questions of Kampuchea and Afghanistan, while the Soviet delegation attempted to confine the talks to strictly bilateral matters. Both sides agreed to continue the consultations alternately in Moscow and Beijing.

Following President Brezhnev's death, Huang Hua (then the Chinese Foreign Minister), who represented China at his funeral in Moscow on Nov. 15, 1982, had talks with Andrei Gromyko, then the Soviet Foreign Minister. Their meeting was the highest-level encounter between Chinese and Soviet ministers since that between Zhou Enlai and Kosygin in 1969. On returning to Beijing on Nov. 18, Huang said that they had discussed ways of removing obstalces to the consultations between their deputies, and that he was optimistic about the prospects for them. Viktor Afanasyev, the editor of *Pravda*, stated on Nov. 16 that "the two sides might promise each other a reduction of military forces in border areas", and that the Soviet troops would eventually be withdrawn from Afghanistan.

A second round of talks took place in Moscow on March 1-15, 1983. According to Chinese sources, the Soviet delegation proposed the signing of a non-aggression pact and measures to restore confidence on the frontier, but refused to discuss Afghanistan or Kampuchea on the ground that these questions involved third countries. The Chinese delegation, on the other hand, held that the signing of such a pact would have little meaning unless the three main obstacles to normal relations were all removed. Before the third round of talks, which was held in Beijing on Oct. 6-30, 1983, a Chinese Foreign Ministry spokesman stated on Oct. 5 that the deployment by the Soviet Union of SS-20 missiles along the border should be included within "the three obstacles", as China hoped that the Soviet Union would reduce its troops along the border, including both conventional and nuclear weapons. Wu Xueqian, Huang Hua's successor as Foreign Minister, said on Dec. 7 that the talks had made no headway because of Moscow's refusal to discuss "the three obstacles". No progress was achieved on these issues at the next two rounds, held in Moscow on March 12-27, 1984, and in Beijing on Oct. 18-Nov. 3.

Mikhail Gorbachev, who was elected General Secretary of the Soviet Communist Party on March 11, 1985, stated on the same day that the Soviet Union would seek "a serious improvement in relations with China". While the sixth round of talks, held in Moscow on April 9-21, 1985, was in progress Deng Xiaoping, the veteran Chinese leader, said on April 17 that "it would be difficult for the Soviet Union to solve all three problems at once", and that the Vietnamese occupation of Kampuchea was the easiest to solve. Although no significant progress was achieved at this round or at the seventh, held in Beijing on Oct. 5-18, it was remarked that for the first time since the talks began the joint communiqué issued on Oct. 20 endorsed an improvement in political relations without explicitly linking it to resolution of "the three obstacles". During the eighth round, held in Moscow in April 1986, the Soviet Foreign Minister, Eduard Shevardnadze, proposed to Qian Qichen on April 14 that Gorbachev and Deng Xiaoping should meet for talks; a Chinese spokesman commented two days later that such a meeting would be unrealistic while "the three obstacles" remained.

Incident on Central Asian Border

The first serious border incident since 1980, a clash between Soviet and Chinese border guards in which a Chinese was killed, occurred on the frontier between Xinjiang and Kazakhstan on July 12, 1986. The Soviet government made a verbal protest on July 14, alleging that a Chinese patrol had entered Soviet territory and opened fire; this was denied by the Chinese Foreign Ministry three days later. After the incident had been reported for the first time by a Japanese newspaper on Aug. 22, the Chinese Foreign Ministry confirmed on the following day that "an isolated incident" had occurred, whilst a Soviet Foreign Ministry said that everything was now quiet on the border. The fact that both governments attempted to minimize the incident was regarded as evidence of their desire to improve relations.

Soviet Concession on Far Eastern Border Question

In a speech in Vladivostok on July 28, 1986, which the London *Financial Times* described as "the most determined attempt by the Soviet Union to improve relations with China since the momentous split in 1960", Gorbachev said that "the Soviet Union is prepared, at any time and at any level, to discuss with China additional measures for creating a good-neighbourly atmosphere". On specific points he stated that the Soviet Union was ready to discuss troop reductions with China; that the number of Soviet SS-20 missiles in Asia would not be increased, and that SS-20s removed from Europe would be liquidated and not transferred elsewhere; that "the question of withdrawing a substantial part of the Soviet troops from Mongolia is being examined jointly with the Mongolian leadership"; that six Soviet regiments would be withdrawn from Afghanistan before the end of the year; and that all the Soviet troops would be withdrawn once a political settlement had been reached.

Gorbachev also made an important concession on the Far Eastern border question in his Vladivostok speech, stating that the official border on the Amur and the Ussuri "might pass along the main ship channel". Elaborating on this point, Mikhail Kapitsa (a Soviet Deputy Foreign Minister) said on Aug. 7, 1986, that this meant that "a number of islands that in 1860 were considered Russian would be beyond the line of the main channel and therefore in the future be transferred to China". According to unofficial reports, the Soviet government had agreed to make this concession, which would involve acceptance of the Chinese claim to Damansky/Zhenbao Island, at earlier border talks, but only as part of a settlement of the whole border issue.

Wu Xuenqian told the Soviet chargé d'affaires on Aug. 13, 1986, that Gorbachev's proposals for improving Sino-Soviet relations, to which China attached importance, were welcome, but fell far short of removing the three major obstacles. He had evaded in particular the question of withdrawing Vietnamese troops from Kampuchea, an issue about which China was most concerned.

Resumption of Border Talks

The Soviet and Chinese Foreign Ministers, Shevardnadze and Wu Xueqian, held extensive discussions on normalizing relations and on international issues at the United Nations on Sept. 25, 1986, at which it was agreed to resume talks on border disputes at Deputy Foreign Minister level in 1987. This agreement was generally believed to have resulted from Gorbachev's initiative in his Vladivostok speech.

The ninth round of talks on normalizing relations was held in Beijing on Oct. 6-14, 1986, the Soviet delegation being led by Igor Rogachev, a Deputy Foreign Minister. At this round the Soviet delegation agreed for the first time to discuss Kampuchea, although Rogachev told the Chinese that China should hold direct talks with Vietnam on the matter, instead of asking the Soviet Union to put pressure on the Vietnamese. A communiqué issued at the end of the talks announced that it had been agreed to resume the boundary negotiations in Moscow in February 1987. In accordance with this agreement, the talks took place on Feb. 9-23, 1987, with the Soviet delegation being headed by Rogachev and the Chinese delegation by Qian Qichen, but no substantive progress was made. A further round of negotiations was held in Beijing on Aug. 7-17, 1987.

CH

China-Taiwan

Taiwan, officially the Republic of China, lies 150-200 kilometres off the south-east Chinese mainland coast and together with certain small islands controlled by the Republic has a total land area of 36,000 sq km and a population of some 19,000,000. Since December 1949 Taiwan has been the seat of the Kuomintang government which fled from mainland China following the Communists' civil war victory, and both regimes have since claimed to be the only legitimate government of all China. (For a map showing the teritorial relationship of China and Taiwan, see page 287.)

Early and Post-War History

The island of Taiwan (also known as Formosa) was occupied in 1624 by the Dutch, who encouraged immigration from China in order to develop its agricultural resources. Supporters of the Ming dynasty, which had been overthrown by the Manchu invaders in 1644, expelled the Dutch in 1661 and used the island as a base for operations against the mainland until 1683, when it was conquered by the Manchus and incorporated into the Chinese empire. Immigration continued throughout the 18th century, and by 1800 the Chinese population far outnumbered the aboriginal inhabitants.

After the Sino-Japanese War of 1894-95 Japan annexed Taiwan and the Pescadores (also known as the Penghu Islands), a group of 48 small islands 30 miles (48 km) west of Taiwan, which had been under Chinese rule since 1281. The 1943 Cairo Declaration issued by Britain, the United States and China laid down that the territories taken from China by Japan should be restored to Chinese sovereignty after the defeat of Japan, and in 1945 the Chinese government took over the administration of Taiwan and the Pescadores pending the conclusion of a peace treaty. Although this change was initially welcomed in Taiwan, the corruption of the new administration led to a serious revolt in 1947.

On the mainland the civil war between the ruling Kuomintang and the Communists culminated in the proclamation of the People's Republic of China in Beijing on Oct. 1, 1949, and the Kuomintang government fled on Dec. 8 from Chengdu, to which it had transferred its capital, to Taiwan, where it established its new capital at Taipeh. It was followed by over

1,500,000 refugees, including about 750,000 members of the armed forces. Since then two regimes have both claimed to be the only legitimate Chinese government—the People's Republic of China, controlling the mainland and 99.7 per cent of Chinese territory, and the Republic of China, controlling Taiwan and a number of offshore islands. Although Hainan, the largest of these, was occupied by the Communists in April 1950, the Kuomintang retained control of (i) the Pescadores; (ii) Quemoy, an island 12 miles (19 km) across, lying about four miles off the mainland port of Xiamen (Amoy), and three smaller islands nearby; (iii) Matsu, off Fuzhou (Foochow); (iv) the Nanchi Islands, about 130 miles (210 km) north of Taiwan; and (v) the Tachen Islands, off the coast of Zhejiang (Chekiang) province, about 200 miles (320 km) north of Taiwan. The Taiwan government also maintained a garrison on Itu Aba, one of the Spratly Islands,[1] in the South China Sea. Gen. Chiang Kai-shek, who had headed the Kuomintang government of China since the late 1920s, became President of Taiwan and retained this post until his death in April 1975.

The People's Republic of China was immediately recognized by the Communist countries, and by January 1950 had also been recognized by 11 other European and Asian countries, including Britain. The process of international recognition, however, was delayed by the outbreak of the Korean War and China's intervention in it. Resolutions in favour of the admission of the People's Republic to the United Nations were submitted annually to the General Assembly from 1950 onwards, but were regularly defeated up to 1969. In consequence, China continued to be represented in the United Nations by the Taiwan government, which held the status of a permanent member of the Security Council, with the right to veto any decision.

Japan renounced all claims to Taiwan and the Pescadores by the peace treaty signed at San Francisco in September 1951, but the treaty did not define to which Chinese government they belonged, and was denounced by both the Chinese governments, neither of which had been invited to the San Francisco conference. In 1952, however, Japan signed a separate peace treaty with the Taiwan government, a document which recognized all residents of Taiwan and the Pescadores who were of Chinese nationality as "nationals of the Republic of China".

The Kuomintang government announced in June 1949 a blockade of all that part of the Chinese coast and territorial waters then under Communist control, which after its withdrawal to Taiwan it extended to the whole coast of mainland China. The blockade led to a number of attacks by Kuomintang warships and aircraft on British and US shipping. On June 27, 1950, two days after the outbreak of the Korean War, President Truman announced that he had ordered the US Seventh Fleet to prevent any attack on Taiwan; that he was calling upon the Taiwan government to cease all air and sea operations against the mainland; and that "the Seventh Fleet will see that this is done". His successor, President Eisenhower, however, announced on Feb. 2, 1953, in his first State of the Union message to Congress, that he had issued instructions that 'the Seventh Fleet shall no longer be employed to shield Communist China".

Zhou Enlai, then Prime Minister of the People's Republic, stated on Aug. 11, 1954, that the "liberation" of Taiwan was an affair that concerned the Chinese people only, and that any attempt by foreign powers to resist it would constitute an infringement on China's sovereignty. John Foster Dulles, then the US Secretary of State, declared on Aug. 24 that the Seventh Fleet would protect Taiwan against any attack from the mainland, as well as other islands the defence of which was intimately connected with that of Taiwan. In defiance of this warning, the Chinese army began a heavy bombardment of Quemoy on Sept. 3, 1954, to which Kuomintang warships and aircraft replied by attacking military targets on the mainland. A mutual security treaty between the United States and the Taiwan government was signed on Dec. 1, 1954, under which the United States undertook to defend Taiwan, the Pescadores and "such other territories as may be determined by mutual agreement" against any armed attack. The Taiwan government gave an undertaking on Dec. 10 that it would not

---

[1]For an account of the Spratly Islands dispute, see pages 374-76.

attack the mainland without prior consultation with the government of the United States.

The small island of Yikiangshan, situated eight miles (13 km) north of the Tachen Islands, was captured by Communist forces on Jan. 18, 1955, and after heavy air attacks the Kuomintang forces evacuated the Tachen and Nanchi Islands in February of that year. At President Eisenhower's request, a resolution authorizing him to employ the armed forces to protect Taiwan and the Pescadores, as well as "such related positions and territories of that area now in friendly hands" as he judged to be appropriate, was adopted by the House of Representatives on Jan. 25 and by the Senate three days later.

The bombardment of the Quemoy group of islands was resumed after a long interval on Aug. 23, 1958. A declaration issued on Sept. 4 of that year extended the limit of China's territorial waters from three to 12 nautical miles, and stated that no foreign warships or aircraft might enter Chinese territorial waters and the airspace above them without permission from Beijing. Although the effect of the declaration was to bring the Quemoys and Matsu within the new 12-mile limit, US warships were used from Sept. 7 to escort supply convoys to Quemoy. The Chinese government suspended the bombardment on Oct. 6, and announced that supplies might be sent to Quemoy on condition that there was no US escort, but resumed the shelling on Oct. 20 on the ground that this condition had not been observed. From Oct. 25, however, shelling was confined to odd dates, to allow supplies to be brought in on alternate days.

Sporadic shelling continued over the next 20 years, although during the latter part of this period the shells largely contained propaganda leaflets. Communist leaders continued to announce their determination to "liberate" Taiwan and Kuomintang leaders their determination to "liberate" the mainland, but neither side made any serious attempt to carry out its threats. Occasional clashes occurred, however, including periodic raids on the coast by Kuomintang commandos and a naval engagement in the Taiwan Strait in 1965 in which each side claimed to have inflicted serious damage on the other.

The People's Republic gradually emerged from its isolation, despite its strained relations with the Soviet bloc after 1960 and the damage to its international reputation caused by attacks on foreign embassies during the Cultural Revolution. During the later 1950s and the 1960s it was recognized by an increasing number of countries, including Egypt in 1956, France in 1964 and Italy in 1970. The 1970 session of the General Assembly voted in favour of the admission of the People's Republic to the United Nations by 51 votes to 49, with 25 abstentions, but the resolution remained inoperative, as the Assembly had previously passed a resolution declaring the Chinese representation issue an 'important question" requiring a two-thirds majority for its adoption.

Impact of US Recognition of Communist China

The dramatic improvement in relations between the People's Republic and the United States from 1971 onwards transformed relations between the People's Republic and Taiwan and between both and the outside world. After it had been announced on July 15, 1971, that President Nixon had accepted an invitation to visit the People's Republic, William Rogers (then Secretary of State) said on Aug. 2 that the United States would support the admission of the People's Republic to the United Nations, while opposing "any action to expel the Republic of China or otherwise deprive it of representation in the United Nations". The General Assembly, however, rejected on Oct. 25, 1971, a US "important question" resolution, and adopted an Albanian resolution recognizing the representatives of the People's Republic as "the only lawful representatives of China to the United Nations" by 76 votes to 35, with 17 abstentions. The People's Republic in consequence replaced the Republic of China (Taiwan) in the General Assembly and the Security Council.

President Nixon paid an official visit to China on Feb. 21-27, 1972, at the conclusion of which he and Zhou Enlai issued a long communiqué in Shanghai. On the Taiwan question this stated: "The Chinese side reaffirmed its position: the Taiwan question is the crucial question obstructing the normalization of relations between China and the United States;

the government of the People's Republic of China is the sole legal government of China; Taiwan is a province of China which has long been returned to the motherland; the liberation of Taiwan is China's internal affair in which no other country has the right to interfere; and all US forces and military installations must be withdrawn from Taiwan. The Chinese government firmly opposes any activities which aim at the creation of 'one China, one Taiwan', 'one China, two governments', 'two Chinas' and 'independent Taiwan', or advocate that 'the status of Taiwan remains to be determined'. The US side declared: The United States acknowledges that all Chinese on either side of the Taiwan Strait maintain that there is but one China and that Taiwan is a part of China. The US government does not challenge that position. It reaffirms its interest in a peaceful settlement of the Taiwan question by the Chinese themselves. With this prospect in mind, it affirms the ultimate objective of the withdrawal of all US forces and military installations from Taiwan. In the meantime, it will progressively reduce its forces and military installations on Taiwan as the tension in the area diminishes."

President Nixon's visit was followed by the recognition of the People's Republic by several major states, including Japan, West Germany, Australia, New Zealand and Spain. During a visit to Beijing in September 1972 the then Japanese Prime Minister, Kakuei Tanaka, signed a joint statement with Zhou Enlai recognizing the government of the People's Republic as the sole legal government of China, and stating that the Japanese government "fully understands and respects" the Chinese government's stand that "Taiwan is an inalienable part of the territory of the People's Republic of China". By July 1974 the People's Republic was recognized by 95 countries, and Taiwan by only 33.

The United States and the People's Republic agreed in 1973 to establish liaison offices in each other's capitals. The movement towards normalization of relations, which developed slowly during the next four years, made rapid progress in 1978, and coincided with a marked softening in the Chinese government's attitude towards Taiwan. In a speech to the National People's Congress on Feb. 26, 1978, Hua Guofeng, then the Prime Minister, declared that "the Chinese People's Liberation Army must make all the preparations necessary for the liberation of Taiwan", but also stated that "it has been our consistent policy that 'all patriots belong to one big family, whether they come over early or late'." A senior Chinese official assured a visiting US Congressman in July 1978 that Beijing did not rule out a negotiated settlement with the Taiwan regime, as the Communist Party and the Kuomintang had worked together in 1924-27 and again during the war with Japan. Deng Xiaoping, then the senior Deputy Premier, told *The New York Times* on Nov. 29 that China would seek a negotiated settlement which took into account the fact that Taiwan's political system differed from that of the mainland, although it would not enter into any pledge to abstain from the use of force, as such a pledge would make the Taiwan authorities refuse to negotiate.

It was announced on Dec. 15, 1978, that the People's Republic and the United States had agreed to recognize each other and to establish diplomatic relations from Jan. 1, 1979. The joint communiqué said: "The USA recognizes the government of the People's Republic of China as the sole legal government of China. Within this context, the people of the USA will maintain cultural, commercial and other unofficial relations with the people of Taiwan. ... The government of the USA acknowledges the Chinese position that there is but one China and Taiwan is part of China."

The two governments at the same time issued statements defining their respective positions on the Taiwan question. The US statement, after announcing that the mutual defence treaty of 1954 would be terminated and that the remaining US military personnel would be withdrawn from Taiwan within four months, emphasized that "the USA continues to have an interest in the peaceful resolution of the Taiwan issue, and expects that the Taiwan issue will be settled peacefully by the Chinese themselves". The Chinese statement said: "The question of Taiwan was the crucial issue obstructing the normalization of relations between China and the USA. It has now been resolved between the two countries in the spirit of the Shanghai communiqué. ... As for the way of bringing Taiwan back to the embrace of the

303

motherland and reunifying the country, it is entirely China's internal affair." President Chiang Ching-kuo of Taiwan commented on Dec. 16, 1978: "Under whatever circumstances, the Republic of China will neither negotiate with the Chinese Communist regime nor compromise with communism, and she will never give up her sacred tasks of recovering the mainland and delivering the compatriots there."

The shelling of Quemoy and Matsu was officially terminated on Jan. 1, 1979, when the Standing Committee of the National People's Congress proposed that the military confrontation between the People's Republic and Taiwan should be "ended through discussion". President Chiang, however, declared on the same day that "our anti-Communist struggle will never cease until the Chinese Communist regime has been destroyed".

The American Institute in Taiwan was incorporated on Jan. 16, 1979, to enable the US and Taiwanese peoples to maintain commercial, cultural and other relations without official government representation or diplomatic relations, and on Feb. 15 the Taiwan government announced the establishment of the Taiwan Co-ordination Council for North American Affairs to act as a liaison office in Washington. An agreement between the two organizations signed on Oct. 2, 1980, provided that they and their staffs would enjoy full diplomatic privileges and immunities. The People's Republic protested against the agreement in a note to Washington of Oct. 15.

Although no progress towards reunification was made during 1979-80, the leaders of the People's Republic continued to refer to the question in conciliatory terms, and ceased to speak of the "liberation" of Taiwan. In contrast to his speech of Feb. 26, 1978, Hua Guofeng merely said when addressing the National People's Congress on Sept. 7, 1980, that "we shall work energetically for the return of Taiwan to the motherland, fulfilling our lofty aim of unifying our homeland at an early date".

The People's Republic announced on April 4, 1980, that it had decided to abolish all customs duties on imports and exports between the mainland and Taiwan, on the ground that Taiwan was part of China. Although in theory exporting goods from Taiwan to China was punishable by severe penalties, trade between Taiwan and the mainland, conducted mainly through Hong Kong, Singapore or Japan, had greatly increased since 1978. According to Hong Kong government figures, the value of Taiwan's exports to China through the colony rose from US$41,000 in 1978 to US$22,000,000 in 1979 and US$222,000,000 in 1980.

The Taiwan Independence Movement

After the flight of the Kuomintang government to Taiwan in 1949 the Legislative *Yuan* (the Chinese Parliament established under the 1946 constitution) was established on the island as its supreme legislative body. As this body supposedly represents the whole of China, the members elected in 1948 to represent mainland constituencies continue to hold their seats, in theory until new elections can be organized on the mainland, which in practice means for life. and only in the Taiwan constituencies are elections held periodically. A similar situation exists in the National Assembly, a body with limited functions, including the election of the President and Vice-President and the adoption of amendments to the constitution.

The political domination of Taiwan by immigrants from the mainland, although they constituted only 13 per cent of the population, led to demands both for the democratization of the regime and for recognition of Taiwan as a state independent of China. An underground Taiwan Independence Movement, which called for self-determination for the island and rejected "all forms of dictatorship—Chinese, Communist or Kuomintang", was responsible for a number of bomb explosions between 1970 and 1976. Although it was effectively suppressed in Taiwan, many of its members being imprisoned as "rebels", it was reported in 1978 to be supported by many Taiwanese in Japan, where it had nearly 10,000 members, and in the United States. The American section of the movement, United

Formosans for Independence, was believed to be responsible for a series of bomb explosions in 1979 at offices of Taiwan government institutions in American cities.

The demand for Taiwanese independence received strong support from the Presbyterian Church, although it had no relations with the Independence Movement and condemned the use of terrorist methods. The church, which has about 200,000 members, published an open letter in 1977 calling for "effective measures whereby Taiwan may become a new and independent country", and appealing to the United States to "guarantee the independence, security and liberty of the people of Taiwan".

As opposition political parties were forbidden under the martial law code in force since 1949, opponents of the Kuomintang regime established during the 1970s a series of magazines which formed a rallying centre for their activities. A number of opposition leaders, including democrats and socialists as well as advocates of Taiwanese independence, founded in August 1979 the monthly *Formosa*, which pressed for a representative parliament, a free press, an amnesty for political prisoners and the ending of martial law, and within two months reached a circulation of over 100,000. After a demonstration organized by *Formosa* on Dec. 10, 1979, in the port of Kaohsiung to celebrate Human Rights Day developed into a riot (the seriousness of which, according to foreign observers, was deliberately exaggerated by the authorities), the magazine was banned. Eight leading dissidents associated with *Formosa* were found guilty on April 18, 1980, of having attempted to seize power and collaborated with exiled advocates of Taiwanese independence, and received sentences ranging from 12 years to life imprisonment.

During the next four years little was heard of the separatist movement, but on April 5, 1984, the Taiwan government declared the League of Formosan Independence a seditious organization, and stated that any activities in collusion with it would be regarded as illegal. The central standing committee of the Kuomintang approved on Oct. 15, 1986, a proposal by President Chiang Ching-kuo to lift martial law, but stipulated that new parties which advocated Taiwanese independence should not be permitted.

1981 Chinese Proposals for Reunification

In a major new development in late 1981, Marshal Ye Jianying (Chairman of the Standing Committee of the Chinese National People's Congress—a post equivalent to head of state) put forward detailed proposals for the peaceful reunification of China and Taiwan. Although the Chinese government had previously suggested that within a reunited China, Taiwan might retain full autonomy as well as its own armed forces and economic system, Marshal Ye's proposal was the first in which the Chinese Communist Party had officially offered to share power with the Kuomintang.

Marshal Ye's nine-point plan, which he put forward in an interview with the New China News Agency on Sept. 30, 1981, was formulated as follows: "(i) In order to bring an end to the unfortunate separation of the Chinese nation as early as possible, we propose that talks be held between the Communist Party of China and the Kuomintang of China on a reciprocal basis so that the two parties will co-operate for the third time to accomplish the great cause of national reunification. The two sides may first send people to meet for an exhaustive exchange of views. (ii) It is the urgent desire of the people of all nationalities on both sides of the straits to communicate with each other, reunite with their families and relatives, develop trade and increase mutual understanding. We propose that the two sides make arrangements to facilitate the exchange of mails, trade, air and shipping services, family reunions and visits by relatives and tourists, as well as academic cultural and sports exchanges, and reach an agreement thereon. (iii) After the country is reunified. Taiwan can enjoy a high degree of autonomy as a special administrative region, and can retain its armed forces. The central government will not interfere with local affairs on Taiwan. (iv) Taiwan's current socio-economic system will remain unchanged, as will its way of life and its economic and cultural relations with foreign countries. There will be no encroachment on the proprietary rights and lawful right of inheritance over private property, houses, land and enterprises, or on foreign investments. (v) People in authority and representative personages of various circles in Taiwan may take up posts of leadership in national political bodies and participate in running the state. (vi) When Taiwan's local finance is in difficulty, the central government may subsidize it as is fit for the circumstances. (vii) For people of all nationalities and public figures of various circles in Taiwan who wish to come and settle on the mainland, it is guaranteed that proper arrangements may be made for them, and there will be no discrimination against them, and that they will have freedom of entry and exit. (viii) Industrialists and businessmen in Taiwan are welcome to invest and engage in various economic undertakings on the mainland, and their legal rights, interests and profits are guaranteed. (ix) The reunification of the motherland is the responsibility of all Chinese. We sincerely welcome people of all nationalities, public figures of all circles and all mass organizations in Taiwan to make proposals and suggestions regarding affairs of state through various channels and in various ways."

Responding to Marshal Ye's proposals, Sun Yun-suan (Taiwan's Prime Minister) said in the Legislative Yuan on Oct. 2, 1981: "The nine-point overture of the Chinese Communists ... has not gone to the heart of the problem, which is whether China should adopt a free and democratic system or a totalitarian and dictatorial one. ... We implement benevolent rule, whereas the Chinese Communists enforce a tyrannical one, so there is no room for compromise." President Chiang Ching-kuo declared at a meeting of the central standing committee of the Kuomintang on Oct. 7: "We shall never negotiate with the Chinese Communists. ... I want to tell our compatriots on the Chinese mainland that we are resolved to remove the yoke that the Communists have imposed upon them."

Despite these rebuffs, Chinese spokesmen continued to elaborate on Marshal Ye's proposals. Peng Deqing, the Minister of Communications, said on Oct. 3, 1981, that his ministry was ready to establish regular passenger and cargo services with Taiwan by sea and air at any time. Zhen Tuobin, Minister of Foreign Trade, on Oct. 7 suggested measures for the expansion of trade between China and Taiwan whereby each would supply the other's needs; China, for example, could supply Taiwan with coal, oil and herbal medicines at preferential prices. Chang Yanqing, vice-president of the Bank of China, proposed on Oct. 10 that exchange transactions and settlement of accounts should be conducted through bank representatives in Hong Kong until direct transactions could be established, and stated that the bank was ready to open savings accounts for Chinese in Taiwan and to guarantee freedom to deposit and withdraw money.

Hu Yaobang, who had succeeded Hua Guofeng as Chairman of the Chinese Communist Party in June 1981, repeated the proposal for co-operation between the Kuomintang and the Communist Party on Oct. 9, in a speech to commemorate the 70th anniversary of the revolution of 1911, which overthrew the Ching dynasty and established the Chinese Republic. Chairman Hu said that the three great tasks confronting China were to modernize agriculture, industry, national defence, and science and technology, to defend world peace, and "to ensure Taiwan's return to the motherland". "The question of Taiwan is entirely China's internal affair", he continued. "It should be settled by the leaders and people on both sides of the strait. The Kuomintang and the Communist Party co-operated twice in history, to complete the northern expedition [in 1926-27] and conduct the war against Japanese aggression. This gave a strong impetus to our nation's progress. Why can we not have a third period of co-operation between the Kuomintang and the Communist Party to build a unified state? It is true that neither of the previous co-operations lasted long, but fair-minded people all admit that the two unfortunate splits were not caused by the Communist Party. We do not wish to settle old accounts here. Let bygones be bygones! Let the past lessons help us to co-operate better in the future!"

He continued: "There is nothing in our present proposal which is unfair or should cause anxiety to the Taiwan side. If the Taiwan side is still worried about something, it may raise questions for study and settlement in the course of negotiations. It is understandable for a certain distrust to exist as a result of long-term separation. But if we do not come into contact and talk things over, how can we remove the barriers and build up mutual trust?" In conclusion, he suggested that the late President Chiang Kai-shek's remains should be brought back to China for burial in his family cemetery, which had been kept in good repair, and invited President Chiang Ching-kuo, Sun Yun-suan and other Kuomintang leaders to visit the mainland, even if they did not wish to enter into talks for the time being. A Taiwan government spokesman described this invitation on the same day as "another joke".

Kuomintang Proposals for Reunification

At the 12th congress of the Kuomintang, held in April 1981, no reference was made to the reconquest of the mainland. Instead, the slogan put forward was "Unify China in accordance with the Three Principles of the People"—i.e. nationalism, democracy and "the people's livelihood", the three principles laid down by Dr Sun Yat-sen, the founder of the Kuomintang and first President of the Republic of China.

Sun Yun-suan elaborated on this slogan and replied to the Chinese government's reunification proposals in a speech of June 10, 1982, in which he suggested that peaceful reunification might become possible as a result of internal changes in Communist China. "The Chinese Communists' peace talks proposals", he said, "have two accompanying preconditions: (i) the government of the Republic of China is to be considered a 'provincial Government' under the jurisdiction of the Chinese Communist regime; (ii) the invasion of Taiwan by force is not ruled out if peace talks fail. In other words, this so-called peace proposal is actually an attempt to annex the Republic of China on Taiwan.

"Even the leadership of the Chinese Communist regime has been compelled to admit openly that mainland China cannot catch up with Taiwan economically", he went on. "The Chinese Communists have tacitly followed the successful experience of the Republic of China in seeking national development. They have imitated our free export processing zones by opening so-called 'special economic zones'. They have introduced foreign capital to help enlarge exports, and readjusted the order of economic construction by giving first priority to agriculture. They recently tried again to adjust the economic structure. While continuing to recognize 'ownership by the whole people' and 'collective ownership', they began in a small way to accept the 'individual economy' of urban and rural workers. All these changes are signs that the consistently dogmatic Chinese Communist regime has been compelled to bow to reality and make an about-face after a series of setbacks.

"In advocating the reunification of China on the basis of the Three Principles of the People we are not trying to embarrass the Chinese Communist regime", Sun declared. "As early as September 1937, soon after the outbreak of the Sino-Japanese War, the Chinese Communists announced: 'Dr Sun Yat-sen's Three Principles of the People are needed today in China, and this party is willing to help carry them out'. In recent years the Chinese Communists have often expressed their respect for Dr Sun Yat-sen. ... They have thus recognized the superiority of the Three Principles of the People. All freedom-loving Chinese sincerely hope that the Chinese Communists will truly return to and identify with Dr Sun Yat-sen's Three Principles of the People, and that they will take earnest action to implement the Three Principles. ... We believe that Chinese reunification should be based on the free will of the Chinese people as a whole. ... If the political, economic, social and cultural gaps between the Chinese mainland and free China continue to narrow, the conditions for peaceful reunification can gradually mature. The obstacles to reunification will be reduced naturally with the passage of time."

Adoption of New Chinese Constitution

A new Chinese constitution adopted by the National People's Congress (NPC) on Dec. 4, 1982, contained a number of passages intended to facilitate the reunification of China and Taiwan on the basis of autonomy for Taiwan. The preamble to the previous constitution, adopted in 1978, had declared: "Taiwan is China's sacred territory. We are determined to liberate Taiwan and accomplish the great cause of unifying our motherland." The corresponding passage of the new constitution, however, stated: "Taiwan is part of the sacred territory of the PRC [People's Republic of China]. It is the lofty duty of the entire Chinese people, including our compatriots in Taiwan, to accomplish the great task of reunifying the motherland." The phrase "liberate Taiwan" was thus omitted, and the possibility of reunifying China in co-operation with "our compatriots in Taiwan" recognized. Whereas the preamble to the 1978 constitution had referred only in general terms to the period of "more than a century of heroic struggle" preceding the Communist revolution of 1949, the 1982 constitution specifically mentioned that "the revolution of 1911, led by Dr Sun Yat-sen, abolished the feudal monarchy and gave birth to the Republic of China".

A completely new article in the constitution (Article 31) stated: "The state may establish special administrative regions when necessary. The systems to be instituted in special administrative regions shall be prescribed by law enacted by the NPC in the light of the specific conditions." Reporting on the work of the committee for the revision of the constitution to the NPC on Nov. 26, 1982, Peng Zhen, vice-chairman of the committee, said that Article 31 would allow Taiwan's current economic and social systems, way of life and economic and cultural relations with foreign countries to remain unchanged after peaceful reunification with the People's Republic.

The Hong Kong Agreement and the Reunification Question—Taiwan's Claim to Mongolia

The Chinese government's views on the form which a future reunification with Taiwan might take were reflected in an agreement with the British government on the future status of Hong Kong which was initialled on Sept. 26, 1984, after two years of negotiations. After receiving the approval of the Standing Committee of the NPC, the British Parliament and the Hong Kong Legislative Council, it was signed by the Chinese and British Prime Ministers in Beijing on Dec. 19, 1984.

Hong Kong Island, which together with adjacent islets have an area of 30.3 square miles (78.4 sq km), was ceded to Britain by China in perpetuity in 1842 by the Treaty of Nanking, signed after the First Opium War. Kowloon, on the mainland opposite, and Stonecutters Island, which together total 4.4 square miles (11.3 sq km), were ceded under the Treaty of Beijing in 1860 after the Second Opium War. The Chinese Communist government, like the Kuomintang government before it, had consistently repudiated the treaties of Nanking and Beijing as "unequal treaties" imposed upon China by force. The New Territories, comprising the hinterland of the Kowloon peninsula and 235 islands, with an area of 375.9 square miles (973.8 sq km), were leased to Britain for 99 years under the Convention of Beijing in 1898. China regarded this agreement as having been signed under duress, and before World War II consistently rejected British proposals for the cession of the territories. The lease was due to expire on June 30, 1997, when the New Territories (without which the economy of Hong Kong Island and Kowloon would not be viable) were due to revert to China.

The 1984 agreement provided that the Chinese government would resume the exercise of sovereignty over Hong Kong from July 1, 1997, and in accordance with Article 31 of the constitution would establish a Hong Kong Special Administrative Region. This would be directly under the authority of the Chinese government but would enjoy a high degree of autonomy, except in foreign and defence affairs, which were the Chinese government's responsibility. It would be vested with executive, legislative and independent judicial power, including that of final adjudication, and the laws currently in force in Hong Kong would remain basically unchanged. The government of Hong Kong would be composed of local inhabitants. "The current social and economic systems in Hong Kong will remain unchanged, and so will the lifestyle", the agreement continued. "Rights and freedoms, including those of the person, of speech, of the press, of assembly, of association, of travel, of movement, of correspondence, of strike, of choice of occupation, of academic research and of religious belief will be ensured by law in the Hong Kong Special Administrative Region.

Private property, ownership of enterprises, legitimate right of inheritance and foreign investment will be protected by law." Hong Kong would retain the status of a free port, a separate customs territory and an international financial centre; its markets for foreign exchange would continue; there would be free flow of capital; and the Hong Kong dollar would continue to circulate and remain freely convertible. Hong Kong would have independent finances, and the Chinese government would not levy taxes there. Hong Kong might maintain and develop economic and cultural relations and conclude relevant agreements with states, regions and relevant international organizations. The Hong Kong government might issue travel documents, and would be responsible for public order in the region. An annex to the agreement stated that the Basic Law of the Hong Kong Special Administrative Region, to be promulgated on July 1, 1997, would stipulate that "the socialist system and socialist policies shall not be practised" and that "Hong Kong's previous capitalist system and lifestyle shall remain unchanged for 50 years".

Zhao Ziyang, the Chinese Prime Minister, said on Sept. 30, 1984, that China was ready to open consultations with Taiwan on reunification, and announced that the "one country, two systems" strategy, which guaranteed the continuation of Hong Kong's economic system, would be applied to Taiwan. President Chiang Ching-kuo, however, described the Hong Kong agreement on Oct. 10 as "nothing but a fraud", and declared that "the Chinese Communists have no right to represent the Chinese people, and any accord bearing their signature is invalid".

The first official contact between Taiwan and China since 1949 occurred as a result of the defection to China on May 3, 1986, of the pilot of an aircraft of Taiwan's state-run China Air Line (CAL). Although CAL initially rejected a Chinese invitation to negotiate on the return of the aircraft and the two other members of its crew, Chinese and CAL officials finally held talks in Hong Kong on May 17-20, following which the aircraft and crew members were returned to Taiwan.

In a statement issued on Jan. 28, 1987, the Taiwan government reiterated its claim, as the legitimate government of China, to sovereignty over the People's Republic of Mongolia (formerly the Chinese province of Outer Mongolia). The statement recalled that the post-World War II Sino-Soviet agreement confirming the independence of the People's Republic of Mongolia had been abrogated by Taiwan in 1953.

CH

China-Vietnam

Major disputes between China and Vietnam have developed since 1975 over four territorial and boundary questions: (i) their common frontier, (ii) territorial waters in the Gulf of Tonkin, (iii) the Paracel Islands and (iv) the Spratly Islands.[1] In 1979 China and Vietnam fought a brief but fierce war in the border area, since when there have been periodic clashes and constant tensions between the two sides.

The Frontier Dispute

The Sino-Vietnamese frontier, 1,200 kilometres long, was defined by a convention between the French government, which then exercised a protectorate over Tonkin, and the

---

[1]The dispute over the Spratly Islands, which are claimed by Taiwan and the Philippines as well as by China and Vietnam, is described on pages 374-76.

Chinese empire signed in Peking in 1887. This was slightly modified by a second convention signed in 1895, stones being erected to mark the frontier. Under the conventions the frontier was not clearly delineated at certain points, where the population living on either side traditionally crossed it freely.

A Vietnamese memorandum of March 15, 1979, claimed that as France had wished to sign a trade agreement with China it had conceded some Vietnamese territory to China under the 1887 convention, and that before the Chinese Communists came to power in 1949 previous Chinese governments had "seized more than 60 places on Vietnamese territory". A commentary issued by the New China News Agency (NCNA) on May 13, 1979, on the other hand, maintained that the 1887 convention had been an "unequal treaty", and that the imperial government had "surrendered to France".

Vietnam was partitioned in 1954 into a Communist state in the north, with its capital at Hanoi, and a pro-Western state in the south, with Saigon as its capital. Until the reunification of the country in 1975, North Vietnam was preoccupied with its relations with its southern neighbour, and in the undeclared war which developed between them it was largely dependent on China for military aid. In these circumstances, North Vietnam was in no position to press its territorial claims against China. In November 1957 the Vietnamese Workers' (Communist) Party proposed that the two countries should maintain the status quo and should settle any border disputes through negotiations, this proposal being accepted by the Chinese Communist Party in April 1958. Vietnamese statements issued in 1979, however, alleged that after 1954 the Chinese government had taken advantage of the situation to carry out a large number of encroachments by sending Chinese to settle on Vietnamese territory, moving the border stones, building roads on Vietnamese territory, altering the border line on maps printed in China for the Vietnamese government, and sending troops to occupy border areas. In particular, it was alleged that during repairs to the international railway line between China and Vietnam in 1955 the Chinese had deliberately moved the junction point more than 300 metres into Vietnamese territory.

Clashes on the border began in 1974. Although no details were published by either side at the time, later Vietnamese statements alleged that the Chinese had been responsible for 179 border incidents and encroachments on Vietnamese territory in that year, whilst Chinese statements accused North Vietnam of making 121 "provocative attacks on the Chinese border" in 1974. The Chinese government proposed on March 18, 1975, that negotiations should take place on the border question, but the North Vietnamese government, while agreeing in principle, suggested on April 12 that they should be postponed, as it was preoccupied with the war in South Vietnam, then approaching its end. According to Chinese sources, the Chinese government repeated its proposal in 1976 and again early in 1977, on both occasions without result.

During a visit to Beijing by Pham Van Dong (the Vietnamese Prime Minister), Li Xiannian, a Chinese Deputy Premier, handed him a memorandum on June 10, 1977, in which he said that although "no big dispute" over the border had arisen before 1974, since that year Vietnam had "continually provoked disputes", and that some shooting incidents had occurred. Admitting that "some of these incidents were caused by violations of our policies by our local personnel", he gave an assurance that measures would be taken to prevent them from crossing the border, and again proposed that negotiations be held, to which Pham Van Dong agreed.

Negotiations between the two countries' Deputy Foreign Ministers opened in Beijing on Oct. 7, 1977. Acording to Chinese reports, the Chinese side put forward the following proposals for a settlement: (i) the two sides should recheck the alignment of the entire boundary and settle all disputes on the basis of the Sino-French conventions; (ii) areas under either side's jurisdiction which lay beyond the boundary line should be returned to the other side unconditionally; (iii) the two sides should settle any differences on the alignment of the boundary through friendly consultations; and (iv) they should then conclude a new boundary treaty, delimit the boundary and erect new boundary markers.

The Vietnamese side submitted on Jan. 12, 1978, a draft agreement as a basis for discussion, the fundamental principles of which were similar to the Chinese proposals. The Chinese in turn put forward on Jan. 24 an enlarged version of their previous proposals, which provided inter alia that "readjustments" to the border might be made in a small number of cases where the two sides agreed. The Vietnamese asked on May 10 for clarifications on this point and a number of others. According to a later Vietnamese Foreign Ministry statement, the Chinese refused to discuss these questions and insisted on discussing only their own proposals of Jan. 24, thus causing a deadlock.

The negotiations were broken off in the summer of 1978 without any agreement having been reached. The Vietnamese memorandum of March 15, 1979, said that they had failed because the Chinese "did not respond to any proposal of the Vietnamese side", whilst the NCNA commentary of May 13, 1979, said that the Vietnamese had "suspended the negotiations under the pretext that its representatives were 'too busy' to negotiate".

Relations between China and Vietnam rapidly deteriorated during 1978 as a result of Chinese support for Kampuchea in its border war with Vietnam, the mass exodus of the Chinese community from Vietnam from April onwards, the admission of Vietnam to the Soviet-led Council for Mutual Economic Assistance (Comecon) in June 1978, the ending of Chinese economic aid to Vietnam in July, and the conclusion of a treaty of friendship and co-operation between Vietnam and the Soviet Union in November. According to diplomatic sources in Hanoi, serious fighting occurred on the border in April 1978, and from September onwards both Vietnam and China frequently reported incidents on the border, a number of which were said to have led to fatal casualties. Eight protests were lodged by Vietnam in the last four months of the year, and six by China.

The situation reached crisis point after Vietnamese troops invaded Kampuchea on Dec. 25, 1978, drove the Chinese-supported government from the capital, Phnom-Penh, and installed a Vietnamese-sponsored government on Jan. 8, 1979. Clashes on the Sino-Vietnamese border increased both in number and in scale during January and the first half of February 1979; the Vietnamese Foreign Ministry said on Feb. 14 that whereas there had been 583 Chinese armed encroachments on Vietnamese territory in 1978, since the beginning of

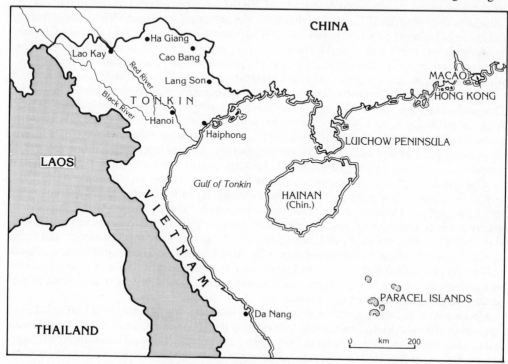

Map 34 The China-Vietnam border.

1979 there had already been 230, in which over 40 people had been killed, hundreds wounded and over 20 abducted to China.

Chinese troops invaded Vietnam along the entire length of the frontier on Feb. 17, 1979, and after a fortnight of heavy fighting entered Lang Son, 11 miles (18 km) south of the border. On March 1 China proposed that the two governments should open negotiations, but Vietnam refused to negotiate until the Chinese had withdrawn to "the other side of the historic borderline". The Chinese government accordingly announced on March 5 that its troops were withdrawing, and on March 16 that their withdrawal had been completed. The Vietnamese government, however, alleged on March 27 that Chinese troops were still occupying 10 points on Vietnamese territory.

Negotiations opened in Hanoi on April 18, 1979, when the Vietnamese side proposed that both sides should establish a demilitarized zone by withdrawing their armed forces to a distance of three to five kilometres from the line of actual control prior to Feb. 17, 1979, and that border problems should be settled on the basis of respect for the borderline laid down in the conventions of 1887 and 1895. The Chinese side put forward as a basis for a settlement an eight-point statement of principles covering the whole field of Sino-Vietnamese relations which included a proposal that, pending a settlement of border disputes on the basis of the Sino-French conventions, each side should strictly maintain the status quo as it existed in 1957-58. The talks were adjourned on May 18, resumed in Beijing on June 28, and continued until Dec. 19, 1979, without any progress having been made. As all Vietnamese proposals for another session were rejected by the Chinese, the head of the Vietnamese delegation left for Hanoi on Feb. 8, 1980, and on March 6 China proposed that the second round of talks should be concluded and a third round held in Hanoi in the second half of the year. Several Vietnamese proposals for the resumption of the talks were subsequently rejected by China.

Since 1979 the two sides have continued to accuse each other of causing border incidents. A Vietnamese statement of Dec. 29, 1980, alleged that during that year the Chinese forces had carried out over 2,500 armed provocations, made repeated raids deep into Vietnamese territory, regularly shelled centres of population, occupied many hilltop positions along the border and killed or wounded hundreds of Vietnamese border guards and civilians. A Chinese note of May 5, 1981, asserted that since the beginning of the year Vietnamese troops had made 241 attacks on Chinese territory, killing over 60 people, and had fired on Chinese territory almost every day. The Vietnamese reply, sent on the following day, rejected the Chinese "slanders", and alleged that since the beginning of the year the Chinese had shelled or made armed incursions into Vietnamese territory on over 700 occasions.

The more intense clashes on the border appeared to coincide with Vietnamese offensives in Kampuchea in support of the Heng Samrin government against the Chinese-backed Khmer Rouge guerillas. In April 1983 the Chinese launched a major shelling campaign, allegedly in retaliation after Vietnamese artillery attacks, at a time when Vietnamese troops were conducting a dry-season offensive against the guerillas. A year later China launched a new cross-border shelling campaign on April 21, 1984, to coincide with a Vietnamese offensive in the Thai border area of Kampuchea which had led to clashes between Vietnamese and Thai troops. A commentary published in *China Daily* on April 6 declared that "the counter-attacks waged by Thailand and China" were necessary "until Vietnam truly expresses a sincere desire to withdraw completely from Kampuchea". Vietnamese spokesmen alleged on May 3 that an offensive by three Chinese regiments against Ha Tuyen province had been repelled with more than 100 Chinese troops killed or wounded, and on May 9 that since April 2 China had fired 50,000 shells at over 100 points situated within 26 of the 28 districts in the six northern provinces. Major clashes continued until July, culminating in a 10-hour battle on July 12 on the border of Ha Tuyen.

After a lull in the fighting, the Chinese renewed their shelling campaign on Nov. 21, 1984, three days after the Vietnamese army had opened its dry-season offensive in Kampuchea, and clashes continued until the end of May 1985. Sporadic shelling and incursions by troops of both sides were reported on a number of occasions between September 1985 and February 1986, although there was no dry-season offensive in Kampuchea during this period. Heavy fighting was reported in October 1986, in which Vietnam claimed on Oct. 20 that 250 Chinese had been "put out of action".

Fighting believed to be the most serious since the Chinese invasion of 1979 occurred on Jan. 5-7, 1987. According to Vietnamese reports, Chinese infantry in divisional strength made repeated attacks on hill positions in Ha Tuyen, all of which were repulsed, nearly 1,500 Chinese being killed. Chinese sources, on the other hand, stated that their forces had counter-attacked in response to Vietnamese incursions, and estimated the number killed at about 500 Vietnamese and "a few dozen" Chinese.

Le Monde described the nature of the fighting as follows in a report of Jan. 11, 1987: "The fighting which the Chinese and Vietnamese have carried on along their frontier for the last eight years is confined to a heavily fortified zone of a few square kilometres, and has taken the form of limited but sometimes murderous trench warfare. In this zone—a mountainous and inaccessible region between Laoshan, in the Chinese province of Yunnan, and Vi Xuyen in the Vietnamese province of Ha Tuyen—modern warfare, with air support and the use of advanced techniques, is out of the question. Generally the two opponents' forces remain dug in to their trenches to protect themselves from the heavy artillery fire."

The Gulf of Tonkin Dispute

The Gulf of Tonkin (known to the Vietnamese as the Bac Bo Gulf and to the Chinese as Beibu Wan) lies between Vietnam to the west, the Chinese mainland to the north, and the Luichow peninsula and the island of Hainan (both Chinese) to the east, and as its greatest extent is 170 nautical miles wide. It has two outlets to the South China Sea, that to the south, which is 125 nautical miles wide at its narrowest point, and another to the east through the Hainan Strait.

The Franco-Chinese convention of 1887 stated that islands in the Gulf lying to the east of longitude 105 degrees 43 minutes east of the Paris meridian (or 108 degrees 03 minutes 13 seconds east of the Greenwich meridian) belonged to China, and islands to the west of this meridian belonged to Vietnam. The Vietnamese maintain that this meridian marks the boundary between the two countries' territorial waters across the entire Gulf. The Chinese, however, contend that both the wording of the convention and the attached map make plain that this article refers only to the offshore islands and does not lay down a sea boundary line.

A statement of the Chinese case published in the Beijing *Guangming Daily* on Dec. 2, 1980, put forward the following aditional arguments: (i) If the line were extended southward to take in the entire Gulf it would be more than 130 nautical miles east of the Vietnamese coast and only about 30 miles west of Hainan, and would give Vietnam two-thirds of the area of the Gulf. (ii) No expert on international law had ever mentioned that the Gulf belonged to Vietnam and China. (iii) Under international law the sea area within a territorial bay was regarded as inland waters (through which ships could pass only with a special permit), but since 1887 neither France nor Vietnam had ever treated foreign ships sailing across the Gulf as ships passing through inland waters. (iv) A French decree on the fishery area in Indo-China laid down that territorial waters extended 20 kilometres from the shore, and made no special provision for the Gulf of Tonkin. (v) Vietnam announced in 1964 that its territorial waters extended 12 nautical miles from the shore, and this was accepted in the latest fishery agreement between China and Vietnam.

The North Vietnamese Foreign Ministry informed the Chinese government on Dec. 26, 1973, of North Vietnam's intention to prospect for oil in the Gulf of Tonkin, and proposed that, as the sea boundary had not been delimited, negotiations should be held on the subject. The Chinese Foreign Ministry accepted this proposal on Jan. 18, 1974, but stipulated that prospecting should not take place in the area between the 18th and 20th parallels and the 107th and 108th meridians, and that third countries should not be involved in the exploration and exploitation of the Gulf. When negotiations opened in Beijing on Aug. 15, 1974, the Vietnamese delegation maintained that the boundary had already been delineated in the 1887 convention, and proposed that it should be officially delineated. As the Chinese refused to accept this contention, the talks were suspended at the end of November 1974 without agreement being reached.

At the negotiations on the land and sea boundaries which began on Oct. 7, 1977, the Chinese refused to discuss the land border unless the Vietnamese gave up their claim that a sea boundary already existed. As a compromise, the Vietnamese suggested that the land border should first be discussed and that each side should maintain its own views on the Gulf of Tonkin, which would be discussed later. As no agreement was reached on the land border, the question of the sea boundary also remained unsettled. A Vietnamese Foreign Ministry statement of Dec. 13, 1979, protested against reports that China had signed contracts with foreign firms to explore for oil in the Gulf of Tonkin as a breach of the convention of 1887.

The Paracel Islands

The Paracel Islands, known to the Chinese as the Xisha (Western Sands) Islands and to the Vietnamese as Hoang Sa, consist of about 130 barren and waterless islands, none larger than a square mile (1.6 sq km) in area, lying about 165 miles (265 km) south-east of the Chinese island of Hainan and 225 miles (360 km) east of the Vietnamese coast. They are divided into two main groups, the Crescent group to the west and the Amphitrite group to the east. The Western name "Paracels" is derived from the Portuguese word for reef.

A Chinese Foreign Ministry document of Jan. 30, 1980, claimed that the islands were discovered by Chinese mariners and were described in Chinese geographical works of the third century AD; that the Chinese Emperor exercised jurisdiction over them in the 11th century; and that they were shown as Chinese territory in official maps of the 18th and early 19th centuries. A Chinese fleet which visited the islands in 1909 set up stone tablets and hoisted the Chinese flag, and two years later they were placed under the administration of Hainan island. The document therefore claimed that "consecutive jurisdiction was exercised over them by successive Chinese governments for more than a thousand years".

A Vietnamese White Book of Sept. 28, 1979, on the other hand, maintained that "the Vietnamese feudal state was the first in history to occupy, claim ownership of, exercise sovereignty over and exploit" the islands, and in support of this claim quoted Vietnamese geographical works of the 17th and 18th centuries. The Emperor of Annam ordered the occupation of the islands in 1816, and his successor in 1836 commanded a survey of them to be carried out and markers to be erected.

The French government, which then exercised sovereignty over Cochin China and a protectorate over Annam and Tonkin, claimed in a note to China in 1931 that the Empire of Annam had a prior title to the islands, and in 1938 the Emperor Bao Dai annexed them to the territory of Thua Thien province. In the following year, however, they were occupied by the Japanese. Japan renounced her claim to them by the peace treaty signed in San Francisco in 1951, but the treaty did not state to whom they belonged. A Chinese official statement commenting on the draft treaty claimed that they had "always been China's territory". At the San Francisco conference, the Vietnamese delegate formally affirmed Vietnam's claim to the islands, whilst in the absence of China, which was not represented, the Soviet delegate described them as China's "inalienable territory".

After Vietnam was divided in 1954 into two states, the South Vietnamese government continued to assert its claim to the Paracels, whereas the North Vietnamese government temporarily accepted China's claim to them. According to the Chinese Foreign Ministry document cited above, North Vietnamese official statements in 1958 and 1965 referred to the islands as Chinese territory, and they were shown and referred to as such in maps and textbooks issued by the North Vietnamese government down to 1974. Both China and South Vietnam exercised control over some of the islands during the period from 1954 to 1974; Woody Island, the main island in the Amphitrite group, was occupied by the Chinese, whilst South Vietnam maintained a small garrison on Pattle Island, the largest of the Crescent group, to man a radio and meteorological station.

After the South Vietnamese government had announced its intention of carrying out surveys for oil off its coast opposite the Paracels, the Chinese Foreign Ministry issued a statement on Jan. 11, 1974, affirming its claim to the islands, this claim being rejected by South Vietnam on the following day. South Vietnamese warships which were sent to the islands withdrew after an engagement with Chinese warships on Jan. 19, and on the following day Chinese troops occupied the three islands still under South Vietnamese control. A North Vietnamese spokesman commented in a non-committal statement on Jan. 21 that "disputes handed down by history, often very complex ones" should be settled through negotiations. Both the United States and the Soviet Union adopted a strictly neutral attitude towards the dispute, and a request by the South Vietnamese government for a meeting of the UN Security Council failed to secure the necessary support for placing the question on the Council's agenda.

Following the overthrow of the Saigon regime in 1975 and the reunification of Vietnam in the following year, the Hanoi government openly laid claim to the Paracels. The Vietnamese White Book of 1979 stated that the question had been discussed between the Vietnamese and Chinese governments in September 1975, and that the latter had admitted that a dispute existed. An official Vietnamese map issued in 1976 showed the Paracels as Vietnamese territory. A government statement of May 20, 1977, said that Vietnamese territorial waters were 12 miles wide and that its exclusive economic zone extended to 200 nautical miles from the coast, and referred to "the islands and archipelagoes belonging to Vietnamese territory and situated outside the territorial waters mentioned" without specifying the islands and archipelagoes in question. In the memorandum which Li Xiannian handed to Pham Van Dong on June 10, 1977 [see above], he accused Vietnam of making the Paracels, "over which there was never any issue", a major subject of dispute. According to Chinese sources, Pham Van Dong replied that "in the war of resistance we of course had to place resistance to US imperialism above everything else", and that earlier Vietnamese statements on the subject must be understood "in the context of the historical circumstances of the time".

Both sides issued a series of statements in 1979 and 1980 reaffirming their claims to the Paracels. At the negotiations held in Hanoi in April and May 1979 the Chinese delegation demanded that Vietnam should recognize China's sovereignty over the islands, this demand being rejected by Vietnam. Following reports that China had signed contracts with foreign companies to prospect for oil around the Paracels, the Vietnamese Foreign Ministry gave warning on Dec. 13, 1979, that companies which conducted exploration in this area without Vietnam's consent "must bear all consequences of their wrongdoings".

Hanoi radio announced on March 3, 1982, that 40 armed Chinese vessels had entered Vietnamese waters to conduct expionage and obstruct fishing, and that after a Vietnamese fishing boat had been damaged "militiamen on board Vietnamese fishing vessels" had set fire to three of the intruders and captured another. The Chinese version of the incident was that Vietnamese gunboats had attacked Chinese fishing boats on the high seas, destroying one, damaging another and capturing a third. In another incident on the following day the Chinese captured what was described as "a Vietnamese reconnaissance boat intruding into China's territorial waters" with its crew of 10, who were released in an exchange of captured intruders on June 21.

Chinese Rejection of Vietnamese Proposals for Talks

Vietnamese proposals for talks were consistently rejected by China. A Chinese statement of Sept. 3, 1981, rejected one such offer on the grounds that Vietnam had "intensified its hostile policy of aggression and expansionism", and that there was no real basis for discussing the normalization of relations. The Vietnamese government renewed its proposal on Jan. 30, 1982, and on the following day welcomed an offer of mediation from Javier Pérez de Cuellar, the UN Secretary-General. The Chinese Foreign Ministry rejected on April 9, 1984, an offer by Nguyen Co Thach, the Vietnamese Foreign Minister, for talks "at any level and anywhere" on easing the border tension, describing it as "hypocritical and wrought with ulterior motives".

Wu Xueqian, the Chinese Foreign Minister, declared on Jan. 29, 1985, that China might have to "teach Vietnam a second lesson" if Vietnamese forces continued their operations in the Thai-Kampuchean border area, and Hu Yaobang, then general secretary of the Chinese Communist Party, said in February that the elimination of "the Vietnamese threat to China" was a major Chinese policy decision. A Chinese Foreign Ministry spokesman denied on Sept. 11, 1985, reports that China and Vietnam were engaged in secret negotiations, stating that there was no chance of an improvement in relations until all Vietnamese troops were withdrawn from Kampuchea.

The official communiqué issued after a meeting on Aug. 17-18, 1986, of the Foreign Ministers of Vietnam, Kampuchea and Laos reaffirmed Vietnam's readiness to enter into talks with China "at any level and anywhere whatsoever". China rejected the offer on Aug. 20, however, on the ground that it could not enter into normalization talks until all Vietnamese forces were withdrawn from Kampuchea. Truong Chinh, then general secretary of the Vietnamese Communist Party, proposed on Oct. 18, 1986, to negotiate an unconditional settlement with China, but the offer was immediately rejected. Armed clashes in border area continued in 1987, with particularly fierce fighting being reported in May, when the Chinese claimed to have repulsed 41 separate Vietnamese assaults.

CH

France-Vanuatu (Matthew and Hunter Islands)

A dispute arose in 1982 over two uninhabited South Pacific islands known as Matthew and Hunter, when the Republic of Vanuatu (the former Anglo-French Condominium of the New Hebrides) declared them to be part of its sovereign territory (and renamed them Umaenupnae and Umaeneag respectively), whereas the French government maintained that they formed part of the French overseas territory of New Caledonia.

The two islands are barren volcanic rocks situated about 350 kilometres south-east of the island of Anatom in Vanuatu and about 450 kilometres due east of the mainland of New Caledonia. The importance of the islands lies principally in the fact that the state exercising sovereignty over them would, under the 200-mile exclusive economic zone system envisaged in the UN Law of the Sea Convention, be entitled to exploitation of some 150,000 square miles (about 390,000 sq km) of the surrounding ocean in respect of fishery, mineral and other resources.

It appeared that no country had ever formally claimed the islands until the 1960s, although maps of the area, including those prepared by the French authorities, had generally shown them as part of the New Hebrides. Following an inconclusive attempt by an Englishman and Frenchman (resident in the New Hebrides and New Caledonia respectively) to claim them jointly as their private property, France laid formal claim in 1975 when a landing party set up a plaque on Matthew Island. In December 1976 a French law declared that they were part of New Caledonia, and a memorandum to that effect was given to the Vanuatu authorities by France and Britain when the Condominium was dissolved prior to independence in July 1980.

The independent government of Vanuatu refused to recognize the French claim, however, and obtained support for its case from pro-independence groups in New Caledonia itself. When it appeared subsequently that a maritime boundary agreement between France and Fiji implied recognition of the French claim, protests from Vanuatu drew assurances from Fiji that the agreement was without prejudice to the Vanuatu claim. In March 1983 a Vanuatu landing party removed the French plaque from Matthew Island and erected a replacement claiming the islands for Vanuatu. French helicopters and ships were reported to be present in the area shortly afterwards, but no confrontation occurred. In May 1983 Vanuatu issued postage stamps depicting Umaenupnae and Umaeneag as part of its territory and gave notice that it intended to pursue its claim in international organizations.

Commenting on Vanuatu's erection of a plaque on Matthew Island, the then French Minister for External Relations, Claude Cheysson, told the defence and armed services committee of the French Senate on May 27, 1983, that this action had "absolutely no effect whatsoever on France's legally indisputable and recognized national sovereignty over those islands". It was reported in March 1985 that France had established a military garrison on Matthew Island.

AJD

India-Pakistan

The dispute between India and Pakistan over the state of Jammu and Kashmir arose from the circumstances in which British India was partitioned in 1947. The accession of the princely states to either India or Pakistan took place smoothly, except in three states in which the religion of the ruler differed from that of the majority of his subjects. After the Moslem ruler of the overwhelmingly Hindu state of Junagadh had announced its accession to Pakistan, with which his territory was nowhere contiguous, the state was occupied by Indian troops and was incorporated into India after a plebiscite, despite Pakistani protests. The Moslem Nizam of Hyderabad, which was entirely surrounded by Indian territory, announced that he wished to maintain its independence, but when order threatened to break down Indian troops moved in and the Nizam agreed to accede to India. The third state was Jammu and Kashmir, generally referred to as Kashmir. (For a map showing the division of Kashmir, see page 267.)

Kashmir before 1947

The state was founded by Gulab Singh, a Hindu military adventurer who in return for his services was created Raja of Jammu by the Sikh ruler Ranjit Singh in 1820, and who conquered Ladakh in 1834. After the defeat of the Sikhs by the British in 1846, Gulab Singh undertook to pay the indemnity of 75,000 rupees demanded by the British from the Sikhs, on condition that he was given Kashmir, then under Sikh rule. This arrangement was confirmed by the Treaty of Amritsar, Gulab Singh being recognized by the British as Maharaja of Jammu and Kashmir.

Jammu and Kashmir has an area of 84,471 square miles (about 220,000 sq km), and borders on India to the south, Pakistan to the west, Afghanistan to the north-west and China to the north and east. According to a census conducted in 1941, it then had a population of 4,023,180, of whom 77.1 per cent were Moslems, 20.1 per cent Hindus, and 2.08 per cent Sikhs, Buddhists and others. The Valley of Kashmir is overwhelmingly Moslem; Hindus constitute the great majority of the population of Jammu, in the south, and also form a considerable part of the population of Srinagar, the capital of the state; the Sikhs are also found mainly in Jammu and Srinagar; and the Buddhists are confined to Ladakh, in the north. Economically, Kashmir is linked with Pakistan by its river system, as its three main rivers, the Indus, the Chenab and the Jhelum, all flow into Pakistan, which is largely dependent on them for its irrigation.

Strong opposition to the autocratic rule of the Maharaja, Sir Hari Singh, developed before World War II under the leadership of Sheikh Mohammed Abdullah, who in 1930 founded the Moslem Conference to agitate for reforms. He broke away from it in 1938, however, to form the Kashmir National Conference, a non-communal organization which maintained close links with the Indian National Congress. He launched an agitation demanding constitutional government in 1945, and was subsequently imprisoned.

The Accession of Kashmir to India

When India and Pakistan became independent on Aug. 15, 1947, it was generally assumed that Kashmir, as a contiguous state with a predominantly Moslem population, would accede to Pakistan. The Maharaja, however, hesitated whether to accede to Pakistan or to India or to seek to maintain Kashmir's independence, and accordingly proposed to both India and Pakistan that both should enter into a standstill agreement with Kashmir. The Indian government asked for further discussions; Pakistan accepted the proposal, but as a means of pressure began an economic blockade of Kashmir, rail and road traffic being discontinued and supplies of food and petrol cut off. Early in October 1947 an armed revolt of the Moslem peasantry in Poonch province, south-west of Srinagar, was joined by many deserters from the Kashmir state forces and by thousands of tribesmen from Pakistan armed with modern weapons supplied by the Pakistan Army, and on Oct. 27 the invaders captured Baramula, only 30 miles north-west of Srinagar.

In a letter to Lord Mountbatten, then Governor-General of India, the Maharaja stated: "With the conditions obtaining at present in my state, and the emergency of the situation, I have no option but to ask for help from the Indian Dominion. Naturally they cannot send the help asked for by me without my state acceding to India. I have accordingly decided to do so, and attach the Instrument of Accession." In his reply accepting Kashmir's accession, Lord Mountbatten wrote: "In consistence with their policy that, in the case of any state where the issue of accession has been the subject of dispute, the question should be decided in accordance with the wishes of the people of the state, it is the government's wish that, as soon as law and order have been restored in Kashmir and her soil cleared of the invader, the question of the state's accession should be settled by reference to the people."

The accession of Kashmir to India was officially announced on Oct. 27, 1947. At the same time Indian troops were flown to the Srinagar front to reinforce the Maharaja's forces, and by the end of the month the invaders, who had advanced to within 18 miles (29 km) of the state capital, had been driven back several miles. Sheikh Abdullah, who had recently been released from prison, was sworn in as Prime Minister on Oct. 31. The rebels meanwhile set up their own "provisional government of Azad (Free) Kashmir", headed by Sardar Mohammad Ibrahim, president of the Moslem Conference.

On Oct. 28, 1947, Jawaharlal Nehru, then Indian Prime Minister, invited the Prime Minister of Pakistan, Liaquat Ali Khan, to meet him in Delhi to discuss the Kashmir question, and proposed that Pakistan should co-operate in preventing the raiders from entering Kashmir. He also gave an assurance that India had no desire to intervene in Kashmir's affairs once the state had been cleared of the raiders, and regarded the question of accession as one solely for the decision of the Kashmiri people. The Pakistan government, however, declared on Oct. 30 that "the accession of Kashmir to India is based on fraud and violence, and as such cannot be recognized". Nehru repeated in a broadcast on Nov. 2 that "we are prepared, when peace, law and order have been established, to have a referendum held under international auspices like the United Nations".

Indian Complaint to the United Nations

On Dec. 22, 1947, the Indian government requested Pakistan to deny to the invading tribesmen all use of its territory for operations against Kashmir, all military and other supplies, and all other aid that might prolong the struggle. As no reply was received, the

318

Indian government made a formal complaint to the UN Security Council on Jan. 1, 1948, stating that the invaders, who included Pakistani nationals, were using Pakistani territory as a base for operations, drew much of their military equipment, transport and supplies from Pakistan, and were being trained and guided by Pakistani officers. Nehru stated on Jan. 2 that in addition to the 50,000 raiders already in Kashmir, another 100,000 were being trained and equipped in Pakistan by the Pakistan Army.

After both sides had put their case before the Security Council, it was agreed on Jan. 20, 1948, that a commission of three members should visit India and Pakistan to investigate the facts and report to the Security Council. Differences arose, however, over two issues. Whereas Pakistan demanded the immediate establishment of an "impartial" administration in Kashmir and the withdrawal of the Indian forces under the commission's supervision, India insisted that Sheikh Abdullah's government should hold a plebiscite under the commission's aegis, and that the Indian forces must stay to ensure external and internal security so long as Kashmir remained acceded to India. The Security Council accordingly adopted on April 21, 1948, a resolution containing the following proposals for the settlement of the dispute:

(1) The commission, whose membership would be increased to five, would place itself at the two governments' disposal to facilitate measures for the restoration of peace and the holding of a plebiscite.

(2) Pakistan would withdraw all her nationals who had entered Kashmir to take part in the fighting, prevent such persons from entering Kashmir and refuse them all aid.

(3) When the commission was satisfied that the tribesmen were withdrawing and an effective ceasefire was in force, India would reduce her forces in Kashmir to the minimum required for the maintenance of order.

(4) The plebiscite would be conducted by a Plebiscite Administration headed by a Plebiscite Administrator appointed by the UN Secretary-General. During the plebiscite the Kashmir state forces and police would be under the supervision of the Plebiscite Administration.

(5) To ensure that the plebiscite was completely impartial, the Kashmir government would be enlarged to include representatives of the major political groups in the state, and the Indian government would undertake to ensure freedom of speech, assembly and movement, the release of all political prisoners, and guarantees against intimidation and victimization.

Both India and Pakistan informed the Security Council that although they were prepared to lend the commission all assistance in their power, they could not commit themselves to accept all the resolution's recommendations. India objected to the proposals for the withdrawal of Indian troops, the control of the state forces by the Plebiscite Administration and the inclusion of members of other parties in the state government, while Pakistan demanded the withdrawal of all Indian troops and maintained that a government headed by Sheikh Abdullah would be unlikely to permit a free plebiscite.

The Ceasefire in Kashmir

The Indian troops meanwhile had cleared the Kashmir Valley of the invaders in November 1947, but in the following month the tribesmen opened a new front in south-west Kashmir, where heavy fighting continued until March 1948. Regular Pakistani troops entered Kashmir early in May to reinforce the tribesmen, and took a major part in a new offensive in north-west and north Kashmir which began in August 1948.

The UN Kashmir Commission, consisting of representatives of Argentina, Belgium, Colombia, Czechoslovakia and the United States, visited India and Pakistan in July, and put forward the following proposals on Aug. 13, 1948:

(1) India and Pakistan would simultaneously issue a ceasefire order, would not augment the military potential of the forces under their control, and would create and maintain an atmosphere favourable to the promotion of further negotiations. The commission would appoint military observers to supervise the observance of the ceasefire.

(2) The Pakistani troops, whose presence constituted "a material change in the situation", the tribesmen and "Pakistani nationals not normally resident therein who have entered the state for the purpose of fighting" would be withdrawn. Pending a final solution, the territory evacuated by Pakistani troops would be administered by the local authority under the commission's surveillance. When the tribesmen had withdrawn and the Pakistani troops were being withdrawn, the Indian government would begin to withdraw the bulk of its forces in stages to be agreed with the commission. India would maintain within the lines existing at the ceasefire those troops which the commission considered necessary for the maintenance of order.

(3) India and Pakistan would enter into consultations with the commission to determine fair and equitable conditions whereby free expression of the will of the people would be ensured.

India accepted the proposals, but Pakistan maintained that only the Azad Kashmir government could issue ceasefire orders. It also demanded that the Azad Kashmir government should continue to administer the territories under its control, that the Azad Kashmir forces should remain intact and that all Indian troops should be withdrawn. As a result the fighting continued until, following further mediation efforts by the UN Commission, a ceasefire was agreed upon on Dec. 31, 1948, and came into force on the following day. Agreement was reached on July 27, 1949, on the ceasefire line, which ran from Manawar on the Pakistan frontier north to Keran, and thence east to the glacier area. Under the agreement troops would remain at least 500 yards from the ceasefire line (to be supervised by a UN observer team), and neither side would introduce fresh troops into Kashmir.

UN Commission's Resolution on Plebiscite

A resolution on the holding of a plebiscite was adopted by the UN Commission on Jan. 5, 1949, and accepted by India and Pakistan, its provisions being as follows:

(1) The accession of Kashmir would be decided through a free and impartial plebiscite, which would be held when the commission found that the ceasefire and truce arrangements set forth in Parts 1 and 2 of the resolution of Aug. 13, 1948, had been carried out and arrangements for a plebiscite completed.

(2) The UN Secretary-General would nominate a Plebiscite Administrator, who would be formally appointed by the Kashmir government.

(3) After Parts 1 and 2 of the resolution of Aug. 13, 1948, had been implemented and the commission was satisfied that peaceful conditions had been restored, the commission and the Plebiscite Administrator would determine in consultation with India the final disposal of the Indian and state armed forces, and in consultation with the local authorities the final disposal of other armed forces.

(4) All Kashmir citizens who had left the state on account of the disturbances would be free to return.

(5) All persons who had entered Kashmir since 1947 for other than lawful purposes would be required to leave.

(6) All authorities in Kashmir would undertake to ensure that there was no intimidation or bribery of voters in the plebiscite, that no restrictions were placed on legitimate political activity, that all political prisoners were released and that minorities were afforded adequate protection.

By agreement with the governments of India and Pakistan, Fleet-Admiral Chester Nimitz, the US naval commander in the Pacific during World War II, was appointed Plebiscite Administrator on March 21, 1949.

As no agreement had been reached on the implementation of the truce, the UN Commission proposed on Aug. 9, 1949, that a joint meeting at ministerial level should discuss the withdrawal of the Pakistani forces, the tribesmen and the bulk of the Indian forces. The Indian government in reply suggested the inclusion of three other items in the agenda: clarification of the phrase "local authority" in the resolution of Aug. 13, 1948, disbanding and disarming of the Azad Kashmir forces, and the administration and defence of the mountainous and sparsely populated regions of northern Kashmir. As the Pakistan government objected to these items, the meeting did not take place. A proposal by the commission that Admiral Nimitz should arbitrate on the differences between them was accepted by Pakistan but rejected by India, on the ground that the disbanding and disarming of the Azad Kashmir forces was "no more a matter for arbitration than the complete withdrawal of Pakistani forces".

Failure of Mediation Attempts

In its third and final report, submitted on Dec. 9, 1949, the commission recommended the appointment of a single person to endeavour to bring India and Pakistan together on all unresolved issues. A resolution adopted by the UN Security Council on March 14, 1950, provided for the dissolution of the commission and the appointment of a mediator, who would supervise a jointly-agreed programme of demilitarization and decide when it had gone far enough to enable a plebiscite to be held. Sir Owen Dixon, an Australian high court judge, was appointed mediator on April 12, 1950.

During talks with both governments in the spring and summer he proposed that a plebiscite should be held only in those areas where the people's desires were uncertain, notably in the Valley of Kashmir, and that those areas where the inhabitants' desires were known should be partitioned between India and Pakistan. This proposal was accepted by India but rejected by Pakistan. A suggestion for a partition of Kashmir without a plebiscite proved impracticable, as it became evident that both parties would in that event insist upon having the Valley of Kashmir.

Following the failure of Sir Owen Dixon's mission, the Security Council adopted a resolution on March 30, 1951, providing for the appointment of a UN Representative for India and Pakistan, who would effect the demilitarization of Kashmir on the basis of the UN commission's resolution. Dr Frank P. Graham, president of North Carolina University, was appointed to the post of UN Representative on April 30. After prolonged negotiations with the Indian and Pakistan governments, he reported to the Security Council on March 27, 1953, that substantial differences still existed on the number of the armed forces which should remain on either side of the ceasefire line, and suggested that India and Pakistan should negotiate directly instead of through a UN mediator as hitherto. Subsequent negotiations and correspondence between Nehru and Mohammed Ali, then Prime Minister of Pakistan, produced no result, and in a final letter of Sept. 21, 1954, the latter declared that as there was no scope left for further direct negotiations the issue should revert to the Security Council.

Constitutional Developments in Kashmir

The question had meanwhile been complicated by constitutional developments in Indian Kashmir. Like all the princely states, Kashmir had acceded to India with regard to defence, communications and foreign policy only, but whereas the other states had since integrated themselves fully with the Indian Union, Article 370 of the Indian constitution, adopted in 1949, limited the Union Parliament's power to legislate for Kashmir to those three subjects and such other matters as the President might by order specify, with the concurrence of the state government.

Despite Pakistani protests, a Kashmir Constituent Assembly was elected in September 1951, and National Conference candidates were returned unopposed in all but two of the constituencies, in which they defeated independent candidates. An agreement between the Indian and Kashmir governments concluded in July 1952 provided that the head of the state would be elected by the State Legislature; that the Indian national flag would have the same position in Kashmir as in other parts of India, but the Kashmir state flag would be retained;

and that although citizenship would be common, the existing law preventing non-residents from acquiring immovable property in Kashmir would remain. Hereditary monarchy was subsequently abolished, and Yuvraj Karan Singh, the son of the former Maharaja, who had been acting as regent since his father left Kashmir in 1949, was elected *Sadr-i-Riyasat* (head of state) by the Constituent Assembly.

The degree to which Kashmir should be integrated with India gave rise to violent controversy inside the state, and the *Praja Parishad*, a Hindu communalist organization, launched an agitation in Jammu demanding the complete accession of Kashmir to India. This was strongly opposed by Sheikh Abdullah (the Prime Minister), who emphasized in his public statements that Kashmir must enjoy complete internal autonomy. After a split in the Cabinet, in which he was opposed by three of his four ministers, he was dismissed by Yuvraj Karan Singh on Aug. 9, 1953, and was arrested later the same day.

The Constituent Assembly finally ratified Kashmir's accession to India on Feb. 15, 1954, and the Indian President issued an order on May 14 greatly extending the application of the Indian constitution to Kashmir. The Indian government was empowered to legislate for Kashmir on the majority of the subjects included in the Union List (i.e. the list of subjects on which only the central government might legislate), but the Concurrent List of subjects on which both the central and the state governments might legislate would not apply to Kashmir, these subjects being reserved for the state government.

Indian Protests against Pakistani Military Alliances

Mohammed Ali announced on Feb. 22, 1954, that Pakistan had asked the United States for military aid, and on Feb. 25 President Eisenhower stated that the United States would comply with this request. In a letter to the Indian Prime Minister, President Eisenhower gave an assurance that this decision was not directed against India, and offered similar assistance to the Indian government, which declined the offer. Nehru said in the Indian Parliament on March 1 that the Kashmir issue "has to be considered from an entirely different point of view, when across the border large additional forces are being placed at the disposal of Pakistan", and called for the withdrawal of the American observers attached to the UN team on either side of the ceasefire line, as they could "no longer be treated by us as neutrals". The American observers were subsequently withdrawn. Admiral Nimitz had previously resigned on Sept. 3, 1953, after Nehru had suggested that the Plebiscite Administrator should be chosen from one of the smaller countries.

In a letter of March 5, 1954, to Mohammed Ali, Nehru said that the granting of US military aid to Pakistan had changed "the whole extent of the Kashmir issue", and continued: "If two countries have actually been conducting military operations against each other in the past, and are in a state of truce, military aid given to either of them is an act unfriendly to the other. .... What was said at a previous stage about the quantum of forces has little relevance. We can take no risks now, as we were prepared to take previously, and we must retain full liberty to keep such forces and military equipment in Kashmir as we may consider necessary in view of this new threat to us." Although in reply Mohammed Ali denied that Pakistan intended to seek a military solution in Kashmir, Nehru continued to uphold his view that US military aid to Pakistan had radically altered the situation.

Indian suspicions were increased by Pakistan's entry into a network of military alliances. On May 19, 1954, a Mutual Defence Assistance Agreement between Pakistan and the United States was signed. At the Manila conference, in which India had refused to take part, Pakistan on Sept. 8, 1954, became a founder member of the South-East Asia Treaty Organization (SEATO), together with the United States, the United Kingdom, France, Australia, New Zealand, the Philippines and Thailand. On June 30, 1955, Pakistan joined the Baghdad Pact alliance, of which the United Kingdom, Turkey and Iraq were already members, and which was subsequently joined by Iran.

A communiqué issued by the SEATO Council on March 8, 1956, called for "an early settlement of the Kashmir question through the United Nations or by direct negotiations".

In a speech on March 20 Nehru commented: "How the question of Kashmir could come within the scope of the SEATO Council is not clear to us. Its reference to Kashmir could only mean that military alliance is backing Pakistan in its disputes with India." Despite this protest, the Council of the Baghdad Pact on April 19 issued a similar call for "an early settlement" of the Kashmir dispute.

Indian Attitude to Plebiscite Plan

The Indian Home Minister, G. B. Pant, said on July 9, 1955, that the conditions for a settlement in Kashmir had been transformed by changes in the situation, including the military alliance between Pakistan and the United States and the "definite decision" taken by the Kashmir Constituent Assembly. In reply to Pakistani protests against this statement, Nehru pointed out on Aug. 22 that at the time of the accession of Kashmir India had made a unilateral declaration that the people of the state would be consulted, no mention being made of a plebiscite. Two years later the UN commission had adopted a resolution (which had been accepted first by India and later by Pakistan) recommending the holding of a plebiscite, provided that certain conditions were fulfilled. There had since been many discussions on the fulfilment of these conditions which had not led to any settlement, and meanwhile there had been developments which would "be taken into consideration".

Following the SEATO Council's pronouncement on Kashmir, Nehru said in the Indian Parliament on March 29, 1956, that the holding of a plebiscite could not be considered until Pakistan had withdrawn all her forces, which still remained in Kashmir eight years after the Security Council had categorically demanded their withdrawal. US military aid to Pakistan had created "not only a new military situation but a new political situation", and that situation had become progressively worse because of the conclusion of the SEATO and Baghdad pacts, which "tend to encircle us". Asked at a press conference on April 2 whether he was no longer in favour of a plebiscite, he said that that inference was "largely correct". He announced on April 13 that he had suggested to the Pakistan government the holding of discussions to settle the question by a demarcation of the border on the basis of the ceasefire line. Chaudhri Mohammad Ali, who had succeeded Mohammed Ali as Prime Minister of Pakistan in 1955, dismissed this proposal on the following day as "preposterous".

The Constituent Assembly adopted on Nov. 17, 1956, a constitution declaring that Kashmir was "an integral part of the Union of India", and that its territories comprised "all territories which on Aug. 15, 1947, were under the sovereignty or suzerainty of the ruler of the state" (i.e. including Azad Kashmir). All sovereignty rested with the state, which had executive and legislative powers in all matters "except those in which [the Indian] Parliament has power to make laws for the state under the provisions of the constitution of India".

In response H. S. Suhrawardy (Chaudhri Mohammed Ali's successor as Prime Minister of Pakistan) declared on Nov. 17, 1956, that Pakistan would never recognize "the right of this or any other such body to represent and legislate on behalf of the people of Jammu and Kashmir", and that by an international agreement, which could not be repudiated by one party to suit its own ends, the question of accession would remain open until it was decided by a free and impartial plebiscite.

Unsuccessful Negotiations, 1957-63

At Pakistan's request, the UN Security Council resumed consideration of the Kashmir question on Jan. 16, 1957. The Pakistani Foreign Minister, F. K. Noon, maintained that the accession to India by the "puppet Constituent Assembly" was "wholly devoid of any legal effect", as the Assembly did not represent Azad Kashmir, its members had been returned unopposed because the population had boycotted the elections, and it had not voted in favour of accession until after Sheikh Abdullah had been imprisoned. He therefore proposed that all Indian and Pakistani forces should be withdrawn from Kashmir, the local forces disbanded and a UN force introduced in preparation for a plebiscite.

The Indian representative, Krishna Menon, maintained in reply that the only problem confronting the Security Council was the Indian complaint about Pakistani aggression. Denying that India was under any legal commitment to hold a plebiscite, he said that the conditions for a truce agreement laid down in the resolution of Aug. 13, 1948, had not been fulfilled by Pakistan, which had not withdrawn its troops, and the Indian government therefore did not consider itself bound by the resolution.

The Security Council adopted on Jan. 24, 1957, a resolution reaffirming the principle that the final disposition of Kashmir would be made through a plebiscite conducted under UN auspices, and declaring that any action taken by the Constituent Assembly would not constitute a disposition of the state in accordance with this principle. At the Council's request the Swedish representative, Gunnar Jarring, visited India and Pakistan in March and April for discussions with the two governments. The Indian government maintained that as Part 1 of the resolution of Aug. 13, 1948, had not been implemented by Pakistan it was premature to discuss the implementation of Parts 2 and 3 or of the resolution of Jan. 5, 1949. The Pakistan government, on the other hand, maintained that it had fully implemented Part 1 of the 1948 resolution, and that the time had come to proceed to the implementation of Part 2.

After considering Jarring's report, the Security Council adopted on Dec. 2, 1957, a resolution directing Dr Graham to visit India and Pakistan and to make recommendations to the two governments for furthering implementation of the UN commission's resolutions. Dr Graham accordingly submitted the following plan to them on Feb. 15, 1958: (i) The two governments would undertake to refrain from statements and actions which would aggravate the situation. (ii) They would reaffirm that they would respect the ceasefire line. (iii) Following the withdrawal of the Pakistan Army from Kashmir, a UN force would be stationed on the Pakistan side of the Kashmir border. (iv) The UN representative would hold discussions with the two governments on the possibility of a plebiscite. (v) A conference of the two Prime Ministers on these questions would be held at the earliest practicable date. These recommendations were accepted in principle by Pakistan, but were rejected by India on the grounds that they bypassed the question of Pakistan's failure to implement the resolution of Aug. 13, 1948, and would "place the aggressor and the aggressed on the same footing".

No major developments in the dispute took place until Jan. 11, 1962, when Pakistan asked for a meeting of the UN Security Council on the question. When the Council met on April 27 (the meeting having been postponed because of the Indian general elections), Sir Muhammad Zafrulla Khan offered on behalf of Pakistan to submit the question to arbitration or to the International Court of Justice, and rejected the Indian claim that a plebiscite was no longer needed as the people of Kashmir had expressed their will in the elections to the Srinagar Assembly. In reply Krishna Menon contended that whatever Lord Mountbatten had written or Nehru had said did not necessarily mean a plebiscite, and pointed out that whereas Pakistan had had no elections in 15 years, there had been three elections in Kashmir since partition (to the Constituent Assembly in 1951 and to the Legislative Assembly in 1957 and 1962). He maintained that the only basis for a plebiscite was the resolution of Jan. 5, 1949, and that the conditions for a plebiscite no longer existed. An Irish resolution reminding the two parties of the principles contained in the commission's resolutions and urging them to enter into negotiations with a view to a settlement was vetoed by the Soviet delegate.

As a result of an Anglo-American initiative, a series of talks were held at ministerial level between Dec. 26, 1962, and May 16, 1963, in preparation for direct talks between Nehru and President Ayub Khan of Pakistan. After India had refused to consider a plebiscite, the two delegations discussed proposals for the partition of Kashmir, but no agreement was reached, as neither side was prepared to abandon its claim to the Kashmir Valley. India offered to transfer to Pakistan about 3,000 square miles (7,750 sq km) west and north of the valley, in addition to those parts of Kashmir already held by Pakistan, totalling about 34,000 square miles (88,000 sq km) out of a total area of 84,471 square miles (220,000 sq km); Pakistan, on the other hand, was prepared to cede to India only about 3,000 square miles in the extreme south of Jammu. In consequence the proposal for talks between Nehru and President Ayub automatically lapsed.

The integration of Kashmir with India was carried a stage farther in 1964, when the provisions of the Indian constitution enabling President's rule to be proclaimed if the constitutional machinery broke down and empowering the Indian Parliament to legislate for a state where President's rule was in force were extended to Kashmir by presidential order. An amendment to the Kashmir constitution adopted by the State Assembly in March 1965 provided that, as in the other Indian states, the *Sadr-i-Riyasat* should be known as the governor, that instead of being elected by the Assembly he should be appointed by the President of India, and that the Prime Minister should be known as the Chief Minister.

The War of 1965 and the 1966 Tashkent Declaration

A major crisis was precipitated when on Aug. 5, 1965, armed infiltrators from Azad Kashmir began entering Indian Kashmir in an unsuccessful attempt to foment a revolt. In order to prevent further raiders from crossing the ceasefire line, Indian troops occupied a number of points on the Pakistani side of the line from Aug. 16 onwards. The Pakistan Army launched an offensive into Jammu on Sept. 1, whereupon the Indian Army invaded Pakistan in three sectors during Sept. 6-8, 1965. Fighting continued until Sept. 23, when a ceasefire came into force at the demand of the UN Security Council.

At the Soviet government's invitation, Lal Bahadur Shastri (who had succeeded Nehru as Prime Minister on the latter's death in 1964) met President Ayub Khan in Tashkent (Uzbekistan) for talks on Jan. 4-10, 1966. In a joint declaration they affirmed their intention to settle their disputes by peaceful means, and stated that they had discussed the Kashmir question against this background. They also agreed that all armed personnel of the two countries should be withdrawn to the positions which they had held before Aug. 5, 1965, and that the two sides would continue meetings "at the highest and other levels on matters of direct concern to both countries".

In accordance with the Tashkent Declaration, talks took place in Rawalpindi on March 1-2, 1966, between Swaran Singh and Zulfiqar Ali Bhutto, the Indian and Pakistani Foreign Ministers respectively. Diplomatic exchanges on the possibility of holding further talks continued throughout the spring and summer, but led to no result, as Pakistan maintained that the most important issue to be discussed was that of Kashmir, whereas the Indian government continued to uphold its view that Kashmir was an integral part of India.

The War of 1971 and the Simla Agreement

During the Indo-Pakistan war of Dec. 3-17, 1971, caused by the civil war in East Pakistan (now Bangladesh), both sides crossed the ceasefire line in Kashmir. Pakistani troops occupied 52 square miles (135 sq km) east of the line in the Chhamb sector, west of Jammu, whilst the Indian forces occupied 480 square miles (1,240 sq km) west and north of the line in the Poonch, Tithwal and Kargil sectors.

At talks in Simla between Indira Gandhi, who had become Indian Prime Minister in 1966, and President (as he then was) Bhutto of Pakistan, it was agreed on July 2, 1972, that "the line of control resulting from the ceasefire of Dec. 17, 1971, shall be respected by both sides without prejudice to the recognized position of either side", and that talks should continue on arrangements for the establishment of a durable peace, including a final settlement of the Kashmir question. Mrs Gandhi said on July 12 that although India continued to regard the Pakistani-held areas of Kashmir as Indian territory, it was prepared to consider any proposal for converting the ceasefire line into a permanent border.

After the Simla talks the Indian government sent a memorandum to the United Nations requesting the withdrawal of the UN observers, on the ground that the former ceasefire line no longer existed. Pakistan asked that they should be retained, however, as the line was still intact except in a few pockets and the issue had not been withdrawn from the United Nations.

Constitutional Status of Indian Kashmir

The constitutional status of Indian Kashmir was defined as follows by an agreement concluded in 1974 between the Indian government and Sheikh Abdullah, who was subsequently reinstated as Chief Minister:

(1) Relations between Kashmir and the Indian Union would continue to be governed by Article 370 of the Indian constitution.

(2) The residuary powers of legislation would remain with the state of Kashmir, although the Union Parliament would continue to have powers to make laws relating to the prevention of activities directed towards the secession of a part of Indian territory from the Union.

(3) Where any provision of the Indian constitution had been applied to Kashmir with adaptations and modifications, these might be altered or replaced by presidential order, but the provisions already applied without modification were unalterable.

(4) The state government might review laws made by Parliament or extended to the state after 1953 on any matter on the Concurrent List, and might decide which of them needed amendment or repeal. The state government would be consulted on the application to Kashmir of laws made by Parliament in future on matters on the Concurrent List.

(5) The President's assent would be necessary for any amendment to the Kashmir constitution passed by the State Legislature relating to the appointment and powers of the Governor, elections and the composition of the Legislative Council (the Upper House of the State Legislature).

Constitutional Status of Azad Kashmir

The constitutional status of Azad Kashmir is anomalous, as Pakistan in theory still regards the whole state as disputed territory. The Pakistani constitution of 1956 said that if the people of Kashmir decided to accede to Pakistan the relationship between Kashmir and Pakistan would be determined by the people of the state, and this wording was imitated in the subsequent constitutions of 1962 and 1973. Azad Kashmir in consequence has never been represented in the Pakistan National Assembly, although until 1974 the Pakistan Cabinet regularly included a Minister for Kashmir Affairs.

Until 1960 the President of Azad Kashmir was elected by the Moslem Conference, but in that year a system of indirect election similar to that then in force in Pakistan was introduced, whereby the President and a State Council of eight members were elected by 1,200 elected members of "basic democracies" in Azad Kashmir and 1,200 elected representatives of Kashmiris settled in Pakistan. This system was abolished by the Azad Kashmir Government Act of 1964, which provided that the President of Azad Kashmir should be appointed by the Pakistani Ministry of Kashmir Affairs and should be responsible to its Joint Secretary. In 1968 it was announced that the President would be elected by the State Council, which was enlarged by the adoption of four nominated members, from among its own members.

Following an agitation in Azad Kashmir against "Pakistani domination", a constitution was introduced in 1970 whereby the President and a 25-member Legislative Assembly were elected by adult franchise. This was replaced in 1974 by a new constitution, which established an Azad Kashmir Council consisting of the Prime Minister of Pakistan as chairman, five Pakistani ministers or members of Parliament nominated by him, and seven members elected by the Azad Kashmir Assembly. The Council would lay down policy and exercise full legislative and executive powers to deal with matters not reserved exclusively for the Pakistan government or the Azad Kashmir Assembly, the Pakistani Ministry of Kashmir Affairs being abolished. The President of Azad Kashmir would be elected by popular vote, and the Prime Minister by the Assembly. After the coup in Pakistan led by Gen. Mohammad Zia ul-Haq in 1977 the Azad Kashmir Assembly was dissolved, like the National and Provincial Assemblies in Pakistan, and in 1978 Gen. Zia, who had assumed the presidency of Pakistan, dismissed the President of Azad Kashmir, replacing him with his own nominee. An agitation in support of demands for a return to democratic rule was suppressed in the later months of 1982, a number of prominent local figures being arrested.

President Zia announced on April 3, 1982, the appointment of observers from the Northern Territories (Gilgit, Hunza and Skardu) to sit in the Federal Advisory Council, which had been established as an interim parliament pending elections to a National Assembly. According to the magazine *India Today*, he said in an interview that these territories were integral parts of Pakistan, and that their representation in the Council was of no relevance to the Kashmir question. The Indian ambassador in Islamabad lodged a protest on April 16, however, pointing out that the territories had not been named as part of Pakistan in the constitution of 1973 or its predecessors, and concern was also expressed in both sectors of Kashmir. Three political leaders in Azad Kashmir warned President Zia in a letter of May 3, 1982, that this development was 'tantamount to a division of the state of Jammu and Kashmir" and would reduce its population by 500,000, to the benefit of "the government of India, which wishes to dominate all Kashmiris". A White Paper issued by the Kashmir state government on May 29 maintained that the Northern Territories were historically an inalienable part of Jammu and Kashmir, and that an arrangement whereby the Maharaja had leased Gilgit to the British in 1935 had not constituted a derogation of his sovereignty over the area.

Recent Developments in Indo-Pakistan Relations, 1980-87

The Soviet intervention in Afghanistan at the end of 1979 led to a temporary improvement in relations between India and Pakistan, notwithstanding each side's suspicion that arms acquisitions by the other indicated an attempt to obtain military superiority. After talks in Islamabad on April 10-14, 1980, between Swaran Singh (by now ex-Foreign Minister of India) and Agha Shahi (who later became Foreign Minister of Pakistan), the latter stated publicly that he had given assurances that "acquisition of arms by Pakistan would be purely for self-defence in view of the new situation [i.e. in Afghanistan] that has arisen", while the former said that both sides should have no difficulty in discussing the Kashmir issue in acordance with the Simla agreement. Moreover, President Zia met Mrs Gandhi for talks in Harare on April 18, 1980, during Zimbabwe's independence celebrations, and the Indian Prime Minister said afterwards that she had withdrawn her objections to Pakistan receiving military aid.

However, relations between the two countries again deteriorated during the summer of 1980, principally because both sides took major steps to strengthen their armed forces, but also because of continuing tensions over the Kashmir issue. A statement issued by the Indian External Affairs Ministry on July 4, 1980, deplored the fact that President Zia had raised the Kashmir question at recent Islamic Conference meetings and described this action as "inconsistent with the spirit of the Simla Agreement". Nevertheless, President Zia again raised the matter in an address to the UN General Assembly on Oct. 1, 1980, when he said that the process of normalizing Indo-Pakistan relations "can and will be further accelerated with a peaceful settlement of the question", and referred to the UN's inability to "redeem its promise to the people of Jammu and Kashmir to enable them to decide their future in accordance with its relevant resolutions".

President Zia publicly suggested on Sept. 15, 1981, that Pakistan and India should enter into negotiations on the conclusion of a non-aggression pact, and this proposal was formally communicated to the Indian government on Nov. 11. India at first reacted with considerable scepticism, as Pakistan had repeatedly refused in the past to discuss Indian offers of a non-aggression pact unless the Kashmir dispute was settled first, and President Zia had made his offer when announcing Pakistan's acceptance of a package of US military aid, including advanced F-16 military aircraft. At the same time, clashes on the Kashmir ceasefire line were reported to have reached their highest level for several years; Mrs Gandhi stated on Nov. 26, 1981, that there had been 55 firing incidents and two minor incursions by Pakistani armed personnel across the line of control in the past three months. The Indian government nevertheless agreed on Dec. 24 to take part in preliminary discussions.

Talks took place in New Delhi on Jan. 29-Feb. 1, 1982, at which it was agreed to hold a second round in Islamabad. On Feb. 19, however, the Pakistani representative at the UN Human Rights Commission made a statement in which he compared Indian-controlled Kashmir to Palestine or Namibia as a region "under foreign military occupation". The Indian government, which held that raising the Kashmir issue in an international forum in a contentious manner was a violation of the spirit of the Simla Agreement, announced on Feb. 25 that in view of these "objectionable statements" the resumption of talks was being postponed indefinitely.

After an emissary from Mrs Gandhi had delivered a letter from her to President Zia, it was announced on June 1, 1982, that discussions would be resumed, and a second round of talks was held at Foreign Secretary level in Islamabad on Aug. 11-12, 1982. Three draft documents were placed before the meeting: (i) a Pakistani draft of a non-aggression pact, (ii) Indian proposals for the establishment of a permanent joint commission and (iii) an Indian draft of a treaty of friendship and co-operation. The Indian draft treaty was reported to include a restriction on the acquisition of weapons beyond limits fixed to correspond to either country's "legitimate defence requirements"; this point reflected India's concern that Pakistan was developing a nuclear weapons capability and that its F-16 aircraft would be so advanced as to upset the military balance in the subcontinent.

The two countries' Foreign Ministers signed an agreement in New Delhi on March 10, 1983, establishing a joint commission to promote co-operation in a range of areas, with the exception of political and military questions. No progress was made, however, on the proposals for a non-aggression pact and a treaty of friendship and co-operation; in particular, Pakistan rejected Indian proposals that all disputes should be solved on a bilateral basis without recourse to international forums such as the United Nations, and that both sides should promise not to provide military facilities for third countries. Indo-Pakistani relations seriously deteriorated in 1984 because of Indian suspicions that Pakistan was assisting a terrorist campaign by Sikh separatists in the Indian state of Punjab, and negotiations between the two countries' Foreign Secretaries and meetings of the joint commission were suspended.

During this period a new outbreak of fighting occurred in Kashmir in the Siachin Glacier region, an area near the Chinese border at an altitude of about 6,000 metres, about 160 miles (250 km) north-east of Srinagar. Neither the 1949 ceasefire line nor the 1971 line of control had demarcated the border in this region, as no fighting had taken place there, and the area was so inhospitable that neither side had thought it likely to become a matter of contention; both agreements merely said that "the line continues northwards" into the glacier region from the last demarcated point just north of the Shyok river. Pakistan claimed that its control over the area was internationally recognized, as was shown by the facts that foreign mountaineering expeditions had obtained the Pakistan government's permission before going there and that reputable map publishers showed the line of control running north-east from the Shyok river to the Karakoram Pass (i.e. with the whole of the Siachin Glacier area under Pakistani control). The Pakistan-China border agreement of 1963[1] fixed the north-eastern terminus of the line of control at the Karakoram Pass, east of the Siachin Glacier; this agreement was not recognized by the Indian government, however, which maintained that Pakistan was "illegally" in control of the area.

Starting in the late 1970s, small units from the Indian High Altitude Warfare School were sent on to the 75 kilometre-long glacier from the Nubra river valley to the south, and early in 1984 a force of 100 Indian troops occupied its northern end. Pakistani troops made unsuccessful attempts to dislodge this force in June 1984, and again in June and September 1985.

Following the assassination of Mrs Gandhi by Sikh separatists on Oct. 31, 1984, President Zia appealed for an improvement in Indo-Pakistani relations. The talks at Foreign Secretary level were subsequently resumed in Islamabad on April 4-5, 1985, and after another meeting in New Delhi on July 30-Aug. 1, at which the proposals for a non-aggression pact and a

[1]See page 285.

treaty of friendship and co-operation were discussed, it was announced that both sides had agreed to "continue efforts aimed at the conclusion of a comprehensive treaty".

At a meeting between President Zia and the new Indian Prime Minister, Rajiv Gandhi, in New Delhi on Dec. 17, 1985, it was agreed that the two countries' Defence Secretaries should meet to find a peaceful solution of the Siachin Glacier issue. The Defence Secretaries subsequently held two meetings, but their discussions remained inconclusive. Five Pakistani soldiers were reported killed in June 1986 in an artillery exchange on the glacier. President Zia told a press conference on Nov. 12, 1986, that the situation there had reached a stalemate, and that this state of affairs would continue until India came to an agreement with Pakistan on the issue.

A tense situation developed on the border after India began winter manoeuvres involving about 200,000 troops in late October 1986, and in December Pakistan began military exercises on a similar scale. The Indian government closed the Punjab frontier on Jan. 23, 1987, accusing Pakistan of preparing to attack, whereupon the Pakistan government proposed immediate talks to reduce tension. Although talks between senior diplomats and army officers opened in New Delhi on Jan. 31, the centre of tension shifted from the Punjab border to Kashmir, where according to Indian sources the army evacuated 100 villages after Pakistani troops shelled part of the area on Feb. 1-2. An agreement was signed on Feb. 4 whereby India and Pakistan would withdraw their troops from the border in stages, beginning with about 50,000 men on each side in Kashmir.

CH

Indonesia-Portugal (East Timor)

The island of Timor to the north-west of Australia was for several centuries divided between Dutch and Portuguese colonial rule in the western and eastern halves of the island respectively. After West Timor had joined with other parts of the Dutch East Indies to become the Republic of Indonesia in 1949, East Timor continued under Portuguese rule until the mid-1970s but was then incorporated into Indonesia in August 1976 following Indonesian military intervention. Whereas the territory is now regarded by Indonesia as its 27th province (called Loro Sae), the Portuguese government and a majority of UN member states have refused to recognize Indonesia's claim to sovereignty over East Timor and have asserted that its people have the right to self-determination of their status.

Background to the Dispute

The territory of East Timor was one of the remnants of the South-East Asian part of the Portuguese empire, most of which was taken over by the Dutch in the 17th century and became the Dutch East Indies; whereas the iatter (including West Timor) became independent as the Republic of Indonesia in 1949, East Timor remained under Portuguese rule throughout this period. During the colonial era East Timor was largely under the influence of Roman Catholic priests, who gave it a Portuguese character and converted to Catholicism about 40 per cent of the local population and thus made it distinct from the Moslem population of Indonesian West Timor. To the Portuguese, East Timor was of value mainly because of the export of sandalwood, most of it to China, but it was never properly developed. In 1974 the territory had no made-up roads outside Díli (the capital); per capita income was about $40 per annum; the illiteracy rate was over 90 per cent (out of a total population officially stated to number 653,211 persons); and there was only one secondary school.

In the wake of the April 1974 revolution in Portugal, which led to the decolonization of Portuguese overseas territories, the population of East Timor was divided over its political future—the options being separate independence, integration with Indonesia or continued links with Portugal—and by 1975 the two main factions were involved in civil war. When it appeared that the territory was going to be ruled by a left-wing liberation movement (the Revolutionary Front for Independence, or Fretilin), East Timor was in December 1975 seized by Indonesian forces (officially described as volunteers), who supported the pro-Indonesian parties in East Timor. The latter set up a provisional government, which asked for East Timor's incorporation in Indonesia, and this subsequently took place in August 1976.

Fretilin, which had set up a rival government of the "Democratic Republic of East Timor", was supported, and the Indonesian action condemned, by a majority of United Nations member states, mainly on the grounds that the population of East Timor had not been consulted on its political future. While guerrilla warfare by Fretilin forces continued on a diminishing scale, the Indonesian authorities began to develop their new province by building roads, restoring the country's infrastructure devastated by the civil war and setting up schools where tuition was in the Indonesian language.

The de facto incorporation of East Timor into Indonesia was gradually accepted by a growing number of governments (though not by a majority of UN member states), those which recognized it de jure including Australia and New Zealand. Under international law as interpreted by the United Nations, Portugal is still regarded as responsible for East Timor and its eventual decolonization, whereas Indonesia claims to have completed the decolonization process in the territory. The governments of the United States and of Australia in particular have made it clear that they do not wish to embarrass the government of Indonesia, a non-communist state in a region where it is desired to exclude communist influence.

Emergence of Political Parties in Portuguese Timor

After the Portuguese revolution of April 1974, the new government of Portugal first discussed the future of East Timor with Indonesian leaders on Oct. 17, 1974, when Dr Antônio de Almeida Santos, then Portuguese Minister for Inter-Territorial Co-ordination, visited Jakarta and said that he did not consider total independence of the territory to be a realistic solution because a majority of its people wished to maintain ties with Portugal. He added that the best way to decolonize Timor would be by a referendum to be held in May 1975, and that a constituent assembly should be elected before that date.

The future of the territory was also discussed in Java early in September 1974 by President Suharto of Indonesia and Gough Whitlam, the then (Labor) Prime Minister of Australia, who were reported to have agreed that annexation by Indonesia would be the best solution for Timor. The Australian government was said to hold the view that an independent Timor would not be able to survive as a state and would be "a potential threat to the region". Both sides agreed to respect the wishes of the Timorese people and not to interfere. A member of the Portuguese Supreme Revolutionary Council, however, declared at the end of May 1975 that the plan to hold a referendum in East Timor had been discarded.

Political parties formed in Portuguese Timor after the Portuguese revolution included (i) the Democratic Union of Timor (*União Democrática de Timor*, UDT), which stood for continued, though looser, connexions with Portugal; (ii) the Timorese Democratic People's Union (Apodeti), which advocated the union of the territory (as an autonomous province) with Indonesia on historical, geographical and ethnic grounds; and (iii) the Timorese Social Democratic Association (ASDT), which stood for full independence of the territory, possibly after a five-year transitional period, on the grounds that 90 per cent of the population were uneducated and without political consciousness and an immediate referendum would therefore give a distorted picture and open the way to corruption and manipulation. The ASDT was eventually superseded by Fretilin, which called for immediate independence and which was widely regarded as pro-communist.

At the end of a conference held in Macao between the Portuguese government, the UDT and Apodeti on June 26-28, 1975, it was affirmed that the people of East Timor had "the right to self-determination with all its consequences, including independence" on "the principle according to which it lies with the people of Timor, and with them alone, to define the political future of the territory". Portuguese sovereignty was to continue until October 1978 unless otherwise agreed by the Portuguese government and the proposed Timorese People's Assembly. In the meantime there was to be a Portuguese-controlled government under a high commissioner and five assistant secretaries (for some of whose posts the Timorese parties would be allowed to submit names of candidates, and of whom three would be Portuguese and the other two probably Timorese). A constitutional law published in Lisbon on July 13, 1975, provided for elections to be held in October 1976 to the People's Assembly, which would draft political and administrative statutes for the territory.

Outbreak of Civil War and Loss of Control by Portugal

The emergence of Fretilin as an anti-Indonesian revolutionary movement aroused a hostile reaction in Indonesia (whose government had stated on Feb. 25, 1975, that it had no territorial ambition and was not planning an invasion of East Timor). In mid-1975 the UDT and Indonesian officials had several meetings in Jakarta and Kupang (the capital of Indonesian West Timor), after which the UDT president, Francisco Xavier Lopes da Cruz, declared that his party would soon take action against Fretilin (which had attacked UDT members in outlying areas), and on Aug. 6 he declared: 'We are realists. If we want to be independent we must follow the Indonesian political line; otherwise it is independence for a week or a month."

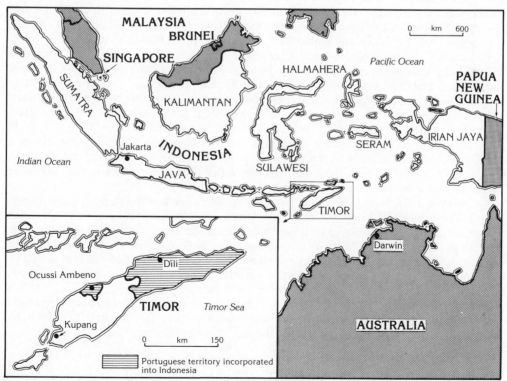

Map 35   East Timor.

331

On Aug. 11, 1975, the UDT staged a coup and gained control of important sectors of Díli. On the following day the UDT demanded immediate independence from Portugal and the imprisonment of all Fretilin members, in response to which the President of Portugal stated in Lisbon on the same day that these demands were unacceptable and claimed that the governor of Portuguese Timor was still in full control. The action of the UDT led to the outbreak of full-scale civil war between the forces of Fretilin on the one hand and on the other those of the UDT, fighting as an Anti-Communist Movement (MAC) and supported by Apodeti and two smaller groups—the Kota and *Trabalhista* (Labour) parties.

On Aug. 21 the Portuguese authorities admitted that they had lost control of the territory. Several hundred Portuguese were evacuated to Australia, where they reported that atrocities had been committed by both sides in the civil war. On Aug. 27 the governor and members of his administration were evacuated to Atauro, an island 30 miles (48 km) north of Díli. By Sept. 1, 1975, Fretilin had taken control of Díli and on Sept. 8 it claimed to have gained complete control of East Timor; it also stated that it was ready for peace talks; that it had dropped its original demand for immediate independence from Portugal; and that it wished to move gradually towards self-government, with the installation of a provisional government early in 1976, the election of a constituent assembly and independence within a few years.

The Indonesian Defence Ministry stated on Sept. 7, 1975, that Indonesian pre-emptive strikes against Fretilin positions might be considered if these were advanced any closer to the Indonesian border; on Sept. 9 it added that it refused to accept any Portuguese move to hand the territory over to a Fretilin government; and on Sept. 13 Dr Adam Malik, the Indonesian Foreign Minister, declared that his country had the right to intervene in East Timor if the war being waged there endangered Indonesian territory, but at the same time he appealed to all factions to cease fighting. Although Fretilin claimed on Oct. 11 that it was in full control of Portuguese Timor and had established a transitional administration, the Indonesian government stated on Oct. 14 that pro-Indonesian forces were holding large sections of the territory and would by the end of October be in control of all of it. It was estimated in Jakarta that since the outbreak of the fighting between 40,000 and 50,000 inhabitants had fled from East Timor and that Díli's population had decreased from 25,000 to about 5,000.

In a memorandum of understanding signed in Rome on Nov. 3, 1975, after a meeting between the Indonesian and Portuguese Foreign Ministers, it was agreed that Portugal represented the legitimate authority in Portuguese Timor and was fundamentally responsible for its decolonization; that there should as soon as possible be a meeting between the Portuguese authorities and all the territory's political parties to bring the fighting to an end; and that Portugal would make "all efforts towards a speedy and orderly implementation of the act of self-determination by the people of Portuguese Timor". Fretilin, however, was on Nov. 6 reported to have refused to recognize the results of the Rome meeting, and on Nov. 14 it asserted that a full Indonesian invasion was imminent (while in Australia it was claimed that it had already begun).

On Nov. 28, 1975, Fretilin declared the territory independent as the Democratic Republic of East Timor, of which Francisco Xavier do Amaral (the Fretilin president) was sworn in as President on Nov. 29, and a government was formed on Dec. 1 under Nicolau dos Reis Lobato as Prime Minister, Fretilin claimed that some 50 Afro-Asian countries had pledged support for an independent East Timor, and on Dec. 1 the new republic was recognized by Mozambique. The four pro-Indonesian parties, on the other hand, declared on Nov. 29 that, as Fretilin's action had "removed the last remains of Portuguese sovereignty in Timor", East Timor was now part of Indonesian territory. The Lisbon government for its part rejected the declarations of both Fretilin and the pro-Indonesian parties, and on Nov. 30 it formally requested United Nations help in settling the East Timor problem.

Indonesian Occupation of East Timor

On Dec. 7, 1975, some 1,000 paratroopers from Indonesia, supported by a naval bombardment, entered East Timor and seized Díli, from which they expelled Fretilin's troops. In Jakarta it was announced that Díli had been "liberated by the people's resistance, spearheaded by Apodeti, the UDT and the Kota and *Trabalhista* parties" and that these resistance forces were "supported by Indonesian volunteers". The Portuguese government on the same day broke off all diplomatic relations with Indonesia (which the latter had in 1964 reduced to consular level because of Portugal's colonial policies) and announced that it would resort to the United Nations with the aim of securing the cessation of "Indonesia's military intervention" as well as a peaceful negotiated solution to the conflict and the decolonization process.

Dr Malik, then Indonesian Foreign Minister, on the other hand said on Dec. 8 that he considered Portuguese sovereignty in Timor to have ended with Fretilin's declaration of independence on Nov. 28; that Díli was being ruled by a coalition of the four pro-Indonesian parties; that Fretilin's resistance had ended; and that Indonesian troops would remain in East Timor only until its people had decided their own future.

The Indonesian Minister of Information said in a statement issued on Dec. 8 that "the presence of Indonesian volunteers in Portuguese Timor" was founded on a number of considerations, among them "the inability of Portugal to control the situation so that the Rome memorandum could not, as a practical matter, be implemented"; a request for help made by the four pro-Indonesian parties; the Indonesian government's "moral responsibility to guarantee the proper, orderly and peaceful decolonization of Portuguese Timor in accordance with the aspirations and desires of all the people in the territory"; the Indonesian government's inability to "permit the situation in East Timor to go on indefinitely and to endanger national security and the stability of the South-East Asian region"; and the need "to take steps to end these continuing developments and safeguard national territorial integrity, to defend the sovereignty of the state and to protect the Indonesian people from disturbances, attacks, invasion, plunder and other provocative acts by Fretilin".

Indonesian and pro-Indonesian forces subsequently consolidated their hold on East Timor, and on Dec. 17 a provisional government was formed with Arnaldo dos Reis Araujo (of Apodeti) as chief executive officer. Four days earlier, the Portuguese enclave of Ocussi Ambeno (on the north coast of Indonesian West Timor) had been officially incorporated in Indonesia; moreover, following the evacuation of the Portuguese governor and his administration from the island of Atauro early in December, the island was occupied by pro-Indonesian forces on Dec. 28, when the Indonesian flag was hoisted on it. The Portuguese presence in East Timor was thus finally ended. Meanwhile, the fighting continued, with Indonesian radio claiming in January 1976 that pro-Indonesian forces controlled two-thirds of East Timor and Fretilin claiming control over 80 per cent of the territory. Francisco Xavier Lopes da Cruz, Vice-Chairman of the provisional government, said in mid-February that up to 60,000 people had lost their lives in East Timor since August 1975.

Incorporation of East Timor in Indonesia

The Indonesian Foreign Ministry announced on March 21, 1976, that the provisional government of East Timor had decided to establish a parliament to approve the merger of the territory with Indonesia and that the United Nations had been informed accordingly. Two months later a petition to integrate East Timor into Indonesia was approved on May 31 by the newly-formed People's Representative Council of 28 members. Of 25 countries invited to send observers to the Council's session, only India, Iran, Malaysia, New Zealand, Nigeria, Saudi Arabia and Thailand did so, while countries which boycotted the session included Australia, Japan, Papua New Guinea, the Philippines, Singapore and the United States.

After the Council's petition had been officially handed over to President Suharto of Indonesia in Jakarta on June 7, 1976, East Timor was symbolically transferred to an Indonesian fact-finding mission on June 24. The United Nations had been invited to take part in this mission but had declined to do so on the grounds that no UN observers had supervised the election of the Council's members who had drawn up the petition. On June 29 the Indonesian government announced its official acceptance of the merger; a bill legalizing East Timor's annexation was passed by the Indonesian Parliament on July 17; and on Aug. 17 East Timor was proclaimed Indonesia's 27th province under the name of Loro Sae, with Arnaldo dos Reis Araujo as its first governor and Francisco Xavier Lopes da Cruz as his deputy.

Guerrilla warfare continued during subsequent years to be conducted by groups of followers of Fretilin and also of the UDT, but many of Fretilin's leaders surrendered or were captured or killed by Indonesian forces, while others represented Fretilin's cause outside East Timor. Following an amnesty offered by President Suharto on Aug. 16, 1977, to all Fretilin supporters who surrendered by the end of that year, large numbers of them were said to have given themselves up, the total being about 60,000, according to Indonesian claims made in mid-1978. Among those who surrendered was Francisco Xavier do Amaral (whom Fretilin had, on Sept. 13, 1977, removed from his posts of president of the organization and President of the Democratic Republic of East Timor, replacing him by Nicolau dos Reis Lobato, who was, however, killed in battle on Jan. 1, 1979). On May 22, 1979, it was reported that President Suharto had appointed the former Fretilin president as deputy governor of the province.

United Nations Condemnation of Indonesia's Action

The UN Trusteeship Committee passed, on Dec. 11, 1975, by 69 votes (including Australia, China and the Soviet Union) to 11 (Benin, India, Indonesia, Iran, Japan, Malaysia, Mauritania, Morocco, the Philippines, Saudi Arabia and Thailand), with 38 abstentions (including the member countries of the European Community, New Zealand, Singapore and the United States) a resolution calling on Indonesia to withdraw from Portuguese Timor immediately and to desist from "further violations of the territorial integrity" of Portuguese Timor. Dr Malik, however, stated on the same day that his country did not feel bound by the resolution and that Indonesia had no troops in the territory except volunteers.

The UN General Assembly, on Dec. 12, 1975, passed, by 72 voltes to 10 with 43 abstentions, a resolution calling on Indonesia to withdraw from East Timor and to enable the latter's people to decide their own future, and condemned the "military intervention of the armed forces of Indonesia". The UN Security Council, meeting at Portugal's request, on Dec. 22 unanimously called on Indonesia to withdraw its forces from East Timor without delay and requested Portugal to co-operate with the United Nations to enable East Timor's people to exercise their right of self-determination. This resolution was also rejected by Indonesia the next day.

Dr Malik said after a visit to Díli on Jan. 9-10, 1976, that his government regarded East Timor as de facto part of Indonesia, but that he had suggested to the provisional government that a consultation of East Timor's people should take place in a year's time. On Jan. 13, however, he stated that the provisional government had invited the Indonesian government to proclaim its sovereignty over East Timor; that they had discarded the idea of consultation; and that they now wanted a law declaring the territory to be part of Indonesia.

Following talks involving Dr Waldheim (the Un Secretary-General) and representatives of Indonesia, Portugal, Australia and Fretilin, a UN special envoy (Vittorio Winspeare Guicciardi, a UN under-secretary-general) visited Lisbon and Jakarta in mid-January and arrived in East Timor on Jan. 18, when Arnaldo dos Reis Araujo was reported to have told him that East Timor had already declared itself part of Indonesia and that a consultation of the people was "superfluous". A proposed visit by the Un special envoy to Fretilin bases in East Timor was called off by Fretilin on Feb. 5 because of Indonesian bombardments and the advance of pro-Indonesian forces.

The UN Security Council, which had debated the situation in East Timor for two weeks, adopted, on April 22, 1976, a resolution sponsored by Guyana and Tanzania and calling on

Indonesia to withdraw all its forces from East Timor without delay and requesting the UN Secretary-General to charge his special envoy with pursuing his mission of fact-finding and consultation with the parties concerned. The resolution was approved by 12 votes to none with two abstentions (Japan and the United States) and without Benin taking part in the vote.

In subsequent years the cause of the right of the people of East Timor to self-determination continued to be defended in the movement of non-aligned countries and at successive sessions of the UN General Assembly. Thus the fifth conference of heads of state and government of the Non-Aligned Movement (NAM) held in Colombo on Aug. 16-19, 1976, included in its political declaration, as demanded by Mozambique, a reaffirmation of the right of self-determination for the people of East Timor. Moreover, a further call for "self-determination for the people of East Timor" was included in the political declaration adopted by consensus on Sept. 9, 1979, by the sixth NAM conference of heads of state and government held in Havana. This was done despite the fact that a special envoy of President Castro of Cuba had stated in Jakarta on April 11, 1979, that the issue of East Timor would not be included in the conference agenda.

Later Australian, New Zealand and Portuguese Attitudes to East Timor Issue

The Australian government's attitude to the conflict developed gradually from criticism of Indonesia's action to acceptance of the incorporation of East Timor in Indonesia as an accomplished fact. In a report released on June 16, 1977, two Australian Foreign Ministry officials accepted the incorporation of East Timor in Indonesia as an "irreversible fact". They found that the towns of the territory and their environs were completely controlled by the provincial authorities; that small areas in the hills were controlled by Fretilin forces; and that the rest of the population was scattered throughout a no-man's land. In their view there was no evidence that Fretilin could mount major operations, but guerrilla harassment could probably be expected for some years.

In an earlier report published on Feb. 21, 1977, James Dunn (a former Australian consul in East Timor and head of the foreign affairs division of the Australian Parliament's research service) estimated that up to 100,000 Timorese had been massacred by Indonesian troops after the 1975 invasion and that those killed had included about 7,000 Chinese (about half East Timor's Chinese population). The Indonesian government objected on March 1 to Dunn's "hostile activities", and Andrew Peacock (Australia's Foreign Minister) stated in Parliament on March 16 that the Dunn report had no official status.

On Jan. 20, 1978, the Foreign Minister of Australia announced that the government had recognized the incorporation of East Timor into Indonesia, although it remained critical of the means by which this integration had been achieved. On Dec. 15 of that year he said that Australia had decided to recognize formally the Indonesian takeover of East Timor, but added: "The acceptance of this situation does not alter the opposition which the government has consistently expressed regarding the manner of the incorporation." Anthony Street, the newly-appointed Australian Foreign Minister, said during a visit to Jakarta on Nov. 14, 1980, that as far as Australia and Indonesia were concerned the East Timor problem had been settled.

The New Zealand ambassador to Indonesia stated on July 20, 1978, that his government supported President Suharto in refusing to tolerate outside interference in East Timor's integration in Indonesia, and that New Zealand would reinforce its support for the integration by participating in the development of Indonesia's newest province.

Portugal's continuing insistence on the East Timor people's right to self-determination was demonstrated when the Portuguese Prime Minister on Sept. 5, 1979, received six leaders of a new National Movement for the Liberation of and Independence of Timor-Díli, which had been formed with the intention of bringing together the UDT, Fretilin and all other Timorese forces in a united effort to achieve the territory's independence under a Christian regime. Moreover, on Sept. 13, 1980, the Portuguese government (of the centre-right

Democratic Alliance) issued a statement announcing that it would seek direct talks with Indonesian officials on independence for East Timor but reaffirming that Portugal remained "faithful to its obligations and responsibilities towards Timor", asserting that the Timorese people had the right to self-determination, the statement added that recognition by Portugal of "the situation created in East Timor" would not be involved in the talks. The Indonesian government rejected the Portuguese proposal on Sept. 21.

Although the Portuguese government continued, during 1981, to claim sovereignty over East Timor, it was disclosed in a report—which was not released in Lisbon until Oct. 16, 1981—that in June 1975 there had been secret talks in Hong Kong between Indonesian and Portuguese officials and that the latter had advised the Indonesians that the Portuguese (left-wing) leaders at the time (President Francisco da Costa Gomes, Prime Minister Vasco Gonçalves and members of the Revolutionary Council) would accept East Timor's incorporation into Indonesia.

Continued Unsettled Situation in East Timor

The Indonesian Foreign Minister (Dr Mochtar Kasumaatmadja) said in London on Oct. 15, 1979, that since 1975 about 60,000 people had died as a result of the civil war and starvation, but added that 200,000 people were benefiting from relief operations and that another 62,000 would be covered by a new Red Cross programme. In November 1979 the population of East Timor was officially stated to total 522,433 people (which meant a decline, since 1974, by more than 130,000, of whom about about 5,000 had left for Australia and an estimated 25,000 for West Timor).

In June 1981 the East Timor People's Representative Council sent to President Suharto of Indonesia a report in which, although "undying gratitude" was expressed for East Timor's incorporation in Indonesia, it was stated that the conduct of Indonesian officials and troops was that of "conquerors towards a conquered people" and that numerous acts of murder, torture and other violence had been committed. According to a letter sent in November 1981 by the head of the Roman Catholic Church in East Timor to the chairman of the Australian Catholic Relief, Indonesian forces had in military operations in July-September 1981 killed many people, including women and children. On Feb. 23, 1982, the Catholic Institute for International Relations stated in London that Indonesian control was "still not unchallenged" in East Timor and that the Indonesian Army was carrying out large-scale operations in the eastern part of the territory.

Fretilin forces, whose strength was variously estimated at between 200 and 6,000 armed men, continued guerrilla activities from 1982 onwards. The Indonesian government conducted no negotiations with the movement, but had since 1977 given amnesty to any surrendering guerrillas.

A revitalized Fretilin command structure, the Revolutionary Council of National Resistance led by José Gusmão Sha Na Na, was in October 1982 reported to be operating under difficult conditions. According to a letter of Feb. 18, 1984, by the Bishop of East Timor, large numbers of Fretilin sympathizers had been arrested and many had been executed. In a letter of Jan. 1, 1985, the Bishop referred to "successive, systematic and regular clean-up operations by Indonesian troops", the recruiting of children to fight Fretilin, and the killing of peasants in reprisal for Fretilin attacks. Amnesty International claimed on June 26, 1985, that since the Indonesian takeover up to 500,000 people in East Timor had been killed or "resettled". The Indonesian Foreign Minister, however, denied that human rights had been violated in East Timor.

At the United Nations, the Secretary-General recommended in 1984 that the General Assembly should again (as in 1983) defer to debate on East Timor, and early in September 1984 this recommendation was endorsed by the UN Decolonization Committee, as negotiations between Indonesia and Portugal (still recognized by the United Nations as the administering power in East Timor) had been in progress since July 1983.

HWD

Japan-South Korea (Tokto)

Since the 1950s a dispute has persisted between Japan and South Korea over the rightful ownership of an outcrop of rocks in the Sea of Japan called Tokto by the South Koreans and Takeshima by the Japanese (and also known internationally as the Liancourt Rocks). Whereas South Korea asserted its jurisdiction over the islets in 1952, Japan has consistently claimed that they form part of its historic national territory. (The location of the islets is shown in the map on page 357.)

Geographical and Historical Background

The disputed rocks are situated in the Sea of Japan about 200 kilometres east of the central South Korean mainland (and some 80 kilometres east-south-east of the South Korean island of Ullung-do) and about 200 kilometres north of the main Japanese island of Honshu (and about 150 kilometres north-north-west of the Japanese island of Oki). There are two main islets (surrounded by a number of reefs) rising about 150 metres above sea level and the total land area is 23 hectares (less than a tenth of a square mile). The islets have substantial phosphate (guano) deposits which have never been developed, not least because there is no safe anchorage and access can only be achieved by small boat in calm weather conditions. The islets had no permanent inhabitants until the South Koreans established a Coast Guard presence on them in 1954.

Japan cites various extant documents and maps which it claims show inter alia that Japanese families exercised title to the islets in the early 17th century (when they were known in Japan as Matsushima) and that subsequently they were consistently regarded as part of Japanese territory. It also points out that in 1905 (the year in which Japan established a protectorate over Korea, prior to outright annexation in 1910) the Japanese government specifically announced the incorporation of the islets into Honshu's Shimane prefecture and that from then until World War II the Japanese authorities regularly issued licences for sea-lion hunting on the islands.

For its part, South Korea claims that the islets have been Korean national territory throughout history and that any early attempts by Japan to exercise authority over them had no legal validity. It regards Japan's incorporation of the islets into Shimane prefecture in 1905 as an act of imperialism characteristic of Japanese policy at that time and essentially as illegal under present-day international law as the subsequent annexation of Korea itself.

Conflicting Views of 1945-47 Territorial Dispositions—1952 Proclamation of South Korean Jurisdiction

South Korea supports its claim to historic sovereignty over the islets with the additional contention that after Japan's defeat in World War II Korean jurisdiction was confirmed by the wartime allies in their dispositions relating to Japanese-held territory. Texts cited by the South Korean side include (i) the declaration issued by the United States and Britain at Potsdam on July 26, 1945, that post-war Japanese sovereignty "shall be limited to the islands of Honshu, Hokkaido, Kyushu and Shikoku [the four main Japanese islands] and such minor islands as we shall determine"; (ii) a memorandum (SCAPIN No. 677) issued on Jan. 29, 1946, by the Supreme Allied Commander in Japan, Gen. Douglas MacArthur, defining Japan as including "the four main islands ... and the approximately 1,000 smaller adjacent islands" and decreeing the cessation of Japanese administration over various non-adjacent territory, including the Liancourt Rocks (i.e. Tokto/Takeshima); and (iii) the peace treaty signed in San Francisco in September 1951 between Japan and the Western allies, under which Japan renounced in perpetuity its formal imperial possessions, including Korea.[1]

---

[1] These texts are also central to the Japan-Soviet Union dispute over a number of islands off northern Japan, for which see pages 339-56.

Japan, on the other hand, contends that none of these texts, nor any other internationally-valid post-war instrument, amounted to a definitive territorial settlement requiring the surrender of its claim to sovereignty over the islets. It maintains in particular that SCAPIN No. 677 was expressly concerned with administrative functions and not with sovereignty, pointing out that the memorandum itself recorded that its content did not indicate allied policy as to the "ultimate determination" of islands being excluded from Japanese administration. Japan also lays stress on the fact that the "MacArthur line" established under SCAPIN No. 677 was abolished by the allies on April 25, 1952 (three days before the entry into force of the San Francisco peace treaty), claiming that at that point the islets legally reverted to Japanese sovereignty as part of Shimane prefecture.

Three months before the Japanese peace treaty came into force and while the Korean war was still in progress,[2] President Syngman Rhee of South Korea on Jan. 18, 1952, proclaimed Korean jurisdiction over waters within a line running an average of 60 nautical miles (and up to 170 miles) from the Korean coast. Aimed principally at excluding Japanese and other fishermen from some of the richest fishing grounds in the Sea of Japan, this so-called "Syngman Rhee line" ran beyond the Tokto islets, which were therefore expressly included within Korean territory. The Japanese government responded on Jan. 28, 1952, by officially protesting against what it described as South Korea's unilateral proclamation of jurisdiction over the high seas and also declaring its non-recognition of the South Korean assumption of rights to the islets, which were described as being "without question Japanese territory".

The South Korean government replied on Feb. 12, 1952, with a Note Verbale recording that it "does not feel inclined to enter into full arguments ... over the ownership of the Liancourt Rocks, known as Tokto in Korea through long centuries, and merely wishes to remind the Japanese government that SCAPIN No. 677 dated Jan. 29, 1946, explicitly excluded the islets from the territorial possessions of Japan and that, further, the same islets were left on the Korean side of the MacArthur line—facts which endorse and confirm the Korean claim to them, which is beyond dispute". This argument was in turn rejected on April 25, 1952, by Japan, which reiterated its contention that, since SCAPIN No. 677 had only directed that Japan should "cease exercising, or attempting to exercise, government or administrative authority over the Liancourt Rocks", it had not decreed the exclusion of the islands from Japanese sovereignty.

1953-54 Incidents at the Islets—Establishment of South Korean Presence

Following what it regarded as the reversion of the islets to Japanese sovereignty in April 1952, the Japanese government laid plans for the re-establishment of actual control, but was precluded from doing so immediately by the fact that the area in question had been designated a US bombing practice zone. (The physical dangers arising from this status had already been demonstrated by an incident near Tokto in June 1948 when 16 Korean fishermen had been killed and four of their boats destroyed by US Air Force planes engaged in bombing practice.) When the designation was eventually lifted by a joint US-Japanese decision of March 19, 1953, the Shimane prefectural authorities began consideration of the issue of licences for fishing and sea-lion hunting at the islets; however, on May 28, 1953, the Japanese marine investigation vessel *Shimane-maru* discovered about 30 Korean fishermen on the islets engaged in collecting seaweed and shellfish. Accordingly, the Japanese government on June 22, 1953, protested to South Korea against "these illegal acts of invasion into Japan's territory committed by Korean nationals" and requested that "adequate and effective measures be taken to prevent the recurrence of a similar case in the future".

The following month, on July 12, 1953, a Japanese patrol boat which ordered the Koreans to leave the islets was fired on by "armed Korean officials" protecting the fishermen. Moreover, a series of notices subsequently erected on the islets by the Japanese, warning

---

[2]For an account of the post-war Korean question, see pages 356-65.

against unauthorized fishing activities, were quickly taken down by the Koreans.

In June 1954 the South Korean Interior Ministry announced that the Korean Coast Guard had established a permanent presence on the islets "to protect them from Japanese aggression", following which a Korean-constructed lighthouse came into operation on Aug. 10. In a further incident on Aug. 23, another Japanese patrol boat was fired at by South Korean personnel stationed on the islets, where according to Japanese accounts they subsequently established various facilities including radio communications, unloading derricks and several buildings.

In view of the tensions around the islets, the Japanese government on Sept. 25, 1954, proposed to South Korea that the sovereignty dispute should be submitted to the International Court of Justice, stating that it would accept whatever decision the Court made and also proposing that in the interim the two sides should consult on steps to prevent any further aggravation of the situation. This proposal was, however, rejected by the South Korean government on Oct. 28, 1954.

Maintenance of Japanese Claim

Although Japan and South Korea normalized their diplomatic relations in 1960, the territorial issue was left unresolved, and Japan has regularly reiterated its claim to Tokto/Takeshima. It followed this practice most recently at a meeting of the two countries' Foreign Ministers held in Tokyo on Sept. 10, 1986, provoking a hostile reaction in the South Korean media and political parties (both government and opposition), some of which demanded that relations with Japan should be broken off if the claim was pursued.

Shortly before the Tokyo meeting, the South Korean government had lodged a strong diplomatic protest with Japan on Sept. 6, 1986, following the publication of an interview in which the Japanese Education Minister, Masayuki Fujio, had suggested that Japan's annexation of Korea in 1910 had been carried out with the consent of the Korean people. Fujio was thereupon dismissed from the Cabinet by the Japanese Prime Minister, Yasuhiro Nakasone, who also sent a formal apology to the South Korean government.

AJD

Japan-Soviet Union

Since 1945 relations between Japan and the Soviet Union have been overshadowed by a territorial dispute over a number of islands off the north-east coast of Japan which were occupied by the Soviet Union in the closing stages of World War II. The islands in question are the Habomai group together with Shikotan, Kunashiri and Etorofu, all of which are regarded by Japan as integral parts of its national territory. Although the two countries normalized their diplomatic relations in 1956, the unresolved dispute over the northern islands has been the main stumbling-block to the conclusion of a formal peace treaty between Japan and the Soviet Union. Indeed, with the passage of time the dispute had become more intractable. Whereas the Soviet Union appeared to be willing in the mid-1950s to return the Habomai islands and Shikotan to Japan provided the latter signed a peace treaty which recognized Soviet sovereignty over Kunashiri and Etorofu, in recent years the Soviet Union has insisted that the territorial issue between the two countries is now closed.

The Disputed Islands

The islands in dispute between Japan and the Soviet Union are the Habomai group (i.e. Suisho, Shibotsu, Yuri Akiyiri and Taraku) as well as Shikotan, Kunashiri and Etorofu—all situated off the north-east coast of Hokkaido, the northern-most of Japan's four main islands. The disputed islands comprise a total land area of 4,996 sq km, of which Etorofu accounts for 3,139 sq km, Kunashiri 1,500 sq km, Shikotan 225 sq km, and the Habomais 102 sq km. In terms of distance, Suisho island in the Habomais is only five kilometres from the nearest point of Nemuro peninsula on the north-east tip of Hokkaido.

Etorofu and Kunashiri are the two most southerly islands in the chain of 20 main islands running south from the Kamchatka peninsula. Whereas Soviet sovereignty over the 18 Kurile islands stretching from Uruppu island northwards is not in dispute, Japan has consistently maintained that Etoforu and Kunashiri are distinct from the Kurile islands and that together with the Habomai group and Shikotan they are historically part of Japan in that until 1945 Russian influence had at no time extended south of Uruppu island. Japan also claims that as regards flora and fauna all the disputed islands are Japanese in botanical character and have a mild climate, whereas the islands from Uruppu to the north are subarctic. For its part, the Soviet Union has contested Japanese versions of the history of the disputed islands in the context of early Russian-Japanese relations and has in any case consistently maintained that its sovereignty over them was clearly established under agreements between the allied powers concluded towards the end of World War II. It also officially describes the disputed islands as the southern Kuriles.

The disputed islands occupy an important strategic position in that the seas around them provide the Soviet Navy with ice-free deep-water access from the Sea of Okhotsk to the Pacific Ocean, while the islands themselves contain several deep-water, ice-free natural harbours as well as large tracts of open land suitable for military bases. Moreover, the waters around the islands are a rich fisheries area traditionally exploited by Japanese fishermen.

Historical Background

Japanese and Russian accounts of the early history of the disputed islands differ as to which side was the first to become the dominant influence in the area in question. They also express conflicting views as to the validity and significance of certain treaties signed by Japan and Tsarist Russia in the 19th and early 20th centuries. Japan maintains in particular that the Treaty of Commerce, Navigation and Delimitation (also known as the Shimoda treaty) signed with Russia in 1855—and also the 1875 Russo-Japanese treaty under which Japan conceded Russian sovereignty over Sakhalin island in exchange for the Kurile islands—both confirmed Japanese sovereignty over the disputed islands. On the other hand, the Soviet Union contends that these treaties have no present-day significance, arguing that Russian territorial concessions to Japan in this period were exacted under duress and specifically that the Japanese aggression against Russia in 1904 nullified all agreements between the two sides.

A document entitled "Japan's Northern Territories" issued by the Japanese Foreign Ministry (and most recently updated in 1987) gives the following account of early Russo-Japanese territorial relations. "The Japanese were aware of Sakhalin and the Kurile islands long before the Russians ever knew of their existence. It was Japan which actually developed these northern regions. But the Japanese had to withdraw from these areas later because of the inroads made by the Russians. Towards the end of the 16th century Russia advanced eastward over the Ural mountains and through Siberia. At the beginning of the 18th century she ruled the Kamchatka peninsula and had discovered Alaska. By that time the Russians were in the northern part of the Kuriles and had come into contact with the Japanese there.

"In 1792 the Russian envoy, Adam Kirilovich Laksman, came to Nemuro in Hokkaido. He was followed by Nikolai Petrovich Rezanov, who came to Nagasaki in 1804 to try to open trade with Japan. The Shogunate [the hereditary military government which ruled Japan from 1192 to 1867], however, refused to respond, by citing Japan's traditional policy of isolationism. In response to these advances made by Russia, the Shogunate conducted surveys of the northern areas by sending Juzo Kondo and Rinzo Mamiya, among others, to the Kuriles and Sakhalin. In governing these islands, the Shogunate endeavoured to build up defences for these regions by establishing guard stations on Etorofu and other islands to the south in order to prevent incursions by foreign explorers or settlers.

"Meanwhile, Russia moved into the Kuriles not only by sending in survey expeditions but also by attempting to colonize the islands through a Russo-American company. Russian influence, however, at no time reached southward beyond Uruppu island because, as mentioned above, the Shogunate had established guard stations on Etorofu and other southern islands to prevent just such incursions. In view of these facts, when the Shogunate concluded the Treaty of commerce, Navigation and Delimitation with Russia in 1855, realizing a new interchange of goods and personnel between the two countries, as it had done earlier with the United States and Britain, the two signatories agreed in Article II of the treaty that thenceforth the boundary between Japan and Russia lay betwen Etorofu and Uruppu, and that the Kurile islands north of Uruppu belonged to Russia. The island of Sakhalin, the treaty also stipulated, was to have no national boundary but to remain a mixed settlement for both nations as before.

"In 1875 Japan decided to abandon all of Sakhalin island in exchange for the Kurile islands ceded by Russia by the Treaty for the Exchange of Sakhalin for the Kurile Islands. Article 2 of this treaty lists the names of 18 islands of the Kuriles, from Shimushu to Uruppu, that were to be handed over from Russia to Japan.

"These facts clearly show that the Habomais, Shikotan, Kunashiri and Etorofu have never been part of the territory of a foreign country but have always been inherent Japanese territory. They also testify to the fact that these islands of the northern territories were already at that time clearly distinguished from the Kurile islands that were ceded by Russia.

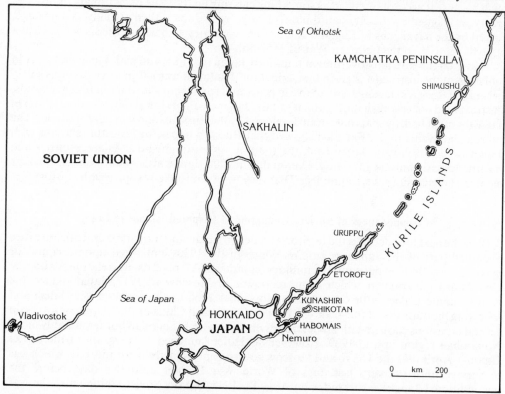

Map 36   The disputed northern islands.

In regard to Sakhalin, incidentally, the Treaty of Portsmouth which concluded the Russo-Japanese War in 1905 gave Japan the southern half of the island, south of 50 degrees north latitude". [Under the other main provisions of the Portsmouth treaty, Korea became a Japanese protectorate (and was annexed by Japan five years later) and Russia ceded to Japan the ice-free port of Port Arthur (now Lushun in China).]

Among many official Soviet refutations of the Japanese version of earlier history as outlined above was one published in September 1981 by *Izvestia* (the newspaper of the Presidium of the USSR Supreme Soviet). As translated by Moscow radio, this analysis included the following: "Absolutely all the arguments used by the [Japanese] authorities today hold no water, and first and foremost this applies to the assertion that the Kuriles are traditionally Japanese territory. Let us recall in this connexion that right up to the mid-19th century the so-called northern territories that Tokyo claims now were not part of Japan proper. What is more, even Hokkaido island, the northern part of present-day Japan, was not part of the country. Only a small peninsula in the southern part of Hokkaido was colonized by the Japanese principality of Matsumae. True, in 1798, the Japanese government proclaimed Hokkaido its territory, but was unable to actually rule it. In 1821 Hokkaido had to be returned to Matsumae principality. Only in 1834 did Japan again proclaim the island its territory, but even then the act was purely nominal. When in 1862 two Americans ... arrived in the south of Hokkaido, they noted that for the Japanese the island was an absolutely enigmatic land.

"So it is not hard to understand, bearing all this in mind, what the claims to the Kuriles are worth, for these islands were peacefully developed by Russia long before even Hokkaido, an island that lies south of the Kuriles, became part of Japan. Claims are being made in Japan that the Russians, by signing in 1855 the Shimoda treaty, recognized Japan's legitimate rights to part of the islands of the Kurile chain. But that is a clear-cut distortion of the historic truth. The Shimoda treaty did not give Japan any legitimate rights and could not recognize such because it was not intended as something clearing up the issue of legitimate rights. The treaty was signed by the Russian diplomat Putyatin in Japan, then actually as a hostage, forced by the naval guns of England and France, countries with whom Russia was then in a state of war [i.e. in the Crimean War of 1853-56].

"Later on the Russian government reminded Japan that Putyatin had signed the treaty in violation of the instructions given him, and if the document was left in force that was solely because of Russia's sincere desire to live in peace and friendship with Japan. In other words, the treaty did not establish the legitimacy of the Japanese rights but signified ceding to Japan a territory that had, by that time, been developed by the Russians and was part of Russia. The subsequent events in the Far East showed that Russia's hopes for peaceful relations with Japan were vain hopes. Japan took the road of aggression against Asian countries and regarded Russia only as an enemy. Eventually, in 1904, Japan attacked Russia, so Russia's territorial concessions were annulled. That they were a mistake was proved by history."

Circumstances of Soviet Occupation of Disputed Islands in 1945

Over the next four decades the territories ceded to Japan under the 1905 and other treaties remained part of the Japanese empire, which in the 1930s embarked upon a course of massive territorial expansion by military conquest. As regards its relations with the Communist government which came to power in Moscow in 1917, Japan signed the Anti-Comintern Pact with Germany in November 1936 (Italy joining a year later) and following the outbreak of full-scale war between Japan and China in 1937 Japanese forces on several occasions clashed with Soviet troops on the Soviet-Mongolian border, notably in the Nomonhan region in mid-1939. However, as Hitler launched his invasion of the Soviet Union in April 1941 the Tokyo and Moscow governments signed a neutrality pact which was to survive until the very last days of World War II. Not until five days before the unconditional Japanese surrender on Aug. 14, 1945, did the Soviet Union enter the war against Japan, whereupon Soviet forces occupied Sakhalin and the islands south of

Kamchatka right down to the northern coast of Hokkaido (meeting no resistance from the now surrendered Japanese). Japanese accounts of this operation show that the Soviet occupation of the islands was not completed until Sept. 3, 1945, i.e. the day after the Japanese surrender instrument was signed on USS *Missouri* in Tokyo Bay.

The Soviet Union's declaration of war on Japan was made on the evening of Aug. 8, 1945 (48 hours after the atomic bomb attack on Hiroshima), and came into effect the following day. The war declaration referred to a "request by the Japanese government to the Soviet government to mediate in the war in Far East" but rejected this proposal in view of Japan's refusal to capitulate unconditionally. It therefore associated the Soviet Union with the proclamation issued at Potsdam the previous month by the United States and Britain (and approved by the Republic of China) calling upon the Japanese to surrender and reaffirming the stipulations regarding Japanese-held territories contained in the earlier Cairo declaration issued by the United States, Britain and China following a summit conference in the Egyptian capital on Nov. 22-26, 1943. It is these documents, together with the agreements reached between the United States, Britain and the Soviet Union at Yalta in February 1945, which are at the centre of the continuing dispute between Japan and the Soviet Union over the northern islands.

The November 1943 Cairo conference brought together President Roosevelt of the United States, Winston Churchill (the British Prime Minister) and Gen. Chiang Kai-shek of China. Their joint declaration recorded that they had "agreed upon future military operations against Japan" and had resolved "to bring unrelenting pressure against their brutal enemies by sea, land and air". It continued: "The three great allies are fighting this war to restrain and punish the aggression of Japan. They covet no gain for themselves and have no thought of territorial expansion. It is their purpose that Japan shall be stripped of all the islands in the Pacific which she has seized or occupied since the beginning of World War I in 1914, and that all the territories that Japan has stolen from the Chinese, such as Manchuria, Formosa and the Pescadores, shall be restored to the Republic of China. Japan will also be expelled from all other territories which she has taken by violence or greed. The aforesaid three great powers, mindful of the enslavement of the people of Korea, are determined that in due course Korea shall become free and independent."

At the Yalta conference of Feb. 4-11, 1945, Roosevelt, Churchill and Stalin agreed in a protocol which remained secret at the time but which was eventually published in Washington, London and Moscow on Feb. 11, 1946, that "in two or three months after Germany has surrendered and the war in Europe has terminated the Soviet Union shall enter into the war against Japan on the side of the allies". Among the specified conditions for this action were (i) that "the status quo in Outer Mongolia shall be preserved" [i.e. its independence would be recognized]; (ii) that "the former rights of Russia violated by the treacherous attack of Japan in 1904 shall be restored", under which heading it was stipulated that "the southern part of Sakhalin, as well as the islands adjacent to it, shall be returned to the Soviet Union"; and (iii) that "the Kurile islands shall be handed over to the Soviet Union". The protocol also recorded that the three leaders "have agreed that these claims of the Soviet Union shall be unquestionably fulfilled after Japan has been defeated".

During the US-UK-Soviet Potsdam conference of July 17-Aug. 2, 1945, the United States and Britain on July 26 issued a proclamation to the Japanese people calling for surrender to avoid the total destruction of Japan. Article 8 of this proclamation (which was approved by radio by Gen. Chiang Kai-shek) specified: "The terms of the Cairo declaration shall be carried out and Japanese sovereignty shall be limited to the islands of Honshu, Hokkaido, Kyushu, Shikoku, and such minor islands as we determine".

In the Soviet view the above agreements between the war-time allies. and particularly the Yalta secret protocol, restored the "historical status quo" in the Far East and confirmed Soviet sovereignty over all the northern islands occupied by Soviet forces at the end of World War II. The sentiments underlying this attitude received forceful articulation Stalin himself when he broadcast to the Soviet people on Sept. 2, 1945, to announce the Japanese surrender and the Soviet occupation of Sakhalin and the Kuriles. In this broadcast the Soviet leader said: "The Japanese invaders inflicted damage not only on our allies—China, the USA and Great Britain—but also most serious damage on our country. Therefore we have a special account of our own to settle with Japan. In February 1904, while negotiations between Japan and Russia were still in progress, Japan took advantage of the weakness of the Tsarist government and treacherously, without declaring war, attacked our country and assaulted a Russian squadron at Port Arthur in order to disable Russian warships and thus to place her own navy in a position of advantage. Characteristically, 37 years later, Japan repeated exactly the same treacherous device against the USA at Pearl Harbour."

Stalin continued: "Russia suffered defeat in the war with Japan, and Japan took advantage of Tsarist Russia's defeat to wrest southern Sakhalin from Russia, to strengthen her hold over the Kurile islands, and in this way to close for our country in the east all outlets to the ocean. But the defeat of 1904 left painful memories in the minds of our people. Our people trusted, waiting for the day to come when Japan would be routed and the stain wiped out. For 40 years we, men of the older generation, have waited for this day. And now it has come. Japan has acknowledged her defeat and signed the act of unconditional surender. This means that southern Sakhalin and the Kurile islands will pass to the Soviet Union, and from now on will not serve as a means for isolating the Soviet Union from the ocean and as a base for Japanese attack on our Far East, but as a means of direct communication for the USSR with the ocean and a base for the defence of our country against Japanese aggression."

On the other hand, Japan has consistently maintained that none of the allied agreements towards the end of World War II specifically mentioned the Habomais, Shikotan, Kunashiri and Etorofu and that therefore they were never intended to confirm Soviet sovereignty over these islands. As regards the 1943 Cairo declaration, Japan argues (in its Foreign Ministry document) that since the Kuriles were ceded to Japan by Russia by "peaceful negotiations" surrounding the 1875 treaty, these islands "can in no way be considered as territories which Japan took 'by violence and greed' ". Moreover, Japan argues, "it is clear that the northern territories, which are distinct from the Kurile islands and are inherent territories of Japan, were not included in the areas thus designated".

As regards the Yalta agreement, the Japanese Foreign Ministry document again stresses that "the names of the islands to be included in the term 'Kurile islands' were not specified", and continues: "From a legal point of view the Yalta agreement was only a declaration of common objectives made by the leaders of Great Britain, the United States and the Soviet Union. On this point, the United States government, one of the participants in this agreement, said in an aide-memoire to Japan dated Sept. 7, 1956 [see below], that it 'regards the so-called Yalta agreement as simply a statement of common purposes by the then heads of the participating powers and not as a final determination by those powers or of any legal effect in transferring territories'. Furthermore, Japan is not a party to the Yalta agreement nor is there any mention of the Yalta agreement in the Potsdam declaration which Japan accepted. Therefore, Japan is not legally bound by it. Likewise, the Soviet Union cannot claim any rights against Japan on the basis of this agreement, which is not binding upon Japan."

On the Potsdam proclamation, the same document makes the following observations: "The final disposition of territories as a result of war is to be made by a peace treaty, and in that sense the stipulations of the Potsdam declaration cannot have any legal effect, as distinguished from that of a peace treaty, with regard to the final disposition of territories. Besides, the declaration merely states 'such minor islands as we determine' and does not specify the names of any islands. Nor can it be interpreted as the expression of a principle which runs counter to the principle of no territorial expansion as contained in the Cairo declaration. As clearly stated in Article 8, the Potsdam declaration is the successor to the Cairo declaration, and Japan accepted it as such at the time of surrender. Further, Soviet participation in the Potsdam declaration can be taken as proof that it admitted the principle of no territorial expansion contained in the Cairo declaration."

A further document of this period which has been cited in the dispute is the memorandum issued on Jan. 29, 1946, by the Supreme Allied Commander in Japan, Gen. Douglas

MacArthur, under the title "Governmental and administrative separation of certain outlying areas from Japan". This memorandum (SCAPIN No. 677) stipulated that "for the purposes of this directive Japan is defined to include the four main islands of Japan and the approximately 1,000 smaller adjacent islands ... and excluding inter alia the Kurile (Chishima) islands, the Habomai island group and Shikotan island". It also stated that "nothing in this directive shall be construed as an indication of allied policy relating to the ultimate determination of the minor islands referred to in Article 8 of the Potsdam declaration".

The MacArthur memorandum thus excluded not only Kunashiri and Etorofu (as covered by the term "Kurile islands") but also the more southerly Habomais and Shikotan from the territorial scope of the allied military administration; for this reason it has been cited by the Soviet Union as further evidence of the intention of the war-time allies that the islands should become Soviet territory. Japan, on the other hand, argues that the memorandum was "an expedient measure to facilitate the administrative functions of the occupation" and had "nothing to do with the final detrmination of the territorial issue", as shown by its reference to Article 8 of the Potsdam declaration.

1951 San Francisco Peace Treaty and Related Developments

At the conclusion of a conference held in San Francisco in September 1951, a peace treaty with Japan was signed on Sept. 8, 1951, by 48 of the 51 wartime allies or associated states represented; the three countries which participated but did not sign were the Soviet Union, Czechoslovakia and Poland (while Burma, India and Yugoslavia did not attend and neither Communist nor Nationalist China was invited to participate). The treaty, which came into force on April 28, 1952, committed Japan inter alia to recognizing the independence of Korea and renouncing all claims to (i) Korea, Formosa (Taiwan) and the Pescadores, (ii) the Kurile islands and "that portion of Sakhalin and the islands adjacent to it over which Japan acquired sovereignty as a consequence of the Treaty of Portsmouth of Sept. 5, 1905", (iii) the Pacific islands formerly mandated to Japan by the League of Nations, (iv) any territory in Antarctica, and (v) the Spratly and Paracel islands. Under the treaty Japan also agreed to place under UN trusteeship, with the United States as the sole administering authority, the Ryukyu Islands south of 29° N (including Okinawa), the Bonin islands, the Volcano islands, Marcus island and some smaller islands.

During the lengthy drafting negotiations associated with the San Francisco treaty, the Soviet Union had repeatedly objected to the procedure being followed and also to certain of the terms generally agreed by the non-communist countries involved. In particular, it had demanded that the treaty should be drawn up by the four major wartime allies (i.e. Britain, China, the USA and the USSR) rather than by the 12-nation Far Eastern Commission, as favoured by the United States and Britain. Soviet spokesmen also, before and after the treaty's signature, criticized its provisions as containing insufficient safeguards against a revival of Japanese militarism and as a US device to convert Japan into a military bridgehead in the Far East.

At the same time, these broad divergences were accompanied by the surfacing of disputation over the particular question of the northern islands. Already, in a speech delivered in Los Angeles on March 31, 1951, John Foster Dulles (then President Truman's foreign affairs adviser) had noted that "South Sakhalin and the Kurile islands were allotted to Russia at Yalta" but had added: "Any peace treaty validation of Russia's title should, we suggest, be dependent on Russia's becoming a party to that treaty." At the San Francisco conference itself, as it transpired that the Soviet Union would not sign the treaty with Japan, Dulles made it clear that the only definition of peace terms binding on Japan and the allies were those contained in the Potsdam declaration and that private understandings among some of the allied powers were not binding upon either Japan or the allies.

In Japan itself the territorial question had become an important issue in the debate over the proposed peace treaty terms. Against a background of demands from opposition deputies in the Diet that the northern islands (as well as the Ryukyu and Bonin islands) should be returned to Japan under the peace treaty, the government submitted materials to the United States intended to show that the Habomais and Shikotan were part of Hokkaido and that Kunashiri and Etorofu had never belonged to a foreign country. Moreover, at the peace conference the Japanese Prime Minister, Shigeru Yoshida, called the attention of the participants to Japan's view that the Soviet-held northern islands were integral parts of Japan proper.

As regards the actual terms of the peace treaty, the Japanese government has consistently pointed out that Japan's renunciation of South Sakhalin and the Kuriles was not accompanied by any stipulation that they should belong to another country and that "unilateral measures" by the Soviet Union to absorb these territories "have no legal effect in transferring title". It has also stressed that in any case the geographical limits of the term "Kurile islands" were again not clearly defined and that therefore "it is quite natural for Japan to consider that the Habomais, Shikotan, Kunashiri and Etorofu are not included in the term".

Following the entry into force of the San Francisco peace treaty on April 28, 1952, the Allied Council for Japan (consisting of representatives of the United States, the British Commonwealth, the Soviet Union and China) was dissolved, whereupon the Japanese government informed the Soviet mission in Tokyo that it no longer had any *raison d'être*. On June 20 the head of the Soviet mission was recalled to Moscow, and since there had been no formal termination of the state of war between Japan and Soviet Union it followed that there could be no diplomatic relations between the two countries.

On the same day as the signing of the San Francisco peace treaty, Japan and the United States entered into a bilateral defence pact under which the Japanese government agreed to the indefinite retention of US forces "in and about Japan" so as to deter any armed aggression against the latter country. Eight years later this pact was replaced by a treaty of mutual co-operation and security (signed on Jan. 19, 1960, and in force from June 23, 1960) under which Japan was no longer treated as the weaker partner but was placed on an equal footing with the United States. The new treaty was clarified by an exchange of notes, in one of which the treaty area was defined as the territory under Japanese rule at any time therefrom, while the parties also agreed to consult together in the event of an armed attack or threat of attack against the islands over which Japan claimed residual sovereignty.

Unsuccessful Japanese-Soviet Peace Treaty Negotiations and 1956 Joint Declaration

In view of the Soviet Union's non-signature of the 1951 peace treaty with Japan, the two sides subsequently entered into discussions on the conclusion of a separate peace treaty, on which formal negotiations eventually opened in London on June 1, 1955. Over the following 14 months the issue of the northern islands became central to these negotiations, and although both sides made concessions on their initial positions it eventually caused the breakdown of the talks in August 1956. On the other hand, agreement was reached on the termination of the state of war between Japan and the Soviet Union and the resumption of diplomatic relations, as set out in a joint declaration signed by the two sides in October 1956.

The opening Soviet conditions put forward in the first round of talks in June-September 1955 included the territorial stipulation that Japan should relinquish all claims to South Sakhalin, the Kurile islands, the Habomais and Shikotan, whereas the Japanese side initially demanded the return of these same territories. When the second round of negotiations began in January 1956 (also in London) the Soviet Union indicated its willingness to return the Habomais and Shikotan to Japanese sovereignty but continued to uphold its claim to South Sakhalin and the Kuriles on the grounds (i) that Japan had renounced all right, claim and title to these territories under the San Francisco peace treaty; and (ii) that the allies had agreed to their cession to the USSR at the Yalta conference. Japan on the other hand maintained (i) that the San Francisco treaty did not determine the ultimate ownership of South Sakhalin and the Kuriles; (ii) that Etorofu and Kunashiri were an integral part of

Japanese territory over which Japanese sovereignty had been recognized by the San Francisco treaty, which had not defined the term "Kuriles"; and (iii) that the Soviet Union could not claim title to these territories by virtue of a treaty which it had not signed. The Japanese government therefore proposed that the southern Kuriles should be returned to Japan and that the future of South Sakhalin should be decided by a conference of the signatories of the San Francisco treaty and the Soviet Union.

The London talks were suspended on March 20, 1956, but negotiations resumed in Moscow on July 31, when the Japanese side immediately announced that Japan had renounced its claim to South Sakhalin and the northern Kuriles but could not relinquish Etorofu and Kunashiri. At the second round of talks on Aug. 3 the Soviet side reaffirmed its view that Etorofu and Kunashiri formed part of the Kuriles, the future of which had been decided at Yalta and San Francisco. Japan responded that it could not be bound by the Yalta agreement, to which it was not a party, and that under the Potsdam and Cairo declarations the Soviet Union had renounced territorial aggrandizement as a war aim. With both sides adhering to their positions, the talks remained deadlocked and were eventually suspended on Aug. 13, 1956, on which date the Japanese Foreign Minister expressed the view at a Moscow press conference that it was advisable for Japan to conclude a peace treaty even on the Soviet terms. But an emergency meeting of the Japanese Cabinet on the same day sent him instructions not to sign the treaty at that stage.

Amid considerable criticism of the proposed terms of the treaty within Japan, the Japanese Prime Minister, Ichiro Hatoyama, sent a personal message to his Soviet counterpart, Nikolai Bulganin, in which he proposed that the territorial question should be temporarily shelved and that negotiations should be resumed on the basis of a five-point plan covering the ending of the state of war between the two countries, the exchange of ambassadors, the repatriation of Japanese war criminals held in the Soviet Union, the conclusion of a 10-year fisheries agreement and Soviet support for the admission of Japan to membership of the United Nations. After talks between Hatoyama and Bulganin in Moscow, a formal agreement was reached on Sept. 29, 1956, that "the negotiations for the conclusion of a peace treaty between the two countries, including the territorial issue, will continue after normal diplomatic relations have been restored between the two countries".

On the basis of these preliminaries, the Japanese and Soviet Prime Ministers proceeded to the signature in the Kremlin on Oct. 19, 1956, of a joint declaration providing for the termination of the state of war between the two countries and the re-establishment of diplomatic relations and also regulating other aspects of their bilateral relations. This declaration, Paragraph 9 of which referred to the territorial issue, was worded as follows:

"(1) The state of war between the USSR and Japan ends on the day the present declaration comes into force, and peace and good-neighbourly relations are established between them.

"(2) Diplomatic and consular relations between the USSR and Japan are re-established, and the two states will exchange ambassadors without delay. The question of the opening of consulates in the Soviet Union and Japan will be settled through diplomatic channels.

"(3) The USSR and Japan confirm that they will be guided by the principles of the UN Charter in their mutual relations, and in particular by the following principles in Article 2 of the Charter: (*a*) to settle their international disputes by peaceful means in such a manner as not to endanger international peace, security, and justice; (*b*) to refrain in their international relations from using the threat of force, or its use, against the territorial integrity or political independence of any state, or from acting in any other manner incompatible with the aims of the United Nations; (*c*) the USSR and Japan confirm that, in accordance with Article 51 of the UN Charter, each of the states enjoys the inalienable right of individual or collective defence; (*d*) the USSR and Japan mutually undertake not to interfere directly or indirectly in each other's internal affairs, whether out of economic, political, or ideological motives.

"(4) The Soviet Union will support Japan's application for membership of the United Nations.

"(5) All Japanese citizens sentenced in the Soviet Union will be freed and repatriated as soon as the joint declaration enters into force. As regards those Japanese whose fate is unknown, the USSR, at Japan's request, will continue to attempt to investigate their fate.

"(6) The Soviet Union waives all claims to reparations against Japan. The USSR and Japan mutually waive all claims for war damages on behalf of the state, its organizations and citizens, against the other state, its organizations and citizens, which may have arisen since Aug. 9, 1945.

"(7) The Soviet Union and Japan agree to start negotiations as soon as possible for the purpose of concluding treaties or agreements with a view to placing their trade, shipping and other business relations on a stable and friendly basis.

"(8) The Convention on Fishing in the Open Seas of the North-West Pacific, and the agreement between the Soviet Union and Japan on mutual co-operation in sea-rescue operations signed in Moscow on May 14, 1956, enter into force simultaneously with the present joint declaration. Taking into consideration the interest of both the Soviet Union and Japan in the preservation and rational utilization of natural fishing resources and other marine biological resources, the two countries will take measures, in a spirit of co-operation, to preserve and develop the fishing resources and to regulate and limit catches in the open sea.

"(9) The USSR and Japan agree to continue, after the re-establishment of diplomatic relations between them, negotiations on the conclusion of a peace treaty. In this connexion, the USSR, meeting the wishes of Japan and taking into account the interests of the Japanese state, agrees to hand over to Japan the Habomai and Shikotan islands, with the reservation that the actual transfer of these islands to Japan is to take place after the conclusion of a peace treaty between the Soviet Union and Japan.

"(10) The present joint declaration is subject to ratification and comes into force when instruments of ratification are exchanged. Exchange of instruments of ratification will take place as soon as possible in Tokyo."

In recent years the Japanese government has consistently cited Paragraph 9 of the 1956 joint declaration to refute the Soviet contention that there is no territorial issue between the two countries. It argues that the negotiations referred to were clearly intended to concern the territorial question, since the major problems normally covered by a peace treaty had been resolved by the joint declaration, and specifically the problem of Kunashiri and Etorofu, since it had already been agreed that the Habomais and Shikotan would revert to Japan on the conclusion of a peace treaty.

Shortly before the signature of the joint declaration a significant development occurred when the United States defined its view on the Japan-Soviet peace treaty negotiations and in particular on the territorial question. An aide-mémoire issued by the US State Department on Sept. 7, 1956, contained the following passages: "The United States regards the so-called Yalta agreement as simply a statement of common purposes by the then heads of the participating powers, and not as a final determination by those powers or of any legal effect in transferring territories. The San Francisco peace treaty (which conferred no rights upon the Soviet Union because it refused to sign) did not determine the sovereignty of the territories renounced by Japan, leaving that question, as was stated by the US delegate at San Francisco, to 'international solvents other than this treaty'. It is the considered opinion of the United States that, by virtue of the San Francisco peace treaty, Japan does not have the right to transfer sovereignty over the territories renounced by it therein. In the opinion of the USA, the signatories of the San Francisco treaty would not be bound to accept any action of this character, and they would presumably reserve all their rights thereunder. The USA has reached the conclusion, after careful examination of the historical facts, that the islands of Etorofu and Kunashiri (along with the Habomai islands and Shikotan, which are part of Hokkaido) have always been part of Japan proper, and should in justice be acknowledged as under Japanese sovereignty. The USA would regard Soviet agreement to this effect as a positive contribution to the reduction of tension in the Far East."

The October 1956 Japanese-Soviet joint declaration and related conventions came into force on Dec. 12, 1956, when instruments of ratification were exchanged between the two governments in Tokyo. During the debate on the agreements in the Japanese Lower House the previous month 58 deputies of the ruling Liberal-Democratic Party absented themselves from the proceedings in protest against the omission of any specific provision in the joint declaration for continued negotiations on Japan's claim to Etorofu and Kunashiri.

Consequent upon the formal ending of the state of war between Japan and the Soviet Union and the restoration of full diplomatic relations between the two countries, a Japanese application for membership of the United Nations was unanimously approved by the Security Council on Dec. 12 and by the General Assembly on Dec. 18, 1956.

Developments in 20 Years following 1956 Joint Declaration

Within a few years of the signing of 1956 joint declaration, the conclusion in January 1960 of the new Japan-US mutual co-operation and security treaty referred to above brought about a hardening of the Soviet stance on the northern islands, any territorial concession on which it now specifically linked with a withdrawal of all foreign (i.e. US) troops from Japanese territory as well as the conclusion of a formal peace treaty. In a memorandum of Jan. 27, 1960, protesting against the new Japan-US treaty, the Soviet government stated that it "perpetuates the actual occupation of Japan, places her territory at the disposal of a foreign power ... and its provisions inevitably lead to the military, economic and political subordination of Japan". In this "new situation" and in view of the fact that the treaty was "directed against the Soviet Union and also against the Chinese People's Republic", the Soviet government could not "allow itself to contribute to an extension of the territory used by foreign armed forces" by handing over the Habomai islands and Shikotan, which would be transferred to Japan "only on condition that all foreign troops are withdrawn from the territory of Japan and a peace treaty is concluded between the USSR and Japan".

The Japanese government responded on Jan. 28, 1960, by accusing the Soviet Union of "interference in Japan's domestic affairs" and of wishing to impose an additional condition on the Soviet undertaking of 1956, thereby revealing "the Soviet attitude of contempt for international pledges". A week later, on Feb. 5, the Japanese government formally rejected the Soviet demand for the withdrawal of foreign troops.

During the latter half of 1961 the US-Japan security treaty and the territorial question formed the subject of correspondence between the Soviet and Japanese Prime Ministers. The exchange opened with a message from Nikita Khrushchev to Nasanosuke Ikeda (delivered by the Soviet First Deputy Prime Minister, Anastas Mikoyan, during a visit to Tokyo in August 1961) in which the Soviet leader appealed to Japan to close "foreign military bases" and end its alliance with the United States, since these two factors did "not help in deepening mutual trust and normalizing relations between Japan and the Soviet Union". In his reply Prime Minister Ikeda rejected Khrushchev's assertions and called on the Soviet Union to restore good relations by settling territorial differences between the two countries and signing a peace treaty. Replying on Sept. 25, Khrushchev categorically refuted Japanese territorial claims, asserting specifically that the status of Kunashiri and Etorofu had been permanently settled "through various international agreements".

In a further letter to Khrushchev on Nov. 15, 1961, the Japanese Prime Minister described the Soviet leader's arguments as "contrary to fact and lacking adequate grounds", adding that Japan could "not remain indifferent" to the fact that the Soviet government was sending more and more Soviet citizens to Kunashiri and Etorofu, whose final status could only be settled in a peace treaty. After saying that the international agreements cited by Khrushchev were "presumably" the Yalta agreement and the 1951 San Francisco peace treaty, Ikeda maintained that the Yalta accord did not determine legally to whom the Kurile islands should belong, even though it contained a statement of common purpose towards them; moreover, Japan had not been a party to the Yalta agreement, while the Potsdam declaration, which Japan had accepted, contained no reference to Yalta. In these circumstances, he continued, Japan was not bound legally or politically by the Yalta decisions, which the Soviet government could therefore not invoke in this question. While accepting that under the San Francisco peace treaty Japan had renounced all rights to South

Sakhalin and the main Kurile group, Ikeda pointed out that the treaty had not laid down the final ownership of these territories and that since the Soviet Union had refused to sign the treaty it could not cite its provisions to support the Soviet case. He also reiterated that Japan had never renounced its claims to Kunashiri and Etorofu, having always contended that the Japanese renunciation had applied to the 18 islands of the main Kurile group, and that the two southern-most islands formed part of Japan proper.

In his reply to Ikeda, which was published on Dec. 12, 1961, Khrushchev again rejected the Japanese arguments. He declared that the Soviet Union would not transfer to Japan its rights over South Sakhalin and the Kuriles, maintaining that they had been acquired under the Yalta agreement, and asserted that Japan was attempting to evade obligations undertaken in international agreements after its unconditional surrender in August 1945.

Over the following decade there were no significant diplomatic developments relating to the basic Japanese-Soviet territorial dispute, but economic relations between the two countries flourished to the extent that the Soviet Union became one of Japan's main trading and economic co-operation partners. In July 1966 Andrei Gromyko became the first Soviet Foreign Minister to pay an official visit to Japan and a joint communiqué issued on that occasion announced that a bilateral consular convention had been signed and that the two countries had agreed to hold regular consultations "both on questions of bilateral Soviet-Japanese relations and on international problems in the solution of which both countries are interested". Without specifically referring to the territorial issue, the communiqué also said that both sides had agreed that it was "possible further to develop relations between Japan and the USSR in all spheres in the spirit of the Soviet-Japanese declaration of 1956" and that the "development of friendly and good-neighbourly relations between Japan and the Soviet Union will greatly contribute to the safeguarding of peace and security in Asia and to the cause of world peace".

Gromyko paid a further visit to Tokyo in January 1972 during which he had extensive talks with his Japanese counterpart, Takeo Fukuda, and also with the Japanese Prime Minister, Eisaku Sato. The principal result of the talks, as recorded in an official communiqué, was a decision to hold further Soviet-Japanese talks later in the year with a view to the conclusion of a peace treaty. Although the communiqué made no specific reference to the question, it was understood that the Japanese side had again raised the issue of the northern islands in relation to a possible peace treaty. When the specified talks took place in Moscow at the level of Foreign Ministers in October 1972, they ended inconclusively amid continued deadlock on the territorial issue. Meanwhile, Japan had on June 26, 1968, secured the reversion of the Bonin and Volcano island groups together with certain smaller islands (under an agreement signed with the United States on April 5, 1968), while on June 17, 1971, a further Japan-US agreement provided for the return to Japanese jurisdiction of the Ryukyo islands (including Okinawa)—the latter agreement being subsequently implemented on May 14, 1972.

In March 1973 the new Japanese Prime Minister, Kakuei Tanaka, sent a letter to the General Secretary of the Soviet Communist Party, Leonid Brezhnev, stressing that the conclusion of a peace treaty was indispensable for the establishment of good-neighbourly relations with the Soviet Union and proposing that further discussion on a peace treaty should be held within the year. After the Soviet leader had responded favourably, Tanaka paid a four-day visit to Moscow on Oct. 7-10, 1973—the first Japanese Prime Minister to do so since Hatoyama's visit in 1956. In a joint communiqué issued after Tanaka's talks with Brezhnev and other Soviet leaders there was again no specific reference to the territorial question, the document containing the following passage: "The two sides recognized that to conclude a peace treaty by resolving the yet unresolved problems remaining since World War II would contribute to the establishment of truly good-neighbourly relations between the two countries and conducted negotiations on matters concerning the content of such a peace treaty. The two sides agreed to continue negotiations for the conclusion of a peace treaty between the two countries at an appropriate time during 1974."

According to the Japanese version of the Tanaka visit to Moscow in October 1973, the question of the northern islands formed the main topic in four meetings between the Japanese Prime Minister and Brezhnev, during which the former twice secured the concurrence of the latter that the territorial issue constituted one of the unsettled post-war issues between the two countries. In the Japanese view, therefore, the talks produced a confirmation that the territorial question, as an unsettled post-war issue, should form the subject of negotiations between the two countries for ultimate resolution in the context of a Japan-Soviet peace treaty.

The next round of talks did not in fact take place until January 1975, when Kiichi Miyazawa (Japanese Foreign Minister) visited Moscow to urge the Soviet government to resume formal negotiations on a peace treaty. On this occasion Gromyko proposed that the two countries should postpone the conclusion of a peace treaty and sign instead a treaty of good-neighbourliness and co-operation, but this suggestion was rejected as inappropriate by Miyazawa. In response to Gromyko's request that Japan should take a "realistic attitude", the Japanese Foreign Minister insisted that if the Soviet Union wished genuinely to establish friendly relations with Japan a truly realistic attitude would be to resolve the territorial issue under a peace treaty. A communiqué issued after Miyazawa's visit repeated the formulation used in the October 1973 text, making no reference to the territorial question as such, but the Japanese Foreign Minister stated that Japan would continue to press its claim.

The new Soviet proposal was repeated in a personal letter from Brezhnev to the Japanese Prime Minister, Takeo Miki, which as delivered on Feb. 13, 1975, suggested that the two sides could conclude a friendship treaty "while continuing negotiations for a peace treaty". This proposal was immediately rejected by the Japanese government, however, on the grounds that a peace treaty was the first requirement and also that the prior conclusion of a friendship treaty would represent a virtual shelving of the northern islands question. An important factor in these new exchanges was the improvement in Sino-Japanese relations which had been underway since the early 1970s and the negotiations then in progress between Japan and China on a bilateral treaty of peace and friendship. The Soviet government repeatedly warned Japan that it would regard the conclusion of such a treaty as an unfriendly act and directed particular criticism at the proposed inclusion of an "anti-hegemony" clause as propounded by China (whose use of this term was generally seen as referring in particular to the Soviet Union). When the China-Japan peace and friendship treaty was eventually signed in Beijing on Aug. 17, 1978—containing in Article 2 a specification that neither side "should seek hegemony in the Asia-Pacific region or in any other region" and that each "is opposed to efforts by any other country or group of countries to establish such hegemony"—the Soviet government delivered a formal protest to the Japanese government and official Soviet sources claimed that Japan had yielded to Beijing's "diktat" by deciding to sign the treaty on China's terms.

Meanwhile, Andrei Gromyko had paid a further visit to Tokyo in January 1976 during which he was reported to have indicated the Soviet Union's willingness to return the Habomais and Shikotan to Japan if the latter agreed to sign a treaty of good-neighbourliness and co-operation with the Soviet Union. However, it was understood that the Japanese government had again rejected this proposal and emphasized Japan's insistence on the return of all the islands in dispute. At the end of the Gromyko visit the Japanese Foreign Minister said that he had made no progress in discussions on the territorial issue, asserting that the Soviet Union appeared to be "obsessed" with the proposed Sino-Japanese treaty and disclosing that Gromyko had not accepted his explanation that the controversial "anti-hegemony" clause in such a treaty would not be directed against the Soviet Union but rather had universal application.

Tensions in Japanese-Soviet Relations, 1976-80

Japanese accounts of the territorial question suggest that from about 1975 the Soviet Union began to take a harder line, in particular by maintaining that the Japanese claim for the return of the northern islands was a "baseless and unwarranted demand made by a small segment of people" and that it was "instigated directly from outside". Such assertions were consistently rejected through diplomatic channels by the Japanese government, which in 1976 also protested when the Soviet Union imposed a requirement that Japanese citizens wishing to visit the graves of relatives on the northern islands should have valid Japanese passports and Soviet visas. Tensions also developed in Japanese-Soviet relations in late 1976 when a Soviet pilot landed a supersonic MiG-25 warplane in Hokkaido on Sept. 7 and was subsequently granted political asylum in the United States; despite Soviet demands for its immediate return, the aircraft was retained for examination by Japanese and US military experts and not returned until mid-November, causing the Soviet Union to take a number of diplomatic and other measures which were interpreted as indicating its displeasure.

Moreover, in December 1976 the territorial issue became directly entangled with questions of fishery rights when on Dec. 10 the Soviet Union proclaimed a 200-mile fishing zone around its coasts and announced that fishing operations could be undertaken by foreigners in this zone only on the basis of agreements or other forms of understanding reached with the Soviet government. The Japanese government responded on Jan. 26, 1977, by extending Japan's territorial waters limit from three to 12 nautical miles (with the exclusion of the three international straits of the region), specifying that the new 12-mile limit would encompass the disputed northern islands. On Feb. 24 the Soviet government announced that it would enforce the 200-mile fishing zone from March 1 and made it clear that the zone would incorporate the waters around the northern islands—this being described by the Japanese government on Feb. 25 as "an unfriendly and regrettable act" and as unacceptable to Japan. However, during talks in Moscow on Feb. 28 between the Japanese Agriculture Minister and the Soviet Fisheries Minister it was agreed that for the time being the Soviet Union would "not apply coercive measures" against Japanese fishing vessels within the zone.

Later in 1977, on May 27, an interim Soviet-Japanese fisheries agreement was signed in Moscow providing for Japanese fishing operations during the rest of the year in seven limited areas within the Soviet 200-mile zone. Moreover, after Japan had itself implemented a 200-mile fishing zone from July 1, 1977, it signed a further interim agreement with the Soviet Union on Aug. 4 granting reciprocal rights to Soviet fishermen within the Japanese zone (this agreement containing a stipulation that nothing in it would impair the positions of either side on any outstanding bilateral or multilateral problem). Negotiations conducted in Moscow between Sept. 29 and Oct. 20, 1977, resulted in the extension for a further year—until the end of 1978—of the two interim Japanese-Soviet fisheries agreements; but as a result of Japan's decision to proceed with the signature of a peace and friendship treaty with China in August 1978 [see above], the Soviet government announced an indefinite postponement of negotiations on a longer-term fisheries agreement with Japan. From the Japanese point of view, this breakdown of co-operation with the Soviet Union over fishing rights was significant not only because of the traditional importance of Japanese fishing operations in waters now within the Soviet economic zone but also because of the relationship between the fisheries and the territorial issues—the failure to resolve the latter being an important underlying factor in tensions over the former. According to official Japanese figures issued in 1977, more than 1,500 Japanese fishing vessels had been seized by the Soviet authorities over the three post-war decades and nearly 13,000 Japanese fishermen had undergone the experience of detention.

During the disputation over fisheries the Japanese and Soviet governments continued diplomatic contacts on the basic peace treaty question, but according to Japanese accounts of these further exchanges the Soviet side from late 1976 took the line that no territorial dispute existed between the two countries. After talks between Sunao Sonoda (Japanese Foreign Minister) and Soviet leaders in Moscow in February 1978 had ended without a communiqué being issued, Sonoda reported on his return to Tokyo that the Soviet side had again denied the existence of a territorial problem and claimed that this was a "unilateral negation" of the undertaking given in the 1973 Tanaka-Brezhnev communiqué. Later in the month the Soviet newspaper *New Times* asserted that a peace treaty could be based "only on a recognition by both sides of the realities that have emerged as a result of World War II".

On Feb. 11, 1978, the Soviet ambassador to Japan, Dmitry Polyansky, presented the Japanese government with a draft treaty of good-neighbourly relations and co-operation between the two countries, but this was immediately rejected by the Japanese Prime Minister (Takeo Fukuda) principally on the grounds that it failed to mention the territorial issue and that such a treaty could not precede a formal peace treaty. This attitude came under strong attack in the official Soviet media, notably in *Pravda*, which on March 3 carried an article claiming that the Japanese government was "closing its eyes to reality" and arousing "revanchist illusions" among the Japanese people.

Throughout the period 1979-80 the Japanese government repeatedly drew attention to what it claimed was a significant build-up of Soviet forces on the northern islands, including the stationing of some 2,000 troops on Shikotan (which had not been militarized since 1960). By May 1980 Soviet military strength in the northern islands was estimated by Japan at some 13,000 troops, compared with about 1,000 in 1976, and Japan also claimed that direct command communications had been established between Kunashiri, Etorofu and Vladivostok (the base of the Soviet Pacific fleet). On Oct. 6, 1979, the Japanese government announced its intention to begin aerial reconnaissance over Shikotan as part of its periodic inspections of the northern islands, this step being condemned as "wild interference" by the Soviet Union.

In a newspaper interview published on March 7, 1980, Dmitry Polyansky said that the Soviet Union would under no circumstances reopen the territorial question. His remarks coincided with the adoption of a resolution by the Japanese House of Representatives calling for an early return of the northern islands and the withdrawal of all Soviet military facilities from them. The resolution, the third of its kind since 1973, called for efforts to consolidate peaceful and friendly relations with the Soviet Union and for the conclusion of a peace treaty. In response to the Soviet claim that the territorial question was now closed, the Japanese Foreign Minister stressed that this was a unilateral decision with which Japan could not agree since in Japan's view the matter had been left as an unresolved issue in the 1956 joint declaration and later communiqués.

On May 7, 1980, Polyansky defended the Soviet military build-up in the region on the grounds that it "should not be considered in isolation from the military and political situation in that area" and that the Soviet Union could not neglect such factors as the anti-Soviet co-operation of Japan and the United States, the strengthening of US-Chinese relations and the instability of the Korean peninsula and Indo-China. On Aug. 19, a Moscow radio broadcast claimed that Japan's "illegal and groundless" claim to the northern islands was largely responsible for what it described as the "stagnant" state of Soviet-Japanese relations, while on Sept. 2 the Soviet news agency Novosti marked the 35th anniversary of Japan's formal surrender at the end of World War II by publishing a strongly-worded article accusing Japan and the United States of falsifying the history of that period and also referring to Japan's "dangerous alliance with American and Chinese hegemonists on the basis of nationalism and anti-Sovietism".

Japanese-Soviet relations deteriorated sharply in early 1980 as a result of the Soviet military intervention in Afghanistan, in protest against which Japan participated in Western sanctions against the Soviet Union and also joined the United States and about 30 other countries in boycotting the 1980 Olympic Games in Moscow. Further aggravation developed in late 1980 when Japanese salvage company began operations to lift the contents of a former Tsarist naval vessel (*Admiral Nakhimov*) which had sunk off the Japanese coast in 1905 with a cargo of gold, platinum and other precious metals whose current value was variously estimated at between US$3,800 million and US$40,000 million. The vessel had been seized by the Japanese during the Russo-Japanese war and had subsequently been sunk outside the former three-mile Japanese territorial waters limit but inside the 12-mile limit introduced in 1977. On Oct. 3, 1980, the Soviet Union claimed proprietary rights over the ship, to which the Japanese government responded (on Oct. 10) that no precedent existed for the return of a ship submerged for so long and (on Oct. 20) that the vessel was rightfully the property of the Japanese government. This in turn brought an angry reaction from the salvage company, which claimed the ship as its own property and which caused some annoyance in Japanese government circles by directly offering the vessel to the Soviet Union in exchange for the return to Japan of the northern islands (the official Japanese view being that only governments could negotiate on the territorial issue).

Developments in the 1980s—Resumption of Foreign Ministers' Meetings

In January 1981 the Japanese government announced that Feb. 7 (the anniversary of the signature of the 1855 Shimoda treaty—see above) had been designated as "Day of the Northern Territories" and would henceforth be the occasion of a national demonstration over the Soviet Union's refusal to recognize the Japanese claim and also over its militarization of the islands. At the same time Japan requested the other countries which had signed the 1951 San Francisco peace treaty not to mark the disputed northern islands as Soviet territory on maps published by them.

Addressing a rally in Tokyo on Feb. 7, 1981, the Japanese Prime Minister, Zenko Suzuki, said that it was "to be deeply regretted, for the sake of promoting peaceful and friendly relations", that the islands had not yet been returned to Japan, and he reiterated the Japanese view that a peace treaty with the Soviet Union could be concluded only on the basis of their return. Following the Japanese government's announcement, the Soviet Foreign Ministry had on Jan. 20 called in the Japanese ambassador in Moscow to protest at the designation of Feb. 7 and had warned him that Japan was thereby undermining the positive achievements of Soviet-Japanese relations. Moreover, a statement from the Soviet news agency Tass on this occasion repeated the Soviet view that no outstanding territorial issue existed with Japan and asserted that Japan was "working to stir up artificially the non-existent territorial issue".

Further forceful expression of the Soviet position was given in an article by the Tokyo correspondent of *Izvestia* published in mid-June 1981 as follows: "The 'territorial problem', which is an invention from beginning to end, is in fact an open infringement of the sovereignty and territorial integrity of the Soviet Union which has been raised to the status of state policy. In the whipping up of barefaced hostility towards a neighbouring state which has always supported good-neighbourliness, peace and equality in mutual relations, it is impossible not to see the revival of a completely different 'tradition'. This tradition was decisively stopped in 1945: by putting their signature to the act of unconditional surrender the then leaders of Japan promised in the name of the Emperor, the government and their ancestors to fulfil the conditions of the Potsdam declaration.

"The shameless campaign of encroachment on Soviet territory which is being carried out at present shows that these obligations are being thrown aside by Tokyo. In fact, not one of the 'arguments' used by the present authorities and their propaganda apparatus to whip up nationalist hysteria around non-existent problems holds water. Least persuasive of all is the assertion that the Kurile islands are supposedly 'age-old Japanese territory'. The USSR's primordial rights to the Kurile islands were acknowledged by its allies long before the defeat of Japanese militarism in World War II. Japan's pledges irrevocably stem from the act signed by its authorized representatives of unconditional surrender in which the validity of the Potsdam declaration, and before it of the Crimea [i.e. Yalta] conference, were recognized. If Tokyo after the event is claiming the role of an unexpectedly far-sighted interpreter of the Yalta decisions, then such attempts can only be interpreted as a desire to revise the results of World War II and to take a kind of propaganda revenge for the defeat of Japanese militarism in 1945.

"In its encroachments on Soviet territories, Japanese ruling circles often receive support from the USA. There are many examples of this, but only one conclusion can be drawn: Washington's repudiation of the war-time understandings on a post-war settlement goes back to the 'cold war' era, when the Truman administration began to throw overboard the legacy of Roosevelt and the USA's pledges of the first post-war years. However, Tokyo's vain attempts to recarve the map of the Far East in alliance with Washington and Beijing are senseless. No matter how hard the enthusiasts of revanchism and their interested benefactors try to turn back the wheel of history, their efforts are doomed to failure.''

Despite this and other indications of Soviet displeasure with the attitude of the Japanese government, Zenko Suzuki and members of his Cabinet embarked on what was officially described as a "tour of inspection" of the northern islands on Sept. 9, 1981, visiting the Nemuro peninsula on the north-eastern tip of Hokkaido and flying by helicopter along the Japanese coast. This action was described as "absurd" and "provocative" by official Soviet sources, which again accused Japanese ruling circles of fanning anti-Sovietism over a non-existent territorial question.

The official Soviet view that no territorial dispute existed with Japan was reiterated by the Soviet Prime Minister, Nikolai Tikhonov, in an interview with Japanese journalists given in Moscow and issued by Tass on Feb. 13, 1982. In answer to a question on the state of Soviet-Japanese relations and the prospects for a peace treaty, Tikhonov said inter alia: "The Soviet Union has been and remains in favour of placing Soviet-Japanese relations on the firm basis of a treaty. It is not our fault that a peace treaty has not been concluded to this day. You know well the reason for its absence. It is the unrealistic stand of the Japanese side. We have declared many times, including at the highest level, that there is no such subject in our relations as the allegedly unsettled 'territorial issue'. Meanwhile, the Japanese side is making attempts to interpret unilaterally in a distorted way certain provisions of the Soviet-Japanese statement of Oct. 10, 1973. That statement ... registered agreement to continue talks on the conclusion of a peace treaty. To assert that the Soviet Union has admitted the existence of the invented 'territorial issue' means deliberately distorting our stand and misleading the Japanese public. These actions of the Japanese side do nothing to bring closer the prospects of reaching agreement on a peace treaty.''

Soviet-Japanese relations continued to be strained by various factors over the next three years, including the shooting down of a South Korean airliner by a Soviet fighter over Sakhalin island in September 1983 and a series of expulsions of alleged spies of the other country. Moreover, Japan continued to criticize what it regarded as a Soviet military build-up in the region, while the Soviet side attacked what it described as "nuclear co-operation" between Japan and the United States. There were also regular protests by Japan against alleged violations of Japanese airspace by Soviet military aircraft, unannounced firing practice by Soviet naval vessels and the unilateral closure of sea areas, including part of Japan's 200-mile fishery zone, for Soviet missile tests.

As regards economic relations, the effect of the Afghanistan-inspired Japanese economic sanctions against the Soviet Union and their partial reactivation in February 1982 over the Polish crisis was to reduce Japan from first to sixth rank among Moscow's capitalist trading partners by 1984; although bilateral trade increased in 1985 over 1984, its value remained well below the levels of the late 1970s. On the other hand, the two countries signed a new fisheries agreement on May 12, 1985 (the first between two governments under the 1982 UN Law of the Sea Convention), governing the fishing operations of each country in the other's economic zones and territorial waters.

On the diplomatic front, the Japanese Foreign Minister, Shintaro Abe, visited Moscow for the funeral of Yury Andropov in February 1984 and had talks with Andrei Gromyko in which the two sides agreed on a resumption of dialogue with a view to improving relations. However, not until the accession to the Soviet leadership of Mikhail Gorbachev in March 1985 was their significant movement, leading to an official visit to Japan on Jan. 15-19, 1986, by the new Soviet Foreign Minister, Eduard Shevardnadze. The latter began the visit (the first by a Soviet Foreign Minister to Japan since the Gromyko visit of 1976) by declaring that he hoped that a "wind of change" would now produce an improvement in relations between the Soviet Union and Japan and that the two countries would become good neighbours.

The January 1986 talks between the Abe and Shevardnadze covered arms control and defence matters as well as prospects for an expansion of trade and economic co-operation. The two ministers also discussed the territorial issue at an unscheduled meeting on Jan. 17, although the matter was not specifically mentioned in the joint communiqué issued on Jan.

19. The main points of this document were (i) that regular consultative meetings of Foreign Ministers would be held alternately in Moscow and Tokyo at least once a year; (ii) that negotiations on the conclusion of a peace treaty would be continued at the next meeting, on the basis of the 1973 Brezhnev-Tanaka statement; and (iii) that bilateral trade and economic relations would be expanded on the basis of mutual benefit. After the talks, Abe said that Japan was determined to negotiate patiently on the territorial issue, using the new communiqué as a starting point.

In an address to the Japanese Diet on Feb. 10, 1986, Prime Minister Nakasone asserted that the continued Soviet "occupation of the northern territories" meant that no formal peace treaty could be signed between Japan and the Soviet Union in the foreseeable future; he also indicated that he would be unwilling to accept the Soviet Union's invitation to visit Moscow (delivered by Shevardnadze the previous month) until "major progress" had been made towards resolving the dispute.

The next Foreign Ministers' meeting took place in Moscow on May 29-31, 1987, during which Abe had talks with Gorbachev as well as with his Soviet counterpart. There was no movement on the Soviet side in respect of the territorial issue, although the visit led to an agreement (which was formalized on July 2, 1986) that Japanese citizens would again be allowed to visit family graves on the northern islands without visas, although they would have to carry identification papers issued by the Japanese government. Arrangements for reciprocal visits to graves on the Soviet and Japanese mainlands were also eased under the agreement.

AJD

The Korean Question

The present boundary between the Democratic People's Republic of Korea (North Korea) and the Republic of Korea (South Korea) is a provisional line established adjacent to the 38°N parallel under the 1953 armistice which brought to an end three years of armed conflict between the Communist North and the US-backed South. Since then both North and South Korea have continued to claim legitimate jurisdiction over all Korea. Periodic initiatives towards the reunification of the country have made no substantive progress. Neither North Korea nor South Korea has become a member of the United Nations. North Korea has no diplomatic relations with Japan, the United States and many other Western countries (but private or unofficial relations exist, especially with Japan). South Korea has no diplomatic relations with Communist countries, but has had governmental and other contacts with China and the Soviet Union.

During World War II an agreement was reached between the Allies to the effect that there was to be, after the defeat of Japan, an independent Korea (a nominally independent Korea having existed until the defeat of Russia by Japan in 1904-05, whereafter Korea had become a Japanese protectorate and had been annexed by Japan in 1910). Under this agreement there was to be a temporary period of Allied control, with the Soviet Union being in charge of the zone north of the 38°N parallel and the United States of the zone to the south of it; in addition, a mixed US-Soviet commission was to set up a provisional Korean government representing all "democratic" parties and mass organizations. In the event, post-war dispositions were made rather differently. In the northern zone, a provisional Communist

Map 37 The division of Korea.

government was set up in February 1946 under the authority of the Soviet occupation forces. In the south, unsuccessful negotiations concerning a possible unified government (in 1946-47) were followed by the establishment of a provisional Legislative Assembly dominated by the Representative Democratic Council (a right-wing nationalist coalition led by Dr Syngman Rhee). Upon an initiative by the United States in 1947, the UN General Assembly resolved, against Soviet objections, that elections should be held under UN supervision throughout Korea; however, the UN supervision commission subsequently appointed was refused permission to enter North Korea in 1948. Separate elections were therefore held (under UN supervision) in the South only in May 1948, and the independent Republic of Korea was established in August of that year.

Soviet forces were withdrawn from North Korea in December 1948 and US forces from South Korea in mid-1949. In June 1950 Soviet-equipped North Korean forces crossed the 38°N line in an attempt to conquer the South and almost succeeded in doing so, although US naval and air support was given to South Korea's forces. An appeal by the UN Security Council for the withdrawal of North Korea's forces was ignored, and the Security Council thereupon recommended (in the absence of the Soviet Union, which was then boycotting the Council) that UN member states should assist South Korea. As a result, 16 UN member states sent contingents to form a UN Command under Gen. Douglas MacArthur of the United States. The UN and South Korean forces, repelling those of North Korea, crossed the 38th parallel in September 1950. The People's Republic of China had earlier issued a warning that it would cross its boundary with North Korea (i.e. the Yalu river) if UN forces moved into North Korea. After Gen. MacArthur had, despite this warning, ordered a "final" offensive against the North, China entered the war in October 1950 and drove the UN forces back into the South.

The war continued until 1953, when an armistice was concluded and a provisional boundary was agreed along a demilitarized zone (DMZ) mainly to the north of the 38th parallel, and to be supervised by UN forces. This armistice line has remained the effective boundary between North and South Korea. A joint military armistice commission consisting of representatives of the North Korean and the United Nations forces (the latter headed by a US officer) has held regular meetings in Panmunjom since 1953.

Unsuccessful Negotiations on Reunification

Proposals for talks on a possible reunification of North and South Korea were made by North Korea on April 12, 1971, but were rejected by South Korea on the grounds that they contained demands which were "utterly impossible to satisfy and quite unreasonable".

However, on July 4, 1972, it was announced that agreement had been reached that "peaceful unification of the fatherland" should be achieved "as early as possible"; that mutual hostile propaganda and armed provocation should cease; and that a North-South co-ordinating committee should be set up. Representatives of the two sides first met at Panmunjom on Oct. 12, 1972, and in November of that year they agreed to establish the proposed North-South co-ordinating committee, which held its first meeting on Nov. 30-Dec. 1, 1972. Further talks were, however, suspended in August 1973.

On June 23, 1973, the South Korean government issued a special foreign policy statement in which it said that it would not object to North Korea becoming a member of international organizations (jointly with South Korea) pending eventual unification, and would open its doors to all countries on a reciprocal basis regardless of their ideologies and systems.

In a statement on Jan. 18, 1974, President Park Chung Hee of South Korea proposed the conclusion of a non-aggression pact between the two governments. At the same time he rejected earlier North Korean proposals for the withdrawal of foreign troops from all of Korea (in effect of the 40,000 US troops still remaining in South Korea), the reduction of each side's armed forces to 100,000 men, a ban on the introduction of foreign military equipment and the abolition of the armistice agreement. His proposal concerning a non-aggression pact was rejected by North Korea on Jan. 26, 1974.

On Aug. 15, 1974, the South Korean government declared three basic principles for peaceful unification—(i) peace should be firmly established on the Korean peninsula; (ii) the two sides should open their doors to each other through constructive dialogue, exchanges and co-operation; and (iii) unification should be achieved through free general elections under fair management and in direct proportion to the indigenous population.

During 1974-75 a number of naval incidents occurred in which gunboats and fishing vessels of both sides were sunk; it was also found that North Korean forces had dug tunnels beneath the demilitarized zone. In an incident in the joint security zone around Panmunjom, two US officers were killed in fighting with North Korean soldiers on Aug. 5, 1976. Under an agreement reached on Sept. 6 of that year the joint security area was divided into two parts by the military demarcation line, and guards were required to remain on their own side of the line.

On Jan. 12, 1977, President Park again proposed the conclusion of a non-aggression pact and added that he could see no objection to the withdrawal of US troops once such a pact had been concluded. His proposal was rejected by North Korea on Jan. 25, when North Korea demanded the unconditional withdrawal of the US forces. On Jan. 1, 1979, President Park called for a resumption of talks between North and South Korea, and three meetings were subsequently held between representatives of the two sides in February and March 1979 but revealed fundamental differences over the level at which talks should be held. A joint US-South Korean proposal for tripartite talks was rejected by North Korea on July 10, 1979.

On Jan. 12, 1980, the North Korean government, for the first time, acknowledged the South Korean government (which it had previously regarded as a "US puppet"). A new effort to revive talks between the two sides was begun in March 1980 and a number of meetings of representatives of both sides took place at Panmunjom. However, relations between North and South Korea then deteriorated sharply as a result of a number of incidents involving the infiltration of North Korean agents into the South and the sinking of naval vessels, leading to the placing on alert of the armies of both North and South Korea by June 25. Early in September 1980 the North Korean Army began to transmit broadcasts calling on the South Korean forces to overthrow President Chun Doo Hwan (who had succeeded President Park after the latter's assassination on Oct. 26, 1979).

On Aug. 11, 1980, it had been reported that North Korea had declared itself ready for peace talks with the United States (which had always refused to negotiate with North Korea without South Korean participation) without prior withdrawal of US troops. On Sept. 14 of that year President Kim Il Sung of North Korea stated that, if the USA agreed to sign a peace treaty with North Korea, the latter would repudiate its military alliances with China and the Soviet Union and would not seek reunification with the South by military means. As regards

President Chun Doo Hwan, however, the North Korean President made a bitter attack on Sept. 25, saying that North Korea was "not prepared to hold talks" with him because he had "no intention" of unifying Korea. South Korea nevertheless again proposed a renewal of the unification talks on Oct. 7, 1980.

President Kim Il Sung declared on Oct. 10, 1980, that the situation in Korea was so strained that there was "a constant danger of war breaking out at any moment" and that this danger could be removed only if the 1953 armistice agreement were replaced by a peace treaty with the United States. He proposed that the North and the South should be reunited as a confederal state in which each side would exercise regional autonomy and would retain its own ideology and social system without trying to impose them on the other. To this end, a "supreme national confederal assembly" should be formed, in which the North and the South would have an equal number of representatives, and should appoint a "confederal standing committee", which would decide on political affairs, defence, foreign affairs and other questions of common concern. Under this proposal, economic co-operation and exchanges between North and South would take place on the basis of a mutual recognition of differing economic systems; however, the northern and southern armies would be combined into a single national army.

These North Korean proposals were officially denounced by the South Korean government on Oct. 15, 1980, on the grounds that they contained conditions which were "preposterous and tantamount to self-destruction" of South Korea. In a New Year broadcast published on Jan. 12, 1981, the South Korean President invited President Kim Il Sung to visit the South Korean capital "without any condition attached and free of any burden", adding that he was prepared to visit North Korea if invited; he also said that it was South Korea's paramount task to reunify the homeland into an independent and democratic state. In North Korea, however, the invitation was rejectd out of hand on Jan. 19 on the grounds that President Chun Doo Hwan was "not a man worthy for us to do anything with".

A draft constitution of South Korea (which came into force on Oct. 27, 1980, after being approved in a referendum held on Oct. 22) made provision inter alia for the creation of an Advisory Council on Peaceful Unification Policy. This council consisted of the 5,277 members of the elected Presidential Electoral College and 3,642 members nominated by the President. It met for the first time on June 5, 1981, when it suggested the following topics for discussion at a meeting of the two countries' Presidents: (i) the easing of tension and prevention of the recurrence of war between North and South Korea; (ii) a comprehensive discussion of the unification formulae advanced by the two sides; (iii) the prevention of waste of national energy stemming from excessive competition in international areas; and (iv) the fostering of international conditions which would promote peaceful unification.

President Chun's 1982 Proposal for Reunification Conference—North Korean Rejection

In a New Year policy speech on Jan. 22, 1982, President Chun of South Korea put forward detailed proposals for reunification through a conference of representatives of both the South and the North, which would draw up a draft constitution. "I would like to make use of this occasion to disclose a new peaceful unification formula that was originally prepared in anticipation of a South-North summit meeting", President Chun said. "I do so with a view to providing the North Korean authorities and the rest of the world with an opportunity to comprehend our genuine intent. It is my conviction that the most reasonable way to peaceful unification is to adopt a constitution of a unified Korea testifying to the commitment of the entire people to unification—a commitment attained through the promotion of national reconciliation—and then to establish a unified state on the terms and conditions laid down in the constitution."

He continued: "I suggest that, to have the said constitution adopted, the South and the North organize a Consultative Conference for National Reunification (CCNR), with participants from the two sides representing the views of the residents in their respective areas, and authorize this body to draft a constitution presenting the terms and conditions of a unified Democratic Republic of Korea committed to the ideals of nationalism, democracy, liberty and individual well-being. I would further suggest that, when such a draft constitution is drawn up, the two sides make it into law through free, democratic referendums held throughout the whole peninsula. The unification of the country can then be accomplished by organizing a unified legislature and establishing a unified government through a general election held under the constitution of the unified Korea. It is my understanding that such issues as the political ideology, the name of the country, the basic domestic and foreign policy directions, the form of government and the methods and dates of the general elections for a unified legislature will have to be discussed and agreed on in the CCNR in the course of drafting the constitution.

"It is our intention to present our own draft of a constitution for a unified country to the CCNR. If North Korea genuinely desires an independent and peaceful unification, they will also have to present a draft constitution for a unified country before the CCNR, so that the two versions can be studied and forged into a single draft.

"It is essential to promote trust between the South and the North and steadfastly eliminate from national life all impediments to unification to facilitate the historic drafting of a unified constitution. Accordingly, the unnatural relations between the South and the North, which have resulted in self-inflicted injuries, must be brought to an end and replaced by normal contacts that promote the national well-being. To achieve this end, I hope that the South and the North will first normalize relations and, within the framework of these normalized relations, take concrete steps to bring about national reconciliation. I therefore propose, as a practical arrangement leading to unification, the conclusion of a provisional agreement on basic relations between South and North Korea featuring the following provisions:

"(1) Relations between South and North Korea shall be based on the principle of equality and reciprocity pending unification.

"(2) The South and the North shall abandon all forms of military force and violence, as well as the threat thereof, as a means of settling issues between them and seek peaceful solutions to all problems through dialogue and negotiation.

"(3) South and North Korea shall recognize each other's existing political order and social institutions and shall not interfere in each other's internal affairs in any way.

"(4) The South and the North shall maintain the existing regime of armistice in force while working out measures to end the arms race and military confrontation in order to ease tension and prevent war on the Korean peninsula.

"(5) In order to eliminate national suffering and the inconvenience resulting from the partition of the land and to promote an atmosphere of national trust and reconciliation, the South and the North shall progressively open their societies to each other through various forms of exchange and co-operation, to substantially advance the interests of the people. The South and the North shall facilitate free travel between the two halves of the peninsula, including the reunion of separated families, and shall promote exchanges and co-operation in the fields of trade, transportation, postal service, communications, sports, academic pursuits, education, culture, news gathering and reporting, health, technology, environmental protection, etc.

"(6) Until unification is achieved, both parties shall respect each other's bilateral and multilateral treaties and agreements concluded with third countries, irrespective of differences in ideologies, ideals and institutions, and consult with each other on issues affecting the interests of the Korean people as a whole.

"(7) The South and the North shall each appoint a plenipotentiary envoy with the rank of cabinet minister to head a resident liaison mission to be established in Seoul and Pyongyang. The specific functions of the liaison missions shall be determined by mutual consultation and agreement, with both parties providing the liaison mission from the other party with all necessary facilities and co-operation to ensure its smooth functioning.

"It is my earnest hope that North Korea will expeditiously accept the proposal for a meeting between the top leaders of the South and the North in order to conduct frank and open-minded discussions on all issues noted above. I propose to North Korea that high-level delegations from the South and the North, headed by cabinet-rank chief delegates, meet together at the earliest possible date in a preparatory conference to work out the necessary procedures for a South-North summit meeting. I want to make it clear that if North Korea is agreeable to the proposal for a preparatory conference, the government of the Republic of Korea has already made the necessary preparations to send a delegation."

The South Korean National Assembly unanimously approved President Chun's proposals on Jan. 23, 1982, and adopted a resolution appealing to the North Korean government to respond favourably to this initiative and to third countries to support the proposals. Vice-President Kim Chong Il of North Korea rejected the proposals on Jan. 26, however, declaring that the only way of solving the reunification question was by the establishment of a confederal republic.

In justification of this rejection, he said: "In the light of the present complicated North-South relations, it is clear to everyone that a possible time for general elections is far off, and moreover it is not logical to hold general elections according to principles of national self-determination and democratic procedure while leaving foreign troops and maintaining the military fascist system in South Korea as they are. As for the formation of a Consultative Conference for National Reunification with those who represent the will of the people, it can only be regarded as mere empty talk under the present state of harsh repression where the conscientious people who speak for the demands of the popular masses are all cast into prison and their political activities banned by law in South Korea . . . . The US troops must be withdrawn from South Korea, democratization carried out there and the anti-communist confrontation policy brought to an end . . . .

"We are ready to meet the present South Korean rulers even tomorrow, if they show their new start by their deeds, by removing these obstacles blocking the way of national reunification. In that case, the reunification consultative body to be organized may take any form—be it a conference for promotion of national reunification or a consultative council for national unification, we will not be nervous about its name. We only hold that the authorities of the North and the South and representatives of different parties and groupings and of all strata at home and abroad should participate in it, and that all reunification proposals to be raised, including the proposal for the establishment of the Democratic Confederal Republic of Koryo and immediate questions for developing North-South relations in the interests of national reunification, should be discussed".

Despite this hostile North Korean reaction, the South Korean Minister of National Unification, Sohn Jae Shik, put forward on Feb. 1, 1982, a list of projects for co-operation between the South and the North. These included the opening of a highway between Seoul and Pyongyang (the respective capitals of South and North Korea); permission for separated families to exchange mail and to meet; establishment of joint fishery and tourist zones; free travel through Panmunjom for overseas Koreans and foreigners; promotion of free trade; ending of "slanderous" broadcasts and jamming; encouragement of sports, cultural and economic exchanges; freedom for journalists to collect material; joint historical and scientific research; joint development and use of natural resources; removal of all military facilities from the demilitarized zone; and establishment of a direct telephone link between the military authorities on each side.

The North Korean Committee for the Peaceful Reunification of the Fatherland put forward alternative proposals on Feb. 10, 1982, for a conference of 50 political figures from the North and 50 from the South, which would discuss all possible proposals for reunification. It also published a list of the proposed participants in the conference; the 50 from the South included well-known political figures, such as ex-Presidents Yun Po Sun (1960-62) and Choi Kyu Hah (1979-80), Kim Dae Jung, Kim Chong Pil, Kim Young Sam and other representatives of the parties dissolved in 1980, but no representatives of any existing parties.

In a statement issued on Feb. 25, 1982, Sohn Jae Shik described the North's action of "arbitrarily announcing a list of figures from the opposite side for a dialogue" as "unprecedentedly brazen", and added that it was "outrageous" for the North Korean

Communists to "pick a quarrel over our political order" while "maintaining a one-man dictatorship for 37 years [and] trying to make this power hereditary" (a reference to the recent recognition of Kim Chong Il as designated successor to this father, President Kim Il Sung), and "mercilessly suppressing en masse" their fellow-countrymen. He proposed that delegations of nine high-ranking officials from each side should meet in Seoul, Pyongyang or Panmunjom to discuss "the holding of talks between the supreme leaders of the North and South Korean authorities to convene a consultative meeting on national unification to formulate a unification constitution and to normalize relations between North and South Korea". At a press conference on the same day he said that the government was prepared to consider the construction of a railway linking North and South Korea.

During the above exchanges between North and South Korea, numerous incidents continued to occur in the border region and at sea. These incidents included the shooting of alleged Northern infiltrators in South Korea, the sinking of alleged South Korean spy ships, and the seizure of South Korean fishing boats by North Korean patrol boats. (In 1982 South Korean sources stated that since 1953 a total of 453 South Korean fishing boats and 3,554 fishermen had been abducted, although most of these had later been returned.)

On Feb. 8, 1983, the Japanese Prime Minister, Yasuhiro Nakasone, said after a meeting with President Chun on Jan. 11-12, 1983, that he approved a South Korean two-stage proposal whereby Japan, and later the United States, would recognize North Korea in return for Chinese, and later Soviet, recognition of South Korea. He added that such a development would depend on the resumption of dialogue on the reunification of North and South Korea.

October 1983 Rangoon Bomb Episode—North Korean Reunification Proposals of 1984

Relations between North and South Korea deteriorated seriously as a result of a bomb explosion in Rangoon (Burma) on Oct. 9, 1983, when 21 persons were killed, among them four visiting South Korean government ministers: It was widely believed that the intention had been to kill President Chun Doo Hwan of South Korea, who arrived on the scene several minutes later. The Burmese government announced on Nov. 4 that the bomb had been planted by North Korean army captains, and that Burma was breaking off its diplomatic relations with North Korea. On Dec. 9, 1983, two North Korean army officers were condemned to death in Rangoon for their part in the bombing.

Notwithstanding the Rangoon episode, the North Korean government renewed its appeal for the "peaceful reunification" of the Korean peninsula when a joint session of the Supreme People's Assembly and the Central People's Committee in Pyongyang approved proposals on Jan. 10, 1984, for "tripartite talks" on this issue with the United States and South Korea, to be held at Panmunjom or in a mutually acceptable third country. As a basis for discussion, the Pyongyang government put forward proposals for (i) the conclusion of a peace treaty with the United States, which would include an agreement for the withdrawal of US troops from South Korea, to replace the armistice agreement of 1953 which ended the Korean war; (ii) the adoption of a non-aggression declaration between North and South Korea which would include a pledge to reduce armed forces and armaments; and (iii) the commencement of a "dialogue of reunification" between the two countries. The North Koreans revived proposals for the establishment of "a confederal state based on a self-governing system, leaving intact the different ideologies and ideas between the North and South", but stressed their "readiness to discuss other proposals". Two letters outlining these suggestions were sent, to the South Korean government in Seoul and to the US Congress, while a third letter to the US administration was delivered personally by Zhao Ziyang, the Chinese Prime Minister, during an official visit to the United States on Jan. 9-16, 1984. It was disclosed by South Korean officials that the North Korean government had raised the issue of a tripartite conference on two previous occasions, namely on Oct. 8 and Dec. 3, 1983.

The January 1984 proposals represented a significant change of policy by the North Korean government in that (i) the regime had hitherto insisted that only the issue of reunification should be discussed, bilaterally, with the South, and that the latter had no role to play in any discussion with the United States on withdrawal of US troops; (ii) it had previously demanded that withdrawal of US troops (estimated to number 30,000-40,000) should be a preliminary to peace talks; (iii) it showed a greater willingness to discuss alternative US or South Korean proposals on reunification; and (iv) the tone of the statement was noticeably muted, with reference being made to the "South Korean authorities" rather than the usual denunciation of the Seoul government as a US "puppet" or "lackey".

The North Koreans had refused to include South Korea in previous proposed negotiations with the United States partly on the grounds that South Korea had not signed the armistice agreement of 1953 and therefore had no legal right to inclusion in such negotiations, and partly because South Korea was in their view "a colonial puppet regime of the USA". The US government, however, had consistently refused to bypass South Korea. President Reagan reiterated this pledge during his visit to the demilitarized zone on Nov. 11-13, 1983, when he promised (i) not to open talks with North Korea without the full and equal participation of South Korea; and (ii) that there would be no attempt to improve US relations with Pyongyang unless corresponding approaches were made to Seoul by countries allied to North Korea.

In its January 1984 statement, the North Korean government asserted that its proposals were a response to the mounting danger of nuclear war on the Korean peninsula, for which it blamed the United States and South Korea, claiming that their aggressive military policies had incited a "war atmosphere" in which "South Korea had become a US powder keg for nuclear war and a nuclear-attack base aimed at the northern half of the Republic". The statement alleged that the USA had already stationed about 1,000 nuclear weapons in South Korea and that in addition it intended to deploy Pershing II and cruise missiles as well as neutron bombs.

South Korean Response to North Korea's 1984 Proposals

Sohn Jae Shik issued a statement on Jan. 11, 1984, which called on the North Korean authorities to admit to and apologize for, either formally or informally, the Rangoon incident and to punish those involved. He went on to renew the South Korean call for bipartite talks between the "highest authorities" of South and North Korea, but also said that the South Korean government would be interested in an "enlarged meeting" at some future date (this being taken as an indication that South Korea would participate in four-way talks including China and the United States, and even six-way talks involving Japan and the Soviet Union as well).

The South Korean government subsequently offered (on Feb. 9, 1984) to meet North Korean representatives directly to present its official reply to the North's proposals for tripartite talks. This meeting took place at the level of officials, on Feb. 14 at Panmunjom when a letter was delivered from Chin Iee Chong, the South Korean Prime Minister, to his newly-appointed North Korean counterpart, Kang Song San. The letter proposed a summit between North and South Korea which could later be expanded to include the United States, China, the Soviet Union and Japan. During the eight-minute exchange the South Korean representatives proposed the resumption of the telephone "hot line" between Seoul and Pyongyang, but the North Korean officials refused to discuss the issue at that meeting. (The telephone "hot line" had been reopened on Feb. 6, 1980, after a three-year break, but had been cut off by the North Koreans on Sept. 25, 1980.)

During a visit to Japan by Hu Yaobang (then General Secretary of the Chinese Communist Party) on Nov. 23-30, 1984, it was agreed that China and Japan would work together to promote peace and stability on the Korean peninsula. The Chinese leader also conveyed assurances from the North Korean President that his country would not invade South Korea, and he added that China had advised North Korea to avoid creating tension in the area.

Talks on possible economic co-operation held by North and South Korean delegations between May 17 and Nov. 20, 1985, remained inconclusive. Interparliamentary talks between the two sides, held between July 23 and Sept. 25, 1985, on the formation of a consultative body to discuss the reunification of Korea led to no agreement on procedure, with the North Koreans proposing the drafting of a constitution for a united Korea, and the South Koreans insisting that a non-aggression pact should be the first step.

Red Cross Negotiations—Sports Meetings

A delegation of the North Korean Red Cross Society had visited Seoul between Aug. 30, 1972, and July 13, 1973, when it was agreed (i) to seek to ascertain the whereabouts and fate of dispersed Korean people (estimated at about 10,000,000); (ii) to facilitate free mutual meetings and visits; (iii) to facilitate free postal exchanges; (iv) to facilitate the reunion of dispersed people according to their wishes; and (v) to discuss other humanitarian issues. However, further Red Cross talks on the reunification of families separated in the war, held in December 1977, had failed to lead to any agreement.

The first new Red Cross meeting was held on Sept. 18, 1984, and discussed details of a flood relief offer made to South Korea by North Korea's Red Cross Society. Such operations were subsequently completed by Oct. 7, 1984.

The North Koreans thereupon suggested the reopening of talks on the reunion of separated families, and at a meeting at Panmunjom held on Nov. 20, 1984, it was agreed to adopt the five-point agenda of 1972-73 [see above]. However, the proposed talks were postponed indefinitely on Jan. 9, 1985, following controversy over a South Korean announcement that annual military exercises of South Korean and US forces would begin on Feb. 1, 1985.

A further visit to Seoul was nevertheless paid by a North Korean Red Cross delegation on May 28-30, 1985, when it was agreed in principle with the South Korean Red Cross Society that there would be an exchange of groups of family members, reciprocal cultural visits and (on a North Korean proposal) "free travel across the demilitarized zone". Detailed agreements in these fields were reached at Panmunjom on July 15 and Aug. 22, 1985. Further discussions followed when a South Korean Red Cross delegation visited Pyongyang between Aug. 27 and Sept. 22, 1985. However, later talks held in Seoul on Dec. 3-4, 1985, ended in disagreement when the South Koreans rejected a North Korean suggestion of free border crossings for people in search of family members (on the ground that this would lead to attempts to "infiltrate trained political agents" into the South), while the North Koreans would not agree to an exchange of letters between family members.

From October 1985 talks were held between representatives of North and South Korea and the International Olympic Committee (IOC) in Switzerland to discuss the question of North Korea's participation in the 24th Olympic Games to be held in Seoul in 1988 and in particular its demand that the events be co-hosted between Pyongyang and Seoul. Whereas South Korea initially took the view that such a division would be a violation of the Olympic Charter, the IOC subsequently put forward proposals for a limited number of events to be held in the North. The 10th Asian Games held in Seoul in September-October 1986 were boycotted by the North because of their alleged "impure political aims".

Deterioration of Relations in 1986—New Initiative by the North

North Korea announced on Jan. 20, 1986, the suspension of all negotiations with the South, in protest against a South Korean announcement of Jan. 18 that the annual "Team Spirit" joint military exercises with US forces would commence the following month, involving over 200,000 troops. On April 24, 1986, the North said negotiations would only be resumed if the South indicated a change in its attitude towards future military exercises and displayed greater tolerance of its internal dissidents. On the same day a South Korean warship sank a North Korean vessel which had allegedly opened fire when challenged but which the North claimed was an unarmed trawler.

A further source of tension during 1986 was the proposed construction of the

Kumgangsan hydroelectric dam on a northern tributary of the Han river about 10 kilometres north of the demilitarized zone. On Nov. 6, 1986, the South Korean Defence Minister warned that his country would be forced to take "self-defence measures" unless work on the dam ceased immediately, claiming that it would have a storage capacity of up to 20,000 millions tonnes of water which, if released, would submerge much of central Korea, including Seoul. The South Korean figures and analysis were subsequently contested by the North, but the South announced on Nov. 26 that work was to begin immediately on a dam of equal size to protect Seoul against the possibility of flooding from the North.

Addressing the North Korean Supreme People's Assembly on Dec. 29, 1986, President Kim Il Sung asserted that the "peaceful reunification of the country" constituted "the most urgent task" currently facing his government. He went on to call for the "founding of a confederal state which would make neither side the conqueror or the conquered" as the long-term solution to the division of the country, and proposed that a joint conference should be established to facilitate "a national dialogue" between the ruling parties and other representative organizations of the North and the South. In January 1987 North Korean ministers followed up the President's initiative by proposing that high-level political and military negotiations should begin forthwith in an effort "to achieve a breakthrough for peace and peaceful reunification".

In response, the South Korean government on Jan. 12, 1987, reiterated its position of rejecting the creation of new channels of communication while those previously set up remained inoperative. President Chun did, however, indicate that he was prepared to have a summit meeting with President Kim in the course of 1987.

North Korean Territorial Claims

At a meeting of the joint military armistice commission on Dec. 1, 1973, the North Korean delegation put forward a claim to the territorial waters around five small islands (Paengyong, Daechong, Sochong, Yonpyong and U) situated six to 10 miles off the North Korean coast, to the west of Panmunjom, which the 1953 armistice agreement had placed under the military control of the UN Command. This claim was not accepted by the other delegations to the committee.

On June 21, 1977, the North Korean government adopted a decree, to come into effect on Aug. 1 of that year, on the extension of the North Korean economic zone to 200 miles from the coast in the Sea of Japan and to the half-way line between North Korea and China in the Yellow Sea, and the exlusion of all foreign vessels from fishing and other economic activities in that zone without previous permission. On Aug. 1, 1977, the North Korean Supreme Command announced that North Korea's military boundary extended up to 50 miles from the coast in the Yellow Sea and up to 200 miles in the Sea of Japan, that foreign military vessels and aircraft were prohibited within this boundary, and that foreign civil shipping and aircraft might operate in it only by prior agreement. These decisions were recognized neither by South Korea nor by Japan.

HWD

Laos-Thailand

The 1,754-kilometre Laos-Thailand border (which follows the watershed between the Mae Nam Nan and Mekong river systems before looping eastwards and then southwards along the Mekong river itself for some 800 kilometres) has been the scene of periodic border incidents in recent years, often involving shooting exchanges across the Mekong. In 1984 a serious territorial dispute arose over three villages on the northern section of the border (west of the Mekong) over which both countries claimed sovereignty.

Historical Background—Laos-Thailand Relations, 1975-82

Siam (the name by which Thailand was known until 1939) invaded the first Lao kingdom (Lan Xang) in 1535, but it was not until 1791 that the three Lao provinces of Vientiane, Luang Prabang and Champassak came under Siamese suzerainty. In 1893 Siam ceded to France Lao-populated territory east of the Mekong, including the islands in the river itself, thereby consolidating French control of Indo-China. A series of treaties and conventions signed by France and Siam in 1902, 1904 and 1907 extended the border of French-controlled Laos to the west of the northern Mekong to include the province of Sayaboury (whose border is at the centre of the current "three villages" dispute).

Throughout the Vietnam War in the 1960s and early 1970s Thailand committed itself to the anti-communist camp and units of Thai irregular soldiers operated in Laos against the pro-communist Pathet Lao (the controlling force in the northern regions following the de facto partition of the country in 1965). Relations between the two countries after the Pathet Lao gained full control of Laos in May 1975 tended to reflect this previous alignment and the fact that Thailand remained in a defence treaty relationship with the United States. The emigration of Lao right-wing forces and politicians to Thailand after the communist victory became a particular source of tension, with Laos consistently accusing successive Thai governments of supporting insurgents based along the border. Thailand has made similar accusations concerning Lao support for communist *Phak Mai* (New Party) guerrillas.

In the months prior to the formation of the Lao People's Democratic Republic (LPDR) in December 1975, clashes across and on the Mekong, particularly in the vicinity of Vientiane (the Laotian captial), resulted in Thailand closing the border to Lao imports and exports, thereby necessitating the airlifting of essential goods to Laos from Vietnam. Nevertheless, Thailand's initial response to the communist victory in Indo-China was essentially conciliatory and resulted in a visit to Vientiane by the Thai Foreign Minister, Pichai Rattakul, on July 31-Aug. 3, 1976. On that occasion a joint statement asserted that bilateral relations should be based on the principles of peaceful co-existence and non-intervention in each other's affairs; it was further agreed to reopen a number of border points and to create a mechanism to hold local meetings in the event of a border incident.

A militantly anti-communist regime under Thanin Kraivichien came to power in Thailand in October 1976 (as the result of a military coup) and throughout the following year a series of border incidents led Thailand to re-impose a partial economic blockade. Lao sources claimed that during April 1977 Thai forces attacked three Lao islands in the Mekong; namely Sang Khi, Con Tam and Singsou. However, a new Thai government which came to power in November 1977, with Gen. Kriangsak Chamanan as Prime Minister, attempted to improve relations with Laos by immediately lifting the partial economic blockade. In March 1978 the Lao Minister of Foreign Affairs, Phoune Sipaseuth, visited Bangkok (the capital of Thailand) and reaffirmed the principles of peaceful co-existence and non-intervention agreed in August 1976. The number of border incidents decreased in 1978, but in December of that year a major skirmish occurred on the Mekong, resulting in the sinking of four military vessels and the deaths of a number of Thai and Lao military personnel.

Gen. Kriangsak visited Vientiane on Jan. 4-6, 1979, following which Kaysone Phomvihane (General Secretary of the ruling Lao People's Revolutionary Party and Chairman of the Council of Ministers) paid a return visit to Bangkok on April 1-4. In a joint communiqué issued at the end of Kaysone's visit, the two leaders described the Mekong as a "river of genuine peace, friendship and mutual benefit" and stated that both countries would adopt "necessary and effective measures to prevent and smash all movements of terrorists using the border areas as hiding places". A memorandum of understanding—providing for the establishment of a border liaison committee, the reduction of armed patrols on the

Mekong and the opening of a fifth official passage across the Mekong—was signed during the visit of a Thai government delegation to Vientiane in August 1979.

Relations again deteriorated after Gen. Prem Tinsulanond succeeded Gen. Kriangsak as Prime Minister of Thailand in March 1980. On June 15 of that year Lao troops fired on a Thai patrol boat operating in the Lao half of the Mekong, killing a naval officer. Thailand responded by closing the frontier for most of July, thereby causing serious food shortages in Vientiane. Another period of tension began on Jan. 20, 1981, when Thai troops reportedly fired on a Lao civilian vessel travelling on the Mekong, killing one crew member; seven days later another Lao boat was attacked and two of its crew were killed. A series of clashes took place in the last week of January and the first three weeks of February 1981, around the small Lao island of Don Sangkhi, in the Mekong near Vientiane. In response, Thai officials closed three points of entry on the border.

A general improvement in relations during 1981 and 1982 was marked by reciprocal ministerial visits. However, shooting incidents across the Mekong recurred in October and November 1981 and in April and June 1982. In the June 1982 incident Thailand alleged that (on June 16) Lao troops stationed on Don Sangkhi island fired on a Thai village, and that the following day Lao forces had shelled Thai patrol boats operating near the island.

The "Three Villages Dispute"

The dispute over the sovereignty of three villages situated near the land border where the western Lao province of Sayaboury meets the northern Thai province of Uttaradit began in March 1984. The disputed villages—Ban Mai, Ban Klang and Ban Sawang—cover an area of some 19 square kilometres and have a combined population of approximately 1,800 Lao-speaking people.

According to Thai sources, Lao troops occupied the three villages in April 1984, having intruded four miles into Uttaradit province during the previous month in an attempt to disrupt Thai construction of a road. This road, described initially by the Thai military as a "strategic" road but later as "developmental", was originally planned to pass near to the three villages but subsequently diverted from the area. Prior to the occupation of the three villages, Lao forces had on April 15 clashed with Thai border patrol police and para-military

Rangers. After another clash in late May, Thai military officials publicized the dispute and on June 6, 1984, Thai troops of the first Cavalry Division took control of the three villages, with little apparent Lao opposition.

The first Lao response to the establishment of Thai military control in the three villages consisted of a series of radio broadcasts blaming the "encroachment" on "ultra-rightist reactionaries in the Thai ruling circles". The same broadcasts linked the latest episode to Thailand's support of the exiled Coalition Government of Democratic Kampuchea (CGDK) as well as to alleged Chinese incursions into Vietnam's northern provinces during April 1984.[1] Lao broadcasts further contended that a direct link existed between Thailand's military occupation of the three villages and a visit to China in May 1984 by Gen. Arthit Kamlang-Ek, the Supreme Commander of the Thai Armed Forces and

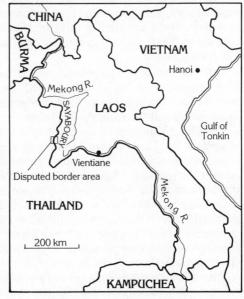

Map 38   The Laos-Thailand border.

---

[1]For an account of Sino-Vietnamese territorial issues, see pages 309-16.

Army C.-in-C. Thailand in turn accused Vietnam of playing a role in aggravating and internationalizing the dispute, with the aim of distracting world attention from the Kampuchea issue. Prasong Soonsiri, the Secretary-General of Thailand's National Security Council, told a press conference on June 22 that "Vietnam's involvement proves beyond doubt that the leaders of the Lao government are being used as a tool".

A Lao delegation visited Bangkok for talks with Thai officials on July 21-24, 1984, and again on Aug. 7-15, but no agreement was reached on the withdrawal of Thai troops from the disputed area, the two sides produced conflicting maps of the area in support of their claims to sovereignty. The Lao map had originally been produced as an addendum to the 1907 border treaty between France and Siam; in addition, the Lao delegation cited the precedent of the Preah Vihear temple dispute between Thailand and Cambodia (Kampuchea) in 1962, when the International Court of Justice had based its ruling on the 1907 Franco-Siamese border treaty. The Thai delegation cited a map published in 1978 (and drawn largely from US aerial reconnaissance photographs, claiming that it showed the three villages to be in Thai territory—i.e. in an area to the west of the Mae Nam Nan-Mekong watershed line (which both countries agreed should form the line of the border). The talks were broken off by Thailand on Aug. 15 after the Lao delegation refused to accept a Thai proposal for a joint technical team to visit the disputed area in order to determine the border.

After Lao troops had in September 1984, killed two border policemen and a mechanic near the disputed area, Air Chief Marshal Siddhi Savetsila (the Thai Foreign Minister) threatened to lodge a complaint to the United Nations. However, in a subsequent address to the UN General Assembly on Oct. 2 he stated that Thai troops were to be withdrawn from the three villages. A Thai Foreign Ministry spokesman announced on Oct. 15 that the withdrawal had been completed, but warned that this step should not be seen as a renunciation of a Thai claim on the three villages. Addressing the same session of the UN Security Council in October 1984, Phoune Sipaseuth described Air Chief Marshal Siddhi's statement as an "attempt to mislead Thai and international public opinion". He also criticized the Thai Foreign Minister's failure to address the questions of Lao villagers allegedly captured by Thai soldiers and of compensation for the "human and material losses suffered by the population".

Lao officials confirmed in late October 1984 that Thai forces had withdrawn from the three villages, but claimed that they continued to occupy strategically important high ground in the vicinity. Lao calls for talks on the dispute in November and December 1984 were rejected by Thailand, which claimed that with the withdrawal of Thai troops the problem had been solved.

Talks on the three villages dispute figured prominently during a visit to Vientiane by a Thai delegation on Juy 29-Aug. 3, 1985. The discussions ended in disagreement, however, with the Lao side insisting on further negotiations at a national level and the Thai delegation maintaining that the issue should be settled at a local level.

The Hong Kong-based *Far Eastern Economic Review* reported on Aug. 22, 1985, that officials in the Thai Foreign Ministry had recently confirmed the existence of a number of previously undisclosed territorial disputes with Laos along their common border. Reports in August 1985 indicated an increase in border hostilities and on Aug. 10 an incident resulted in the death of a Thai border patrol policeman.

On June 14, 1986, Thai government officials announced that 40 Lao troops had crossed the northern land border and launched an attack on a makeshift encampment of illegal Lao immigrants, near the town of Chiang Kham, killing 35 and seriously wounding a number of others. A formal Thai protest to the United Nations was rejected by Laos as a "pretext for creating tension" along the border.

Thereafter, relations between the two countries appeared to improve, beginning in early August 1986, when Kaysone sent a letter of congratulations to Gen. Prem on his reappointment as Thailand's Prime Minister, expressing a wish for better relations. On Sept. 24, 1986, Laos delivered a memorandum to the Thai ambassador in Vientiane proposing that both countries should appoint high-level working groups to prepare for future ministerial talks, this being agreed the following day during talks at the United Nations in New York.

A senior Thai delegation led by Arun Panupong (a Foreign Ministry adviser) visited Vientiane on Nov. 27-29, 1986, and during talks both sides reportedly agreed to stop propaganda attacks against each other. Talks at governmental level continued on March 24-28, 1987, when a Lao delegation led by the deputy Foreign Minister, Souban Salitthilat, paid a visit to Bangkok. Prior to these talks, on Feb. 18, the Thai Foreign Trade Department had issued an order reducing the number of "strategic goods" banned for export to Laos from 273 to 61. Further armed clashes were reported on the border in May and June 1987.

DS

Malaysia-Philippines (Sabah)

A territorial claim to Sabah—known as British North Borneo until September 1963 and constituting the north-eastern part of the island of Borneo, and bordering on Indonesian territory—was first enunciated by the government of the Philippines in 1961, when plans were being formulated by Britain and Malaya for the formation of a Federation of Malaysia, which was eventually to embrace Malaya, Singapore, Sarawak and Sabah. The Philippine claim, based largely on historical grounds, was rejected by both Britain and Malaya, and later by Malaysia, but it was pursued by the Philippines with the result that for three years diplomatic relations between Malaysia and the Philippines were suspended. The formation of the Association of South-East Asian Nations (ASEAN) in 1967 led to an improvement in relations between the two countries, and 10 years later the Philippine President announced that as a contribution to the unity of the organization his government would cease actively prosecuting its claim to Sabah. However, a further 10 years later efforts to achieve a negotiated resolution of the dispute were still in progress.

Philippine Declarations regarding Sabah and British Response, 1961-63

Following the approval by the governments of Britain and Malaya (as announced in a joint statement issued on Nov. 23, 1961) of a plan for the formation of a Federation of Malaysia, a press campaign was launched in the Philippines against the proposed incorporation of British North Borneo in the projected Federation. The arguments put forward in support of the Philippine claim to Sabah, and the legal position as seen by the British side, reflected contrasting interpretations of the historical background to the dispute, as given in the following outline (itself based on an account published at the time in *The Times* of London).

In 1877 and 1878 the Sultans of Brunei and Sulu agreed to transfer their rights in North Borneo to a British syndicate formed by Alfred Dent (later Sir) and Baron Gustavus de Overbeck. The concession was taken over in 1881 by the British North Borneo Company, which was incorporated by Royal Charter in that year, and remained so until 1946, when North Borneo became a British colony after having been a British protectorate since 1883. The 1878 deed provided that the Sultan of Sulu, on behalf of himself and his heirs and successors, "granted and ceded" to Dent and Baron de Overbeck, "for ever and in perpetuity, all rights and powers ... over all the territories and lands tributary [to the Sultan] on the mainland of Borneo ... with all islands within three marine leagues of the coast". In return, the Sultan and his heirs and successors were guaranteed an annual payment of $5,000 (Malayan). In 1903 the Sultan signed a confirmatory deed stating that "all the islands that

369

are near the territory" (of North Borneo) had been ceded "to the government of British North Borneo" and specifically enumerating the islands affected, because their names had not been individually mentioned in the 1878 agreement. At the same time the annual payment to the Sultan was increased by a further $300 (Malayan).

The Philippines based its claim to North Borneo on the contention that the whole transaction was illegal *ab initio*, since the Sultan of Sulu had no right to dispose of the territory; alternatively, it was argued that if the Sultan had such a right, he intended to lease the territory and not sell it outright. In the latter respect, argument centred on the translation of the Malay word *padak*, a vaguer term than the official translation "grant and cede" (although the original deed also included the phrase "for ever and in perpetuity"). As regards the legality or otherwise of the cession, the Philippine contention was that Spain, and not the Sultan, was sovereign in the area of North Borneo and the Sulu archipelago. Treaties concluded between Spain and the Sultan of Sulu in 1836, 1851 and 1864 were, however, not recognized by Britain on the grounds that Spain was unable to control the Sultan, and in 1885 Spain signed a treaty with Britain and Germany renouncing in Britain's favour sovereignty over the territories "on the continent of Borneo formerly belonging to the Sultan of Sulu". In return, Britain recognized Spanish sovereignty over the Sulu archipelago, a group of islands midway between Mindanao (the southernmost of the Philippine islands) and North Borneo. As North Borneo was then under the control of the British North Borneo Company, the 1885 treaty in effect legalized the position then existing.

Following the Spanish-American War of 1898 the United States replaced Spain as the sovereign power in the Philippines, and by an Anglo-American convention of 1930 the US government recognized that North Borneo was under British protection. This convention

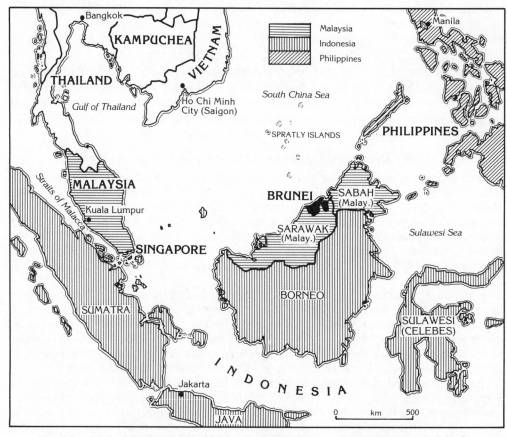

Map 39   Territorial relationship of Malaysia and Philippines, showing the Spratly Islands.

was expressly cited in 1946 when President Truman proclaimed the independence of the Philippine Republic. Supporters of the Philippine claim contended, however, that the Philippine Republic could not be bound by undertakings previously entered into with a colonial power.

On the death of the then Sultan of Sulu, the government of the Philippines (then under US sovereignty) declared that it would recognize the Sultanate's authority over the Sulu archipelago, the Philippines thereby assuming power in place of the Sultan and his heirs and successors. Thus the Sulu archipelago was under Philippine sovereignty when the independent Philippine Republic came into existence in 1946.

In a resolution adopted unanimously by the Philippine House of Representatives on April 30, 1962, it was declared: "The claim of the Philippine Republic upon a certain portion of the island of Borneo and adjacent islands is valid." The House accordingly requested President Diosdado Macapagal of the Philippines to "take the necessary steps consistent with international law and procedure" for the recovery of the territory. Accordingly, on June 22, 1962, the Philippine government sent a note to the British government, asking for talks on the question of North Borneo and expressing the hope that disputes between the two countries would be settled peacefully and in an atmosphere of goodwill. The British government agreed, in a note sent to the Philippines on Aug. 7, 1962, that such talks should be held but reiterated that in its view the status of North Borneo was not in dispute.

Earlier, President Macapagal had proposed, on July 27, 1962, the formation of an independent Greater Malaya, comprising the Philippines, Malaya, Singapore, North Borneo, Sarawak and Brunei, and superseding "the British-sponsored Federation of Malaysia". Declaring that "Asians should not accept a European project as a substitute for an Asian project planned and carried out by Asians themselves in the true and enduring interests of the Asian world", he said that "the great arc of islands consisting of the Philippine archipelago, North Borneo, Singapore and the Malayan peninsula would form a formidable geographical, cultural, economic and political unity that would be a powerful force for freedom, progress and peace".

In a statement issued on Jan. 28, 1963, the Philippine President described North Borneo as essential to Philippine national security in the light of the continuing communist danger in South-East Asia. At the same time he emphasized that his government, while claiming British North Borneo, also recognized the principle of self-determination, and he therefore urged that the people of North Borneo should be allowed to declare—perhaps in a referendum under United Nations auspices—whether they wished to be independent, part of the Philippines, or "placed under another state".

At the end of talks which were held in London on Jan. 28-Feb. 1, 1963, between Emmanuel Pelaez, then Philippine Vice-President and Minister of Foreign Affairs, and Lord Home, then British Foreign Secretary, it was stated inter alia that the Philippine delegation had made a detailed statement of their government's claim to North Borneo, whilst the British government had explained why this claim "could not be accepted"; that it had been agreed to exchange copies of documents relating to the legal position; and that the British government hoped that after the establishment of the Federation of Malaysia it would be possible for Britain and the Philippines to reach agreement.

North Borneo Majority Decisions in favour of Incorporation in the Federation of Malaysia

The North Borneo Legislative Assembly unanimously approved the entry of the territory into the proposed Federation on Sept. 12, 1962. In elections held to local councils (on the basis of adult suffrage) in North Borneo in December 1962, a total of 95 out of the 110 seats were won by supporters of the proposed Federation. The newly-elected council members subsequently took part in the indirect (three-tier) elections of a new Legislative Council. During 1963 it was established, both by the British government and by the United Nations, that a majority of the inhabitants of North Borneo approved the proposed incorporation of the territory in the Federation of Malaysia.

A commission of inquiry, appointed by the British government on Jan. 17, 1962, under the chairmanship of Lord Cobbold (a former governor of the Bank of England) to ascertain the views of the people of Sarawak and North Borneo on the proposed Federation, stated in its unanimously adopted report (published on Aug. 31, 1963) inter alia that about one-third of the population of the two territories strongly favoured early realization of the Federation, that another third also favoured it, although under various safeguards and conditions, and that the last third included a "hard core, vocal and politically active", which would oppose Malaysia on any terms unless it was preceded by independence and self-government; this "hard core" was estimated to amount to "near 20 per cent in Sarawak and somewhat less in North Borneo".

A UN mission sent to Sarawak and North Borneo to establish whether the 1962 elections had been properly conducted and reflected the wishes of the population regarding Malaysia found (in its report published on Sept. 14, 1963) that in properly conducted elections a majority of the voters had shown their desire to join the Federation. The mission had been joined by observers from Indonesia and the Philippines, and on arrival in North Borneo it had been greeted by a mass demonstration in favour of Malaysia and opposed to rule by Indonesia.

Period of "Confrontation" between Malaysia and the Philippines, 1963-66

The Federation of Malaysia came into being on Sept. 16, 1963, when North Borneo officially took the name of Sabah. The newly-established Federation was, however, not recognized by Indonesia (which entered upon a period of "confrontation" with Malaysia), while the government of the Philippines downgraded its embassy in Kuala Lumpur (the Malaysian capital) to the status of a consulate. Tunku Abdul Rahman, the Malaysian Prime Minister, thereupon announced on Sept. 17 that (in addition to the severance of diplomatic relations with Indonesia) all of Malaysia's diplomatic staff had been withdrawn from Manila on the ground that the Philippine decision to reduce the status of its embassy was "not acceptable".

Although diplomatic relations between Malaysia and the Philippines subsequently remained suspended, there was some improvement in relations between the two countries as a result of a meeting in Pnom-Penh (Kampuchea) on Feb. 10-12, 1964, between Tunku Abdul Rahman and President Macapagal, who stated afterwards that they had "cleared the air" in their dispute; that they had agreed to consider the mutual establishment of consulates as a step towards the resumption of normal diplomatic relations; and that the two governments would consider the "best way" to settle the Philippine claim to Sabah, including the possible reference of the question to the International Court of Justice. Consular relations between the two countries were thereafter restored on May 8, 1964. Following an agreement concluded on June 1, 1966, on the ending of the three-year "confrontation" between Malaysia and Indonesia, full diplomatic relations were officially resumed between Malaysia and the Philippines on June 3, 1966.

Renewed Suspension of Diplomatic Relations following Revival of Philippine Claim in 1968

The Philippine claim to Sabah was revived in 1968, when it was discussed by Malaysia and Philippine officials meeting in Bangkok (Thailand) from June 17 to July 16. At this meeting Leon Maria Guerrero, the Philippine chief delegate, upholding his country's claim to the territory, demanded that the dispute should be referred to the International Court of Justice, whereas Tan Sri Ghazali bin Shafie, the Malaysian chief delegate (and later Foreign Minister), rejected the Philippine claim as neither legally nor politically valid. As no agreement was reached the Malaysian delegation left the talks on July 16. The Philippine government thereupon withdrew its ambassador from Kuala Lumpur in protest against "Malaysia's intransigence" and its "abrupt rejection of the Philippine claim" to Sabah.

On Aug. 26, 1968, the Philippine House of Representatives passed a bill including Sabah within the national boundaries of the Philippine Republic, and this bill was signed by President Ferdinand Marcos on Sept. 18 of that year. On the same day Tunku Abdul Rahman, at the end of a Malaysian cabinet meeting, denounced the bill as "a violation of Malaysia's sovereignty and territorial integrity" and "a highly provocative act tantamount to aggression". On the following day Malaysia suspended its diplomatic relations with the Philippines and abrogated an anti-smuggling agreement between the two countries, under which some Philippine customs officers had been stationed in Sabah.

Narciso Ramos, then Philippine Secretary for Foreign Affairs, on Oct. 15, 1968, reiterated his country's demand that the Sabah question should be referred to the International Court of Justice and added that his government would accept the Court's judgment, although until the question was settled the Philippine government would not recognize the authority of the Malaysian government to represent the people and territory of Sabah. This refusal to recognize Malaysia's right to speak for Sabah was restated by the Philippine government on Oct. 16. Tunku Abdul Rahman thereupon announced on Oct. 23 that diplomatic status had been removed from the remaining staff at the Philippine embassy in Kuala Lumpur, and on Nov. 19 it was announced in Manila that the Philippine government had decided to withdraw its entire diplomatic staff from the Malaysian capital.

Resumption of Diplomatic Relations in 1969—Moderation of Philippine Position in 1977

Following the formation of the Association of South-East Asian Nations (ASEAN) in August 1967, with both Malaysia and the Philippines being members of this organization, it was announced at a meeting of ASEAN member countries' Foreign Ministers in Malaysia on Dec. 16, 1969, that the two sides had agreed to resume their diplomatic relations. The Sabah question was not raised again by the Philippines during the following years, and at the second meeting of the Heads of State and Government of the ASEAN member countries, held in Kuala Lumpur, President Marcos declared on Aug. 4, 1977, that as a contribution to the unity of the ASEAN, the Republic of the Philippines intended to renounce its claim to Sabah.

As a result, the President and Datuk Hussein bin Onn, the Prime Minister of Malaysia, agreed to establish joint border patrols between Sabah and the Philippines in order to prevent piracy, smuggling and drug traffic, while Malaysia also undertook to prevent Malaysian extremist Moslems from smuggling weapons to Moslem separatists in the southern Philippines. As a result of continued warfare between Philippine armed forces and the Moro National Liberation Front in the southern islands of the Philippines, over 90,000 Moslems were said to have reached Sabah by the end of 1978.

Inconclusive Negotiations on Resolution of Sabah Dispute

Notwithstanding President Marcos's 1977 statement of intent, a final resolution of the Sabah dispute remained outstanding over the next decade, during which Malaysian-Philippine relations were from time to time strained by the continued use of bases in Sabah by Moslem separatists opposed to the Manila government. Moreover, the Philippine Defence Minister warned on Oct. 1, 1985, of a possible confrontation with Malaysia, following reports that Malaysian gunboats and helicopter gunships engaged in anti-piracy operations had killed or abducted over 50 people in an attack on the Philippine island of Maddanas (1,000 kilometres south of Manila).

In May 1986 the two governments agreed to set up a two-member panel of Foreign Ministry officials to seek a resolution of the Sabah issue. Following the panel's first meeting the following month (in Manila), the then Malaysian Foreign Minister was reported to have stated on July 3 that he had "reached an understanding" with his Philippine counterpart on the Sabah issue, although no details could yet be published. However, a government minister in Manila declared shortly afterwards that the Philippines was not yet ready to waive its claim to Sabah.

HWD

The Spratly Islands

The Spratly Islands (known to the Chinese as the Nansha Islands, to the Vietnamese as the Truong Sa and to the Philippines as Kalayaan) are a group of islets, coral reefs and sandbars in the South China Sea dispersed over 600 miles (965 km), which are claimed, either in whole or in part, by the People's Republic of China, the Republic of China (Taiwan), Vietnam, the Philippines and Malaysia.(A map showing the location of the Spratly Islands appears on page 370.)

Geographical and Historical Background—Contending Post-War Claims

The Spratly Islands lie nearly 300 miles (480 km) west of the Philippine island of Palawan, slightly over 300 miles east of Vietnam and about 650 miles (about 1,050 km) south of Hainan, the nearest Chinese territory. All the islands are very small; the largest, Itu Aba (known to the Chinese as Taiping), has an area of only 90 acres (36 hectares). They occupy a position of strategic importance, however, as they command the sea passage from Japan to Singapore. Oil was discovered in 1976 at Reed Bank, midway between Palawan and the Spratlys, and has been developed by the Philippines since 1979.

The two Chinese governments claim that the islands were discovered by Chinese navigators, were used by Chinese fishermen for centuries and came under Chinese administration in the 15th century, and that China's sovereignty over them was never disputed until the 1930s. They also claim that the Spratlys form a continuation of the Paracel Islands, which are claimed by both China and Vietnam.[1] Vietnam maintains that the Spratlys became part of the Empire of Annam in the early 19th century, and that they had not previously been under the administration of any country. The Philippines bases its claim on proximity and administrative control, but has laid no claim to Spratly Island itself, which lies over 200 miles (320 km) south-west of the main group of islands. For its part, Malaysia published an official map in December 1979 showing a southern portion of the Spratly archipelago as part of its continental shelf.

The French government, which then ruled Vietnam, annexed the Spratlys in 1933, despite protests from China and also from Japan, which claimed to have been in continuous commercial occupation of them since 1917. The islands were occupied and annexed by Japan in 1939. Following the defeat of Japan in World War II, a naval expedition sent by the Chinese (Kuomintang) government formally took possession of them in 1946, and left a garrison on Itu Aba. Japan renounced her claim by the peace treaty signed in San Francisco in 1951, but the treaty did not state to whom the islands belonged. The Vietnamese delegate to the San Francisco peace conference declared that Vietnam had recovered her sovereignty over them, but this claim was rejected by both Chinese governments, neither of which was represented at the conference. After the division of Vietnam into two states in 1954, the South Vietnamese government continued to uphold its claim to the islands.

The Chinese Communist government reaffirmed its claim in a statement on its territorial seas issued on Sept. 4, 1958. Pham Van Dong, then the Prime Minister of North Vietnam, informed the Chinese government of North Vietnam's support for this declaration in a note of Sept. 14. of that year.

In May 1956, after a private Philippine expedition had surveyed and occupied a number of the islands, the Philippine government laid claim to them for the first time. This claim was disputed by China, Taiwan and South Vietnam, and a South Vietnamese garrison occupied Spratly Island in August 1956. After the Taiwan garrison on Itu Aba had fired on a Philippine fishing boat, the Philippine government sent a note in July 1971 demanding their withdrawal. At a press conference on July 10, 1971, President Marcos of the Philippines maintained that after Japan renounced its sovereignty over the islands they had become a de

---

[1]For an account of this dispute, see pages 314-15.

facto trusteeship of the allied powers, and that this trusteeship precluded the setting up of garrisons on any of them without the allies' consent. He stated that the Philippines were in effective control of three of the larger islands, however, and according to news agency reports Philippine troops were landed on these islands.

The South Vietnamese government issued a decree in September 1973 incorporating the Spratly Islands into Phuoc Tuy province. As contracts for offshore oil exploration and exploitation off Phuoc Tuy had previously been granted to four foreign companies, the decree made it legally possible for other contracts to be granted in the area off the Spratlys. A Chinese Foreign Ministry statement of Jan. 11, 1974, denounced the decree as "a wanton infringement of China's territorial integrity and sovereignty". After the expulsion of the South Vietnamese garrison from the Paracel Islands by the Chinese a few days later, South Vietnamese troops occupied several of the Spratly Islands.

During the civil war in Vietnam the North Vietnamese government and the Communist South Vietnamese provisional revolutionary government adopted a neutral attitude towards the dispute, in order to avoid friction with their Chinese allies, but in April 1975, shortly before the surrender of Saigon, Vietnamese Communist troops took possession of the islands previously occupied by South Vietnamese garrisons. When the Philippine government announced in May 1976 that a consortium of Swedish and Philippine companies had contracted to explore for oil in the area, the provisional revolutionary government, which had effectively ruled South Vietnam since the fall of Saigon, declared that "the Republic of South Vietnam again reaffirms its sovereignty over the Spratly archipelago and reserves the right to defend this sovereignty". Similar protests were issued by the Chinese and Taiwan governments. The reunification of Vietnam in July 1976 brought the Hanoi government into direct confrontation with China on the issue.

The Philippine government set up a military command on Palawan in March 1976, and by March 1978 had established garrisons on seven of the islands. It reached an agreement with Vietnam in January 1978 to solve the dispute "in a spirit of conciliation and friendship", however, and concluded a similar agreement with China in the following March. At a press conference on Sept. 14, 1979, President Marcos made it clear that the Philippines confined its claim to the seven islands under its occupation. These islands, he declared, were "unoccupied, unowned and unpossessed islands" which had not even been shown on maps before World War II, and the Philippines had therefore occupied them as "new territory or res nullius". In August 1980 the Vietnamese Foreign Ministry protested to the Philippines over what it described as the latter's "occupation" of the Comodor Reef in "the Vietnamese archipelago of Truong Sa".

Progress of the Dispute since 1975

The dispute was a major factor in the deterioration of relations between China and Vietnam after 1975. Whereas before that year North Vietnam had not openly disputed China's claim, an official Vietnamese map issued in 1976 showed the Spratly Islands as Vietnamese territory. A Chinese Foreign Ministry statement of Dec. 29, 1978, declared that the islands had "always been part of China's territory" and that claims to sovereignty over them by any foreign country were all illegal and null and void. The Vietnamese Foreign Ministry rejected these "arrogant allegations" on the following day, but added that it advocated a policy of settling all international disputes by peaceful methods. During talks between China and Vietnam held in Hanoi in April and May 1979 the Chinese delegation demanded that Vietnam should recognize and respect China's sovereignty over the islands, this demand being rejected by Vietnam. The Vietnamese government reaffirmed its claim to sovereignty in a White Book issued on Sept. 28, 1979, to which the Chinese Foreign Ministry replied at length in a document published on Jan. 30, 1980. The Taiwan government also reiterated its claim to sovereignty in a statement of July 25, 1980.

Following the publication (in December 1979) of the official Malaysian map showing a southern part of the Spratly archipelago as falling within Malaysia's continental shelf, the

Chinese Foreign Ministry on May 30, 1980, handed the Malaysian ambassador in Beijing a memorandum taking exception to this claim to "Chinese territories and territorial waters", reiterating that China "has the indisputable sovereignty over the Nansha Islands and their neighbouring sea waters", and asserting that such "unilateral demarcation without negotiating with the Chinese government" constituted "violation of China's sovereignty". Nevertheless, on Sept. 4, 1983, a Malaysian naval unit was reported to have landed on a southern atoll (named as Terumbu Layang Layang) of the Spratly Islands, provoking protests from both China and Vietnam. On Sept. 14, 1983, the Malaysian Foreign Ministry asserted that the atoll (and also the Vietnamese-occupied coral reef of Pulau Kecil Amboyna, some 65 kilometres to the south-east) lay within Malaysia's 200-mile exclusive economic zone and had "always been marked as Malaysian territory on maps of the area". However, on Oct. 3 of that year it was announced that the Foreign Ministers of Malaysia and Vietnam had agreed to conduct "friendly negotiations" on their respective claims. Subsequently, the Chinese southern fleet undertook naval exercises which were reported to have threatened Vietnamese positions on the islands on May 1, 1984, at a time of increased tension on the Sino-Vietnamese border.

Meanwhile, the then Prime Minister of the Philippines, César Virata, made an inspection tour of some of the islands under Philippine occupation in May 1982, and said afterwards that the Philippines would defend these strategically important places, with their rich underground resources, and would not allow encroachment by China or any other country. He also claimed that during a recent visit to the Philippines, Caspar Weinberger (the US Secretary of Defence) had guaranteed that in accordance with the joint defence treaty between the two countries the United States would assist the Philippines if the latter's territories, including the Spratly Islands, were invaded by any other country.

In a statement issued on April 15, 1987, the Chinese Foreign Ministry again took issue with Vietnam over the Spratly Islands, claiming that Vietnamese troops had recently occupied another island (named by the Chinese as Bojiao), demanding their immediate withdrawal from this and nine other islands in the archipelago and reserving "the right to recover these islands at an appropriate time". Noting that Soviet-Vietnamese economic co-operation had identified continental shelf oil exploitation as "a key project", the Chinese statement claimed that "Vietnam's purpose in illegally dispatching troops to Bojiao island is to occupy the continental shelf nearby and pave the way for its future exploitation of oil". The statement also made common cause with Taiwan against Vietnam, recalling that since 1946 Taiping island (Itu Aba) had been "guarded by the KMT" (i.e. by the Kuomintang forces of Taiwan) and asserting that "as long as the KMT and CCP [Chinese Communist Party] armies take unanimous action against their enemies, it is absolutely possible to stop Vietnam's expansionist atrocity and even to punish it severely".

A statement issued by the Vietnamese Foreign Ministry on April 16, 1987, categorically rejected the Chinese assertions and reaffirmed Vietnam's claim to sovereignty over the islands. Moreover, on June 13, 1987, the Vietnamese Foreign Ministry claimed that since early the previous month China had "repeatedly sent many ships to survey and conduct illegal activities in the sea area of the Vietnamese archipelago Truong Sa", including military exercises from May 16 to June 6; these actions were described as a "brazen violation of Vietnam's territorial sovereignty, causing tension in Sino-Vietnamese relations and endangering peace and stability in South-East Asia".

CH

5. THE AMERICAS AND ANTARCTICA

Introduction

Nearly every country in Latin and Central America has or has had claims to territory of a neighbouring state. The majority of these claims date back to the colonial era and in particular to the many uncertainties attached to the boundaries of the independent nations which emerged in the 19th century, for the most part on the basis of old Spanish administrative divisions. Although the successor states subscribed to the principle of *uti possidetis juris* (under which they were presumed to possess sovereignty within the relevant Spanish administrative areas), the eventual development of remoter areas revealed that the old boundaries were usually unclear or, in some cases, non-existent. In recent years, moreover, competing claims to newly-discovered or potential economic resources such as minerals or hydro-electricity have given added dimension to many such territorial uncertainties.

Like other regional groupings, the Organization of American States (OAS) has aspired to provide a forum and mechanism for the peaceful resolution of border and territorial disputes between member states. The organization also specifically excludes from membership applicant states which are involved in a territorial dispute with an existing member. Such constraints have had some effect in preventing armed conflict over territorial claims, of which there have been few instances in recent years between OAS member states. Nevertheless, a number of such disputes remain unresolved and constitute a serious source of actual or potential strain between various states of the region.

Important factors determining whether and when these situations develop into open confrontation include the domestic political circumstances of the government or governments involved and also the particular constellation of political forces in the area concerned. In the latter respect, for example, the current struggle in Central America between revolutionary movements and states on the one hand and traditionalist forces on the other has generally relegated territorial dispute to the background, although in at least one instance it has exacerbated territorial tensions between states in opposing camps.

It should also be noted that most Latin American states have a much longer independent history than many former colonial territories in other parts of the world. This has meant that in many cases territorial disputes originally deriving from colonial uncertainties have had time to acquire strong nationalist overtones, especially where Latin American countries have in the past gone to war over territorial issues. In this sense, some Latin American territorial disputes bear a close resemblance to those familiar from the pre-1945 history of Europe.

Nationalism is also a crucial factor in another category of disputes dealt with in the following section, namely those between Latin American states and external powers which retain dependencies or responsibilities in the region. Some longstanding issues of this type have been settled in recent years (e.g. the Panama-US dispute over the Panama Canal Zone); others remain extremely contentious (e.g.

Guatemala's claim to the whole of the former British colony of Belize); and in April 1982 one such dispute—that between Argentina and the United Kingdom over the Falkland Islands—escalated into open military conflict. Furthermore, conflicting claims in Antarctica—frozen at the moment, appropriately enough, but basically unresolved—also involve the United Kingdom in territorial dispute with both Argentina and Chile.

Argentina-Chile

The small islands of Picton, Lennox and Nueva, situated at the eastern entrance to the Beagle Channel (off Tierra del Fuego and north of Cape Horn), have been at the centre of a territorial dispute between Argentina and Chile dating from the late 19th century. A 1977 ruling by a court of arbitration confirming Chilean sovereignty over the islands was rejected by Argentina, as were papal mediation proposals presented to both governments in December 1980. Following the restoration of civilian rule in Argentina, the Vatican's mediation proposals (again awarding the islands to Chile and establishing respective maritime boundaries) were accepted by both sides under a treaty signed in November 1984 and ratified in March the following year. However, the Argentinian ratification was accomplished against strong opposition from the armed forces and the political right.

History of the Dispute

When Argentina achieved independence from Spain in the early 19th century, it assumed sovereignty over territory east of the Andes which had previously been administered by the Viceroyalty of La Plata. Chile's territory (west of the Andes) was controlled by the Viceroyalty of Peru until Chile declared independence in 1810, and even then the fierce Araucanian Indians prevented new settlement in the far south until well into the 19th century. In the 1840s Chile established settlements on Brunswick peninsula (at Puerto del Hambre and Punta Arenas) against Argentinian protests but no real dispute emerged at the time. In 1855 the Argentine Confederation and Chile signed a treaty of friendship, commerce and navigation which provided that both sides recognized as their boundaries those which had existed on independence in 1810.

The dispute over ownership of the southern territory developed in the 1870s, when guano deposits were found in the region and Chile regarded them as being on its own territory, this leading to clashes and incidents. To clarify the delimitation of their frontier (which stretched for nearly 3,000 miles or some 4,800 km), the two countries signed a treaty on July 23, 1881, in Buenos Aires. In the south, this assigned to Chile all islands west of Tierra del Fuego and south of the Beagle Channel down to Cape Horn, while Chile renounced claims to Patagonia, and the Magellan Strait remained neutral for shipping. Chile has since based its claim to the disputed islands on the 1881 treaty, which also laid down that Staten Island (off the eastern tip of Tierra del Fuego), the small neighbouring islands, and other islands which could be said to be in the Atlantic, east of Tierra del Fuego and off the east coast of Patagonia, would belong to Argentina.

Argentina, however, claimed that a so-called "bi-oceanic" principle was established in an 1893 supplement to the 1881 treaty, which stated (in Article 2) that Argentina could claim no territory (land or waters) on the Pacific side and Chile none on the Atlantic side, the division being a meridian passing through Cape Horn. In contrast, Chile maintained that this principle applied only for the purposes of the formal exchange of territorial rights laid down in the 1881 treaty.

With Chilean authority established de facto over the islands, Argentinian fears grew in the 20th century that access to the Atlantic from its naval base at Ushuaia (on the northern side of the Beagle Channel), as well as to its Antarctic bases, might be threatened if Chile used its position on the islands to obtain direct access to the Atlantic. In recent years, the potential economic resources of the South Atlantic and Antarctic regions (oil, minerals, fish and krill) constituted an important factor in the dispute, which was also complicated by the fact that Argentina and Chile have overlapping claims in the Antarctic.[1]

---

[1] For an account of competing claims in Antarctica, see pages 439-42.

The 1977 Arbitration Award

Under a treaty of May 28, 1902 (renewable every 10 years), the British Crown was made responsible for arbitrating in territorial disputes between Chile and Argentina (in connexion with disputes at that time over more northerly sectors of the border). When called upon in 1971 to intervene in the Beagle Channel affair, Britain in July of that year, after consultations with the two parties, referred the dispute to arbitration by five former judges of the International Court of Justice (ICJ).

In the meantime, Argentina announced in March 1972 that it did not intend to renew the 1902 treaty when it expired in September of that year; accordingly the Foreign Ministers of the two countries signed an agreement in Buenos Aires on April 5, 1972, to the effect that any dispute between them which could not be solved by direct negotiations should be referred directly to the ICJ. It was established that the signature of the new agreement would not affect the arbitration currently in progress and that the 1902 treaty would remain in force with respect to that arbitration until its conclusion.

The five judges (from Britain, France, Nigeria, Sweden and the United States) sat in Geneva under the chairmanship of the British judge, Sir Gerald Fitzmaurice, and studied 28 volumes of evidence and more than 400 maps submitted to them by the two parties. They also visited the area as guests of both Chile and Argentina. Finally, on Feb. 18, 1977, they delivered their findings to the British government, which made them public on May 2, 1977, in the form of a declaration from Queen Elizabeth II ratifying the unanimous decision of the court of arbitration and recognizing the sovereignty of Chile over Picton, Lennox and Nueva and other islands in the area of the Beagle Channel.

The award document included a hydrographic chart on which a red line established the boundary between the territorial and maritime jurisdictions of the two countries in the area, being set approximately at the middle of the Beagle Channel. It established that all the islands, islets, reefs, banks and shoals situated north of the red line belonged to Argentina and those south of the line to Chile, citing as examples the Bacasses islets (Argentina) and Snipe islet (Chile), and that the Beagle Channel's southern arm, the Goree Channel, was not, as claimed by Argentina, part of the main channel. Furthermore, the ICJ's report on the tribunal's findings laid down that Chile's title (in terms of the 1881 treaty) to the southern islands would automatically also "involve jurisdiction over the appurtenant waters and continental shelf and adjacent submarine areas ... by the applicable rules of international law".

The Chilean government immediately announced officially (on May 2, 1977) that it would "closely observe the conditions of the award". However, Argentina stated that it intended to review its own position over the next nine months (i.e. before the award was due to enter into force on Feb. 2, 1978). Before the end of this period of deliberation, Argentina stated formally on Jan. 25, 1978, that it had "decided to declare null and void the decision of Her Britannic Majesty on the Beagle Channel question". Argentina cited among the reasons for its rejection (i) that the court had ruled on other islands whose status was not a matter within its jurisdiction, (ii) that there had been contradictions of reasoning, faulty legal interpretation, and geographical and historical errors, and (iii) that the arguments and proofs advanced by each party had not been fairly evaluated. Accordingly, the government reasserted Argentina's sovereignty "over all islands, maritime areas, continental shelves and seabed which belong to it beyond any doubt since they are located in the Atlantic Ocean, east of the Cape Horn meridian, in line with the spirit and letter of the 1881 and 1893 treaties and the 1902 treaty". It also announced that it would "implement all measures necessary to defend its rights in the area up to Cape Horn", while stressing that it wished to seek a peaceful solution.

Chile stated in response on Jan. 26, 1978, that Argentina's unilateral rejection was contrary to international law and bilateral treaties, that the court's ruling remained mandatory and fully valid, and that it had submitted to Argentina a rejection of the Argentinian declaration containing also a reaffirmation of Chilean rights. Chile in the meantime published a map delineating Chilean jurisdiction over waters in the South Atlantic based on the court's ruling and accompanied by a decree which extended Chilean claims outside the arbitration area and over waters in the south. This provoked a protest from Argentina, which in August 1977 had placed a navigational beacon on the island of Barnevelt (over which Chile had traditionally had sovereignty) in symbolic opposition to Chilean penetration of the Atlantic and the effective extension of its sea limits and its claims over the Antarctic.

Submission of Dispute to Vatican Mediation—Rejection of Papal Proposals by Argentina

The two countries in late 1977 began what appeared to be preparations for a military confrontation in the area (Argentina being in military terms the stronger). Warlike gestures over the next few months included the inspection of troops in border regions, army and naval manoeuvres in sensitive areas, and also the arrest by Argentina of many Chileans in January 1978 in the provinces of Chubut and Mendoza, bordering on Chilean territory. President Videla of Argentina and President Pinochet of Chile met in Mendoza (Argentina) on Jan. 19, 1978, for several hours of talks on "matters of joint concern, especially with regard to the southern area", a communiqué stating that they had "laid the basis for reaching an agreement". A second meeting was postponed after Argentina formally rejected the court ruling, but the two Presidents met again in Puerto Montt (Chile) on Feb. 20 and signed an act as the first step towards creating "a harmonious atmosphere which may lead to a peaceful solution of our controversies and, subsequently, to determining our two nations' respective rights under the legal system".

Under the Act of Puerto Montt, a joint negotiating commission was set up and was allocated 180 days to resolve the dispute. The act listed the main areas of disagreement, proposed a plan of work, and noted the interest of the two sides in the physical integration of

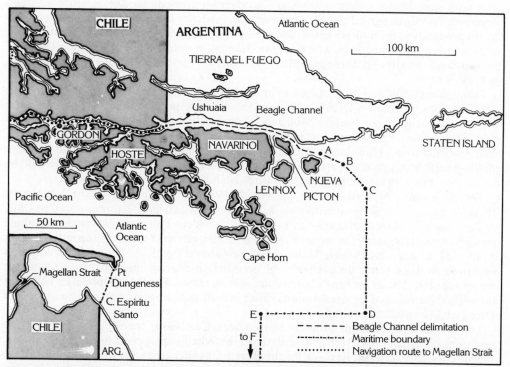

Map 40 **Argentina-Chile: Beagle Channel delimitation confirmed in 1984, also showing maritime boundaries in southern sea and at eastern entrance to Magellan Strait (inset).**

the area and also the mutual desire to defend legal rights in the Antarctic, while ensuring that citizens of both countries, especially those living in the border areas, should regard each other as brothers.

During the 180-day period six rounds of negotiations took place, but preparations for war continued and Argentina enforced certain transit restrictions against Chile. On the expiry of the 180-day period on Nov. 2, 1978, the two countries announced that, while agreement had been reached on the joint economic development of the region and on the co-ordination of their Antarctic policies, they had not resolved the delimitation of their maritime zones. On the same day the Chilean Foreign Minister (Hernán Cubillos Sallato) noted in a communication to the Argentinian government that "positive results" had been achieved regarding some of the points at issue; but he also noted the lack of agreement on "the final demarcation of the Chilean and Argentinian jurisdiction in the southern region" and on navigational rights in the Magellan Strait. He therefore proposed that a "friendly government" should be asked to mediate in the dispute. Argentina agreed on Nov. 8, 1978, that the conflict should be submitted to arbitration, and on Dec. 11 the two countries' Foreign Ministers met in Buenos Aires to designate a mediator.

There was no immediate agreement, however, and further military confrontations were already at this stage taking place in southern waters, while Argentina was carrying out blackout and civil defence exercises in various cities. Argentina protested to the UN Security Council on Dec. 21, 1978, that Chile had illegally deployed troops and artillery on the Beagle Channel islands. Chile stated in response that Argentina had generated tension by committing numerous violations of air, sea and land areas which belonged to Chile and that it was trying to change the status of islands which had "long been under the peaceful and effective sovereignty of Chile".

Tension was defused when both Argentina and Chile accepted (on Dec. 21, 1978) an official offer from the Vatican to mediate in the conflict. Cardinal Antonio Samore, a former papal nuncio to various Latin American countries, accordingly held preliminary contacts with both sides before a declaration was signed in Montevideo on Jan. 8, 1979, whereby Argentina and Chile agreed (i) not to have recourse to force in their mutual relations, (ii) to return gradually to the military situation existing at the beginning of 1977, and (iii) to refrain from adopting any measures which might disturb "harmony in any sector". Cardinal Samore was formally appointed as mediator in April 1979 and negotiations opened in Rome in May 1979.

Throughout 1979 and 1980 Argentinian and Chilean delegations held meetings with Cardinal Samore, and on Dec. 12, 1980, proposals were presented at the Vatican to the Chilean and Argentinian Foreign Ministers, respectively René Rojas Galdames and Brig.-Gen. Carlos Washington Pastor. Details of the proposals were not officially disclosed but were reported to contain plans to make the area surrounding the disputed islands into a jointly-controlled zone of peace from which all military installations and weapons would be withdrawn, but with sovereignty over the three islands being retained by Chile.

The Argentinian government on March 25, 1981, communicated to the Vatican its effective rejection of the papal proposals, acceptance of which had been announced by Chile on Jan. 8 and confirmed officially on Feb. 13 by President Pinochet. A period of strained relations ensued following the arrest of two Argentinian officers by the Chilean authorities in April 1981, as a result of which the border was closed on April 29. Although the situation improved in June (after an exchange of prisoners including the two officers and the reopening of the border on June 12), tension again increased sharply in September 1981 over the alleged intrusion of an Argentinian cruiser into disputed waters south of the islands of Deceit and Hershcel.

The Argentinian Foreign Minister (now Oscar Camillión) travelled to Rome at the beginning of September 1981 to deliver alternative mediation proposals to Cardinal Samore, which reportedly included (i) plans for the Beagle Channel area to become a demilitarized zone under Argentinian jurisdiction (rather than the "sea of peace" said to have been proposed by the Pope) and (ii) plans for the establishment of cross-border development areas in southern Argentina (including the disputed area) and also in the northern border region.

The Argentinian Foreign Ministry on Jan. 21, 1982, announced the unilateral termination of the 1972 agreement committing both sides to seeking ICJ arbitration in their dispute, on the grounds that it had proved ineffective and was no longer serving Argentina's national interests. The treaty had been due to expire in December 1982 but was renewable unless either side gave notice of abrogation in the preceding six months. Argentina reaffirmed its confidence in the papal mediation process as the sole appropriate channel for the achievement of a just and peaceful solution, expressed willingness to draw up a new treaty with Chile for resolving disputes, and also proposed that both sides should suspend arms purchases from abroad. Talks resumed between the Chilean and Argentinian delegations and Cardinal Samore in Rome on Feb. 1, 1982, after a 13-month break.

In a further naval incident on Feb. 19, 1982, an Argentinian naval patrol boat anchored off Deceit to provide support for boats taking part in an international yacht race, but was ordered to leave by a Chilean torpedo boat. Warning shots were said to have been fired by the Chilean boat before naval vessels of both countries converged on the area, while Chile said that two Argentinian combat aircraft had flown low over Chilean ships "in an act of open provocation".

Acceptance of Papal Mediation Proposals by Argentina and Chile—Signature of 1984 Treaty of Peace and Friendship

While talks between Argentinian and Chilean representatives continued under Vatican auspices, the issue was complicated by the Falklands/Malvinas war between Argentina and the United Kingdom in April-June 1982.[2] Officially Chile adopted a neutral stance in the conflict, but an incident on May 26, 1982, when a British military helicopter on an undisclosed mission made a landing near Punta Arenas (in southern Chile) contributed to a widespread belief in Argentina that Chile was actively assisting the British task force.

The fall of the Galtieri government at the end of the Falklands war resulted in Argentina adopting a more conciliatory approach, as evidenced by its signature on Sept. 15, 1982, together with Chile, of an undertaking that the 1972 arbitration agreement would be extended (this being accomplished at the personal request of Pope John Paul II). However, relations between the two countries deteriorated again in mid-1983 over a further naval incident which generated renewed rumours of impending war over the territorial issue. In the incident, an Argentinian naval patrol landed on the Hermanos islet (adjacent to Picton island) on Aug. 18; although it withdrew when Chilean military helicopters flew over the islet, the Chilean Foreign Minister made an official protest to the Argentinian government.

In the political sphere, opposition groups in both countries maintained close observance of governmental actions in the dispute. On Aug. 18, 1982, the Democratic Alliance in Chile and the Multipartidaria in Argentina issued a joint call for "the speedy signing of a peace treaty" and expressed their gratitude to the Pope for his mediating role. In addition, they stated their belief that "on regaining democracy, our peoples will be in a better condition to consolidate peace, to move towards the integration of their economies and to defend their respective rights in the Antarctic, as well as reaching an effective recognition of the rights of Argentina over the Malvinas".

The new civilian government elected in Argentina in December 1983 under Raúl Alfonsín of the Radical Civic Union (which had been a component of the Multipartidaria) placed particular emphasis on the need to resolve the Beagle Channel dispute (not least because it wished to introduce major cuts in military expenditure) and immediately announced its acceptance of the papal proposals as "a basis for negotiations". Subsequent talks between the two sides made speedy progress, with the result that a draft treaty of peace and friendship was signed in the Vatican on Jan. 23, 1984, by the respective Foreign Ministers of Argentina and Chile. Work then began on incorporating a settlement of territorial issues into the draft,

---

[2]For an account of the Argentinian-UK territorial dispute, see pages 387-97.

still under papal mediation. This process culminated in the signature of a definitive treaty on Nov. 29, 1984 (also in the Vatican).

The treaty contained 19 articles and two annexes, the first on conciliation and arbitration procedures (41 articles) and the second on navigation (13 articles); it also incorporated a number of maps as integral parts of the treaty. Its most important provision was to confirm Chilean sovereignty over Picton, Lennox and Nueva islands, while at the same partially recognizing the "bi-oceanic" principle by limiting Chilean rights in Atlantic waters in favour of Argentina.

The award of the three disputed islands to Chile was enshrined in Article 7 of the treaty, which defined the boundary of respective sovereignties over sea, soil and sub-soil in the southern zone sea "starting from the end of the existing delimitation in the Beagle Channel", this area being delimited between six points A to F (see map). The same article contained a declaration that the exclusive economic zones (EEZ) of Argentina and Chile would extend respectively east and west of this delimitation to limits determined under international law. Under Article 8 the parties agreed that in the sea area between Cape Horn and the easternmost point of Staten Island they would each recognize the other as having territorial rights up to three nautical miles (measured from their respective baselines), although vis-à-vis third states each party might claim the maximum extent of territorial waters permitted under international law.

Established jurisdictions were also recognized under Article 10, which delimited the eastern mouth of the Magellan Strait by a line traced from Point Dungeness in the north to boundary marker 1 on Cape Espiritu Santo on the southern side, with Argentina having exclusive rights to the east of this line. Two declarations of wider international interest were incorporated in respect of the Magellan Strait, namely (i) that the delimitation in no way altered the principle laid down in the 1881 Argentina-Chile treaty whereby the Strait was neutralized in perpetuity and unrestricted navigation assured to the flags of all states; and (ii) that Argentina agreed to respect, at all times and under any circumstances, the right of ships of all flags to sail freely and unimpeded through its waters to and from the Strait of Magellan.

Under Article 12 the parties decided to establish a permanent bi-national commission to enhance economic co-operation and physical integration, it being specified that they would seek to develop initiatives concerning a global system of ground communications, reciprocal improvements of ports and customs-free zones, land transport, aviation, electricity connexions and telecommunications, development of natural resources, environmental protection and tourist facilities.

The treaty's second annex on navigation regulated in particular procedures for vessels using the shorter and more protected route from Argentinian Beagle Channel ports to the Magellan Strait via Chilean inland waters (i.e. avoiding the more exposed oceanic routes). This annex granted Argentina navigation facilities solely for passage through a clearly demarcated route and with a Chilean pilot on board. The Argentinian authorities were obliged to notify the relevant Chilean authorities at least 48 hours in advance of transit passages, which were required to proceed in a continuous and uninterrupted manner (subject to *force majeure*). All vessels making the passage would be subject to the rules of international law and were required to refrain from any activity which might disturb the security and communications of Chile. The annex also stated that submarines and other submersible vehicles must proceed on the surface with their lights on, and that all vessels must fly their flag. It was further specified that only three Argentinian warships could be using this route at any one time and that they should not be carrying landing units.

The second annex also laid down rules of navigation and pilotage in the Beagle Channel, stating that the parties would have unrestricted freedom of navigation on both sides of the demarcation line. In that area, merchant ships of third countries would enjoy the right of free passage subject to the rules established in the annex; however, warships of third-party states heading for a port in the area belonging to either party (i.e. Argentina or Chile) could only do so with prior authorization from that party, which was required to notify the other party of the arrival and departure of such warships.

The treaty specified that its general provisions (Articles 1-6) were to be applicable to the Antarctic territories of the parties, thus establishing a potential procedure for the peaceful resolution of their overlapping claims in that area. It was expressly stated, however, that all other provisions of the treaty would in no way affect the parties' sovereignty, rights, legal positions or delimitations in Antarctica or its adjacent areas.

Ratification of 1984 Treaty—Military and Political Opposition in Argentina

As regards the ratification of the 1984 treaty, it was agreed between the parties that the document had to be approved or rejected in its entirety and that no changes or amendments could be proposed. This proved to be a straightforward process in Chile, where the military junta, as the legislative authority, ratified the treaty on April 14, 1985, notwithstanding earlier criticism by one of its members (the Navy Commander, Admiral José Toribio Merino) that its terms were "detrimental to Chile". Among the Chilean opposition, a leader of the Democratic Alliance criticized the regime for not consulting the people on the treaty.

In Argentina the people were consulted, in an advisory referendum held on Nov. 25, 1984, when in a turnout of 73 per cent the initial results showed 77 per cent voting in favour and 21 per cent against (although the result was later modified when about 600,000 negative votes, about 4 per cent of those cast, were reclassified as abstentions). Subsequently, the treaty obtained ratification in the Argentinian Senate on March 15, 1985, by the narrow margin of 23 votes in favour to 22 against, with one abstention. Strong opposition to the treaty was expressed by the (Peronist) Justicialist National Movement and by elements within the armed forces, as well as by some small left-wing groups.

The Argentinian and Chilean Foreign Ministers exchanged instruments of ratification of the treaty on May 2, 1985. The final ceremony was held in the Vatican to mark the apparently successful conclusion of six years of papal mediation in the dispute.

JB/EG

Argentina-Paraguay

A dispute has existed since the 19th century over the exact position of the north-eastern part of the border between Argentina and Paraguay, which is theoretically constituted by the course of the Pilcomayo river (which has its source in Bolivia). The dispute has centred on the fact that the course of the river has from time to time changed by up to $1\frac{1}{2}$ kilometres towards either side.

In 1974 Argentina and Paraguay signed an agreement to conduct studies on how the Pilcomayo's flood waters could best be exploited. Argentina subsequently carried out certain works designed to control the movement of the river and to lessen flood damage, but it claimed that this work had led to no change in the border. Early in November 1980 the Paraguayan government alleged that Argentina was unilaterally using water from a portion of the Pilcomayo river shared with Paraguay. Elpidio Acevedo, Paraguay's Deputy Minister of Foreign Affairs, stated in Buenos Aires that his government had proof that over the past two years Argentina had deliberately been altering the course of the river and that this action was contrary both to the principles of international law and to agreements entered into by the two governments.

This allegation was rejected in a statement issued by the Argentinian Foreign Ministry on Nov. 9, 1980, declaring inter alia: "The portion [of the river] shared with Paraguay is

385

changing course as a result of the very special geological formation of the area and the sediment carried by the river. As a result the waters have drained into Argentinian and Paraguayan territories at three different points .... The situation has been duly studied by the Argentinian and Paraguayan governments and agreement has been reached to implement the appropriate measures to dam up the above-mentioned drainage so that the waters can return to their normal course as soon as possible .... Seeking an effective and equitable use of the waters of the Pilcomayo river, the Argentinian, Bolivian and Paraguayan governments are conducting a joint study with the co-operation of the Organization of American States within a framework of a project for multiple use of the Pilcomayo."

In Argentina fears were expressed that the timing of the revival of the dispute by Paraguay might lead to delays in the construction of a proposed joint Argentinian-Paraguayan hydroelectric project at Yacyretá on the Paraná river, on which Argentina and Paraguay had signed an agreement on Aug. 30, 1979.

Under an agreement signed on Aug. 22, 1985, it was decided to expedite the demarcation of the boundary where it followed the Pilcomayo river. Argentina also proposed the demarcation of clear boundaries in the Paraná and Paraguay rivers and the determination of sovereignty over islands which would be permanently above water because of the effect on the river level of the hydroelectric projects.

HWD

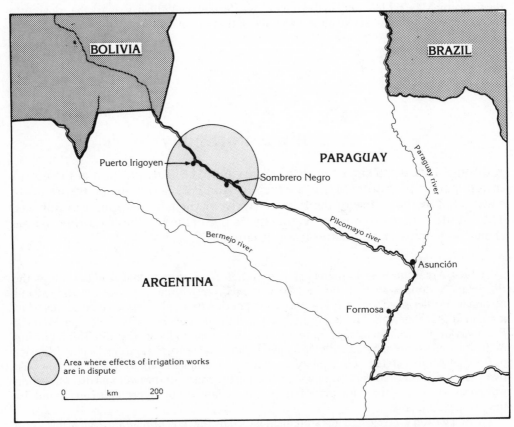

Map 41   The Pilcomayo waters dispute between Argentina and Paraguay.

Argentina-United Kingdom (Falklands, South Georgia and South Sandwich Islands)

British sovereignty over the Falkland Islands in the South Atlantic has been consistently disputed by Argentina ever since they became a British possession in 1833. Argentina's claim to the islands (which it calls Las Malvinas) is based on their proximity to its coast, Argentinian possession of them for several years in the early 19th century and what it regards as the colonial nature of their acquisition and continued possession by Britain. The British claim is based on early settlement, reinforced by formal claims in the name of the Crown and completed by "open, continuous, effective and peaceful possession, occupation and administration of the islands since 1833". Britain also lays stress on the fact that the exercise of UK sovereignty has been in accordance with the express wish of the islanders, in which connexion UK governments have cited the fundamental principles of the self-determination of peoples enshrined in the UN Charter and other international covenants.

After several years of inconclusive negotiations between the two governments on the sovereignty and other issues, the military regime then in power in Argentina launched a surprise invasion of the Falklands on April 2, 1982, its forces overwhelming a small garrison of Royal Marines and installing an Argentinian military governor. Britain responded by dispatching a powerful naval task force to the South Atlantic, where a fierce conflict ensued, resulting in the recapture of the islands by British troops by mid-June 1982 and the restoration of British

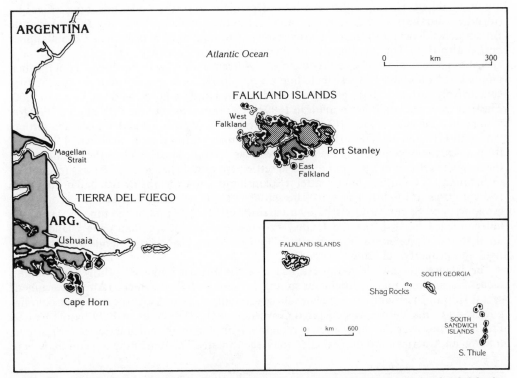

Map 42   The disputed Falkland Islands (Malvinas), South Georgia and the South Sandwich Islands.

administration. Notwithstanding its military defeat (which led directly to the restoration of civilian government in Buenos Aires), Argentina has continued to assert its claim to sovereignty over the Falklands/Malvinas. However, the British government, while seeking a normalization of relations with Argentina, has refused to enter into negotiations involving the question of sovereignty and has maintained a substantial British military presence in and around the Falkland Islands.

Under new constitutional arrangements introduced in 1985, South Georgia and the South Sandwich Islands ceased to be direct dependencies of the Falkland Islands and became British dependencies in their own right. Argentina also claims these South Atlantic islands within the framework of its claims to the Falklands themselves and to certain islands of the British Antarctic Territory.[1] In the 1982 conflict only South Georgia was occupied by Argentinian forces (and subsequently repossessed by the British).

Geographical, Political and Historical Background

The Falklands/Malvinas lie some 300 miles (480 km) to the east of Argentina, almost opposite the eastern entrance to the Magellan Strait. They have a land surface area of 4,618 square miles (12,000 sq km) and a civilian population, largely of British descent, of about 2,000 (which was declining before 1982 but was showing a slight increase by 1986). Executive power is vested in a Crown-appointed Governor acting with an Executive Council, the latter elected from among its members by a Legislative Council itself elected by universal adult suffrage.

South Georgia, an island of about 1,450 square miles (3,750 sq km), is situated some 800 miles (1,285 km) east-south-east of the Falklands and houses a British scientific base. The South Sandwich Islands lie about 470 miles (750 km) to the south-east of South Georgia and are uninhabited. Having until 1985 been dependencies of the Falklands, South Georgia (together with the nearby Shag Rocks) and the South Sandwich Islands now form a separate British dependency, although the Governor of the Falklands acts as their Commissioner (and is also High Commissioner of the British Antarctic Territory).

Although navigators of several countries have been credited with the discovery of the then uninhabited Falkland Islands (including a Captain Davis of the *Desire* in 1592), the first conclusively authenticated sighting was made by the Dutch sailor Sebald van Weert in 1600. The first recorded landing was made in 1690 by Captain Strong of the English ship *Welfare*, who named the islands after the then Navy Treasurer, Viscount Falkland. French settlers landed in 1764 and named the islands "Les Malouines" (after their home town of St Malo), from which the Argentinian name Las Malvinas is derived. The French settlers relinquished their rights to Spain in 1766, but a British settlement established in 1765-66 was recognized by Spain in 1771—although only after a Spanish move to expel the British had brought the two countries to the brink of war. The settlement was withdrawn in 1774 on grounds of economy, and Spain withdrew its own garrison in 1811, so that at the time of Argentine independence in 1816 (as the United Provinces of the River Plate) the islands were uninhabited. However, the British left a plaque declaring that the Falklands were the "sole right and property" of King George III.

The islands meanwhile became a base for the British and US sealing and whaling industries, and temporary settlements sprang up there. In 1820 the Buenos Aires government sent a ship to the islands to proclaim its sovereignty as successor to the former colonial power, and Luis Vernet was declared Governor of the Falklands in 1829 by the United Provinces; however, in 1831, after complaints from sealers about interference with their trading, an American warship expelled the Argentinians. The remaining Argentinians were

---

[1]For conflicting Argentinian, Chilean and UK territorial claims in Antarctica, see pages 439-42.

expelled by a British warship in 1832, and British sovereignty was established early the following year.

The first recorded landing on South Georgia was made by Captain James Cook in 1775 (although it had been sighted at least twice during the previous 100 years), and the South Sandwich Islands were discovered during the same voyage. Argentina first made formal claim to South Georgia in 1927 and to the South Sandwich Islands in 1948.

Inconclusive Negotiations between Argentina and Britain, 1966-80

Negotiations between Britain and Argentina began in 1966 after the UN General Assembly had in December 1965 approved a resolution noting the existence of a dispute over the Falklands and inviting the two countries to enter into negotiations "with a view to finding a peaceful solution to the problem", bearing in mind the interests of the islanders.

After a period in which negotiations were mainly concerned with technicalities such as communications between the islands and the Argentinian mainland, the Argentinian government in 1973 (on the return to power of Gen. Juan Perón) again brought up the question of sovereignty over the Falkland Islands. In a note to the UN Secretary-General (Dr Kurt Waldheim) on Nov. 5, 1973, Argentina called for an end to the "colonial situation", accused Britain of "paralysing" talks on sovereignty, and said that Britain's "anxiety to respect the right of self-determination of the inhabitants of the islands would be more praiseworthy and legitimate" if the population had been consulted when the islands were annexed in the 19th century. The UN General Assembly subsequently in December 1973 adopted a resolution (3160/XXVIII) calling on both countries to "arrive at a peaceful solution of the conflict of sovereignty between them" in order to "put an end to the colonial situation".

The following year, amid reports that the British government was considering granting oil exploration rights off the Falkland Islands to a Canadian company, there were calls from certain political and press sectors in Argentina for an invasion of the islands and for the severance of trade and communications links. In January 1975 Argentina extended its control over air travel to the Falkland Islands (which was operated solely by the Argentinian Air Force from Argentina) by making it obligatory for all travellers to obtain clearance from the Argentinian Foreign Ministry, in contravention of a July 1971 communications agreement between Britain and Argentina which stated that only Argentinians travelling to the Falklands needed a special tourist card.

In October 1975 the Argentinian ambassador was recalled from London after Argentina objected to the dispatch of a British mission to the islands, headed by Lord Shackleton, to carry out an "economic and fiscal" survery at the request of the Falkland Islands Executive Council and to assess prospects and make recommendations on developments in "oil, minerals, fisheries and alginates" as well as to advise on capital expenditure needs over the next five years. Argentina warned that both sides had agreed in 1964 to "abstain from unilateral innovations in fundamental aspects of the question" and that the exploitation of natural resources would not be possible, since they belonged to Argentina.

When the Shackleton mission nevertheless arrived in Port Stanley (the Falklands capital) aboard the Royal Navy ice patrol ship *Endurance* in January 1976, travelling from an undisclosed Latin American country because the Argentinian government had refused to let the team members use the normal air route via Buenos Aires, the Argentinian Foreign Ministry expressed the opinion that the UK ambassador to Buenos Aires should be withdrawn on the basis of (i) the presence of the mission in the Falklands, (ii) the refusal of the British government to resume negotiations on the sovereignty issue, and (iii) a note from the UK Foreign and Commonwealth Secretary on Jan. 12, 1976, to the effect that the sovereignty dispute was "sterile" and calling for talks on economic co-operation. The ambassador accordingly left for London on Jan. 19, 1976.

During February 1976 another British ship engaged in scientific research in the South Atlantic (the *Shackleton*) was intercepted by an Argentinian destroyer which fired shots across its bows and tried to effect an arrest; however, the *Shackleton* (on the orders of the Falklands Governor) ignored the attempt and sailed directly to Port Stanley, with the destroyer following closely. Argentina claimed in a letter to the UN Security Council on Feb. 11, 1976, that the ship was searching for oil when challenged, while Britain protested to the Security Council at the "provocative" action of Argentina and urged the latter to stop harassing peaceful vessels in contravention of international law. The *Shackleton* left Port Stanley to continue its research on Feb. 17 after talks had been held in New York between British and Argentinian government representatives on ways of resuming negotiations and normalizing relations.

In accordance with UN Resolution 31/49 of Dec. 1, 1976—which urged Britain and Argentina to "expedite the negotiations concerning the dispute over sovereignty" in line with Resolutions 2065/XX and 3160/XXVIII and called on both parties to refrain from taking decisions which implied the introduction of unilateral modifications in the situation—a UK Foreign Office Minister of State in the then Labour government, Edward Rowlands, visited Buenos Aires in February 1977 with a view to seeking formal talks. Prior to the actual visit, Rowlands went to the Falklands "to hear from the islanders at first hand how they view their future". On his way back to Buenos Aires Rowlands said in a statement that his delegation would attempt to work out terms of reference with Argentina for subsequent formal negotiations on political relations and economic co-operation, and that such talks would have to take into account "the broad issues affecting the future of the islands, including sovereignty"; he maintained that Britain's intention to seek a basis for negotiation had the approval of the Falkland Islands Councils. At the same time, the Argentinian Foreign Ministry issued a statement to the effect that the intention of Argentina in the forthcoming talks remained the recovery of the Falklands, and that discussions about the economy remained subordinate to this.

The Rowlands talks took place on Feb. 22-23, 1977, a joint communiqué stating afterwards that they had been held "in a constructive spirit" and that the two delegations now needed to consult with their governments over certain points. It described the talks as considering "all aspects of the future of the Falkland Islands, the South Georgias and the South Sandwich Islands and Anglo-Argentinian co-operation in the south-west Atlantic area, and to explore the possibility of establishing terms of reference for subsequent negotiations".

Further rounds of talks were held in 1977 in Rome and New York, and after the latter round the two sides agreed to set up two working groups "on political relations, including sovereignty, and on economic co-operation". A third round was held in Lima (Peru) in February 1978.

Full diplomatic relations were resumed between Argentina and Britain (now under a Conservative government) in late 1979. The new Minister of State at the Foreign and Commonwealth Office, Nicholas Ridley, had talks in New York in April 1980 with Air-Commodore Carlos Cavandoli (the Argentinian Under-Secretary of State for Foreign Relations) and also with a representative of the Falklands Legislative Council, Adrian Monk. Later in that year (Nov. 22-29) Ridley visited the Falklands for talks with the islanders on how best to approach the dispute with Argentina over status; en route he also paid a courtesy call on Air-Commodore Cavandoli in Buenos Aires. While the visit was in progress the Falkland Islands Office in London asserted publicly that one of several options being put to the islanders by the British minister was that of a transfer of sovereignty to Argentina coupled with a lease-back of the islands (this, according to the Office, being the option most favoured by Whitehall). Lord Carrington, the UK Foreign and Commonwealth Secretary, stressed on Nov. 26, however, that there was no question of Britain's acting against the wishes of the islanders.

Escalation of Dispute into Military Conflict—Argentinian Occupation and British Repossession of the Islands

In January 1981 the Falkland Islands Legislative Council passed a resolution stating that, although it was not pleased with any of the ideas presented by Nicholas Ridley regarding the sovereignty issue, it agreed that the British government should continue talks with Argentina and that the Legislative Council should be represented; furthermore, it urged that the British delegation should try to reach an understanding to freeze the dispute for an indefinite period. An Argentinian Foreign Ministry spokesman replied that Argentina would negotiate only with Britain on the islands and that the resolution (a copy of which had been presented by the British ambassador) was therefore of no concern to it.

Representatives of the islands' Legislative Council took part in the next three rounds of talks, which were held in New York in April 1980, February 1981 and February 1982. A joint communiqué issued after the February 1982 talks—the first to take place under the new Argentinian military government of Gen. Leopoldo Galtieri, which had taken office on Dec. 22, 1981—said that they had been held in a "cordial and positive spirit" and that the two sides had reaffirmed their resolve to find a solution to the dispute. Nevertheless, the Argentinian Foreign Ministry issued a statement only two days later (on March 1) warning that, unless a speedy negotiated settlement was reached, Argentina would "put an end" to negotiations, "seek other means" of resolving the dispute, and feel free to choose "the procedure which best corresponds to its interests".

The conflict between Britain and Argentina escalated sharply soon afterwards, following the illegal landing on South Georgia on March 19, 1982, of a party of about 60 Argentinian scrap merchants with an apparently valid commercial contract to dismantle disused whaling installations. The British Antarctic Survey team on South Georgia ordered them to leave and to seek permission from the British authorities if they wished to continue their work, following which most of the party subsequently departed on March 21, lowering the Argentinian flag which they had raised. However, the Galtieri government, which claimed to have no prior knowledge of the landing, refused a British request that it should make arrangements for the removal of the remaining dozen men, to whom supplies were delivered by an Argentinian naval vessel on March 25. The British Ministry of Defence confirmed on March 24 that the *Endurance* was in the area and was ready to give assistance if required; the presence of Argentinian warships and naval vessels was reported in the area soon afterwards.

Despite a UN Security Council meeting on April 1, 1982, and last-minute diplomatic efforts, Argentinian troops invaded the Falklands on April 2, on which day the Argentinian junta announced the "recovery of the Malvinas, the Georgias and the South Sandwich Islands for the nation". The small detachments of Royal Marines on the Falklands and South Georgia were overwhelmed, and the British Governor was deported and replaced by an Argentinian military governor, Maj.-Gen. Mario Benjamin Menéndez. In an address to the nation on April 2, President Galtieri said that the decision to recover the islands "was prompted by the need to put an end to the interminable succession of evasive and dilatory tactics used by Britain to perpetuate its dominion over the islands and their zone of influence". There were no British casualties in this phase of the conflict.

The UN Security Council on April 3, 1982, adopted by 10 votes to one (Panama) with four abstentions (China, Poland, Spain and the Soviet Union) a resolution (502) demanding the immediate cessation of hostilities and an immediate withdrawal of all Argentinian forces from the Falklands, and calling on the Argentinian and British governments to seek a diplomatic solution and to respect fully the UN Charter.

The British government reacted to the Argentinian invasion by dispatching a large naval task force to the South Atlantic, the main body of which had arrived in Falklands waters by late April 1982. During the approximately three weeks taken by the British warships to complete the 8,000-mile journey to the South Atlantic, intensive diplomatic exchanges took place, with the US government acting as principal intermediary, in an effort to resolve the dispute by negotiation. However, the Argentinian government refused to yield on its fundamental claim to sovereignty over the islands (which it garrisoned with some 12,000 troops), while Britain insisted on an Argentinian military withdrawal as the basic requirement for a peaceful resolution of the immediate crisis. Unsuccessful mediation attempts were also made by the Peruvian government and by the UN Secretary-General.

As the task force sailed for the South Atlantic, the UK Defence Secretary (John Nott) announced in the House of Commons on April 7, 1982, that a 200-nautical-mile "maritime exclusion zone" (MEZ) would be established around the Falkland Islands as from April 12 and that any Argentinian warships or naval auxiliaries found within the zone would be treated as hostile and would therefore be liable to be attacked. On April 28 the UK Defence Ministry announced that as from April 30 the MEZ would become a "total exclusion zone" (TEZ) applicable to both naval and merchant vessels "operating in support of the illegal occupation of the Falkland Islands" and also to both military and civil aircraft. On May 7 the TEZ was extended by Britain up to a line 12 nautical miles from the Argentinian coast and a warning was issued that ships or aircraft transgressing this line would be liable to attack.

International reactions to the escalating conflict included the adoption by a special Foreign Ministers' meeting of the Organization of American States (OAS) in Washington on April 26-28, 1982, of a resolution recognizing Argentinian sovereignty over the Falklands/Malvinas and calling on Britain to cease hostilities in the South Atlantic; the voting was 17 to none with four abstentions (Chile, Colombia, Trinidad and Tobago, and the United States). As regards the European Community member states, they showed solidarity with Britain by unanimously imposing a one-month ban on Argentinian imports from April 16 (although the following month Ireland and Italy refused to continue the sanctions, which were eventually lifted on June 22, 1982).

In the South Atlantic theatre, British forces recaptured South Georgia on April 25, 1982, causing the Argentinian Foreign Minister to declare that his country was now "technically at war" with Britain (although no such formal declaration was ever made by either side). In the first, and most controversial, naval engagement of the conflict, the Argentinian battle-cruiser *General Belgrano* was torpedoed and sunk by a British submarine on May 2 some 30 miles outside the TEZ, it being claimed by Britain that the warship and her escorts "posed a major threat to our ships". Two days later, on May 4, the destroyer HMS *Sheffield* became the first Royal Navy loss in the conflict when it was struck by an Exocet missile launched from an Argentinian warplane. Other British warships and auxiliaries were sunk or disabled by the Argentinian Air Force during and after a landing of British troops in force at Port San Carlos on East Falkland on May 21. Nevertheless, in subsequent heavy land fighting, during which the British established further bridgeheads, the Argentinian forces were pushed back to Port Stanley (the capital of the Falklands), where an unconditional Argentinian surrender was secured with effect from midnight on June 14-15, 1982.

The UK government subsequently announced, on June 20, 1982, the surrender the previous day of a small group of Argentinians stationed on Southern Thule (in the South Sandwich Islands), where Argentina had established a base in December 1976 without British authorization. Whereas Argentina had described the base as a scientific station, the Argentinians who surrendered were all found to be military personnel.

During the later stages of the fighting, Britain and the United States on June 4, 1982, had vetoed a UN Security Council resolution calling on both sides to institute a ceasefire, it being pointed out by the UK government that a ceasefire would have left Argentina in military possession of key areas of the Falklands, including the capital. Nine Security Council members voted in favour of the resolution and four abstained (France, Guyana, Jordan and Togo). It later transpired that the US vote against the resolution should have been an abstention but that instructions to that effect had been received too late.

British casualties in the Falklands conflict included 254 task force personnel (236 service and 18 civilian) and three islanders killed. Argentinian fatalities were unofficially estimated to have been about three times higher (including about 370 lost in the *General Belgrano* sinking).

Aftermath of 1982 Hostilities—Argentina's Reaffirmation of Right to Sovereignty

In Argentina the Falklands defeat resulted in the fall of the Galtieri government on June 17, 1982, and the assumption of the presidency by Gen. Reynaldo Bignone. The new government indicated its acceptance that military hostilities had ended de facto (thus enabling Britain to repatriate approaching 12,000 Argentinian prisoners of war); however, then and subsequently Argentina refused to issue an unconditional declaration of cessation of hostilities. In a note to the UN Security Council on June 18, Argentina asserted that "the total cessation of hostilities will only be achieved when the United Kingdom agrees to lift its air and sea blockade and the economic sanctions, and when it withdraws the military occupation forces from the islands"; the note added that "only negotiations within the United Nations framework can lead to a definitive solution to the conflict, eliminating a situation of illegitimate colonial domination, sustained by force, which in itself constitutes a permanent threat to peace".

Britain lifted the TEZ and the coastal blockade of Argentina on July 22, 1982, but requested Argentina to ensure that its warships and military aircraft did not enter a 150-mile (240-km) protection zone around the Falklands; moreover, Argentinian civil aircraft and shipping were asked not to enter the zone without prior agreement with Britain and to "stay clear of other British dependencies in the South Atlantic". Most of the ships and troops making up the British task force were withdrawn from the South Atlantic during June-August 1982, but a garrison of some 4,000 soldiers was retained on the Falklands and a significant naval presence was maintained in Falklands waters. It was confirmed in June 1983 that a new strategic airfield would be constructed on the Falklands to enable the British garrison to be reinforced by air in an emergency (the airfield, at Mount Pleasant, being subsequently opened in May 1985).

In December 1982 the UK government announced a £31,000,000 programme for the economic development of the islands over a six-year period, including the creation of a Falkland Development Corporation. On March 28, 1983, a British Nationality (Falkland Islands) Amendment Bill was enacted, conferring British nationality on about 400 islanders who had not acquired it under the 1981 British Nationality Act.

The UK Prime Minister, Margaret Thatcher, paid a five-day visit to the Falklands on Jan. 8-12, 1983, this being described by the Argentinian government as "an act of provocation and arrogance" and as "yet another flagrant violation of Argentina's sovereign rights". During a debate in the House of Commons on Jan. 25-26, 1983, on the Franks Report (on how ministerial responsibilities had been discharged in the period before the Argentinian invasion), Mrs Thatcher said that if the Falklands were at present a fortress this was "purely and simply a state of affairs caused by the Argentinian aggression of April 2 and by our determination that that aggression will not be repeated". She continued: "Our policy is to create conditions in which the islanders can live happy, prosperous and free lives under a government of their choosing .... The Argentinian government must commit themselves formally and unequivocally to a cessation of hostilities .... If and when Argentina makes a clear declaration that hostilities are at an end, there will have to be a period in which I hope that they will be prepared to work towards full normalization of our bilateral relations .... At this stage ... it is obvious that the Argentines see negotiations solely as a means of achieving the direct transfer of sovereignty over the Falklands Islands and the dependencies to Argentina. That is totally unacceptable to us and the islanders, and no amount of pressure will induce me to enter negotiations on that basis."

Consideration of Falklands/Malvinas Question by UN General Assembly, 1982-86

The principal international forum in which Argentina sought to exert pressure on the UK government to resume negotiations on the sovereignty question was the UN General Assembly, to which Argentina formally resubmitted the Falklands/Malvinas question on Aug. 16, 1982. The subsequent 37th Assembly session on Nov. 4, 1982, adopted by 90 votes (including the United States) to 12 (Britain, 10 Commonwealth states and Oman) with 53 abstentions a resolution, tabled by Argentina and other Latin American countries, requesting Britain and Argentina to resume negotiations in order to find as soon as possible a peaceful solution to the sovereignty dispute and also asking the UN Secretary-General to undertake a renewed mission of good offices to assist the parties. The UK representative stated that the resolution was unacceptable because it placed no obligation on Argentina to affirm that the hostilities which it had initiated were finished or to renounce the use or threat of force in the future; nor did it acknowledge that the Falkland islanders were the most important party to the dispute. In response, the Argentinian Foreign Minister asserted that the dispute was about territorial integrity rather than self-determination, in that the islanders did not have legitimate ties with the territory and therefore did not possess the right to self-determination; maintaining that Britain and Argentina were the sole parties to the dispute, he added that Argentina would never cede its right to sovereignty over the islands.

At the 38th General Assembly session a similar resolution was adopted on Nov. 16, 1983, by 87 votes to nine (Britain, seven Commonwealth states and Oman) with 54 abstentions. Virtually the same formula was also incorporated into the Falklands/Malvinas resolution adopted at the 39th session on Nov. 1, 1984, by 89 votes to nine with 54 abstentions. However, at the 40th Assembly session a two-day debate on the issue concluded with the adoption on Nov. 27, 1985, of a resolution (drafted by a group of non-aligned countries and supported by Argentina) requesting Argentina and the United Kingdom "to initiate negotiations with a view to finding the means to resolve peacefully and definitively the problem pending between both countries, including all aspects of the future of the Falklands (Malvinas)". In that this resolution did not mention the word sovereignty, it secured adoption by 107 votes to four (Britain, Belize, Oman and the Solomon Islands) with 41 abstentions; countries which had previously abstained but which now voted in favour included three European Community members (France, Greece and Italy) and several Commonwealth states (including Australia and Canada).

At the 41st Assembly session, an identical resolution was adopted on Nov. 25, 1986, by 116 votes to four (Britain, Belize, Oman and Sri Lanka) with 34 abstentions. Those in favour in 1986 again included Australia, Canada, the United States, France, Greece, Italy and Spain (now a member of the European Community); the Netherlands (previously an abstainer) became the fifth European Community member to vote in favour.

Developments following Return to Civilian Rule in Argentina

Prospects of direct negotiations appeared to increase with the inauguration on Dec. 10, 1983, of a civilian Argentinian government under President Raúl Alfonsín, following which the UK government indicated its willingness to enter into talks without a formal declaration of cessation of hostilities having been made by Argentina. However, Britain's continued refusal to discuss the question of sovereignty meant that Argentina's essential condition for entering into direct negotiations was not met.

In his first major policy statement on the Falklands/Malvinas, President Alfonsín on Jan. 3, 1984, described the British military presence on the islands as "illegal and forcible" and stressed what he called the "permanent will of the Argentinian people to reverse that situation and to obtain restitution of the Malvinas, South Georgia and the South Sandwich Islands". He called on the UK government to negotiate the peaceful transfer of the islands to Argentinian sovereignty, offering in return a "special statute" in which Argentina would guarantee the "interests" of the islanders.

The UK government replied on Jan. 4, 1984, that it was ready for immediate negotiations on the restoration of normal relations, particularly economic and commercial links, but that there could be no discussions on sovereignty.

The UK Foreign and Commonwealth Office disclosed on Feb. 2, 1984, that secret UK-Argentinian contacts had been in progress since December 1983 through the Swiss embassy representing British interests in Buenos Aires and the Brazilian embassy representing Argentinian interests in London. It further disclosed on Feb. 17, 1984, that Argentina had replied officially to a UK proposal (advanced on Jan. 26) for the normalization of diplomatic, economic and cultural relations, the return of the bodies of Argentinian soldiers buried on the Falklands and the restoration of air links between the islands and Argentina and between Argentina and the United Kingdom.

The Argentinian reply was made in the form of counter-proposals, namely (i) that Argentina would not end hostilities before negotiations started; (ii) that Argentina would not negotiate on the return of the bodies of war dead, although a humanitarian gesture would be accepted; (iii) that the British garrison on the islands should be replaced by a UN peace-keeping force; (iv) that the protection zone should be lifted before a declaration of an end to hostilities; and (v) that talks should be held without preconditions set by either side and on the basis of an open agenda. The Argentinian Foreign Minister said that as "the maximum concession possible" the sovereignty issue could be left until the second round of talks, although the question of the British military presence would be raised at the first round.

During a visit to Spain in mid-June 1984, President Alfonsín was party to a joint "Declaration of Madrid" issued on June 13 in which it was asserted that Spain and Argentina were both "victims of an anachronistic colonial situation" and accordingly supported their respective claims to Gibraltar and the Malvinas "to restore the integrity of their national territories through peaceful means in conformity with the relevant resolutions of the United Nations".[1]

A meeting between senior Argentinian and British diplomats, arranged by the Swiss Foreign Ministry was held in Berne (Switzerland) on July 18, 1984. The two sides had originally agreed to hold a two-day meeting on the understanding that the UK side would refuse to discuss the sovereignty issue but that Argentina would be free to raise any issue it chose. This formula produced the expected result. The talks ended abruptly after the first day when the Argentinian delegation raised the sovereignty issue.

In a report published on Dec. 12, 1984, the all-party select committee on foreign affairs of the UK House of Commons found, on the basis of an examination of the British and Argentinian claims to the Falklands, that "the historical and legal evidence demonstrates such areas of uncertainty that we are unable to reach a categorical conclusion on the legal validity of the historical claims of either country". Describing the principle of self-determination as a "political axiom" rather than a legal right (but conceding that the Argentinian invasion had "greatly strengthened that axiom" in the case of the Falkland islanders), the report suggested that in the long run "a solution acceptable to the Falklands' immediate neighbours is essential to the islanders themselves", since "their prosperity must depend on having decent relations with Argentina". On the issue of sovereignty, the report said that the UK-Argentinian negotiations between 1967 and 1982 belied the suggestion that successive governments had no doubts about British sovereignty over the Falklands and pointed out that even after the 1982 invasion the UK government had been prepared to admit the possibility of talks on sovereignty but had later changed its position to insist on non-negotiable sovereignty. The report also noted that it was currently costing "about one thousand times as much to defend each inhabitant of the Falklands as it costs to defend each inhabitant of the United Kingdom". In a response to the report, the UK government regretted the committee's "reluctance to reach a categorical conclusion of the legal validity" of the British title to the islands, adding that the fact that UK governments had been prepared to seek a negotiated solution "should not be taken as a reflection of any doubts about the British title".

The introduction in 1985 of a new Falkland Islands constitution, containing in its preamble an explicit reference to the islanders' right to self-determination, drew strong criticism from Argentina on the grounds that it implied disregard for UN resolutions calling on both sides to refrain from unilateral actions which modified the existing situation. A

---

[1] For an account of the Spanish-UK dispute over Gibraltar, see pages 90-101.

statement by the Argentinian Foreign Ministry on Feb. 16, 1985, added that the new constitution blocked efforts to find a peaceful solution to the sovereignty dispute by enshrining the right to self-determination, thus in effect giving the islanders the power to veto over parliamentary decisions and enabling them to extend the "colonial status" of the islands indefinitely.

Under the new constitution the title of Governor of the Falklands was restored in place of that of High Commissioner (introduced after the 1982 conflict), it being stated by the UK Foreign and Commonwealth Office that the islanders had strongly requested this change; at the same time, the position of Military Commissioner (also created in 1982) was abolished, the head of UK forces on the islands becoming Commander, British Forces, Falkland Islands, and ceasing to have joint executive authority with the Governor. The new arrangements also provided for the establishment of South Georgia and the South Sandwich Islands (hitherto dependencies of the Falklands) as separate dependencies of the United Kingdom, although in response to concern among the islanders over the potential significance of this separation the British government agreed that for the present the Governor of the Falklands would also be Commissioner of South Georgia and the South Sandwich Islands and that the Falkland islanders would have consultative rights as regards decisions concerning these islands.

Partial Normalization of UK-Argentinian Trade Relations—Continuing Impasse on Sovereignty Question—Establishment of Fisheries Protection Zone

With effect from midnight on July 8-9, 1985, the UK government lifted the ban on Argentinian imports imposed in the wake of the April 1982 invasion of the Falklands, asserting at the same time its desire for a restoration of normal commercial and economic relations between the two countries. The Argentinian Foreign Minister responded that the British decision had no real bearing on the question of a normalization of relations and (in a statement on July 10, 1985) offered to declare a formal end to hostilities if Britain agreed to resume bilateral talks, including the sovereignty issue, within 60 days. This offer was, however, rejected by the UK Foreign Secretary, who said on July 12 that Argentina's continued insistence on discussing sovereignty was "neither realistic nor constructive".

Although no official announcement was made by Argentina on the lifting of its reciprocal ban on British imports, UK-Argentinian trade relations were subsequently reported to have become "near normal" by April 1986. In an earlier development, the Argentinian government had stated on Jan. 2, 1985, that it would refuse to recognize any oil exploration permits granted by Britain in the Falklands area; this announcement followed confirmation being given that an oil exploration contract had been signed between the Falklands administration and a US company in July 1984.

During 1985-86 various contacts took place between British and Argentinian political representatives at non-governmental level, notably within the framework of the Inter-Parliamentary Union. Moreover, two British opposition leaders, Neil Kinnock of the Labour Party and David Steel of the Liberal Party, had talks with President Alfonsín in Buenos Aires in September and October 1985 respectively during which both agreed on the need for direct UK-Argentinian negotiations from which the question of the sovereignty of the Falklands should not be excluded. At the government level, however, the two sides remained at an impasse, as was demonstrated by the failure of a mediation attempt in April-May 1986 by the UN Secretary-General, who was told by President Alfonsín that the sovereignty question must be included on the agenda of any negotiations and by Mrs Thatcher that sovereignty was not negotiable.

A further divide in UK-Argentinian relations opened on Oct. 29, 1986, when the British Foreign Secretary announced the creation as from Feb. 1, 1987, of a new 150-mile fisheries protection zone around the Falkland Islands (i.e. co-terminous with the existing naval protection zone). Described as an "interim conservation and management zone", the new arrangement was intended to curtail what the British and Falklands governments regarded as the development of serious over-fishing in the area, notably by factory ships from Japan, Spain, the Soviet Union and other Soviet-bloc countries. As from Feb. 1, 1987, all foreign ships wishing to fish in the zone would require licences, the aim being to reduce the number of such vessels to about 250 as compared with over 600 in the 1986 season.

The UK Foreign Secretary stated that the new zone would be policed by two Royal Navy fisheries protection vessels based at the Falklands and made it clear that other forces remained available "to deter Argentine aggression and maintain the integrity of the protection zone". He also gave notice of "the entitlement of the Falklands, under international law, to a fisheries limit of 200 miles, subject to delimitation with Argentina"—with whose own 200-mile limit a 200-mile Falklands limit would overlap—and asserted "our rights to jurisdiction over the continental shelf up to the limits prescribed by the rules of international law".

President Alfonsín responded by convening an emergency meeting of ministers and military leaders on Oct. 29, 1986, following which all military leave was cancelled. A government statement condemned the UK move as "juridically and politically unacceptable since it is asserted over maritime areas in respect of which the Argentine Republic exercises rights of sovereignty and jurisdiction". The statement added that the British decision "will be the cause of very serious tensions and conflicts with still unpredictable consequences, which may even affect the interests of third states". International support subsequently given to Argentina included the unanimous adoption by a special meeting of OAS states (including the United States) in Guatemala City on Nov. 9 of a resolution criticizing Britain for introducing a "new element of tension and potential conflict".

In the course of November 1986 Argentina launched a new diplomatic initiative to gain US and West European support for its case on the Falklands/Malvinas. On Nov. 18, coinciding with a visit to Washington by President Alfonsín, Argentina offered to make a formal declaration of a cessation of hostilities with Britain in return for the lifting of the Falklands protection zone, without making British agreement to sovereignty negotiations as such a precondition for such action. However, this new proposal was dismissed by the UK government as "an exercise in megaphone diplomacy" and as representing no real change in the established Argentinian position that direct negotiations must include the sovereignty issue.

During a visit to the Falklands in early January 1987 the UK Defence Secretary reiterated Britain's commitment to the effective defence of the islands. He said that the current British troop strength of some 4,000 would be reduced by about half by the end of 1987, but pointed out that the new Mount Pleasant military airfield gave the local military commander a rapid reinforcement capacity in time of emergency. On Feb. 1, 1987, the new Falklands fisheries protection zone came into effect without incident, some 230 licences having been issued to foreign ships for the forthcoming fishing season.

JB/SM

Belize-Guatemala

The British Crown Colony of Belize (formerly British Honduras) became independent in September 1981, notwithstanding the existence of an unresolved Guatemalan claim to its territory dating back to 1859. Under the Guatemalan constitution of 1945 Belize was regarded as the 23rd department of that country, and Guatemala thus claimed that the granting of self-determination to Belize would disrupt its own national unity and territorial integrity. While the British government had been ready to grant full independence to the colony much earlier, Belize feared that in the event of a British withdrawal without adequate defence guarantees Guatemala would invade to implement its claim. However, following an overwhelming vote at the United Nations in November 1980 in favour of the independence of Belize, the British government decided to proceed with granting independence and convened a constitutional conference followed by tripartite negotiations in which the basis for Guatemalan acceptance of Belize's independence appeared to have been established. Although it later transpired that Guatemala had not substantially modified its position, Belize nevertheless proceeded to full independence as a constitutional monarchy on Sept. 21, 1981, with British troops continuing to be stationed there for an indefinite period. Since then Guatemala has maintained a territorial claim against Belize, while indicating since 1983 a willingness to accept a compromise settlement giving it improved access to the Caribbean Sea.

Mexico also has a dormant claim to the northern half of Belize and had previously stated that it would reactivate this claim "in the event of any change in the colony's status which is not in accordance with the right of its inhabitants to self-determination".

History of the Dispute

Extending over an area of 8,866 square miles (23,000 sq km), British Honduras was granted internal self-government in 1964 and changed its name to Belize on June 1, 1973. It had become a Crown Colony in 1871, having been a British colony since 1862 and under British sovereignty since 1798.

The first settlers were English timbercutters and their black slaves in the mid-17th century. Under the 1670 Treaty of Madrid, Spain conceded certain rights to the timbercutters who, over the previous 30 years, had established themselves on the uninhabited shores of the Belize river. The British government did not, however, lay claim to the territory officially. Over the next 130 years the territory was subjected to repeated attacks by Spain, which claimed sovereignty over it. Finally, a Spanish naval flotilla was defeated by a small Belizean boat fleet at the Battle of St George's Cay on Sept. 10, 1798, and British sovereignty over Belize was explicitly recognized by the Peace of Amiens in 1802.

When Mexico and Guatemala became independent in 1821 they both claimed sovereignty over Belize as successors to the Spanish Crown in the region. Their claims were rejected by Britain, however, in view of the fact that British settlers had by this time already established themselves as far south as the Sarstoon river (the present southern boundary). Mexico recognized British Honduras in 1826 and renounced claims to it in 1893 by treaty; the United States recognized it in 1850 (together with British Guiana) as exceptions to the Monroe Doctrine. However, Guatemala continued to regard Belize as part of its territory.

In 1859 Britain tried to settle the territorial dispute between Guatemala and British Honduras by means of a frontier convention, one of whose articles provided for the joint construction of a means of communication between Guatemala and the Caribbean across Belize; this article was never implemented and has remained a bone of contention. A supplementary convention was signed in 1863 under which the British government undertook to pay a substantial amount towards the cost of a road, although this never came to fruition despite the later renewal of the offer by Britain.

Guatemala on Sept. 24, 1945, conveyed to the British government the text of a draft decree declaring the 1859 convention null and void and inserting into its own constitution a clause laying claim to the whole of British Honduras as Guatemalan territory. Its claim was based on the contention that, as the 1859 convention on communications had never been implemented, the whole convention was null and void and that Guatemala therefore had a claim to the whole of British Honduras, or at least to the southern part. The claim was wholly rejected by Britain, which said that even had the convention lapsed this would be no reason why any part of the territory should belong to Guatemala, since Britain had been in possession for 150 years (i.e. since before the convention was signed or Guatemala became independent). In January 1946 Britain invited Guatemala to submit the dispute to the International Court of Justice, and repeated the invitation on subsequent occasions, but Guatemala never took it up.

British Honduras achieved internal self-government on Jan. 1, 1964, following a constitutional conference in London on July 10-22, 1963, at which only British Honduras and Britain were represented. Guatemala (ruled at that time by Col. Enrique Peralta) broke off diplomatic relations with Britain on the last day of the conference, claiming that the British government's decision to move towards the independence of British Honduras was "a unilateral action which is a flagrant violation of the inalienable and sovereign rights of Guatemala". Prior to this, President Ydigoras Fuentes of Guatemala had raised the issue of sovereignty in December 1961 and talks on the issue had taken place in Puerto Rico in April 1962 at the instigation of Britain. Among matters agreed on this occasion were the creation

Map 43   Present territorial relationship of Belize and Guatemala and also of El Salvador and Honduras.

of mixed committees of representatives of Guatemala, Britain and British Honduras on mutual relations, and on economic and social development.

In July 1965 Britain and Guatemala requested the United States to mediate in their dispute. Accordingly, President Johnson commissioned a report from a New York lawyer, Bethuel M. Webster, who on April 18, 1968, proposed that Britain and Guatemala should conclude a treaty, and that the former should endeavour to persuade British Honduras to accede to it on becoming independent. It was proposed that the treaty should contain the following conditions: (i) that British Honduras should attain independence by Dec. 31, 1970, with the probable name of Belize; (ii) that there should be unrestricted trade, travel and other contacts between Guatemala and British Honduras; and (iii) that a road should be constructed between the two countries.

George Price, the Prime Minister of British Honduras, declared on May 9, 1968, that his government rejected Webster's proposals because they failed to recognize the colony's right to sovereignty. Britain thus responded on May 20 that since the British Honduras government, with the endorsement of its House of Representatives, had asked Britain not to accede to such a treaty with Guatemala, and since the dispute with Guatemala could only be settled in accordance with the wish of the British Honduras people, it could not endorse the mediator's proposals.

Developments in the 1970s

In 1971 Guatemalan troop movements in the border area gave rise to fears of a Guatemalan invasion of British Honduras. Guatemala subsequently protested over a British military training exercise held there in February 1972 to coincide with British naval manoeuvres in the Caribbean, and the outcome was that Guatemala in March 1972 broke off informal talks on the Belize issue. At the end of the troop exercise Britain decided to increase the size of its permanent British garrison in Belize from one to two companies (i.e. to about 700 men), giving rise to another protest from Guatemala. The presence of an increased number of troops proved a stumbling block to further talks, which did not resume until February 1975. On their resumption, Britain rejected Guatemalan proposals envisaging the cession of the southern quarter of Belize (south of latitude 16°30'), including an area thought to contain oil deposits, in return for the renunciation by Guatemala of its claim to the rest of the colony. The talks broke down in July 1975.

Reports of increased Guatemalan military activity in the border areas in October 1975 led Britain in November 1975 to send reinforcements to its garrison in Belize at George Price's request. By Nov. 8 its military strength in the colony had been increased to over 1,000 men, supported by six Hawker Harrier vertical takeoff aircraft and a frigate, which patrolled offshore with a detachment of Marines aboard. The UK Foreign and Commonwealth Secretary in the then Labour government, James Callaghan, told the House of Commons in a statement on Nov. 6 that the British garrison in Belize had been strengthened because of the increased Guatemalan military activity on the border and because of "statements by Guatemalan ministers of their intention to incorporate Belize in Guatemala". He said that he had informed Guatemala in September that "if there were an invasion of a British colony which is seeking to become independent and whose independence is denied only by the Guatemalan claim, we would fulfil our responsibilities to that colony".

Despite Guatemalan opposition to the reinforcement of the British miliary presence in Belize, however, no further action was taken by Guatemala, and at the end of November 1975 Britain and Guatemala agreed to hold fresh talks, with Belizean participation, early the following year.

The UN General Assembly on Dec. 8. 1975, adopted a resolution on Belize (3432/XXX)—with Mexico abstaining and Guatemala not participating—which had already been adopted by the UN Trusteeship Committee on Nov. 21. This resolution (i) reaffirmed the "inalienable right of the people of Belize to self-determination and independence"; (ii) declared that the "inviolability and territorial integrity of Belize must be preserved"; (iii) called upon all states to respect the right of the people of Belize to self-determination, independence and territorial integrity and to facilitate the attainment by them of their goal of a secure independence"; (iv) called upon Britain as the administering power, acting in close consultation with the government of Belize, and on Guatemala, to "pursue urgently their negotiations for the earliest possible resolution of their differences of opinion concerning the future of Belize in order to remove such obstacles as have hitherto prevented the people of Belize from exercising freely and without fear their inalienable right to self-determination and independence"; and (v) declared that "any proposals for the resolution of these differences of opinion that may emerge from negotiations between the administering power and the government of Guatemala must be in accordance with paragraphs (i) and (ii) above".

A similar resolution (31/50) was adopted by the General Assembly on Dec. 1, 1976, urging all states to refrain from any action threatening the territorial integrity of Belize, on which Mexico again abstained. Panama, which had previously supported Guatemala's claim, voted in favour of Resolution 31/50, causing Guatemala to sever diplomatic relations with Panama in May 1977.

Meanwhile, George Price's People's United Party (PUP), which was returned to power in Belize in the October 1974 general elections after calling for early independence, tried during 1975 to internationalize the sovereignty issue, winning the support of the Non-Aligned Movement and being backed by various independent Caribbean states including Jamaica, Cuba, Guyana, and Trinidad and Tobago. The Belize government also decided to seek UN support for its cause, and invited the opposition United Democratic Party (UDP) to join the PUP in formulating a case. The UDP accepted, after agreeing to a formula which affirmed its own commitment to Belize's right to self-determination while reserving its position on the timing of independence (to which it adopted a more gradualist approach).

Talks recommended between the three parties in April 1976 (after delays due to the earthquake in Guatemala in February 1976) and more talks were held in June and September 1976, the latter (in Panama City) being followed in October by the first ever bilateral meeting between Belizean and Guatemalan officials (in Honduras). At this stage (the end of 1976) Guatemala was said to have agreed to certain economic co-operation proposals including the use of free-port facilities in Belize City, but it still refused to abandon its claim to that part of Belize south of latitude 16°30′. No progress was made on the fundamental issue of Belizean territorial integrity.

In July 1977 the British military presence was again strengthened in Belize because of tension between the colony and Guatemala; the latter's troops were reported to be massing on the border, and Guatemalan leaders spoke of the possibility of an armed conflict with Britain. A Royal Navy frigate took up position off Belize, British forces were moved to within two miles of the border, and the Hawker Harrier detachment (which had been withdrawn just before the April 1976 talks) was again deployed in the colony. Despite the military tension, however, further tripartite talks were held in July 1977 in Washington.

While in Washington, the British and Guatemalan delegates also had separate talks on the Belize issue with Cyrus Vance, the US Secretary of State in the Carter Administration. George Price said on July 8 that he would welcome a US endorsement of Belize's right to "complete independence" and he called for a US defence guarantee after independence if Britain continued to decline to undertake such a commitment.

In line with a commitment made in a joint communiqué after the Washington talks, a British Foreign Office minister (Edward Rowlands) visited Guatemala in July 1977 while the military alert was still in force along the border with Belize. At a press conference in Guatemala City on July 28 he said that he had personally assured President Laugerud that "the British government is not an aggressor, will not be an aggressor and will not intimidate or apply intimidating pressure on the negotiations", which would be resumed on an unspecified date. President Laugerud, however, said in a speech at the end of July that no further negotiations could take place until the British reinforcements were withdrawn from Belize, where the British military presence constituted "a physical aggression against Guatemalan territory".

Negotiations leading to Independence of Belize

Over the next two years (i.e. until the end of 1979) no substantial progress was made towards a settlement, although the parties concerned had numerous contacts and negotiations. The United States assumed an active role, and an increasing number of countries of the region came to support Belize's position.

Following talks in London in January 1978 involving Dr David Owen (then UK Foreign and Commonwealth Secretary), George Price and Edward Rowlands, Dr Owen told the House of Commons on Jan. 25 that "various proposals including the possibility of territorial adjustments" had recently been discussed between Britain and Guatemala. Price himself emphasized at a press conference later on Jan. 25 that no Belizean territory could be ceded. He revealed for the first time that during the past six months the British government had been considering various proposals for the cession to Guatemala of an area of Belize's southern territory which had been progressively reduced in size over that period, ranging from about 2,000 square miles (comprising land south of Monkey River plus seabed) to about 1,000 square miles (land south of the Moho river plus seabed between the Moho river and Ranguana cays, where oil prospecting was in progress); this latest proposal would give Guatemala sovereignty over an alternative access route (by sea) to its Caribbean port of Puerto Barrios. Price's own view was that the cession of land would create not solve problems and, since the latest London talks had failed to produce an acceptable basis for settlement, Belize would now seek security guarantees from Caribbean countries.

Accordingly, in February and March 1978 George Price had contacts with the Bahamas, Barbados, Grenada, Guyana, Jamaica, and Trinidad and Tobago, and told a press conference in March that certain countries had indicated their readiness to participate in "multilateral security arrangements which would defend the territorial integrity of an independent Belize"; his government had, however, ruled out the possibility of asking for Cuban military aid, in order to avoid problems with the USA.

Belize's aim at this stage appeared to be the stationing of a security force in Belize which would be strong enough to allow Belize to attain independence without having to negotiate a settlement with Guatemala first. However, the Guatemalan government indicated in mid-May 1978 (while a further round of Anglo-Guatemalan talks was in progress) that it was maintaining its demand for a territorial concession and was also demanding in the current talks the formation of a joint Guatemala-Belize military staff and joint consultations on Belize's external relations.

Subsequently, at a meeting in New York in June 1978, Dr Owen, Price and Dean Lindo (the UDP leader) drew up a "memorandum of understanding" whereby (i) Britain undertook to invite the Belize government and opposition to participate in all future talks with Guatemala, (ii) Britain agreed to submit any agreement reached at such talks to a national referendum in Belize and (iii) Price and Lindo agreed to "put the issue of the Anglo-Guatemalan dispute above party politics and treat the search for a solution as a national objective".

After Maj.-Gen. Fernando Romeo Lucas García became President of Guatemala on July 1, 1978, fresh talks involving representatives of the new government opened in September in New York; in December, however, Guatemala rejected British settlement proposals whereby Belize would after independence have refrained (i) from introducing measures regarding its offshore jurisdiction in the Bay of Amatique which would block Guatemala's sea access to its Caribbean ports, and (ii) from entering into any pacts with third countries without Guatemalan agreement. Guatemala would for its part have been granted preferential customs treatment for trade through the port of Belize City, and Britain would have financed the construction of a new road from Guatemala through Belize to the Caribbean. The UN General Assembly on Dec. 13, 1978, adopted a resolution (33/36) urging a settlement to the dispute on the basis of Belize's "right to self-determination, independence and territorial integrity"; the resolution was supported by 128 states, this time including Costa Rica and Colombia (which had voted against a previous resolution on Nov. 27, 1977). On a further resolution (34/38) adopted on Nov. 21, 1979, referring to the inviolability and territorial integrity of Belize, Latin American countries voting for the first time in favour of Belize's right to self-determination included Brazil, Dominican Republic, Ecuador and Nicaragua.

Tripartite talks opened in May 1980 at which Britain was reported to have taken the line that, if mutually acceptable agreement could not be reached, Britain would unilaterally move the territory towards independence. Guatemala's position in 1980 was considerably weaker than it had been hitherto due to the deterioration of Guatemala's internal security situation, which led the United States and also Mexico to wish to seek a stable solution to the Belize issue in the interests of regional security. Washington was also anxious at this stage that Britain should continue to exercise its defence commitment to Belize after eventual independence.

On Nov. 11, 1980, the UN General Assembly adopted by 139 votes (including the United States) to none, with seven abstentions and with Guatemala absent, a resolution (35/20) to the effect that Belize should be granted independence by the end of 1981, calling upon Britain to convene a constitutional conference to prepare for Belizean independence; and urging Britain to "continue to ensure the security and territorial integrity of Belize". It also called on Guatemala and independent Belize to "work out arrangements for post-independence co-operation on matters of mutual concern". The British government accordingly announced on Dec. 2, 1980, that it intended to convene a constitutional conference in the near future.

At a round of talks involving Britain, Guatemala and a Belizean delegation in London beginning on March 5, 1981, all three delegations accepted 16 heads of agreement, whose text was formally signed on March 16 by ministerial representatives of the three countries as follows:

"The United Kingdom and Guatemala, in order to settle the controversy between them over the territory of Belize, have reached agreement on the following points:

"(1) The United Kingdom and Guatemala shall recognize the independent state of Belize as an integral part of Central America, and respect its sovereignty and territorial integrity in accordance with its existing and traditional frontiers, subject, in the case of Guatemala, to the completion of the treaty or treaties necessary to give effect to these heads of agreement.

"(2) Guatemala shall be accorded such territorial seas as shall ensure permanent and unimpeded access to the high seas, together with rights over the seabed thereunder.

"(3) Guatemala shall have the use and enjoyment of the Ranguana and Sapodilla [Zapotillo] cays, and rights in those areas of the sea adjacent to the cays, as may be agreed.

"(4) Guatemala shall be entitled to free port facilities in Belize City and Punta Gorda.

"(5) The road from Belize City to the Guatemalan frontier shall be improved; a road from Punta Gorda to the Guatemalan frontier shall be completed. Guatemala shall have freedom of transit on these roads.

"(6) Belize shall facilitate the construction of oil pipelines between Guatemala and Belize City, Dangriga and Punta Gorda.

"(7) In areas to be agreed an agreement shall be concluded between Belize and Guatemala for purposes concerned with the control of pollution, navigation and fishing.

"(8) There shall be areas of the seabed and the continental shelf to be agreed for the joint exploration and exploitation of minerals and hydrocarbons.

"(9) Belize and Guatemala shall agree upon certain developmental projects of mutual benefit.

"(10) Belize shall be entitled to any free port facilities in Guatemala to match similar facilities provided to Guatemala in Belize.

"(11) Belize and Guatemala shall sign a treaty of co-operation in matters of security of mutual concern, and neither shall permit its territory to be used to support subversion against the other.

"(12) Except as foreseen in these heads of agreement, nothing in these provisions shall prejudice any rights or interests of Belize or of the Belizean people.

THE AMERICAS AND ANTARCTICA

"(13) The United Kingdom and Guatemala shall enter into agreements designed to re-establish full and normal relations between them.

"(14) The United Kingdom and Guatemala shall take the necessary action to sponsor the membership of Belize in the United Nations, the Organization of American States, Central American organizations and other international organizations.

"(15) A joint commission shall be established between Belize, Guatemala and the United Kingdom to work out details to give effect to the above provisions. It will prepare a treaty or treaties for signature by the signatories to these heads of agreement.

"(16) The controversy between the United Kingdom and Guatemala over the territory of Belize shall therefore be honourably and finally terminated."

George Price said in a nationwide broadcast on March 17, 1981, that "Belize has gained its overwhelming objectives while protecting the basic rights of the Belizean people and adhering fully to the UN resolutions that protect our sovereignty and territorial integrity". In Guatemala, the government presented the heads of agreement as an honourable means of settling the dispute in the face of strong international pressure.

The Mexican government was reported to be happy with the agreement and to have no intention of pressing its dormant claim, but the Honduran government made an official protest to Britain over the status of the Sapodilla cays, to which it had a longstanding dormant claim. Honduras also claimed a right to participate in the proposed negotiations on the grounds that "the delimitation of sea areas could lead to situations of conflict to the detriment of Honduras's legitimate rights".

The British government formally announced on March 20, 1981, that a constitutional conference would begin in London on April 6. However, the UDP continued to oppose the heads of agreement as a sell-out of Belizean interests, and mounted an anti-government campaign which developed into public disorders and led to the declaration of a state of emergency in Belize from April 2 to 24. In view of the emergency George Price did not attend the London constitutional conference, the Belize delegation being led by Carl Rogers, the deputy leader of the PUP. The UDP boycotted the conference.

Negotiations on a treaty to give formal effect to the heads of agreement were held in New York from May 20 to 28, 1981, by a tripartite commission of British, Guatemalan and Belizean government representatives. A further round held in New York on July 6-10 became deadlocked after Guatemala reportedly insisted that its interpretation of the heads of agreement would allow the establishment of naval facilities on Ranguana and Sapodilla cays, this being rejected by Britain and Belize.

In the absence of agreement on a treaty, and following Belize-UK talks in London on July 19-23, 1981, it was announced on July 26 that independence would be granted to Belize notwithstanding on Sept. 21 and that British troops would continue to be stationed there for "an appropriate period" thereafter. Guatemala responded by restating its intention to "reserve its legal and historic rights" over Belize, although it made it clear that no attempt would be made to occupy Belizean territory by force after independence. On Sept. 7 Guatemala broke off all remaining diplomatic links with Britain, severed commercial ties, and closed its border with Belize. Independence Day on Sept. 21, 1981, was declared a day of national mourning in Guatemala, and the ceremony in Belize was boycotted by the UDP. At the request of George Price (who became the first Prime Minister of independent Belize), the ceremonial lowering of the British flag took place in total darkness to symbolize the fact that Britain was not wholly relinquishing its responsibilities towards Belize.

A schedule to the Belize constitution defined the territories of the new independent country with reference to (i) the Guatemalan frontier prescribed by the UK-Guatemala treaty of 1859, and (ii) the Mexican frontier prescribed by the UK-Mexico treaty of 1893. Belize's offshore reefs, islands and islets were listed, together with "their adjacent waters as far as the outer limits of the territorial seas appertaining to them".

Continuation of Dispute in Post-Independence Period—Guatemala's Apparent Willingness to accept Compromise Settlement

Belize was admitted to the United Nations on Sept. 25, 1981, its application being sponsored by Mexico, which subsequently became the first non-Commonwealth country to establish diplomatic relations with Belize. The Guatemalan government stated (on Sept. 25) that it would "continue to struggle, in a peaceful manner, to defend its rights by diplomatic means and international law". In December 1985, apparently in response to local economic pressures, Guatemala reopened one border crossing to Belize.

A statement by the Price government that Belize would apply for full membership of the Non-Aligned Movement was welcomed by the movement's then chairman, President Castro of Cuba, who urged all member countries to "offer their rapid recognition" of the new state. As regards the Organization of American States (OAS), Belize submitted a formal application in October 1981 but stated that it did not wish to be considered for membership immediately (its admission being effectively blocked under the OAS rule requiring the exclusion of applicant states currently involved in territorial disputes with existing members). Nevertheless, Belize was invited to send observer delegations to subsequent OAS conferences. Belize's first post-independence bilateral friendship agreement was concluded with Costa Rica in November 1981.

Following the accession to power in Guatemala of Gen. Efraín Ríos Montt in March 1982, a new attempt was mounted to solve the territorial issue. Although the new regime maintained Guatemala's refusal to recognize the independence of Belize, the Guatemalan Foreign Minister formally proposed in July 1982 (via the Swiss embassy, which was then representing British interests in Guatemala) that Britain and Guatemala should resume negotiations, it being subsequently announced that tripartite talks would open in New York in January 1983. Initially Guatemala had proposed bilateral talks with Britain, which had objected on the grounds that Belize was now an independent country and should therefore be fully represented.

Prior to the new talks, President Ríos Montt announced on Jan. 13, 1983, that whereas Guatemala had previously claimed the whole territory of Belize "now the Guatemalan position has changed: we want the district of Toledo to form part of our territory". He said that the Guatemalan claim to this area—about one-fifth of the total area of Belize and including the southern port of Punta Gorda—was based on considerations of cultural traditions, geography and national security, adding that if the claim were met Guatemala would recognize the independence of Belize. However, this Guatemalan offer (which was reported to have been encouraged by the US government) was immediately rejected by the Belize government.

The tripartite negotiations opened in New York on Jan. 24, 1983, but broke down after only one day. Belize refused to make any territorial concessions, while Guatemala rejected counter-proposals under which it would have gained a sector of Belize's territorial waters transit rights through the south of Belize and participation in a joint development zone on either side of the Sarstoon river to a width of five kilometres.

After a further Guatemalan military coup in August 1983, the new regime reverted to claiming the whole of Belize, thus apparently withdrawing the Ríos Montt compromise proposal of January 1983. Meanwhile, a contingent of some 1,800 British troops remained in Belize, their presence being regarded as even more essential by the Belize government in the light of the Argentinian invasion of the Falkland Islands in April 1982. In the Belize general elections of December 1984 (which resulted in a defeat for Price's PUP and the formation of a UDP government led by Manuel Esquivel) both major parties supported the retention of the British troops and also rejected suggestions emanating from the UK government that US troops might replace them.

The UDP government was represented at a further round of talks in New York in February 1985, when the Guatemalan side was reported to have again indicated a willingness to accept a compromise territorial settlement. In May 1985 the Guatemalan Constituent

Assembly, in drawing up a new civilian constitution, approved an article empowering the government to take appropriate action to resolve the dispute "in conformity with national interests", thus effectively dropping the previous constitution's assertion that Belize was part of Guatemala. On Dec. 17, 1985, the new civilian President-elect of Guatemala, Vinicio Cerezo, publicly advanced the possibility of Guatemala extending recognition to Belize in return for territorial concessions which would improve Guatemalan access to the Caribbean Sea.

In August 1985 Manuel Esquivel visited London in an attempt to secure a commitment that British troops would remain in Belize until the territorial dispute with Guatemala had been finally resolved. He later stated that the UK government had reiterated its pledge to retain its forces for "as long as necessary" but had declined to give an indefinite commitment to the defence of Belize. It was agreed, however, that Britain would assist in the training and expansion of the 600-strong Belize Defence Force and would provide aid for economic and infrastructural development.

Having resumed consular relations on Aug. 19, 1986, Britain and Guatemala resumed full diplomatic relation on Dec. 29, 1986—a development which was welcomed by the Esquivel government as potentially facilitating Guatemala's recognition of the independence of Belize. On April 29-30, 1987, further Belize-Guatemala-UK talks (held in Miami) were officially described as "cordial" but again failed to result in any substantive progress towards a resolution of the territorial issue.

JB/AJD

Bolivia-Chile
(Lauca River Waters)

A dispute over the use of the waters of the River Lauca (which has its source in Chile and flows on to the Andean plateau of Bolivia), which had existed for several years, reached a critical point in 1962 after Bolivia had warned Chile on March 22 of that year that the diversion of water from the river by Chile would be regarded as an act of aggression, as such a diversion could not be undertaken without the agreement of both countries.[1] (For a map illustrating this dispute, see page 409.)

Despite the Bolivian warning, the Chilean President on April 14, 1962, ordered that the sluice gates of a new dam on the Lauca river should be opened to supply an irrigation scheme and a new hydroelectric project in Chile. Bolivia in turn contended that this action reduced the flow of the Lauca river waters into Bolvia and broke off its diplomatic relations with Chile on April 16.

The Bolivian government also appealed to the Council of the Organization of American States (OAS) to find a solution to the dispute. The Council unanimously decided on May 24, 1962, to call on Bolivia and Chile to come to an agreement by making use of any of the peaceful means for settling disputes contained in the 1947 Inter-American Treaty for Reciprocal Assistance (the Treaty of Rio). Bolivia and Chile, however, failed to agree on such means, with Bolivia favouring mediation by five Latin American states and Chile

---

[1]For the separate dispute between Bolivia, Chile and Peru over the question of Bolivian access to the sea, see pages 407-11.

wishing to call for arbitration by the International Court of Justice, on the grounds that the issue was a legal and not a political matter.

On Sept. 3, 1962, however, the Bolivian government temporarily withdrew from participation in the activities of the OAS, stating that it had acted "in strict accordance with the terms of the [OAS] resolution of May 24", whereas the Chilean government appeared not to intend to contribute to the reaching of an immediate solution because it was "the beneficiary of the present illegal situation". Bolivia also claimed that the humidity in the area had already been reduced, that the salinity of Lake Coipasa (into which the Lauca river flows) had been raised, that difficulties had been created in agriculture and cattle-raising in three provinces, and that Chile was also attempting to divert waters from the Caquena river (which like the Lauca rises in Chile and flows into Bolivia).

After the OAS had studied the question for over a year without reaching a solution, the Bolivian government announced on June 12, 1963, that it would withdraw permanently from the OAS, which it called "an incompetent organ" as it had failed to solve the dispute. However, this decision was not carried out and a few months later Bolivia resumed its participation in the work of the OAS.

The first dialogue between Bolivia and Chile for 12 years was held by (the right-wing) Presidents Hugo Banzer Suárez of Bolivia and Augusto Pinochet Ugarte of Chile in Brasilia (in the presence of President Ernesto Geisel of Brazil) on March 16, 1974, and President Pinochet stated afterwards that Chile was ready to resolve the dispute. A Chilean proposal made in 1976 and providing for an exchange of territory whereby Bolivia would acquire a corridor to the sea also contained a clause under which Bolivia was to grant Chile the use of the Lauca river waters. Although President Banzer at first accepted these proposals as "a global basis for negotiation", they were generally rejected in Bolivia.

On March 17, 1978—by which date no progress had been made in negotiations concerning Bolivia's access to the sea—the Bolivian government again broke off diplomatic relations with Chile, following which relations between the two countries deteriorated further during 1979. Although in the mid-1980s the two governments achieved a degree of rapprochement, no announcement has been made on any progress towards a solution of the Lauca river waters dispute.

HWD

Bolivia-Chile-Peru

Bolivia has been landlocked since losing its coastal territory in the Pacific War of 1879-84, when Chile seized the then Bolivian port of Antofagasta and the surrounding coastline. Peru, which joined the war in support of Bolivia, lost its own southern provinces of Tacna and Arica to Chile but retrieved Tacna in 1929 under the Treaty of Ancón. Bolivia's efforts to regain an outlet to the Pacific Ocean have since been hampered by a provision in the Treaty of Ancón to the effect that no Chilean territory formerly belonging to Peru could be surrendered to a third country without the consent of Peru. Bolivia also failed, in the Chaco War of the early 1930s, to obtain proper access to the Atlantic Ocean via the Paraguay river. Bolivia has as a national policy aim the regaining of access to the Pacific and in April 1987 put forward new proposals to that end involving the cession of territory by Chile.

History of the Dispute

The exact border between Chile and Bolivia was not defined when the two countries became independent from the (Spanish) Viceroyalty of Peru—independence being accomplished by Chile in 1810 and by Bolivia (which was formerly encompassed by the Audiencia of Charcas) in 1824. In 1866 the two countries reached an agreement setting their boundary along the 24°S parallel of latitude to the south of Antofagasta (in the Atacama desert) but providing that the proceeds from nitrate and guano deposits extracted from a common zone between the 23rd and 25th parallels should be equally divided.

After Bolivia had broken an agreement signed with Chile at Sucre in 1874 by placing fresh taxes on Chilean firms already exploiting nitrates in the common zone, a Chilean expeditionary force in February 1879 took possession of Antofagasta and Mejillones (on the coast) and Caracoles (inland). Chile called on Peru to proclaim its neutrality in the conflict, and, when the latter refused, declared war on both Peru and Bolivia. Peru thereupon joined forces with Bolivia under a treaty concluded secretly in February 1873, but a joint Peruvian-Bolivian army was defeated at Tarapacá in November 1879 and the Peruvians retreated to Tacna, losing the whole of Tarapacá nitrate area to Chile. After this Bolivia played little further part in the Pacific war, although Peru fought on, with the result that Lima and Callao were occupied by Chilean troops in 1881.

Chilean forces remained in Lima in strength until 1883, when General Miguel Iglesias was elected President of Peru with Chilean backing and then proceeded to sign the Treaty of Ancón on Oct. 20, 1883. The treaty ceded to Chile in perpetuity and unconditionally the province of Tarapacá and provided that the provinces of Tacna and Arica would remain in Chilean possession and subject to Chilean administration for 10 years, at the end of which time a plebiscite would be held to decide whether the territories should remain in Chilean hands or revert to Peru.

The last Chilean forces withdrew from Lima in August 1884, and the same year (in April) a separate truce was signed between Chile and Bolivia, terminating the state of war between them and providing that, while the truce remained in force, Chile was to administer the territory from the 23rd parallel to the south of the Loa river on the Pacific. This meant that Bolivia lost not only its seaports but also its nitrate territory. In October 1904 a treaty was signed in implementation of the 1884 truce agreement, re-establishing peace between Chile and Bolivia, confirming the absolute and perpetual sovereignty of Chile over the former Bolivian territory occupied since the Pacific War, and demarcating the Bolivian-Chilean border from north to south through 96 points.

Article 3 of the 1904 treaty established that the port of Arica would be linked with the plateau above La Paz (Bolivia) by means of a railway which was to be built at Chile's expense, while in Article 6 Chile recognized in perpetuity Bolivia's free and full right of commercial transit through Chilean territory and ports on the Pacific seaboard. In return, under a supplementary protocol of November 1904, Bolivia recognized Chile's absolute and perpetual dominion over the territory between the 23rd and 24th parallels from the Pacific to the Argentinian border. By 1913 the railway was completed and Bolivia was due to come into ownership of its own section in 1928 under the terms of the 1904 treaty. The Peruvian government protested at the bilateral treaty between Chile and Bolivia and warned that such a treaty did not diminish its own rights to the provinces of Tacna and Arica.

In 1918 Bolivia demanded an outlet to the sea by means of a port in either Tacna or Arica provinces, to which it asserted that neither Peru nor Chile had a conclusive right. It stated its preference for Arica on the grounds of geographical proximity, economic considerations and the fact that Arica (as well as Tacna) had been part of the Charcas Audiencia before independence. Furthermore, in 1920 Bolivia called on the League of Nations to obtain a revision of the 1904 treaty on the grounds that it had been imposed by force, that Chile was not carrying out some of its fundamental provisions, that a permanent threat of war existed in the current situation, and that it had no access to the sea. The League ruled, however, that a treaty could only be modified by the parties to it.

Meanwhile, on expiry of the 10-year period stipulated under the Treaty of Ancón, no attempt was made by Chile to hold a plebiscite in Tacna and Arica. By the early 1920s, when the USA was asked to intervene, the areas had already become Chileanized. When registration of voters was eventually carried out in preparation for the holding of a plebiscite, it was found that most Peruvians had failed to enrol, so that the plan to hold a plebiscite was abandoned. Peru and Chile in 1929 resumed diplomatic relations, which they had broken off some 20 years earlier, and on June 3, 1929, an agreement also known as the Treaty of Ancón was signed in Lima, returning the territory of Tacna to Peru and leaving Arica in Chilean hands. A complementary protocol of the same date stated that neither government could without the consent of the other cede to any third party any or all of the territory previously in dispute, or build new international railways across it.

Tacna was handed back to Peru at a ceremony on Aug. 28, 1929, and the following year Arica was incorporated by Chile into the province of Tarapacá, its northern boundary forming the frontier with Peru.

The Chaco War

From the late 1870s Bolivia sought the settlement of an old claim to part of the vast and largely uninhabited Chaco territory, including an area between the Pilcomayo and Verde rivers awarded to Paraguay as against Argentina in November 1878. Aspiring partly to gain an outlet to the Atlantic, Bolivia based its claim on the proposition that the Audiencia of Charcas had always exercised jurisdiction as far east as the Paraguay river. A number of agreements on delimitation of territory in the Chaco were signed but not ratified between Bolivia and Paraguay over the next few years, including the Soler-Pinilla protocol of Jan. 12, 1907.

In 1928 the two sides attacked each other's outposts in the Chaco and, despite attempts at arbitration by other South American countries, fighting took place sporadically in 1930-31,

Map 44 The above map illustrates the dispute over Bolivian access to the sea, and also the separate dispute between Chile and Bolivia over the Lauca river waters.

breaking out in earnest in 1932. The Bolivian forces were greater in number and better equipped than the Paraguayans, but many of them were Indians accustomed to high altitudes and they died in large numbers on the lower hot plains of the Chaco. Paraguay, on the other hand, was fighting on familiar ground; its forces under Col. José Félix Estigarribia advanced steadily and by the end of 1934 had captured thousands of square miles of territory beyond Bolivia's line of outposts. After some 100,000 men had died, a truce entered into force in 1935 and peace talks were held in Buenos Aires. A final boundary was established in 1938, whereby most of the territory was ceded to Paraguay, and Bolivia was granted the right of rail access to the Paraguay river.

Renewed Bolivian Claims to Sea Outlet—Bolivia's 1987 Proposals

In 1962 Bolivia broke off diplomatic relations with Chile after the latter was accused of reducing the flow of the Lauca river waters into Bolivia,[1] and relations were not resumed until 1975. In the 1970s with General Hugo Banzer in office in Bolivia and General Augusto Pinochet in power in Chile, the question of access to the sea was elevated to a major nationalistic issue in Bolivia, and in 1974 Bolivia and Chile initiated high-level contacts for the first time in 12 years.

In December 1975 Chile put forward a series of proposals aimed at resolving Bolivia's sea access problem. They required, however, that Bolivia should (i) relinquish an equal amount of her own territory (reportedly in a mineral-rich area of Potosí department in south-west Bolivia) in exchange for a corridor to the sea; (ii) purchase from Chile the Chilean sector of the Arica-La Paz railway; (iii) allow Chile full use of the Lauca river waters; (iv) undertake to keep any land corridor demilitarized; and (v) pay compensation for the use of port facilities. President Banzer accepted the proposals as a basis for negotiation but they were generally ill-received in Bolivia.

Chile itself later declined to consider a set of Peruvian proposals put forward in November 1976 whereby (i) Bolivia should be granted a corridor of land 8½ miles (13½ km) wide along the Chilean-Peruvian frontier, two miles north of Arica-La Paz railway; (ii) an international zone should be set up under the joint control of Chile, Peru and Bolivia where the corridor reached the coast; (iii) port facilities at Arica should be administered by all three countries; (iv) Bolivia should be allowed to establish a port under its sole sovereignty in the international zone; and (v) the sea area around the zone should be Bolivia's territorial waters.

Thereafter, relations between Peru and Chile continued to be strained over the question of Bolivian access to the sea. Moreover, in March 1978 President Banzer of Bolivia again broke off relations with Chile on the grounds that it was not showing sufficient flexibility over the issue. The centenary of the outbreak of the Pacific War (in 1979) was marked in Bolivia by emotional demonstrations in support of the regaining of access to the Pacific Ocean.

In the 1980s the prospects of movement on the Bolivia-Chile-Peru territorial issue appeared to become linked with the Argentina-Chile territorial dispute in their southern border region, and with the Argentina-UK dispute over the Falklands/Malvinas.[2] Following its defeat in the 1982 South Atlantic war with Britain, Argentina sought to secure Chilean diplomatic support on the Falklands by finally accepting Chile's claims in the Beagle Channel. Further, Argentina reportedly sought to ensure Bolivian and Peruvian support by making its concessions to Chile conditional upon the latter making concessions on the access to the sea question. In the event, however, Chile denied that any such linkage existed under the 1984 treaty with Argentina confirming Chilean sovereignty over the disputed Beagle Channel islands.

Nevertheless, Chile thereafter responded to Bolivian attempts at a diplomatic rapprochement by accepting the appointment of a Bolivian consul in Santiago in February

---

[1]For an account of this dispute, see pages 406-7.
[2]For accounts of these disputes, see pages 379-85 and 387-97 respectively.

1986 and by entering into direct talks in New York at the level of Foreign Ministers. These resulted in the signature on Sept. 30, 1986, of a 30-point agreement on the development of socio-economic and political relations, although the impact of the agreement was somewhat diminished by the simultaneous announcement by Chilean National Railways that it had suspended the Arica-La Paz service because of Bolivia's outstanding debts.

Thereafter, further talks on the access to the sea question took place in various American capitals, culminating in a meeting of Foreign Ministers in Montevideo (Uruguay) on April 21, 1987, at which the Bolivian side formally presented detailed proposals envisaging that Chile would cede either (i) a narrow strip of territory on its northern border with Peru, north of Arica and stretching eastwards to the current Bolivian border, or (ii) one of three identified coastal enclaves further south, with assured communications to Bolivia proper. It was further proposed that under any of these alternative scenarios Bolivia would make appropriate compensation and that Bolivia and Chile, together with Peru where appropriate, would establish an institutional framework for the economic development of their border regions.

The first of these alternatives envisaged that Bolivia would have full sovereignty, ownership and use in perpetuity of a demarcated strip of territory on the present Chile-Peru border, with full maritime rights off the coast of the ceded territory. Bolivia would also have various permanent rights of access to adjacent communications facilities which would remain in Chilean or Peruvian territory, with Bolivia undertaking to respect all existing private rights in the territory ceded. The three coastal enclaves identified in the alternative Bolivian proposals were a 42-kilometre area north of Pisagua (totalling 1,068 sq km), a 47-kilometre segment north of Tocopilla (1,238 sq km) and a 50-kilometre stretch north of Mejillones (1,500 sq km). An essential Bolivian requirement was that any such enclave ceded by Chile should contain utilizable maritime transport facilities, i.e. it should contain a serviceable port.

The Bolivian proposals met with a negative response from the ruling military junta in Chile, among whose members the Navy Commander, Admiral José Toribio Merino Castro, publicly rejected any arrangement involving the cession of Chilean territory to Bolivia. It was also pointed out in Chilean ruling circles that any modification of the 1904 treaty with Bolivia would require legislative enactment and might also need to be endorsed in a national plebiscite. A Chilean Foreign Ministry spokesman said on June 9, 1987, that his government was willing to continue exploratory talks with Bolivia on possible solutions to the territorial issue but stressed that any further Bolivian proposals should "not alter the Chilean territory". The following day the Bolivian consul was withdrawn from Santiago and the Bolivian government announced that it was considering suspending trade relations with Chile.

JB/EG

Colombia-Nicaragua

The new Sandanista government of Nicaragua on Feb. 4, 1980, unilaterally declared null and void a 1928 treaty under whose terms Colombian sovereignty had been confirmed over the Caribbean archipelago of San Andrés and Providencia, held by Colombia since the 19th century. San Andrés and Providencia, as well as the cays of Roncador, Quitasueño and Serrana (whose sovereignty is also in dispute), are all situated within 200 miles (320 km) of Nicaraguan shores on the Nicaraguan Rise (an undersea bank between Nicaragua and Jamaica) in an area which is thought to contain hydrocarbon deposits. Their distance from Colombia is considerably further, although they are somewhat nearer to Panama, which was a province of

Colombia until 1903 and which has a dormant claim to the islands. San Andrés, Providencia, Roncador, Serrana and Quitasueño are currently administered as part of Colombian territory.

The new regime in Nicaragua (installed in July 1979 after the overthrow of President Anastasio Somoza) claims that the islands and cays are part of its 200-mile continental shelf, jurisdiction over which it asserted in December 1979. It bases the delimitation of its territory on the "natural boundaries" principle enshrined in the 1826 Declaration of Independence of the United Provinces of Central America and endorsed in 19th-century Nicaraguan constitutions. It also points out that, in the many bilateral treaties signed by Nicaragua with other countries in the 19th and early 20th centuries, no mention was ever made of a Colombian right to these islands until the Bárcenas Meneses-Esguerra treaty was signed in 1928 under US coercion.

Colombia bases its claim to the islands and cays on a royal order of 1803. According to this, the Spanish Crown delegated to the Viceroyalty of Sante Fé de Bogotà (of which present-day Colombia and also Panama were then a part) the defence of San Andrés and Providencia and the Mosquito (i.e. Atlantic) coast to prevent pirate incursions. Nicaragua, however, claims that the 1803 order was purely military and points out that under a further royal order of 1806 responsibility for the defence of the areas was restored to the Captaincy-General of Guatemala (under which Nicaragua was administered at the time); it states

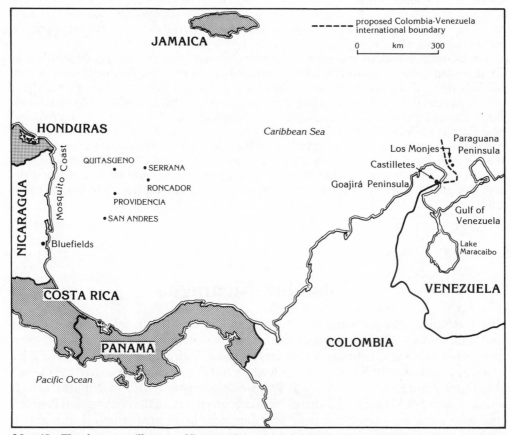

Map 45   **The above map illustrates Nicaragua's territorial claims against Colombia, and also the latter country's dispute with Venezuela over delimitation of the Gulf of Venezuela.**

furthermore that only royal decrees and not royal orders were juridically applicable as regards border questions. Nicaragua also disputes Colombia's assertion that the cays have always been considered, geographically and juridically, as part of the San Andrés archipelago, and rejects a 1972 treaty signed in Bogotá on Sept. 8 between the USA and Colombia under which the former recognized Colombian sovereignty over the three cays. The 1972 treaty was not ratified by the US Senate until July 31, 1981, following which instruments of ratification were exchanged on Sept. 17 of that year.

History of Dispute

Nicaragua was a focus of interest for the colonial powers in the 19th century because of the possibility of constructing an interoceanic canal across its territory. In the 18th century Britain had established a protectorate on the Mosquito coast (including part of present-day Honduras), known as the Miskito "kingdom", and its presence in the area was not finally ended until 1894. The 1905 Altamirano-Harrison treaty between Britain and Nicaragua subsequently recognized full Nicaraguan sovereignty over the coast.

The United States tried unsuccessfully to annex Nicaragua to the southern slave states in the mid-19th century and intervened militarily there in 1912-25 and again in 1926-33. It first proposed to Nicaragua that a treaty should be concluded recognizing Colombian sovereignty over San Andrés and Providencia in 1925 (apparently as a recompense to Colombia for the loss of Panama, whose independence in 1903 the USA had supported), but it was not until the second term of office of President Adolfo Díaz of Nicaragua (1926-28) that the Bárcenas Meneses-Esguerra treaty was signed with Colombia on March 24, 1928. The treaty stated that Colombia recognized Nicaraguan sovereignty over the Mosquito coast in exchange for Nicaraguan recognition of Colombian sovereignty over San Andrès and Providencia (but expressly excepted Roncador, Quitasueño and Serrana). It was not ratified until March 6, 1930, however, when President Moncada of the Liberal Party was in power in Nicaragua.

Just after the signature of the treaty, the USA and Colombia on April 10, 1928, came to an agreement regulating the juridical status of Roncador, Quitasueño and Serrana—the USA having earlier taken over the cays (in 1919) under the "Guano law" whereby islands considered by the USA as *terrae nullius* became its property if guano was discovered there. The agreement (in the form of an exchange of notes) laid down that in view of the claims of both countries over the islands the status quo should be maintained. Colombia should continue to fish around the islands and the USA should maintain navigational aids in the area.

In support of its contention that Colombia had no well-founded claim to the Mosquito coast or the adjacent islands, Nicaragua has cited a number of treaties concluded between Nicaragua and other countries, or between other countries. These have included (i) the Molina-Gual treaty of 1825 between Colombia and the United Provinces of Central America, which pledged that both sides would "guarantee the integrity of each other's respective territories ... on the same basis as they naturally occurred before the present war of independence"; and (ii) the Nicaraguan-Spanish treaty of 1850, which recognized the independence of Nicaragua and its adjacent islands, stating that Spain "renounced in perpetuity in the most formal and solemn manner for itself and its successors the sovereignty, rights and actions which correspond to it over the American territory situated between the Atlantic Ocean and the Pacific with its adjacent islands, formerly known under the denomination of the Province of Nicaragua and now a Republic of the same name".

Nicaragua has also claimed that its sovereignty over the Mosquito coast was recognized implicitly in the 1850 Clayton-Bulwer and 1852 Crampton-Webster treaties (both concluded between Britain and the USA), which stated that only the Central American states themselves could exercise sovereignty over Central American territory. Moreover, explicit Nicaraguan sovereignty over the Mosquito coast was recognized in the 1860 Treaty of

Managua, concluded between Britain and Nicaragua when the British settlement still existed on the coast.

On the basis of an 1894 treaty between Nicaragua and Honduras which declared that both were sovereign masters of their countries, it was later established between the two states that they had full sovereignty over their Atlantic coasts and adjacent islands. As stated above, Britain also recognized Nicaraguan sovereignty over the Mosquito coast and hence over its adjacent islands in the 1905 Altamirano-Harrison treaty.

Nicaragua also points out that when the Bárcenas Meneses-Esguerra treaty was signed and ratified, the constitution in force was that of 1911, which stated in Article 1 that Nicaraguan territory included "the adjacent islands". Article 2 stated that, since sovereignty was "inalienable and imprescriptible and resides essentially with the people", treaties should not be concluded "which are opposed to national independence and integrity or which affect its sovereignty in any war", except such as tended towards union with one or more of the Central American republics. The subsequent constitution of 1939 contained largely similar provisions, while the 1948 constitution also included Nicaragua's continental shelf and the stratosphere as under Nicaraguan jurisdiction.

Current State of Dispute

In unilaterally abrogating the Bárcenas Meneses-Esguerra treaty in 1980 Nicaragua stressed that the measure was not intended as a sign of aggression against a neighbour nation whose people it had always respected, nor was it claiming a part of Colombia's continental shelf, but rather territory which was geographically, historically and juridically an integral part of Nicaragua. It said that the circumstances of Nicaragua's history since 1909 had prevented it from defending its rights to the continental shelf, the jurisdictional waters and the island territories, and that treaties disadvantageous to Nicaragua such as the Bárcenas Meneses-Esguerra treaty and the earlier Chamorro-Bryan agreement of 1914 (which was later abrogated) were signed under duress and therefore lacked legal validity.

In response to Nicaragua's moves the Colombian government reinforced its military presence in and around San Andrés and recalled its ambassador for consultations. The two countries agreed to hold talks (pending which they maintained their original positions) and Colombia also referred its case to the UN Law of the Sea conference. In February 1982 Colombia reaffirmed its sovereignty over the disputed islands by "implementing" the 1972 treaty with the United States.

In April 1986 the Nicaraguan Foreign Minister, Miguel d'Escoto, reiterated his government's denunciation of the 1928 Bárcenas Meneses-Esguerra treaty with Colombia and stated that Nicaragua intended to have recourse to international law to have it declared illegal. On Oct. 23, 1986, the Colombian Senate approved a maritime delimitation treaty with Honduras (signed on Aug. 2) which endorsed Colombia's sovereignty over the areas in dispute with Nicaragua.

JB/AJD

Colombia-Venezuela

The boundary between Colombia and Venezuela—originally based on that between the (1810) Spanish captaincies-general of Venezuela and Granada—was not properly determined until 1932, when the final implementation was achieved of an arbitration award made on March 24, 1922, by the Swiss Federal Council, to which the two countries had in 1916 decided to submit their long-standing dispute for arbitration. Notwithstanding this land border settlement the two countries have in recent years been at issue over the delimitation of their respective sovereignties in the Gulf of Venezuela and the area around the Los Monjes Islands to the north-east of the Goajirá Peninsula. (For a map of the region, see page 412.)

Under a treaty signed in Bogotá (the capital of Colombia) on April 24, 1894, but not subsequently ratified, Colombia had ceded to Venezuela certain territories, including settlements on the east coast of the Goajirá Peninsula (i.e. the west coast of the Gulf of Venezuela). In a previous arbitration award of March 16, 1891, by the King of Spain, the whole of that peninsula had been awarded to Colombia.

In connexion with the discovery of oil resources in the area of the Gulf of Venezuela and Lake Maracaibo, a new dispute arose in the 1920s on the question of sovereignty over the waters and resources of the Gulf of Venezuela and the area around the islands of Los Monjes. The latter are situated to the north-east of the Goajirá Peninsula and were occupied by Venezuela under the dictatorship of President Pérez Jiménez in 1953-58.

In December 1965 it was alleged in Venezuela that Colombia had granted certain US oil companies concessions for prospecting for oil in Venezuelan territory. The two governments nevertheless agreed in that year to engage in talks on the "delimitation of marine and submarine areas" between their two countries. In 1968 the Venezuelan Foreign Minister defined his government's position as follows: "The submarine areas of the Gulf of Venezuela south of the parallel through Castilletes and Punta Salinas [i.e. roughly 12° N] in their entirety form part of Venezuelan territory [and] are in no case the object of negotiations, and therefore we recognize no kind of concessions in this area". In Bogotá it was claimed in April 1973 that the islands of Los Monjes did not have their own continental shelf, and in the same month the talks were broken off by Colombia.

On July 20, 1975, President López Michelsen of Colombia declared that the Gulf of Venezuela was "a historic bay, a condominium of the two riparian states—Colombia and Venezuela". He also quoted a statement which he had made in August 1974, as follows: "Our right to the continental shelf and the waters which cover it is derived from the geographical fact that this bay is not exclusively surrounded by Venezuelan territory." His thesis was, however, utterly rejected in Venezuela.

On Jan. 28, 1976, it was reported that the Colombian government would not submit its claim regarding the Los Monjes Islands area to the International Court of Justice but was ready to discuss it in direct talks with Venezuela on the delimitation of marine and submarine areas in the Caribbean Sea. At the same time, the Venezuelan Foreign Minister was reported to have stated that Venezuela's sovereignty over the Los Monjes Islands was unquestionable.

The Colombian Foreign Minister disclosed on Nov. 17, 1978, that talks were being held with Venezuela "in a spirit of cordiality and understanding" on the dispute over marine and submarine areas in what he called the Gulf of Maracaibo (i.e. of Venezuela) and added that Colombia rejected the appointment of a tribunal to arbitrate in the dispute. This idea was also rejected by the Venezuelan Foreign Minister during talks held in Bogotá on Dec. 11-13, 1978.

On March 14, 1979, President Luis Herrera Campíns of Venezuela was reported to have appointed a commission to travel to Colombia to resume negotiations on the demarcation in the Gulf of Venezuela. In response to a statement by the Colombian Council of State recognizing Venezuelan sovereignty over the Los Monjes Islands, the Venezuelan Foreign Ministry issued, on March 30, a statement welcoming this announcement as "a positive factor" in the talks but noting that the status of the islands had never been the subject of debate during marine and submarine demarcation talks between the two countries.

The talks were continued until it was announced in a broadcast in Bogotá on Oct. 21, 1980, that agreement had been reached on a draft treaty on the delimitation of marine areas, including "internal waters" and "exclusive economic zones". The draft treaty provided inter alia for the "innocent passage" of all merchant vessels using ports of the two countries and that of their warships and non-commercial state-owned vessels. It reaffirmed that the Los Monjes Islands were part of Venezuela but recognized limited Colombian rights in the Gulf. On the question of oil production the draft treaty laid down (in Article 4) that "if a hydrocarbons field extends to both sides of the boundary line established in this treaty each party will explore and exploit the deposit within its own marine areas and will receive one-half of the hydrocarbons extracted but will also be responsible for one-half of the corresponding cost" and that "those deposits that do not cross the boundary line will be developed unilaterally by the country in which they are found".

The draft treaty was strongly opposed by certain circles in both countries, but particularly in Venezuela (where there was widespread hostility towards Colombians, of whom several hundred thousand had entered Venezuela in search of work in recent years). Those opposing what they called "the ceding of Venezuelan waters to Colombia" included some members of the ruling Christian Social Party (COPEI), leading members of the opposition *Acción Democrática* (but not ex-President Carlos Andrés Pérez, who publicly supported the draft treaty), all left-wing parties and, above all, the armed forces.

President Herrera Campins had stated after its publication that the treaty would not be signed unless a clear consensus existed on its terms. At the same time the Venezuelan Minister of Energy assured Colombia that Venezuela would not drill for oil in the disputed area until the issue was settled. Further talks between representatives of the two governments on the boundary issue were suspended in November 1980, and it was only at a meeting of the two countries' Presidents in Venezuela on Oct. 2, 1981, that the possibility of renewed talks on the sea boundary dispute was mentioned, but there was no indication of the terms on which it might eventually be settled.

Regarding the two countries' common land border, the Colombian Foreign Minister announced on Jan. 29, 1982, that Colombia and Venezuela would begin to demarcate the border on Feb. 1. In Venezuela it was stated on Jan. 29 that the demarcation would take some nine months and that, as there was no problem of delineation, the purpose of the demarcation was merely to prevent confusion among the people living in the area and to comply with international agreements.

At a meeting held on June 14, 1985, the two countries' Presidents expressed their determination to find a peaceful solution to the dispute over the delimitation of their countries' maritime border.

The Venezuelan Foreign Minister, however, stated in June 1986 that as long as Venezuela existed as a state it would continue to exercise its sovereignty over the Los Monjes islands, and he described as "absurd" a recent "draft amendment on the status of the islands" drawn up by a Colombian magistrate. On June 16, 1986, it was reported that the commanders of the two countries' navies had undertaken "to handle prudently any isolated incidents and to prevent friction between the two governments" while agreements were being sought through diplomatic channels.

Following a reported border incursion by Colombian soldiers in late April 1987, the Venezuelan Defence Ministry on May 1 deployed additional troops to reinforce security positions along the entire length of the southern frontier with Colombia. Moreover, in mid-August serious tensions developed over an alleged incursion into Venezuelan waters by a Colombian naval vessel, whose activities were described as a "provocation" by Venezuela.

HWD

Cuba-United States

The US Guantánamo base in Cuba is the only US base in the world on communist territory. It was leased to the United States for a nominal rent in 1903 as a naval and coaling base by the newly formed Republic of Cuba, the United States being granted full jurisdiction and control over the territory containing the base in return for recognizing Cuban sovereignty over the area. The agreement on the lease was confirmed by a treaty of 1934. In 1960, following a deterioration in US-Cuban relations after Fidel Castro came to power, President Eisenhower issued a statement to the effect that the agreement could only be modified or abrogated with the consent of both parties, and that the USA had no intention of taking any such step. Diplomatic relations between the two countries were severed in January of the following year, and in 1964 the United States made the base self-sufficient after Cuba cut off fresh water supplies on Feb. 6 of that year. Cuba regards the base as being illegally occupied and has not cashed any of the rent payment cheques since 1960.

The Guantánamo base is located on the southern coast of the eastern end of the island of Cuba, at the foot of the Sierra Maestra mountains, in an area of 117 square miles (300 sq km), one-third of which is taken up by Guantánamo Bay. The bay, the third largest in Cuba, is a deep, sheltered inlet in a strategic location, which was considered at the time of its acquisition as fundamental to the maintenance of US interests in the Caribbean, South America and Central America, as well as for control of the Panama Canal.

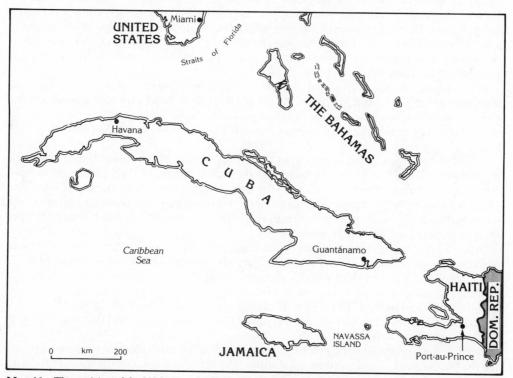

Map 46   **The position of the US base at Guantánamo in Cuba, also showing the position of Navassa Island (US), which is claimed by Haiti.**

417

Historical Background

Cuba was a Spanish colony from the 15th century until 1898, except for a brief period of British occupation in 1762-63. Cuban rebels fought to achieve the island's independence in the latter half of the 19th century, and the latest of these independence revolts (in 1895) led to the intervention three years later of the United States, which had shown interest in the island from the beginning of the century. A brief war ensued, after which Spanish dominion over Cuba was transferred to the USA with the signature on Dec. 10, 1898, of the Treaty of Paris.

Before the United States declared war on Spain, a joint resolution was passed by the US Congress on April 1898, authorizing the USA to intervene. The resolution declared that "the United States hereby disclaims any disposition or intention to exercise sovereignty, jurisdiction or control over said island except for the pacification thereof, and asserts its determination, when that is accomplished, to leave the government and control of the island to its people". It also stated that "the people of the island of Cuba are, and of right ought to be, free and independent"; and that "it is the duty of the United States to demand, and the government of the United States does hereby demand, that the government of Spain at once relinquish its authority and government in the island of Cuba and withdraw its land and naval forces from Cuba and Cuban waters".

Cuba remained under US military jurisdiction from 1898 to 1902, when the government of Cuba was handed over to the island's first President under the terms of the Platt Amendment (named after a Connecticut senator, Orville H. Platt, who presented it to the US Senate, although its text was drawn up by the Secretary of War, Elihu Root). The amendment authorized the US President to relinquish the government and control of the island of Cuba to its people "as soon as a government shall have been established in said island under a constitution which, either as a part thereof or in an ordinance appended thereto, shall define the future relations of the United States with Cuba".

The amendment also stated, however, "that the government of Cuba consents that the United States may exercise the right to intervene for the preservation of Cuban independence, the maintenance of a government adequate for the protection of life, property and individual liberty, and for discharging the obligations with respect to Cuba imposed by the Treaty of Paris on the United States, now to be assumed and undertaken by the government of Cuba".

Furthermore, Article VII stated that "to enable the United States to maintain the independence of Cuba, and to protect the people thereof, as well as for its own defence, the government of Cuba will sell or lease to the United States the lands necessary for coaling or naval stations at certain specified points to be agreed upon with the President of the United States".

The Platt Amendment was approved by the Cuban constitutional convention by a narrow majority on June 12, 1901, notwithstanding the earlier failure of the Cuban side to have certain qualifications attached to it and in the face of the US threat to continue to occupy the island if it was rejected. The amendment was attached to the new 1901 constitution, but Cuba has regarded it ever since as contradicting the 1898 joint resolution, which committed the USA to respect for Cuban independence.

In line with Article VIII of the Platt Amendment, which said that the provisions of Article VII would be embodied in a treaty with the USA, a Permanent Treaty was signed on May 22, 1903, between Cuba and the United States, providing for the perpetual lease of lands for coaling and naval stations. It became operative through an agreement signed by Cuba on Feb. 16, 1903, and by the USA on Feb. 23 of that year, which stated that Cuba and the USA were desirous to "execute fully Article VII of the Platt Amendment" and that they had thus reached agreement as follows:

"*Article I*. The Republic of Cuba hereby leases to the United States, for the time required for the purposes of coaling and naval stations, the following described areas of land and water situated in the island of Cuba: (i) in Guantánamo ... and (ii) in north-western Cuba in Bahía Honda .... *Article II*. The grant of the foregoing article shall include the right to use and occupy the waters adjacent to said areas of land and water, and to improve and deepen the entrances thereto and the anchorages therein, and generally to do any and all things necessary to fit the premises for use as coaling or naval stations only, and for no other purpose. Vessels engaged in the Cuban trade shall have free passage through the waters included within this grant. *Article III*. While on the one hand the United States recognizes the continuance of the ultimate sovereignty of the Republic of Cuba over the above described areas of land and water, on the other hand the Republic of Cuba consents that during the period of the occupation by the United States of said areas under the terms of this agreement the USA shall exercise complete jurisdiction and control over and within said areas with the right to acquire (under conditions to be hereafter agreed upon by the two governments) for the public purposes of the United States any land or other property therein by purchase or by exercise of eminent domain with full compensation to the owners thereof."

On Dec. 10, 1903, the USA took possession of the land and sea areas leased for the establishment of the base at Guantánamo at a price of US$2,000 a year in US gold throughout the period it occupied and used the areas.

On May 29, 1934, Cuba and the USA signed a Treaty on Relations which abrogated the 1903 treaty and the Platt Amendment, although Article II of the new treaty provided the following: "Until the two contracting parties agree to the modification or abrogation of the stipulations of the agreement in regard to the lease to the USA of lands for coaling and naval stations signed ... in 1903 ... the stipulations of that agreement with regard to the naval station of Guantánamo shall continue in effect .... So long as the USA shall not abandon the said naval station of Guantánamo or the two governments shall not agree to a modification of its present limits, the station shall continue to have the territorial area that it now has, with the limits that it has on the date of the signature of the present treaty."

Developments since 1960

Since the advent of Fidel Castro to power in 1959, the sharp deterioration in relations between Cuba and the USA has elevated the US presence at Guantánamo to a major subject of contention. At the UN General Assembly on Sept. 26, 1960, Dr Castro described the US presence on the island as "the most tragic case in the entire history of the bases now scattered over the world" and the base as being "forcibly placed in what is undeniably our territory, a good distance from the coasts of the United States, against Cuba and against the people, imposed by force and constituting a threat to and concern for our people". In a speech on July 26, 1962, the Cuban leader said that the naval base was "a dagger stuck in the heart of Cuba" and a piece of land which Cuba would not reclaim by force but would never renounce.

President Eisenhower, however, stated on Nov. 1, 1960: "Our rights in Guantánamo are based on international agreements with Cuba and include the exercise by the United States of complete jurisdiction and control over the area. These agreements with Cuba can be modified or abrogated only by agreement between the two parties .... Our government has no intention of agreeing to the modification or abrogation of these agreements and will take whatever steps may be appropriate to defend the base. The people of the United States, and all of the peoples of the world, can be assured that the United States' presence in Guantánamo and the use of the base pose no threat whatever to the sovereignty of Cuba, to the peace and security of its people, or to the independence of any of the American countries. Because of its importance to the defence of the entire hemisphere, particularly in the light of the intimate relations which now exist between the present government of Cuba and the Sino-Soviet bloc, it is essential that our position in Guantánamo be clearly understood."

The US government broke off relations with Cuba on Jan. 3, 1961, after Cuba demanded a substantial reduction in the number of US personnel at the US embassy in Havana. Other major crises erupted (i) in April 1961, when a small force of anti-Castro exiles financed by the US Central Intelligence Agency (CIA) landed in the Bay of Pigs in an abortive attempt to overthrow the regime; and (ii) in October 1962, when the presence of Soviet missile bases was discovered in Cuba. Dr Castro in February 1961 said that relations between the USA and

Cuba could only be normalized if a number of conditions were met by the former, one of these being the withdrawal of the USA from the Guantánamo base.

Cuba has based its demand for the withdrawal of the USA from Guantánamo not only on historical considerations but also on UN General Assembly resolutions, notably (i) Resolution 2105/XX of Dec. 20, 1965, which calls on colonial powers to dismantle military bases in the colonial territories and to refrain from setting up new ones, and (ii) Resolution 2344/XXII of Dec. 19, 1967, which calls on the UN Disarmament Committee to renew its study of the means of eliminating foreign military bases in the Asian, African and Latin American countries in line with Resolution 2105/XX. The Cuban position has also been supported in resolutions approved at conferences of the Non-Aligned Movement.

In 1976 Cuba adopted by referendum a new constitution, Article X of which states: "The Republic of Cuba rejects and considers illegal and null and void all treaties, pacts and concessions which were signed in conditions of inequality or which disregard or diminish its sovereignty over any part of the national territory."

JB

Ecuador-Peru

For over 150 years a large area of the Amazon Basin in what is now the north Peruvian department of Loreto has been claimed by Ecuador. The dispute over the area evolved after various territorial reorganizations under Spanish colonial rule left Ecuador, on its independence, without access to either the Amazon river or the region's other major waterway, the Marañon, and thus without direct access to the Atlantic. After engaging in hostilities over the issue in 1941, the two sides signed an internationally agreed protocol in Rio de Janeiro the following year under which the whole of the disputed territory was allocated to Peru. This protocol was unilaterally declared null and void in 1960 by the Ecuadorean government of the day, and since then successive governments have reaffirmed Ecuador's rights over the Amazon Basin, while official Ecuadorean maps show the territory as being within Ecuador's frontiers. Peru, however, has regarded the border problem as being regulated by the Rio Protocol and is not prepared to consider sacrificing more territory after losing large areas to Chile and Brazil in the 19th century. In 1981 the dispute flared up again with a five-day war between the two countries, and has remained unresolved since then.

The area currently in dispute covers 125,000 square miles (325,000 sq km) and includes the Amazon and Marañon rivers. It contains Iquitos, a fast-developing city on the west bank of the Amazon, and also Peru's main inland oil-producing region (in territory between the Tigre and the Corrientes rivers in the north).

Peru has an area of 496,224 square miles (1,285,000 sq km) and a population of 20,000,000 people; its armed forces are among the strongest and best-equipped in Latin America (numbering some 100,000 men) and the country produces about 10,000,000 tonnes of oil annually. Ecuador has an area of 270,000 square miles (700,000 sq km), a population of 9,500,000 and armed forces numbering only about 40,000 men. Nearly half its territory falls within the area of application of the Amazon Co-operation Treaty (on the harmonious development of the Amazon Basin)—the largest proportion in relation to surface area of any of the treaty's signatories, which also include Brazil and Peru; however, its route to the Atlantic is of necessity via Pacific ports and the Panama Canal. Ecuador claims to have discovered the Amazon, maintaining that the expedition led by Francisco de Orellano set out from Quito in 1542 (although this is also disputed by Peru). Ecuador produces about 14,000,000 tonnes of oil annually and is a member of the Organization of the Petroleum Exporting Countries (OPEC).

History of the Dispute

The main area of contention between Ecuador and Peru was the province of Maynas, although parts of Tumbes and Jaén provinces were also at issue. Under Spanish rule Maynas was part of the area ruled as the Audiencia of Quito by the Viceroyalty of Peru, whose southern border (according to a Spanish Royal Decree of 1740) ran along the Marañon and Amazon from Tumbes, on the Pacific coast, to the borders of the Portuguese territories (Brazil). The Audiencia of Quito was in 1739 attached as an integral territory to the Viceroyalty of Nueva Granada (also known as Sante Fé de Bogotà).

In further administrative changes under a Spanish Royal Decree of 1802, the government and commandancy-general of Maynas were separated from Nueva Granada and reattached to the Viceroyalty of Peru, together with the government of Quijos province. In the 1802 decree (wherein Peru also incorporated Tumbes, Jaén, and the Maynas commandancy-general into its own constitution), the frontiers of the commandancy-general of Maynas were described as extending along the Marañon to the frontiers of the Portuguese colonies and also along all the other rivers which entered the Marañon on its northern and southern banks, and other smaller streams, up to where those rivers ceased to be navigable because of falls or insurmountable rapids.

Peru thus contended that at the time of its own independence in 1821 Maynas was administered by the Viceroyalty of Peru, and it points out that Ecuador did not exist as such at the time (being until 1830 part of the Gran Colombia federation into which the

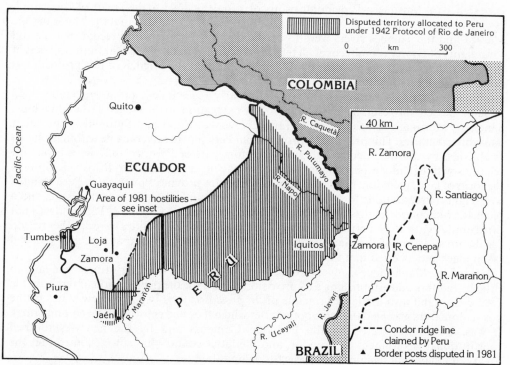

Map 47   Ecuador's territorial claim against Peru, with inset showing area of 1981 hostilities.

Viceroyalty of Nueva Granada was converted on its liberation from the Spanish). Ecuador, on the other hand, maintained that the 1802 decree separated only certain military and ecclesiastical aspects of Maynas province from the administration of Nueva Granada, and that Maynas was thus still part of the Viceroyalty of Nueva Granada at that time, and not under Peruvian jurisdiction. Ecuador has since based its claim to the disputed area largely on (i) an 1829 peace and border treaty, signed between Peru and Gran Colombia, and (ii) an 1830 protocol to this treaty, whose existence is disputed by Peru.

The 1829 Treaty of Guayaquil was concluded in an effort to settle the territorial conflict which had erupted into a crisis in 1828 after Peru reasserted a claim to Jaén province and also to the whole of Maynas by convening elections there in 1826. Gran Colombia opposed the Peruvian claim to Jaén at this stage on the grounds that Jaén had requested to be reincorporated into the Gran Colombia federation in 1824 despite having earlier become independent; as for Maynas, Peru had previously restricted itself to convening elections in the southern part of that province.

On expiry of an ultimatum to Peru to relinquish Jaén and southern Maynas, Gran Colombia declared war on Peru in July 1828, and in September of that year Peru blockaded Gran Colombia's ports. The Peruvian Navy captured Guayaquil in 1829 and the Army occupied the Colombian province of Loja, but was eventually defeated. The immediate conflict ended with a Colombian victory over Peru at Tarqui in February 1829 and a preliminary peace agreement was concluded. Following a change of government in Peru in June 1829, a truce was signed at Piura in July and talks took place, resulting in the signature of the Guayaquil Treaty on Sept. 22, 1829, which stated that both parties recognized as their territorial limits "those of the old viceroyalties". Peru regards this treaty as null and void because it was concluded with Gran Colombia and says that, even had it been valid, it would have been superseded by a later treaty of alliance and friendship, signed with Ecuador in 1832 in Lima, which stated that the existing boundaries should be recognized until a boundary convention was negotiated.

On Aug. 11, 1830—just before Ecuador emerged as a separate state—Gran Colombia and Peru signed the Mosquero-Pedemonte protocol, supplementary to the Treaty of Guayaquil, establishing guidelines for the delimitation of their borders. It stated that the Marañon, the Macará and the Tumbes rivers were to be the definitive borders and recognized the full sovereignty of Gran Colombia over all territory on the left bank of the Marañon, and that of Peru over all territory on the right bank. Peru claims that the original of this protocol has never been exhibited by Ecuador.

Efforts to negotiate a boundary treaty in the early 1840s failed, and in November 1853 Ecuador passed a law establishing its right to free navigation on rivers such as the Chinchipe, Santiago, Morona, Pastaza, Tigre, Curaray, Naucana, Napo and Putomayo, and other Amazon tributaries. This provoked a protest from Peru that the rivers came within the limits established by the 1802 decree and were therefore part of Peru. In 1857 Peru broke off relations with Ecuador after Ecuador decided to pay off certain debts to British creditors in the form of land, including parts of Quijos and Canelos provinces over which Peru claimed sovereignty. Preparations for war were made by Peru and Ecuador over this issue, and a blockade of Ecuador's ports was decreed in 1858 by President Castilla of Peru and was not lifted until August 1859. Peru subsequently claimed that these hostilities were another reason for the invalidation of the Guayaquil Treaty, but Ecuador denied that a proper war had taken place and asserted that the treaty remained in force.

In 1860 the Mapasingue Convention was signed, annulling Ecuador's transfer of land to British creditors and establishing as a provisional basis for the delimitation of territory the 1802 decree and also the legal principle of *uti possidetis juris* (whereby new states of the post-colonial era accepted the same boundaries which they had enjoyed under colonial rule). It was, however, rejected by the Peruvian Congress and by the newly-established constitutional government of Ecuador, and the latter country has since claimed that the Treaty of Guayaquil remained the basis for delimitation.

In 1887 the two sides signed the Espinosa-Bonifaz Treaty, which established that they wished to solve amicably any border questions and that any such issues should be submitted to the King of Spain for arbitration. On the basis of this treaty, therefore, arbitration began in 1904, but when Ecuador in 1910 learned the apparently adverse outcome of the findings (which were not officially published) it decided not to accept them. Negotiations recommenced in 1936 to seek a settlement of the border issue on the basis of a status quo established in advance as well as a de facto line regarding territorial positions; however, these negotiations proved fruitless and were adjourned after two years.

The 1941 War and the 1942 Rio Protocol

On July 5, 1941, despite efforts by Argentina, Brazil, and the United States to forestall a conflict, hostilities broke out between Peru and Ecuador, the immediate cause being the stationing of garrisons in disputed border areas; incidents continued sporadically until September, when Peru gained the upper hand. The mediatory nations at that point established a demilitarized zone (under the Talara Agreement of Oct. 2, 1941) and, in a memorandum of Oct. 4, called upon the two sides to withdraw their troops not less than 10 miles (16 km) behind the 1936 status quo line as a prior condition to negotiating a settlement.

The Protocol of Rio de Janeiro was concluded on Jan. 29, 1942, between Peru and Ecuador with the participation of the mediatory nations after negotiations which began on Jan. 13. It was ratified by the Congresses of both Peru and Ecuador on Feb. 26, 1942, and it established the border between the two countries as internationally recognized today.

Its main provisions were as follows:

"*Article 1.* The governments of Peru and Ecuador solemnly affirm their determined intention to maintain between the two peoples relations of peace and friendship, understanding and goodwill and to abstain each in respect of the other from any act capable of disrupting these relations.

"*Article 2.* The government of Peru will within 15 days withdraw its military forces to the line described in Article 8 of this protocol.

"*Article 3.* The United States, Argentina, Brazil and Chile will co-operate by means of military observers in order to adjust to the circumstances the evacuation and withdrawal of troops under the terms of the previous article.

"*Article 4.* The military forces of the two countries will remain in their positions until the definitive demarcation of the frontier line. Until then, Ecuador shall have civil jurisdiction only in the zones which Peru shall evacuate, which remain in the same state as was the demilitarized zone of the Act of Talara.

"*Article 5.* The negotiation of the USA, Argentina, Brazil and Chile shall continue until the frontiers between Ecuador and Peru have been definitively demarcated, and this protocol and its execution shall remain under the guarantee of [these] four countries.

"*Article 6.* Ecuador shall enjoy the same concessions for navigation on the Amazon and its northern tributaries as Brazil and Colombia, beyond those which are agreed in a treaty on commerce and navigation designed to facilitate navigation on these rivers.

"*Article 7.* Any doubt or disagreement which may arise over the execution of this protocol shall be resolved by the parties with the collaboration of the representatives of the USA, Argentina, Brazil and Chile within the shortest possible time."

Article 8 established the border line with reference to named points.

"*Article 9.* It is understood that the line described above shall be accepted by Ecuador and Peru for the establishment by technicians in that field of the frontier between the two countries. The parties shall nevertheless, in proceeding with their plan of terrain, be able to grant each other reciprocal concessions which they consider proper in order to adjust to the geographical reality. Such rectifications shall be carried out with the collaboration of representatives of the USA, Argentina, Brazil and Chile."

Considerable problems of demarcation ensued, notably in the southern sector, where the Rio Protocol specified that the border should follow the line of the watershed between the Zamora and Santiago rivers (running to the north-west and east respectively of the Condor mountains). Matters were complicated by the discovery in 1947 (by US aerial photographers) of a new river system, the Cenepa, running north-south into the Marañon between the Zamora and Santiago rivers and separated from each by a natural watershed. In the view of Ecuador, this discovery invalidated the relevant clause of the protocol, which was now shown to have referred to a non-existent single watershed, and entitled Ecuador to additional territory to the south and east of the line of the Condor ridge which Peru regarded as the proper boundary. This view was strongly asserted by President Galo Plaza Lasso in a message to the Ecuadorian Congress in August 1951, when he said that his government could only accept a border in this sector which recognized "the alienable Amazonian right of Ecuador" and allocated it "a proper and sovereign right to the Marañon river".

Demarcation of the frontier then stopped, leaving a 50-mile (80-km) stretch in the southern sector uncharted, and with the line adopted by Peru strongly disputed by Ecuador. Ecuadorian proposals that a special mixed commission should study the geography of the area were rejected by Peru, as was a mediation offer made at Ecuador's request by the four guarantor states. In consequence, in 1960 President José Velasco Ibarra of Ecuador declared the entire Rio Protocol null and void, arguing that acquisition of territorial rights by force was proscribed under the 1933 Montevideo Convention on the Rights and Duties of States and that Ecuador had been coerced into signing the protocol against its wishes. Nevertheless, on Dec. 7, 1960, Ecuador's repudiation of the protocol was declared invalid by the four guarantor powers.

The 1981 Hostilities and Subsequent Developments

Over the two decades following Ecuador's repudiation of the Rio Protocol with Peru, co-operative relations between the two countries developed within the framework of various multilateral regional agreements, notably the Andean Pact (created in 1969) and the Amazon Co-operation Treaty (signed in 1978). Nevertheless, Ecuador continued to assert its claim to territorial rights in the Amazon Basin, in which connexion its then Foreign Minister, Alfredo Pareja Diezcanseco, stated on May 21, 1980, that "a territorial conflict does exist between Ecuador and Peru", which Ecuador wished to resolve in accordance with international law. On that occasion, President-elect Fernando Belaúnde Terry of Peru responded that he rejected "the thesis that Peru has territorial conflicts with Ecuador"; however, the new Ecuadorian Foreign Minister, Alfonso Barrera, stressed on Oct. 28 of that year his country's need to obtain "an outlet to the Atlantic via the Amazon", particularly in view of the growing congestion in the Panama Canal.

Early the following year, the situation deteriorated sharply in the Condor mountains sector when on Jan. 23, 1981, a Peruvian military helicopter was said by Ecuador to have violated its airspace and to have fired on one of its border posts, and by Peru to have been fired on by Ecuadorian soldiers while on a routine flight. Five days later, on Jan. 28, fighting erupted on the ground as Peruvian forces engaged Ecuadorian troops who had apparently occupied three military posts—Paquisha, Mayayco and Machinaza—several kilometres east of the Condor ridge line which Peru regarded as the international frontier in this sector. The border between the two countries was immediately closed, both sides declared states of emergency and large numbers of troops were mobilized by both sides. After five days of hostilities, a ceasefire came into force on Feb. 2, by when Peru claimed to have driven the Ecuadorian forces out of the three border posts.

The ceasefire was established in response to a call by representatives of the four guarantors of the Rio Protocol (the United States, Argentina, Brazil and Chile), meeting in Brasília on Feb. 1, 1981, when it was also agreed in consultation with Ecuador and Peru that a military commission of the four countries would supervise the disrupted area. A further serious incident occurred on Feb. 20, when a Peruvian helicopter was shot down in the border area, causing Peru's President to issue a warning on Feb. 22 that "any new infiltration" by Ecuador would be "regarded as an act of war". However, the four guarantor countries announced on Feb. 26 that Ecuador and Peru had agreed to pull their troops 15 kilometres back on either side of the disputed border and to enter into discussions on "a formula for assuring harmony and opening the way to broader agreements". These talks began immediately and resulted in a firm agreement on March 5 on the withdrawal of forces; at the same time, the two sides undertook to maintain peaceful relations and also requested the guarantor countries to propose a solution to their underlying dispute.

No such solution was found in the succeeding years, however, and tensions have surfaced periodically between the two countries, notably in January 1984 when one Ecuadorian soldier was killed in a clash with Peruvian border guards at a frontier post on the Corrientes river about 400 kilometres south-east of Quito. The official Peruvian position as reiterated on May 11, 1985, by Prime Minister Sandro Mariategui, is that no territorial dispute exists between the two countries and that the Ecuador-Peru border is a "natural geographical boundary . . . legally established in the Rio de Janeiro Protocol". For its part, Ecuador has consistently refused to abandon its demand for a revision of the 1942 agreement, and especially for "a fair and honourable" solution to the particular problem of what it regards as the undemarcated border in the Condor mountains sector.

JB/AJD

El Salvador-Honduras

A treaty demarcating two-thirds of the 343-kilometre common frontier between El Salvador and Honduras was signed in 1980 as a major step towards ending a border dispute dating back to the 19th century, when both countries attained independence as separate nations. As well as terminating the effective state of war which had existed between them since they engaged in brief hostilities in July 1969, the treaty contained an undertaking to reach agreement within five years on the remaining disputed stretch of border including the border pockets (*bolsones territoriales*) which formed part of a demilitarized zone set up in 1970. In the absence of such an agreement, however, the two sides agreed in May 1986 to submit outstanding issues to the judgment of the International Court of Justice. (For a map of the region, see page 399.)

Efforts to resolve Border Issue in 19th Century

Both El Salvador and Honduras belonged to a federation of Central American states until this was dissolved in 1838. According to Honduras's first political constitution, decreed on Dec. 11, 1825, the country's territorial area corresponded to that covered under Spanish rule by the "Bishopric of Honduras", while El Salvador's first two constitutions (1824 and 1841) specified that its own territorial area corresponded to certain Spanish administrative areas and established its frontiers broadly as the River Paz (in the west), the inlet of Conchagua (in the east), the province of Chiquimula (in the north) and the Pacific Ocean to the south.

A number of local border disputes had already emerged by 1884, and on April 10 of that year the two sides signed a border convention in San Miguel (El Salvador). In the light of the data available to them on territorial claims, this convention fixed land and sea limits from the Gulf of Fonseca (in the Pacific) to the Guatemalan frontier. However, Honduras regarded the convention as prejudicing the rights of Hondurans because it had not taken into account the claims of certain localities on the frontier; thus the Honduran Congress on Feb. 7, 1885, abrogated the convention—although Honduras agreed the following month to take all the necessary measures to arrive at a permanent solution to the border problem.

To this end, representatives of the two governments met on Sept. 28, 1886, in Tegucigalpa (Honduras) and decided to set up commissions to determine the delimitation of the border by mutual agreement, it being agreed (i) that both governments would respect the outcome; (ii) that if no agreement was reached the dispute would be submitted to a friendly nation for arbitration; and (iii) that, while the new border line was being drawn, the 1884 line, regarded as the status quo, would be respected.

The two commissions set to work in late 1888 but could only reach agreement on the section of the frontier "constituted by the Goascorán river, from its mouth in La Unión bay (Gulf of Fonseca) upriver to where it flows into the Guajiniquil river", this section being declared "undisputed and indisputable". The commissions were then dissolved without further agreement being reached, and although the two governments agreed in San José de Costa Rica on Jan. 3, 1889, to put the dispute to the President of Costa Rica for arbitration, no such step was taken.

On Jan. 19, 1895, the Bonilla-Velasco border convention was signed in San Salvador, under the terms of which representatives of the two countries met on Nov. 13, 1897, to work out the delimitation of the frontier between Opatoro and Santa Ana (Honduras) and Lislique and Poloros (El Salvador). The treaty bore little fruit, however, since it was ratified by neither country, and there were few further developments during the period of the treaty's subsequent extension up to 1916. Moreover, no significant progress towards solving the border issue was made over the next 50 years.

The 1969 Football War and its Aftermath

Although the immediate cause of the 1969 war was football violence following World Cup qualifying matches between the two countries' national teams, the major underlying cause was a deep-rooted conflict over Salvadorean immigration to and settlement in Honduras. From the 1920s onwards thousands of Salvadoreans left their densely-populated country and took over pieces of land in Honduras for cultivation; although a bilateral migration agreement was signed in 1965 giving them the opportunity to regularize their position in Honduras, the latter country estimated that less than 1 per cent of the migrants took advantage of this facility.

In January 1969 the Honduran government applied an agrarian reform which meant that thousands of Salvadoreans were expelled from the land on which they had lived. With 300,000 facing deportation, and with the homeward exodus of Salvadoreans gathering force and placing increasing strains on the Salvadorean economy, the latter country's military government in June 1969 broke off diplomatic relations with Honduras following the football incidents, and full-scale fighting began on July 14 after a series of border incidents in the preceding two weeks. The Salvadorean armed forces occupied an area of Honduran territory and bombarded towns and border areas before hostilities ceased on July 18 under a truce negotiated by the Organization of American States (OAS).

The OAS on Oct. 27, 1969, passed seven resolutions regarding bilateral relations between El Salvador and Honduras, covering (i) peace and treaties, (ii) free transit, (iii) diplomatic and consular relations, (iv) border questions, (v) the Central American Common Market, (vi) claims and differences and (vii) human and family rights. These were to form the basis of the general peace treaty signed in October 1980. In the meantime, however, a bilateral working group with a Uruguayan moderator was set up to work towards solving their differences, and met throughout 1970 and 1971.

On June 4, 1970, a "Plan for the Establishment of a Zone of Security with a View to Pacification" was signed on San José de Costa Rica, creating a three-kilometre-wide demilitarized zone on each side of the traditional border, and measures were adopted to put this into effect not only on land but also at sea and in the airspace above the demilitarized zone. OAS military observers were designated to supervise the execution of the plan, and Guatemala, Nicaragua and Costa Rica became its guarantors. However, although the plan was designed to allow the inhabitants of both countries to return to the frontier area in safety, its content was stated to have no bearing on any border claim.

Contacts between representatives of the two countries continued over the next few years and work progressed towards the elaboration of a treaty on the basis of the seven OAS resolutions. In July 1976 there were fresh military incidents on the border which led to meetings between the Foreign Ministers of the guarantor nations of the San José plan, and subsequently to the signature on Aug. 9, 1976, of the Act and Protocol of Managua, which placed OAS military observers on the frontier itself. The protocol specified the areas where incidents had frequently occurred as Dolores, Sabanetas, Sazalapa and Las Pilas (in Honduras) and Sazalapa and Monteca (in El Salvador).

The 1980 Lima Peace Treaty

After four years of negotiation under the mediation of Dr José Luis Bustamante y Rivero (a former President of Peru and also of the International Court of Justice in The Hague), a general peace treaty was signed in Lima (Peru) on Oct. 30, 1980, by the Salvadorean and Honduran Foreign Ministers, respectively Fidel Chávez Mena and Col. César Elvir Sierra. Instruments of ratification were subsequently exchanged on Dec. 10, 1980, at a ceremony in Tegucigalpa.

Section IV of the treaty, covering border questions, described the delimitation of the 225 kilometres of border over which there was no controversy (Article 16) and stated that the border was "invariable in perpetuity". The demarcation of this section of the border, the delimitation of that in the disputed areas and the determination of the juridical situation with regard to islands and maritime areas were referred to a mixed border commission set up on May 1, 1980, which was to complete its task within five years (Articles 18-19).

To delimit the border in the disputed areas (among which were parts of the Chalatenango and La Unión provinces of El Salvador and the Goascorán river delta), the mixed commission was authorized to use as a basis documents issued by the Spanish Crown or by any other Spanish secular or ecclesiastical authority during the colonial epoch which dealt with jurisdictional areas or territorial limits; other evidence would be taken into account of a legal, historical or human nature, or of a kind recognized under international law (Article 26). Each new delimitation required the approval of both governments in the form of additional protocols to the treaty (Article 27), and if there was a disagreement within the border commission itself the case would be referred to both governments for a pronouncement to be made within 60 days (Article 28). It was further established that if no agreement was reached on the areas in dispute within the five years laid down, the case would be submitted to the International Court of Justice (Article 31).

Until the frontier had been fully delimited, the two parties undertook not to alter the status quo which existed in the disputed areas prior to July 14, 1969, and to re-establish the status quo in so far as it had been modified, in order to guarantee peace in the areas in question (Article 37). During the five-year period of work of the border commission neither side could unilaterally have recourse to other peaceful means of solving the conflict or place it before international bodies (Article 38), with the proviso that if both sides agreed it could be submitted to the International Court of Justice within the five years (Article 39).

The other major provisions of the treaty were that both sides agreed to maintain "firm and lasting peace, solid fraternity and permanent constructive co-operation" (Article 2); that they would allow free transit across their territory of each other's goods and nationals (Articles 7-9); that they would restore diplomatic relations fully without further formalities (Articles 10-14); that they would contribute to the restructuring of the Central American Common Market (Articles 40-41); that they would not claim compensation for damages incurred in or just before July 1969 (Article 42); and that they would respect the rights of each other's nationals and allow them to reside freely in their countries (Articles 44-45).

Progress of Relations in the 1980s—Submission of Border Dispute to International Court of Justice

The border between El Salvador and Honduras was reopened on Dec. 11, 1980, and thereafter relations between the two countries improved as Honduras gave increasing support to the Salvadorean government in its struggle against left-wing insurgents and both countries backed US-sponsored actions against the left-wing Sandinista regime in Nicaragua. Talks on the demarcation of the disputed border areas were resumed by a joint border commission on July 20, 1982, and on Aug. 23 of that year an agreement was signed providing for the restoration of trade links from Sept. 1 in accordance with Article 41 of the 1980 Lima treaty. It was stated that both countries were committed to the policy objectives of the new Central American Democratic Community (CDC) established in January 1982 (and also including Costa Rica).

Nevertheless, underlying suspicions arising from the border dispute were apparent when the Honduran Army opposed a US plan, announced in May 1983, for a training base for Salvadorean soldiers to be established at Puerta Castilla (on the northern Honduran coast). Even after a contingent of 120 US advisers arrived at Puerta Castilla in mid-June 1983, the Honduran government continued to insist that the project was being negotiated to ensure that the Honduran military had full control of the command and operation of the base. Eventually, on Sept. 30, 1984, the Honduran authorities announced the suspension of training at the base, relating this decision to the lack of substantive progress on the border issue.

Notwithstanding regular meetings of the joint border commission (and talks between the Salvadorean Presidents in October 1984 and July 1985), it was apparent by the end of the five-year period specified in the 1980 agreement that most key issues remained to be resolved. Accordingly, Presidents Duarte of El Salvador and Azcona of Honduras signed an agreement on May 24, 1986 (during a Central American summit meeting in Guatemala), providing for the submission of the dispute to the International Court of Justice (ICJ). This agreement entered into force on Oct. 1, 1986, and on Dec. 11 of that year the two governments formally notified the ICJ of their decision.

During talks in El Salvador on July 30-31, 1986, the Salvadorean and Honduran Presidents undertook to implement fully the ICJ's eventual ruling. They also agreed on the advisability of creating a special commission to study and propose solutions to the human, civil and economic problems which might arise once the border dispute had been resolved.

JB/AJD

France-Suriname

Suriname (until 1975 a Dutch overseas dependency) and the French overseas department of Guiana are currently in dispute over the sovereignty of a triangular area of land totalling some 5,000 square kilometres and lying between two upper tributaries of the Maroni river. The dispute bears some resemblance to that between Suriname and Guyana [see pages 431-34] in that it centres on uncertainties over the course of a river which both countries agree in principle to be their joint boundary, but which is still in its upper reaches somewhat inaccessible and under-developed in terms of natural resources. The area in question is thickly forested, mountainous and has many fast-flowing rivers which originate in the Tumac-Humac range forming the border with Brazil in the south. At present the economic importance of the area in dispute is uncertain, though explorations for bauxite and for gold are believed to have been undertaken by the French. Early disputes over the course of the lower reaches of the river have been settled at various times, but the outstanding disagreement over its upper course, and hence over the sovereignty of the land concerned, seems unlikely to be settled in the near future despite the renewal of efforts to this end during the 1970s. Indeed, the intensification of domestic security problems in Suriname in the mid-1980s has increased its government's suspicions that its opponents are receiving support from within French Guiana.

Historical Background to the Dispute

France and the Netherlands, as colonial powers controlling the area, first reached an agreement in 1688 specifying that the Maroni river should form the boundary between their respective colonies. At this stage, however, neither country attached great importance to the largely uncharted interior of the territory, preferring to concentrate on the more easily accessible lands in the coastal regions and on the Maroni estuary, which is navigable for a distance of some 25 miles (40 km). The lower 100 miles (160 km) of the Maroni have since then always been agreed to form the boundary between the two colonies; differences arose, however, in the early 19th century as to whether the boundary further inland should follow the Tapanahoni river (originating in the south-west in what is now Suriname) or the Awa (or

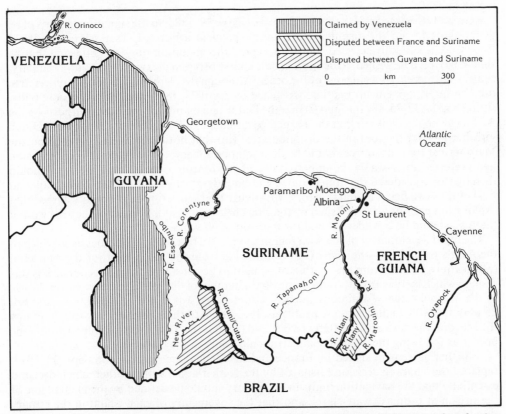

Map 48 Suriname's territorial disputes with France (French Guiana) and Guyana, also showing Venezuela's claim to the Essequibo region of Guyana.

429

Lawa) river (flowing from the south), these two rivers being of comparable length (although the Awa is wider at the confluence).

Dutch colonists had by this time begun the exploration and settlement of the area between the Tapanahoni and the Awa, although there was also a limited French presence in the area. The boundary question remained vague for many years, but acquired a new currency in 1815 when France and Portugal concluded a basic agreement on a dispute over the sovereignty of part of northern Brazil (colonized at that time by Portugal but claimed by France). In establishing the French Guiana/Brazilian border under Article 107 of the 1815 Congress of Vienna settlement, Portugal allowed French Guiana all of the territory to the west of the Oyapock river, which still forms the department's south-eastern border with Brazil. It was agreed at the Congress of Vienna that Article 107 was to be implemented by a subsequent convention; this convention, signed by France and Portugal on Aug. 28, 1817, also defined French Guiana's western boundary as following the Maroni and Tapanahoni rivers, but this arrangement was reached without the consultation of the Netherlands, which protested against the decision.

On Nov. 9, 1836, the colonial governors of Cayenne and Suriname reached a formal agreement which declared that the western boundary of French Guiana was to be the right bank of the Maroni river from its source. The failure of this agreement to define the source as either the Tapanahoni or the Awa gave it little credibility, however, and in 1849 the Dutch government declared that it had not settled the boundary question. The governors of the two colonies therefore set up a mixed commission in 1861 to decide on the main course of the river, but it reported that it had been unable to decide on a main course and that the name Maroni could not legitimately be applied to any part of the river above the confluence of the Tapanahoni and the Awa. Discussions on the matter continued thereafter but eventually lapsed in 1876.

Renewed efforts to resolve the dispute led on Nov. 29, 1888, to the signature in Paris of an undertaking to put the dispute before an independent arbitrator. Tsar Alexander III of Russia was eventually selected, but he accepted the invitation only on condition that he should be free, if he wished, to define a middle course between the two rivers as the boundary, rather than merely choosing one or the other. Although the Netherlands initially objected to this condition, agreement was finally reached on April 28, 1890, and the arbitration body, sitting on May 13-25, 1891, found (i) that the Dutch had maintained military outposts on the Awa since about 1700; (ii) that the French government had on occasions recognized Dutch jurisdiction over negroes in the disputed area; (iii) that both parties had agreed that the Maroni river from its source should be their joint boundary; (iv) that the 1861 commission had preferred the Awa as the upper course of the Maroni; and (v) that the Awa should therefore be considered the upper course and boundary between the two colonies, all land west of the Awa being Dutch territory. In August 1891 a meeting of governors agreed that exploration permits already issued by the French government in respect of the area west of the Awa should be considered valid for a period of 40 years.

The rapid development of the Awa region soon led to further uncertainties as to which of the Awa's tributaries—the Itany (Litani), flowing from the south-west, or the Marouini (Marowijni), flowing from the south-east—ought to be considered its main course: it is this dispute which is still current. At the same time a number of disagreements arose over the use of the Maroni estuary, and consequently a conference was called at the Hague on April 25-May 13, 1905, to discuss these problems. It reported (i) that the boundary should follow the Maroni, the Awa and the Itany rivers, and (ii) that the Thalweg principle (defining the border as following the deepest channel) should apply to the estuary.

A further agreement signed by France and the Netherlands in Paris on Sept. 30, 1915, replaced the Thalweg decision (disputed by the Netherlands) with another which declared essentially that the navigation limits in the estuary should be defined by the median line of the stream at ordinary water level, and that the sovereignty of each island in the estuary should be determined according to whether the greater part of its area lay on the Suriname or the French Guiana side. It was also agreed that all minerals obtained from the river should be shared equally between the two colonies and that any important project capable of changing the course of the stream or of affecting shipping should be subject to the approval of both sides.

Developments since Independence of Suriname

Despite the 1905 recommendations, however, the area between the Marouini and the Itany continued to be claimed by the Netherlands, and discussions since then have reached no positive results on the issue. Suriname took over the claim to the disputed territory when it achieved its independence from the Netherlands in 1975, and negotiations conducted in November 1975 and February 1977 resulted in the formulation of a treaty between France and Suriname whereby the latter would recognize French sovereignty over most of the area still in dispute in return for French development aid totalling some 500,000,000 francs for the joint development of any resources in the area. The treaty was initialled on Aug. 15, 1977, but despite further meetings in August 1978 it has not been signed or ratified, and there have been no indications of any intention on the part of Suriname to proceed with it.

The relationship between the two countries has deteriorated sharply since 1980, as a consequence of the military coup in Suriname which unseated the Prime Minister Henck Arron and brought the relatively unstable administration of Col. Desi Bouterse to power. A series of often bloody political upheavals in 1981-85 forced many of the regime's political opponents into exile across the border in French Guiana, from where rebel forces, led after mid-1986 by former minister Ronnie Brunswijk, made increasingly successful raids into the interior of Suriname. By November 1986 it was reported that Brunswijk's forces, aided by the dispossessed bush negroes of Suriname, had gained control of practically all the eastern half of the country (excluding the military bases of Moengo and Albina), and that they also held much of Brokopondo district. Suriname has repeatedly claimed that the insurgents are receiving complicit support from the French Guiana authorities.

In December 1986 Suriname also alleged that French troops were massing along the Maroni in readiness for an imminent invasion of Suriname, to which France responded that its troops were engaged in "strictly humanitarian" assistance to Surinamese refugees displaced by the fighting in the interior. The two countries have, however, been able to agree on the reopening of the Surinamese consulate in French Guiana, and on the inauguration of a joint border patrol on the Maroni, aimed at preventing the massive trade in smuggled goods into Suriname.

MW

Guyana-Suriname

Relations between Guyana (formerly British Guiana) and Suriname (formerly Dutch Guiana) have been periodically strained by a still unresolved dispute dating from the late 19th century over the sovereignty of a triangular area of land lying within the territory currently administered by Guyana. The area in dispute, comprising some 6,000 square miles (15,000 sq km), is situated between two tributaries of the Corentyne river and is bordered on the third and southern side by the watershed which marks the boundary shared by Guyana and Suriname with Brazil. Numerous attempts to reach a peaceful bilateral settlement of the issue have taken place since 1966, but a 1970 agreement on the mutual demilitarization of the

431

disputed land does not appear to have been implemented. (For a map illustrating this dispute, see page 429.)

The origins of the dispute lay largely in the extreme inaccessibility of the terrain in the foothills of the Guiana Highlands, and in consequent confusion over the true course of certain tributaries of the Corentyne river. Whereas a boundary agreement signed between two Dutch colonial governors in 1800 had referred only to the main course of the Corentyne, subsequent investigations established in 1871 that its longest course was not, as hitherto believed, along the Cutari and Curuni rivers running down from central southern Suriname, but rather along the so-called New river, which rises in Guyana well to the west of the Cutari/Curuni, joining the lower reaches of the Corentyne between the third and fourth parallels. Guyana adheres to the original (i.e. Cutari/Curuni) interpretation of the main course, while Suriname maintains that the New river (which it has unilaterally designated the Upper Corentyne) represents its true western boundary, and claims the New River Triangle as its sovereign territory.

At present the disputed area has little economic importance, since no significant mineral deposits have yet been located (bauxite mining being the major source of export revenue for both countries); however, the many freely flowing rivers in the area offer considerable scope for hydroelectric development, and balata (a form of ersatz rubber) is extracted from trees in the area below the high southern savannah.

Early Agreements and Explorations

The first recorded disputes between Suriname and Berbice (now the easternmost county of Guyana) over the ownership of land west of the Corentyne took place in the late 18th century in the form of a domestic conflict (in that both Suriname and Berbice had been Dutch possessions since the mid-17th century). The land then at issue was coastal territory largely comprising fertile cotton plantations, and the metropolitan government in Amsterdam ruled in 1794 that the territory of Berbice extended as far as the west bank of the Corentyne river.

By 1799 both Berbice and Suriname had been acquired by the British, but the Dutch governors of the two colonies (A. I. van Imbyse van Battenburg and J. F. Frederici respectively) were retained in office. The two men sought agreement on the confirmation of the west bank as the eastern boundary of Berbice, and a proclamation to this effect was published by the Governor and Councils of Berbice on Feb. 7, 1800. Guyana has since claimed that, although bilaterally agreed, the proclamation did not in itself constitute a boundary agreement; for its part Suriname has maintained that the agreement was subsequently confirmed by the 1815 Peace of Paris. Suriname also claims, contrary to Guyana's assertions, that the Peace of Paris made a definite ruling on the sovereignty of the river itself, giving the entire width of the river up to but not including the west bank, as well as all islands, to Suriname.

Meanwhile, the Dutch had regained control of both colonies in 1802, although the following year the British recaptured Berbice and in 1831 the colonies of Berbice, Essequibo and British Demerara were united to form British Guiana.

In 1841 the government commissioned Robert Schomburgk, an explorer, to investigate the boundaries of British Guiana; the Suriname authorities were invited to send a commissioner with him on his exploration of the (hitherto uncharted) Corentyne but explained that they had no authority from the Netherlands to do so. Schomburgk reported on his return that the Curuni and Cutari rivers were the main tributaries of the Corentyne, and mapped these rivers as constituting the boundary between Suriname and British Guiana; this interpretation formed the basis of all British and most Dutch maps for the remainder of the century, despite the discovery made in 1871 by a British geologist, Barrington Brown, that the New river was in fact larger than the Curuni/Cutari. Barrington

432

Brown expressed the view that the Curuni/Cutari might in fact be only a tributary, but, like Schomburgk, he mapped it as the source of the Corentyne.

Dutch claims to the New river as the source of the Corentyne arose at the time of an 1899 arbitral tribunal investigating British Guiana's border with Venezuela.[1] The British government reacted by describing the Cutari as "a definite and always easily ascertainable boundary ... [which] should not be upset by geographical discoveries made long subsequent to the original adoption of the boundary and by theories so uncertain as those which are held to determine the true source of a river".

Dutch Moves towards Settlement of the Border Dispute

The controversy over the New river subsided somewhat over the next 30 years as the Netherlands government adopted a more conciliatory attitude to the dispute. A prominent Dutch geographer, Dr Yzerman, told the Dutch Royal Geographical Society in 1924 of his opinion that the Cutari river basin was considerably larger than that of the New river, and his arguments were in 1925 and 1926 repeatedly cited by Dutch government ministers resisting Dutch claims to the disputed land on the grounds that no adequate information justifying such claims was available.

In 1926 the British government concluded a treaty with Brazil for the demarcation of the latter's common border with British Guiana. The treaty avoided exact reference to the area in dispute between Suriname and British Guiana by means of the following formulation: "The British Guiana/Brazil frontier shall lie along the watershed between the Amazon basin and the basins of the Essequibo and Corentyne rivers as far as the point of junction or convergence of the frontier of the two countries with Dutch Guiana".

The Dutch government suggested to the United Kingdom in 1929 that a treaty should be formulated establishing the Suriname/British Guiana border, and on Aug. 4, 1930, offered to settle on the definition of the border as "the left bank of the Corentyne and the Cutari up to its source, which rivers are Netherland territory". This firm Dutch claim to the whole width of the Corentyne and Curuni/Cutari contrasted with the de facto situation in that, in the absence of a universally accepted border treaty, the actual boundary had normally been treated by both countries as following the middle of the river. Nonetheless, Britain declared its willingness to negotiate on this basis, and a final draft of a border treaty was formulated; however, it was never signed because of the outbreak of World War II in 1939. More successful was the fixing in 1936 of a tri-junction point (as provided for in the treaty with Brazil mentioned above), which was established in accordance with the Netherlands' suggestion that a boundary line should be drawn from the source of the Cutari, leading over a particular named rock, and that the tri-junction point should be the intersection of such a line with the Brazilian watershed. A definitive map was drawn up and was signed by Brazil, the United Kingdom and the Netherlands.

Revival of Dutch and Surinamese Claims to the New River Triangle

After World War II the Dutch attitude hardened considerably, and in 1962 the Netherlands presented a revised draft border definition which discarded the Curuni/Cutari line and revived the claim to the New River Triangle. British Guiana was offered the sovereignty of the Corentyne and New rivers up to mid-stream, and Suriname designated the New river as the Upper Corentyne, a step currently described by Guyana as having no significance in international law. The United Kingdom rejected the Dutch proposals and Suriname, in anticipation of Guyana's achievement of independence (which finally took place in May 1966), called on the British government in April 1966 to place on record that the boundary of Suriname and Guyana was in dispute.

Representatives of Guyana and Suriname met in London in June 1966 to discuss the

---

[1]For an account of the Guyana-Venezuela territorial dispute, see pages 435-38.

dispute, but subequently presented widely varying accounts of the meeting. Suriname described it as one between "good friends and neighbours" (May 1968), but the then Guyanese Minister of State for Foreign Affairs, S. S. Ramphal QC, reported in February 1968 that there had been a "free and frank exchange of views during which Guyana asserted its rights to the New river area and sought to demonstrate how utterly indefensible was the Suriname contention that the boundary could be otherwise than on the Cutari".

The situation deteriorated markedly in December 1967, when Guyana expelled from the disputed area a group of Surinamese who were thought to be involved in surveys for a new hydroelectric dam. (Suriname later received the support of the World Bank for a hydroelectric project situated outside the disputed area but dependent on water whose origin is in dispute.) Suriname described the expulsion as an inadmissible use of force, and prolonged diplomatic exchanges followed during which Suriname was alleged to have threatened the expulsion of all 2,000 Guyanese workers from its territory. S. S. Ramphal replied on Feb. 2, 1968, that Guyana would not surrender its sovereignty over the New River Triangle, but offered to re-open negotiations with Suriname, and in 1970 new discussions took place, leading to an agreement on economic, social and cultural co-operation and on the demilitarization of the Upper Corentyne. Although a joint standing commission was established the following November to examine the issue and to enforce the demilitarization, it quickly became apparent that neither side intended to make concessions.

A serious incident developed in August 1969, when Guyana alleged that armed Surinamese workers had been driven from the New River Triangle while attempting to set up a landing strip and military camp. Suriname dismissed the report, claiming instead that Guyanese troops had landed at the Tigri aerodrome in Suriname and occupied it, adding later that Guyanese forces had illegally occupied a frontier post in the disputed area.

Suriname maintained its claim to the New River Triangle after its attainment of independence from the Netherlands in November 1975, and a series of minor incidents continued to trouble relations between the two countries despite renewed efforts to reach agreement. In September 1977 the Guyanese authorities confiscated four trawlers, one of which was part-owned by the Suriname government, alleging that they had been fishing in Guyana's exclusive 200-mile fisheries zone without payment of the appropriate fee. Suriname retaliated on Jan. 1, 1978, by withdrawing fishing licences from about 100 Guyanese who had traditionally worked the Corentyne river, and was said to have used gunboats to harass loggers on the river. Talks were opened in February 1978 in Paramaribo, the capital of Suriname, leading in mid-1978 to the settlement of the fisheries dispute and to the return of the Surinamese trawler.

Forbes Burnham, Prime Minister (later President) of Guyana, and Henck Arron, then Prime Minister of Suriname, held talks in Barbados in April 1979, during which the two countries signed a fishing agreement and agreed to reopen negotiations on the border dispute. The Arron government was subsequently overthrown on Feb. 25, 1980, by a military coup in Suriname, but the new regime continued Suriname's contacts with Guyana through a civilian government installed on March 15, 1980. Nevertheless, Suriname's growing internal security and economic problems (which it blamed Guyana for exacerbating in various ways) led to a deterioration of relations in the 1980s.

The death of Forbes Burnham in 1985 was followed by some improvement in Guyana-Suriname relations under his successor, Desmond Hoyte, who adopted a generally more pragmatic approach to current issues. However, the territorial dispute between the two countries remained unresolved in mid-1987.

MW

Guyana-Venezuela

During the 19th century Venezuela and Guyana (then British Guiana) claimed overlapping areas of territory covering about 50,000 square miles (130,000 sq km), consisting mainly of dense tropical rain forest which had discouraged early colonization and development. Despite an 1899 ruling by an international court of arbitration which awarded much of the disputed territory to British Guiana, Venezuela in the 1960s reasserted its claim to Guyana's present territory west of the Essequibo river. In 1970 Venezuela and Guyana signed a protocol declaring a 12-year moratorium on the border issue, which has nevertheless remained a source of friction between the two countries, but on its expiry in 1982 renewed border tensions became apparent. The following year the UN Secretary-General was requested to mediate by the two governments, who subsequently developed closer economic relations with the aim of creating the basis for a peaceful settlement of the territorial issue. (For a map illustrating this dispute, see page 429.)

The colony of British Guiana (incorporating former Dutch possessions) was established in 1831; it obtained internal self-government in 1961, became fully independent on May 26, 1966, and has been a co-operative republic within the Commonwealth since 1970; it has an area of 83,000 square miles (215,000 sq km) in its present boundaries. Venezuela, with a present land area of 352,000 square miles (910,000 sq km), declared itself an independent republic in 1811 after three centuries of Spanish rule and separated from the Gran Colombia federation in 1830.

Historical Background to Dispute

The British claim prior to 1899 was to the drainage basin of the Cuyuni river (in the eastern part of what is now Bolivar state, Venezuela) up to within a few miles of the Orinoco and Caroni rivers. The Venezuelan claim was, and remains, to all territory west of the Essequibo river (i.e. about two-thirds of present-day Guyana).

The major issue at the centre of the claim was the degree of control exercised by the Dutch in the area west of the Essequibo prior to British rule, which Guyana claimed was extensive. It said that the Dutch settlement of Kykoveral (established in 1616) had controlled the Essequibo; that the Dutch had controlled trade as well as the indigenous population by means of trading posts established on the upper Essequibo as well as on the Pomeroon, Barima and Cuyuni rivers; and that the provinces of Essequibo and Berbice had been recognized as Dutch possessions under the 1648 Treaty of Münster (Westphalia) which ended the Spanish-Dutch wars.

Venezuela said in support of its own claim that the Essequibo formed the most natural eastern frontier for Venezuela and pointed to the geographical unity of the land between the Orinoco and the Essequibo. It claimed that Spain had first discovered, explored and settled the British Guiana region and had exercised political control over it, and it produced evidence of the activity of Spanish missions in the area (which Guyana disputed).

The boundaries of British Guiana were established in the mid-19th century on the basis of explorations carried out by Robert Schomburgk, a surveyor and botanist engaged by the British government for that purpose. Starting in 1841, Schomburgk surveyed most of the colony's territory in the disputed and other areas, preparing as he went maps on which he marked the boundary line he had established. According to the Schomburgk line, the boundary between British Guiana and Venezuela began at the mouth of the Amacuro river, followed it to its source in the Imataca mountains, ran along the crest of the ridge to the sources of the Acarabisi creek, then to the junction of the Cuyuni river with the Venamo (Wenamu), and finally to the Venamo's source in the Mount Roraima.

Further surveys were later carried out by two British geologists, James Sawkins and Barrington Brown, from 1867 to 1871. They travelled over the present North-West district of Guyana, as well as the Demarara and Essequibo rivers, the Rupununi and Mahu savannas, and the Takatu and Kwitaro rivers. Brown alone explored the whole of the southern district, discovering the Kaieteur Fall in 1870, and the two men surveyed the Corentyne, Berbice and Mazaruni rivers together, before leaving the colony in 1871.

In the early 1880s the boundary issue was raised after the British government discovered that the Venezuelan government had made two grants of land in the Amacuro region within the Schomburgk line. The whole area granted (including part of Venezuela proper, islands at the mouth of the Orinoco, the whole of the coastal district between the Orinoco and Pomeroon, and the area between all that section and the Essequibo) was destined to be part of a new federal territory. Britain immediately took steps to reassert British claims and in 1866 declared the boundaries of British Guiana officially, also issuing a map showing the Schomburgk line.

After Britain had proclaimed the borders of its colony, it took further steps to pre-empt Venezuelan claims to the Barima and Amacuro areas, where British colonists had already settled, by proclaiming the region the North-West district of British Guiana. Gold was discovered there in the 1890s, much of the activity centring on the Barima and Arakaka.

After an incident in 1895, in which two inspectors of the British Guiana police were seized by Venezuelan police from a station on a tributary of the Cuyuni river, President Grover Cleveland of the USA (who was supporting Venezuela in its territorial claim) warned Britain that any unilateral action by Britain would constitute an infringement of the Monroe Doctrine (under which the USA regarded any attempt by European powers to reassert or extend their influence in the Americas as dangerous to its peace and security); to avert such a possibility, he demanded that the dispute should be submitted to arbitration. After a period of strained relations between Britain and the United States, Britain agreed, and an arbitration treaty was signed in 1897 with Venezuela, both countries agreeing to accept the tribunal's award as a "full, perfect and final settlement". The tribunal which was appointed consisted of two Americans, two British members and a Russian president.

The ruling of the court of arbitration, announced in 1899, awarded to British Guiana most of the territory within the Schomburgk line and to Venezuela a valuable portion at the mouth of Orinoco river. British Guiana lost some land in the North-West district and much of the Cuyuni basin, the loss amounting to about 5,000 square miles (13,000 sq km). A mixed border commission appointed by the two governments met and demarcated the border, an agreement recording the demarcation line being signed in 1905.

In the meantime, the King of Italy had been asked to arbitrate on British Guiana's border dispute with Brazil. His pronouncement in 1901 again followed the Schomburgk line, although British Guiana lost some territory.

Reopening of the Border Issue in 1951—1970 Port of Spain Protocol

In 1951 Venezuela questioned the validity of the 1899 ruling and demanded the reopening of the border issue on the basis of the posthumous publication of a memorandum by Sevro Mallet-Prevost, an American counsel, which alleged that the award had been an illegal compromise and that international political pressures had been used to obtain it. This was denied by the British government, but Venezuela raised the issue at the 17th session of the UN General Assembly in 1962, stating that it could no longer accept the arbitral award and wished to put it on record before British Guiana became independent that Venezuela did not accept that the border issue was settled. Accordingly, Britain agreed to engage in talks with Venezuela and British Guiana to re-examine all the documentary evidence on the border question, but stressed that this did not constitute an offer to engage in substantive talks about a revision of the frontier.

The talks led to the signature on Feb. 17, 1966, of the Geneva Agreement between Britain and Venezuela, establishing procedures for the settlement of their dispute. Article 1 provided for the setting up of a mixed commission to seek satisfactory solutions for the practical settlement of the controversy; Article 2 provided that within two months of the entry into force of the agreement each country would appoint two representatives to the commission; Article 3 required the commission to present six-monthly reports on progress; and Article 4 said that if full agreement had not been reached within four years from the date of the agreement, any outstanding questions would be referred to the respective governments, which would then "without delay choose one of the means of peaceful settlement provided in Article 33 of the UN Charter". Article 5 provided that no new or enlarged claim might be asserted while the agreement was in force, except within the mixed commission.

The work of the mixed commission was repeatedly interrupted by border incidents. In October 1966 Forbes Burnham, then Prime Minister of Guyana, said that about 100 Venezuelans had entered the Guyanese section of Ankoko island (on the Venamo river) and had begun mining operations; and in July 1968 Venezuela published a decree declaring territorial rights over waters nine miles beyond Guyana's three-mile limit—i.e. affecting waters to the west of the mouth of the Essequibo. This decree was immediately declared null and void by the Guyana Parliament, while the British government informed the Venezuelan ambassador in London of its concern over the decree. Finally, in February 1970 Guyana protested to Venezuela over "military attacks against Guyanese territory", whereupon Venezuela denied that its troops had opened fire near the disputed Ankoko island and said that Guyanese units had provoked the incidents.

After receiving in June 1970 the final report of the mixed commission, which had failed to settle the dispute, the governments of Britain, Guyana and Venezuela on June 18, 1970, signed the Protocol of Port of Spain. This protocol, which was supplementary to the Geneva Agreement (Article 4 of which was suspended while the protocol was in force), placed a 12-year moratorium on the territorial dispute. Article 1 stated that "so long as this protocol remains in force and subject to the following provisions, the government of Guyana and the government of Venezuela shall explore all possibilities of better understanding between them and their peoples and in particular shall undertake periodical reviews, through normal diplomatic channels, of their relations with a view to promoting their improvement and with the aim of producing a constructive advancement of the same".

Article 2 stated that as long as the protocol remained in force "no claim whatever arising out of the contention referred to Article 1 of the Geneva Agreement shall be asserted by Venezuela to territorial sovereignty in the territories of Guyana or by Guyana to territorial sovereignty in the territories of Venezuela". Article 5 stated that the protocol would remain in force for an initial period of 12 years which would be renewable thereafter for successive 12-year periods.

In October 1978 President Carlos Andrés Pérez became the first Venezuelan head of state to visit Guyana; he and Forbes Burnham afterwards indicated only that they had established "an intelligent understanding on the border dispute". However, after an official visit to Venezuela early in April 1981 Forbes Burnham (who had been installed as the first executive President of Guyana in January 1981) said that his country would "not cede an inch" of the Essequibo region to Venezuela, whereas President Luis Herrera Campins of Venezuela reiterated his country's claim to the region and denied reports of a proposed extension of the 12-year moratorium under the Protocol of Port of Spain, due to expire in June 1982.

On June 2, 1981, the Venezuelan President disclosed that he had told President Burnham that the Venezuelan government was committed to "keeping alive the historic claim to the Essequibo territory"; that there was, for the time being, no possibility of continuing to implement the Port of Spain Protocol; and that Venezuela had "to continue to study the Geneva Agreement [of 1966] for a way to reach a satisfactory solution which would permit a practical settlement of the issue". He claimed that the Geneva Agreement was not only "the law of the Republic" (of Venezuela) but had also been signed by the governments of Great Britain, Guyana and Venezuela, who were "committed to comply with it". Venezuela notified Britain on Dec. 11, 1981, that it would not extend the Port of Spain moratorium when it expired.

In January 1981 the government of Cuba officially expressed its support for Guyana's territorial integrity. This was strongly resented in Venezuela, whereupon the Cuban Communist Party's organ *Granma* on May 9, 1981, denounced what it called the "anti-Cuban manoeuvres of Luis Herrera Campin's government in connexion with the border dispute between Venezuela and Guyana.

Continuation of Dispute in the 1980s—1987 Hoyte-Lusinchi Agreement on Closer Co-operation

Tensions over the Essequibo dispute increased over an alleged border incursion by Venezuelan soldiers on May 10, 1982, following which Guyana lodged a formal protest with the UN Security Council. Two more protests were made in September 1982, when Guyana claimed that on Sept. 3 a Venezuelan helicopter carrying military personnel had tried to land at an airstrip 70 kilometres inside the Guyanese border, and that on Sept. 5 Venezuelan troops had tried to enter Guyanese territory at Eteringbang on the western bank of the Essequibo river. The following month Guyana appeared to be preparing for a possible armed conflict with Venezuela, by signing a substantial arms supply agreement with Brazil and agreeing that some Guyanese troops should receive military training in Brazil.

Against this background, the Guyanese Foreign Minister, Rashleigh Jackson, proposed to the UN General Assembly on Oct. 12, 1982, that either the Assembly or the International Court of Justice should be asked to select a procedure for resolving the dispute, to which his Venezuelan counterpart, José Alberto Zambrano Velazco, responded with a counter-proposal that the UN Secretary-General should be asked to act as a mediator. The Venezuelan proposal was eventually accepted by Guyana on March 28, 1983, but no immediate progress was made towards an accomodation.

Following the accession to the Venezuelan presidency of Dr Jaime Lusinchi in February 1984, Venezuela adopted a more conciliatory approach to the Essequibo dispute. A new Venezuelan Foreign Minister, Dr Isidro Morales Paúl, visited Guyana on Feb. 6-9, 1985, and agreed with Rashleigh Jackson that a "new spirit of friendship and co-operation" now infused relations between the two countries, and also that the UN Secretary-General should be invited to send a special envoy to both capitals to mediate. This special envoy, Diego Cordóvez, duly visited Caracas and Georgetown in March 1985 and announced afterwards that the groundwork for resolving the dispute had been laid.

Two years later, President Desmond Hoyte of Guyana paid a four-day visit to Caracas on March 24-27, 1987, during which he agreed with President Lusinchi that their respective governments would continue bilateral contacts in order "to assist the work of the UN Secretary-General" in seeking a solution to the Essequibo dispute. Various economic and other co-operation agreements were concluded during the visit, these being described as potentially creating the climate for an eventual resolution of the dispute. Nevertheless, President Hoyte warned that "no-one should feel that we will, by sleight of hand, settle in a few days a problem that is rooted in the remote colonial past".

JB/AJD

Haiti-United States (Navassa Island)

A longstanding dispute exists between Haiti and the United States over the sovereignty of Navassa Island, a small uninhabited outcrop of rock situated in the Jamaica Channel about 32 miles (50 km) west of Haiti. The US claim to the island under a 19th-century Guano Act has been periodically contested by Haiti, although the issue has never been formally submitted to arbitration. Dormant for many years, the dispute resurfaced in mid-1981 when the island was symbolically (and briefly) "occupied" by a group of Haitian nationals with official backing. (For the location of Navassa Island, see map on page 417.)

Navassa Island, with an area of about two square miles (5 sq km), is claimed by the United States under the "Guano Island C Act" of the 1860s, one of a series proclaiming sovereignty over uninhabited islands in the Caribbean and Pacific with a view to exploiting their deposits of guano (seabird droppings), a valuable source of nitrogen fertilizer. During World War II the United States built a lighthouse on the island, while in the 1950s Haiti built a church there for use by passing fishermen (although the island is difficult to land on by boat).

On July 18, 1981, a group of six Haitian radio hams (i.e. amateur enthusiasts) landed on Navassa by helicopter with the intention of transmitting from the island under its rarely-used call prefix (as had been achieved two years previously by a group of US hams). Although the permission of the US Coastguard was normally required to land on the island, the Haitian hams declined to seek such approval on the grounds that Navassa belonged to Haiti, depicting their action as a symbolic occupation of the island. Official government approval of the landing was indicated by the fact that the then President of Haiti, Jean-Claude Duvalier, made three helicopters available to the group, who were accompanied by a camera crew from the Haitian national television station. At the same time the Haitian Communications Authority allocated a Haitian radio call prefix to the island, hitherto identified by an American prefix.

On landing on the island, the Haitian party was greeted by a detachment of six US Marines, who took down the names and addresses of the hams before returning by helicopter to a nearby US Navy vessel. The camera crew then recorded a ceremonial raising of the Haitian flag on the island.

AJD

Antarctica

The question of territorial claims in the Antarctic south of 60°S latitude was frozen for 30 years—until 1991—under a treaty which was signed by 12 countries in 1959 and which entered into force in 1961. Seven of the signatories have claims to territory in the Antarctic (Argentina, Australia, Chile, France, New Zealand, Norway and the United Kingdom) and the claims of three of these—Argentina, Britain and Chile—overlap.

The Antarctic mainland covers 5,350,000 square miles (13,900,000 sq km) and its ice mass represents about three-quarters of the world's store of fresh water. The area is believed to contain oil, gas, hydrocarbons, iron, coal and other minerals (in quantities not yet ascertained), as well as substantial resources of fish and krill (a protein-rich crustacean which is most dense around the Antarctic Convergence). The main harvesters of krill in the area are the USSR, Japan, Chile, Norway, Poland, South Korea, East and West Germany and Taiwan.

A number of Antarctic islands are claimed by more than one country. The South Shetlands are claimed by Argentina, Britain and Chile, while the South Orkneys are disputed by Argentina and Britain.[1] The South Shetlands and South Orkneys currently form part of the British Antarctic Territory (established on March 3, 1962), having previously been dependencies of the (British) Falkland Islands. This territory includes that part of Antarctica lying between 20° W and 80° W longitude stretching south of 60° S to the South Pole, plus the islands, and covers a total land and sea area of about 3,000,000 square miles (7,750,000 sq km) including the Weddell Sea.

In December 1947, after an Argentinian naval expedition had landed on the South Shetlands and South Orkneys and had established bases in territory claimed by Britain, the UK government proposed the submission of contending claims (which also involved Chile) to the International Court of Justice (ICJ). Although this proposal was rejected by both Argentina and Chile (on the grounds of their "indisputable rights" to the "South American Antarctic"), Britain unilaterally submitted the dispute to the ICJ on May 4, 1955, pointing out that British claims to the territories had been formally confirmed and defined in Letters Patent issued in 1908 and 1917. However, the ICJ decided on March 17, 1956, not to give a hearing to the British application on the grounds that both Argentina and Chile had declared beforehand that they would not submit to the Court's jurisdiction.

The following countries have established scientific research bases in Antarctica since 1944: Argentina, Australia, Britain, Chile, France, Japan, New Zealand, Poland, South Africa, the Soviet Union, the United States and Uruguay.

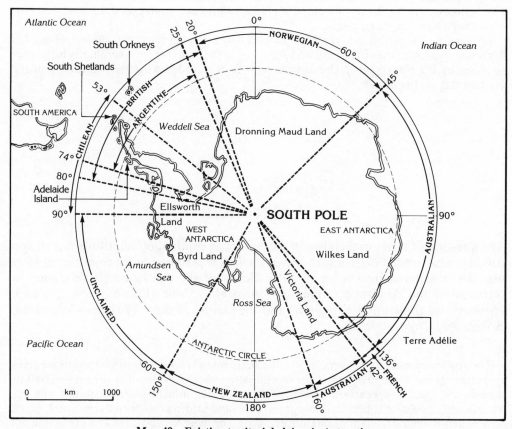

Map 49   Existing territorial claims in Antarctica.

---

[1]For an account of the Argentinian-UK dispute over the more northerly British dependencies of the Falkland Islands, South Georgia and the South Sandwich Islands, see pages 387-97.

The United States and the Soviet Union both stressed in 1959 that, although they had no specific territorial claims to parts of the Antarctic, they did not relinquish the right to make such claims nor did they necessarily recognize the claims of other powers.

The Treaty of the Antarctic

The treaty was signed on Dec. 1, 1959, at the conclusion of a conference on peaceful international scientific co-operation in the Antarctic, which had first been proposed by President Eisenhower in 1958 for International Geophysical Year. It entered into force on June 23, 1961, after its ratification by all 12 original signatories, namely Argentina, Australia, Belgium, Chile, France, Japan, New Zealand, Norway, South Africa, the Soviet Union, the United Kingdom and the United States. Other countries which subsequently became parties to the treaty were Brazil (1975), Bulgaria (1978), China (1974), Cuba (1984), Czechoslovakia (1962), Denmark (1965), Finland (1984), East Germany (1974), West Germany (1979), Hungary (1984), India (1983), Italy (1981), the Netherlands (1967), Papua New Guinea (1981), Peru (1981), Poland (1981), Romania (1971), Spain (1982), Sweden (1984) and Uruguay (1980).

Apart from freezing all territorial claims for its 30-year duration, the treaty set the region aside for peaceful scientific research, made all installations liable to inspection by any other signatory, banned all military activities and proclaimed the region nuclear-free. The preamble to the treaty stated that the signatory governments recognized "that it is in the interest of all mankind that Antarctica shall continue forever to be used exclusively for peaceful purposes and shall not become the scene or object of international discord".

Article I provides (i) that Antarctica shall be used for peaceful purposes only and that any measure of a military nature, such as the establishment of military bases and fortifications, the carrying out of military manoeuvres, as well as the testing of any type of weapons, shall be prohibited; and (ii) that the treaty shall not prevent the use of military personnel or equipment for scientific research or for any other peaceful purpose. Article II specifies that freedom of scientific investigation in Antarctica and co-operation toward that end, as applied during the International Geophysical Year, shall continue, subject to the provisions of the treaty.

Article IV contains the following provisions: (i) nothing contained in the treaty shall be interpreted as (*a*) a renunciation by any contracting party of previously asserted rights of or claims to territorial sovereignty in Antarctica, (*b*) a renunciation or diminution by any contracting party of any basis of claim to territorial sovereignty in Antarctica which it may have, whether as a result of its activities or those of its nationals in Antarctica, or otherwise, (*c*) prejudicing the position of any contracting party as regards its recognition or non-recognition of any other state's right of, or claim or basis of claim to, territorial sovereignty in Antarctica; (ii) no acts or activities taking place while the treaty is in force shall constitute a basis for asserting, supporting or denying a claim to territorial sovereignty in Antarctica, or create any rights of sovereignty in Antarctica, and no new claim, or enlargement of an existing claim, to territorial sovereignty in Antarctica shall be asserted while the treaty is in force.

Article V provides (i) that any nuclear explosions in Antarctica and the disposal there of radioactive waste material shall be prohibited; and (ii) that in the event of the conclusion of international agreements concerning the use of nuclear energy, including nuclear explosions and the disposal of radioactive waste material, to which all of the contracting parties whose representatives are entitled to participate in future consultative meetings are parties, the rules established under such agreements shall apply in Antarctica. Article VI specifies that the provisions of the treaty shall apply to the area south of 60° S latitude, including all ice shelves, but nothing in the treaty shall prejudice or in any way affect the rights, or the exercise of the rights, of any state under international law with regard to the high seas within that area.

Article VII establishes that each contracting party has the right to designate observers to carry out inspection with complete freedom of access to all areas of Antarctica. Aerial observation can be carried out at any time and notice has to be given of all expeditions to and within Antarctica, all stations occupied by a country's nationals, and any military personnel or equipment intended to be introduced into it subject to Article I of the treaty. Article XI provides that any dispute which cannot be settled by consultation among the signatories themselves should be submitted to the International Court of Justice.

At the time of the treaty's signature, Argentina and Chile stated that, while agreeing to the freezing of territorial claims for 30 years under its terms, they did not thereby relinquish claims to the territory included within British Antarctica. In January 1985 it was officially confirmed by the UK government that, under an unpublicized agreement of the previous year, Britain had transferred to Chile a base on Adelaide Island (in a sector claimed by Britain, Argentina and Chile); the government explained that this change had "no legal effect on the sovereignty position of either the United Kingdom or Chile in Antarctica" and would have "no direct bearing on any future review of the [Antarctic] treaty".

Since the signature of the treaty, a series of consultative meetings have been held by the adherent countries, mainly to discuss the protection of the Antarctic environment and other eco-systems dependent on it. The problem of regulating the exploitation of minerals after 1991 (when the signatories will be freed from the constraints under the treaty) has also been discussed as a potential source of conflict in the future. In this latter respect, many Third World countries have expressed dissatisfaction over what they view as the intention of the treaty countries to dominate minerals exploitation in the Antarctic and have put forward, in the United Nations and elsewhere, proposals for the treaty arrangement to be superseded by some form of broader international control for the benefit of the whole world community.

JB/AJD

Select Bibliography

Al-Baharna, Husain M.—*The Arabian Gulf States: Their Legal and Political Status and Their International Problems* (2nd revised edition, Beirut 1975).

Allsebrook, Mary—*Prototypes of Peacemaking: The First Forty Years of the United Nations* (Harlow 1986).

Bernstein, Itamar—*Delimitation of International Boundaries: A Study of Modern Practice and Devices from the Viewpoint of International Law* (Tel Aviv 1974).

Blum, Y. Z.—*Secure Boundaries and Middle East Peace in the Light of International Law and Practice* (Jerusalem 1971).

Brownlie, Ian—*African Boundaries: A Legal and Diplomatic Encyclopaedia* (London & Los Angeles 1979).

Burrell, R. M.—*The Persian Gulf* (New York, 1972).

Cukwurah, A. O.—*The Settlement of Boundary Disputes in International Law* (Manchester 1967).

Dodd, C. H., & Sales, M. E.—*Israel and the Arab World* (London 1970).

East, W. G., & Moodie, A. E. (eds)—*The Changing World: Studies in Political Geography* (London 1956).

East, W. G., & Prescott, J. R. V.—*Our Fragmented World: An Introduction to Political Geography* (London 1975).

East, W. G., Spate, O. H. K., & Fisher, C. A. (eds)—*The Changing Map of Asia* (5th edition, London 1971).

Gilbert, Martin—*The Arab-Israeli Conflict: Its History in Maps* (London 1974).

Gross, Feliks—*World Politics and Tension Areas* (New York 1966).

Horrell, Muriel—*The African Homelands of South Africa* (Johannesburg 1973).

Hoskins, Catherine—*Case Studies in African Diplomacy 2: The Ethiopia-Somalia-Kenya Dispute, 1960-67* (Dar es Salaam 1969).

International Boundary Studies—series published by the Geographer of the US Department of State, Washington DC.

Ireland, Gordon—*Boundaries, Possessions and Conflicts in South America* (Cambridge, Mass. 1938).

Kelly, J. B.—*Eastern Arabian Frontiers* (New York 1964).

Kratochwil, Friedrich, *et al.–Peace and Disputed Sovereignty: Reflections on Conflict over Territory* (Columbia 1985).

Leng, Lee Y.—*The Razor's Edge: Boundary Disputes in Southeast Asia* (London 1980).

Luard, D. E. T. (ed.)—*The International Regulation of Frontier Disputes* (London 1970).

McEwen, A. C.—*International Boundaries of East Africa* (Oxford 1971).

Marchant, Alexander—*Boundaries of the Latin American Republics: An Annotated List of Documents, 1493-1943* (Department of State, Washington 1944).

Prescott, J. R. V.—*The Geography of Frontiers and Boundaries* (London 1965).

Prescott, J. R. V.—*Map of Mainland Asia by Treaty* (Melbourne 1975).

Prescott, J. R. V.—*Boundaries and Frontiers* (London 1978).

Sharma, Surya P.—*International Boundary Disputes and International Law* (Bombay 1976).

Stuyt, A. M.—*Survey of International Arbitrations, 1794-1970* (Leiden 1972).

Touval, Saadia—*The Boundary Politics of Independent Africa* (Cambridge, Mass. 1972).

Widstrand, Carl Gösta (ed.)—*African Boundary Problems* (Uppsala 1969).

Index

Anglo-Irish Treaty (1921), 57, 62
Anjouan, *see* Comoros
Ankoko Island, 437
Annam, Emperor of, 314
Annunzio, Gabriele d' (Italy), 74
Antarctica, 378, 439-42; map, 440
Anti-Comintern Pact (Germany-Italy-Japan), 342
Antofagusta, 407, 408
Antonescu, Ion (Romania), 88, 90
Antrim, *see* Ireland, Northern
Aozou strip, 113-16; map, 114
Apartheid, 184
Aqaba, Gulf of, 209, 212, 221, 232; map, 213
Arab-Israeli conflict, 196, 197-226, 232-4; maps, 213, 233
Arab League, 132, 195, 204, 206, 218, 221, 224, 225, 226, 227, 239, 243, 246
Arafat, Yassir (Palestine), 211, 225
Ardagh, Sir John (UK), 284
Argentina
  Antarctica, territorial claim, 439ff; map, 440
  Chile, dispute with, 379-85; map, 381
  Paraguay, dispute with (Pilcomayo river), 385-6; map, 386
  United Kingdom, dispute with (Falklands), 383, 387-97; map, 387
Argun river, 296
Arica, 407ff
Armagh, *see* Ireland, Northern
Arron, Henck (Suriname), 431, 434
Arthit Kamlang-Ek (Thailand), 367
Arun Panupong (Thailand), 369
Arunachal Pradesh, 279, 281, 282, 283; map, 279
Arusha Agreement (Kenya-Somalia, 1967), 147
Assad, Hafez el- (Syria), 239
Assam, 264, 279, 280, 281
Association of South-East Asian Nations (ASEAN), 261, 369, 373
Atatürk, Kemal (Turkey), 46, 256
Atkins, Humphrey (UK), 67
Audja, Wadi al-, 249
Audu, Ishaya (Nigeria), 111
Austin, Warren (USA), 206
Australia
  Antarctica, territorial claim, 439ff; map, 440
  East Timor issue, policy towards, 330, 335
Austria
  Italy, dispute with (South Tyrol), 1, 10-15; map, 10
Austro-Hungarian empire, 11, 52, 73, 88
Awa river, 429, 430; map, 429
Ayub Khan, Mohammed (Pakistan), 269, 271, 324, 325
Azad Kashmir, *see* Kashmir
Azcona del Hoyo, José (Honduras), 428

B

Badoglio, Pietro (Italy), 74
Baghdad Pact, 259, 322, 323
Bahrain
  Iran, dispute with, 226-9; map, 231
  Qatar, dispute with (Hawar Islands), 229-31; map, 231
Bajpai, K. S. (India), 286
Bakali, Mahmut (Yugoslavia), 8, 9
Bakassi peninsula, 111; map, 139
Balfour declaration (1917), 199, 211
Balkan Federation, 82
Balkan Pact, 4, 83
Balkan Wars (1912-13), 3, 81
Baluchistan, 263, 264, 270ff
Bamana, Younoussa (Mayotte), 121, 125
Ban Klang, 367, 368
Ban Mai, 367, 368
Ban Sawang, 367, 368
Banda, Hastings (Malawi), 156
Bandaranaike, Sirimavo (Sri Lanka), 282
Bangladesh
  India, dispute with (New Moore/South Talpatty Island), 277-8
Bantu Authorities Act (1957), 184
Bantu Land Act (1913), 184
Bantu Self-Government Act (1959), 184
Bantu Trust and Land Act (1936), 184
Banzer Suárez, Hugo (Bolivia), 407, 410
Bárcenas Meneses-Esguerra Treaty (1928), 412, 413, 414
Barrera, Alfonso (Ecuador), 424
Bashev, Ivan (Bulgaria), 83
Basic Treaty (East Germany-West Germany), 37-8
Basra province, 244, 245, 246
Basri, Driss (Morocco), 165, 182
Bassas da India, 132-6; map, 119
Basutoland (Lesotho), 151-3
Batin, Wadi al-, 249
Beagle Channel, 379ff; map, 381
Beaux, Henri (France), 121
Bedjaoui, Mohammed (ICJ Judge), 108
Begin, Menahem (Israel), 218, 219, 220, 223
Beijing, Convention of (1898), 308
Beijing, Treaty of (1860), 289ff, 308
Beirut, 223
Belaúnde Terry, Fernando (Peru), 424
Béli region, 105-6,
Belize, Guatemalan claim to, 397-406; map, 399
Bengal, 264
Ben-Gurion, David (Israel), 208
Berbice, 432, 435
Bérenger, Paul (Mauritius), 136, 160
Berlin
  Berlin wall, construction (1961), 40-2
  quadripartite agreement (1971), 43-4
  status of, 30, 34, 35, 36, 38ff